Roman Civilization
Volume II

ROMAN CIVILIZATION

SELECTED READINGS

Edited by
Naphtali Lewis and Meyer Reinhold

VOLUME II
THE EMPIRE

THIRD EDITION

COLUMBIA UNIVERSITY PRESS • NEW YORK

COLUMBIA UNIVERSITY PRESS
New York   Chichester, West Sussex
copyright © 1990 Columbia University Press

Library of Congress Cataloging-in-Publication Data

*Roman civilization : selected readings / edited by Naphtali Lewis and
Meyer Reinhold. — 3d ed.*
p.   cm.
Includes bibliographical references.
Contents: v. 1. The Republic and the Augustan Age — v. 2. The Empire.
ISBN 0-231-07133-7
1. Rome—Civilization—Sources.   I. Lewis, Naphtali.
II. Reinhold, Meyer
DG13.L4   1990
937—dc20   *90-33405*
                                                          CIP

*Casebound editions of Columbia University Press books are
printed on permanent and durable acid-free paper.*

Printed in the United States of America
c 10 9 8 7 6 5 4 3 2 1
p 10

CONTENTS

ABBREVIATIONS USED IN
CITING SOURCES

AE *L'Année Epigraphique* (Paris, 1888–)

CIL *Corpus Inscriptionum Latinarum* (16 vols., Berlin, 1862–)

Dessau H. Dessau, *Inscriptiones Latinae Selectae* (3 vols., Berlin, 1892–1916)

Dittenberger W. Dittenberger, *Sylloge Inscriptionum Graecarum* (3d ed., 4 vols., Leipzig, 1915–1924)

E-J V. Ehrenberg and A. H. M. Jones, *Documents Illustrating the Reigns of Augustus and Tiberius* (3d ed., Oxford, 1976)

ESAR T. Frank, ed., *An Economic Survey of Ancient Rome* (5 vols., Baltimore, 1933–1940)

FIRA *Fontes Iuris Romani Antejustiniani* (2d ed., 3 vols., Florence, 1940–1943)

IG *Inscriptiones Graecae* (14 vols., Berlin, 1873–)

IGRR *Inscriptiones Graecae ad Res Romanas Pertinentes* (3 vols., Paris, 1906–1927)

LCL Loeb Classical Library

Mitteis "Juristischer Teil, Zweite Hälfte: Chrestomathie," in L. Mitteis and U. Wilcken, *Grundzüge und Chrestomathie der Papyruskunde* (Leipzig and Berlin, 1912)

OGIS W. Dittenberger, *Orientis Graeci Inscriptiones Selectae* (2 vols., Leipzig, 1903–1905)

SB *Sammelbuch Griechischer Urkunden aus Ägypten* (Strasbourg and elsewhere, 1915–)

SEG *Supplementum Epigraphicum Graecum* (Leiden, 1923–)

Select Papyri A. S. Hunt and C. C. Edgar, *Select Papyri* (2 vols., London, 1932–1934; Loeb Classical Library)

Wilcken "Historischer Teil, Zweite Hälfte: Chrestomathie," in L. Mitteis and U. Wilcken, *Grundzüge und Chrestomathie der Papyruskunde* (Leipzig and Berlin, 1912)

ROMAN CIVILIZATION
VOLUME II

The Empire

THE ROMAN PEACE (A.D. 14–192): IMPERIAL POLICY AND ADMINISTRATION

The century and a half from the accession of Tiberius to the renewal of barbarian incursions during the reign of Marcus Aurelius is known traditionally as the era of the *Pax Romana* (Roman Peace). This designation is the product of imperial propaganda, contemporary laudations (cf. § 90), and modern idealization of the ecumenical character of the Roman Empire and the orderliness of civilized life within its frontiers. "You see," says Epictetus (A.D. c. 50–120) in one of his *Discourses* (III. xiii. 9), "that the emperor appears to provide us with profound peace, that there are no longer wars nor battles nor extensive brigandage nor piracy, but at any hour we may travel the roads or sail from the rising of the sun to its setting." In modern times Gibbon, for example, was moved to proclaim, "If a man were called to fix the period in the history of the world, during which the condition of the human race was most happy and prosperous, he would, without hesitation, name that which elapsed from the death of Domitian to the accession of Commodus."

But more recent scholarship has sought to strike a more realistic balance by emphasizing that the "limitless majesty of the Roman Peace" rested upon the might of Roman arms and the collaboration of the propertied classes in all parts of the Empire; that the masses of the laboring people remained in the main an apolitical multitude only lightly touched by Roman culture, rigidly controlled, and systematically exploited; and that the economy of the Empire even at its height was highly unstable and generative of growing socioeconomic maladjustments which were to erupt in the massive crisis of the third century (chapter 6).

1. AUGUSTUS' SUCCESSOR

With Tiberius firmly established in the last years of Augustus' life as coregent and designated successor (vol. 1, § 210), the transfer of power on Augustus' death proceeded without incident. Any stirrings of wishful hope for a return to republican government that might have been entertained by unrealistic members of the nobility were promptly dissipated. On the other hand Tiberius, himself of noble family, continued the Principate essentially on the pattern laid down by his predecessor, going out of his way particularly, at least in the first part of his reign, to encourage the senate to exercise its "partnership" in the government (cf. § 12).

Cassius Dio, *Roman History* LVII. vii–ix (abridged)

As long as Germanicus lived[1] Tiberius exercised the imperial office in the following general manner. He did little or nothing on his own responsibility but brought all matters, even the slightest, before the senate and consulted that body as a partner. In the Forum had been erected a tribunal, on which he sat and administered justice in public; and he always acted with advisers,[2] after the manner of Augustus—in fact, he would take no important step without first consulting the others. After setting forth his own opinion he would not only grant everyone complete freedom to express disagreement but even tolerated it when some occasionally voted in opposition to him. . . .

In all other matters, too, he acted in this same manner. He would not allow freemen to call him master, nor any but the soldiers to call him *imperator*. The title of "father of his country" he rejected absolutely. That of Augustus he did not assume—in fact, he never permitted it even to be voted him—but he did not object to hearing it spoken or to reading it in writing, and whenever he sent messages to kings he would regularly include it in his letters. Generally he was called Caesar, sometimes Germanicus (from the exploits of Germanicus) or, in accordance with ancient usage, *princeps senatus* [see vol. 1, p. 555] (which he himself used, too). He often used to say, "I am master of the slaves, *imperator* of the soldiers, and *princeps* of the rest." He would pray, whenever some such occasion arose, to live and rule as long as it might be advantageous to the state. And he was likewise so democratic in all matters that he

1. Germanicus, Tiberius' nephew and adopted son, died A.D. 19. For honors to the dead Germanicus see § 162.
2. Cf. vol. 1, chapter 9, note 12.

would permit no unusual celebration on his birthday[3] and would not allow people to swear by his Fortune,[4] and if anyone after swearing by it was accused of perjury he would not prosecute. . . . No sacred precinct was set apart for him in those days either by his own choice or otherwise; and no one was allowed to set up an image of him, for he promptly and expressly forbade any city or private citizen to do so. To this prohibition, it is true, he attached the proviso "unless I grant permission," but he added, "I will not grant it."[5] He would have no truck with charges that he had been insulted or accorded insufficient respect by someone (they were already calling even such things lese majesty and were bringing many cases to trial on that charge), and he accepted no such indictment as to himself, although he upheld the majesty of Augustus in this respect, too. At first he did not even punish any of those accused in regard to the latter, and he even released some who had been accused of perjuring themselves when swearing by the Fortune of Augustus; but as time went on he put very many to death [cf. § 6].

2. THE PROBLEM OF THE SUCCESSION

For half a century after the death of Augustus, while there existed members of the Julio-Claudian (i.e., Augustan-Tiberian) house, the succession to the Principate remained within that family, though not without dynastic intrigue and murders. The decisive power of the armed forces was apparent from the start, when the prefect of the Praetorian Guard was the first after the consuls to swear allegiance to Tiberius, and it was not long before the military intervened openly in emperor making. The Praetorian prefects were the leaders in the assassination of Caligula, and, though Claudius was next in the line of succession, it was the Praetorians who placed him on the throne (A.D. 41). In A.D. 68 Nero's doom was sealed by the disaffection of legions and Guard. With Nero's death the Julio-Claudian line was extinct, and in the ensuing year four generals in different parts of the Empire were proclaimed emperor by their respective forces. Thus, in Tacitus' classic remark *(Histories* I. iv), "was revealed a secret of the imperial power, that the emperor could be created elsewhere than at Rome." Vespasian, who emerged the victor at the end of the "Year of the Four Emperors," was succeeded by his two sons, Titus and Domitian, in turn; this dynasty, the Flavian, ended with Domitian's assassination in

3. In contrast to Augustus; cf. vol. I, § 207.
4. On such oaths cf. chapter 4, note 111.
5. On Tiberius' attitude to emperor worship, see § 143, first and second selections.

A.D. 96. Thereafter, a series of emperors without sons of their own put into practice the policy, hastily but futilely extemporized by Galba in 69, whereby the emperor adopted the ablest man available as his son, chief aide, and successor. Marcus Aurelius, the last of these so-called Good Emperors, whose reigns covered nearly a century (A.D. 96–180), reverted to the dynastic principle, designating his son Commodus as his successor despite his awareness of the young man's many shortcomings. In 192 Commodus, too, was slain, and the throne became once again the plaything of the armies (see chapter 6).

THE LEGIONS PROCLAIM VESPASIAN EMPEROR

Tacitus, *Histories* II. lxxix–lxxxi (abridged)

The first step in transferring the imperial power to Vespasian was taken at Alexandria by Tiberius Alexander, who promptly on July 1 administered to his legions the oath of allegiance to him.[6] That day was thereafter celebrated as the first day of Vespasian's principate, even though the army of Judaea took the oath before him in person on July 3. . . . All was done by the impulsive action of the soldiers, without a formal meeting, without a massing of the legions. . . . One day, as Vespasian emerged from his bedchamber, a few soldiers standing by in the usual formation for saluting a legate, saluted him as emperor; then others ran up, calling him Caesar and Augustus and heaping on him all the titles of the Principate. Their minds had passed from apprehension to confidence in fortune's favor. Vespasian showed no elation, arrogance, or change at the turn of events. As soon as he dispelled the mist which such exaltation had spread before his eyes, he spoke as befitted a soldier and listened to the joyful intelligence pouring in from every quarter. For Mucianus,[7] who was waiting for precisely this, now administered to his eager soldiers the oath of allegiance to Vespasian. . . . Before July 15 all Syria had sworn the same allegiance. . . . All the provinces washed by the sea as far as Asia and Achaea, and all the territory extending inland to Pontus and Armenia, took the oath.

---

6. Tiberius Julius Alexander, a Jewish apostate, was prefect of Egypt. The year is A.D. 69.

7. Governor of the province of Syria, and henceforth the spearhead of Vespasian's successful bid for the throne.

THE PRINCIPLE OF ADOPTION

Tacitus, *Histories* I. xv–xvi

We are told that Galba, taking hold of Piso's hand, spoke to this effect: "If I were a private man, and were now adopting you under the curiate law before the pontiffs, as our custom is, it would be a high honor to me to introduce into my house a descendant of Gnaeus Pompey and Marcus Crassus; and it would be a distinction to you to add to the nobility of your lineage the honors of the Sulpician and Lutatian houses. As it is, I who have been called to the imperial power by the unanimous agreement of gods and men am moved by your splendid endowments and patriotism to offer to you, a man of peace, the Principate over which our ancestors fought, and which I myself obtained by war. I am following the example of the deified Augustus, who placed on an eminence next to his own first his nephew Marcellus, then his son-in-law Agrippa, afterwards his grandsons, and finally his stepson Tiberius Nero. But Augustus looked for a successor in his own family. I look for one in the state, and not because I have no relatives or companions of my campaigns. But it was not by campaigning for office that I myself received the imperial power, and the proof of my decision may be found in the connections—not only mine but yours as well—that I have passed over for you. You have a brother, as noble as yourself and older, who would be well worthy of this fortune, were you not worthier. . . .

"Could the vast frame of this Empire have stood and preserved its balance without a directing spirit, I was not unworthy of inaugurating a republic. As it is, matters have long since come to the pass where my age can confer no greater boon on the Roman people than a good successor, your youth no greater than a good emperor. Under Tiberius, Gaius, and Claudius, we were the inheritance, so to speak, of a single family. The exercise of choice which begins with us will be a substitute for freedom.[8] Now that the house of the Julians and the Claudians has come to an end, adoption will discover the worthiest successor in each case. To be begotten and born of princes is a mere accident, and is reckoned as no more. In adoption there is nothing that need bias the judgment, and if you wish to make a choice, a unanimous opinion points out the man.[9] Let Nero be ever before your eyes, swollen with

8. By "freedom" Tacitus means a Republican constitution.

9. Tacitus wrote this in the reign of Trajan, one of the "Good Emperors," brought to the throne by the adoption principle (cf. introduction to this section). The flattery in these words is obvious.

the pride of a long tine of Caesars. . . . I have no need to advise you
further at this time; all my purpose is fulfilled if I have made a good
choice in you. The most practical and the shortest method of distinguishing between good measures and bad is to think what you yourself
would or would not like under another emperor. Here, unlike nations
ruled by kings, we do not have one particular family of masters and the
rest slaves. You will have to rule over men who can bear neither
complete slavery nor complete freedom."

Cassius Dio, Roman History LXVIII. iii. 4–iv. 2

Nerva, therefore, finding himself held in such contempt [by the Praeto-
rians] because of his old age, ascended the Capitol and proclaimed aloud,
"May it be auspicious to the Roman senate and people and to myself: I
adopt Marcus Ulpius Nerva Trajanus." . . . Thus Trajan became Caesar[10]
and later emperor, even though there were relatives of Nerva living.
But Nerva did not esteem family relationship above the welfare of the
state, and though Trajan was a Spaniard and not an Italian or an Italiote,
he adopted him nonetheless despite that. No foreigner had previously
held the Roman sovereignty; but Nerva believed in judging a man by
his ability and not by his nationality.

Cassius Dio, Roman History LXIX. xx. 1–xxi. i; Adapted from LCL

Hadrian convened at his house the most prominent and most respected
of the senators and . . . spoke to them as follows: "I, my friends, have
not been permitted by nature to have a son, but you have made it
possible by legal enactment. Now there is this difference between the
two methods—that a begotten son turns out to be whatever sort of
person heaven pleases, whereas one that is adopted a man takes to
himself by his own choice. Thus by the process of nature a maimed and
witless child is often given to a parent, but by deliberate selection one of
sound body and sound mind is certain to be chosen. For this reason I
formerly selected Lucius Commodus before all others—I could not even
have prayed to have such a child myself. But since heaven has bereft us
of him. I have found an emperor for you in his place, whom I now give
you. He is noble, mild, tractable, prudent, neither so young as to do

---

10. The official title of the emperor designate. The reigning emperor used this title along with that
of Augustus.

anything reckless nor so old as to neglect aught. He has been brought up according to the laws and has held commands in accordance with our ancestral customs, so that he is not ignorant of any matters pertaining to the imperial office but can handle them all effectively. I refer to Aurelius Antoninus here. Although I know him to be the least inclined of men to become involved in public affairs and far from any such desire, still I feel sure he will not deliberately disregard either me or you but will accept the office even against his will."

So it was that Antoninus became emperor. And since he had no male offspring, Hadrian adopted for him Commodus' son Commodus, and in addition to him Marcus Annius Verus; for he wished to designate as far ahead as possible even those who were afterward to be emperors.

THE BREAK WITH THE PRINCIPLE OF ADOPTION

Cassius Dio, *Roman History* LXXII. i; From *LCL*

Commodus was not naturally wicked but, on the contrary, as guileless as any man that ever lived. His great simplicity, however, together with his cowardice, made him the slave of his companions, and it was through them that he at first, out of ignorance, missed the better life and then was led on into lustful and cruel habits, which soon became second nature. And this, I think, Marcus [Aurelius] clearly perceived beforehand. Commodus was nineteen years old when his father died, leaving him many guardians, among them the best of the senators; but Commodus rejected their suggestions and counsels.

3. EXPRESSIONS OF ALLEGIANCE TO THE EMPEROR

Upon the accession of a new *princeps* appropriate celebrations were proclaimed throughout the Empire. In addition, following the precedent established by Augustus (cf. vol. 1, § 201), the military forces and the entire civilian population took an oath of allegiance to the new emperor and renewed this oath on each anniversary of his accession. And every year on January 3 prayers were offered in the Capitol in Rome and in the military camps and the provinces throughout the Empire for the health and safety of the emperor during the year ahead. It is worth noting how the language of these declarations grows in fulsomeness with the increasing autocracy of the regime (cf. § 7).

Tacitus, *Annals* I. vii. 3

The oath of allegiance to Tiberius Caesar was sworn first by the consuls, Sextus Pompeius and Sextus Appuleius, then in their presence by Seius Strabo and Gaius Turranius, prefects of the Praetorian cohorts and of the grain supply, respectively, and then by the senate, the soldiers, and the people.

CIL, vol. II, no. 172 (=Dessau, no. 190); A.D. 37

To Gaius Ummidius Durmius Quadratus, legate of the Emperor Gaius Caesar Germanicus with rank of praetor.

Oath of the Aritensians

I solemnly swear that I will be an enemy to those who I learn are enemies to Gaius Caesar Germanicus. If anyone brings or shall bring danger to him and his welfare, I will not cease to pursue him with arms and deadly war on land and on sea till he has paid the penalty to him; I will hold neither myself nor my children dearer than his welfare; and I will regard as enemies of mine those who have hostile intentions against him. If I knowingly swear or shall swear falsely, then may Jupiter Best and Greatest and the deified Augustus and all the other immortal gods cause me and my children to be deprived of fatherland, safety, and all good fortune.

May 11 [11] in Old Aritium [in Lusitania in Spain], in the consulship of Gnaeus Acerronius Proculus and Gaius Petronius Pontius Nigrinus, in the magistracy of Vegetus son of Tallicus and . . . ibius son of . . . arionus.

Dittenberger, no. 797; A.D. 37

In the consulship of Gnaeus Acerronius Proculus and Gaius Pontius Petronius Nigrinus.

11. This oath was taken fifty-two days after the death of Tiberius. The time it took for the news of an emperor's accession to be brought from Rome to the governors of the different provinces varied considerably with all sorts of circumstances. The two papyrus texts given later in this section show that Nero's accession was made known in Middle Egypt thirty-five days after it took place in Rome, whereas in the case of Pertinax it was sixty-four days before the governor of the province (who was in Lower Egypt) knew of the event. Other papyri reveal that in Middle and Upper Egypt Trajan was thought to be still alive some four months after his death.

Decree of the Assians on Motion of the People[12]

Whereas the rule of Gaius Caesar Germanicus Augustus, hoped and prayed for by all men, has been proclaimed and the world has found unbounded joy and every city and every people has been eager for the sight of the god since the happiest age for mankind has now begun, it was decreed by the council and the Roman businessmen among us and the people of Assus [a city in the province of Asia] to appoint an embassy chosen from the foremost and most distinguished Romans and Greeks[13] to seek an audience and congratulate him, and beg him to remember the city with solicitude, as he personally promised when together with his father Germanicus he first set foot in our city's province.[14]

Oath of the Assians

We swear by Zeus the Savior and by the deified Caesar Augustus and by the ancestral Holy Maiden[15] to be loyal to Gaius Caesar Augustus and all his house and to regard as friends whomever he chooses and as enemies whomever he censures. If we remain faithful to our oath may it go well with us; if we swear falsely, the opposite.

Oxyrhynchus Papyrus No. 1,021 (= *Select Papyri,* no. 235); A.D. 54; From *LCL*

The Caesar who was owed to his ancestors, god manifest, has gone to join them, and the emperor whom the world expected and hoped for has been proclaimed; the good genius of the world and source of all blessings, Nero Caesar, has been proclaimed. Therefore ought we all wear garlands and with sacrifices of oxen give thanks to all the gods. Year 1 of Nero Claudius Caesar Germanicus, the 21st of the month New Augustus.[16]

12. There was not, as in the case of most municipal decrees, merely an individual mover (as, for example, in vol. 1, § 207, third selection).

13. The envoys' names, appended in the document but omitted here, show that one Roman and four Greeks were chosen.

14. The distortion of the facts in this adulation is striking. Germanicus' visit to Asia occurred in A.D. 18. At that time Caligula was only six years old and was not even in line for the succession, since his elder brothers Nero and Drusus were still living.

15. Athena Polias. Tiberius is not named here along with Augustus because he was not deified. On Tiberius' attitude toward emperor worship see § 1 and § 162, first and second selections.

16. November 17; cf. note 11. The Egyptian month Hathyr was renamed New Augustus in honor of Tiberius, who was born in November (cf. vol. 1, § 207, last selection). The text of this document is not an official proclamation received from Rome or from the prefect of Egypt but a local proclamation

Pliny, *Letters* book x, nos. 52–53

[Pliny to the Emperor Trajan][17]

The day, my lord, on which you preserved the Empire by taking up the imperial power, we celebrated with all the joy you deserve, praying the gods to keep you safe and prosperous for the human race, whose protection and security rest upon your welfare. We administered the oath of allegiance both to our fellow soldiers, who rendered it in the customary manner, and to the people of the province, who emulated them with the same devotion.

[The Emperor Trajan to Pliny]

I was pleased to learn from your letter, my dear Pliny, with what dutifulness and joy my fellow soldiers and the provincials celebrated under your leadership the day of my accession.

Berlin Papyrus No. 646 (= *Select Papyri*, no. 222); A.D. 193

Mantennius Sabinus to the *strategi* of the Heptanomia[18] and of the Arsinoite Nome, greeting. I have ordered a copy of the edict sent by me to the most illustrious Alexandria to be appended hereto, so that you may all be informed and may hold festival for the like number of days. I wish you good health. Year 1 of the Emperor Caesar Publius Helvius Pertinax Augustus, Phamenoth 10.[19]

Copy of edict: It is meet, people of Alexandria, that you should hold festival for the most fortunate accession of our lord the Emperor Publius Helvius Pertinax Augustus, *princeps* of the sacred senate, father of his country, and of Publius Helvius Pertinax his son, and of Flavia Titiana Augusta [his wife], offering public sacrifice and prayer en masse on behalf of his enduring rule and of all his house, and wearing garlands for fifteen days beginning from today.

---

issued upon receipt of the news in the village of Oxyrhynchus; cf. the prefect's edict in the last selection of this section.

17. The date of these letters is A.D. 111–13; cf. vol. 1, p. 27.

18. The "Seven Nomes" region of Middle Egypt. Mantennius Sabinus was the prefect of Egypt.

19. March 6; cf. note 11. Pertinax, for whose "enduring rule" the prefect orders fifteen days of celebration, was slain by a band of Praetorians on March 28.

In addition to oaths of allegiance and festivities to mark the accession of a new emperor, cities and provinces often sent letters congratulating him and asking him to reaffirm privileges and benefits granted by his predecessors. The following papyrus contains Trajan's reply to such a letter from Alexandria.

Oxyrhynchus Papyrus No. 3,022; A.D. 98

The Emperor Caesar Nerva TRAJAN Augustus Germanicus, *pontifex maximus,* holding the tribunician power for the second year, to the city of Alexandria. [Being fully aware of] your city's outstanding loyalty to the emperors and mindful of the benefactions which my deified father conferred upon you among the first acts of his rule, and in addition to these claims [of yours] having myself personally a favorable disposition towards you, I have commended you first of all to myself and then also to my friend and prefect [of Egypt] Pompeius Planta, so that he may take every care in providing for your unbroken peace and your food supply and your common and individual rights. From which it will be clear that. . . . [The rest is lost.]

4. THE POWERS OF THE EMPEROR

Each emperor was constitutionally invested with his powers by the formality of a decree passed in the Senate, followed by a comprehensive law enacted in the popular assembly. This bronze tablet—the sole extant document of its kind—contains the end of the law of investiture which conferred the imperial powers upon Vespasian, enumerating the various rights that had in one way or another accrued to the emperor during the first century of the Principate. The formulas of this enactment, however, are mainly those of a decree of the Senate rather than of a law. The explanation lies in the fact that the Senate first decreed the *imperium* to Vespasian, about December 20, A.D. 69, and the assembly subsequently incorporated this decree of the Senate in its own statute, enacted early in January, A.D. 70. Vespasian, however, dated the beginning of his reign from July 1, A.D. 69, when he was acclaimed emperor by the legions in Egypt (cf. § 2, first selection).

CIL, vol. VI, no. 930 (= *FIRA,* vol. 1, no. 15)

. . . that he shall have the right, just as the deified Augustus and Tiberius Julius Caesar Augustus and Tiberius Claudius Caesar Augustus Germanicus had,[20] to conclude treaties with whomever he wishes;

20. Only these three predecessors of Vespasian are named because Nero had been officially declared

And that he shall have the right, just as the deified Augustus and Tiberius Julius Caesar Augustus and Tiberius Claudius Caesar Augustus Germanicus had, to convene the senate, to put and refer[21] proposals to it, and to cause decrees of the senate to be enacted by proposal and division of the house;

And that when the senate is convened [in special session] pursuant to his wish, authorization, order, or command, or in his presence, all matters transacted shall be considered and observed as fully binding as if the meeting of the senate had been regularly convoked and held;

And that at all elections especial consideration shall be given to those candidates for a magistracy, authority, *imperium,* or any post whom he has recommended to the Roman senate and people or to whom he has given and promised his vote;[22]

And that he shall have the right, just as Tiberius Claudius Caesar Augustus Germanicus had, to extend and advance the boundaries of the *pomerium* [see vol. 1, § 6] whenever he deems it to be in the interest of the state;

And that he shall have the right and power, just as the deified Augustus and Tiberius Julius Caesar Augustus and Tiberius Claudius Caesar Augustus Germanicus had, to transact and do whatever things divine, human, public, and private he deems to serve the advantage and the overriding interest of the state;

And that the Emperor Caesar Vespasian shall not be bound by those laws and plebiscites which were declared not binding upon the deified Augustus or Tiberius Julius Caesar Augustus or Tiberius Claudius Caesar Augustus Germanicus, and the Emperor Caesar Vespasian Augustus shall have the right to do whatsoever it was proper for the deified Augustus or Tiberius Julius Caesar Augustus or Tiberius Claudius Caesar Augustus Germanicus to do by virtue of any law or enactment;

And that whatever was done, excuted, decreed, or ordered before the enactment of this law by the Emperor Caesar Vespasian Augustus, or by anyone at his order or command, shall be as fully binding and valid as if they had been done by order of the people or plebs.[23]

"of damned memory," and Caligula was practically so regarded; the brief reigns of Galba, Otho, and Vitellius were considered ephemeral.

21. Other interpretations, less satisfactory, of the Latin *remittere* are "withdraw from consideration," "return for further consideration."

22. The earlier emperors possessed the right of *commendatio,* but more restricted than that here granted to Vespasian. Such candidates of the emperor appear in § 13.

23. This omnibus clause was especially necessary in Vespasian's case because of the interval of six

Sanction

If anyone in consequence of this law has or shall have acted contrary to laws, enactments, plebiscites, or decrees of the senate, or if he shall have failed to do in consequence of this law anything that it is incumbent on him to do in accordance with a law, enactment, plebiscite, or decree of the senate, it shall be with impunity, nor shall he on that account have to pay any penalty to the people, nor shall anyone have the right to institute suit or judicial inquiry concerning such matter, nor shall any [authority] permit proceedings before him on such matter.

5. An Imperial Triumph

One of the most coveted honors of the Republic, the celebration of a triumph by victorious generals (cf. vol. 1, § 90), came to an end in the reign of Augustus. The precedent for this was set by Augustus's ablest general, Marcus Agrippa, who refused all triumphs voted him. The last triumph recorded in the Calendar of Triumphs (vol. 1, pp. 233–34) occurred in 19 B.C. Thereafter this honor was reserved for the emperors and the imperial family. As a substitute, conquering generals were awarded *ornamenta triumphalia* (triumphal decorations). One of the most spectacular triumphs of the imperial period was celebrated jointly by Vespasian and Titus in A.D. 71 after the Jewish War.

Josephus, *Jewish War* VII. v. 122–156 (abridged); Adapted from *LCL*

Previous notice having been given of the day on which the triumphal procession would take place, not a soul among the countless multitude in the city remained at home; all issued forth and occupied every position where it was at all possible to stand, leaving only room for the necessary passage of those upon whom they were to gaze.

The troops, while it was still night, had all marched out in centuries and cohorts under their commanders. . . . About the time dawn was breaking Vespasian and Titus issued forth, crowned with laurel and clad in the traditional purple robes, and proceeded to the porticoes of Octavia; for here the senate and the chief magistrates and those of equestrian rank were awaiting their coming. A platform had been erected in front

---

months between his elevation by the eastern legions and his formal accession (cf. introduction to this section).

of the porticoes, with chairs of ivory placed for them upon it; to these they mounted and took their seats. Instantly, acclamations rose from the troops, all bearing ample testimony to their valor. The princes were unarmed, in silk robes, and crowned with laurel. Vespasian, having acknowledged their acclamations, which they wished to prolong, gave the signal for silence. Then, amidst profound and universal stillness, he rose and, covering most of his head with his mantle, recited the customary prayers, Titus also praying in like manner. . . . The princes . . . having donned their triumphal robes and sacrificed to the gods . . . sent the procession on its way, driving off through the theaters, in order to give the crowds a better view.

It is impossible adequately to describe the multitude of those spectacles and their magnificence . . . for the collective exhibition on that day of almost everything that men who have ever been blessed by fortune have one by one acquired . . . displayed the majesty of the Roman Empire. . . .

The war was shown in numerous representations, in separate sections, affording a very vivid picture of its episodes. Here was to be seen a prosperous country being devastated, there whole battalions of the enemy slaughtered; here a party in flight, there others being led into captivity; walls of surpassing size demolished by engines, mighty fortresses overpowered; cities with well-manned defenses completely mastered and an army pouring within the ramparts, an area all deluged with blood, the hands of those incapable of resistance raised in supplication; temples being set on fire, houses pulled down over their owners' heads; and, after general desolation and woe, rivers flowing, not over a cultivated land, nor supplying drink to man and beast, but across a country still on every side in flames. . . .

The spoils in general were borne in promiscuous heaps; but conspicuous above all stood out those captured in the temple at Jerusalem. These consisted of a golden table, many talents in weight, and a candelabrum, likewise made of gold. . . .[24] After these, and last of all the spoils, was carried a copy of the Law of the Jews. Then followed a large party carrying images of victory, all made of ivory and gold. Behind them drove first Vespasian, followed by Titus; while Domitian rode alongside them, in magnificent apparel and mounted on a horse that was a remarkable sight.

24. The table of the shewbread and the seven-branched menorah. These, together with other spoils from the temple, appear on the reliefs depicting this triumphal procession on the inner walls of the extant Arch of Titus, erected at the edge of the Forum shortly after Titus' death.

The triumphal procession ended at the temple of Jupiter Capitolinus, on reaching which they halted, for it was a time-honored custom to wait there until the execution of the enemy's general was announced. This was Simon bar Giora, who had just figured in the procession among the prisoners,[25] and then, with a noose around him and scourged meanwhile by his escorts, had been dragged to the spot abutting on the Forum, where Roman law requires that malefactors condemned to death should be executed.[26] After the announcement that Simon was no more and the shouts of universal applause which greeted it, the princes began the sacrifices and, having duly offered these with the customary prayers, withdrew to the palace.

CIL, vol. VI, no. 944 (=Dessau, no. 264)[27]

The Roman senate and people [dedicated this] to the Emperor Titus Caesar Vespasian Augustus, son of the deified Vespasian, *pontifex maximus,* holding the tribunician power for the tenth year, acclaimed *imperator* seventeen times, consul eight times, father of his country, their *princeps,* because with the guidance and plans of his father, and under his auspices, he subdued the Jewish people and destroyed the city of Jerusalem, which all generals, kings, and peoples before him had either attacked without success or left entirely unassailed.

6. LESE MAJESTY

The law on treason was revised under Augustus to embrace affronts to the majesty of the emperor (cf. vol. 1, §§ 200, 202). But lack of specificity as to what constituted "impairment" of his majesty made the law—as administered by some emperors, at least—an insidious instrument of terror; and the high rewards offered for convictions (usually one fourth of the property of the condemned) brought into being a host of spies, professional informers *(delatores),* and agents provocateurs. Tacitus dwells on the pernicious extension of the law's scope and the unrestrained encouragement of informers as leading characteristics of the reign of Tiberius. But recent scholarship has shown that Augustus' successor was in the

---

25. Seven hundred Jewish prisoners were paraded in the triumph, together with the two Zealot leaders, Simon bar Giora ("son of the proselyte") and John of Gischala. The latter was imprisoned for life.

26. The Roman state prison at the foot of the Capitoline Hill.

27. From an arch in Rome, no longer extant, erected in A.D. 80–81.

main correct and moderate in his application of the law (cf. § 1). It seems clear that Tacitus retrojected to the times of Tiberius the reign of terror through which he lived under Domitian.

NEW APPLICATIONS OF THE LAW OF TREASON

Tacitus, *Annals* I. lxxii–lxxiii

Tiberius gave new impetus to the law of treason. This law had the same name in olden times, but other matters came under its jurisdiction— betrayal of an army, or inciting the plebs to sedition, in short, any public malfeasance which diminished the majesty of the Roman people [on this phrase cf. vol. 1, pp. 89, 189]. Deeds alone were subject to accusation then, words went unpunished. Augustus was the first to conduct trials for libel within the scope of this law, provoked to it by Cassius Severus' wanton defamation of respectable men and women in his impudent writings. Next Tiberius, when consulted by the praetor Pompeius Macer as to whether such trials for treason should be placed on the calendar, replied that the laws must be enforced. He too had been exasperated by verses, which were circulated anonymously, attacking his cruelty, his arrogance, and his estrangement from his mother.

It will not be without value to relate the first experiments in such charges, made in the cases of two unpretentious Roman *equites,* Falanius and Rubrius. . . . Against Falanius the accuser alleged that he had admitted among the votaries of Augustus . . . a certain Cassius, a mime of unnatural vice, and that when selling some gardens he had included a statue of Augustus in the sale. Against Rubrius it was charged that he had violated the divinity of Augustus by perjury. When these charges came to Tiberius' attention he wrote to the consuls that a place in heaven had not been decreed to his father in order that the honor might be turned to the destruction of the citizens. Cassius the actor had, along with others of the same occupation, taken part in the games which his own mother had consecrated to the memory of Augustus; nor was it sacrilegious to let statues of Augustus, like the effigies of other divinities, go with the property in sales of gardens and houses. As to [Rubrius'] oath, it should be treated exactly as if he had deceived Jupiter; the gods' injuries were the gods' concern.[28]

---

28. In other words, in these first "trial balloon" cases of A.D. 15, Tiberius rejected the idea that the actions alleged constitute lese majesty. The last clause, incidentally, was a maxim of Roman law; cf. the constitution of Alexander Severus of A.D. 223, cited in Justinian *Code* iv. i. 2: "Scorn for the sanctity of an oath has its own sufficient avenger in the god."

A ROMAN HOLIDAY FOR INFORMERS

Tacitus, *Annals* I. lxxiv. 1–2

Caepio took up a way of life which the miseries of the age and the impudence of men soon rendered popular. Indigent, unknown, and restless, he first wormed his way, by means of his private reports, into the confidence of his pitiless sovereign. It was not long before he had become a terror to the entire nobility. He acquired the favor of one man[29] and the hatred of all, and those who followed the example that he set rose from beggary to riches, from objects of contempt to objects of fear, till at last they crowned the ruin of others by their own.

Tacitus, *Annals* IV. xxx. 3–5

It was proposed that informers should receive no rewards when a person accused of treason took his life by his own hand before the completion of the trial. The motion was on the point of being carried when Tiberius, with considerable asperity and unusual frankness, spoke up for the informers, complaining that the laws would be ineffective and the state brought to the brink of disaster. "Better," he said, "subvert the constitution than remove its guardians." Thus the informers, a breed invented for the public ruin and never adequately curbed even by penalties, were lured on by rewards.

AGENTS PROVOCATEURS

Epictetus,[30] *Discourses* IV. xiii. 5; From *LCL*

In this fashion the rash are ensnared by the soldiers in Rome. A soldier, dressed like a civilian, sits down by your side and begins to speak ill of Caesar, and then you, too, just as though you have received from him some guarantee of good faith in the fact that he began the abuse, tell likewise everything you think, and the next thing is—you are led off to prison in chains.[31]

29. The Emperor Tiberius. This passage is from Tacitus' narrative of A.D. 15; the passage that follows refers to A.D. 23.

30. A teacher of Stoic philosophy (A.D. c. 50–120) who taught at Nicopolis in Epirus after Domitian's expulsion of philosophers from Rome. He is the author of the famous *Enchiridion,* or *Manual*.

31. We are told in a fragment of Cassius Dio's fifty-eighth book: "Tiberius put to death a man of

SUBVERSIVE HISTORY

Tacitus, *Annals* IV. xxxiv–xxxv

In the consulship of Cornelius Cossus and Asinius Agrippa, Cremutius Cordus was arraigned on a new and hitherto unheard-of charge—that he had published a history in which he praised Marcus Brutus and called Gaius Cassius the last of the Romans.[32] His accusers were Satrius Secundus and Pinarius Natta, creatures of Sejanus.[33] That was enough to ruin the accused; in addition, the emperor listened with angry mien to his defense, which Cremutius, resolved to give up his life, began thus:

"It is my words, Conscript Fathers [senators], which are here impeached, so innocent am I of any guilty act. And even these words are not against the emperor or the emperor's mother, who are alone comprehended under the law of treason. I am said to have lauded Brutus and Cassius, whose careers so many have described and no one mentioned without praise. Titus Livius, whose reputation for eloquence and truthfulness is second to none, extolled Gnaeus Pompey in such laudatory terms that Augustus called him "the Pompeian," yet this was no obstacle to their friendship. Scipio, Afranius,[34] this very Cassius, this same Brutus, he nowhere describes as brigands and traitors—the terms now applied to them—but repeatedly as illustrious men. Asinius Pollio's writings hand down a glorious account of them, and Messalla Corvinus used to speak with pride of Cassius as his general; yet both these men prospered to the end with wealth and preferment.[35] To that book of

---

consular rank on the charge of having carried in his bosom a coin bearing the emperor's likeness when he retired to a latrine."

32. Cremutius Cordus was a historian of note, whose works are lost. His trial, which took place in A.D. 25 before the Senate with the emperor present, has become through Tacitus' brilliant rhetoric a *cause célèbre*. Actually, since Brutus and Cassius had been legally proclaimed traitors and outlaws, it is doubtful whether Cordus' trial appeared to his contemporaries as a particularly radical extension of the types of trials for libel mentioned in the first selection of this section. Similarly, drinking to the memory of Brutus and Cassius on their birthdays and writing a laudatory biography of Cato the Younger were among the crimes that brought death in Nero's reign to Publius Clodius Thrasea Paetus. Domitian put to death the author of a biography praising Paetus, and his books, like Cordus', were publicly burned. On the burning of books under Augustus, see vol. 1, pp. 404, 611.

33. Lucius Aelius Sejanus was prefect of the Praetorian Guard and was a veritable viceroy in this period of Tiberius' reign. He plotted to secure the succession for himself, and before his dramtic fall in A.D. 31 he was able to put even members of the imperial household, including the heir apparent, out of the way on charges of treason.

34. Scipio and Afranius were Pompey's father-in-law and lieutenant, respectively.

35. Asinius Pollio and Messalla Corvinus were both prominent men of letters and affairs of the Augustan period.

Marcus Cicero's in which he praised Cato to the skies, what other answer did Caesar the dictator make but an oration written in reply, as if he were pleading before a jury? The letters of Antony, the harangues of Brutus contain invectives against Augustus, false to be sure, but extremely violent; the poems of Bibaculus and Catullus,[36] crammed with abuse of the Caesars, are still read—and the deified Julius and the deified Augustus themselves bore all this and let it pass. . . . To every man posterity gives his due honor, and if a fatal sentence hangs over me there will be no lack of people to remember me as well as Cassius and Brutus."

He then left the senate and ended his life by starvation. The senators decreed that his books should be burned by the aediles; but they survived in concealment and were afterwards republished—which disposes one all the more to laugh at the folly of men who suppose that tyranny in the present can actually cause the succeeding age to forget. On the contrary, the persecution of genius fosters its influence; foreign despots, and all who have imitated their barbarity, have merely begotten infamy for themselves and glory for their victims.

7. EVOLUTION OF THE PRINCIPATE: FROM "FIRST CITIZEN" TO BENEVOLENT DESPOT

The "partnership in government" with the Senate which was inherent in the Augustan conception of the Principate quickly proved to be unworkable. The Senate receded into impotence (cf. § 12), and the emperor's domination became more and more complete. From all quarters of the Empire we hear a chorus of praise for the ruler of the Roman world, swelling in volume and adulation as we pass from the Julio-Claudians and Flavians of the first century to the "Good Emperors" of the second. We find it in poetry, history, philosophy, and other writings, as well as in the language of officialdom (cf., for example, § 3). The dominant theme in this constant paeaning is the enjoyment of peace and prosperity under the protection of an all-wise, all-powerful, all-virtuous, divinely ordained ruler. Opposition of subject peoples to Roman rule was not completely dead, however. It manifested itself in sporadic revolts and in the continued production of popular anti-Roman literature (cf. vol. 1, § 147; vol. 2, § 90).

---

36. The famous poet Gaius Valerius Catullus, c. 84 B.C.–54 B.C. Bibaculus was his contemporary.

Strabo, *Geography* iv. iv. 2 (at end); From *LCL*

Italy—though it has often been torn by faction, at least since it has been under the Romans—and Rome itself have been prevented by the excellence of their form of government and of their rulers from proceeding too far in the ways of error and corruption. But it would be a difficult thing to administer so great a dominion otherwise than by turning it over to one man, as to a father. At all events, never have the Romans and their allies thrived in such peace and plenty as that which was afforded them by Augustus Caesar from the time he assumed the absolute authority and is now being afforded them by his son and successor, Tiberius, who is making Augustus the model of his administration and decrees.

Velleius Paterculus, *Compendium of Roman History* ii. cxxvi. 2–5; From *LCL*

Credit has been restored in the Forum, strife has been banished from the Forum, canvassing for office from the Campus Martius,[37] discord from the senate house; justice, equity, and industry, long buried in oblivion, have been restored to the state; the magistrates have regained their authority, the senate its honor, the courts their dignity; rioting in the theater has been suppressed; all have either been imbued with the wish to do right or have been forced to do so. Right is now honored, evil is punished; the humble man looks up to the great but does not fear him, the great has precedence over the lowly but does not despise him. When was the price of grain more reasonable, the blessings of peace greater? The Augustan peace, which has spread to the regions of the east and of the west and to the bounds of the north and of the south, preserves every corner of the world safe from the fear of brigandage. The munificence of the Emperor [Tiberius] takes upon itself the accidental losses not merely of individual citizens but of whole cities. The cities of Asia have been restored,[38] the provinces have been freed from the oppression of their magistrates. Honor ever awaits the worthy; for the wicked

---

37. In A.D. 14. Tiberius discontinued the election of magistrates by the Centuriate Assembly in the Field of Mars (vol. 1, § 27) and transferred this prerogative to the Senate, which was thereafter the sole electoral organ of the state.

38. A series of earthquakes in A.D. 17 caused great damage in Asia Minor. Tiberius sent Sardis a gift of 10,000,000 sesterces, and at his bidding the Senate granted that city a five-year remission of taxes (cf. § 20). Similar assistance was given to the other stricken cities. In A.D. 23 two earthquake-stricken cities (one in Asia, one in Greece) were accorded a three-year remission of taxes. Similar cases are recorded under other emperors.

punishment is slow but sure; fair play now has the upper hand over influence, and merit over campaigning for office, for the best of emperors teaches his citizens to do right by doing it himself, and though he is the greatest among us in power, he is still greater by his example.

PLINY'S ENCOMIUM ON TRAJAN

Under the Principate the consulship (now mainly an honorary distinction) and other high offices were attained upon nomination by the emperor. It was customary for the consul on entering office to deliver a speech thanking the emperor for this preferment and mark of favor. An extant example of these fulsome panegyrics is that delivered by Pliny the Younger in A.D. 100, when he held the consulship for two months. In the reworked and expanded form in which he published this panegyric it runs to some 18,000 words. In it Pliny celebrates the career, acts, and virtues of the Emperor Trajan.

Pliny, *Panegyric Addressed to the Emperor Trajan* lxv–lxxx (abridged)

You[39] have spontaneously subjected yourself to the laws, to the laws which, Caesar, no one ever drafted to be binding upon the *princeps*.[40] But you desire to have no more rights than we; and the result is that we would like you to have more. What I now hear for the first time, now learn for the first time, is not, "The *princeps* is above the laws," but "The laws are above the *princeps,* and the same restrictions apply to Caesar when consul as to others." He swears fidelity to the laws in the presence of attentive gods—for to whom should they be more attentive than to Caesar? . . .

Hardly had the first day of your consulship dawned when you entered the senate house and exhorted us, now individually, now all together, to resume our liberty, to take up the duties of imperial administration shared, so to speak, between yourself and us, to watch over the public interests, to rouse ourselves. All emperors before you said about the same, but none before you was believed. People had before their eyes the shipwrecks of many men who sailed along in a deceptive calm and foundered in an unexpected storm. . . . But you we follow fearlessly and happily, wherever you call us. You order us to be free: we will be.

39. Trajan. Pliny shifts back and forth in his panegyric, addressing now the emperor, now the Senate.

40. Cf. Justinian, *Digest* I. iii. 32 (quoting Ulpian): "The emperor is not bound by the laws."

You order us to express our opinions openly: we will pronounce them. It is neither through any cowardice nor through any natural sluggishness that we have remained silent until now; terror and fear and that wretched prudence born of danger warned us to turn our eyes, our ears, our minds, away from the state—in fact, there was no state altogether. But today, relying and leaning upon your right hand and your promises, we unseal our lips closed in long servitude and we loose our tongues paralyzed by so many ills. . . .

Here is the picture of the father of our state as I for my part seem to have discerned it both from his speech and from the very manner of its presentation. What weight in his ideas, what unaffected genuineness in his words, what earnestness in his voice, what confirmation in his face, what sincerity in his eyes, bearing, gestures, in short in his whole body! He will always remember his advice to us, and he will know that we are obeying him whenever we make use of the liberty he has given us. And there is no fear that he will judge us reckless if we take advantage unhesitatingly of the security of the times, for he remembers that we lived otherwise under an evil *princeps*.[41]

It is our custom to offer public prayers[42] for the eternity of the Empire and the preservation of the emperor . . . "if [he] has ruled the state well and in the interest of all." . . . You reap, Caesar, the most glorious fruit of your preservation from the consent of the gods. For when you stipulate that the gods should preserve you only "if you have ruled the state well and in the interest of all," you are assured that you do rule the state well since they preserve you.[43] And so you pass in security and joy the day which tortured other emperors with worry and fear when in suspense, thunderstruck, uncertain how far they could rely on our patience, they awaited from here and there the messages of public servitude. . . .

In judicial inquiries, what soft severity [you display], what clemency without weakness! You do not sit as judge intent on enriching your privy purse,[44] and you want no reward for your decision other than to have judged rightly. Litigants stand before you concerned not for their

---

41. Domitian, whose reign of terror Pliny is here contrasting with the enlightened rule of Trajan.

42. Annually on January 3; cf. introduction to § 3.

43. This recalls a prayer of Augustus reported by Suetonius (*Life of Augustus* xxviii. 2): "May I be permitted to set the state on a safe and sound base and to reap from that act the fruit I seek, so that I may be called the creator of the best of governments and bear with me when I die the hope that the foundation of the state which I have laid will remain unshaken."

44. Nero, Vespasian, and Titus carried out large-scale confiscations of private estates (cf. § 25), many of them belonging to persons convicted of treason. In one famous case, Nero is said to have put

fortunes, but for your good opinion, and they fear not so much what you may think of their case as what you may think of their character. O care truly that of a *princeps,* and even of a god, to reconcile rival cities, to calm peoples in ferment, less by imperial command than by reason, to impede the injustices of magistrates, to annual everything that ought not have been done, in fine, in the manner of the swiftest star to see all, hear all, and like a divinity be present and be helpful forthwith wherever invoked! Such, I imagine, are the things that the father of the world [Jupiter] regulates with a nod when he lets his glance fall upon the earth and deigns to count human destinies among his divine occupations. Henceforth free and released in this area he can attend to the sky alone, since he has sent you to fill his role toward the human race. You fulfill that function, and you are worthy of him who entrusted it to you, since each of your days is devoted to our greatest good, to your greatest glory.

THE BLESSINGS OF IMPERIAL RULE

Plutarch, *Precepts of Statecraft* xxxii

The greatest blessings that cities can enjoy are peace, prosperity, popu-lousness, and concord. As far as peace is concerned the people have no need of political activity, for all war, both Greek and foreign, has been banished and has disappeared from among us. Of liberty the people enjoy as much as our rulers allot them, and perhaps more would not be better. A bounteous productiveness of soil; a mild, temperate climate; wives bearing "children like to their sires" [Hesiod, *Works and Days* 233], and security for the offspring—these are the things that the wise man will ask for his fellow citizens in his prayers to the gods.

Aelius Aristides,[45] *To Rome* xxix–xxxiii, lx (abridged); From the translation of S. Levin (Glencoe, Illinois, 1950)

Extensive and sizable as the Empire is, perfect policing does much more than territorial boundaries to make it great. . . . Like a well-swept and fenced-in front yard . . . the whole world speaks in unison, more dis-

---

out of the way six wealthy landowners who together possessed half the area of the province of Africa, so that he could acquire their properties; see pp. 85–86.

45. Publius Aelius Aristides (A.D. 117–c. 185) was one of the celebrated Greek rhetoricians of his day. A native of Mysia, he traveled and lectured in many places. Two of his treatises and over fifty of

tinctly than a chorus; and so well does it harmonize under this director-in-chief that it joins in praying this Empire may last for all time. All everywhere are ruled equally. The mountain people are lowlier in their submissiveness than the inhabitants of the most exposed plains. The owners and occupants of rich plains are your peasants. Continent and island are no longer separate. Like one continuous country and one people, all the world quietly obeys. Everything is carried out by command or nod, and it is simpler than touching a string. If a need arises, the thing has only to be decided on, and it is done. The governors assigned to cities and provinces govern their various subjects; but among themselves and in relation to one another, all of them alike are governed . . . [by] the supreme governor, the chief executive. They are convinced that he knows what they are doing better than they know it themselves. They fear and respect him more than any slave could fear his master standing over him personally and giving orders. None of them are so proud that they can sit still if they so much as hear his name. They leap up, praise him, bow, and utter a double prayer—to the gods on behalf of him, and to him on their own behalf. If they feel the slightest doubt about their subjects' lawsuits, public or private, or whether petitions should be granted, they immediately send to him and ask what to do, and they wait for a signal from him, as a chorus from its director.[46] No need for him to wear himself out making the rounds of the whole Empire, or to be in one place after another adjusting the affairs of each people whenever he sets foot in their country. Instead, he can very easily sit and manage the whole world by letters, which are practically no sooner written than delivered, as if flown by birds. . . . The constitution is a universal democracy under the one man that can rule and govern best.

THE BENEVOLENT DESPOT

The following excerpts[47] from the works of two Pythagoreans, apparently of the second century, present philosophical rationales of the intermediate stage that the position of the Roman emperor had then reached in its

---

his speeches are extant. This panegyric idealizing the Roman emperor and Empire was delivered by him in Rome about the year 150. A comprehensive study of the oration, with translation and detailed commentary, is published by J. H. Oliver in *Transactions of the American Philosophical Society* (1953), vol. 43, part 4.

46. Pliny's letters to the Emperor Trajan, a number of which appear in this volume, afford a vivid illustration of this statement.

47. Preserved by John of Stobi (Joannes Stobaeus; fifth[?] century) in his *Anthology* iv. vii. 61, 64.

evolution from *primus inter pares* to absolute monarch by divine right. Though both treatises are strongly imbued with Stoic doctrine, they reveal an interesting difference in concept. "Diotogenes admits the divinization of the king rather than his divinity. It is the majesty of his function and the resemblance of terrestrial royalty to divine royalty that give him a divine aspect: he is the lieutenant of God on earth, and his imitator. . . . The ideal of Diotogenes is human rather than divine." But for the more mystical Ecphantes the king was created by the supreme god in his own image, to govern mankind as the god governs the universe (cf. the selection from Pliny's *Panegyric,* earlier). His king is divine by nature, and his function stems from his divinity, while Diotogenes' king derives divinity from his function. Under either concept, however, "the king or emperor, presented in the guise of a mediator and savior . . . promises the human community to bring about an order of things which, by reproducing the [perfect] organization of the universe, corresponds to the will of God and assures the salvation of humanity." (The quotations are translated from L. Delatte, *Les Traités de la royauté d'Ecphante, Diotogène et Sthénidas* [Liège, 1942], pp. 289–290.)

Diotogenes, *On Kingship* (fragment); Adapted from the translation of E. R. Goodenough, *Yale Classical Studies* (1928), 1:66–68

The duties of a king are threefold: military leadership, the dispensing of justice, and the cult of the gods. . . . Accordingly, the perfect king must be a good commander, judge, and priest, for these are fitting and proper to a king's supremacy and virtue alike. For the task of a pilot is to save the ship, of a charioteer to save the chariot, of a physician to save those who are ill, while the task of a king and captain is to save those who are in danger in war. . . . In dispensing and distributing justice, whether as a whole in public law or to individuals in private law, it is right for a king to act as does God in his reign and command over the universe— in public matters by harmonizing the whole with his single rule and reign, and in individual matters by bringing details into accord with this same harmony and reign. The king is also occupied in being good and beneficent to his subjects, and that according to justice and law. The third duty, that is the worship of the gods, is no less fitting for a king. For the Best should be honored by the best man, and the Reigning Principle by the man who reigns. Now God is the best of the things most honored by inherent nature, and the king is best in the earthly and human realm. And king bears the same relation to state as God to universe; and state is to universe as king is to God. For the state, made up as it is by the harmonizing of many different elements, is an imitation of the order and harmony of the universe, while the king, who has absolute rule and is himself Animate Law, has been transfigured into a god among men.

Ecphantes, *On Kingship* (fragment); Adapted from the translation of E. R. Goodenough, *Yale Classical Studies* (1928), 1:76–78

The king is like the rest [of mankind] in his earthly tabernacle, inasmuch as he is formed out of the same material; but he is fashioned by the supreme artificer, who in making the king used himself as archetype. Accordingly the king, as a copy of the higher king, is a single and unique creation, for he is on the one hand always intimate with the one who made him, while to his subjects he appears in the light of royalty. . . . And the very fact that a divine being rules well causes the king's subjects to be ruled well by him. So then I suppose that the earthly king can in no particular fall short of the virtue of the heavenly king; but just as the king is an alien and foreign thing which has come down from heaven to mankind, so one would suppose his virtues also were the work of divinity and his through divinity.

8. FOREIGN AND FRONTIER POLICY

The foreign policy of the Roman Empire in the first two centuries A.D. was substantially that bequeathed to it by Augustus—nonaggressive imperialism, defense and security of the borders, with prime attention to the watch on the Rhine–Danube frontier against the restless Germanic tribes, and on the desert–river–mountain frontier in Syria and Asia Minor against the Parthian Empire. To achieve this policy with an economy of means, imposed by the limited financial and military resources of the Empire, succeeding emperors adhered, with rare exceptions (see § 10), to Tiberius' "policy of conducting foreign affairs by astute diplomacy and of keeping war at a distance" (Tacitus, *Annals* VI. xxxii. 1), though occasional campaigns were initiated to consolidate and shorten frontier lines. In addition to buffer zones of client states, the emperors relied on the traditional Roman policy of "divide and rule," fostering internal conflicts and discord among the peoples beyond the borders and winning over some of their leaders to a pro-Roman orientation. "May the tribes," prayed Tacitus, writing in A.D. 98, "ever retain if not love for us, at least hatred for each other; for while the fate that overtakes empires is at our heels, fortune can

grant no greater boon than discord among our foes" *(Germany* xxxiii).[48]
From the end of the first century on, further protection was provided
along the land frontiers of the Empire by the construction of *limites,*
continuous massive barriers guarded by forts and observation towers,
the most impressive remains of which is "Hadrian's Wall" in northern
Britain.

Appian, *Roman History* Preface. vii; Adapted from *LCL*

Possessing the best part of the earth and sea, they have, on the whole,
aimed to preserve their Empire by diplomacy rather than to extend their
sway indefinitely over poor and profitless tribes of barbarians, some of
whom I have seen at Rome negotiating and offering themselves as
subjects; but the emperor would not accept them because they would be
of no use to him. They give kings to a great many other peoples whom
they do not need to have under their rule. To some of these subject
peoples they make disbursements in addition, deeming it dishonorable
to give them up even though they are costly. They surround the Empire
with great armies and they garrison the whole stretch of land and sea
like a single stronghold.

THE PEOPLES ON THE FRONTIERS

The *Germany* of Tacitus is the most extensive ancient account of a people
with whom the Romans were in contact on the frontiers of their Empire.
Only a few excerpts from this monograph are given here. A brief glimpse
of the lower Danube frontier a century earlier is contained in one of the
works written by the poet Ovid during his exile at Tomis (modern
Constanta in Romania) on the Black Sea.

Tacitus, *Germany* vii, xi, xiii–xiv, xvi, xxvi; Adapted from *LCL*

They obtain their kings on the basis of birth, their generals on the basis
of courage. The authority of their kings is not unlimited or arbitrary.
Their generals control them by example rather than command, and by
means of the admiration which attends upon energy and a conspicuous
place in the front line. But capital punishment, imprisonment, even

---

48. Cf. Tacitus, *Agricola* xii: "Our most effective weapon against the most powerful tribes (in
Britain) is that they have no common policy. Seldom do two or three peoples come to an agreement to
repel a common danger; thus, they fight singly, and all are conquered."

flogging are permitted only to the priests, and then not as a penalty or under the general's orders but as an inspiration from the god whom they suppose to accompany them on campaign. Certain totems, in fact, and emblems are fetched from groves and carried into battle. The strongest incentive to courage lies in this, that neither chance nor casual grouping makes the squadron or wedge, but family and kinship. . . .

On small matters the chiefs consult, on larger questions the community, but with this limitation, that even the matters whose decision rests with the people are first handled by the chiefs. They meet, unless there is some unforeseen and sudden emergency, on specified days—when the moon, that is, is new or at the full. They regard this as the most auspicious herald for the transaction of business. They count not by days as we do, but by nights. . . . It is a failing of their freedom that they do not meet at once, when commanded, but waste a second and a third day by dilatoriness in assembling. When the throng is pleased to begin, they take their seats carrying arms. Silence is called for by the priests, who thenceforward have power also to coerce. Then kings or chiefs are listened to, in order of age, birth, glory in war, or eloquence, with the prestige that belongs to their counsel rather than with any prescriptive right to command. If the advice tendered is displeasing, they reject it by shouting; if it pleases them, they clash their spears. . . .

They transact no business, public or private, without arms in their hands. Yet the custom is that no one takes arms until the state has endorsed his competence. Then, in the assembly itself, one of the chiefs or his father or his relatives equip the young man with shield and spear. This corresponds with them to assuming the toga [of manhood] and is a youth's first public distinction. Before this he was regarded as a member of his household, but now as a member of the state. Conspicuously high birth or signal services on the part of ancestors confer the rank of chief, even in the case of very young men; they mingle with others of maturer strength and long-tested valor, who are not ashamed to be seen among their retinue. In the retinue itself degrees are observed, depending on the judgment of him whom they follow. There is great rivalry among the retainers to decide who shall have the first place with his chief, and among the cheiftains as to who shall have the largest and most spirited retinue. To be surrounded always by a large band of chosen youths means rank, strength, glory in peace, protection in war. . . .[49]

49. Medieval feudalism grew, in part, from the institution here described by Tacitus.

Should it happen that the community where they are born is inactive with long years of peace and quiet, many of the high-born youths voluntarily seek those tribes which are at the time engaged in some war. For peace is unwelcome to this people, and they distinguish themselves more readily in the midst of dangers. Besides, a great retinue cannot be maintained except by war and violence, for it is to the generosity of their chief that they look for the war horse and the murderous and masterful spear. Banqueting and a certain rude but lavish munificence take the place of pay. . . .

It is well known that none of the German tribes lives in cities and that they do not even allow houses to touch one another. They live separately and scattered, according as spring, meadow, or grove appeals to each man. They lay out their villages not, after our fashion, with buildings contiguous and connected; everyone keeps a clear space round his house. . . .

Land is taken up by a village as a whole, in quantity according to the number of the cultivators. They then distribute it among themselves on the basis of rank, such distribution being made easy by the extent of the domain occupied.

Ovid, *Laments* v. vii. 11–20, 39–56; From *LCL*

Though upon this coast there is a mixture of Greeks and Getans, it derives more from the scarce-pacified Getans. Great hordes of Sarmatians and Getans go and come upon their horses along the roads. Among them is not one who does not bear quiver and bow, and darts yellow with viper's gall. Harsh voices, grim countenances, veritable pictures of Mars, neither hair nor beard trimmed by any hand, right hands not slow to stab and wound with the knife which every barbarian wears fastened at his side. . . .

I busy my mind with studies beguiling my grief, trying to cheat my cares. What else am I to do, all alone on this forsaken shore, what other resources for my sorrows should I try to seek? If I look upon the country, 'tis devoid of charm, nothing in the whole world can be more cheerless; if I look upon the men, they are scarce men worthy of the name; they have more of cruel savagery than wolves. They fear not laws; right gives way to force, and justice lies conquered beneath the aggressive sword. With skins and loose breeches they keep off the evils of the cold; their shaggy faces are protected with long locks. A few retain traces of the Greek tongue, but even this is rendered barbarous by a Getic twang. . . . I, the Roman bard . . . am forced to utter most things in the Sarmatian tongue.

A PRO-ROMAN GERMAN CHIEFTAIN

Tacitus, *Annals* i. lvii. 6–lix. 8

Segestes himself was also present,[50] a stately sight, unafraid, secure in the knowledge that he had been a good ally. His speech was to this effect: "This is not the first day of my steadfast loyalty toward the Roman people. From the time I was granted citizenship[51] by the deified Augustus, I have chosen my friends and enemies in accordance with your interests, not from hatred of my fatherland . . . but because it was my conviction that the Romans and Germans have the same interests and that peace is better than war. Therefore I accused Arminius, the ravisher of my daughter, the violater of your treaty, before Varus [cf. vol. 1, § 203, second selection], who was then in command of the army. . . . I threw Arminius into chains and I endured the same at the hands of his followers. And now at last that I have access to you, I declare my preference for the old over the new, for peace over disorder, not for a reward, but to absolve myself of the charge of bad faith and at the same time to be a suitable mediator for a German tribe, if they show preference for repentance rather than destruction. . . ."

When news of Segestes' surrender and of his favorable reception was spread, it was received with hope or grief, according as each was against or desirous of war. . . . Arminius rushed about among the Cheruscans demanding war against Segestes, war against Caesar. And he did not restrain his taunts: "Let Segestes dwell on the conquered bank; let him restore to his sons his priesthood for the worship of men [i.e., of the emperors]; the Germans will never quite excuse the fact that they saw the *fasces* and toga between the Elbe and the Rhine. . . . If you prefer your fatherland, your ancestors, and your ancient traditions to masters and new colonies, follow Arminius as your leader to glory and freedom rather than Segestes to disgraceful servitude."[52]

50. The time is A.D. 15, during Germanicus' unauthorized invasion of Germany. Segestes, leader of the pro-Roman party in Germany, is here addressing Germanicus, who had just rescued him from Arminius (i.e., Hermann), chief of the Cheruscans, who was married to Segestes' daughter, Thusnelda.

51. The granting of Roman citizenship both to client kings and to prominent native leaders was established policy in the late Republic and during the Empire.

52. In recording the assassination of Arminius in A.D. 19 by his own kinsmen, Tacitus (*Annals* ii.

9. CLIENT STATES

The borders of the Empire were cushioned at various points by vassal states ruled by client princes invested with their power by the emperor (cf. vol. 1, § 203). These client kings contributed to the security of the frontiers by restraining their own peoples (cf. Tacitus, *Agricola* xiv: "the old, long-established policy of the Roman people of employing kings too as instruments of enslavement") and by repelling attacks from beyond their own borders. Gradually most of the client kingdoms in North Africa, Syria, Asia Minor, and Thrace were absorbed into the provincial system during the first century of the Principate. From the time of the Flavian emperors it was principally on the Rhine–Danube frontiers and along the Euphrates that such buffer states were retained. Early in the Principate occasional subsidies were granted to client states, but in time such payments came to be expected, and by the second century they were made annually. Later, such subsidies were paid to border peoples to buy off their threatened attacks against the Empire (see §§ 11, 110).

In the first year of the principate of Caligula the city of Cyzicus, a prosperous commercial center on a large island in the Propontis off the coast of the province of Asia, decreed honors to the neighboring royal dynasties of Thrace and Pontus.

IGRR, vol. IV, no. 145

Whereas the new Sun god Gaius Caesar Augustus Germanicus [CALI-GULA] has desired that the kings too, bodyguards of the empire, should join in giving illumination by their own rays, so that the majesty of his immortality should be the more venerable in this respect also, the kings being unable even if they strongly strove to find equal return for the benefactions they received from the favor of such a god; and whereas he has restored the sons of Cotys, namely Rhoemetalces and Polemo and Cotys, who were brought up with him and were his companions, to the kingdoms due them from their fathers and forefathers; and whereas they, enjoying the abundance of immortal favor, are greater than those of the past in that those took succession from their fathers whereas these have become kings by grace of Gaius Caesar to have joint rule with such gods; and whereas the favors of the gods differ from human successes as much as the sun from the night and immortal from human nature; and

---

lxxxviii. 3–4) calls Arminius "assuredly the liberator of Germany, who challenged the Roman people not only in the early stage, like other kings and leaders, but at the height of their Empire. . . . He is still a theme of song among the barbarian tribes."

whereas Rhoemetalces and Polemo, having become greater than the great and more marvelous than the illustrious, have come to our city to join in worshiping and participating in the festival with their mother as she conducts the games for the goddess the New Aphrodite Drusilla [Caligula's sister], coming not simply as to a friendly land but as if to their own native land; and whereas their mother Tryphaena, both the daughter of kings and mother of kings, regarding this as her native land, has set down here the hearth and the blessing of her life, in order to bestow blessings free from divine disfavor for the kingdoms of her children; and whereas the people, considering their presence to be most pleasing, with all zeal directed the magistrates to introduce a decree of welcome to them through which they should give thanks to them through their mother Tryphaena for the benefactions she desired to give to the city, and to make plain also the attitude of the people to them;

Therefore the people voted to praise the kings Rhoemetalces and Polemo and Cotys and their mother Tryphaena, and that on their entrance the priests and priestesses, having opened the sacred precincts and adorned the images of the gods, should pray for the eternal permanence of Gaius Caesar and for their safety; and that all the people of Cyzicus, having revealed their goodwill towards them, meeting them with the magistrates and crown-wearers, should greet them and welcome them and invite them to consider the city as their native land and to become the source of all blessing for it; and that for the welcome the ephebarch should bring the ephebes and the supervisor of education all the free boys; and that this decree is for piety to the emperor and honor to the kings.

Cassius Dio, *Roman History* LX. viii. 1–3; From *LCL*

Next Claudius restored Commagene to Antiochus, since Caligula, though he had himself given him the district, had taken it away again; and Mithridates the Iberian, whom Caligula had summoned and imprisoned, was sent home again to resume his throne. To another Mithridates, a descendant of Mithridates the Great, he granted the kingdom of Bosporus, giving to Polemo some land in Cilicia in place of it. He enlarged the domain of Agrippa of Palestine, who, happening to be in Rome, had helped him to become emperor, and he bestowed on him the rank of consul; and to his brother Herod he gave the rank of praetor and a principality. And he permitted them to enter the senate and to express thanks to him in Greek.

Tacitus, *Germany* xli–xlii

Closer to us—to follow the course of the Danube now, as I previously followed that of the Rhine—lies the state of the Hermundurians, which is loyal to the Romans. Accordingly, they are the sole Germans with whom trade is carried on not on the river bank but far within our territory, and even in the most flourishing colony [Augusta Vindelicorum (modern Augsburg)] of the province of Raetia. They cross over everywhere unguarded; and while to other tribes we display only our arms and camps, to these we have thrown open our houses and villas, for they do not covet them. . . .

Next to the Hermundurians dwell the Naristians, and then the Marcomannians[53] and the Quadians. The Marcomannians are especially famous and powerful. . . . Nor are the Naristians and Quadians inferior to them. This area is, as it were, the van of Germany, as far as it is bounded by the Danube. The Marcomannians and the Quadians down to our time still had native kings, of the noble line of Maroboduus and Tudrus; now they accept even foreign kings, but the power and sovereignty of the kings stem from Roman authority. On occasions they are aided by our armed forces, more often by subsidies, but their domestic power is not thereby reduced.[54]

THE CORONATION OF TIRIDATES

In the reign of Nero, Roman suzerainty over the vassal state of Armenia, long a bone of contention between Rome and Parthia, was challenged by Vologeses, ruler of the Parthian empire, who placed his brother Tiridates on the throne of Armenia. By a major stroke of diplomacy Tiridates was permitted to retain the kingdom, provided he acknowledged Roman overlordship and received his crown from Nero. This compromise between the two great powers, symbolized by the coronation of Tiridates in Rome in A.D. 66, assured a half century of stability and peace on the eastern frontier. The name of a Roman centurion discovered carved on a mountain face in Azerbaijan—farther east than any previously known Roman inscription—attests the presence of Roman soldiery by the western shore of the Caspian Sea in A.D. 89–96.

---

53. Their name signifies "men of the mark," that is, "border people."
54. For the invasions of the Empire by these Germanic peoples during the reign of Marcus Aurelius, see § 11, second selection.

Cassius Dio, *Roman History* LXIII. i. 2–v. 4 (abridged); Adapted from *LCL*

Tiridates set out for Rome, bringing with him not only his own sons but also those of Vologeses, Pacorus, and Monobazus.[55] Their progress all the way from the Euphrates was like a triumphal procession. . . . The prince covered the whole distance as far as Italy on horseback, and beside him rode his wife, wearing a golden helmet in place of a veil, so as not to go counter to her native customs by letting her face be seen. In Italy he was conveyed in a chariot sent by Nero and met the emperor at Naples. . . . He refused, however, to obey the order to lay aside his sword when he approached the emperor, but fastened it to the scabbard with nails. Yet he knelt upon the ground, and with arms crossed called him master, and did obeisance. . . .

After this Nero conducted him to Rome and set the diadem upon his head. The entire city had been decorated with torches and garlands, and great crowds of people were to be seen everywhere, the Forum being especially full. . . . Everything had been prepared during the night; and at daybreak Nero, wearing the triumphal garb and accompanied by the senate and the Praetorian Guards, entered the Forum. He ascended the *Rostra* and seated himself upon a chair of state. Next Tiridates and his retinue passed between lines of armed troops drawn up on either side, took their stand before the *Rostra,* and did obeisance to the emperor as they had done before. At this a great roar went up, which so alarmed Tiridates that for some moments he stood speechless, in terror of his life. Then, silence having been proclaimed, he recovered courage and quelling his pride made himself subservient to the necessities of the occasion, caring little how humbly he spoke, in view of the prize he hoped to obtain. These were his words: "Master, I am the descendant of Arsaces, brother of the kings Vologeses and Pacorus, and thy slave. And I have come to thee, my god, to worship thee as I do Mithras.[56] Whatever destiny thou spinnest for me shall be mine; for thou art my fate and my fortune." Nero replied to him as follows: "Well hast thou done to come hither in person, that meeting me face to face thou mayest enjoy my grace. For what neither thy father left thee nor thy brothers gave and preserved for thee, this do I grant thee. King of Armenia I now declare thee, that both thou and they may understand that I have the power to take away kingdoms and to bestow them." At the close of

---

55. Pacorus was a brother of Tiridates; Monobazus was king of Adiabene, a client state of Parthia.
56. For the worship of Mithras in the Roman Empire, see introduction of § 165.

these words he bade him ascend by the approach which had been built in front of the *Rostra* expressly for this occasion, and when Tiridates had been made to sit beneath his feet, he placed the diadem upon his head.

10. TERRITORIAL EXPANSION

Only two significant departures from the nonaggressive foreign policy of the Empire occurred in the first two centuries. The conquest of Britain was undertaken in the reign of Claudius primarily to protect the security of Gaul by removing a formidable focus of Celtic national independence across the Channel; southern Britain was rapidly overrun and organized into a province (A.D. 43–47), though prolonged military operations, lasting about a century, were required to end native resistance. At the beginning of the second century a radical extension of the long-established borders was projected by the soldier-emperor Trajan, who launched successive wars across the two most critical points of the frontiers and carved out the new provinces of Dacia, north of the Danube, and of Armenia, Mesopotamia, and Assyria, east of the Euphrates. At his death in A.D. 117 the Empire stood at its greatest territorial extent. But Trajan's aggressive policy had overtaxed the manpower and financial resources of the Empire; Hadrian upon his accession promptly returned to the traditional defensive policy, abandoning Trajan's annexations beyond the Euphrates but retaining Dacia because of its economic advantages.

THE CONQUEST OF BRITAIN

Cassius Dio, *Roman History* LX. xix. 1–xxii. 1 (abridged); Adapted from *LCL*

Aulus Plautius, a senator of great renown, made a campaign against Britain; for a certain Bericus [a British chieftain], who had been driven out of the island as the result of an uprising, had persuaded Claudius to send a force there. . . . [The Roman forces] put in to the island and found none to oppose them. For the Britons as a result of their inquiries had not expected that they would come and had therefore not assembled beforehand. And even when they did assemble, they would not come to close quarters with the Romans but took refuge in the marshes and the forests, hoping to wear them out in fruitless effort, so that, just as in the days of Julius Caesar [see vol. 1, § 87], they should sail back with nothing accomplished.

Plautius, accordingly, had a great deal of trouble in searching them out; but when at last he did find them, he first defeated Caratacus and then Togodumnus, the sons of Cunobellinus,[57] who was dead. (The Britons were not self-governing, but were divided into groups under various kings.) After the flight of these kings he gained by capitulation a part of the Bodunnians, who were ruled by the Catuvellanians; and leaving a garrison there, he advanced farther. . . .

Though Togodumnus perished, the Britons were far from yielding, but united all the more firmly to avenge his death. Plautius became afraid, and instead of advancing farther, proceeded to guard what he had already won, and sent for Claudius. For he had been instructed to do this in case he met with any stubborn resistance. And, in fact, extensive equipment, including elephants, had already been assembled for the expedition.

When the message reached him, Claudius . . . set out for the front. He sailed down the river to Ostia, and from there he was conveyed to Marseilles; thence, advancing partly by land and partly along the rivers, he came to the ocean and crossed over to Britain, where he joined the legions that were waiting for him near the Thames. Taking over the command of these, he crossed the stream, and engaging the barbarians, who had gathered at his approach, he defeated them in battle and captured Camulodunum [the site of modern Colchester], the capital of Cunobellinus. Thereupon he brought over to his side numerous tribes, some by treaty, others by force, and was acclaimed *imperator* several times, contrary to precedent (for no one man may receive this appellation more than once for one and the same war). He deprived the conquered of their arms and handed them over to Plautius, bidding him also subjugate the remaining districts. Claudius himself now hastened back to Rome,[58] sending ahead the news of his victory. . . . The senate on learning of his achievement gave him the title Britannicus and granted him the celebration of a triumph.

CIL, vol. VI, no. 920 (=Dessau, no. 216)[59]

To Tiberius Claudius Caesar, son of Drusus, Augustus Germanicus, *pontifex maximus,* holding the tribunician power for the eleventh year, consul five times, acclaimed *imperator* . . . times, father of his country, the Roman senate and people [dedicated this] because he received the

---

57. Cunobellinus (Cymbeline) had built up a powerful Belgic empire in Britain. His death in A.D. 42 led to internal disorders that facilitated Roman intervention.

58. Claudius spent only sixteen days in Britain.

59. From an arch in Rome erected A.D. 51–52.

surrender of eleven kings of Britain conquered without any reverse and because he was the first to subject to the sovereignty of the Roman people barbarian tribes across the ocean.

TRAJAN'S ANNEXATION OF DACIA

Cassius Dio, *Roman History* LXVIII. vi. 1, xiii. 1–xiv. 3; From *LCL*

After spending some time in Rome, Trajan made a campaign against the Dacians; for he took into account their past deeds and was grieved at the amount of money they were receiving annually, and he also observed that their power and their arrogance were increasing. . . .

Trajan constructed over the Danube a stone bridge for which I cannot sufficiently admire him.[60] Brilliant, indeed, as are his other achievements, this surpasses them. For it has twenty piers of squared stone 150 feet in height above the foundations and sixty in width, and these, standing at a distance of 170 feet from one another, are connected by arches. How, then, could one fail to be astonished at the expenditure made upon them, or at the way in which each of them was placed in a river so deep, in water so full of eddies, and on a bottom so muddy? . . . The very fact that the river in its descent is here contracted from a great flood to such a narrow channel, after which it again expands into a greater· flood, makes it all the more violent and deep, and this feature must be considered in estimating the difficulty of constructing the bridge. This, too, then, reveals the magnitude of Trajan's designs, though the bridge is of no use to us; for merely the piers are standing, affording no means of crossing. . . . Trajan built the bridge because he feared that some time when the Danube was frozen over war might be made upon the Romans on the farther side, and he wished to facilitate access to them by this means. Hadrian, on the contrary, was afraid that it might also make it easy for the barbarians, once they had overpowered the guards at the bridge, to cross into Moesia, and so he removed the superstructure.

Trajan, having crossed the Danube by means of this bridge, conducted the war with safe prudence rather than with haste; and eventually, after a hard struggle, vanquished the Dacians. . . . Decebalus,[61]

60. Trajan's famous bridge at Drobetae (Turnu-Severin, Romania), erected in A.D. 106, was the work of the Syrian architect Apollodorus. Some of the piers are still *in situ*.
61. King of the Dacians, who had unified the region during the reign of Domitian. His inroads into the province of Moesia led to a campaign by Domitian against Dacia, but the threat of attacks by

when his capital and all his territory had been occupied and he was himself in danger of being captured, committed suicide; and his head was brought to Rome. In this way Dacia became subject to the Romans,[62] and Trajan founded cities there.

HADRIAN RETURNS TO A DEFENSIVE POLICY

"Historia Augusta," *Life of Hadrian* v. 1–3; From *LCL*

On taking possession of the imperial power Hadrian at once resumed the policy of the early emperors and devoted his attention to maintaining peace throughout the world. For the nations that Trajan had conquered began to revolt; the Moors, moreover, began to make attacks, and the Sarmatians to wage war, the Britons could not be kept under Roman sway, Egypt was thrown into disorder by riots, and finally Libya and Palestine showed the spirit of rebellion. Whereupon he relinquished all the conquests east of the Euphrates and the Tigris, following, as he used to say, the example of Cato, who urged that the Macedonians, because they could not be held as subjects, should be declared free and independent.

11. THE DANUBE FRONTIER

The weakest part of the northern frontiers remained the Danube. Continued payment of subsidies to peoples beyond the borders for help in guarding the frontiers and Trajan's effort to drive a wedge between Rome's enemies by occupying Dacia failed to stabilize the area. Early in the Principate a drastic policy was introduced—the settlement of barbarian tribes on the Roman side of the frontier in exchange for border military service. From the middle of the second century the pressures on the Empire's frontiers grew in intensity, and the "philosopher-king," Marcus Aurelius, was compelled to spend nearly his entire reign at war. New impetus was given by Marcus Aurelius to the assignment to barbarians of lands in border provinces, and this policy was continued by succeeding emperors, notably Pertinax and the Severi (see § 110). This practice introduced increasing numbers of Germans into the Roman provinces and armed forces, with far-reaching consequences for the future.

---

other trans-Danubian tribes induced Domitian to grant Decebalus a favorable peace (A.D. 89), including huge subsidies.

62. The dates of Trajan's Dacian Wars are A.D. 101–102, 105–106. Scenes from his campaigns in Dacia are depicted on the reliefs of the famous Column of Trajan in Rome.

CIL, vol. XIV, no. 3,608 (=Dessau, no. 986)[63]

To Tiberius Plautius Silvanus Aelianus son of Marcus, of the Aniensian tribe, pontiff, priest of Augustus, member of the board of three for minting bronze, silver, and gold, quaestor of Tiberius Caesar, legate of the Fifth Legion in Germany, urban praetor, legate and member of the staff of Claudius Caesar in Britain [cf. § 10, first selection], consul [A.D. 45], proconsul of Asia, legate with the rank of praetor in Moesia [probably early in Nero's reign]. To this province he transplanted—and forced to pay tribute—more than 100,000 Transdanubians with their wives and children, chiefs and kings. He suppressed an incipient disturbance of the Sarmatians, although he had sent a great part of his army to the expedition against Armenia. Kings hitherto unknown or hostile to the Roman people he brought to the bank which he guarded, to honor the Roman standards. He restored to the kings of the Bastarnians and the Rhoxolanians their sons, and to the king of the Dacians his brothers, who had been captured or rescued from the enemy. From other kings he received hostages. By these measures he both strengthened and advanced the peace of the province. He also dislodged the king of the Scythians from the siege of Chersonesus,[64] which is beyond the Dnieper River. He was the first to add to the grain supply of the Roman people a great quantity of wheat from that province [Moesia]. While he was legate in Spain he was recalled to assume the prefecture of the city, and during his prefecture the senate honored him with triumphal decorations on motion of the Emperor Caesar Augustus Vespasian, whose address contained the words recorded below:

"He governed Moesia so ably that the bestowing of triumphal decorations on him should not have been delayed to my time, save only that in the course of the delay he obtained a more distinguished honor, namely the prefecture of the city."

The Emperor Caesar Augustus Vespasian made him consul for a second time [A.D. 74] while he held the said prefecture of the city.

---

63. From the mausoleum of the Plautian family at Tibur (modern Tivoli), Italy.
64. This flourishing city was near modern Sevastopol in the Crimea.

Cassius Dio, *Roman History* LXXI. iii. 1–2, xi. 1–xii. 2; From *LCL*

Marcus Aurelius himself fought for a long time, in fact almost his entire life, one might say, with the barbarians in the region of the Danube, with both the Iazyges and the Marcomannians, one after the other, using Pannonia as his base. . . .

Many of the Germans, too, from across the Rhine advanced as far as Italy and inflicted many injuries upon the Romans. They were in turn attacked by Marcus Aurelius, who opposed to them his lieutenants Pompeianus and Pertinax; and Pertinax (who later became emperor) greatly distinguished himself. Among the corpses of the barbarians there were found even women's bodies in armor. . . .

Marcus Aurelius remained in Pannonia in order to give audience to the embassies of the barbarians; for many came to him at this time also.[65] Some of them, under the leadership of Battarius, a boy twelve years old, promised an alliance; these received money and succeeded in restraining Tarbus, a neighboring chieftain, who had come into Dacia and was demanding money and threatening to make war if he should fail to get it. Others, like the Quadians, asked for peace, which was granted them, both in the hope that they might be detached from the Marcomannians, and also because they gave him many horses and cattle and besides promised to surrender all the deserters and captives—13,000 at first, and later all the others as well. The right to attend the markets,[66] however, was not granted them, for fear that the Marcomannians and the Iazyges, whom they had sworn not to receive and not to let pass through their territory, should mingle with them and, passing themselves off for Quadians, should reconnoiter the Roman positions and purchase provisions. Besides these that came to Marcus many other envoys were sent, some by tribes and some by peoples, offering surrender. Some of them were sent on campaigns elsewhere, as were also the captives and deserters who were fit for service; others received land in Dacia, Pannonia, Moesia, the province of Germany, and in Italy itself. Those who were settled at Ravenna made an uprising and even went so far as to seize possession of the city; for this reason Marcus did not again bring any of the barbarians into Italy but even banished those who had previously come there. . . .

65. The campaign of A.D. 169–170 is the subject of this passage. The Column of Marcus Aurelius, still standing in Rome, commemorates victories won in the campaigns against various tribes in 172–175.

66. That is, in the towns (usually fortress towns) on the Roman side of the Danube.

The Astingians, led by their chieftains Raüs and Raptus, came into Dacia with their entire households, hoping to secure both money and land in return for their alliance. . . . In response to urgent supplications addressed to Marcus Aurelius they received from him both money and the privilege of asking for land in case they should inflict some injury upon those who were fighting against him.

12. THE ROLE OF THE SENATE

The Senate was maintained by the emperors of the first two centuries as a major governmental organ alongside the imperial administration. It elected the magistrates (cf. note 37), enacted legislation, and served as a trial bench for major offenses (cf. § 6). But the elections now became increasingly a routine formality as the candidates were more and more designated by the emperors; and the Senate's legislative function rapidly degenerated into voicing perfunctory assent to motions submitted by the emperor either in person or through the consuls. Thus, though the emperors in general were careful to maintain and even increase the visible prestige and dignity of the order, the Senate was no longer an independent, policy-making body but only a legislative and administrative instrument of the *princeps*. Indeed, it waited upon the emperor's initiative and performed his will with such sedulous servility that it even evoked his open scorn. "What men—ready for slavery!" is said to have been Tiberius' comment on senate meetings (Tacitus, *Annals* III. lxv). The history of the Senate under the Principate is one of increasing subservience and decreasing importance proceeding *pari passu* with the increasing autocracy of the emperor (cf. § 7). In the Augustan Age few senators came from outside Italy, and even as late as the early third century a majority of them were Italians and natives of the western provinces.

Berlin Papyrus No. 611, col. 3, lines 10–22 (=*FIRA,* vol. I, no. 44); A.D. 42–51

The following is an excerpt from an address on trial procedures delivered in the senate by the Emperor Claudius.

If these proposals meet with your approval, Conscript Fathers, say so at once, frankly and honestly. If, however, you disapprove, find another solution, but do it here in this temple. Or if you want to take more time to consider the matter at greater leisure, take it, so long as you remember that, in whatever order you are called, you must state your own view. For, Conscript Fathers, it is altogether unbecoming to the majesty of this body to have one man alone, the consul designate, state his view here, copying it word for word from the motion of the consuls; and the rest of you utter but one word, "I agree," and leave saying, "Well, we spoke."

Pliny, *Letters* book II, no. II. 1–19 (abridged)

Gaius Plinius to his dear Arrianus, greeting.[67]

It is always a source of pleasure to you when something is done in the Senate that is worthy of that order. . . . Learn then what took place in the last few days—something memorable in view of the prominence of the person involved, salutary in the severity of the example, everlasting because of the importance of the affair.

Marius Priscus[68] was accused by the people of Africa, which he had governed as proconsul. Without making any defense he asked that the case be referred to a senatorial trial commission. Cornelius Tacitus and I, assigned as counsel for the provincials, felt obliged in good conscience to inform the Senate that because of Priscus' barbarity and fiendishness the charges against him were beyond the competence of such a commission, since he had accepted bribes to condemn and even execute innocent persons. . . .[69]

The case was adjourned to the next meeting of the Senate, which presented a most awesome spectacle. The emperor himself presided, since he was consul. In addition it was the month of January, when the Senate, like everything else [in Rome], is at its most crowded. . . . Picture to yourself our concern and anxiety at having to speak on so important a matter before such a gathering, and in the presence of the emperor. I have spoken in the senate on more than one occasion, you know—nowhere, indeed, do I have a friendlier audience. Yet this time I was perturbed by a novel anxiety, as if everything were new to me. Besides the considerations already mentioned, I was aware of the difficult nature of the case. There stood before me a man until lately of consular rank, until lately a member of the board of seven for conducting religious banquets, and now neither of these. It was an exceedingly onerous task to prosecute a convicted man. . . .[70]

---

67. This letter was written in A.D. 100.

68. This is the Marius of the classic remark of Juvenal quoted in vol. 1, p. 401.

69. Capital crimes were excluded from the purview of this special senatorial trial commission; cf. vol. 1, § 202.

70. Before this trial on the bribery charge Priscus had already been convicted of practicing extortion in his province and stripped of his honors.

However, I collected my spirits and wits as best I could and launched into my speech, and the approval of the listeners was as great as my own concern had been. I spoke for almost five hours, and four water-clocks were added to the twelve of largest size which had been allowed me. Indeed the very factors that had appeared as difficulties and impediments when I was waiting to speak proved advantageous when I was actually speaking. The emperor showed such solicitude, such care (it would be too much to say concern) for me, that he frequently urged a freedman of mine standing behind me to have me spare my voice and breath, thinking I was exerting myself beyond what my slight frame could bear.

Claudius Marcellinus replied in behalf of Marcianus.[71] The Senate then adjourned to the following day, for the next speech could not have been begun without being interrupted by nightfall. . . .[72] It was a fine thing, like olden times, to see the Senate interrupted by the night, called together three days in a row, held in session three days in a row. Cornutus Tertullus, consul designate, an excellent man ever firm in the cause of truth, moved that Marius pay into the public treasury the 700,000 sesterces he had accepted, and that Marius be banished from Rome and Italy and Marcianus from Africa in addition. He concluded with the further motion that, whereas Tacitus and I had faithfully and vigorously discharged the role of advocate assigned to us, the Senate judged that we had acted in a manner worthy of the duty entrusted to us.

13. SENATORIAL CAREERS

The senatorial order remained under the Principate the highest social and political class of the Roman state. But the noble families of the Republic, decimated by the civil wars and by persecution under the Julio-Claudian emperors, provided a steadily declining portion of the membership. To make up the full complement the emperors adopted the policy of bringing in new members from other classes, especially *equites* and upper-class provincials. The minimum property qualification for belonging to this nobility was 1,000,000 sesterces. The senatorial order provided the men of praetorian and consular rank, who held the higher magistracies at Rome and most of the top posts in the army and in the administration of the

71. One of the men accused of bribing Priscus.
72. The Senate could not legally act after nightfall; cf. vol. 1, p. 432.

provinces, imperial as well as senatorial. Tombstones and statue bases with inscriptions recording the careers of men of senatorial rank are extant in great numbers. A small but representative selection is given below, in chronological order ranging from the time of Augustus to the middle of the second century (cf. also the first selection in § 11). In these inscriptions, offices and honors are usually listed in chronological sequence—either in the order in which they were obtained, following an ascending order of importance, or in descending order, beginning with the last and highest.

CIL, vol. IX, no 2,845 (=Dessau, no. 915)

[Histonium, Samnium]

Publius Paquius Scaeva son of Scaeva and Flavia, grandson of Consus and Didia, great-grandson of Barbus and Dirutia; quaestor; member— after his quaestorship, in accordance with a decree of the Senate—of the board of ten for judging lawsuits; member—after his quaestorship and membership on the board of ten for judging lawsuits, in accordance with a decree of the Senate—of the board of four for capital cases; tribune of the plebs; curule aedile; criminal-court judge; praetor of the treasury; as proconsul governed the province of Cyprus; commissioner of the roads outside the city of Rome for five years in accordance with a decree of the Senate; proconsul extraordinary a second time by authority of Augustus Caesar, and by decree of the Senate sent to restore order in the remainder of the province of Cyprus; fetial; cousin and also husband of Flavia daughter of Consus, granddaughter of Scapula, great-grand-daughter of Barbus, laid to rest [here] together with her.

CIL, vol. X, no. 5,182 (=Dessau, no. 972)

[Casinum, Latium]

To Gaius Ummidius Durmius Quadratus[73] son of Gaius, of the Teretine tribe; consul; member of the board of fifteen for performing public sacrifices; legate of Tiberius Caesar Augustus in the province of Lusi-tania; legate of the deified Claudius in Illyricum, and of the same and of Nero Caesar Augustus in Syria; proconsul of the province of Cyprus; quaestor of the deified Augustus and of Tiberius Caesar Augustus; curule aedile; praetor of the treasury; member of the board of ten for judging lawsuits; curator of the public archives; prefect for distributing grain in accordance with a decree of the senate.

73. This is the same man who appears as governor of Lusitania in § 3, second selection.

CIL, vol. III, no. 4,013 (=Dessau, no. 1,005)

[Andautonia, Pannonia Superior]

Dedicated in gratitude to our patron, Lucius Funisulanus Vettonianus son of Lucius, of the Aniensian tribe; military tribune of the Legion VI Victrix; quaestor of the province of Sicily; tribune of the plebs; praetor; legate of the Legion IV Scythica; prefect of the public treasury; commissioner of the Aemilian Way; consul; member of the board of seven for conducting religious banquets; legate with rank of praetor in the province of Dalmatia, likewise in the province of Pannonia, likewise in Moesia Superior; decorated by the Emperor Domitian Augustus Germanicus[74] in the Dacian War with four crowns (the mural, the rampart-storming, the naval, and the golden), four parade spears, and four detachment banners.[75]

CIL, vol. XI, no. 5,211 (= Dessau, no. 991)

[Fulginiae, Umbria]

Dedicated in gratitude to our excellent patron Gnaeus Domitius . . . Curvius Tullus son of Sextus; consul; proconsul of the province of Africa; fetial; prefect of all auxiliary forces against the Germans; who, when he was praetor designate as candidate of the emperor, [cf, note 22], was detailed by the Emperor Vespasian Augustus as legate with rank of praetor to the army stationed in Africa and was raised to praetorian rank *in absentia;* decorated by the Emperor Vespasian Augustus and by Titus Caesar, son of the emperor, with the mural, rampart-storming, and golden crowns, with three parade spears, and three detachment banners; enrolled among the patricians; tribune of the plebs; quaestor of Caesar Augustus; military tribune of the Legion V Alauda; member of the board of ten for judging lawsuits.

74. The name of Domitian is effaced. This was the regular practice with the names of emperors declared "of damned memory" after death; cf. note 79.

75. Vettonianus was apparently cited four times for bravery, receiving as decorations on each occasion a military crown, an untipped spear, and the "company colors." These military crowns are described in Aulus Gellius, *Attic Nights* v. vi. 16–19: "The mural crown is that which is awarded by a commander to the man who is first to mount the wall and force his way into an enemy's town; therefore it is ornamented with representations of the battlements of a wall. A camp [rampart-storming] crown is presented by a commander to the soldier who is first to fight his way into an enemy's camp; that crown has a palisade as its insigne. The naval crown is commonly awarded to the armed man who is first to board an enemy ship in a sea fight; it is decorated with representations of the beaks of ships. The mural, camp, and naval crowns are regularly made of gold." (Adapted from the Loeb Classical Library.)

14. EQUESTRIAN CAREERS

Certain key posts, such as the great prefectures (see introduction to vol. 1, § 198), and most of the middle-grade administrative and military offices were assigned to men of the equestrian class, which, unlike the Senate, with its nostalgic memory of Republican rule, was wholehearted in its support of the imperial regime. Thus, there developed a public career for *equites* paralleling the senatorial career, and eventually encroaching upon it.

A major segment of the equestrian career was the civil service. The basis of the civil service organization was laid by the Emperor Claudius, who divided the record keeping and related routine operations of his administration into five or more departments and placed one of his most trusted freedmen in charge of each. One department handled the voluminous correspondence in Latin and Greek that passed between the emperor and all parts of the Empire in the form of letters, reports, resolutions, memoranda, and so forth. The functionary in charge of this office *(ab epistulis)* was thus a kind of secretary general to the emperor. The accounting office *(a rationibus)* handled the finances of the fisc, or privy purse, into which flowed the revenues from the emperors' many estates all over the Empire, from the imperial provinces, and—increasingly as financial control was progressively centralized in the hands of the emperor—even from the senatorial provinces. Requests and petitions to the emperor were the concern of the secretary *a libellis,* while the secretary *a cognitionibus* prepared all papers bearing on judicial cases coming before the emperor for decision. The secretary *a studiis* probably took care of the emperor's private library and provided him with references and material for speeches and edicts. The Flavian emperors and their successors retained and expanded this organizational structure, but, leaving the menial and clerical jobs to slaves and freedmen, they appointed with increasing frequency *equites* to the administrative posts, including the important and influential departmental secretaryships, which ranked just under the equestrian prefectures. Under the Emperor Hadrian the civil service was given its definitive organization, with fixed salaries for each rank and a fixed course of promotion. Moreover, completely separate careers were henceforth available in the civil and the military services. This separation, a departure from the age-old tradition of Roman public life, while it doubtless made for efficiency through specialization, was like Hadrian's military reorganization (§§141–143) fraught with long-term consequences for the future.[76]

76. "The separation of the civilian from the military career was dangerous, not because it deprived

The financial qualification for the equestrian order was a minimum worth of 400,000 sesterces. Admission was by birth or through promotion by the emperor. Except in individual cases this promotion was withheld from freedmen but readily granted to their sons. The following is a sampling from the numerous extant inscriptions recording equestrian careers of the first two centuries; as in the senatorial careers, the offices are generally arranged in ascending or descending order. It is noteworthy that the last of these inscriptions is a completely civilian career.

CIL, vol. VI, no. 31,856 (= Dessau, no. 1,327)

[Rome]

Lucius Julius Vehilius Gratus Julianus; prefect of the Praetorian Guard; prefect of the grain supply; financial secretary to the emperor; prefect of the praetorian fleet of Misenum; prefect of the praetorian fleet of Ravenna; imperial procurator placed in command of a detachment at the time of the war in Britain; imperial procurator of the province of Lusitania and Vettonia; imperial procurator placed in command of a detachment in . . . . ; imperial procurator and prefect of the Black Sea fleet; imperial procurator placed in command of a detachment in Achaea and Macedonia and [sent] into Spain against the rebellious Castabocans and Moors; commander of detachments at the time of the German and Sarmatian wars; prefect of the Tampian Company; prefect of the Herculean Company; tribune of the First Ulpian Cohort of the Pannonians; prefect of the Third Augustan Cohort of the Thracians; honored with military decorations by the Emperors Antoninus [MARCUS AURELIUS] and Verus for the victory in the Parthian War, likewise by Antoninus and Commodus for the victory in the German and Sarmatian wars. . . . [The rest is lost.]

CIL, vol. VI, no. 798 (= Dessau, no. 1,448)

[Rome]

Gnaeus Octavius Titinius Capito;[77] prefect of a cohort; military tribune; honored with the parade spear and the rampart-storming crown; secretary general to the emperor[78] and procurator of the imperial estate

---

men engaged in administration of some slight acquaintance with the army, but because . . . a bureaucracy of civilians was likely to be confronted before long with a more formidable body of men whose occupation was wholly military. And so it befell. In the conflict which began before the end of the second century the civilians were helpless before the army, power passed to men whose distinction in war was their only fame." (Quoted from *Cambridge Ancient History,* 11:432.)

77. He is mentioned by Pliny in his *Letters* as a gentleman and man of letters of the period.

78. Domitian, whose name is deliberately omitted; cf. note 79.

bureau; again secretary general of the deified Nerva, and on his motion awarded the insignia of praetorian rank by decree of the senate; a third time secretary general of the Emperor Caesar Trajan Augustus Germanicus; prefect of the night patrol; dedicated this thank offering to Vulcan.

CIL, vol. VI. no. 1,625b (= Dessau, no. 1,340)

[Rome]

To Marcus Petronius Honoratus son of Marcus, of the Quirine tribe; prefect of the First Cohort of the Raetians; military tribune of the dutiful and faithful Legion I Minervia; prefect of the dutiful and faithful Augustan Company of the Thracians; procurator of the mint; procurator of the five-percent tax on inheritances; procurator of the provinces of Belgium and the two Germanies; financial secretary to the emperor; prefect of the grain supply; prefect of Egypt [A.D. 147–148]; minor pontiff. The oil merchants from Baetica [dedicated this to him], their patron.

CIL, vol. X, no. 7,584 (=Dessau, no. 1,359)

[Carales, Sardinia]

To Marcus Cosconius Fronto son of Marcus, of the Pollian tribe; chosen aide-de-camp by the consul; prefect of the first cohort. . . ; military tribune of the Legion I Italica; imperial procurator for Pontus, Bithynia, Interior Pontus, and Paphlagonia for the revenue of the five-percent tax on inheritances; imperial procurator for Asia, Lycia, Phrygia, Galatia, and the Cyclades islands, likewise for the revenue of the five-percent tax on inheritances; subprefect of the grain supply of the city [of Rome]; imperial procurator for the revenue of the iron mines of Gaul; imperial procurator and prefect of the province of Sardinia. Lucretius, imperial freedman, keeper of records of the province of Sardinia, [dedicated this to him], his excellent and most just chief.

Dessau, no. 9,200

[Baalbek, Syria]

To Gaius Velius Rufus son of Salvius; first centurion of Legion XII Fulminata; prefect of detachments of Legions IX . . . , I Adiutrix, II Adiutrix, II Augusta, VIII Augusta, IX Hispana, XIV Gemina, XX Victrix, and XXI Rapax; tribune of the thirteenth urban cohort; general of the African and Mauretanian army [sent] to subdue the peoples which are in Mauretania; decorated in the Jewish War by the Emperor Vespasian and the Emperor Titus with the rampart-storming crown, collars, breastplates, and armlets, likewise decorated with the mural crown, two parade spears, and two detachment banners, and in the war of the Marcomannians, Quadians, and Sarmatians, against whom he made an expedition through the kingdom of King Decebalus of the Dacians, with the mural crown, two parade spears, and two detachment banners; procurator of the Emperor Caesar Augustus [Domitian] Germanicus in the province of Pannonia and Dalmatia; likewise procurator of the province of Raetia, with power of life and death. He was sent into Parthia and brought back to the Emperor Vespasian Epiphanes and Callinicus, the sons of King Antiochus [of Commagene], together with a large number of tribute-paying persons. Marcus Alfius Olympiacus son of Marcus, of the Fabian tribe, standard bearer, veteran of Legion XV Apollinaris [erected this].

CIL, vol XIV, no. 2,922 (=Dessau, no. 1,420)

[Praeneste, Latium]

To Titus Flavius Germanus son of Titus; superintendent of the most fortunate second German triumph of the Emperor Caesar Lucius Aurelius Commodus Augustus;[79] honored by the same with the most illustrious priesthood of minor pontiff; procurator of the five-percent tax on inheritances; procurator of the imperial estate bureau; procurator of the Great Games; procurator of the Morning Games;[80] procurator of the districts of the city with the added charge of paving streets in two parts of the city; procurator of the five-percent tax on inheritance for Umbria, Etruria, Picenum, and the district of Campania; procurator for child assistance[cf. § 70] in Lucania, Bruttium, Calabria, and Apulia; commissioner of public works and religious edifices in good repair; aedile; *duovir;* flamen of the deified Augustus; *duovir quinquennalis* [cf. vol. 1,

79. Commodus, like Nero and Domitian, was upon his death declared "of damned memory"; hence his name, as well as the words "by the same," were chiseled out of this inscription: cf. note 74. Such effacement of imperial names from subsequent inscriptions in this volume will not be indicated.

80. The Great, or Roman, Games were annual votive games to Jupiter Capitolinus, instituted, according to Roman tradition, by the ancient king Tarquinius Priscus (vol. 1, p. 60). At the height of their popularity, in the early Empire, these games were celebrated for fifteen days in September. The occasion of the Morning Games is not known; it is known from references in literature, however, that when circus games were being held, the combats with wild animals were customarily held in the mornings (cf. § 40, second selection).

chapter 7, note 44]; patron of the colony. Cerdo, his freedman, [dedicated this to him], patron incomparable, together with his sons, Flavius Maximinus, Germanus, and Rufinus, honored with equestrian rank.

15. Extension of Roman Citizenship

Under the Principate, Roman citizenship spread gradually to the provinces, progressively leading the Empire in the direction of cultural unity. Augustus' conservative policy with regard to the extension of Roman citizenship to non-Italians was, in part, a reaction to the unpopularity in Italy of Julius Caesar's granting of citizenship to a number of wealthy and influential men among the various Gallic tribes and his enrollment of some of these new citizens in the Roman Senate. With the advent of the Emperor Claudius a more liberal policy of extending citizenship to urban communities in the Romanized provinces was initiated. Claudius thus laid the basis of the systematic process, widely extended by the Flavian emperors, which, with Trajan and Hadrian, brought to the Principate emperors born of Roman families in Spain, and which by the beginning of the third century led to almost universal enfranchisement (see § 106). In this process Roman citizenship was conferred by the emperors upon entire communities in the provinces by the grant of colonial or municipal status, and upon meritorious individuals (cf. the similar grants under the Republic: vol. 1, §§ 103, 135, 152). In a special class was the grant of Roman citizenship to individuals as a reward for military service (see § 150). Newly enfranchised citizens customarily adopted the family name of the emperor who authorized the grant; hence the large number of persons named Claudius, Flavius, and Aelius in the first two centuries A.D. The inscriptions reveal many persons of provincial origin who attained the senatorial and equestrian careers. In the process of expansion "the value and meaning of the franchise change; it becomes a *passive* citizenship, in Mommsen's phrase, and is no longer sought for its political significance but as an honour, or out of sentiment; the old privileges and duties of *civis Romanus* are effaced, and the extension of the citizenship becomes the sign of the unification of the Empire within one abiding system of law" (A. N. Sherwin-White, *The Roman Citizenship,* p. 168).

ENFRANCHISEMENT OF ALPINE TRIBES

The Anaunians, Tulliassians, and Sindunians were peoples living under the jurisdiction of the municipality of Tridentum (modern Trento) in the Italian Alps. In the reign of Claudius it was discovered that, though they had for some time been conducting their affairs as Roman citizens, they had never been granted such status *de jure*. To avoid the confusion that would result from the invalidation of property titles, marriages, and other such economic and social relationships contracted in good faith, the emperor in A.D. 46 issued an edict formally granting Roman citizenship to these peoples. The edict is preserved on a bronze tablet found at Val di Non near Trento.

CIL, vol. V, no. 5,050 (= *FIRA,* vol. I, no. 71)

The edict of Tiberius Claudius Caesar Augustus Germanicus which is recorded below was issued in the consulship of Marcus Junius Silanus and Quintus Sulpicius Camerinus, on March 15, in the imperial villa at Baiae.

Tiberius Claudius Caesar Augustus Germanicus, *pontifex maximus,* holding the tribunician power for the sixth year, acclaimed *imperator* eleven times, father of his country, designated consul for the fourth time, declares:

Whereas, owing to ancient unsettled disputes which were of long standing even in the times of my uncle Tiberius Caesar—disputes which concerned only the people of Como and the Bergaleians, as far as my memory serves—Tiberius sent Pinarius Apollinaris for the settlement of the same; and whereas the latter at first because of the obstinate retirement of my uncle, and then because in the Principate of Gaius he was not requested by him to make a report, not unwisely neglected to do so; and whereas subsequently Camurius Statutus reported to me that a good many fields and woodlands are subject to my jurisdiction;[81]

I have for the matter under consideration sent Julius Planta, my friend and adviser. And since he has investigated and examined the matter with the utmost care, in consultation with my procurators, both those who were in the vicinity and those in other parts of the region, with regard to all other matters I grant him permission to make decision and render judgment in accordance with the facts laid before me in the memorandum prepared by him.

But with regard to the status of the Anaunians, the Tulliassians, and the Sindunians, some of whom, as the informer is said to have proved, are merely attributed[82] to the Tridentines, while some do not even have such connection, although I am aware that persons of this category do

---

81. That is, these lands belonged to the imperial estates.
82. That is, these peoples were subject to the jurisdiction of the municipality but did not enjoy full civic rights in the community.

not have too strong a basis for Roman citizenship; nevertheless, since they are said to have been in possession thereof by long usage and are so amalgamated with the Tridentines that they cannot be separated from them without serious harm to the flourishing municipality, I permit them by my indulgence to retain the legal status which they believed was theirs. And I am all the more inclined to do this because a number of this group are said to be actually serving in my Praetorian Guard, several indeed to have held officer rank, and some are said to be judging cases enrolled as members of jury panels at Rome.

And in granting them this benefaction, I order that all acts performed or done by them acting as if Roman citizens, whether among themselves or in relations with the Tridentines or others, shall be valid, and I allow them to keep the names which, when acting as if Roman citizens, they previously used.

ADMISSION OF PROVINCIALS TO THE SENATE

In A.D. 48 Claudius, acting as censor, proposed to fill some of the vacancies in the Roman Senate with prominent citizens from the Gallic provinces. Despite the opposition of various senators, Claudius persevered, and thereby provided the impetus that led gradually to the transformation of the senate into a body whose members were recruited from the entire Empire. The following account of Tacitus is a paraphrase of the address delivered by Claudius in the Senate. Part of the actual address is preserved in a bronze inscription found at Lyons. This inscription begins in the middle of a lengthy historical disquisition, here omitted, to show that innovations were characteristic of Roman history and that earlier Romans were liberal in their policy toward foreigners. A detailed comparison of the Lyons inscription with Tacitus' text is made by K. Wellesley in *Greece and Rome* (1954), 1:13–33.

Tacitus, *Annals* XI. xxiii. I–xxv. I

In the consulship of Aulus Vitellius and Lucius Vipstanus, when the question of filling up the membership of the senate was debated, the leading men of Gallia Comata, as it is called,[83] who had long before attained the rights of allies and Roman citizenship, sought the privilege of obtaining public offices at Rome. There was much talk of every kind

83. Literally, "long-haired Gaul," a name derived from a custom of the natives in the three Gauls conquered by Julius Caesar (see vol. 1, p. 84).

on this issue, and a variety of arguments in opposition was expressed before the emperor. "Italy," some asserted, "is not so feeble that it is unable to furnish its capital with a senate. . . . Let [the Gauls] by all means enjoy the title of citizens, but let them not cheapen the distinctions of the senators and the honors of the magistracies."

The emperor was not impressed by these and similar arguments. He at once spoke out in opposition, and, convening the senate, he addressed them as follows: "[The experience of] my ancestors . . . induces me to employ the same policy in governing the state, namely that of transferring to this city all outstanding persons, wherever found. I am fully aware that the Julian family came from Alba, the Coruncanian from Camerium, the Porcian from Tusculum, and, not to search into the past, that members have been brought into the senate from Etruria, Lucania, and the whole of Italy, that Italy itself finally was extended to the Alps,[84] so that not only individuals but even regions and tribes were amalgamated into our state. We had stable peace at home, and our foreign relations were in an excellent state in the days when the people beyond the Po were admitted to citizenship, and when, under the pretext of settling our legions throughout the world, we reinforced our exhausted Empire by joining to ourselves the most vigorous of the provincials. Do we regret that the Balbian family came over from Spain, and others not less illustrious from Narbonese Gaul? Their descendants are still here, and are not second to us in patriotism. . . .

"If you review all our wars, none was ended in a shorter time than that with the Gauls. Thenceforth there has been an unbroken and loyal peace. Mingled with us as they are now, in their way of life, in their culture, and by intermarriage, let them bring us their gold and wealth rather than keep it in isolation. Everything, members of the senate, which is now considered to be of the highest antiquity was once new. Plebeian magistrates came after patrician, Latin magistrates after the plebeian, magistrates of other peoples of Italy after the Latin. This practice, too, will establish itself, and what we are this day defending by precedents will itself be a precedent."

The emperor's address was followed by a decree of the senate, and the Aeduans were the first to obtain the right of becoming senators at Rome.

---

84. By Caesar, who granted citizenship to the inhabitants of the Po Valley (Cisalpine Gaul) at the beginning of the Civil War, in 49 B.C..

CIL, vol. XIII, no. 1,668, col. 2 (=*FIRA,* vol. I, no. 43)

. . . Surely both my great-uncle, the deified Augustus, and my uncle, Tiberius Caesar, were following a new practice when they desired that all the flower of the colonies and the municipalities everywhere—that is, the better class and the wealthy men—should sit in this senate house. You ask me: Is not an Italian senator preferable to a provincial? I shall reveal to you in detail my views on this matter when I come to obtain approval for this part of my censorship. But I think that not even provincials ought to be excluded, provided that they can add distinction to this senate house.

Look at that most distinguished and that most flourishing colony of [Gallic] Vienna [modern Vienne], how long a time already it is that it has furnished senators to this house! From that colony comes that orna-ment of the equestrian order—and there are few to equal him—Lucius Vestinus, whom I cherish most intimately and whom at this very time I employ in my affairs. And it is my desire that his children may enjoy the first step in the priesthoods, so as to advance afterwards, as they grow older, to further honors in their rank. . . . I can say the same of his brother, who because of this wretched and most shameful circum-stance cannot be a useful senator for you.

The time has now come, Tiberius Caesar Germanicus,[85] now that you have reached the farthest boundaries of Narbonese Gaul, for you to unveil to the members of the senate the import of your address. All these distinguished youths whom I gaze upon will no more give us cause for regret if they become senators than does my friend Persicus, a man of most noble ancestry, have cause for regret when he reads among the portraits of his ancestors the name Allobrogicus.[86] But if you agree that these things are so, what more do you want, when I point out to you this single fact, that the territory beyond the boundaries of Narbonese Gaul already sends you senators, since we have men of our order from Lyons and have no cause for regret. It is indeed with hesitation, mem-bers of the senate, that I have gone outside the borders of the provinces with which you are accustomed and familiar, but I must now plead openly the cause of Gallia Comata. And if anyone, in this connection, has in mind that these people engaged the deified Julius in war for ten years, let him set against that the unshakable loyalty and obedience of a

---

85. Claudius here addresses himself.

86. An honorary name derived from the Allobroges, a Gallic tribe over whom one of Persicus' ancestors probably won a military victory.

hundred years, tested to the full in many of our crises. When my father Drusus was subduing Germany, it was they who by their tranquillity afforded him a safe and securely peaceful rear, even at a time when he had been summoned away to the war from the task of organizing the census which was still new and unaccustomed to the Gauls. How difficult such an operation is for us at this precise moment we are learning all too well from experience, even though the survey is aimed at nothing more than an official record of our resources. [The rest is lost.]

CITIZENSHIP FOR AN EGYPTIAN

Pliny, *Letters* book x, nos. 5–7

[Pliny to the Emperor Trajan]

Last year, my lord, when I was attacked by a very serious illness and in danger of my life, I called in a therapist, whose solicitude and devotion I can adequately reward only by your gracious benevolence. I therefore beg you to grant him Roman citizenship; for he is of alien status, the freedman of an alien woman. His name is Harpocras, and his patroness, now long since dead, was Thermuthis, daughter of Theo.

I beg you also to grant full citizen rights[87] to Hedia and Harmeris, freedwomen of Antonia Maximilla, a lady of the highest rank, at whose instance I make this request of you.

[Pliny to the Emperor Trajan]

I thank you, my lord, for your ready compliance in bestowing full citizen rights on the freedwomen of the lady related to me, and Roman citizenship on Harpocras, my therapist. But as I was preparing a declaration, as you had directed, of his age and census rating, I was advised by persons more informed than myself that, since he is an Egyptian, I should have obtained for him first Alexandrine citizenship, then Roman. Not realizing that there was any difference between Egyptians and other aliens,[88] I had contented myself with writing you only that he had been manumitted by an alien woman and that his patroness had long since died. Still, I do not regret this ignorance of mine, since it has resulted in my being further obligated to you on behalf of the same man.

87. Slaves manumitted by a woman, even though she possessed Roman citizenship, acquired only the lesser Latin status; cf. vol. 1, § 205, and vol. 2, introduction to § 64.

88. On the special disabilities of Egyptians, see § 79. They were rigidly excluded from both Roman and Alexandrine status, being forbidden to marry even a freedman of an Alexandrian.

And so, that I may enjoy your benefaction in proper form, I beg you to confer upon him both Alexandrine and Roman citizenship. That your kindness may encounter no further delay, I have already sent his age and census rating to your freedmen[89] as you had directed.

[Trajan to Pliny]

Following the precedent set by the emperors it is my policy not to grant Alexandrine citizenship indiscriminately. But, since you have already obtained Roman citizenship for Harpocras, your therapist, I cannot deny you this further request. You will have to let me know from what nome he comes, so that I may send a letter for you to my friend Pompeius Planta, the prefect of Egypt.

CITIZENSHIP FOR AN AFRICAN HEADMAN

The first of these three documents inscribed on a bronze tablet is a letter written in or c. 168 by the Emperors Marcus Aurelius and Lucius Verus to the governor of Mauretania Tingitana in response to his request that Roman citizenship be granted to one Julianus (I), a leading local figure, and to his wife and children, the eldest of whom was also named Julianus (II). The second document, of A.D. 177, is a similar grant of Roman citizenship to the wife and children of Julianus (II), who had succeeded his father as headman. The third document, bearing a date equivalent to July 6, 177, is an extract from the imperial register *(commentarius)* of such grantees; from it we learn that the grant was authenticated by the signatures of the twelve members of the emperors' advisory council *(consilium)*, one of them being the learned jurist Quintus Cervidius Scaevola and all of them past holders of the consulship or other high office; the exactitude of the copy is attested by the imperial freedman in charge of that archive.

By these grants this North African family added Roman citizenship to its existing local status; this is explicitly stated by the proviso "with the law of their people remaining intact." Such dual citizenships are in evidence from the time of Augustus (cf. vol. 1, § 202). But the wording of the proviso in this inscription is new, and it helps us to a better understanding of the imperfectly preserved similar clause in Caracalla's universal grant of Roman citizenship (§ 106).

89. That is, secretaries. The Emperor Claudius entrusted the operation of his most important administrative departments to a number of freedmen of the imperial household, who, as a result, became veritable powers behind the throne and amassed tremendous fortunes, including landed estates. Pallas was the financial secretary and second in importance only to Narcissus, who was a kind of secretary-general (cf. introduction to § 14).

AE, 1971, no. 534 (=*Journal of Roman Studies* [1973], 63:86–87)

Copy of a letter of our Emperors Antoninus [Marcus Aurelius] and Verus Augusti to Coiedius Maximus. We have read the petition of Julianus the Zegrensian which was attached to your letter, and although Roman citizenship, except when it has been evoked by very great services, is not normally granted to members of those peoples by imperial indulgence, nevertheless since you affirm that he is one of the leading men of his people and is most loyal in his ready assistance to our interests, and since we do not think that many clans among the Zegrensians can make equal assertions regarding their services (although we desire that very many may be impelled by the honor conferred by us upon his house to emulate Julianus), we do not hesitate to grant to him himself, his wife Ziddina, likewise their children Julianus (II), Maximus, Maximinus, and Diogenianus, Roman citizenship with the law of their people remaining intact.

Copy of a letter of our Emperors Antoninus [Marcus Aurelius] and Commodus Augusti to Vallius Maximianus. We have read the petition of the headman [Julianus II] of the Zegrensian peoples and we have noted with what favor of Epidius Quadratus your predecessor he is aided. Induced by the testimonial of the latter and by his own merits and examples which he adduces, we have granted to his wife and children Roman citizenship with the law of their people remaining intact. So that this may be recorded in our register, find out what the age of each is and write us.

Copied and verified from the register of those granted Roman citizenship by the deified Augustus, by Tiberius Caesar Augustus, by Gaius Caesar, by the deified Claudius [and all the other emperors to Commodus except Otho and Vitellius], which [register] the freedman Asclepiodotus presented [for inspection], the following extract: In the consulship of the Emperor Caesar Lucius Aurelius Commodus Augustus and Marcus Plautius Quintilius, the day before the Nones of July, at Rome.

Faggura, wife of Julianus (II) headman of the Zegrensian people, aged 22 years, Juliana 8 years,[90] Maxima 4 years, Julianus (III) 3 years, Diogenianus 2 years, the children of the aforementioned Julianus (II).

90. It appears that Faggura was already married and a mother when she was fourteen years old.

At the request of Aurelius Julianus (II) headman of the Zegrensians by petition, and on the recommendation of Vallius Maximianus by letter, we have granted them Roman citizenship with the law of their people remaining intact and without any reduction of the tribute and taxes [payable] to the [Roman] people and the imperial treasury.

> Done the said day, said place, under the said consuls. I, Asclepio-dotus, freedman, have verified.
>   Signatures:

[The twelve notables of the Emperors' *consilium:* cf. Introduction.]

16. SOCIAL POLICY AND URBANIZATION

Through the evolution of inherent socioeconomic forces and the conscious policy of the emperors (especially Augustus, Claudius, Vespasian, and Trajan) the Roman Empire at its height assumed the appearance of a vast aggregate of cities. The policy of extending Roman citizenship to merito-rious individuals and groups in Romanized areas and of converting ad-vanced rural areas into urban communities was calculated to achieve two fundamental aims: to develop an Empire-wide base of privileged support-ers of the regime, and to spread the burdens of administration and tax collection among the numerous self-governing municipalities (cf. §§ 63–69). A further result, however, was the eventual polarization of society into two strata, *honestiores* (a propertied, educated, office-holding upper class) and *humiliores*.

  Most of the evidence on these imperial policies is to be found in archaeological and epigraphical remains. The following is an idealized, rhetorical evaluation of the Empire in the middle of the second century. (For Aelius Aristides, see note 45).

Aelius Aristides, *To Rome* lix–lx, lxiii–lxxi, xciii–civ; Adapted from the translation of
S. Levin (Glencoe, Illinois, 1950)

Most noteworthy by far and most marvelous of all is the grandeur of your concept of citizenship[?]. There is nothing on earth like it. For you have divided all the people of the Empire—when I say that, I mean the whole world—in two classes: the more cultured, better born, and more influential everywhere you have declared Roman citizens and even of the same stock; the rest vassals and subjects. Neither sea nor any inter-

vening distance on land excludes one from citizenship. No distinction is
made between Asia and Europe in this respect. Everything lies open to
everybody; and no one fit for office or a position of trust is an alien.
There exists a universal democracy under one man, the best *princeps* and
administrator. . . .

You have not made Rome a world's conceit, by letting nobody else
share in it. No, you have sought out the complement of citizens it
deserves. You have made the word "Roman" apply not to a city but to
a universal people. . . .

So, of course, things as they are satisfy and benefit both poor and
rich. No other way of life remains. There is one pattern of government,
embracing all. Under you, what was formerly thought incapable of
conjunction has been united, rule of an Empire at once strong and
humane, mild rule without oppression[?]. Thus towns are free of garrisons, whole provinces are adequately guarded by battalions and cavalry
companies, which are not stationed in force in the various cities of each
people but scattered through the countryside among a multitude of the
population, so that many provinces do not know where their garrison
is.[91]

But if a city anywhere, through excessive bigness, has outgrown its
capacity to use self-restraint, you do not withhold from such the men
needed to take charge of and watch over it.[92]

Moreover, all people are happier to send in their tribute to you than
anyone would be to collect it for himself from others. . . .

Instead of quarreling over empire and primacy, through which all
wars formerly broke out, some of your subjects . . . relax in utmost
delight, content to be released from troubles and miseries, and aware
that they were formerly engaged in aimless shadow-boxing. Others do
not know or remember what territory they once ruled. . . . But they
accepted your leadership fully, and in a flash revived. How they came to
this they cannot say; they know nothing, except to look with awe upon
the present state of affairs. . . . Whether there ever were wars is now
doubted; most people hear of them in the category of empty legends.
Whenever they occurred somewhere along the frontiers, as is natural in
a vast, measureless empire . . . then just like legends the wars passed by
quickly and so did talk of them. Such profound peace has come to you,
although war is your ancestral way of life. . . .

91. On the garrison army of the second century, see §§ 142–144.

92. For the agents of the central administration who served as curators of municipalities in the
second century, see § 69.

Were there ever so many cities, inland and maritime? Were they ever so thoroughly modernized? Could a person in the past travel thus, counting up the cities by the number of days on the road, sometimes even going past two or three of them . . . ?

The upshot is that not only were former empires so inferior at the top, but also the peoples whom they ruled were none of them on a par, in numbers or in caliber, with those same peoples under you. You may contrast the tribe of the past with the city there today. Indeed, it may be said that they were virtually kings of wilderness and fortresses, while you alone govern cities.

The whole world, as on a holiday, has doffed its old costume—of iron—and turned to finery and all festivities without restraint. All other competition between cities has ceased, but a single rivalry obsesses every one of them—to appear as beautiful and attractive as possible. Every place is full of gymnasia, fountains, gateways, temples, shops, and schools. . . . Gifts never stop flowing from you to the cities; and because of your impartial generosity to all, the leading beneficiaries cannot be determined. Cities shine in radiance and beauty, and the entire country-side is decked out like a pleasure ground. . . . Festivity, like a holy, unquenchable fire, never fails, but goes around from one place to the next and is always somewhere, for it fits in with the universal prosperity. And so, only those outside your Empire, if there are any, are fit to be pitied for losing such blessings. . . . Greek and barbarian can now readily go wherever they please with their property or without it. It is just like going from their own to their own country. Neither the Cilician Gates nor the narrow, sandy approaches through Arabia to Egypt present any danger. Nor do impassable mountains, vast stretches of river, or inhospitable barbarian tribes. For safety, it is enough to be a Roman, or rather, one of your subjects. . . .

You have surveyed the whole world, built bridges of all sorts across rivers, cut down mountains to make paths for chariots, filled the deserts with hostels, and civilized it all with system and order. . . .

One might thus appraise and evaluate the state of things before your rule and under you: before it, they were all mixed up topsy-turvy, drifting at random. But with you in charge, turmoil and strife ceased, universal order and the bright light of life and government came in, laws were proclaimed, and the gods' altars acquired sanctity. . . . Now, universal and manifest freedom from fear has been granted to all—the earth itself and its inhabitants. It appears to me that they are wholly rid of oppression, while getting many opportunities for good guidance, and that the gods, looking benevolently on your empire, helped in ordering it and have vouchsafed you secure possession of it.

17. TAXATION: THE GRAIN SUPPLY OF ROME (ANNONA)

Famine was an ever-present threat in antiquity, especially in the large urban centers, and bread riots were a common phenomenon (cf. § 68). In Rome the food problem became especially acute with the decline of Italian cereal production in the second century B.C. (cf. vol. I, p. 474). Thereafter, one of the chief tasks of the government was the *cura annonae*—keeping the capital city supplied with grain from overseas provinces and maintaining normal market prices. Under the Republic this was one of the duties of the aediles, but it was found necessary on several critical occasions to appoint special grain commissioners. Augustus made the *cura annonae* one of the emperor's permanent responsibilities, and it remained a department of the imperial administrative structure for over five hundred years. At its head was the prefect of the grain supply. In addition to its headquarters and central storehouses in Rome the department had substations at the Italian harbors of Puteoli and Ostia, where the new harbor of Portus was built in A.D. 42 especially to provide improved facilities for handling the grain supply. There were also agents, offices, and storehouses in other important ports of the Empire, and in the prime grain-producing provinces, Egypt and Africa. Altogether this far-flung organization conducted the largest single shipping operation in the Empire, and the emperors enacted special measures to assure a sufficiency of bottoms for the transportation of the *annona*. While no comprehensive statistics are available, one ancient source records that under Augustus Rome received 20,000,000 *modii* a year from Egypt, and another states that in the first century the Egyptian grain tribute fed the city for four months. On the grain fleet, see further §§ 28–29.

Tacitus, Annals III. liv.6–8

The following is a part of Tacitus' paraphrase of a letter from the Emperor Tiberius to the senate, A.D. 22.

But no one makes any proposal about the fact that Italy is dependent on supplies from abroad, that the life of the Roman people is tossed every day at the mercy of wave and wind. And if the harvests of the provinces ever fail to come to the aid of our masters, slaves, and fields, then our parks and villas [in Italy] will support us forsooth. This, Conscript Fathers, is one of the services that the emperor assures; if neglected, this will drag the state down in utter ruin.

"A HUNGRY PEOPLE DOES NOT LISTEN TO REASON"

Tacitus, *Annals* VI. xiii. 1–2, XII. xliii [93]

The excessive price of grain led practically to insurrection, and for several days the theater was the scene of many demands shouted with greater boldness than was customary toward the emperor. Aroused by this, Tiberius upbraided the magistrates and the senators for failing to restrain the populace by the authority of the state, and reminded them of the provinces from which he imported the supply of grain and of how much greater a supply it was than Augustus had provided.

.   .   .   .

Many prodigies occurred in that year. . . . A shortage of grain again and the resulting famine were regarded as a portent. And people did not merely grumble in private, but they surrounded Claudius with mutinous clamor as he sat in judgment, drove him to the edge of the Forum, and kept jostling him about until the arrival of a band of soldiers made it possible for him to force his way through the hostile throng. It was ascertained that the city had provisions for fifteen days, no more, and the desperate situation was relieved only by the great mercy of the gods and the mildness of the winter. And yet, by heaven, in former times Italy used to export supplies for the legions into far-distant provinces, and even now it does not suffer from infertility, but it is we who prefer to cultivate Africa and Egypt and commit the life of the Roman people to ships and all their risks.

Suetonius, *Life of Claudius,* xviii–xix; Adapted from *LCL*

Claudius always gave scrupulous attention to the care of the city and the supply of grain. . . . When there was a scarcity of grain because of long-continued droughts, he was once stopped in the middle of the Forum by

---

93. These selections refer to the years 32 and 51, respectively. The quotation in the caption is from Seneca, *On the Shortness of Life,* xviii. 5. The same thought is also given pithy expression by Seneca's nephew, the poet Lucan, in his *Pharsalia* III. 55–58: "The grain supply provides the mainsprings of hatred and popularity. Hunger alone sets cities free, and reverence is purchased when rulers feed the lazy mob: a hungry populace knows no fear." For other food riots see § 68. In addition to supplying food, the emperors relied on spectacles and circus games to keep the Roman populace quiet; cf. § 40

a mob and so pelted with abuse and at the same time with pieces of bread that he was barely able to make his escape to the palace by a back door. After this experience he resorted to every possible means to bring supplies to Rome, even in the winter season. To the importers he held out the certainty of profit by assuming the expense of any loss that they might suffer from storms.[94] To those who built merchant ships he accorded great benefits adapted to the conditions of each, namely, to a citizen, exemption from the Papian–Poppaean Law; to one of Latin rights, full citizenship; to women, the privileges of mothers of four children.[95] And all these provisions are in force today.

TRANSPORTING THE GRAIN TO ROME

Seneca speaks of the workaday cares of the functionaries who "see to it that the grain pours into the storehouses unadulterated through fraud or negligence on the part of those who transport it, that it does not collect moisture and become heated and spoiled, that it tallies in measure and weight" (*On the Shortness of Life* xix. 1). An example of the precautions taken in the collection of the *annona* is afforded by the following text, written on a small pottery jar which contained a sealed sample of a shipment of grain loaded on two river boats in Middle Egypt for transportation to Alexandria. There the sample would be opened and compared with the cargoes to make sure the latter had not suffered adulteration or spoilage en route; if they had, the loss would have to be made good by the region of origin. The soldiers who accompanied the shipment guarded both the sealed sample and the cargoes against tampering and theft; in the second century this duty was transferred, in Egypt at least, to civilians as a compulsory public service. From Alexandria the *annona*—except for a small part retained for feeding the administration and the soldiers stationed in the province—was transshipped to Rome, doubtless under similar precautions. The second text below is a letter from a man who made the trip from Egypt to Italy on a grain ship as a member of the crew or possibly as one of the soldiers of the guard. (See further § 28.)

---

94. Cf. the similar arrangement during the Second Punic War, in vol. 1, §§ 92–93. Tiberius, besides fixing grain prices, granted a subsidy of two sesterces per *modius* to grain merchants (Tacitus, *Annals* ii. lxxxvii). For special privileges accorded to shipowners engaged in the grain trade, see §§ 29, 116.

95. For the significance of these different privileges, see vol. 1, §§ 204 and 205, and vol. 2, §§ 46 and 91.

Journal of Juristic Papyrology (1950), 4:106–115; 2 B.C.

From the Oxyrhynchite Nome

Ammonius son of Ammonius, pilot of a government boat with the emblem . . . attached to him as escort being Lucius Oclatius, soldier of Legion XXII, second cohort, century of Maximus Stoltius; and Hermias son of Petalus, pilot of a second boat with the emblem *Egypt,* attached to him as escort being Lucius Castricius, soldier of Legion XXII, fourth cohort, century of Titus Pompeius. This is a sample of the cargo we have loaded from the harvest of the 28th year of Augustus—Ammonius, 433¼ artabs of wheat, loaded to the rail; Hermias, likewise 433¼ artabs of wheat—a total of 866½ artabs of wheat consigned by Leonidas and Apollonius, *sitologi* of the Lower Toparchy, Eastern Division, plus the supplement of one half artab of wheat per hundred. We loaded from the 2d of Hathyr to the 4th of the same month, and we have sealed [this jar] with both our seals, Ammonius' with a figure of Ammon, Hermias' with a figure of Harpocrates. Year 29 of Augustus, Hathyr 4.

Berlin Papyrus No. 27 (= *Select Papyri,* no. 113); second or third century A.D.

Irenaeus to Apollinarius, his dearest brother, many greetings. I pray continually for your health, and I myself am well. I want you to know that I reached land [probably at Ostia-Portus] on the 6th day of the month Epeiph [June 30], and we finished unloading on the 18th of the same month [July 12]. I went up to Rome on the 25th of the same month [July 19], and the place received us as the god willed.[96] We are daily expecting our discharge, so that up to today nobody in the grain fleet has been able to leave. I salute your wife warmly, and Serenus, and all who love you, each by name. Farewell. Mesore 9 [August 2].

18. Taxation: Customs Duties and Transit Tolls

In addition to direct taxes on land *(tributum)* and other personal property, the central government imposed a variety of indirect taxes *(vectigalia)* upon the inhabitants of the Empire. The most important of the indirect taxes were the customs dues *(portorium)* exacted at harbors and at certain

---

96. This noncommittal phrase suggests that the visit was not an unmitigated success.

points along the road system. For the collection of this impost the Roman Empire was divided, probably under Tiberius, into about ten large customs districts. At the land and sea frontiers of these districts customs dues were exacted on goods entering or leaving, and at certain points within these districts (e.g., at bridges or ferries) transit tolls were collected. The *portorium* was not a protective tariff, since it was payable on exports and imports alike; its purpose was simply to provide another source of revenue for the imperial fisc. Except on the eastern frontier of the Empire, where the rich oriental luxury trade was taxed at the rate of 25 percent, the rate at the district borders was generally 2 or 2.5 (in some cases 5) percent *ad valorem;* the tolls collected inside customs districts were generally at a much lower rate. In addition to this imperial duty, many towns had the right to collect local *octrois* and transit tolls for their municipal treasuries.

RIGHT OF SEARCH

The following is part of the regulations of a customs bureau.

Pseudo-Quintilian, *Declamations* ccclix[97]

Except for means of transportation, all articles shall be subject to a tax of 2½ percent, payable to the tax farmer. The tax farmer has the right of search. Undeclared articles shall be confiscated. The person of a matron may not be searched.

The following is a fragment of the regulations governing the collection of duties payable at the customs barrier either at Memphis (for Nile-borne traffic) or at one of the Red Sea ports of Egypt.

Oxyrhynchus Papyrus No. 36 (= Wilcken, no. 273); second or early third century

. . . if the customs collector requires the boat to be unloaded, the merchant shall unload. If anything other than what he declared is found, it shall be liable to confiscation; but if nothing is found, the customs collector shall reimburse the merchant for the expense of unloading . . . and they shall receive from the tax farmers a written certification, so that they may be unmolested thereafter. . . . [The rest is lost.]

Malpractices on the part of customs collectors in connection with clearance of cargoes are revealed in this fragment from an edict of the prefect of Egypt.

97. From one of two collections of *declamationes* (cf. introduction to § 55), transmitted under Quintilian's name but of uncertain authorship; cf. vol. 1, p. 23.

Princeton Papyrus No. 20 (= *SB*, no. 8,072); second century

. . . prefect of Egypt declares: I am informed that the tax farmers have employed exceedingly clever devices against those passing through the country and, in addition, are fraudulently demanding charges not due them and are laying hold of those who are in haste, so that some may buy from them a speedier departure. I therefore order them to desist from such greed. . . . [The rest is fragmentary.]

THE TARIFF OF COPTUS

This inscription, dating from A.D. 90, contains a schedule, not of customs dues (as formerly thought), but of toll fees charged various categories of persons and goods for permits to use one of the roads connecting the caravan terminal of Coptus on the Nile with Red Sea ports. These roads were provided by the government with water stops, caravanserais, and protective garrisons, and the charges were doubtless intended to defray the expense of maintaining these services.

IGRR, vol. I, no. 1,183 (= *OGIS*, no. 674)

By order of Mettius Rufus[?], prefect of Egypt. Lucius Antistius Asiaticus, prefect of Mt. Berenice, has had engraved on this stone the sums which must be exacted in accordance with the regulations by the tax farmers of the toll fees subject to the jurisdiction of the customs controller in Coptus.

For a captain in the Red Sea trade	8 drachmas
For . . .	6 drachmas
For a lookout officer	10 drachmas
For a guard	10 drachmas
For a sailor	5 drachmas
For a shipwright's helper	5 drachmas
For an artisan	8 drachmas
For courtesans	108[a] drachmas
For sailors'[?] women	20 drachmas
For soldiers' women	20 drachmas

[a] This high fee represents not (as usual to be thought) an attempt to discourage prostitution, but a form of tax upon that occupation.

For a permit for a camel	1 obol
For seal on permit	2 obols
For each permit for a man outbound up country[a]	1 drachma
For [permits for] all women, at the rate of	4 drachmas
For a donkey	2 obols
For a covered wagon	4 drachmas
For a mast	20 drachmas
For a yardarm	4 drachmas
For a funeral (going and return)	1 drachma 4 obols

The ninth year of the Emperor Caesar Domitian Augustus German-icus, Pachon 15.

[a] In addition to toll fees, an extra charge was made for the requisite official permit.

The ninth year of the Emperor Caesar Domitian Augustus Germani-cus, Pachon 15.

19. THE IMPERIAL POST

One of the enduring innovations of Augustus was the establishment of an imperial post *(cursus publicus)* for official dispatches and personages. The burden of maintaining and financing the relays of horses and carriages, the posting stations, and the hostels for official travelers was imposed upon the cities and towns on the trunk roads in all parts of the Empire through which the service ran. Protests by communities against the heavy costs and against irregularities in the requisitioning of the services led to various relief measures by the emperors. In the second century a separate imperial bureau was established to administer the imperial post. Though under Hadrian and Septimius Severus the entire costs were temporarily assumed by the fisc, by the end of the third century responsibility for the mainte-nance of the post became one of the compulsory duties of local officials.

Suetonius, *Life of Augustus* xlix. 3

To enable what was going on in every province to be reported and known more speedily and promptly, Augustus stationed at short inter-vals along the military roads first young men, and later conveyances. The latter arrangement appeared the more convenient, since the same man brings a dispatch all the way from its source and can, if occasion demands, be questioned as well.

CIL, vol. III, no. 7,251 (= Dessau, no. 214)

[Tegea, Greece, A.D. *49/50]*

Tiberius Claudius Caesar Augustus Germanicus, *pontifex maximus,* holding the tribunician power for the ninth year, acclaimed *imperator* sixteen times, father of his country, declares:

Whereas I have often tried to lighten for the colonies and municipalities not only of Italy but also of the provinces, and likewise for the communities of every province, the burdens of providing conveyances; and whereas it seems to me that I have devised many and sufficient remedies, still . . . men's negligence. . . . [The rest is lost.]

Pliny, *Letters* book x, nos. 45–46, 120

[Pliny to the Emperor Trajan]

I beg, my lord, that you write and free me from uncertainty about permits to use the imperial post which have expired — whether you wish them to be honored at all and for how long. For I fear that I may err through ignorance in one of two directions — either approving illegal permits or blocking necessary ones.

[Trajan to Pliny]

Travel permits which have expired must not be in use. I therefore make it an especial rule to send out new permits to all the provinces before there can be any need of them.

[Pliny to the Emperor Trajan]

Up to this time, my lord, I have granted permits to use the imperial post to no one and for no purpose except in your service. This fixed rule of mine has been broken by an emergency. My wife, hearing of her grandfather's death, wanted to rush to her aunt, and I thought it hard to refuse her a permit, as the amenities of such an obligation depend on speed, and I knew that you would approve the reason for a journey dictated by filial devotion. I write you this because it seemed to me I should be ungrateful not to confess that along with other benefits I owe this too to your kind favor that, in reliance upon it, I did not hesitate to

act as if I had consulted you, when I should have acted too late had I
waited to consult you.

[Trajan's reply consists of one sentence approving Pliny's action.]

20. REMISSION OF TAXES

Among the forms of help granted by the emperors to distressed areas was
a remission of, or moratorium on, the payment of taxes. In the second
century, as the Roman Empire proved unable to produce year in and year
out the revenues demanded by the imperial regime, the emperors began
to resort on occasion to wholesale cancellation of tax arrears. By this
palliative they attempted to achieve a kind of economic "pump priming"
and thereby strengthen the allegiance of the peoples of the Empire. Thus,
in addition to the erection of the following inscription at Rome, Hadrian's
tax remission was celebrated also by the issuance of coins bearing the
legend: "Nine hundred million sesterces in old arrears canceled."

CIL, vol. VI, no. 967 (=Dessau, no. 309); A.D. 118

[Dedicated by] the Roman Senate and people to the Emperor Caesar
Trajan HADRIAN Augustus, son of the deified Trajan Parthicus, grandson
of the deified Nerva, *pontifex maximus,* holding the tribunician power
for the second year, twice consul, the first and only one of all the
emperors to cancel 900,100,000 sesterces owed to the fisc and by this
liberality to render not only the citizens now living but also their descendants free from worry.

"Historia Augusta," *Life of Hadrian* vii. 6

Hadrian canceled a countless sum of money owed to the fisc by private
debtors in Rome and Italy, and also vast sums of arrears in the provinces, and he burned the records of indebtedness in the Forum of the
deified Trajan in order to strengthen the general sense of security.

Cassius Dio, *Roman History* LXXI. xxxii. 2

Marcus Aurelius remitted all debts incurred by anyone to the imperial
fisc or to the state treasury over a period of forty-five years in addition
to the fifteen years of Hadrian,[98] and he ordered all the records relating
to these debts to be burned in the Forum.

98. That is, Hadrian's remissions extended to A.D. 133, and Marcus Aurelius forgave arrears from
178 back to 133.

21. IMPERIAL LARGESS

From the time of Augustus, the distribution of largess to the soldiery and the populace of Rome was reserved for the emperors. This policy of keeping the army and people contented and loyal through repeated donatives to the soldiers and through *frumentationes* (grain doles) and *congiaria* (gifts of money) to the Roman populace was maintained for centuries and constituted a heavy drain on the imperial fisc. It has been estimated that in the 250 years between the dictatorship of Caesar and the accession of Septimius Serverus about 1,500,000,000 *denarii* were expended by the emperors on *congiaria* alone. In time the soldiers came to consider such donatives a regular emolument, and quickly became disaffected from an emperor who neglected to distribute donatives they considered due them. In A.D. 68–69, and again in 193, when the Principate was disputed by several claimants, the Praetorian Guard readily transferred their support to the highest bidder (see §§ 104–105).

Cassius Dio, *Roman History* LIX. ii. 1–4

By paying to the others all the bequests made by Tiberius as if they were his own, Caligula gained among the masses some reputation for generosity. And together with the senate he immediately inspected the Praetorian Guards when they were drilling, and distributed to them the 1,000 sesterces apiece which had been bequeathed to them, and he added an equal amount to this on his own account. And to the people he paid the 45,000,000 sesterces which had been bequeathed to them, and in addition the 240 sesterces apiece which they had not received on the occasion of his assuming the toga of manhood, together with an additional 60 sesterces in interest. He also honored the bequests to the urban cohorts, to the night patrol, to those on the army rolls who were outside Italy, and to any other group of citizen troops who were in the smaller garrisons, the urban cohorts receiving 500 sesterces apiece, and all the rest 300. . . . In some instances it was through fear of the people and the soldiers that he did this, but for the most part on principle.[99]

99. Cf. Suetonius, *Life of Claudius* x. 4: [When he was acclaimed emperor by the Praetorian Guard], "Claudius permitted the armed assembly to swear allegiance to him and promised 15,000 sesterces to each man, the first of the Caesars to secure the fidelity of the soldiery by bribery"; Cassius Dio, *Roman History* LX. xiii. 4: "On the first anniversary of the day he had been declared emperor, Claudius did nothing out of the ordinary except to give the Praetorians one hundred sesterces, a thing he did every year thereafter."

22. PUBLIC WORKS

An enormous number of public works in Rome, Italy, and the provinces was erected out of the funds of the imperial fisc. The remains of many of these are still to be seen in all parts of the Empire. Characteristically utilitarian, the public monuments of the imperial builders, both religious and civic, were executed on a grandiose scale. An important purpose of the extensive public works programs of the emperors was to provide employment for surplus labor. An anecdote relates that when a mechanical engineer offered to transport heavy columns inexpensively, Vespasian refused to permit the labor-saving device to be used, declaring, "You must allow me to feed my poor commons" (Suetonius, *Life of Vespasian* xviii).

Suetonius, *Life of Claudius* xx; Adapted from *LCL*

The public works which Claudius completed were great and essential rather than numerous; they were in particular the following: an aqueduct begun by Caligula; also the drainage channel of Lake Fucinus[100] and the harbor at Ostia, although in the case of the last two he knew that Augustus had refused the former to the Marsians in spite of their frequent requests, and that the latter had often been considered by the deified Julius but given up because of its difficulty. He brought to the city on stone arches the cool and abundant springs of the Claudian aqueduct . . . and at the same time the channel of the New Anio, distributing them into many beautifully ornamented fountains. He made the attempt on the Fucine Lake as much in the hope of gain as of glory, inasmuch as there were some who offered to drain it at their own cost provided the land that was drained be given them. He finished the drainage canal, which was three miles in length, partly by leveling and partly by tunneling a mountain, a work of great difficulty requiring eleven years, although he had 30,000 men at work all the time without interruption. He constructed the harbor at Ostia [cf. § 17] by building curving breakwaters on the right and left, while before the entrance he placed a mole in deep water. To give this mole a firmer foundation he first sank the ship in which the great obelisk had been brought from

100. In central Italy, in the Marsian region. The engineering work, not completed until A.D. 52, was only partially successful. The complete drainage of the lake was not achieved until the nineteenth century.

Egypt,[101] and then securing it by piles built upon it a very lofty tower
after the model of the Pharus at Alexandria, to be lighted at night and
guide the course of the ships.

"Historia Augusta," *Life of Hadrian* xix, 9–13; From *LCL*

He built public works in all places and without number, but he inscribed
his own name on none of them except the temple of his father Trajan.
At Rome he restored the Pantheon, the voting enclosure, the Basilica of
Neptune, many temples, the Forum of Augustus, the Baths of Agrippa,
and dedicated all of them in the names of their original builders.[102] Also
he constructed the bridge named after himself, a tomb on the bank of
the Tiber,[103] and the temple of the Bona Dea. With the aid of the
architect Decrianus he lifted the Colossus[104] and, keeping it in an upright
position, moved it away from the place in which the Temple of Rome
now stands, though its weight was so vast that he had to furnish for the
work as many as twenty-four elephants. This statue he then consecrated
to the Sun after removing the features of Nero,[105] to whom it had
previously been dedicated, and he also planned with the assistance of the
architect Apollodorus [cf. note 60] to make a similar one for the Moon.

ROAD BUILDING

The construction and maintenance of the highway network that spanned
the Empire, serving military, administrative, and commercial needs, was
a perennial task. The manual labor was usually performed by common
laborers recruited locally, but in addition the soldiers stationed in the

101. From Heliopolis, in the reign of Caligula. This is the obelisk that now stands before St.
Peter's, in the Vatican. The ship in which it was transported to Rome is described in Pliny, *Natural
History* xvi. cci–ccii.

102. All the structures mentioned by name in this sentence were bult in the principate of Augustus,
all but the Forum by Agrippa. The restored Pantheon bears the inscription "Marcus Agrippa son of
Lucius, consul three times, built this" (*CIL,* vol. VI, no. 896).

103. The famous Mausoleum of Hadrian, now called Castel Sant' Angelo, still stands as one of the
familiar landmarks of modern Rome.

104. A colossal bronze statue of Nero, over 100 feet high.

105. This is an error. The rededication of the statue to the Sun had taken place during the reign of
Vespasian.

provinces were frequently detailed to road building and repair. The emperor in whose reign construction or repair took place was honored by appropriate commemorative inscriptions; his name appeared also on the milestones placed along the roads. A few representative specimens of the hundreds of these inscribed stones, which have been found throughout the Mediterranean world, follow.

CIL, vol. III, no. 7,203

[Asia Minor, near Smyrna, A.D.75]

The Emperor Caesar VESPASIAN Augustus, *pontifex maximus,* holding the tribunician power for the sixth year, acclaimed *imperator* thirteen times, father of his country, consul six times, designated consul for a seventh time, censor, saw to the repair of the roads.

CIL, vol. III, no. 8,267

[Right bank of Danube, A.D. 100[106]]

The Emperor Caesar Nerva TRAJAN Augustus Germanicus, son of the deified Nerva, *pontifex maximus,* holding the tribunician power for the fourth year, father of his country, consul three times, built this road by cutting through mountains and eliminating the curves.

CIL, vol. III, no. 14,149 (21–22) (=Dessau, no. 5,834)

[Road to Petra, A.D. 111]

The Emperor Caesar Nerva TRAJAN Augustus Germanicus Dacicus, son of the deified Nerva, *pontifex maximus,* holding the tribunician power for the fifteenth year, acclaimed *imperator* six times, consul five times, father of his country, after reducing Arabia to the status of a province, through the agency of Gaius Claudius Severus, imperial legate with rank of praetor, opened and paved a new road from the border of Syria to the Red Sea.

54th [mile]

---

106. Inscribed on a cliff between Viminacium and Retiaria (in modern Serbia), about 20 miles west of Trajan's bridge across the Danube into Dacia (cf. § 10, third selection).

CIL, vol. IX, no. 6,075 (= Dessau, no. 5,875)

[Appian Way, A.D. 123]

The Emperor Caesar Trajanus HADRIAN Augustus, son of the deified Trajan Parthicus, grandson of the deified Nerva, *pontifex maximus,* holding the tribunician power for the seventh year, consul three times, rebuilt the Appian Way for 15¾ miles where it had become unusable through age, adding 1,147,000 sesterces to the 569,100 sesterces which the landowners contributed.[107]

IGRR, vol. I, no. 1,142

[Antinoöpolis, Egypt, A.D. 137]

The Emperor Caesar Trajanus HADRIAN Augustus, son of the deified Trajan Parthicus and grandson of the deified Nerva, *pontifex maximus,* holding the tribunician power for the twenty-first year, twice acclaimed *imperator,* three times consul, father of his country, built from Berenice to Antinoöpolis through secure and level country the New Hadrian Way, with copious cisterns, resting stations, and garrisons at intervals along the route. Year 21, Phamenoth 1.

AE, 1904, no. 21

[North Africa, A.D. 152]

The Emperor Caesar Titus Aelius Hadrianus Augustus [ANTONINUS] PIUS, *pontifex maximus,* holding the tribunician power for the fifteenth year, consul four times, restored the road through the Numidian Alps, when it had broken down because of age, by rebuilding the bridges, draining swamps, and strengthening the sections which had sunk. [The work was carried out] under the direction of Marcus Valerius Etruscus, his legate with rank of praetor.

CIL, vol. II, no. 4,712

---

107. *On the Conditions of Fields,* a work on surveying by Siculus Flaccus, who lived in the second half of the first century A.D., has an instructive passage in this connection (C. Thulin, *Opuscula agrimensorum veterum* [Leipzig, 1923], p. 110): "There are, first, public roads, which are built at state expense and named after their originators. These roads are under the supervision of commissioners, who let the construction to contractors. For certain of these roads, however, a certain sum of money is levied periodically on the landowners of the region." Actually, the major expense of road building under the Empire was borne not by the impoverished state treasury but by the imperial fisc.

[Córdoba, Spain, A.D. 35/36]

TIBERIUS Caesar Augustus, son of the deified Augustus, grandson of the deified Julius, *pontifex maximus,* consul five times, acclaimed *imperator,* holding the tribunician power for the thirty-seventh year. [Road] from Janus Augustus at the Baetis [Guadalquivir] river to the [Atlantic] Ocean.

64th [mile]

CIL, vol. VIII, no. 10,048

[North Africa, A.D. 123]

The Emperor Trajanus HADRIAN Augustus, grandson of the deified Nerva, son of the deified Trajan Parthicus, *pontifex maximus,* holding the tribunician power for the seventh year, consul three times, had the road from Carthage to Theveste paved by the Legion III Augusta under the command of Publius Metilius Secundus, imperial legate with rank of praetor.

85th [mile]

CIL, vol. II, no. 4,906

[Road from Spain to Aquitaine, A.D. 134]

The Emperor Caesar HADRIAN Augustus, son of the deified Trajan Parthicus, grandson of the deified Nerva, *pontifex maximus,* holding the tribunician power for the eighteenth year, acclaimed *imperator,* consul three times, father of his country.

From Cara: 3 miles

2

THE ROMAN PEACE (A.D. 14–192): ECONOMIC LIFE

23. ECONOMIC RESOURCES OF THE EMPIRE

Evidence on the natural resources, products, and trade of the different parts of the Empire is abundant, but it consists in large part of isolated data scattered throughout the sources. The following selections contain a number of representative examples on which good texts are available. Particularly important sectors of the economy—such as agriculture, mining, and trade—and various types of business activity are treated separately in this chapter. For a more extensive treatment of the sources on the economic life of the Roman Empire the reader is referred to T. Frank, ed., *An Economic Survey of Ancient Rome,* Vols. 2–5

SPAIN

The chief importance of Spain in the economy of the Empire lay in her rich mineral deposits. "Almost all Spain," says Pliny (*Natural History* III. iii. 30), abounds in mines of lead, iron, tin, silver, and gold." For the imperial administration of the mines of the Iberian Peninsula, see § 26.

Diodorus of Sicily, *Historical Library* v. xxxv–xxxviii (abridged); From *LCL*

Since we have set forth the facts concerning the Iberians, we think that it will not be foreign to our purpose to discuss the silver mines of the land; for this land possesses, we may venture to say, the most abundant and most excellent known sources of silver, and to the workers of this silver it returns great revenues. . . . The Iberians, having come to know the peculiar qualities possessed by silver, sank notable mines, and as a consequence, by working the most excellent and, we may say, the most abundant silver to be found, they received great revenues. The manner, then, in which the Iberians mine and work the silver is as follows. The mines being marvelous in their deposits of copper and gold and silver, the workers of the copper mines recover from the earth they dig out a fourth part of pure copper, and among the unskilled workers in silver there are some who will take out a Euboeic talent [about 57 lb. avoirdupois] in three days; for all the ore is full of solid silver dust which gleams forth from it. Consequently, a man may well be filled with wonder both at the nature of the region and at the diligence displayed by the men who labor there. Now at first unskilled laborers, whoever might come, carried on the working of the mines, and these men took great wealth away with them, since the silver-bearing earth was convenient at hand and abundant; but at a later time, since the Romans made themselves masters of Iberia, a multitude of Italians have swarmed to the mines and taken away great wealth with them, such was their greed.[1] For they purchase a multitude of slaves whom they turn over to the overseers of the working of the mines; and these men, opening shafts in a number of places and digging deep into the ground, seek out the seams of earth which are rich in silver and gold; and not only do they go into the ground a great distance, but they also push their diggings many stades in depth and run galleries off at every angle, turning this way and that, in this manner bringing up from the depths the ore which gives them the profit they are seeking. . . .

The slaves who are engaged in the working of the mines produce for their masters revenues in sums defying belief, but they themselves wear out their bodies both by day and by night in the diggings under the earth, dying in large numbers because of the exceptional hardships they endure. For no respite or pause is granted them in their labors, but compelled beneath blows of the overseers to endure the severity of their plight, they lose their lives in this wretched manner, although certain of them who can endure it, by virtue of their bodily strength and their persevering souls, suffer such hardships over a long period; indeed death in their eyes is more to be desired than life, because of the magnitude of the hardships they must bear. . . .

Tin also occurs in many regions of Iberia, not found, however, on the surface of the earth as certain writers continually repeat in their

1. Diodorus describes here conditions prevailing during the last decades of the Roman Republic. At first state property, the mines in the Iberian Peninsula had by the first century B.C. passed into private ownership. During the first century of the Empire all mines were gradually brought under the imperial fisc and administration (see § 26).

histories, but dug out of the ground and smelted in the same manner as silver and gold. For there are many mines of tin in the country above Lusitania and on the islets which lie off Iberia out in the Ocean and are called because of that fact Cassiterides.[2] And tin is brought in large quantities also from the island of Britain to the opposite Gaul, whence merchants transport it on horses through the interior of Celtica both to Marseilles and to the city of Narbonne.

GAUL

The Gallic provinces were famous for their foodstuffs, yielded large quantities of building stones, and possessed vigorous mining, pottery, and textile industries.

Strabo, *Geography* IV. i. 2, ii. 1–2 (abridged); From *LCL*

The whole of this country is watered by rivers: some of them flow down from the Alps, the others from the Cemmenus [Cévennes] and the Pyrenees; and some of them are discharged into the Ocean, the others into Our Sea. Further, the districts through which they flow are plains, for the most part, and hilly lands with navigable watercourses. The river beds are by nature so well situated with reference to one another that they afford transportation from either sea into the other; for the cargoes are transported only a short distance by land, with an easy transit through plains, but most of the way they are carried on the rivers —on some into the interior, on the others to the sea. The Rhone offers an advantage in this regard; for not only is it a stream of many tributaries . . . but it also connects with Our Sea, which is better than the Outer Sea [Ocean], and traverses a country which is the most favored of all in that part of the world. For example, the same fruits are produced by the whole of the province of Narbonese Gaul as by Italy. As you proceed toward the north and the Cemmenus [Cévennes] mountains, the olive-planted and fig-bearing land indeed ceases, but the other things still grow. Also the vine, as you thus proceed, does not easily bring its fruit to maturity. All the rest of the country produces grain in large quantities, and millet, and nuts, and all kinds of livestock. And none of the

2. That is, "Tin Islands," the location of which is much debated; the name probably applies to all the North Atlantic tin lands, especially Cornwall in Britain and the nearby Scilly Islands. The importance of Cornish tin in the economy of the Mediterranean fell off during the Empire because of the competition of the Spanish tin deposits.

country is untilled except parts where tilling is precluded by swamps and woods. . . .

Most of the Ocean coast of the Aquitanians is sandy and thin-soiled, thus growing millet, but it is rather unproductive of other products. Here, too, is the gulf [Bay of Biscay] which, along with the Galatic Gulf [Golfe du Lion], which is within the coastline of Narbonese Gaul, forms the isthmus. . . . The gulf is held by the Tarbellians, in whose land the gold mines are most important of all; for in pits dug only to a slight depth they find slabs of gold as big as the hand can hold, which at times require but little refining; but the rest is gold dust and nuggets, the nuggets, too, requiring no great amount of working. . . . Among the Petrocorians there are fine iron works, and also among the Bituriges Cubi; among the Cadurcians, linen works; among the Rutenians, silver mines; and the Gabalians also have silver mines. The Romans have given the "Latin right"[3] to certain of the Aquitanians, such as the Auscians and the Convenians.

ITALY

Though Italy was primarily an importer and consumer, especially of basic foodstuffs and luxury products (see §§ 17, 27–31), it continued during the Empire to be a heavy producer of wine, olive oil, and livestock and, in addition, maintained flourishing pottery, glass, metal-ware, and textile industries.

Cisalpine Gaul

Strabo, *Geography* v. i. 12; From *LCL*

As for the excellence of the regions, it is evidenced by their goodly store of men, the size of their cities, and their wealth, in all of which respects the Romans there have surpassed the rest of Italy. For not only does the tilled land bring forth fruits in large quantities and of all sorts, but the forests have acorns in such quantities that Rome is fed mainly on the herds of swine that come from there. And the yield of millet is also exceptional, since the soil is well watered; and millet is the greatest preventive of famine, since it withstands every unfavorable weather and can never fail, even though there be scarcity of every other grain. The country has wonderful pitch works, also; and as for the wine, the quantity is indicated by the jars, for the wooden ones are larger than

3. See vol. 1, § 205, and introduction to vol. 2, § 64.

houses; and the good supply of pitch helps much toward the excellent smearing the jars receive. As for wool, the soft kind is produced by the regions round Mutina [Modena] and the river Scoltenna (the finest wool of all); the coarse, by Liguria and the country of the Symbrians, from which the greater part of the households of the Italians is clothed; and the medium, by the regions around Patavium [Padua], from which are made the expensive carpets and covers and everything of this kind that is woolly either on both sides or only on one. But as for the mines, at the present time they are not being worked here as seriously as before— perhaps on account of the fact that those in the country of the Transalpine Gauls and in Spain are more profitable.

The Iron Mines at Elba

Diodorus of Sicily, *Historical Library* v. xiii. 1–2; Adapted from *LCL*

Off the city of Etruria known as Populonia there is an island which men call Aethalia [the Greek name of Elba]. It is about 100 stades distant from the coast and received the name it bears from the smoke *(aethalus)* which lies so thick about it. For the island possesses a great amount of iron ore, which they quarry in order to melt and cast and thus secure the iron, and they possess a great abundance of this ore. Now those who are engaged in the working of the ore crush the rock and burn the lumps which they have thus broken in certain igneous furnaces; and in these they smelt the lumps by means of a great fire and form them into pieces of moderate size which are in their appearance like large sponges. These are bought up by traders in exchange [for money or goods] and are then transported to Puteoli[4] or the other trading stations, where there are men who purchase such cargoes and who, with the aid of a multitude of artisans in metal whom they have collected, work it further and manufacture iron objects of every description. Some of these are worked into the shape of armor, and others are ingeniously fabricated into shapes well suited for two-pronged forks and sickles and other such tools; and these are then transported by traders to every region, and thus many parts of the inhabited world have a share in the usefulness which accrues from these products.

---

4. In Campania, where the iron-fabricating industry of Italy was concentrated; the modern Puzzuoli.

GREECE

Strabo, *Geography* IX. i. 23; From *LCL*

Of the mountains [of Attica], those which are most famous are Hymettus, Brilessus, and Lycabettus; and also Parnes and Corydallus. Near the city are most excellent quarries of marble, the Hymettian and Pentelic. Hymettus also produces the best honey. The silver mines in Attica were originally valuable, but now they have failed. Those who worked them, when the mining yielded only meager returns, melted again the old refuse, or dross, and were still able to extract from it pure silver, since the workmen of earlier times had been unskillful in heating the ore in furnaces. But though the Attic honey is the best in the world, that from the district of the silver mines is said to be much the best of all.

BITHYNIA AND PONTUS

Strabo, *Geography* XII. iii. 12–13, 40; Adapted from *LCL*

Both Sinopitis and all the mountainous country extending as far as Bithynia and lying above the aforesaid seaboard have shipbuilding timber that is excellent and easy to transport. Sinopitis produces also the maple and the mountain nut, the trees from which they cut the wood used for tables. And the whole of the tilled country situated a little above the sea is planted with olive trees.

After the mouth of the Halys comes Gazelonitis, which extends to Saramene; it is a fertile country and is everywhere level and productive of everything. It has also a sheep industry, that of raising flocks covered with skins and yielding soft wool,[5] of which there is a very great scarcity throughout the whole of Cappadocia and Pontus. The country also produces gazelles, of which there is a scarcity elsewhere. . . .

Mount Sandaracurgium,[6] not far away from Pimolisa . . . is hollowed out in consequence of the mining done there, since the workmen have excavated great cavities beneath it. The mine used to be worked by publicans, who used as miners the slaves sold in the market because of their crimes; for, in addition to the painfulness of the work, they say that the air in the mines is both deadly and hard to endure on account of

5. This ancient custom of protecting fine wool by tying hides around the sheep is still practiced in Asia Minor.

6. The name means "realgar mine" (realgar is red sulfide of arsenic).

the grievous odor of the ore, so that the workmen are doomed to a quick death. What is more, the mine is often left idle because of the unprofitableness of it, since the workmen [required] number more than two hundred and are continually spent by disease and death.

ASIA

Strabo, *Geography* XII. viii. 14, 16 (abridged); From *LCL*

Synnada is not a large city; but there lies in front of it a plain planted with olives, about sixty stadia in circuit[?]. And beyond it is Docimaea, a village, and also the quarry of "Synnadic" marble (so the Romans call it, though the natives call it "Docimite" or "Docimaean"). At first this quarry yielded only stones of small size, but on account of the present extravagance of the Romans great monolithic pillars are taken from it, which in their variety of colors are so nearly like the alabastrite marble; so that, although the transportation of such heavy burdens to the sea is difficult, still, both pillars and slabs, remarkable for their size and beauty, are conveyed to Rome. . . .

The country round Laodicea produces sheep that are excellent not only for the softness of their wool, in which they surpass even the Milesian wool, but also for its raven–black color, so that the Laodiceans derive rich revenue from it, as do also the neighboring Colossians from the color which bears the same name.[7]

SYRIA AND JUDAEA

Strabo, *Geography* XVI. ii. 9, 23, 42 (abridged); From *LCL*

Then one comes to Laodicea, situated on the sea. It is a city most beautifully built, has a good harbor, and has territory which, besides its other good crops, abounds in wine. Now this city furnishes most of the wine to the Alexandrians, since the whole of the mountain which lies above the city and is possessed by it is covered with vines almost as far as the summits. . . .

The Tyrian purple has proven itself by far the most beautiful of all; the shellfish are caught near the coast, and the other things requisite for dyeing are easily got; and although the great number of dye works makes the city unpleasant to live in, yet it makes the city rich through the superior skill of its inhabitants. . . .

7. "Colossian" wool was dyed purple or madder-red.

Lake Sirbonis[8] is large; in fact, some state that it is 1,000 stadia in circuit; however, it extends parallel to the coast to a length of slightly more than 200 stadia, is deep to the very shore, and has water so heavy that there is no use for divers, and any person who walks into it and proceeds no farther than up to his navel is immediately raised afloat. It is full of asphalt. The asphalt is blown to the surface at irregular intervals from the midst of the deep. . . . They reach the asphalt on rafts and chop it and carry off as much as they each can.

EGYPT

Besides being one of the principal grain-producing regions of the Empire, Egypt was—as it had been from Pharaonic times—the center of the cultivation of the papyrus plant and of the manufacture therefrom of the paper of antiquity.

Pliny, *Natural History* XIII. xxii-xxiii. 71–77

Papyrus grows in the marshes of Egypt, or in the sluggish waters of the Nile, where they have overflowed and lie stagnant in pools that do not exceed about three feet in depth. The root, which lies obliquely, has the thickness of a man's arm; the stalk is triangular and tapers gracefully upward to a height of not more than about fifteen feet. . . . The natives employ the roots as wood—not only for firewood but also for making various utensils and vessels. From the plant itself, by plaiting it, they also construct boats, and from the inner bark they make sails and mats, and also cloth, as well as coverlets and ropes; they chew it also, both raw and boiled, though they swallow only the juice. . . .

Paper is made from the papyrus plant by separating it with a needle point into very thin strips as broad as possible. The choice quality comes from the center, and thence in the order of slicing. The choice quality, in former times called "hieratic" because it was devoted only to religious books, has, out of flattery, taken on the name of Augustus, and the next quality that of Livia, after his wife, so that the "hieratic" has dropped to third rank.

The next has been named "amphitheatric" from its place of manufacture.[9] At Rome, Fannius' clever workshop took it up and refined it by

8. The name used by Strabo is erroneous, for he proceeds to describe the Dead Sea (Lake Asphaltites).

9. That is, near the amphitheater of Alexandria. Manufacture took place near the source of the raw

careful processing, thus making a first-class paper out of a common one and renaming it after himself; the paper not so reworked remained in its original grade as "amphitheatric."

Next is the "Saitic," so called after the town where it is most abundant, made from inferior scraps, and from still nearer the rind the "Taeneotic," named after a nearby place. This is sold, in fact, by weight, not by quality. The "emporitic," being useless for writing, provides envelopes for papers and wrappings for merchandise, and its name accordingly comes from [the Greek for] merchants. After this there is (only) the papyrus stalk, and its outermost husk is similar to a rush and useless even for rope except [for those used] in moisture.

The various kinds of paper are processed upon a board moistened with Nile water, the muddy liquid of which has the effect of glue.[10] First, an upright layer is spread upon the board, the full length of the papyrus available being used after the strips have been trimmed off at either end; after which cross strips are used, producing a lattice work effect. Next, the sheets are pressed with presses, and then dried in the sun; after which they are joined together. The quality of each succeeding sheet is progressively inferior down to the poorest. There are never more than twenty sheets to a roll.[11]

NORTH AFRICA

Pliny, *Natural History* XVIII. xxi

Nothing is more prolific than wheat. Nature has given it this attribute since she nourishes man chiefly on it. A single *modius* of wheat, if the soil is suitable, like that of the Byzacium plain in Africa, yields 150 *modii*. From that region the deified Augustus received from his procurator—incredible as it seems—a shipment of almost 400 shoots grown from a single grain (the correspondence on this matter is still extant).[12]

---

material in the Delta region of the Nile, where were located also the town of Saïs and the Taenea district (near Alexandria) mentioned later.

10. Actually, any water has the same effect. Two layers of raw papyrus strips, if pressed together when moist, will adhere to each other upon drying.

11. This refers, of course, to the standard rolls of blank paper as prepared in the workshops for shipment and sale. The user would then cut from these rolls as much paper as required for specific purposes, or, if the roll were not long enough, as for a book, additional sheets from another roll would be glued on.

12. Josephus (*Jewish War* II. xvi. 383) informs us that Africa supplied the city of Rome annually with grain sufficient for eight months, a quantity estimated at 40,000,000 *modii*; see further introduction to § 17.

Nero, similarly, received 360 stalks grown from one grain. The plains of Leontini and elsewhere in Sicily, the whole of Baetic Spain, and especially Egypt, yield wheat a good hundredfold.[13]

24. AGRICULTURE: THE LARGE ESTATE; RISE OF TENANCY

The agricultural economy of the Roman world had been persistently evolving since late republican times (see vol. 1, § 166) in the direction of large estates. During the first two centuries of the Principate, both in Italy and in the provinces, latifundia, the most important of which were the imperial domains (see § 25), were the basic form of agricultural organization, though small-scale husbandry persisted in many areas. Despite contemporary moralizing denunciations of the mushrooming of the latifundia, Italian agriculture, which continued to concentrate on olive and wine production, does not appear to have been in a state of economic decay. Throughout most parts of the Empire, absentee landowners, through the development of more efficient and intensive exploitation of land and labor force, derived comfortable profits from their estates. But in the first century there began a momentous transformation in the agricultural labor force, which was to have far-reaching consequences. Powerful economic and social forces converged to render slave labor in this area of the economy relatively unprofitable. To ensure a cheap and stable labor supply, latifundists increasingly leased their estates in smaller parcels to the growing class of free tenant farmers *(coloni)*, often ex-slaves. By the second century, slave-operated latifundia were becoming obsolete and tenancy was becoming prevalent. Gradually formalized by imperial legislation, this institution, called the colonate, contained the seeds of manorial serfdom and was one of the most significant heritages of the Roman world to feudal times (cf. § 130).

"THE LATIFUNDIA HAVE RUINED ITALY"

Pliny, *Natural History* XVIII. vii. 35

The men of olden times believed that above all moderation should be observed in landholding, for indeed it was their judgment that it was better to sow less and plow more intensively. Vergil, too, I see agreed with this view. To confess the truth, the latifundia have ruined Italy,

---

13. The yields mentioned in this passage, if accurate, must be taken as exceptional occurrences.

and soon will ruin the provinces as well. Six owners were in possession of one half of the province of Africa at the time when the Emperor Nero had them put to death.

MANAGEMENT OF A LARGE ESTATE

It is instructive to compare these directions with those of Cato and Varro (vol. 1, § 166). It is apparent that Columella, writing in the first century, had in view much larger estates than these writers of the two preceding centuries.

Columella, *On Agriculture* 1. vi–ix (abridged); Adapted from *LCL*

The size of the villa and the number of its parts should be proportioned to the whole enclosure, and it should be divided into three groups: the *villa urbana* (manor house), the *villa rustica* (farmhouse), and the *villa fructuaria* (storehouse). . . .

As for the situation of the farmhouse and the arrangement of its several parts, enough has been said. It will be necessary, next, that the farmhouse have the following near it: an oven and a mill, of such size as may be required by the number of tenant farmers; at least two ponds, one to serve for geese and cattle, the other in which we may soak lupines, elm withes, twigs, and other things suitable for our needs. There should also be two manure pits, one to receive the fresh dung and keep it for a year, and a second from which the old is hauled; but both of them should be built shelving with a gentle slope, in the manner of fish ponds, and built up and packed hard with earth, so as not to let the moisture drain away. . . .

After all these things have been obtained or constructed, the master must give special attention, among other things, to laborers; and these are either tenant farmers or slaves (unfettered or in chains). He should be civil in dealing with his tenant farmers, should show himself affable, and should be more exacting in the matter of work than of payments, as this gives less offense yet is, generally speaking, more profitable. For when land is carefully tilled, it usually brings a profit, and never a loss except when it is assailed by unusually severe weather or robbers; and therefore the tenant does not venture to ask for reduction of his rent. But the master should not be insistent on his rights in every particular to which he has bound his tenant, such as the exact day for payment of money, or the matter of demanding firewood and other trifling contributions; attention to such matters causes country folk more trouble than expense. . . . I myself remember having heard Publius Volusius, an old man who had been consul and was very wealthy, declare that estate to be most fortunate which had natives of the place as tenant farmers and which held them by reason of long association, even from the cradle, as if born on their own father's property. So I am decidedly of the opinion that repeated re-letting of a farm is a bad thing, but that a worse thing is the tenant farmer who lives in town and prefers to till the land through his slaves rather than by his own hand. Saserna[14] used to say that from a man of this sort the return was usually a lawsuit instead of income, and that for this reason we should take pains to keep with us tenants who are country-bred and at the same time diligent farmers, when we are not able to till the land ourselves or when it is not feasible to cultivate it with our own household; though this does not happen except in districts which are desolated by the severity of the climate and the barrenness of the soil. But when the climate is moderately healthful and the soil moderately good, a man's personal attention never fails to yield a larger return from his land than does that of a tenant. Even reliance on an overseer yields a larger return, except in the event of extreme carelessness or greed on the part of that slave. There is no doubt that in general both these offenses are either committed or fostered through the fault of the master, inasmuch as he has the authority to prevent such a person from being placed in charge of his affairs or to see to it that he is removed if so placed. On far-distant estates, however, which it is not easy for the owner to visit, it is better for every kind of land to be under free farmers than under slave overseers, but this is particularly true of grain land. To such land a tenant farmer can do no great harm, as he can to vineyards and trees, while slaves do it tremendous damage: they let out oxen for hire, and they keep them and other animals poorly fed; they do not plow the ground carefully, and they charge the account with far more seed than they have actually sown; what they have committed to the earth they do not foster so that it will make the proper growth; and when they have brought it to the threshing floor, every day during the threshing they lessen the quantity either by trickery or by carelessness. For they themselves steal it and do not guard against the thieving of others, and even when it is stored away, they do not enter it honestly in their accounts. The result is that both manager and hands are offenders, and the land pretty often gets a bad name. Therefore my

14. Hostilius Saserna, a writer on agriculture of the late Republican period.

opinion is that an estate of this sort should be leased if, as I have said, it cannot have the presence of the owner.

The next point is with regard to slaves—over what duty it is proper to place each, and to what sort of tasks to assign them. So my advice at the start is not to appoint an overseer from the sort of slaves who are physically attractive, and certainly not from that class which has been engaged in the voluptuous occupations of the city. This lazy and sleepy-headed class of slaves, accustomed to idling, to the Field of Mars, the circus and the theaters, to gambling, to taverns, to bawdy houses, never ceases to dream of these follies; and when they carry them over into their farming, the master suffers not so much loss in the slave himself as in his whole estate. A man should be chosen who has been hardened by farm work from his infancy, one who has been tested by experience. . . . He should be of middle age and of strong physique, skilled in farm operations or at least very painstaking, so that he may learn the more readily; for it is not in keeping with this business of ours for one man to give orders and another to give instruction, nor can a man properly exact work when he is being tutored by an underling as to what is to be done and in what way. Even an illiterate person, if only he have a retentive mind, can manage affairs well enough. Cornelius Celsus [see chapter 3, note 123] says that an overseer of this sort brings money to his master oftener than he does his book, because, being illiterate, he is either less able to falsify accounts or is afraid to do so through a second party, because that would make another aware of the deception.

But be the overseer what he may, he should be given a woman companion to keep him within bounds and moreover in certain matters to be a help to him. . . . He must be urged to take care of the equipment and the iron tools, and to keep in repair and stored away twice as many as the number of slaves requires, so that there will be no need of borrowing from a neighbor; for the loss in slave labor exceeds the cost of articles of this sort. In the care and clothing of the slave household he should have an eye to usefulness rather than appearance, taking care to keep them fortified against wind, cold, and rain, all of which are warded off with long-sleeved leather tunics, garments of patchwork, or hooded cloaks. If this be done, no weather is so unbearable but that some work may be done in the open. He should be not only skilled in the tasks of husbandry but should also be endowed, as far as the servile disposition allows, with such qualities of mind that he may exercise authority without laxness and without cruelty, and always humor some of the better hands, at the same time being forbearing even with those of lesser worth, so that they may rather fear his sternness than detest his cruelty. . . .

In the case of the other slaves, the following are, in general, the precepts to be observed, and I do not regret having held to them myself: to talk rather familiarly with the country slaves, provided only that they have not conducted themselves unbecomingly, more frequently than I would with town slaves; and when I perceived that their unending toil was lightened by such friendliness on the part of the master, I would even jest with them at times and allow them also to jest more freely. Nowadays I make it a practice to call them into consultation on any new work, as if they were more experienced, and to discover by this means what sort of ability is possessed by each of them and how intelligent he is. Furthermore, I observe that they are more willing to set about a piece of work on which they think that their opinions have been asked and their advice followed. Again, it is the established custom of all men of caution to inspect the slaves in the prison, to find out whether they are carefully chained, whether the places of confinement are quite safe and properly guarded, whether the overseer has put anyone in fetters or removed his shackles without the master's knowledge. . . . And the investigation of the householder should be the more painstaking in the interest of slaves of this sort, that they may not be treated unjustly in the matter of clothing or other allowances, inasmuch as, being subject to a greater number of people, such as overseers, taskmasters, and jailers, they are the more liable to unjust punishment, and again, when smarting under cruelty and greed, they are more to be feared. Accordingly, a careful master inquires not only of them, but also of those who are not in bonds, as being more worthy of belief, whether they are receiving what is due them under his instructions. He also tests the quality of their food and drink by tasting it himself and examines their clothing, mittens, and foot covering. In addition, he should give them frequent opportunities for making complaints against those persons who treat them cruelly or dishonestly. In fact, I now and then avenge those who have just cause for grievance, as well as punish those who incite the slaves to revolt or who slander their taskmasters; and, on the other hand, I reward those who conduct themselves with energy and diligence. Also, to women who are unusually prolific, and who ought to be rewarded for the bearing of a certain number of offspring, I have granted exemption from work and sometimes even freedom after they have reared many children: a mother of three children received exemption from work,[15] a mother of more, her freedom as well. Such justice and consideration on the part of the master contributes greatly to the increase of his estate. . . .

This, too, I believe: that the duties of the slaves should not be confused to the point where all take a hand in every task. For this is by no means to the advantage of the husbandman, either because no one regards any particular task as his own or because, when he does make an effort, he is performing a service that is not his own but common to all, and therefore shirks his work to a great extent; and yet fault cannot be fastened upon any one man because many have a hand in it. For this reason plowmen must be distinguished from vine dressers, and vine dressers from plowmen, and both of these from men of all work. Furthermore, squads should be formed, not to exceed ten men each, which the ancients called *decuriae* and approved of highly, because that limited number was most conveniently guarded while at work and the size was not disconcerting to the person in charge as he led the way. Therefore, if the field is of considerable extent, such squads should be distributed over sections of it and the work should be so apportioned that men will not be by ones or twos, because they are not easily watched when scattered; and yet they should not number more than ten, lest, on the other hand, when the band is too large, each individual may think that the work does not concern him. This arrangement not only stimulates rivalry, but also discloses the slothful; for, when a task is enlivened by competition, punishment inflicted on the laggards appears just and free from censure.

THE PROFITABLENESS OF AGRICULTURE

Columella, *On Agriculture* III. iii (abridged); Adapted from *LCL*

Now, before discoursing on the planting of vines, I think it not out of place to lay down, as a sort of foundation for the coming discussion, the principle that we should carefully weigh and investigate in advance

---

15. Cf. in vol. I, § 204, the similar privileges for the free and freedman classes enacted by Augustus. During the Pax Romana slaveowners turned more and more to breeding and rearing slaves in their homes and on their estates—practices they scorned in the heyday of their conquests, when huge supplies of war captives were dumped into the slave markets. Cf. the exaggerated but realistic evidence in Petronius' *Satyricon* liii. 1–2: "His bookkeeper read aloud . . . 'July 26, born on the Cumaean estate belonging to Trimalchio, slave boys 30, girls 40.' "

whether viticulture will enrich the proprietor. . . . And most people would be doubtful on this point, to such an extent that many would avoid and dread such an ordering of their land and would consider it preferable to own meadows and pastures, or woodland for cutting. . . .

Those devoted to the study of agriculture must be informed of one thing first of all—that the return from vineyards is a very rich one. . . . We can hardly recall a time when grain crops, throughout at least the greater part of Italy, returned a yield of four to one.[16] Why, then, is viticulture in disrepute? Not, indeed, through its own fault, but because of human failings. . . . Most people, in fact, strive for the richest possible yield at the earliest moment; they make no provision for the time to come, but, as if living merely from day to day, they put such demands upon their vines and load them so heavily with young shoots as to show no regard for succeeding generations. After committing all these acts, or at any rate most of them, they would rather do anything at all than admit their own guilt; and they complain that their vineyards do not yield them a return—vineyards which they themselves have ruined through greed, or ignorance, or neglect. But if any who combine painstaking care with scientific knowledge receive not forty or at least thirty amphoras per *iugerum* according to my reckoning but, using a minimum estimate as Graecinus[17] does, twenty, they will easily outdo in the increase of their ancestral estates all those who hold fast to their hay and vegetables. And he is not mistaken in this, for, like a careful accountant, he sees, when his calculations are made, that this kind of husbandry is of the greatest advantage to his estate. For, admitting that vineyards demand a very generous outlay, still seven *iugera* require the labor of not more than one vine dresser, upon whom people in general set a low value, thinking that even some malefactor may be acquired from the auction block; but I, disagreeing with the opinion of the majority, consider a high-priced vine dresser of first importance. And supposing his purchase price to be 6,000—or better, 8,000—sesterces, when I estimate the seven *iugera* of ground as acquired for just as many thousand sesterces,[18] and that vineyards . . . with their stakes and withes

16. A very low rate indeed, reflecting the continuing decline of cereal culture in Italy. The yield in the provinces, and even in parts of Italy in the preceding century, was many times higher (cf. § 23, last selection).

17. Julius Graecinus, a senator, who wrote a work on viticulture in the early first century.

18. That is, 7,000 sesterces. The price of the slave is deliberately set very high; cf. introduction to §35.

are set out for 2,000 sesterces per *iugerum,* still the total cost, reckoned to the last penny, amounts to 29,000 sesterces. Added to this is interest at six percent per annum, amounting to 3,480 sesterces for the two-year period when the vineyards, in their infancy as it were, are delayed in bearing. The sum total of principal and interest thus comes to 32,480 sesterces. And if the husbandman will enter this amount as a debit against his vineyards just as a moneylender does with a debtor, in order that the owner may realize the aforementioned six-percent interest on that total as a perpetual annuity, he must take in 1,950 sesterces every year. By this reckoning the return from seven *iugera,* even according to the [minimum] estimate of Graecinus, exceeds the interest on 32,480 sesterces. For, assuming that the vineyards are of the very worst sort, still, if taken care of, they will yield certainly one *culleus*[19] of wine to the *iugerum;* and even though every forty urns are sold for 300 sesterces, which is the lowest market price, still seven *cullei* bring a total of 2,100 sesterces—a sum far in excess of the interest at six percent. And these figures, as we have given them, are based on the calculations of Graecinus. But our own opinion is that vineyards which yield less than three *cullei* to the *iugerum* should be rooted out. And, even so, we have made our calculations up to this point as if there were no quicksets to be taken from the trenched ground; though this item alone, at a favorable price, would clear the entire cost of the land, if only the land belongs not to the provinces but to Italy.[20]

THE GROWTH OF TENANCY

Pliny, *Letters* book III, no. 19

Gaius Plinius to his dear Calvisius Rufus, greeting.

As usual, I call on you to advise me about my property. Lands adjoining my property, and even jutting into it, are for sale. Many

19. A bulk liquid measure, equivalent to twenty amphoras.

20. Examples of exceptionally profitable viticulture through intensive cultivation are cited in Pliny, *Natural History* xiv. v. Here, as in olive culture, Italy in the first century was already feeling the competition of the provinces. Cf. Pliny, *Natural History* xiv. viii. 71: "In the Spanish provinces the vineyards of Laeetanum are renowned for their abundant yield, while for quality those of Tarragona, Lauron, and the Balearic Islands bear comparison with the choice vintages of Italy"; Columella, *On Agriculture* preface 20: "And so, in 'this Latium and this Saturnian land,' where the gods had taught their progeny the fruits of the fields, we now auction off contracts for the importation of grain from the overseas provinces, so as not to suffer from hunger, and we store away wines from the Cyclades Islands and from the Baetic and Gallic regions."

things in them tempt me, but there are some factors—hardly minor ones—which deter me. First, I am tempted by just the attractiveness of rounding out my estate; second, because it would be at once convenient and pleasurable. For the same work could go on in both places, they could be visited at the same traveling expense, and they could be kept under the same overseer and practically the same agents, and while one villa is cared for and kept fully equipped, the other can be merely looked after. One should add in the reckoning the cost of the furnishings, the cost of the stewards, the gardeners, the artisans, and even the equipment for hunting. It makes the greatest difference whether one assembles these in one place or disperses them in several. On the other hand, I am afraid that it is risky to expose so much property to the same storms, the same contingencies; it seems safer to make trial of the uncertainties of fortune by distributing one's investments. Also, much pleasure is afforded by the change in climate and by the actual travel between one's estates.

Now the chief reason for my deliberation is the following: while the property is fertile, rich, and well supplied with water, and consists of meadows, vineyards, and woods that produce an income from timber which though modest is steady, this fertility of the soil is plagued by the cultivators' lack of means. For the previous owner a number of times sold the securities [for their leases], and while he thus reduced the arrears of the tenant farmers for the time being, he drained their resources for the future, the lack of which caused the arrears to mount again. A number of them, therefore, have to be supplied with industrious slaves; for I myself have none in chains anywhere, nor does anyone in those parts.

Finally, you should know at what price the property can, apparently, be bought—3,000,000 sesterces, though at one time the price was 5,000,000. But on account of the impoverishment of the tenant farmers and the general distress of the times, the returns from landed property as well as prices have dropped. You ask whether I can easily get together this 3,000,000 sesterces. Indeed, practically all my investments are in real estate, though I do have some money out at interest, and it will not be difficult for me to borrow. I can get the money from my mother-in-law, whose purse I use as if it were my own. Do not therefore be concerned about this, if there are not hindrances on the other counts, to which I want you please to give your most careful consideration. For in the planning of investments, as in everything else, you have an abundance of experience and foresight. Farewell.

Pliny, *Letters* book x, no. 8. 5–6

[Pliny to the Emperor Trajan]

I beg . . . that you grant me a leave of absence. . . .[21] For the leasing of the lands which I possess in the same region[22] cannot possibly be postponed, particularly since the rent is over 400,000 sesterces,[23] and the new tenant should attend to the pruning, which is close at hand. More-over, repeated bad seasons oblige me to think of reductions in rents, the accounting of which I cannot undertake except in person. I shall there-fore be indebted to your indulgence, my lord . . . for the opportunity of settling my private affairs, if you grant me . . . a leave of absence for thirty days. For I cannot specify a shorter time, since both the munici-pality and the lands to which I refer are over 150 miles away.

Pliny, *Letters* book ix, no. 37 (abridged)

Gaius Plinius to his dear Paulinus, greeting.

. . . I am detained by the necessity of leasing my estates so as to set them in order for several years. In which connection I am obliged to adopt new arrangements. For in the last five-year period, despite large reductions [of rent], the arrears mounted. Hence several tenants no longer have any concern to reduce a debt which they despair of being able to pay off; they even seize and consume whatever is produced, acting like people who think they no longer have to be thrifty since it is not their own property. The growing evils, therefore, have to be faced and relieved. There is one method of remedying them—to lease not for a rent in money but on shares, and then to place some of my men to superintend the work and guard the produce. . . . It is true that this requires great integrity, keen eyes, and many hands. However, I must try the experiment and, as in a chronic disease, try and see what help a change may bring.

LEASE OF LAND

The following lease illustrating tenancy arrangements is representative of a large number of such documents extant among the papyri from Egypt.

21. Pliny held a minor office at Rome at this time, probably A.D. 99.
22. Probably Tifernun-on-Tiber; cf. § 71, last selection.
23. It is not clear whether this amount is the annual rent or covers a period of years.

Amherst Papyrus No. 91; A.D. 159

To Hero son of Sarapio, a minor, with his guardian Ischyrio son of Herodes, and with the concurrence of the minor's mother, Heroïs, from Aphrodisius son of Acusilaus, of the metropolis [Arsinoë]. I wish to lease the eleven arouras or thereabouts of vineland belonging to Hero in one parcel near the village of Euhemeria for two years from the current twenty-third year of the lord Antoninus Caesar, at a total yearly rent for all the arouras, not including seed, of forty artabs of wheat by the four-*choinix-dromus* measure, subject to no charge or risk. I will perform the annual operations: [maintaining] the embankments, irrigation, plowing, hoeing, dredging of irrigation canals, sowing, weeding, and all else that is fitting, at my own expense and at the proper seasons, doing nothing injurious. I will sow the arouras in the first year with any crops I choose except *cnecus*,[24] and in the second year one half with wheat and the other half with light crops.[25] The annual expense of transporting [produce delivered] to the state shall be borne by me, Aphrodisius, but all the other state charges by Hero. I will pay the yearly rent in the month of Payni,[26] new, pure, unadulterated, and unmixed with barley, at the village of Theadelphia; and at the end of the period I will deliver the arouras with the produce, after being sown as aforesaid, duly harvested, and free from rushes, coarse grass, and refuse of all sorts, if you consent to the lease. Aphrodisius, aged forty years, with a scar in the middle of his forehead. Year 23 of the lord Antoninus Caesar, Hathyr 12.

25. IMPERIAL ESTATES AND AGRARIAN POLICY

By far the biggest landowner in the Roman Empire was the emperor. As *princeps* he possessed estates all over the Empire, some inherited from various local dynasties on their extinction, others bequeathed by or confiscated from private owners. Each estate was operated under the supervision of a resident imperial procurator, who carried out the general policies laid down by the emperors within the framework of local conditions and traditions. While specific details might thus vary from place to place even within a single province, certain general features do stand out. We are best informed about the estates in Africa and Egypt, the two major sources of

---

24. The safflower, an oleaginous plant still grown in Egypt.
25. Such rotation of crops is frequently specified in ancient leases of land.
26. That is, May–June (cf. introduction to § 34), the height of the harvest season in Egypt.

Rome's food supply. The general procedure in both these provinces was to lease parcels of the estate to tenant farmers *(coloni)* for varying periods; a significant difference is seen in the fact that in Africa the tenant's obligations under the lease were to deliver a certain share of the crops and furnish a number of days' labor to the lessor, while in Egypt the leases were for a stipulated rental payable in kind. In some places the procurators leased large tracts to lessees-in-chief *(conductores),* who cultivated part themselves and sublet the rest to *coloni.* While slaves were undoubtedly used to some extent as agricultural laborers, they appear more often as household or administrative assistants (bailiffs, secretaries, etc.) of the chief lessees or procurators, who were themselves often imperial freedmen.

Like other large estates, those of the emperor were affected in the first two centuries by the growing shortage of agricultural manpower. In Egypt (and doubtless elsewhere as well), when not enough voluntary tenants appeared, the remaining land was assigned to neighboring individuals or villages for compulsory cultivation. In addition, the emperors began to offer the tenant farmers special inducements to stimulate and assure production. The Mancian Law, dating probably from the late first century and confirmed and liberalized by Hadrian, offered two major concessions to *coloni* who took possession of waste or abandoned land on imperial or private estates and established domiciles thereon: (1) quasi-ownership of any such land as long as they kept it under cultivation, limited only by inability to sell, and (2) rent-free occupation for the first five or ten years, depending on the crops grown. Thus, like the Gracchi and their followers in Republican times (cf. vol. i, §§ 96–99), but with considerably greater success,[27] the Roman emperors attempted to create a solid and stable class of tenant farmers on the land. Then, as time passed and the *coloni* handed on their holdings to their heirs, both the holding and the "owner's" status came to be regarded as hereditary; thus, the *coloni* became the forerunners of the praedial serfs of the Middle Ages (cf. §§ 117, 130).

IMPERIAL ESTATES IN AFRICA

The following two inscriptions come from the Bagradas (modern Medjerda) valley in North Africa. They are open to varying interpretations on a number of points of detail, owing to the physical mutilation of the stones, the barbarity of the stonecutters' Latin, and the uncertainty of the

---

27. We are informed by extant texts that in the late fifth century, under Vandal rule, there were still "Mancian fields" in North Africa.

specific connotation of some terms. Where different possibilities exist, our translation gives, usually without further comment, what we regard as the sense most congruent with the known facts.

CIL, vol. VIII, no. 25,943, cols. 1–3, supplemented by no. 26,416; (= *FIRA*, vol. I, no. 101, supplemented by no. 102)

[The Inscriptions of Ain-el-Jemala and Ain Wassel, A.D. 117–138]

[Petition of tenant farmers to the procurators of the estate:] . . . we ask, procurators, that through the foresight which you exercise in the name of Caesar, you be minded to have regard for us and for his advantage, and grant us the land which is swampy and wooded to plant with olive orchards and vineyards on the terms in force on the neighboring Neronian estate in accordance with the Mancian Law. . . .

Statement of the procurators of the Emperor Caesar HADRIAN Augustus: Since it is the order of our Caesar, in the untiring care with which he assiduously watches over mankind's interests, that all parts of the land suitable for olives and vines as well as for grains be brought under cultivation, therefore by the grace[?] of his foresight the right is granted to all to take possession even of those parts among the leased-out surveyed parcels of the Blandian and Udensian estates and of those parts of the Lamian and Domitian estate adjoining[28] the Tuzritan estate which are not being exploited by the chief lessees. Those who so take possession are granted the right—comprehended in the law of Hadrian on waste lands and fields which have lain uncultivated for ten successive years—of possessing and enjoying the usufruct of the land, and of leaving it to their heirs. No greater shares of produce shall be exacted from the Blandian and Udensian estate than tenant farmers pay by virtue of Caesar's supreme beneficence: anyone who takes possession of places neglected by the chief lessees shall give one third of the crops, which is the share customarily given; also from those sections of the Lamian and Domitian estate adjoining the Tuzritan he shall give the same. From olive trees which anyone sets out or grafts onto wild olive trees, no share of the crops obtained shall be exacted for the next ten years; of fruits no share shall be exacted for the next seven years, and no fruits shall ever be subject to division other than those sold by the possessors.

---

28. Or "attached to." The name that follows is spelled Thusdritan in *CIL*, vol. VIII, no. 26,416. The same name appears a few lines below.

Whatever shares of the dry produce anyone must give he shall give for the next five years to the person in whose leasehold he occupies a field, and after that time to the account of the fisc.

CIL, vol. VIII, nos. 10,570 and 14,464, col. 2, line 1–col. 4, line 8 (= *FIRA,* vol. I, no. 103)

[The Inscription of Sûk-el-Khmis, A.D. 180–183]

[Petition to the emperor from Lurius Lucullus on behalf of estate tenants:] . . . that you may know of the collusion[?] which your procurator has practiced without limit not only with Allius Maximus, our adversary, but with practically all the chief lessees, in violation of right and to the detriment of your fisc. As a result he has not only refrained for so many years past from investigating when we petitioned and pleaded and cited your divine order, but he has even yielded to the wiles of the said Allius Maximus, the chief lessee, who stands so high in his favor, to the point of sending soldiers into the said Burunitan estate and ordering some of us to be seized and tortured, others fettered, and some, including even Roman citizens, beaten with rods and cudgels; and the only thing we did to deserve this was that, in the face of injury so palpable and so oppressive in relation to the measure of our insignificance, we had resorted to sending a letter of complaint beseeching your majesty's aid. The evidence of our injury, Caesar, can be judged from the fact that . . . perform work. . . . This has driven us, most wretched of men, now again to implore your divine providence, and we therefore ask you, most sacred Emperor, to come to our aid. Let the procurators also, not to mention the chief lessee, be deprived of the right, as they are deprived by the section of the law of Hadrian cited above, of increasing to the tenant farmers' detriment the shares of crops or the labor or teams to be furnished, and, as provided in the records of the procurators deposited in your archives of the Carthaginian district, let us owe annually per man not more than two days' work at plowing, two at cultivating, and two at harvesting, and let there be no dispute about this, inasmuch as it has been inscribed in bronze and observed as the established practice down to the present day by absolutely all our neighbors on every side and confirmed to be such by the abovementioned records of the procurators. Succor us, and—since we are poor peasants sustaining life by the toil of our hands and no match, in our relations with your procurators, for the chief lessee, who stands very high in their favor because of his lavish gifts and is well known to each of them in succession by virtue of the lease—have pity on us, and deign to instruct by your sacred rescript that we are to perform no more service than we are obligated to in accordance with the law of Hadrian and with the records of your procurators, that is, three periods of two days' work per man, so that through the benefaction of your majesty we, your own peasants, born and raised on your estates, may be harassed no further by the chief lessees of lands belonging to the fisc.

The Emperor Caesar Marcus Aurelius COMMODUS Antoninus Augustus Sarmaticus Germanicus Maximus to Lurius Lucullus and the others represented by him: In view of established tradition and my order, procurators will see to it that nothing more than three periods of two days' work per man[29] is unjustly exacted from you in violation of established practice.

IMPERIAL ESTATES IN EGYPT

Information about the imperial estates in Egypt is provided by a considerable body of papyri. The following two documents illustrate their economic operations and the history of their ownership. The first emperors distributed large numbers of these estates to members of the imperial family and to favored associates; but in the era of confiscations initiated by Nero and intensified by Vespasian and Titus (cf. chapter 1, note 44), these estates were practically all repossessed by the emperor.

Milan Papyrus No. 6; A.D. 25

To Aphrodisius son of Zoilus, lessee of the estate of Julia Augusta[30] and the children of Germanicus Caesar, from Harthotes son of Marres. If I am granted the right to gather papyrus and rush from the marsh [in an area extending] from the limits of Theoxenis to the boundaries of Philoteris, and to weave mats therefrom and sell them in any villages of the nome I choose during the twelfth year of TIBERIUS Caesar Augustus, I engage to pay four drachmas of silver and fifteen obols together with the appropriate supplemental and receipt fees, which I will remit in three installments in Epeiph, Mesore, and the month of Augustus[31] next year if you see fit to grant me this on the aforesaid terms. Farewell. Year 12 of TIBERIUS Caesar Augustus, Payni 24.

---

29. The words "more than . . . per man" were probably not in the emperor's rescript but were inserted by the *coloni* who set up the inscription.

30. The name of Livia, Augustus' wife, after his death.

31. Not our month August, but the first month of the Egyptian calendar, Thoth (August 29–

Rylands Papyrus No. 171; A.D. 56/57

To Euschemo, agent of the estate of Tiberius Claudius Doryphorus, formerly owned by Narcissus,[32] in the Arsinoite nome, from Papus son of Trypho, of Heraclia in the Themistes division, living in the farmstead of Antonia wife of Drusus. . . .[33] I desire to lease for four years from the coming third year of the Emperor NERO Claudius Caesar Augustus Germanicus twenty-seven arouras . . . in the vicinity of the said village . . . in two parcels . . . bounded as follows: on the south, crown land;[34] on the north, crown land on the lake shore; on the west, grounds of Pa . . . ; on the east, grounds of the estate of Maecenas. . . . I will pay a total yearly rental of . . . artabs per aroura, including the one artab of wheat per aroura which I receive for seed. . . . [The rest is lost.]

AN IMPERIAL CATTLE RANCH IN ITALY

The following inscription concerns a cattle-raising imperial estate in the mountains of central Italy. It contains orders protecting the lessees of the estate against molestation by the local authorities and provides incidentally one of the earliest evidences for the exercise of the police power in Italy by the Praetorian Prefect.

CIL, vol. IX, No. 2,438 (= *FIRA,* vol. I, no. 61); A.D. 169–172

Bassaeus Rufus and Macrinius Vindex to the magistrates of Saepinum, greeting. We have appended a copy of a letter written to us by Cosmus, freedman of the emperor and financial secretary [cf. introduction to § 14], together with that which was subjoined to his, and we warn you to refrain from abusing the lessees of the flocks of sheep to the serious detriment of the fisc, lest it be necessary to investigate the matter and punish the act, if the facts are as reported.

Letter of Cosmus, freedman of the emperor and financial secretary, written to Bassaeus Rufus and Macrinius Vindex, prefects of the Prae-

---

September 27), which was renamed in honor of Augustus, who was born in September; cf. chapter 1, note 16.

32. Narcissus was the freedman and secretary general of the Emperor Claudius. Nero had deprived him of the estate and granted it to his own freedman and notorious favorite, Doryphorus.

33. Nero Claudius Drusus, brother of the Emperor Tiberius, married the younger Antonia, daughter of Mark Antony. Germanicus and the Emperor Claudius were born of this marriage.

34. Land belonging to the emperor's privy purse, so called because inherited by him from the Ptolemaic dynasty of Egypt.

torian Guard, *eminentissimi viri:* I have appended a copy of a letter written to me by Septimianus, my fellow freedman and assistant, and I beg that you be good enough to write to the magistrates of Saepinum and Bovianum to refrain from abusing the lessees of the flocks of sheep, who are under my supervision, so that by your kindness the account of the fisc may be secured against loss.

Letter written by Septimianus to Cosmus: Since the lessees of the flocks of sheep, who are under your supervision, are now repeatedly complaining to me that they frequently suffer injury along the paths of the mountain pasturages at the hands of the imperial police[35] and magistrates at Saepinum and Bovianum, inasmuch as they detain in transit draught animals and shepherds that they have hired, saying that they are runaway slaves and have stolen draught animals—and under this pretext even sheep belonging to the emperor are lost to them in such disturbances—we considered it necessary to write them again and again to act more temperately, so that the imperial property might suffer no loss. And since they persist in the same insolence, saying that they will pay no attention to my letters and that it will do no good even if you write to them, I request, my lord, that, if you deem fit, you notify Bassaeus Rufus and Macrinius Vindex, prefects of the Praetorian Guard, *eminentissimi viri,* to issue letters to the said magistrates and police. . . . [The rest of this concluding sentence is fragmentary.]

26. OPERATION AND ADMINISTRATION OF MINES

Most mines were government property. Under the Republic their exploitation had been leased by the censors, like other public contracts, to companies of publicans (cf. vol. 1, p. 417). Under the Empire the publican system was progressively replaced, in mining as in other activities, by more direct governmental operation. Like the imperial estates, the mining districts were placed under the control of resident procurators, each of whom issued his own local rules to implement general imperial policies. The mining villages were usually not organized along municipal lines; instead, the procurator, like his counterpart on a landed estate, personally exercised the administrative and judicial authority in the village and district. Gangs of slaves and convicts (cf. § 159) constituted the traditional labor force of mines in antiquity.

---

35. *Stationarii.* These were soldiers stationed at guard posts, which were placed along the roads throughout the Empire to serve as local gendarmeries.

The two inscriptions that follow come from the copper- and silver-mining district of Vipasca (near modern Aljustrel, Portugal). The first details the conditions of mine tenure and operation; the second, given here only in part, contains some of the procurator's regulations governing a variety of other economic activities in the mining district.

FIRA, vol. I, no. 104 and *Iura* (1951), 2:127–133; A.D. 117–138

. . . to his dear Ulpius Aelianus,[36] greeting.

. . . he shall make immediate payment. If anyone does not do so and is convicted of having smelted ore before paying the price as specified above, his share as occupier shall be confiscated and the entire diggings shall be sold by the procurator of the mines. Anyone who proves that the tenant has smelted ore before paying the price of the half share belonging to the fisc shall receive one fourth.

Silver[37] diggings must be worked in accordance with the details contained in these regulations. Their prices will be kept in accordance with the liberality of the most sacred Emperor Hadrian Augustus, whereby the ownership of the share belonging to the fisc belongs to the first person to offer the price for the diggings and pay down to the fisc the sum of 4,000 sesterces.

If anyone strikes ore in one out of five diggings, he shall, as stated above, carry out the work in the others without interruption. If he does not do so, another shall have a legal right to take possession. If anyone after the twenty-five days granted for raising working capital actually begins regular operations but then stops operations for ten consecutive days, another shall have the right to take possession. If a diggings sold by the fisc is idle for six consecutive months, another shall have a legal right to take possession on condition that when the ore is extracted therefrom one half shall be, according to customary practice, reserved to the fisc.

The occupier of diggings shall have the right to have any partners he wishes on condition that each partner contribute his proportionate share of the expenses. If anyone does not do so, then the one who covers the expenses shall have an account of the expenses covered by himself posted on three consecutive days in a most frequented place in the

36. The procurator of the Vipasca mines, an imperial freedman as shown by his bearing the family names of Trajan and Hadrian; cf. introduction to § 44. The sender, whose identity is lost in the preceding lacuna, was some higher official, perhaps the provincial procurator.

37. The preceding paragraph presumably refers to copper mines; cf. the arrangement in the last two paragraphs.

forum, and shall demand of his partners through the public crier that each contribute his proportionate share of the expenses. If anyone does not thus contribute or does anything with malice aforethought to avoid contributing or to deceive one or more of his partners, he shall not have his share of such diggings, and that share shall belong to the partner or partners who cover the expenses. Alternatively, tenants who cover expenses in such diggings in which there are many partners shall have a legal right to recover from their partners anything that is shown to have been expended in good faith. Tenants shall have the right to sell among themselves, at as high a price as they can, even shares of diggings purchased from the fisc and paid for. Anyone who wishes to sell his share or buy shall submit a declaration to the procurator who is in charge of the mines; otherwise he shall not be allowed to buy or sell. Anyone who is a debtor of the fisc shall not be allowed to give away his share.

Ore extracted and lying at the diggings must be conveyed to the smelters by those to whom it belongs between sunrise and sunset; anyone convicted of having removed ore from the diggings after sunset in the night shall have to pay to the fisc the sum of 1,000 sesterces. A stealer of ore, if he is a slave, shall be whipped by the procurator and sold on this condition, that he shall be kept perpetually in chains and not tarry in any mine or mining district; the price of the slave shall belong to the owner. If the thief is a free man, the procurator shall confiscate his property and debar him forever from the mining district.

All diggings shall be carefully propped and reinforced, and the tenant of each diggings shall provide new and suitable replacements for rotten material. It shall be forbidden to touch or damage pillars or props left for reinforcement, or to do anything with malice aforethought to render the said pillars or props unsafe or. . . . If anyone is convicted of having injured, weakened, or damaged[?] a diggings, or of having done anything with malice aforethought to render such diggings unsafe, if he is a slave he shall be whipped at the discretion of the procurator and sold by his master on this condition, that he shall not tarry in any mine [or mining district]; if he is a free man, the procurator shall appropriate his property to the fisc and debar him forever from the mining district.

Anyone who operates copper diggings shall avoid the ditch that drains the water from the mines and leave a space of not less than fifteen feet on either side. It shall be forbidden to damage the ditch. The procurator shall permit the driving of a drift from the ditch for the purpose of discovering new mines, on condition that the drift be not more than four feet in width and depth. It shall be forbidden to look for or chop out ore within fifteen feet on either side of the ditch.[38] If anyone is convicted of having done anything different in the drifts, if he is a slave he shall be whipped at the discretion of the procurator and sold by his master on this condition, that he shall not tarry in any mine [or mining district]; if he is a free man, the procurator shall appropriate his property to the fisc and debar him forever from the mining district.

Anyone who operates silver diggings shall avoid the ditch that drains the water from the mines and shall leave a space of not less than sixty feet on either side. He shall work the diggings occupied by him or allotted to him within the boundaries prescribed, and shall not advance beyond nor collect leavings nor drive drifts outside the limits of the diggings allotted. . . . [The rest is lost.]

CIL, vol. II, no. 5,181 (= Dessau, no. 6,891 = *FIRA,* vol. I, no. 105); second century

OF THE MANAGEMENT OF THE BATHS. The lessee of the baths or his partner shall, in accordance with the terms of his lease running to June 30 next, be required to heat the baths and keep them open for use entirely at his own expense every day from daybreak to the seventh hour for women, and from the eighth hour to the second hour in the evening for men, at the discretion of the procurator in charge of the mines. He shall be required to provide a proper supply of running water for the heated rooms, to the bath tub up to the highest level and to the basin, for women as well as for men. The lessee shall charge men one half *as* each and women one *as* each. Imperial freedmen or slaves in the service of the procurator or on his payroll are admitted free; likewise minors and soldiers. At the expiration of the lease the lessee, or his partner or agent, shall be required to return in good condition all the bath equipment consigned to him, excepting any rendered unusable through age. He shall be duly required to wash, dry, and coat with fresh

---

38. Diodorus, in his account of mining in Spain (see § 23), gives the following description of mine drainage (*Historical Library* v. xxxvii. 3): "Now and then down deep they come upon rivers flowing underground, the force of which they overcome by diverting their inundating streams through transverse channels. For, driven as they are by fully justified expectations of profits, they push their several enterprises to the very limit and, most surprising of all, they draw off the streams of water by means of Egyptian screws, as they are called, which Archimedes of Syracuse invented when he visited Egypt. By means of these they carry the water in successive lifts to the mouth and dry up the bottom of the mine." Several of these ancient Archimedean pumps have actually been found in the mining region of southern Spain. The standard screw was a wooden cylinder twenty inches in diameter and fourteen feet long, but since it was worked on an incline it achieved a net vertical lift of only five feet.

grease every thirty days the bronze implements which he uses. If any needed repair prevents the proper operation of the baths, the lessee shall be entitled to prorate the rental for that period; beyond this, whatever else he may do for the purpose of operating the said baths, he shall be entitled to no reduction of rental. The lessee shall not be allowed to sell wood except for branch trimmings unsuited for fuel;[39] if he does anything in violation of this, he shall have to pay to the fisc 100 sesterces for each sale. If these baths are not properly kept open for use, then the procurator of the mines shall have the right to fine the lessee up to 200 sesterces every time they are not kept open properly. The lessee shall at all times have on hand a supply of wood sufficient for . . . days.

OF THE SHOEMAKING TRADE. Anyone who makes any of the shoes or thongs which shoemakers customarily handle, or who drives or sells shoemaker's nails, or who is convicted of selling within the district anything else which shoemakers are entitled to sell, shall have to pay double to the concessionaire, or to his partner or agent. The concessionaire shall sell nails in accordance with the regulations of the iron mines. The concessionaire, or his partner or agent, shall have the right to obtain security. No one will be allowed to repair shoes, except to mend or repair his own or his master's[?]. The concessionaire shall be required to offer all types of shoes for sale; if he does not, everyone shall have a legal right to purchase wherever he wishes.

OF THE BARBERING TRADE. The concessionaire shall be entitled to operate with the assurance that no one else in the village of the Vipasca mines or within the district thereof shall practice barbering for profit. Anyone who so practices barbering shall have to pay the concessionaire, or his partner or agent . . . *denarii* for each use of the razors, and the said razors shall be forfeited to the concessionaire. Slaves attending to their masters or their fellow slaves are excepted. Itinerant barbers not sent by the concessionaire shall not have the right to practice barbering. The concessionaire, or his partner or agent, shall have the right of obtaining security; anyone who hinders his receiving security shall have to pay five *denarii* for each such act. The concessionaire shall engage one or more skilled workers in proportion [to the need].

---

39. Because the bath fuel was supplied by the government or—more likely—to prevent the lessee of the baths from infringing the monopoly of the firewood concessionaire.

OF THE FULLERS' SHOPS. No one to whom the concessionaire, or his partner or agent, has not leased or granted the right shall be allowed to do work on new or used clothing for pay. Anyone convicted of any violation of this shall have to pay the concessionaire, or his partner or agent, three *denarii* for each garment. The concessionaire, or his partner or agent, shall have the right to obtain security. . . .

SCHOOLTEACHERS. It is decreed that schoolteachers are exempt from taxation at the hands of the procurator of the mines.[40]

CLAIMS TO DIGGINGS, OR PERMIT FEE[?]. Anyone who, in accordance with the regulations issued for the mines,[41] stakes a claim to or occupies a diggings or a diggings site within the district of the Vipasca mines with a view to maintaining a legal right shall within the next two days after such claim or occupancy declare to the farmer of this revenue, or his partner or agent. . . . [The rest is lost.]

A LABOR CONTRACT

The following contract, written on a waxed tablet found in the gold-mining district of Dacia, illustrates the use of free labor in mining operations.

CIL, vol. III, p. 948, no. X (= *FIRA,* vol. III, no. 150*a*); A.D. 164

In the consulship of Macrinus and Celsus, May 20. I, Flavius Secundinus [probably a clerk in the mine office] at the request of Memmius son of Asclepius (because he declared that he was illiterate)[42] have here recorded the fact that he declared that he had let, and he did in fact let, his labor in the gold mine to Aurelius Adjutor from this day to November 13 next for seventy *denarii* and board. He shall be entitled to receive his wages in installments. He shall be required to render healthy and vigorous labor to the above-mentioned employer. If he wants to quit or stop working against the employer's wishes, he shall have to pay five sesterces for each day, deducted from his total wages. If a flood hinders operations, he shall be required to prorate accordingly.[43] If the employer

---

40. On the tax exemption of teachers in the Roman Empire see § 56.
41. The reference is presumably to the regulations preserved in part in the preceding inscription.
42. But he could sign his name, which is affixed at the end of the contract.
43. This prorated reduction probably did not apply to board but only to wages.

delays payment of the wages when the time is up, he shall be subject to the same penalty after three days of grace.

Done at Immenosum Maius.

[Signed] Titus son of Beusans, also known as Bradua; Socratio son of Socratio; Memmius son of Asclepius.[44]

27. INTERNAL TRADE

The unity of the Empire during the Roman Peace, and its excellent harbor facilities and road system, produced an expansion of commercial activity unequaled until modern times. Internal trade, far more important than foreign commerce (see § 30), was predominantly in products of prime necessity—grain, and raw materials, especially for military purposes. In the first century, Italy was the great consuming center, and the capital city of Rome the principal market. Later, with the growing economic development of the provinces, Italy lost this dominant commercial position as an intense interprovincial and intraprovincial trade sprang up. Most of the traffic of the Roman Empire was waterborne, since overland transportation was cumbersome and costly. Shipping was in the hands mostly of the peoples of the eastern Mediterranean, the most active of whom in this sphere were the Syrians. The common carrier was a ship (or riverboat) owner who sailed his own vessel, carrying cargoes on his own account or on consignment for others. Shippers often joined in partnerships or associations (cf. § 29), and some of these established importing and distribution agencies, often with their own docks and warehouses, at Rome, in the ports serving Rome, and in other important harbors of the Empire.

AE, 1967, no. 480; mid-second century

With good fortune! Lucius Antonius Albus, proconsul, declares: If it is necessary for the greatest metropolis of Asia and for practically the whole world that its port, which receives people drawn to it from everywhere, not be impeded, I, upon learning how it is being damaged, deemed it necessary, by [this] edict, both to put a stop to it and to ordain an appropriate penalty for those disobeying. I therefore order those importing wood or stone not to stack their wood or to saw stone by the shore, for the ones by the weight of their cargoes damage the piles installed for the protection of the harbor, and the others by producing

---

44. Since the last signature is that of the laborer being hired in this contract, the first two signatories were presumably agents or partners acting for the employer rather than witnesses.

and dumping stone dust fill up the deep water and choke the free flow, and both render the shore impassable. Therefore . . . let them know that if anyone ignores my edict and is caught doing any of the forbidden acts, he will pay a penalty of _____[45] to the renowned city of Ephesus, and in addition he personally will answer to me for his disobedience; for when our greatest emperor has concerned himself with the protection of the port and has repeatedly sent letters about this, it is not just that those who destroy it should discharge their guilt by merely paying money.

Post in public.

Pliny, Letters book x, no. 41

[Pliny to the Emperor Trajan]

. . . In the territory of the city of Nicomedia[46] there is a very extensive lake, over which marbles, produce, firewood, and timber are transported by ship to the trunk road at modest cost and effort. Thence they are conveyed in wagons to the sea with great labor and greater expense. The Nicomedians therefore desire to connect the lake with the sea.[47] This project requires many hands; but these, on the other hand, are available, for the countryside, and particularly the city, is exceedingly populous. And one may definitely hope that everybody will very gladly engage in a project which will be profitable to all.

It only remains for you to send, if you deem proper, a civil engineer or an architect to examine carefully whether the lake lies above sea level; the experts of this region maintain that it is about sixty feet higher. I find there is in the same vicinity a trench which was cut by one of the kings. But as it is unfinished, it is uncertain whether it was for the purpose of draining the adjacent lands or of connecting the lake with the river;[48] it is equally doubtful whether it is unfinished because of the intervening death of the king or abandonment of the hope of completing the project. But—you will forgive my being ambitious for your glory —I am urged on by this very fact and ardently desire that what kings merely began should be brought to completion by you.

---

45. The reason the amount was not filled in must remain a matter of speculation.
46. The capital of the province of Bithynia, situated on the trunk road connecting the Danube provinces with the eastern frontier. The city carried on a large export trade with Rome.
47. This sentence gives the sense of an obvious lacuna in the text.
48. The ancient Sangarius (modern Sakriya), which flows into the Black Sea.

Dittenberger, no. 1,229 (= *IGRR*, vol. IV, no. 841)

[Hierapolis, Phrygia, second century?]

Flavius Zeuxis, merchant, who sailed seventy-two trips around Cape Malea [see note 56] to Italy, built this tomb for himself and his children, Flavius Theodorus and Flavius Theudas, and for any to whom they grant permission.

> Excavations in the Bay of Naples area in recent decades have yielded scores of waxed wooden tablets containing business records — loans, receipts, bonds, and so on. The following example is particularly instructive in its details about the storage facilities at the port of Puteoli and on the degree to which some slaves conducted their masters' business.

AE, 1969–70, no. 100; July 2, A.D. 37

In the consulship of Gaius Caesar Germanicus Augustus and Tiberius Claudius Nero Germanicus, six days before the Nones of July. I, Diognetus slave of Gaius Novius Cypaerus, have written at the bidding and in the presence of my master Cypaerus that I have rented to Hesicus slave of Evenus, freedman of Tiberius Julius Augustus, Warehouse No. 12 in the middle block of the Bassian public warehouses at Puteoli, in which is stored rice-wheat [shipped] from Alexandria which he [Hesicus] received as security this day from Gaius Novius Eunus; likewise he [Hesicus] received as security from the said Eunus two hundred sacks of beans, which he has stored in the said warehouses, lower block, between the pillars. From the Kalends of July [rent] per month one thousand sesterces, cash. Done at Puteoli.

A TYRIAN AGENCY AT PUTEOLI

> The financial straits of this agency of Tyrian merchants at Puteoli, the chief port of Italy in republican times, reflects the sharp drop in business at this Campanian port not only because of the successful competition of the harbor at Ostia, nearer Rome, but because of the general decline of Italian commerce in the second century.

IG, vol. XIV, no. 830, lines 1–19 (= OGIS, no. 595 = IGRR, vol. I, no. 421);
A.D. 174

Letter written to the city of Tyre, the sacred, inviolable and autonomous metropolis of Phoenicia and of other cities, and mistress of a fleet. To the chief magistrates, council, and people of their sovereign native city, from the [Tyrians] resident in Puteoli, greeting.

By the grace of the gods and the good fortune of our lord the emperor [Marcus Aurelius] there is many a commercial agency in Puteoli, as most of you know, and ours excels the others both in adornment and in size. In the past this was cared for by the Tyrians resident in Puteoli, who were numerous and wealthy; but now this care has devolved on us, who are few in number, and since we pay the expenses for the sacrifices and services to our ancestral gods consecrated here in temples, we do not have the means to pay the agency's annual rent of 250 *denarii,* especially as the expenses of the Puteoli Ox-Sacrifice Games[49] have in addition been imposed on us. We therefore beg you to provide for the agency's continued existence. And it will continue if you make the 250 *denarii* paid annually for rent your concern; for the remaining expenses, including those incurred to refurbish the agency for the birthday festival of our lord the emperor, we set down to our own account, so as not to burden the city [i.e., Tyre]. And we remind you that the agency here— unlike the one in the capital, Rome—derives no income either from shipowners or from merchants. We therefore appeal to you and beg you to make provision for this unfortunate circumstance.

Written in Puteoli, July 23, in the consulship of Gallus and Flaccus Cornelianus.

> [The letter is followed by an extract from the minutes of the meeting of the council of Tyre held on December 8, A.D. 174, at which, after it was pointed out that the agency at Rome had always paid the Puteoli agency's rent from its receipts, the council voted that this practice be continued.]

AGENCIES AT OSTIA

The excavations at Ostia have uncovered a large piazza flanked on three sides by porticoes containing over sixty offices of shipping agencies and other organizations connected with the port's commerce. In front of each

---

49. Nothing further is known about these games.

office was a mosaic pavement executed in a design appropriate to the business of the house. A number of mosaic floors also contained inscribed legends; those sufficiently well preserved are given here (the arabic numerals are editorial additions to indicate the position of each office in sequence around the piazza). Most of the mosaics date from the time of Commodus.

CIL, vol. XIV, no. 4,549

1. Clodius Primigenius, Claudius Crescens, *quinquennales*. Caulkers, ropemakers.
2. Association of pelt-dealers of Ostia and Portus here.
3. Ships' carpenters association.
10. Shipowners of Misua[50] here.
12. Shipowners from Hippo Diarrhytus.
14. Agency of Sabrata.
15, 16. Shipowners and merchants, at their own expense.[51]
17. Shipowners of Gummi, at their own expense.
18. Shipowners of Carthage, at their own expense.
19. Shipowners of Turris.
21. Shipowners and merchants of Carales.
23. Shipowners of Syllecthum.
32. Shipowners of Narbo.
34. Shipowners of Curubis, at their own expense. Agency of the grain merchants of the colony of Curubis.
43. Tiber boatmen, at their own expense.

SPEED OF TRAVEL

The speeds in the voyages mentioned here average better than 100 miles a day, or five knots, slightly better than half the normal speed of tramp steamers used in the grain trade today. The average speed of Roman cargo vessels was about three knots with a favoring wind. Comparative figures for overland transport may be found in § 30, second selection, according to which an Arabian caravan averaged twenty-three Roman miles a day; and in Pliny's statement (*Natural History* VII. xx. 84) that the Emperor

---

50. The towns named in nos. 10–18, 23, and 34 were in North Africa; those in nos. 19 and 21 were in Sardinia; Narbo, in no. 32, was the capital and commercial center of southern Gaul *(Gallia Narbonensis)*.

51. Since the office space in the portico was provided by the imperial government, "at their own expense" here and later probably refers to the cost of laying the mosaic pavement.

Tiberius "completed by carriage the longest twenty-four hours' journey on record when hastening to Germany to his brother Drusus, who was ill: this covered two hundred [Roman] miles."

Pliny, Natural History xix. i. 3–4

Two prefects of Egypt, Galerius and Balbillus, made the passage from the Straits of Sicily to Alexandria in under seven and six days, respectively. Fifteen years later Valerius Marianus, a senator of praetorian rank, made Alexandria from Puteoli in less than nine days, in summertime, on a very light breeze. To think that [commerce] brings Cádiz, by the Strait of Gibraltar, within seven days of Ostia, Hither Spain within four days, the province of Narbonese Gaul within three, and Africa, even on a very gentle breeze, within two (as happened to Gaius Flavius, legate of the proconsul Vibius Crispus)!

28. The Grain Fleet

The two selections given here are our most detailed ancient descriptions of the size of the vessels of the Alexandrian grain fleet and of the routes by which they reached Italy. The usual route was to follow the prevailing winds north to Asia Minor, thence west via Crete to Malta, and thence north to Puteoli or Ostia, the ports of Rome. The burden of the ship described by Lucian has been variously estimated; the most recent study puts it at 1,200 to 1,300 tons. The average merchantman had a draught of 50 tons.

Lucian,[52] The Ship i–ix (abridged)

Lycinus: Timolaus . . . [you're a] tireless sightseer.

Timolaus: Well, Lycinus, what do you expect of a person who has nothing to do and hears that such an unusually large ship has put into Piraeus,[53] one of the grain ships from Egypt to Italy? What is more, I believe that you and Samippus there came down from the city for no other reason but to see the ship.

---

52. Lucian of Samosata on the Euphrates was born A.D. c. 120 and died after 180. He was a traveling lecturer and wrote about eighty pieces in Greek, mostly satirical dialogues. *The Ship* was written *c.* 165.

53. The point is that vessels of the Alexandrian grain fleet were not often seen in Piraeus. This ship (the *Isis*) had encountered foul winds on its course westward from Asia Minor, and the skipper decided to lay over in the harbor of Athens. When the *Isis* arrived there, the Athenians streamed down to the harbor to see the unusual sight.

Lycinus: So we did, and Adimantus . . . came along with us; only I don't know where he is—he got lost in the crowd of spectators. We came together to the ship and went on board. . . .

Timolaus: I remember now, Samippus, where it was we lost Adimantus. It was when we were standing all that time looking up at the mast, counting the layers of hides, and watching in amazement the sailor going up the reefs, then running up there on the yardarm, perfectly safe, supporting himself by the yardarm tackling. . . .

Samippus: Incidentally, what a big ship! About 180 feet long, a shipbuilder would say, and something over a quarter of that in beam; and the maximum depth from deck to keel, through the hold, about 44 feet. And then the height of the mast; what a huge yardarm is has; and what a forestay it requires to secure it! And how the stern rises with its gentle curve, with its gilded beak, balanced at the opposite end by the long rising extension of the prow, with [a figure of] the name-goddess of the ship, Isis, on either side! Now, as to the other ornamental details, the paintings and the fiery bright topsail, I was more astonished by the anchors, and the capstans and windlasses, and the stern cabins. The size of the crew could be compared to that of an army. And they were saying she carried enough grain to feed everybody in Attica for a year. . . .

Timolaus: They set sail with a moderate wind from the Pharus [the lighthouse of Alexandria, Egypt], and sighted Acamas[54] on the seventh day. Then a west wind blew up, and they were carried off their course as far as Sidon. On their way thence they fell in with a heavy gale, and on the tenth day came through the straits to the Chelidon Isles;[55] and there they all nearly went to the bottom . . . on a pitch dark night. However, the gods were responsive to their lamentation and showed them a fire from Lycia, which enabled them to identify that place, and a bright star—either Castor or Pollux—appeared at the masthead and guided the ship into the open sea on their left, just as she was making straight for the cliff. Thence, having once fallen off their proper course, they sailed through the Aegean beating up against adverse Etesian winds until they came to anchor in Piraeus yesterday, the seventieth day out from Egypt, so far off their course were they carried. Whereas if they had properly taken Crete on their right, they would have sailed beyond Malea[56] and been in Italy by this time.

---

54. The northwestern promontory of Cyprus, modern Hagios Epiphanios.
55. Off the southern coast of Asia Minor, between Cyprus and Rhodes.
56. The southern promontory of the Peloponnese, famous for its treacherous weather and seas. To

SAINT PAUL'S VOYAGE TO ITALY

Acts of the Apostles 27. 1–28. 13 (abridged); Adapted from the New Testament, an
American Translation

When it was decided that we were to sail for Italy, Paul and some other
prisoners were turned over to a centurion of the Augustan Cohort,
named Julius.[57] We went on board an Adramyttian ship bound for the
ports of Asia, and put to sea. We had a Macedonian from Thessalonica,
named Aristarchus, with us. The next day we put in at Sidon, and Julius
kindly entrusted Paul to his friends, to whom he went to be taken care
of. Putting to sea from there, we sailed under the lee of Cyprus, as the
wind was against us, and after traversing the Cilician and Pamphylian
waters, we reached Myra in Lycia. There the centurion found an Alexandrian [grain] ship bound for Italy, and put us on board her. For a
number of days we made slow progress and had some difficulty in
arriving off Cnidus. Then, as the wind kept us from going on, we sailed
under the lee of Crete, off Cape Salmone, and with difficulty coasted
along it and reached a place called Fair Havens, near the town of Lasea.

As a great deal of time had now passed, and navigation had become
dangerous,[58] for the Day of Atonement was already over, Paul began to
warn them. . . . But the centurion was more influenced by the pilot and
the shipowner than by what Paul had to say, and as the harbor was not
fit to winter in, the majority favored putting to sea again, in the hope of
being able to reach and winter in Phoenix, a harbor in Crete facing west-
south-west and west-north-west. When a moderate south wind sprang
up, thinking their object was within reach, they weighed anchor and ran
close along the coast of Crete. But soon a very violent wind—the
Euroclydo [Northeaster], as it is called—rushed down upon it. The ship
was caught by it and could not face the wind, so we gave way and let
her run before it. As we passed under the lee of a small island called
Cauda, we managed with great difficulty to secure the ship's boat. After
hoisting it on board, they used ropes to brace the boat, and as they were
afraid of being cast on the Syrtis banks [of North Africa], they lowered

---

reach Italy from Piraeus the *Isis* would have to double Cape Malea, a danger to which ships keeping
the usual course south of Crete were not exposed.

57. The place is Caesarea in Judea; the time is A.D. 60.

58. Shipment of grain from Egypt to Italy (cf. § 17) was suspended during the winter because of
the danger.

the gear and let the ship drift. The next day, as the storm continued to be violent, they began to throw the cargo overboard, and on the next they threw the ship's tackle overboard with their own hands. For a number of days neither the sun nor the stars were visible, and the storm continued to rage, until at last we gave up all hope of being saved. . . .

It was the fourteenth night of the storm, and we were drifting through the Adriatic, when about midnight the sailors began to suspect that there was land ahead. On taking soundings they found a depth of twenty fathoms, and a little later, taking soundings again, they found a depth of fifteen. Then, as they were afraid we might go on the rocks, they dropped four anchors from the stern and waited anxiously for daylight. The sailors wanted to escape from the ship, and actually lowered the boat into the sea, pretending that they were going to run out anchors from the bow, but Paul said to the centurion and the soldiers, "You cannot be saved unless these men stay on board." Then the soldiers cut the ropes that held the boat and let it drift away. Until daybreak Paul kept urging them all to take something to eat. . . . We were about seventy-six souls on board.[59] When they had had enough to eat, they threw the wheat into the sea, in order to lighten the ship.

When daylight came they could not recognize the coast, but they saw a bay with a beach and determined to run the ship ashore there if possible. So they cast off the anchors and left them in the sea; at the same time they undid the lashings of the rudders, and hoisting the foresail to the wind they made for the beach. But they struck a shoal and ran the ship aground. The bow stuck and could not be moved, while the stern began to break up under the strain. The soldiers proposed to kill the prisoners, for fear some of them might swim ashore and escape, but the centurion wanted to save Paul, so he prevented them from doing this, and ordered all who could swim to jump overboard first and get to land, and the rest to follow on planks or other pieces of the wreckage of the boat. So they all got safely to land.

After our escape we learned that the island was called Malta. The natives showed us remarkable kindness, for they made a fire and welcomed us all, because of the rain that had come on and the cold. . . . Three months later we sailed on an Alexandrian ship with Castor and Pollux as its figurehead which had wintered at the island. We put in at

59. A variant reading gives the number on board as 276. The lower figure is probably to be preferred.

Syracuse and stayed there three days; then we weighed anchor and reached Regium. A day later a south wind sprang up, and the following day we arrived at Puteoli.[60]

29. PRIVILEGES FOR SHIPOWNERS

"Those are called *navicularii* (shipowners)," says a scholiast on Cicero's oration *In Favor of the Manilian Law,* "who transport grain to the city or wherever the emperor is." Because the imperial government relied on private shippers to transport supplies to Rome and the military forces, *collegia* of shipowners were the first trade associations to be granted official recognition and privileges, chiefly exemption from compulsory municipal services. These associations, with which it was more convenient for the government to contract than with individual shipowners, are first known in great numbers from about the time of Hadrian; they remained free agents until the third century, when, with increasing encroachment of the state in all areas, they were absorbed into the imperial service (see §§ 116, 129).

Gaius, Institutes I. xxxiic

Likewise, by an edict of Claudius, Latins acquire Roman citizenship if they build a seagoing vessel of a capacity of not less than 10,000 *modii* of grain, and if that ship, or another in its place, carries grain to Rome for six years.[61]

Justinian, Digest L. vi. 6

Merchants who assist in provisioning the city with grain, and also shipowners who service the grain supply of the city, obtain exemption from compulsory public services as long as they are engaged in activity of this sort. For it has been properly decided that their risks should be compensated, or rather encouraged, by rewards, in order that those who perform services abroad that are both of a public nature and accompanied by danger and effort may be free from annoyances and expenses at home. For it is not even too much to say that they are absent on public business while they serve the grain supply of the city.

60. For a description of the arrival of an Alexandrian grain fleet at Puteoli and the attendant bustle, see Seneca, *Letters* LXXVII. 1–3.

61. For other privileges enacted by Claudius to encourage shipowners to enter the grain trade, see § 17, third selection.

A fixed pattern has been given to the exemption granted to shipowners—this exemption only they themselves possess; it does not extend either to their children or to their freedmen. This is set forth in imperial enactments. The deified Hadrian stated in a rescript that only shipowners of maritime vessels who serve the grain supply of the city possess exemption.

Although anyone may belong to the association of shipowners, nevertheless a person who does not own one or more ships and does not meet all the requirements provided by the imperial enactments cannot avail himself of the privileges granted to shipowners. And the deified brothers [Emperors Marcus Aurelius and Lucius Verus] stated the following in a rescript: "There are some persons who claim to be shipowners engaged in transporting grain and olive oil to the markets of the Roman people and therefore exempt, and who demand release from compulsory services, but who neither actually sail nor have the greater part of their property invested in shipowning and commercial activities. Such persons shall be deprived of exemption." . . .

The deified [Antoninus] Pius also stated in a rescript that whenever a question arose as to any shipowner, an investigation should be made as to whether he is assuming the role of a shipowner for the purpose of avoiding compulsory services.

30. FOREIGN TRADE

In its trade with regions beyond its borders, especially the Far East, from which it imported large quantities of luxury goods, the Roman Empire showed an adverse trade balance which resulted in a sizable and steady drain of specie (cf. introduction to § 43). From the northern and eastern shores of the Black Sea came slaves, hides, salt fish, shipbuilding timber, linen, hemp, wax, and pitch. With the Baltic region there was a lively commerce in amber. The oriental trade brought aromatics from Arabia (which the inhabitants of the Roman Empire consumed in enormous quantities for ceremonial and personal use), spices, cotton, Chinese silk, and numerous other luxuries from India. Several important caravan routes led overland from Central Asia to the Syrian ports of the Mediterranean, but as these passed through the Parthian Empire and were subject to its tolls, the bulk of the Empire's Indian and Arabian wares was carried by water to the Red Sea ports of Egypt, and thence down the Nile to Alexandria, the central clearinghouse of this eastern trade. The fourth selection below is from a kind of "Trader's Guide to the Red Sea and

Indian Ocean," written in the middle of the first century A.D. by a Greek merchant of Egypt actively engaged in the India trade. Striking recent discoveries are an ivory statuette of the Indian goddess Lakhshmi at Pompeii, and Italian pottery and other evidences of settlements of Roman merchants in Indian ports.

THE AMBER TRADE

Pliny, *Natural History* XXXVII. xi

It is certain that amber is a product of the islands of the Northern Ocean, and that it is the substance called by the Germans *glaesum*. . . . Amber is imported by the Germans into Pannonia especially, and thence the Veneti . . . a people very close to Pannonia and dwelling on the shores of the Adriatic, first made it famous. . . .[62] At the present day the peasant women of the region beyond the Po wear necklaces of amber, primarily as ornaments but also for its medical value; for amber, indeed, is believed to be good for tonsils and throat ailments. . . .

From Carnuntum[63] in Pannonia to the coast of Germany from which the amber is imported is a distance of about 600 miles—a fact which has only recently been ascertained. And there is still alive a Roman *eques* who was sent there by Julianus, the manager of the gladiatorial exhibitions for the Emperor Nero, to procure this product. Journeying along the coasts and through markets there, he brought back such great quantities of amber that the nets which are used for holding back the wild beasts and for protecting the podium[64] were studded with amber. The arms, too, the litters,[65] and all the equipment of one particular day [of spectacles] were decorated with amber, to vary the display of each separate day. The largest piece of amber that this personage brought to Rome weighed thirteen pounds.

62. Archaelogical discoveries have shown that amber had been transported along this route from the Baltic to the Mediterranean since very ancient, perhaps prehistoric times. During the Principate, Aquileia in northern Italy was the principal manufacturing and distributing center for amber goods.

63. A key Roman frontier fortress on the Danube, between Vienna and Bratislava.

64. Where the emperor and nobles sat in the amphitheater.

65. On which slain gladiators were removed.

INCENSE FROM ARABIA

Pliny, *Natural History* XII. xxxii. 63–65; From *LCL*

Frankincense after being collected is conveyed to Sabbatha[66] on camels, one of the gates of the city being opened for its admission; the kings have made it a capital offense to turn aside [camels so laden] from the high road. At Sabbatha a tithe estimated by measure and not by weight is taken by the priests for the god they call Sabis, and the incense is not allowed to be put on the market until this has been done; this tithe is drawn upon to defray what is a public expenditure, for actually on a fixed number of days the god graciously entertains guests at a banquet. It can only be exported through the country of the Gebbanites,[67] and accordingly a tax is paid on it to the king of that people as well. Their capital is Thomna, which is 1,487½ [Roman] miles distant from the town of Gaza in Judaea on the Mediterranean coast; the journey is divided into sixty-five stages with halts for camels. Fixed portions of the frankincense are given to the priests and the king's secretaries, but beside these the guards and their attendants and the gate keepers and servants also have their pickings. Indeed all along the route they keep on paying, at one place for water, at another for fodder, or the charges for lodging at the halts, and the various *octrois;* so that expenses mount up to 688 *denarii* per camel before the Mediterranean coast is reached; and then again payment is made to the tax farmers of our Empire [cf. § 18]. Consequently the price of the best frankincense is six, of the second best five, and the third best three *denarii* a pound.

66. The capital of the kingdom of Saba—the Sheba of the Bible—in the southwestern part of the Arabian peninsula (Arabia Felix).

67. This is, by camel caravan. Much of the traffic also went by sea to Egypt, as Strabo (*Geography* XVI. iv. 14) tells: "Now the cargoes [of aromatics] are conveyed from Leuce Come to Petra, and thence to Rhinocolura, which is in Phoenicia near Egypt, and then to the other peoples; but at the present time they are for the most part transported on the Nile to Alexandria; and they are brought from Arabia and India to Myus Hormus, and they are conveyed by camels over to Coptus in the Thebaid, which is situated on a canal of the Nile, and then to Alexandria."

THE INDIA TRADE

Pliny, *Natural History* VI. xxvi. 100–106; From *LCL*

Such was the route followed by the fleet of Alexander the Great; but subsequently it was thought that the safest line was to start from Syagrus,[68] a promontory of Arabia, with a west wind (the name for which in those parts is Hippalus[69]) and make for Patale,[70] the distance being reckoned as 1,332 [Roman] miles. The following period considered it a shorter and safer route to start from the same cape and steer for the Indian harbor of Sigerus, and for a long time this was the course followed, until a merchant discovered a shorter route, and the desire for gain brought India nearer; indeed, the voyage is made every year, with companies of archers on board, because the seas used to be very greatly infested by pirates. And it will not be amiss to set forth the whole of the voyage from Egypt, now that reliable knowledge of it is for the first time accessible. It is an important subject, in view of the fact that in no year does India absorb less than 50,000,000 sesterces of our Empire's wealth, sending back merchandise to be sold with us at a hundred times its original cost.

Two miles from Alexandria is the town of Juliopolis. The voyage up the Nile from there to Coptus is 309 miles, and takes twelve days when the midsummer trade winds are blowing. From Coptus the journey is made with camels, stations being placed at intervals for the purpose of watering; the first, a stage of 22 miles, is called Hydreuma [i.e., "Watering Place"]; the second is in the mountains, a day's journey on; the third at a second place named Hydreuma, 85 miles from Coptus; the next is in the mountains; next we come to Apollo's Hydreuma, 184 miles from Coptus; again a station in the mountains; then we get to New Hydreuma, 230 miles from Coptus. There is also an Old Hydreuma, known by the name of Trogodyticum, where a garrison is stationed on

68. Ras Fartak, on the south coast of Arabia, at the entrance to the Gulf of Aden.

69. The Indian Ocean monsoon, called Hippalus by the Greeks and Romans, after the mariner who discovered that these seasonal winds could be used for direct passage between the mouth of the Red Sea and India. The date of Hippalus' discovery is generally placed c. 100 B.C. or A.D. c. 50. The earlier date, preferred by the most recent scholarship, would explain the great increase in Alexandrian shipping to India in the reign of Augustus, when, according to Strabo (*Geography* II. v. 12), "as many as 120 vessels were sailing from Myus Hormus [on the Red Sea] to India, whereas formerly, under the Ptolemies, only a very few ventured to undertake the voyage and to carry on traffic in Indian merchandise."

70. The Indian ports and market towns mentioned in this and the following selection were located along the west coast of the Indian subcontinent.

outpost duty [for such a garrison see § 143, second selection], at a caravanserai accommodating two thousand travelers; it is 7 miles from New Hydreuma. Then comes the town of Berenice, where there is a harbor on the Red Sea, 257 miles from Coptus.[71] But as the greater part of the journey is done by night because of the heat, and the days are spent at the stations, the whole journey from Coptus to Berenice takes twelve days.

Traveling by sea begins at midsummer before the Dog Star rises or immediately after its rising [i.e., in July], and it takes about thirty days to reach Ocelis in Arabia or Cane in the frankincense-producing district; there is also a third port named Muza, which is not called at on the voyage to India, and is used only by merchants trading in frankincense and Arabian perfumes.[72] . . . The most advantageous way of sailing to India is to set out from Occlis; from that port it is forty days' voyage, if the Hippalus is blowing, to the first trading station in India, Muziris— not a desirable port of call, on account of the neighboring pirates, who occupy a place called Nitriae, nor is it specially rich in articles of merchandise; and furthermore the roadstead for shipping is a long way from the land, and cargoes have to be brought in and carried out in boats. . . . There is another more serviceable port, belonging to the Nelcyndian tribe, called Becare. . . .

Travelers set sail from India on the return voyage at the beginning of the Egyptian month of Tybi, which is our December, or at all events before the sixth day of the Egyptian Mechir, which equals January 13 in our calendar—so making it possible to return home within a year. They set sail from India with a southeast wind [actually, the Northeast monsoon] and after entering the Red Sea continue the voyage with a southwest or south wind.

Anonymous, *Navigation of the Erythraean Sea* xlix, lvi

Into this trading port [of Barygaza] come wine, principally Italian but also Laodicean and Arabian; copper, tin, and lead; coral and peridot; all kinds of clothing, plain and patterned; multicolored girdles a cubit wide; storax, yellow sweet clover, raw glass; realgar, sulphide of antimony;

71. Still another road led from Coptus to the Red Sea port of Myus Hormus. Later, a third led to Berenice from Antinoöpolis on the Nile (see § 22). For the toll fees charged for the use of these roads, see § 18.

72. Of the three Arabian ports mentioned in this sentence, Muza corresponds to modern Mocha, on the Red Sea coast; Ocelis was located c. 50 miles to the south, near Pirim Island; and Cane was on the south coast, c. 200 miles east of Aden.

Roman gold and silver money, which is exchanged at some profit against the local coinage; and ointment, inexpensive but not much of it. For the king in times past there were imported silverware of great price, musician slaves, beautiful girls for concubinage, fine wine, clothing expensive though undecorated, and choice ointment. Exported from this region are nard, costus, bdellium, ivory, onyx . . . agate; all kinds of cloth, Chinese [silk], *molochinon,* and yarn; long pepper; and the wares brought here from the trading stations in the area. . . .

Ships in these trading ports [Muziris and Nelcynda] sail fully laden because of the great bulk and quantity of pepper and *malabathrum.*[73] Here come especially great sums of money; peridot; clothing, plain and not much of it; multicolored textiles; sulphide of antimony; coral; raw glass; copper, tin, lead; wine, not much but about as much as in Barygaza; realgar; orpiment; and grain, just enough for the shipping personnel, since the local merchants do not use it. The principal export is pepper, produced in quantity uniquely in one region near these trading ports. . . . Exported also are a quantity of fine-quality pearls; ivory; Chinese [silk] cloth; nard brought down the Ganges; *malabathrum* brought here from the interior; transparent gems of all kinds; diamonds; sapphires; and tortoise shell.

ALEXANDRIA, THE CROSSROADS OF THE WORLD

Dio Chrysostom, *Discourses* XXXII. 36, 40; From *LCL*

Your city is vastly superior in point of size and situation, and it is admittedly ranked second among all cities beneath the sun. For not only does the mighty land of Egypt constitute the framework of your city— or, more accurately, its appanage—but the peculiar nature of the river [Nile], when compared with all others, defies description with regard to both its marvelous habits and its usefulness [cf. § 80], and furthermore, not only have you a monopoly of the shipping of the entire Mediterranean by reason of the beauty of your harbors, the magnitude of your fleet, and the abundance and the marketing of the products of every land, but also the outer waters that lie beyond are in your grasp, both the Red Sea and the Indian Ocean, whose name was rarely heard in former days. The result is that the trade, not merely of islands, ports, a few straits and isthmuses, but of practically the whole world is yours. For Alexandria is situated, as it were, at the crossroads of the whole

---

73. A famous cinnamon aromatic of antiquity (Indian *tamala patram*).

world, of even the most remote nations thereof, as if it were a market serving a single city, a market which brings together into one place all manner of men, displaying them to one another and, as far as possible, making them a kindred people. . . . For I behold among you, not merely Greeks and Italians and people from neighboring Syria, Libya, Cilicia, not merely Ethiopians and Arabs from more distant regions, but even Bactrians and Scythians and Persians and a few Indians.

31. ROME THE EMPORIUM OF THE WORLD

Aelius Aristides,[74] *To Rome* xi–xiii

Around [the Mediterranean] lie the continents far and wide, pouring an endless flow of goods to you. There is brought from every land and sea whatever is brought forth by the seasons and is produced by all countries, rivers, lakes, and the skills of Greeks and foreigners. So that anyone who wants to behold all these products must either journey through the whole world to see them or else come to this city. For whatever is raised or manufactured by each people is assuredly always here to overflowing. So many merchantmen arrive here with cargoes from all over, at every season, and with each return of the harvest, that the city seems like a common warehouse of the world. One can see so many cargoes from India, or, if you wish, from Arabia Felix, that one may surmise that the trees there have been left permanently bare, and that those people must come here to beg for their own goods whenever they need anything. Clothing from Babylonia and the luxuries from the barbarian lands beyond arrive in much greater volume and more easily than if one had to sail from Naxos or Cythnos to Athens, transporting any of their products. Egypt, Sicily, and the civilized part of Africa are your farms. The arrival and departure of ships never ceases, so that it is astounding that the sea—not to mention the harbor—suffices for the merchantmen. . . . And all things converge here, trade, seafaring, agriculture, metallurgy, all the skills which exist and have existed, anything that is begotten and grows. Whatever cannot be seen here belongs completely to the category of nonexistent things.

74. See chapter 1, note 45.

32. THE FINANCIAL PANIC OF A.D. 33

Julius Caesar, when dictator, in order to check the hoarding of currency and the decline in real estate values caused by the unsettled conditions of the Civil War, had passed a law that apparently required owners of capital to invest a certain portion or amount in the purchase of Italian land. Thereafter the law fell into desuetude until the Emperor Tiberius revived it in A.D. 33, with the apparent double purpose of supporting sagging real estate prices and of reducing luxury spending (cf. § 43). This sudden enforcement of the law caused a wholesale calling in of loans, and the immediate result was a wave of forced sales, a precipitous collapse of property values, and widespread financial ruin. Land could be picked up cheaply by those with ready cash, and this undoubtedly contributed further to the growth of latifundia in Italy (§ 24). To restore credit and enable debtors to discharge their debts without losing their land, Tiberius then created a temporary "land bank" authorized to make interest-free loans in amounts up to one half the value of the land offered as security. Tacitus' account of the episode, given here, is characteristically dramatic and moralizing.

Tacitus, *Annals* VI. xvi–xvii

Informers in great numbers pounced upon those who kept increasing their liquid assets through loans at interest in violation of the law of the dictator Caesar which sets up regulations for moneylending and land-holding within Italy — a law which had long since become a dead letter because the public welfare is subordinated to private profit. The curse of moneylending has, to be sure, been an inveterate one in the city, and a very frequent cause of civil discord and dissension. . . . On this occasion Gracchus, the praetor to whom the investigation of this matter had fallen, was impelled by the great number of persons endangered to lay the matter before the senate. The senators, in alarm (for no one was free from guilt in the matter), begged the emperor for indulgence; and with his consent everyone was allowed the next year and six months in which to arrange his finances in accordance with the requirements of the law.

The result was a scarcity of money, since all debts were called in at the same time and because, with so many persons condemned and their property sold off, specie was accumulating in the fisc or the state treasury.[75] To obviate this the senate had directed everyone to invest two

75. Tacitus cannot resist adding this second causal clause, one of his favorite themes (cf. § 6), even though it is alien to the immediate subject.

thirds of his loan principal in lands anywhere in Italy.[76] But creditors were calling for payment in full, and it did not suit those called upon to impair their credit [by defaulting]. So at first there was a mad scramble and pleading [for loans], then the praetor's tribunal was in an uproar. The buying and selling that had been devised as a remedy had the contrary effect, for the moneylenders had stored up all the money needed for the purchase of land. The abundance of land offered for sale caused a drop in prices; the more heavily burdened with debt a man was, the harder he found it to sell off, and many a fortune toppled; financial ruin dashed rank and reputation headlong. At length the emperor came to the rescue by distributing 100,000,000 sesterces among the banks and affording an opportunity of borrowing for three years without interest if the debtor offered the state twice the amount in land as security. Thus credit was restored, and little by little private lenders too reappeared on the scene.

33. REAL ESTATE TRANSACTIONS

RESTRICTIONS ON SPECULATION

This bronze tablet from Herculaneum records a decree of the Roman Senate from the reign of Claudius. It forbids the deliberate, profit-motivated destruction of buildings in Rome and Italy. (Similar provisions were applied in provincial municipalities: cf. vol. 1, pp. 448, 456; vol. 2, § 64). Strabo, writing a few decades earlier, describes the prevalence of such activity (*Geography* v. iii. 7): "They build incessantly because of the collapses and fires and repeated sales, which go on incessantly, too. Indeed, the repeated sales are intentional collapses, so to speak, since they tear down some and build others in their place to their heart's desire."

CIL, vol. X, no. 1,401 (= Dessau, no. 6,043 = FIRA, vol. I, no. 45);

A.D. 45/46 and 56

In the consulship of Gnaeus Hosidius Geta and Lucius Vagellius, September 22. Decree of the senate.

Since the foresight of our excellent emperor has made provision also for the permanence of the buildings of our city and of all Italy, which he

---

76. According to Suetonius (*Life of Tiberius* xlviii. 1) the Senate had also provided that debtors need pay only two thirds of their debts when due.

has himself benefited not only by his most august precept but also by his own example, and since protection to public and private structures alike is fitting and appropriate to the happiness of the approaching age,[77] and since all ought to refrain from a most vicious kind of speculation and not bring about an appearance most incompatible with peace by the demolition of homes and villas; the senate decrees that if anyone purchases any building as a speculation, in order by tearing it down to obtain more than the price at which he purchased it, then he shall pay to the state treasury double the sum at which he bought the said property and the matter shall nonetheless be laid before the senate. And since a sale involving such evil precedent is no more admissible than such purchase, in order that sellers who knowingly and with malice aforethought sell contrary to this expressed will of the senate may also be restrained, the senate decrees that such sales shall be invalid. The senate affirms, however, that [this decree] shall in no wise affect owners who with the intention of remaining in possession of their properties transfer parts from one to another of the said properties, provided this is not done for the purpose of speculation.

Adopted. Present in the senate: 383.[78]

RENTAL ADVERTISEMENTS

These are among the numerous notices found painted on house walls at Pompeii; other texts from Pompeii's walls will be found in vol. 1, p. 463, and below, §§ 65, 74.

CIL, vol. IV, nos. 138 and 1,136 (= Dessau, nos. 6,035, 5,723 =; *FIRA,* vol. III, no. 143)[79]

i

In the Arrius Pollio block owned by Gnaeus Alleius Nigidius Maius, to let from the fifteenth of next July, shops with their stalls, high-class second-story apartments, and a house. Prospective lessees may apply to Primus, slave of Gnaeus Alleius Nigidus Maius.

---

77. This refers to the imminent celebration by Claudius of the Secular Games, signaling the advent of a new era (cf. § 161, last selection).

78. The total membership of the Senate at this time was about 600.

79. These inscriptions date, at the latest, from A.D. 79, the year in which Pompeii was buried in the famous eruption of Vesuvius.

ii

On the property owned by Julia Felix, daughter of Spurius, to let from the thirteenth of next August to the thirteenth of the sixth August hence, or five consecutive years, the élite Venus Baths, shops, stalls, and second-story apartments. Interested parties may apply to the lessor in the matter.[80]

CIL, vol. VI, no. 33,860 (= Dessau, no. 5,913 = FIRA, vol. III, no. 145b)

This inscription, found at Rome and dating from the second century, must have been affixed to the wall of a warehouse.

In this private warehouse[81] of Quintus Tineius Sacerdos Clemens [perhaps the consul of A.D. 158] . . . for rent from this day or from July 1[82] storerooms, magazines, passageways, chests, floor sections, and storage space for chests.

SALE OF PART OF A HOUSE

Michigan Papyrus No. 257; A.D. 30

I, Didyme daughter of Petesuchus son of Chambuchis, with my husband Harpuonsis son of Orseus as guardian, acknowledge that I have sold to Marres son of Dionysius son of Cambuchis the one-third share that I own in one fourth of a three-story house and courtyard and all their appurtenances,[83] common and undivided, in Talei.[84] The boundaries of the entire house and courtyard are: on the south of the house, the house of Petermuthis son of Orseus, the smith; on the south of the courtyard, the courtyard of Zeno son of Ptolemaeus; on the north, the house of Anubio and his brother, the fuller; on the west, the courtyard of Zeno son of Ptolemacus; on the east, the royal road. And I have received from Marres the entire agreed-upon contract price of the sold share in full, by hand, out of the house,[85] and I will guarantee the sale as

80. The last sentence is conjectural. In familiar or formulaic expressions like this the Romans commonly abbreviated by writing only the initial letter of each word. Although the meaning of many such abbreviations is known with certainty, many others still remain riddles for which scholars have proposed various solutions.

81. There were also in Rome imperial granaries and warehouses in which storage space could be rented by private individuals.

82. Annual leases in Rome commonly ran from July 1 to June 30.

83. That is, the right of ingress and egress, and possibly other privileges as well.

84. A village in the Arsinoite nome of (Lower) Egypt.

85. The phrase "out of the house" does not refer to the object of the sale; it is part of the Graeco-Egyptian formula for immediate cash payment.

aforesaid with every guarantee against all public and private encumbrances and every kind of tax. Herodes son of Herodes wrote for them because they are illiterate.

[Signature] Marres son of Dionysius son of Cambuthis [sic]. The sale has been made to me as aforesaid. Diodorus son of Ptolemaeus wrote for him because he is illiterate.

LOAN ON MORTGAGE

Oxyrhynchus Papyrus No. 2,134, lines 8–35; A.D. 170

Helene, minor, daughter of Psosnaus and Eudaemonis, with her son Diodorus, also known as Longinus son of Amois son of Diodorus, inhabitant of Chusis, as her guardian[86] and surety for the payment of all that is secured under this mortgage, to Spartas son of Pausanias (son of Sarapio) and Didyme, inhabitant of the city of Oxyrhynchus, greeting. I acknowledge that I have received from you the sum of 1,800 silver drachmas of the imperial coinage, to which nothing has been added, with interest at the rate of 3 obols per mina per month[87] from the present month of Mecheir to the month of . . . in the coming twelfth year, or 189 drachmas altogether, making a total of principal and interest of 1,989 silver drachmas, on the security of four arouras in full, of rectangular shape, of catoecic[88] grain-bearing, arable land out of the five arouras . . . belonging to me near the said Chusis in the Hermopolite nome and forming part of a total of twenty arouras, joint and undivided, held with Chesphibis son of Petosiris and others. [The description of the boundaries is here omitted.] And I will repay the total sum of 1,989 silver drachmas to you or your agents with no delay on Phaophi 30 in the coming twelfth year of the lord [MARCUS AURELIUS] Antoninus Caesar Armeniacus Medicus Parthicus Maximus, and if I do not repay as stated, you shall in place thereof have the ownership of the aforesaid arouras, and it shall be lawful for you to make use of and dispose of them in whatever way you choose, and I will perforce guarantee them completely against all claims with every guarantee, free from liability to cultivate royal or domain land and every other obligation henceforth, and whenever you please it is lawful for you to make your claim to the

---

86. Here is an extreme example of the kind of situation that could arise from the early marriage of Egyptian girls: Helene, though still a minor (i.e., under twenty-five), had a son old enough to serve as her legal representative and sign on her behalf.

87. This comes to 0.5 percent per month, or 6 percent per annum; cf. introduction to § 34.

88. Land originally granted by the Ptolemies to Greek and Macedonian military settlers *(catoeci)*. See also chapter 4, note 110.

mortgage and to the said arouras through the property record office of the Hermopolite nome without requiring my presence or concurrence. If I violate any of these provisions, it shall be invalid, and I will furthermore forfeit in respect of any kind of violation the damage and, in addition thereto, a penalty of six hundred silver drachmas and an equal sum to the public treasury, with no disturbance to their validity, and the mortgage, which is done in duplicate in identical terms without erasure or insertion by the hand of me, Diodorus also known as Longinus, shall nonetheless remain valid. Year 10 of the Emperor Caesar MARCUS AURELIUS Antoninus Augustus Armeniacus Medicus Parthicus Maximus, Mecheir 24.

[Signatures] I, Helene, minor, have received from you, Spartas, the 1,800 drachmas with interest at the rate of 3 obols amounting to 189 drachmas on the security of the four arouras, and I will repay the principal with the total interest on Phaophi 30 in the coming year or else you shall have the ownership of the said arouras, and I will guarantee them as aforesaid. I, Diodorus, also known as Longinus son of Amois, have been appointed my mother's guardian, and wrote for her because she is illiterate, and I am surety for the payment of what is secured under the mortgage, the same date.

34. LOANS

Credit operations, large and small, formed an important part of the private and business life of the Roman world. Numerous extant documents, especially among the papyri, illustrate the different types of contracts in use—loans in money or in kind, secured or unsecured, running for a fixed term or payable on demand. The standard interest rate on money loans was 1 percent per month (but often half that rate for real-estate mortgages); that on loans in kind, which were usually repayable after the next harvest, was (in Egypt, at least) 50 percent. For a mortgage loan, see the selection immediately preceding.

The following texts were inscribed on waxed tablets found in the Dacian goldmining district.[89] The first records the formation of a lending partnership. One of the partners appears as an individual lender in the second.

---

89. These documents were normally written on a triptych, or unit of three tablets, in duplicate "inner" and "outer" texts separated by the signatures.

A LOAN COMPANY

CIL, vol. III, pp. 950, 2,215, no. XIII (= *FIRA,* vol. III, no. 157); A.D. 167

Between Cassius Frontinus and Julius Alexander a moneylending partnership from last December 23 in the consulship of Pudens and Pollio to April 12 next coming was agreed to on the following terms, namely, that they would be obligated to assume in equal shares whatever accrued from the capital in this partnership, whether profit or loss occurred.

To this partnership Julius Alexander contributed 500 *denarii* in cash and on loan, and Secundus, slave and agent of Cassius Palumbus, contributed 267 *denarii* for Frontinus. . . .

In this partnership, if either one is found to have perpetrated a fraud with malice aforethought, he shall have to pay the other 1 *denarius* for each *as* . . . and 20 *denarii* for each *denarius.* . . . And when the contract period is completed, they shall each recover the aforesaid sums less loans outstanding, and shall divide any surplus. Cassius Frontinus demanded the formal acknowledgment that this would be given, done, and warranted, and Julius Alexander formally promised.[90]

Of this agreement two sets of tablets have been signed and sealed [i.e., two copies, one for each party]. Likewise, 50 *denarii* are due to Cossa, which he shall be entitled to receive from the above-named partners.[91]

Done at Deusara on March 28 in the consulship of Verus (for the third time) and Quadratus. [Signatures illegible.]

A DEMAND LOAN

CIL, vol. III, p. 934, no. V (= *FIRA,* vol. III, no. 122); A.D. 162

Julius Alexander demanded the formal acknowledgment that 60 *denarii* of good coin[92] would be duly paid on any day he demanded it, and Alexander son of Cariccus formally promised that it would be paid. And he declared that he had received the aforementioned 60 *denarii* in cash as a loan, and that he owed this sum. And Julius Alexander demanded the formal acknowledgment that the interest thereon at the rate of 1 percent

---

90. This was the Roman formula of oral contractural agreement known as *stipulatio.* In the presence of witnesses one contracting party gave his *promise* or *assent* thereto. Cf. the similar language in the three texts following this.

91. There is no indication of the nature of this obligation.

92. Or perhaps, as later, *properly* is meant—that is, "be properly and duly paid."

per thirty days from this day would be paid to Julius Alexander, or to whomever the right thereto might in the future belong, and Alexander son of Cariccus formally promised that it would be paid. Titius Primitius stood surety for the due and proper payment of the aforementioned principal together with the interest [cf. note 80].

Done at Alburus Major on October 20 in the consulship of Rusticus (for the second time) and Aquilinus.

[Signatures] of Lucius Vasidius Victor . . . ; Bato son of . . . ; Titius Primitius; Alexander son of Cariccus, the debtor himself.

35. SLAVE SALES

The prices of ordinary slaves attested in the first and second centuries range roughly from 200 to 1,000 *denarii*. Talented or specially desirable slaves of course fetched much higher prices. The first contract below is, like those in § 34, a waxed triptych from the Dacian goldmining district; the second is a papyrus found in the Arsinoite nome of Egypt but executed in Syria.

CIL, vol. III, pp. 940, 2,215, no. VII (= *FIRA*, vol. III, no. 88); A.D. 142

Dasius, a Breucian,[93] purchased and received by legal transfer for 600 *denarii* from Bellicus son of Alexander, with Marcus Vibius Longus acting as surety, the boy Apalaustus, or whatever other name he may have, of Greek origin. . . .

It is warranted that this boy has been handed over in good health, that he is guiltless of theft or other delict, and that he is not a vagrant, a runaway, or an epileptic.[94] And if anyone evicts from his possession the said boy in question or any part [cf. § 50, last selection] of him, thereby preventing the aforementioned purchaser or anyone to whom the said property may in the future belong from duly using, enjoying, having, and possessing it, Dasius the Breucian demanded the formal acknowl-

---

93. The Breucians were an Illyrian people settled by the Save River in Lower Pannonia.

94. Such warranties are provided for in the edict of the curule aediles of Rome, which reads: "Any persons who sell slaves shall inform the purchasers of what disease or fault each has, who is a runaway or a vagrant, or is under indictment for a delict; and all this they shall openly and duly declare when they sell such slaves. . . . Likewise, if any slave has committed a capital offense, or has made any attempt to commit suicide, or has been sent into the arena to fight with wild animals, they shall openly declare this at the sale; for we will grant a trial for such causes. Furthermore, if anyone is said to have sold contrary to these provisions knowingly and with malice aforethought, we will grant a trial" (Justinian, *Digest* XXI. i. 1. 1.)

edgment that in that case he would be duly paid in good coin [cf. note 92] double any amount thus evicted from his possession, and Bellicus son of Alexander formally promised that it would be paid, and Vibius Longus likewise stood surety for the same.[95]

And Bellicus son of Alexander declared that he had received and had from Dasius the Breucian 600 *denarii* as the price for the said aforementioned boy.

Done in the camp town of Legion XIII Gemina on May 16 in the consulship of Rufinus and Quadratus.

[Signatures] of Appius Proclus, veteran of Legion XIII Gemina; Antonius Celer; Julius Viator; Ulpius Severinus; Lucius Firmius Primitivus; Marcus Vibius Longus, surety; Bellicus son of Alexander, seller.

Columbia Papyrus inv. 551 verso (= *SB*, no. 7,533); A.D. 160/161

To the market commissioners of _____ from Sarapio son of Zoilus son of Apio. I swear by the Emperor Caesar Titus Aelius Hadrianus ANTONINUS Augustus PIUS that I have sold to Agathus Daemo, freedman of Heraclides and of Sarapio also known as Dorio both sons of Sarapio, of the same city, the houseborn slave Didymus belonging to me by inheritance from my said father, who was my paternal uncle and father by adoption, the late Zoilus, sold just as is and not to be taken back except for epilepsy or third-party claim; [and I swear] that he is mine and not mortgaged or alienated to others in any way, and that I have received the price of one thousand three hundred drachmas, and I guarantee it. If I swear well may it go well with me, swearing falsely the opposite. I, _____, wrote for him because he is illiterate.

> [A copy of the deed of sale is subjoined. It recites the terms as above, adding the detail that the buyer gave the seller a gold ring as deposit and received it back when he paid the purchase price.]

FIRA, vol. III, no. 132; A.D. 166

Gaius Fabullius Macer, subaltern of the trireme "Tigris" of the praetorian fleet of Misenum, purchased from Quintus Julius Priscus, soldier of the same trireme in the same fleet, a boy of trans-Euphrates origin named Abbas, also known as Eutyches or by whatever other name he is called, about seven years old, at a price of 200 *denarii* and the customs

---

95. On this formulaic procedure, cf. note 90.

duty per head.[96] Fabullius Macer demanded the formal acknowledgment in accordance with the edict that the boy was in good health, and that if anyone evicted from his possession the said boy or any part of him the whole sum would be duly repaid without the formality of notification, and Quintus Julius Priscus formally promised. Gaius Julius Antiochus, private of the trireme "Virtue," stood surety and warranty for the same.

And the seller, Quintus Julius Priscus, stated that he had received and had from Gaius Fabullius Macer, the purchaser, the said aforementioned 200 *denarii* in good coin duly paid in cash, and that he had transferred to him the aforementioned slave Eutyches on satisfactory terms.

Done at Seleucia Pieria in the winter camp of the detachment of the praetorian fleet of Misenum on May 24 in the consulship of Quintus Servilius Pudens and Aulus Fufidius Pollio.

[Signatures and a docket follow.]

36. AN APPRENTICESHIP CONTRACT

Oxyrhynchus Papyrus No. 275; A.D. 66

Trypho son of Dionysius son of Trypho, his mother being Thamunis daughter of Onnophris, and Ptolemaeus son of Pausirio son of Ptolemaeus, weaver, his mother being Ophelous daughter of Theo, both parties being inhabitants of Oxyrhynchus, mutually agree that Trypho has apprenticed to Ptolemaeus his son Thoönis, whose mother is Saraëus daughter of Apio and who is not yet of age, for a period of one year from this day to serve him and perform all the duties given him by Ptolemaeus in connection with the weaving trade in all its branches as he himself knows it. The boy is to be fed and clothed during the whole period by his father Trypho, who is also to be responsible for all the taxes upon the boy, on condition that Ptolemaeus shall pay him 5 drachmas per month on account of victuals and 12 drachmas on account of clothing at the termination of the whole period.[97] Trypho shall not

96. See § 18. The boy Abbas was obviously taken captive in Mesopotamia in the period of the Roman operations against Parthia under Lucius Verus, brought back by his captors to Greek-speaking Syria, and given a Greek name, Eutyches ("Good Luck").

97. These specific arrangements varied, of course, from contract to contract. In Oxyrhynchus Papyrus No. 725 (A.D. 183), for example, the apprentice also lives at home, and the father undertakes to "produce him to attend the teacher for the stipulated period [five years] every day from sunrise to sunset"; in addition, the apprentice is allowed "twenty holidays a year on account of festivals without any deduction from his wages," and the contract also provides for no salary for the first two years and

have the right to withdraw the boy from Ptolemaeus until the completion of the period, and if there are any days during it on which he fails to fulfill his obligation he shall produce him for an equal number of days after the period or shall pay a penalty of 1 silver drachma for each day; the penalty for withdrawing him within the period shall be 100 drachmas, and an equal sum to the public treasury. If Ptolemaeus on his part fails to instruct the boy thoroughly he shall be liable to the same penalties. This contract of apprenticeship is valid. Year 13 of Emperor NERO Claudius Caesar Augustus Germanicus, month of Augustus [see note 33], the 21st.

I, Ptolemaeus son of Pausirio son of Ptolemaeus, my mother being Ophelous daughter of Theo, will carry out all the provisions in the one year. I, Zoilus son of Horus son of Zoilus, my mother being Dieus daughter of Soceus, wrote for him because he is illiterate. Year thirteenth of the Emperor NERO Claudius Caesar Augustus Germanicus, month of Augustus, the 21st.

---

seven months, and for wages increasing from twelve to sixteen to twenty-four drachmas a month over the rest of the five-year period. As for the reference to taxes in the present contract, since the boy was a minor (under fourteen) he would not be subject to the poll tax but only to the tax on trades; early in the second century the prefect Vibius Maximus rescinded the trades tax on minors.

3

THE ROMAN PEACE (A.D. 14–192):
SOCIETY AND CULTURE

37. The Grandeur of Rome

With these descriptions should be compared § 134, which, though composed at a later date, lists monuments and landmarks most of which were already in existence in the first and second centuries.

Pliny, *Natural History* III. v. 66–67

In the principate and censorship of Vespasian and Titus, in the 826th year after the city's foundation [A.D. 73], the walls of Rome, embracing the seven hills, measured 13.2 miles in circumference. The city itself is divided into fourteen districts, and has 265 intersections with guardian *Lares*.[1] A measurement running from the milestone set up at the head of the Roman Forum [see chapter 6, note 90] to each of the city gates—which today number thirty-seven if the Twelve Gates are counted as one and the seven of the old gates that no longer exist are omitted—gives a total of 20.765 miles in a straight line. But the measurement of all the thoroughfares block by block, from the same milestone to the outermost edge of the buildings including the Praetorian Camp,[2] totals a little more than sixty miles. And if one should consider in addition the height of the buildings,[3] he would assuredly form a fitting appraisal and

1. There were little shrines of these household gods at the central crossroads of each neighborhood. The division of the city into fourteen districts was organized by Augustus; cf. vol. 1, § 208, second selection.

2. The Praetorian cohorts, stationed partly in Rome and partly in neighboring towns by Augustus, were concentrated by Tiberius in a permanent camp just outside the Viminal Gate.

3. "To reduce the number of collapses Augustus lowered the height of new buildings and forbade that they be raised higher than seventy feet on the public streets" (Strabo, *Geography* v. iii. 7).

would admit that no city has existed in the whole world that could be compared with Rome in size. On the east it is enclosed by the Rampart of Tarquin the Proud, a work among the leading wonders of the world, for he raised it as high as the walls where the approach was level and the city most exposed. On the other sides it was protected by lofty walls or steep hills, but the increasing spread of buildings has added many suburbs.

Strabo, *Geography* v. iii. 8; Adapted from *LCL*

So much, then, for the blessings with which nature supplies the city; but the Romans have added still others, which are the result of their foresight. For if the Greeks had the repute of being most felicitous in the founding of cities, in that they aimed at beauty, strength of position, harbors, and productive soil, the Romans had the best foresight in those matters which the Greeks took but little account of, such as the construction of roads and aqueducts, and of sewers that could wash out the filth of the city into the Tiber. . . . The sewers, vaulted with close-fitting stones, have in some places left room enough for wagons loaded with hay to pass through them. And water is brought into the city through the aqueducts in such quantities that veritable rivers flow through the city and the sewers; and almost every house has cisterns and service pipes and copious fountains—with which Marcus Agrippa concerned himself most, though he also adorned the city with many other structures.[4] In a word, the early Romans took but little account of the beauty of Rome, because they were occupied with other—greater and more necessary—matters; whereas the later Romans, and particularly those of today and in my time, have not fallen short in this respect either but have filled the city with many beautiful structures. Pompey, the deified Caesar, Augustus, his sons and friends, and wife and sister, have outdone all others in their zeal for buildings and in the expense incurred.[5]

4. Pliny says (*Natural History* XXXVI. xv. 121) that "Agrippa in his aedileship . . . created 700 cisterns, 500 fountains, and 130 reservoirs, many of them magnificently adorned. Upon these structures he erected 300 statues of bronze or marble and 400 marble columns." Like modern writers, almost every ancient writer who talks about Rome singles out the aqueducts and water supply for admiring praise. The most complete and detailed information on this subject is contained in *The Water Supply of Rome* by Sextus Julius Frontinus, who became water commissioner in A.D. 97. His book gives the name, date, and type of construction, length, and purpose (drinking, washing, etc.) of each of the nine aqueducts; describes the maintenance of the system by slave gangs; tells of water rates, fraudulent diversion of public water to private uses, fines for unlawful use, damage, or pollution, and a host of other matters. Selections from this work are given in vol. 1, § 208.

5. This passage was apparently written before the death of Augustus, since, unlike Caesar, he is

The Campus Martius contains most of these, and thus, in addition to its natural beauty, it has received still further adornment as the result of foresight. The size of the Campus is awe-inspiring, since it affords space at the same time for chariot races and every other equestrian exercise unhindered by the great multitude of people exercising themselves by playing ball, trundling hoops, and wrestling; and the works of art situated around the Campus Martius, and the ground covered with grass throughout the year, and the crowns of the hills that rise above the river and extend as far as its bed, presenting the appearance of a stage painting —all this affords a spectacle from which it is hard to tear one's self away. And near this Campus is still another,[6] and colonnades around it in very great numbers, and sacred precincts, and three theaters, and an amphitheater, and very costly temples in close succession to one another. . . . Believing this place most sacred, they erected in it also the tombs of their most illustrious men and women. The most noteworthy is the one called the Mausoleum, a great mound near the river on a lofty foundation of white marble, thickly covered with evergreen trees to the very summit. On top is a bronze image of Augustus Caesar; beneath the mound are the tombs of himself and his kinsmen and intimates;[7] and behind the mound is a large sacred precinct with wonderful promenades; and in the center of the Campus around his crematorium is a wall, this too of white marble, surrounded by a circular iron fence and planted with black poplars inside. And again if, on passing to the Old Forum, one should see forum after forum ranged alongside it, and basilicas, and temples, and should see also the Capitol and the works of art there and those on the Palatine and in Livia's Promenade, one would easily forget the things outside. Such is Rome.

38. THE GREAT FIRE AT ROME

In A.D. 64 Rome was gutted by a disastrous fire that raged for nine days (July 18–26). Though there is no credible evidence for the familiar charges that Nero was responsible for setting fire to the capital or that he "fiddled while Rome burned," contemporary public opinion was receptive to such

not called "deified"; among subsequent emperors, Hadrian was particularly noted for the number and sumptuosity of his public works (cf. § 22 and note 7).

6. Actually, this is part of the Campus Martius.

7. Imperial burials filled the Mausoleum of Augustus by the time of Hadrian, who erected a new mausoleum on the opposite bank of the Tiber; cf. chapter 1, note 103.

rumors because of Nero's previous crimes and because in rebuilding the city he appropriated a sizable area in the center of the city for a new imperial palace, the *Domus Aurea* (Golden House). To silence the hostile talk, Nero found a scapegoat in the adherents of the tiny Christian sect; thus began the first persecution of Christians, on which see §§ 167–172.

Tacitus, *Annals* xv. xxxviii–xliv (abridged)

A disaster followed, whether the result of accident or of the emperor's guile is uncertain, as authors have given both versions, but graver and more dreadful than any other which has befallen this city through the ravages of fire. It started first in that part of the Circus which adjoins the Palatine and Caelian Hills, where, amid the shops containing inflammable wares, the conflagration broke out, instantly gathered strength, and, driven by the wind, swept down the length of the Circus. There were no residences fenced with masonry, or temples surrounded by walls, or anything else to act as an obstacle. The blaze in its fury ran first through the level portions of the city, rose to the hills, then again devastated the lower places, outstripping all remedial measures, so rapid was the scourge and so completely was the city at its mercy owing to the narrow winding lanes and irregular streets which characterized old Rome. . . .

Nero at this time was at Antium and did not return to the city until the fire approached the house which he had built to connect the palace and the Gardens of Maecenas.[8] It could not, however, be stopped from consuming the palace, the house, and everything around. But, for the relief of the homeless and roving populace, he threw open the Campus Martius, the public structures of Agrippa, and even his own gardens, and put up temporary structures to receive the destitute multitude. The necessities of life were brought up from Ostia and neighboring towns, and the price of grain was reduced to three sesterces a *modius*. These acts, though popular, were of no effect, because a rumor had spread about that, at the very time when the city was in flames, the emperor had mounted his private stage and sung of the destruction of Troy, comparing present misfortunes with the calamities of the past.

At last, on the sixth day, the conflagration was brought to an end at the foot of the Esquiline Hill by the demolition of the buildings over a vast area, so that the uninterrupted violence of the fire encountered clear ground and open sky, as it were. But before people had laid aside their

---

8. These gardens were on the Esquiline Hill and were connected with the imperial palace (on the Palatine) by the *Domus Transitoria* (Passage House).

fears or regained hope, the fire attacked again, mostly in the less congested parts of the city; as a result, though there was less loss of life, the temples of the gods and the porticoes devoted to enjoyment were destroyed on a wider scale. . . .

Rome is divided into fourteen districts [cf. note 1]; of these, four remained untouched, three were leveled to the ground, and in the other seven were left only a few shattered, half-burned relics of houses. . . . But Nero profited by his country's desolation, and erected a mansion in which the jewels and gold, objects long familiar and vulgarized by our extravagance, were not so much the marvels as were the fields and pools, the woods on one side and the open spaces and views on the other to provide a sense of isolation. . . .

The parts of the city unoccupied by the mansion were built up, not as was the case after the burning by the Gauls [vol. 1, § 14], without any discrimination or order but with regular rows of streets and broad thoroughfares, with a restriction on the height of buildings [cf. note 3], with open spaces, and with porticoes added to shade the fronts of the tenement blocks. Nero promised to erect these porticoes at his own expense and to hand over the building sites to the owners cleared of debris. He also offered bounties in proportion to each person's rank and financial resources, and fixed a time within which they could obtain them if they completed their houses or tenement blocks. He gave orders for the rubbish to be dumped in the marshes of Ostia, and for the ships which had brought up grain by the Tiber to sail down loaded with rubbish. The buildings themselves were to be solidly constructed to a specified extent of stone from Gabii or Alba, without wooden beams, because that rock[9] is impervious to fire; and they were to be enclosed not by party walls but each by its own walls. Then, to make the water supply, which individuals had illegally tapped, more abundant and available for public use in more places, guards were appointed; and everyone was to keep aids for putting out fires in the open air. These changes, which were welcomed for their utility, also added beauty to the new city. There were, however, some who thought that its old appearance had been more conducive to health, since the narrow lanes and high roofs were not so much penetrated by the sun's rays, while now the open space, unprotected by any shade, burned with a more oppressive heat. . . .

But all human efforts, all the largesses of the emperor, all the propi-

9. The volcanic peperino, found in the hills near Rome.

tiations of the gods, failed to dispel the sinister belief that the conflagration had been ordered. Consequently, to scotch the rumor, Nero fastened the guilt and inflicted the most exquisite tortures upon a group hated for their abominations,[10] whom the populace called Christians. Christus, from whom the name had its origin, had been condemned to death in the reign of Tiberius by the procurator Pontius Pilate, and the pernicious superstition, thus suppressed for the moment, was breaking out again not only in Judaea, the original source of this evil, but even in Rome, where all things horrible or shameful from all parts of the world collect and become popular. First, then, those who confessed membership were arrested; then, on their information, great numbers were convicted, not so much of guilt for the conflagration as of hatred of the human race. And mockery was added to their deaths: they were covered with the skins of wild beasts and torn to death by dogs, or they were nailed to crosses and, when daylight failed, were set on fire and burned to provide light at night. Nero had offered his gardens for the spectacle, and was providing circus games, mingling with the populace in the dress of a charioteer or driving a chariot. Hence, though they were deserving of the most extreme punishment, a feeling of pity arose as people felt that they were being sacrificed not for the public good but because of the savagery of one man.

39. ROMAN BATHS

The famous Roman baths *(thermae)*, grandiosely and sumptuously executed, served as vast community, recreation, and social centers not only in Rome itself but in every municipality of the Empire. The utilitarian character of much of Roman architecture is summed up in the classic remark of Frontinus (*The Water Supply of Rome* I. vi): "With so many indispensable structures for so many aqueducts, compare, if you will, the idle pyramids or the useless, though famous, works of the Greeks."

Lucian,[11] *Hippias, or The Bath* (abridged); From *LCL*

The building suits the magnitude of the site, accords well with the accepted idea of such an establishment, and shows regard for the principles of lighting. The entrance is high, with a flight of broad steps of

10. The early Christians were commonly believed by their contemporaries to practice infanticide, incest, and other horrors; cf. §§ 167–169.

11. See chapter 2, note 52.

which the tread is greater than the pitch, to make them easy to ascend. On entering, one is received into a public hall of good size, with ample accommodations for servants and attendants. On the left are the lounging rooms, also of just the right sort for a bath, attractive, brightly lighted retreats. Then, besides them, a hall, larger than need be for the purposes of a bath, but necessary for the reception of richer persons. Next, capacious locker rooms to undress in, on each side, with a very high and brilliantly lighted hall between them, in which are three swimming pools of cold water; it is finished in Laconian marble, and has two statues of white marble in the ancient style, one of Hygeia, the other of Aesculapius.

On leaving this hall, you come into another which is slightly warmed instead of meeting you at once with fierce heat; it is oblong, and has an apse on each side. Next to it, on the right, is a very bright hall, nicely fitted up for massage, which has on each side an entrance decorated with Phrygian marble, and receives those who come in from the exercising floor. Then near this is another hall, the most beautiful in the world, in which one can stand or sit with comfort, linger without danger, and stroll about with profit. It also is refulgent with Phrygian marble clear to the roof. Next comes the hot corridor, faced with Numidian marble. The hall beyond it is very beautiful, full of abundant light and aglow with color like that of purple hangings. It contains three hot tubs.

When you have bathed, you need not go back through the same rooms, but can go directly to the cold room through a slightly warmed chamber. Everywhere there is copious illumination and full indoor daylight. . . . Why should I go on to tell you of the exercising floor and of the cloak rooms? . . . Moreover, it is beautified with all other marks of thoughtfulness—with two toilets, many exits, and two devices for telling time, a water clock that makes a bellowing sound and a sundial.

Seneca, *Moral Epistles* lvi. 1–2

I live over a bathing establishment. Picture to yourself now the assortment of voices, the sound of which is enough to sicken one. When the stronger fellows are exercising and swinging heavy leaden weights in their hands, when they are working hard or pretending to be working hard, I hear their groans; and whenever they release their pent-up breath, I hear their hissing and jarring breathing. When I have to do with a lazy fellow who is content with a cheap rubdown, I hear the slap of the hand pummeling his shoulders, changing its sound according as the hand is laid on flat or curved. If now a professional ball player comes along and begins to keep score, I am done for. Add to this the arrest of a brawler or a thief, and the fellow who always likes to hear his own voice in the bath, and those who jump into the pool with a mighty splash as they strike the water. In addition to those whose voices are, if nothing else, natural, imagine the hair plucker keeping up a constant chatter in his thin and strident voice, to attract more attention, and never silent except when he is plucking armpits and making the customer yell instead of yelling himself. It disgusts me to enumerate the varied cries of the sausage dealer and confectioner and of all the peddlers of the cook shops, hawking their wares, each with his own peculiar intonation.

40. "Bread and Circus Games": Gladiatorial Shows, Chariot Races, Prize Fights

"The people which once bestowed *imperium, fasces,* legions, everything, now foregoes such activities and has but two passionate desires: bread and circus games"—Juvenal's classic sarcasm (x. 78–81) is merely the best-known and most trenchant of a host of witnesses in literature, inscriptions, and papyri, to the Roman populace's "enthusiasm for actors and passion for gladiators and horses . . . the talk at home . . . and in the schools" (Tacitus, *Dialogue on Oratory* xxix). The most important features of the Roman games were chariot races, wild animal fights, and gladiatorial combats; in the last-named, slaves and condemned criminals were pitted, equipped with varying amounts of armor, against other gladiators or against wild beasts. The emperors provided these amusements with lavish hand, as a means of keeping the populace amused and out of mischief: under the Empire circus games were held at Rome on fifty days of the year. In addition, there was a revival, under imperial encouragement and patronage, of the Greek athletic meets, which had declined after the heyday of the Greek city-states. These were now introduced in Italy as well, while Roman spectacles spread to the cities of the Hellenistic East, as famous festivals of the past were restored to their old splendor and many new ones organized throughout the Empire. An Empire-wide athletes' guild, with Hercules as patron divinity, was organized with imperial sanction and favor. Its members, professional athletes mainly from the Hellenized eastern provinces, toured the Empire, competing at the various meets. Athletes enjoyed extraordinary honors and privileges at home and abroad, including the right of obtaining pensions from their native cities as rewards for important victories. Many of these professional athletes accumulated considerable wealth. Galen, however, in his *Exhortation on the Choice of a Profession* (ix–xi), gives us the other side of the picture, stressing their overindulgence in food and sleep, their battered and disfigured bodies, their tendency toward early obesity, and their resultantly shorter-than-average life expectancy. Some of the following texts date from the third century, but they are in most particulars equally applicable to the period of this chapter.

Fronto, *Elements of History* xvii

It was the height of political wisdom for the emperor not to neglect even actors and the other performers of the stage, the circus, and the arena, since he knew that the Roman people is held fast by two things above all, the grain supply [cf. § 17] and the shows, that the success of the government depends on amusements as much as on serious things. Neglect of serious matters entails the greater detriment, of amusements the greater unpopularity. The money largesses [*congiaria;* cf. § 21] are less eagerly desired than the shows; the largesses appease only the grain-doled plebs singly and individually, while the shows keep the whole population happy.[12]

> In 46 B.C. and at least twice in the two following decades, members of senatorial and equestrian families had been forbidden to appear on the stage or in gladiatorial combats. Ignored with impunity, those bans were repealed in A.D. 11. But eight years later the Emperor Tiberius had the Senate order an end to such scandalous conduct.

AE, 1978, no. 145 (= *Journal of Roman Studies* [1983], 73:97–115); A.D. 19

Decree of the senate [meeting] on the Palatine in the portico adjoining the temple of Apollo. Present at the writing were Gaius Ateius Capito [a leading jurist] son of Lucius, of the Aniensian tribe, [and six others named]. Whereas Marcus Silanus and Lucius Norbanus Balbus, the consuls, state that they had, as the matter was given to them, drafted a memorandum pertaining to the obscenity of women or those who, contrary to the dignity of their order, appear or rent their services on the stage or in games, and [whereas] the senate's decrees on this subject which were passed in previous years enjoined what it desired should be

---

12. The last two words are supplied to complete the apparent sense.

done when through a circumvention they lessened the majesty of the senate;

Regarding this matter the senate decreed: No one shall present on the stage or engage by contract to fight with animals or put on the feathers or take up the wooden practice-sword of gladiators, or manage in any other activity of similar kind a senator's son, daughter, grandson, grand-daughter, great-grandson or great-granddaughter, or a man whose father, grandfather (paternal or maternal), or brother or any woman whose husband or father or grandfather (paternal or maternal) or brother ever had the right of sitting in the seats reserved for members of the equestrian order; nor shall hire anyone [of the above] if he offers himself; nor shall any [of the above] hire himself out. In this matter special care shall be taken so that if they who have the right to sit in the equestrian seats persist with malice aforethought, to make a mockery of the authority of that order, and even go so far as to resign voluntarily from their equestrian order and then contract themselves out to appear on the stage, they shall receive public disgrace or be condemned in a judgment of infamy. If any of those listed above acts [thus] contrary to the dignity of his order, he shall not have burial rites, except if the person appearing on the stage or renting out his services in the arena is the son or daughter of an actor, gladiator, trainer, or procurer. As is written in the decree of the senate passed on the motion of the consuls Manius Lepidus and Titus Statilius Taurus [A.D. 11], freeborn females less than twenty years old and freeborn males less than twenty-five shall not be permitted to contract themselves or let out their services for arena, stage, or obscene lucre, except any who were consigned to games, stage, or obscene lucre by the deified Augustus or by Tiberius Caesar Augustus. [The rest is lost.]

GLADIATORIAL SHOWS

Seneca, *Moral Epistles* vii. 3–5

I chanced to stop in at a midday show, expecting fun, wit, and some relaxation, when men's eyes take respite from the slaughter of their fellow men. It was just the reverse. The preceding combats were merciful by comparison; now all trifling is put aside and it is pure murder. The men have no protective covering. Their entire bodies are exposed to the blows, and no blow is ever struck in vain. . . . In the morning men are thrown to the lions and the bears, at noon they are thrown to their spectators. The spectators call for the slayer to be thrown to those who in turn will slay him, and they detain the victor for another butchering. The outcome for the combatants is death; the fight is waged with sword and fire. This goes on while the arena is free.[13] "But one of them was a highway robber, he killed a man!" Because he killed he deserved to suffer this punishment, granted. . . . "Kill him! Lash him! Burn him! Why does he meet the sword so timidly? Why doesn't he kill boldly? Why doesn't he die game? Whip him to meet his wounds! Let them trade blow for blow, chests bare and within reach!" And when the show stops for intermission, "Let's have men killed meanwhile! Let's not have nothing going on!"

TOMBSTONE OF AN IMPRESARIO

Excavations in the Vatican under St. Peter's basilica have in recent years uncovered an ancient cemetery with numerous mausoleums, burial urns, and funerary inscriptions, the following among them.

Zeitschrift für Papyrologie und Epigraphik (1986), 65:248–249; third(?) century

To Aurelius Nemesius, spouse most dear and well deserving, who lived 53 years 9 months 11 days, who with the highest praise for his art served as master of chorus, dance and pantomime. To him his wife Aurelia Eutychiane has dedicated and erected [this stone].

CAREER OF A FAMOUS CHARIOTEER

This monument to the charioteer Diocles was erected by admirers and stablemates, perhaps upon his retirement at the age of forty-two after twenty-four years of driving in races. Only the first part of this long inscription is given here.

---

13. That is, during an intermission in the scheduled program; cf. the end of this selection.

CIL, vol. VI, no. 10,048 (= Dessau, no. 5,287)

[Rome, A.D. 146]

Gaius Appuleius Diocles, charioteer of the Red Stable,[14] a Lusitanian Spaniard by birth, aged 42 years, 7 months, 23 days. He drove his first chariot in the White Stable, in the consulship of Acilius Aviola and Corellius Pansa. He won his first victory in the same stable, in the consulship of Manius Acilius Glabrio and Gaius Bellicius Torquatus. He drove for the first time in the Green Stable in the consulship of Torquatus Asprenas (for the second time) and Annius Libo. He won his first victory in the Red Stable in the consulship of Laenas Pontianus and Antonius Rufinus.[15]

Grand totals: He drove chariots for 24 years, ran 4,257 starts,[16] and won 1,462 victories, 110 in opening races.[17] In single-entry races[18] he won 1,064 victories, winning 92 major purses, 32 of them (including 3 with six-horse teams) at 30,000 sesterces, 28 (including 2 with six-horse teams[19]) at 40,000 sesterces, 29 (including 1 with a seven-horse team[20]) at 50,000 sesterces, and 3 at 60,000 sesterces; in two-entry races he won 347 victories, including 4 with three-horse teams at 15,000 sesterces; in three-entry races he won 51 victories.[21] He won or placed 2,900 times, taking 861 second places, 576 third places, and 1 fourth place at 1,000 sesterces;[22] he failed to place 1,351 times.[23] He tied a Blue for first place 10 times and a White 91 times, twice for 30,000 sesterces.[24] He won a

14. There were four organized chariot-racing "stables" *(factiones)* at Rome (and later at Constantinople), known by their colors as the Blues, Greens, Reds, and Whites.

15. These consulships correspond to A.D. 122, 124, 128, and 131, respectively.

16. This comes to an average of 177 races a year for the twenty-four years of Diocles' career, or an average of three to four races on each of the fifty circus days of the year.

17. Literally, "from the procession." Before the races began there was a grand parade *(pompa)* through the streets to the circus; a special distinction apparently attached to the opening race after the parade.

18. Races in which each of the four stables ran only one chariot. In these star events, which offered the biggest purses, the stables naturally entered only their topnotch drivers.

19. Farther on the inscription tells that both these victories were won on the same day, an unprecedented record.

20. "A number of horses never before this exhibited at the games," the inscription later informs us.

21. This sentence gives a breakdown of Diocles' 1,462 victories by types of races. A breakdown according to his racing feats is given below.

22. The sum is specified to make it clear that his one fourth place was a prize-winning finish. Fourth place did not win a prize when there were only four chariots in the race.

23. These figures add up to 4,251 of the 4.257 total recorded above. The remaining six races are mentioned a few lines below.

24. These ties are obviously included in the above tabulations of wins.

total of 35,863,120 sesterces. In addition, in races with two-horse teams for 1,000 sesterces he won three times, and tied a White once and a Green twice.[25] He took the lead and won 815 times, came from behind to win 67 times, won under handicap 36 times, won in various styles 42 times, and won in a final dash 502 times[26] (216 over the Greens, 205 over the Blues, 81 over the Whites). He made nine horses 100-time winners, and one a 200-time winner.

[The remainder of the inscription (about three fifths), under the heading "His Records," lists in great detail, naming record-holding drivers and horses, the various records which Diocles broke: "the champion of all charioteers . . . he excelled the charioteers of all the stables who ever participated in the races of the circus games."]

CERTIFICATE OF MEMBERSHIP IN THE ATHLETES' GUILD

The certificate proper, signed by various guild and meet officials, is preceded by the texts of three imperial rescripts, which are recited as evidence of the favor which earlier emperors accorded the guild.

British Museum Papyrus No. 1,178 (= Wilcken, no. 156), in part; A.D. 194

The Sacred Hadrianic Antoninian Septimian Traveling Athletes' Guild[27] Dedicated to Hercules and the presider-over-games[28] and the Emperor Caesar Lucius SEPTIMIUS SEVERUS Pertinax Augustus, to the members of the said guild, greeting. Know ye that Herminus, also known as Morus, from Hermopolis, boxer, about . . .[29] years old, is a fellow member of our guild and has paid the entire regulation initiation fee of 100 *denarii* in

25. These are the six races that complete Diocles' grand total of 4,247; cf. note 23. It is noteworthy that while these six races are included in his total number of starts, they are not included in arriving at the total of 1,462 wins enumerated above and below.

26. The figures in this sentence up to this point give another breakdown of the total of 1,462 wins. The "final-sprint" victories were presumably the most highly regarded, since they are further broken down by opposing stables in the following parentheses.

27. In *IG*, vol. XIV, no. 956 (early fourth century) the name is given as "The Sacred World-wide Traveling Athletes' Guild."

28. In classical Greece this epithet referred mostly to Hermes, sometimes also to Zeus, Poseidon, and Apollo. Since there is no evidence connecting the Athletes' Guild with any of these gods, perhaps the preceding *and* in the Greek text was written by mistake and the epithet is intended for Hercules, the guild's patron god.

29. This notice of membership was obviously a form letter, with the member's name, origin, athletic speciality, and age to be inserted in the appropriate place. In this case the space for the age was never filled in.

full. We have therefore written to you, so that you may be informed. Farewell.

Done at Naples, Italy, at the forty-ninth quadrennial performance of the great Augustan Italian Roman Games, in the consulship of Lucius SEPTIMIUS SEVERUS Pertinax Augustus (for the second time) and Claudius Septimius Albinus Caesar (for the second time), September 23,[30] the following being high priests of athletic meets everywhere, lifetime athletic-meet presidents, and overseers of imperial baths: Marcus Aurelius Demostratus Damas,[31] citizen of Sardis, Alexandria, Antinoöpolis, Athens, Ephesus, Smyrna, Pergamum, Nicomedia, Miletus, Lacedaemon, and Tralles,[32] pancratiast,[33] twice clean-sweep winner,[34] undefeated boxing champion, star performer, and Marcus Aurelius Demetrius, citizen of Alexandria, of Hermopolis, pancratiast, clean-sweep winner, wrestler, star performer, and Marcus Aurelius Chrysippus . . . citizen of Smyrna, of Alexandria, wrestler, clean-sweep winner, star performer; the lifetime president officiating at the meet being Marcus Aurelius Demetrius, high priest and overseer of imperial baths; the presidents of the guild being Alexander II son of Athenodorus, citizen of Myra and Ephesus, wrestler, pancratiast, star performer, and Prosdectus son of . . . citizen of Mytilene, runner, star performer; the treasurer being C . . . ctabenus son of Proclus, citizen of Ephesus, trainer, star performer; the secretary of the guild being Publius Aelius Euctemo, chief secretary of the meet.

AN ATHLETE CLAIMS HIS PENSION

Hermopolis Papyri Nos. 52–56, col. 4 (= *Select Papyri*, no. 306); A.D. 267

To the most excellent council of Hermopolis, the great, ancient, most august, and most illustrious city, from Aurelius Leucadius, Hermopolitan, victor in sacred games, pancratiast, through Aurelius Appianus, also known as Demetrius, Hermopolitan, appointed his executor. I request that an order be issued me for payment of the following sums from the municipal account toward my pension: For the victory and

30. This was the birthday of Augustus. Little seems to be known about these Augustan Games at Naples, which are mentioned here and in the document following this.

31. His career is recorded in the next selection.

32. In addition to their native citizenship famous athletes were granted honorary citizenships in other cities, in much the same way as visiting notables today are granted the "keys of the city."

33. A competitor in the *pancratium*, a combined boxing-and-wrestling match.

34. This term, which may be translated more literally as "complete-cycle winner," designated an athlete who had been victorious in the four great Greek games—the Olympic, Pythian, Isthmian, and Nemean—in a row.

crown which I won at the sacred iselastic[35] games, for the period from Phamenoth [1] of the tenth year to Mecheir 30 of the fourteenth year, or forty-eight months at 180 drachmas per month:[36] 1 talent 2,640 drachmas. And for the victory and crown which I won at the sacred iselastic world-championship juvenile games, ranking with the Olympic Games, held in the colony of Sidon, for the period from Phamenoth 6 of the eleventh year to and including Mecheir of the fourteenth year, or thirty-five months and twenty-five days at 180 drachmas per month: 1 talent 450 drachmas. This makes a total claim of two talents three thousand ninety drachmas of silver (2 tal. 3,090 dr. silv.), without prejudice to any right of the city and the council in the matter.

Year 14 of the Emperor Caesar Publius Licinius GALLIENUS Germanicus Maximus Persicus Maximus Pius Felix Augustus, Phamenoth.

41. THE SATURNALIA AT ROME

This poem commemorates a celebration of the Saturnalia in the reign of Domitian. This seven-day festival, which began annually on December 17, was characterized by merriment, revelry, and exchange of gifts; in addition, for one day slaves were released from their duties and regaled by their masters.

Statius,[37] *Silvae* I. vi (abridged); From *LCL*

Hence, father Phoebus and stern Pallas! Away, ye Muses, go, keep holiday; we will call you back at the New Year. But Saturn, slip your fetters and come hither, and December tipsy with much wine, and laughing Mirth and wanton Wit, while I recount the glad festival of our merry Caesar and the banquet's drunken revel.

Scarce was the new dawn stirring, when already sweetmeats were raining from the line,[38] such was the dew the rising east wind was scattering; the famous fruit of the Pontic nut groves, or of Idume's

35. Games so designated entitled a victor to a triumphal entry into and a pension for life from his native town.

36. For comparative purposes it may be noted that at this time skilled labor and legionary soldiers (even after the 50-percent increase granted the latter by Caracalla) were paid at the rate of about 60 drachmas a month.

37. Publius Papinius Statius (A.D. c. 40–c. 95), born at Naples, was a prominent court poet of the Flavian period. His most important works were occasional poems entitled *Silvae* and two epics, the *Thebaid* and the *Achilleid*.

38. Dainties were scattered among the populace from a rope stretched across the amphitheater.

fertile slopes [Palestinian dates], all that devout Damascus grows upon its boughs [Damson (Damascene) plums] or thirsty Caunus ripens [figs] falls, gratis, in a generous profusion. Biscuits and melting pastries, Amerian fruit [apples and pears] not overripe, must cakes, and bursting dates from invisible palms were showering down. . . . Let Jupiter send his tempests through the world and threaten the broad fields, while our own Jove sends us showers like these!

But lo! another multitude, handsome and well dressed, as numerous as that upon the benches, makes its way along all the rows. Some carry baskets of bread and white napkins and more luxurious fare; others serve languorous wine in abundant measure. . . . Thou dost nourish alike the circle of the noble and austere and the folk that wear the toga, and since, O generous lord, thou dost feed so many multitudes, haughty Annona knoweth nought of this festival. . . .[39] One table serves every class alike, children, women, common people, knights, and senators: freedom has loosed the bonds of awe. Nay even thyself—what god could have such leisure, or vouchsafe as much?—thou didst come and share our banquet. And now everyone, be he rich or poor, boasts himself the emperor's guest.

Amid such excitements and strange luxuries the pleasure of the scene flies quickly by: women untrained to the sword take their stand, daring, how recklessly, men's battles! . . . Then comes a bold array of dwarfs. . . . They give and suffer wounds, and threaten death—with fists how tiny! . . . .

Now as the shades of night draw on, what commotion attends the scattering of largess! Here enter maidens easily bought; here is recognized all that in theaters wins favor or applause for skill or beauty. Here a crowd of buxom Lydian girls are clapping hands, here tinkle the cymbals of Cádiz, there troops of Syrians are making uproar, there are theater folk, and they who barter common sulphur for broken glass [i.e., junk dealers]. Countless voices are raised to heaven, acclaiming the emperor's Saturnalia festival; with loving enthusiasm they salute their lord. This liberty alone did Caesar forbid them. . . .[40]

For how many years shall this festival abide! Never shall age destroy so holy a day! While the hills of Latium remain and Father Tiber, while thy Rome stands and the Capitol thou hast restored to the world, it shall continue.

39. That is, there is such an abundance that the usual problems of the grain supply of Rome do not exist.

40. That is, the liberty to address him as "lord" *(dominus)*. Cf., however, introduction to § 162.

42. THE WORLD METROPOLIS: WEALTH AND MISERY

Juvenal, *Satires* iii (abridged)

Although distressed at the departure of my old friend, yet I commend him for determining to fix his abode at unfrequented Cumae [on the coast of Campania]. . . . It is the gateway to Baiae, a pleasant seashore delightful to retire to. I prefer even Prochyta to the Suburra.[41] For what place have we seen so wretched, so lonely that you would not think it worse to be in dread of fires, the perpetual collapse of houses, the thousand dangers of the cruel city—and poets reciting in the month of August? . . .

"Let those remain," [said my friend], "who turn black into white, to whom it comes easy to contract for work on temples, rivers, harbors, cleaning sewers, carrying corpses to funeral pyres, and to put up slaves for sale at auction. These men, formerly hornblowers and constant attendants of the municipal amphitheaters, with their puffed-out cheeks well-known from town to town, now produce gladiatorial shows, and when the mob turns its thumbs up kill off anyone you like to please the people. . . . What should I do in Rome? I know not how to lie; if a book is bad, I cannot praise it and ask for a copy; I am ignorant of astrology; I neither will nor can promise the death of a father; I never inspected the entrails of frogs. Let others know how to carry to a married woman the presents and messages of her lover. . . .

"What people is now most in favor with our rich men, and what people I would particularly shun I will hasten to tell you, nor shall shame prevent me. I cannot bear, Romans, a Greek Rome; and yet, how small a portion of our dregs is from Greece! Long since Syrian Orontes [the longest river of Syria] has flowed into the Tiber and has brought with it its language and manners. . . . The coming of the Greek has brought us a Jack-of-all-trades—grammarian, rhetorician, geometrician, painter, wrestling manager, prophet, ropewalker, physician, magician; he knows everything. Bid the hungry Greekling go to heaven, he will go. . . . Shall I not shun the purple robes of these fellows? Shall such a one sign his name before me and recline at dinner propped up on

41. Prochyta (modern Procida) is a barren island off the west coast of Italy; Suburra was a disreputable quarter in Rome.

a better couch,[42] though imported to Rome by the same wind as plums and figs! . . .

"What, moreover—to speak plainly—are the services of the poor man, what are his good offices worth here, if he takes pains to hurry in his toga before daybreak, when a praetor is urging on his lictor and bidding him go with all speed, since the childless matrons have been long awake, for fear his colleague be beforehand in paying his morning respects to Albina and Modia?[43] Here the son of freeborn parents walks on the left of a rich man's slave; another gives to Calvina or Catiena, to enjoy her favors once and again, as much as tribunes in the legion receive; but you, [poor man], when the face of a dressed-up harlot pleases you, hesitate and are doubtful. . . . 'How many slaves does he keep? How many *iugera* of land does he possess? How numerous and how large are the dishes at his dinners?' The credence accorded a man is in proportion to the amount of money he keeps in his strongbox. . . . Why add that this same poor man furnishes everybody with material and occasions for jest, if his cloak is dirty and torn, if his toga is a trifle shabby and one of his shoes shows a break in the leather, or if more than one tear reveals the coarse, recently applied thread where the rent has been sewn together? There is nothing about unhappy poverty that is crueler than this, that it makes men ridiculous. . . . The poor among the Romans ought to have emigrated in a body long ago. Not easily do those emerge from obscurity whose noble qualities are cramped by domestic poverty. But at Rome the attempt is still harder for them; a great price must be paid for a wretched lodging, a great price for slaves' keep, a great price for a modest little dinner. A man is ashamed to dine off earthenware. . . . Here splendor of dress is carried beyond people's means; here something more than is enough is occasionally borrowed from another man's strongbox. This vice is common to all of us; here all of us live in a state of pretentious poverty. In a word, in Rome everything costs money. . . .

"Who fears or ever has feared the collapse of a house at cool Praeneste, or at Volsinii situated among the wooded hills, or at simple Gabii, or on the heights of sloping Tibur?[44] We inhabit a city supported to a

42. This refers to the ancient custom of reclining on couches at dinner parties. Certain locations on the couches were considered places of honor.

43. Legacy hunting is one of the most frequently mentioned vices of imperial Rome. The patron–client relationship of the early Republic (cf. vol. 1, § 8) had by this time been reduced to the formality of having the client attend the morning "greeting" *(salutatio)* in the reception room of his patron and receive a gift *(sportula)* of food or money.

44. These are representative country towns in Latium and Etruria.

great extent by slender props; for in this way the bailiff saves the houses from falling. And when he has plastered over the gaping hole of an old crack, he bids us sleep securely, with ruin overhanging us. The place to live in is where there are no fires, no noctural alarms. . . . Already your third story is smoking; you yourself know nothing about it; for if the alarm begins from the bottom of the stairs, the last man to know there is a fire will be the one who is protected from the rain only by the roof tiles, where the gentle doves lay their eggs. . . . A wretched man has lost the little he had; but the crowning point of his misery is this, that though he is naked and begging for scraps, no one will help him with food, no one with the shelter of a roof. If the great house of Asturicus has been destroyed, we have the matrons and nobles in mourning, the praetor adjourns his court; then we groan over the accidents of the city, then we detest fires. The fire is still burning, and already someone runs up to make a present of marble, to contribute to the expenses of rebuilding. One will contribute nude white statues, another some masterpieces of Euphranor or Polyclitus; some lady will give antique ornaments of Asiatic gods; another man, books and bookcases and a statue of Minerva to put among them; another, a bushel of silver plate. Persicus, most sumptuous of childless men, replaces what is lost by choicer and more numerous objects and is in fact with reason suspected of having himself set fire to his own house. If you are able to tear yourself away from the circus games, an excellent house can be bought at Sora, or Fabrateria, or Frusino, for the same price at which you now rent a dark hole for a year. . . .

"Many a sick man dies here from want of sleep, the sickness itself having been produced by undigested food clinging to the fevered stomach. For what rented lodgings allow of sleep? It takes great wealth to sleep in the city. Hence the origin of the disease. The passage of carriages in the narrow winding streets, and the abuse of the drivers of the blocked teams would rob even [the heaviest sleepers] of sleep.

"If a social duty calls him, the rich man will be carried through the yielding crowd and will speed over their heads on his huge Liburnian litter bearers; he will read on his way, or write, or even sleep inside, for a litter with closed windows induces sleep. Yet he will arrive before us. We in our hurry are impeded by the wave in front, while the multitude which follows us presses on our back in dense array; one strikes me with his elbow, another with a hard pole, one knocks a beam against my head, another a wine jar. My legs are sticky with mud; before long I am

trodden on all sides by large feet, and the hobnails of a soldier stick into
my toe. . . .

"Observe now the different and varied dangers of the night. What a
height it is to the lofty roofs, from which a tile brains you, and how
often cracked and broken utensils fall from windows—with what a
weight they mark and damage the pavement when they strike it! You
may well be accounted remiss and improvident about sudden accidents
if you go out to supper without making a will. There are just so many
fatal chances as there are wakeful windows open at night when you are
passing by. Hope, then, and carry this pitiable prayer about with you,
that they may be content merely to empty broad wash basins over you.
The drunken and insolent fellow who has not chanced to fall on someone suffers tortures. . . . But though heated with wine, he keeps clear of
the man whom the scarlet cloak, the very long train of attendants, the
many torches, and the bronze lamp point out as one to be avoided. Me,
whom the moon or the brief light of a candle whose wick I regulate and
adjust is wont to escort home, he despises. Mark the preliminaries of the
wretched brawl, if brawl it be, where you strike and I alone am beaten.
He stands facing you, and orders you to stand; you must obey, for what
are you to do when a madman forces you, and moreover one stronger
than yourself? . . . It is all one whether you try to say anything or draw
back in silence. They beat you in either case; then in anger they make
you post bail. This is the liberty of a poor man: after being beaten, he
prays, and after being thrashed with fisticuffs he entreats, to be allowed
to retire from the scene with a few teeth left him. Nor yet are such
things all you have to fear, for there will not be wanting one to plunder
you after the houses are shut, and all the shops everywhere are quiet,
their shutters closed fast with bolts. Sometimes, too, the swift footpad
plies his business with a weapon, as often as the Pomptine marshes and
the Gallinarian forest are kept safe by an armed guard and all these
fellows run from there to this place just as to a game preserve. . . .

"The greatest amount of iron is used in making chains, so that one
may fear that there will not be enough to make plows, and that there
will be a shortage of mattocks and hoes. Happy our remote ancestors!
Happy one may call the ages which in days of yore, under kings and
tribunes, saw Rome content with a single prison."

43. THE SPREAD OF LUXURY

Luxurious living became a feature of Roman upper-class life in the last centuries of the Republic, as the wealth from conquest flowed in upon the capital (cf. vol. 1, §§ 170–172). But luxury attained unprecedented heights in the first two centuries of the Empire, spreading not only among the upper classes but also among the large class of *nouveau-riche* freedmen, whose vulgar taste in conspicuous consumption is a stock theme in contemporary literature (cf. also § 48). "At the lowest reckoning," says Pliny the Elder (*Natural History* XII. xli. 84), "India, China, and the Arabian peninsula drain our Empire of 100,000,000 sesterces every year—that is what our luxuries and womenfolk cost us." Latin literature continues, as before, to be full of moralizing strictures on the decline from the sturdy ancestral mores, but the few attempts by the government to curb such excesses, such as Tiberius' attempt to revive and enforce the sumptuary legislation of Augustus, were at best only partially and temporarily successful.

Tacitus, Annals III. lii. i–liv. 5

Gaius Sulpicius and Decimus Haterius were the next consuls [A.D. 22]. It was a year free from disturbance in foreign affairs, but at home there was an uneasy anticipation of stern measures against the luxury which had broken all bounds in everything on which wealth is lavished. Some expenditures, though considerable, were kept secret, generally by concealing the true prices; but the costly preparations for gluttony and dissipation had become the subject of endless gossip and aroused concern lest an emperor of old-fashioned frugality react with too drastic reforms. In fact, when Gaius Bibulus raised the subject, the other aediles too had argued that the sumptuary law was disregarded,[45] that illegal prices for necessities were rising daily and could not be stopped by halfway measures; and the senate, when its counsel was sought, had referred the matter without discussion to the emperor.

Tiberius, after repeated deliberation as to whether such extravagant desires could be kept in check, whether such restraint might not cause yet greater harm to the state, and how ill-advised it would be to attempt something that he would not achieve or that, if enforced, would entail

45. Probably the most recent of the sumptuary laws is meant, that of Augustus of 22 B.C. (see vol. 1, p. 496).

the degradation and disgrace of men of distinction, finally wrote the senate a letter to the following effect:

". . . What am I to start with prohibiting and cutting down to the standard of old? The vast size of the country manors? The number of slaves of every nationality? The weight of silver and gold? The marvels in bronze and painting? The indiscriminate dress of men and women,[46] or that luxury peculiar to the women alone which, for the sake of jewels, diverts our riches to foreign and even hostile peoples?

"I am not unaware that at dinner parties and social gatherings these excesses are condemned and a limit is demanded. But let anyone enact a law imposing penalties, and those very same persons will clamor that the state is being subverted, that this means ruin for every member of high society, that no one is guiltless. . . . The many laws devised by our ancestors, the many passed by the deified Augustus, are dead letters, the former buried in oblivion, the latter—to our greater shame—in contempt. And this has made luxury bolder. For when you crave something not yet forbidden, you are in fear that you may be forbidden it; but when you have once crossed forbidden ground with impunity, neither fear nor shame is left. Why then did frugality prevail in olden times? Because everyone practiced self-control, because we were all citizens of one city. Even when we were masters of Italy alone, we did not have the temptations of today. Victories in foreign wars taught us to devour the substance of others, victories in civil wars, our own. . . ."

Seneca, Moral Epistles lxxxvi. 1–7 (abridged)

I am resting at the very country house that once belonged to Scipio Africanus. . . . It was therefore a great pleasure to me to contrast Scipio's ways with our own. In this tiny recess the "terror of Carthage," to whom Rome owes the fact that she was captured only once,[47] used to wash clean his body wearied with work in the fields. For he kept himself occupied and cultivated the soil with his own hands, as was the practice among the Romans of old. Beneath this dingy roof he stood, this cheap floor bore his weight.

But who nowadays could bear to bathe in such fashion? We think

---

46. There is an echo here of Tiberius' legislation six years earlier when he "forbade men to wear silk clothing and also forbade anyone to use golden tableware except for religious purposes" (Cassius Dio, *Roman History* LVII. xv. 1).

47. That is, only by the Gauls in 390 B.C., and not also by Hannibal.

ourselves poor and mean if our walls are not resplendent with large and costly mirrors; if our marbles from Alexandria are not set off by mosaics of Numidian stone, if they are not covered all over with an elaborate coating variegated to look like painting; [48] if our vaulted ceilings are not concealed in glass; if our swimming pools—into which we lower our bodies after they have been drained weak by copious sweating—are not lined with Thasian marble, once a rare sight in a temple, or if the water does not flow from silver spigots. I have so far been speaking of ordinary installations; what shall I say when I come to the baths of freedmen? What a host of statues, of columns that support nothing but are set up as decorations merely for the sake of spending money! What masses of water that fall crashing in cascades! We have become so luxurious that we will tread upon nothing but precious stones.

Pliny, *Natural History* XIII. xxix. 92; From *LCL*

There still exists a table that belonged to Marcus Cicero for which with his slender resources and, what is more surprising, at that date, he paid half-a-million sesterces, and also one is recorded as belonging to Asinius Gallus that cost a million. Also two hanging tables were sold at auction by King Juba, of which one fetched 1,200,000 sesterces and the other a little less. A table that was lately destroyed in a fire came down from the Cethegi and had changed hands at 1,300,000 sesterces—the price of a large estate, supposing somebody preferred to devote so large a sum to the purchase of landed property.

Pliny, *Natural History* IX. lviii. 117–118

I have seen Lollia Paulina [49] at an ordinary betrothal banquet covered with emeralds and pearls interlaced with each other and shining all over her head, hair, ears, neck, and fingers, their total value amounting to 40,000,000 sesterces, and she herself ready at a moment's notice to show the bills of sale in proof of ownership: they were not presents from an extravagant emperor but heirlooms acquired actually with the spoils of provinces. This is the outcome of plunder, it was for this that Marcus

48. Marble was tinted by being rubbed with a mixture of oil and wax.

49. The Emperor Caligula's third wife, whom he took from her husband in A.D. 38 and divorced the following year. Ten years later this millionairess was a strong but unsuccessful candidate for the hand of the Emperor Claudius.

Lollius disgraced himself by taking gifts from kings throughout the East[50] . . . that his granddaughter might glitter in the lamplight covered with 40,000,000 sesterces!

A SUMPTUOUS DINNER

The following selection is from the best-known part of the *Satyricon*—the long account of the banquet at the house of Trimalchio, a millionaire freedman pictured as living in riotous splendor in a town in Campania (cf. § 48, second selection). Though characterized by ironical and scornful exaggeration to emphasize the vulgarity of the man and his class, the description is instructive nonetheless.

Petronius, *Satyricon* xxxi. 3–xxxiv. 4

At length we took our places, and slaves from Alexandria poured iced water on our hands and other attendants for the feet came in and pared our toenails very carefully. And even during this unpleasant duty they were not silent, but continued to sing the whole time. I wanted to see whether the whole slave ménage could sing, so I asked for a drink. A slave supplied it at once, singing every bit as shrilly, as did anyone you asked to give you something; you would have thought it a theatrical troupe rather than a dining room in a private gentleman's house. All the same, the appetizer course was very elegantly served; for all but Trimalchio had now taken their places, the chief seat being reserved for the host after the latest fashion. Well, on the tray of relishes stood an ass made of Corinthian bronze, with two panniers, which contained white and black olives. This figure was flanked by two dishes, which had Trimalchio's name and the weight of the silver engraved on their edge; and on them were mounted salvers in the shape of little bridges, laden with dormice sprinkled with honey and poppyseed.[51] There were also sausages smoking-hot on a silver gridiron, with damsons and pomegranates sliced up and placed beneath it.

We were engaged in discussing these delicacies, when Trimalchio himself was carried in to a flourish of music. His appearance, bolstered up as he was among tiny cushions, made those who weren't expecting

---

50. Marcus Lollius, an early senatorial supporter of Octavian, was the first legate sent by Augustus, in 25 B.C., to govern the newly formed province of Galatia.

51. The sumptuary laws vainly forbade the use of dormice as food. They are still a delicacy in modern Italy.

it burst into laughter. For he had poked his close-shaven pate out of his scarlet mantle and had wrapped up his neck, already well-covered with clothes, in a napkin with a broad purple stripe and fringes all around. He was wearing as well a huge, lightly gilded[52] ring on the little finger of the left hand and actually had on the last joint of the next finger a smaller ring, which I thought was of solid gold but was as a matter of fact picked out with star-like designs in iron. And to show that he had other costly trinkets besides, he had drawn back his sleeve and bared his right arm, which was adorned with a gold band and an ivory circlet fastened by a plate of shining metal.

Then, picking his teeth with a silver toothpick, he vouchsafed the following remark: "My friends, I did not really want to come to dinner just yet, but I have sacrificed my own convenience so as not to keep you waiting any longer by my absence. Still, you will allow me to finish my game." A slave followed him carrying a draughtboard of juniper wood and draughts of crystal; and I noticed one most elegant refinement, namely the use of gold and silver coins instead of the usual black and white counters. Meanwhile, as he continued the game, using all manner of coarse expressions,[53] a tray was placed before us, as we were still busy with the appetizers, containing a basket in which there was a hen carved in wood with her wings spread out round her just as if she were sitting on eggs. Up stepped two slaves and, while the band played a loud fanfare, they began to rummage in the straw, dividing among the guests the peahen's eggs which they dug out one after the other. Trimalchio, turning to this exhibition, remarked: "My friends, I ordered pea-hens' eggs to be set under a hen, and by Jove I am afraid they are half-hatched already; but let us try whether we can still suck them." Spoons weighing at least half a pound each were handed to us and we broke the eggs, which were made of rich pastry. To tell the truth I nearly threw my share away, for I thought it had developed into a chick already. But I heard one of the other guests, who was an old hand at these tricks, say, "There ought to be something good here"; so I broke up the shell in my hand and found a fine, plump beccafico,[54] well seasoned with pepper, hidden inside the yolk.

Trimalchio had interrupted his game, and had already had all the same dishes served him; and he had in a loud voice invited anyone of us who wished to take a second glass of mead, when all of a sudden, at a

---

52. To give the appearance of the gold ring that was the sign of equestrian rank.
53. Literally, "weavers' expressions," emphasizing Trimalchio's lowly origins.
54. The "figpecker," still an Italian delicacy.

signal given by the band, the appetizer trays were quickly removed, likewise by a singing troupe. But in the middle of the scurry an entrée dish was dropped, and when a slave picked it up from the ground Trimalchio abused him and ordered his ears boxed, and told him to throw the dish down again. In came one of the slaves in charge of dishes and with a broom began to sweep away the silver dish along with the rest of the litter. He was followed by two hairy Ethiopian slaves carrying little wineskins, like those used to sprinkle the sand in the amphitheater,[55] and they poured wine over our hands—for no one so much as offered water.

44. A RICH MAN'S COUNTRY RESIDENCE

In this letter Pliny gives a detailed description of his suburban seaside villa at Laurentum, where he lived in the winter. In other letters he describes a villa in Etruria, where he spent his summers, and two villas on Lake Como, near his native town. These sumptuous residential villas have little in common with the villas of agricultural estates.

Pliny, *Letters* book II, no. 17 (abridged)

Gaius Plinius to his dear Gallus, greeting.

You are surprised that I am so fond of my Laurentine villa . . . but you will cease to be when you come to know the charm of the villa, the convenience of its location, and the extent of the shoreline. It is only seventeen miles from the city; so that after getting through with business you can be here with the day's work safely done and disposed of. Two roads give access to it: the Laurentine and Ostian roads lead to it, but you must turn off the Laurentine road at the fourteenth milestone, off the Ostian road at the eleventh. Both of them are sandy part of the way, and somewhat heavy and tedious for a team, but short and easy on horseback. The scenery on all sides is varied: at times the path is hemmed in by woods, at others it extends and opens over broad meadows, where many flocks of sheep and many herds of horses and cattle, driven down from the mountains by the winter, fatten on the grass and vernal warmth.

The villa is spacious enough for my needs, and the upkeep is not expensive. In the first part of it the entrance room is plain but not mean. Next there are colonnades that come together in a form very much like

---

55. Saffron was sprinkled in the amphitheaters to make the air sweeter.

the letter D, enclosing a small but pleasant area. This affords an excellent retreat in bad weather, as it is protected by windows, and much more by the overhanging roof. . . .

To the left of this dining room, somewhat recessed, is a large salon, then a second smaller one, one of whose windows faces east, the other west, also affording a view of the sea but a more unstudied one. The angle formed by the projection of this room and the dining room retains and increases the warmth of the very clear sunlight. This serves as a winter retreat, and also as a gymnasium for my household; here there are no winds except those which bring unsettled weather, and it is not until the fair weather is gone that the place loses its usefulness. Attached to the angle is another chamber with a bay window, whose windows admit sun all day long. Set in the wall of this room is a closet like a bookcase containing books that should be reread, not merely read. Attached to this is a bedroom connected to a passageway with a hollow floor and walls fitted with pipes from which it receives hot air circulated in all directions at a healthful temperature. The rest of this side of the house is reserved for the use of the slaves and freedmen, most of the rooms being elegant enough to accommodate guests. . . .

Next comes the spacious and expansive cold room of the baths, in the opposite walls of which are two bath tubs curving outward as if forced out of the wall; these are quite roomy, when you consider how near the sea is. Adjacent are the anointing room, the furnace room, and also the steam room; then come two small chambers, tasteful rather than sumptuous. Attached to these is a splendid warm pool, where one may swim and have a view of the sea. Close by is the ball court, which receives the very hot afternoon sun. . . .

Next, a covered gallery extends, almost large enough for a public structure. It has windows on both sides, more on the side facing the sea, fewer on the garden side, there being one here for every two on the other side. When the day is fair and serene, these are all kept open; but if it is windy, those on the side where the wind is gentle are kept open without discomfort. Before the covered gallery is a terrace perfumed with violets. The warmth is intensified by the reflection of the sun beating on the gallery, which both absorbs the sun's heat and checks and keeps off the northeast wind; and it is as warm in front as it is cool in the rear. In the same manner it checks the southwest wind, and thus it breaks the force of and halts winds blowing from any direction. This is the charm of this spot in the winter; but it is greater in the summer. For in the morning the terrace, and in the afternoon the nearest part of the promenade and garden, are made comfortably shady by it, and as the days grow longer or shorter, the shade that is cast is now shorter, now longer in one place or the other. The covered gallery itself is then shadiest when the sun is hottest and falls directly on the roof. In addition, when the windows are open, westerly breezes come in and blow through, and it never becomes close with stale and stagnant air.

At the head of the terrace and the gallery is a garden apartment, my favorite, really my favorite, for I had it constructed myself. It contains a sun parlor, one side of which has a view of the terrace, the other of the sea, and both are exposed to the sun; and also a bedroom with a view of the covered gallery from its folding doors and of the sea from a window. Opposite the center wall is my retreat, very neatly recessed, which by its glazed windows and by opening or drawing the curtains can be joined to or shut off from the bedroom. It contains a couch and two chairs. Below is the sea, behind are villas, above are woods. These varied views can be seen from the windows either separately or in one panorama. Adjoining the retreat is a chamber for sleeping and napping. Neither the voices of the servants nor the murmur of the sea, nor even the fury of storms penetrate this, nor lightning, nor even daylight, unless the windows are open. . . . When I retire to this apartment, I fancy myself far away even from my own villa, and I take particular pleasure in it especially at the Saturnalia, when the remaining parts of the house resound with the license and the festive shouting of those days [see § 41], for I don't hinder their festivities, and they don't disturb my studies.

Among these conveniences and pleasures there is one drawback— lack of running water, but there are wells, or rather springs, for they are on the surface. And the nature of this coast is quite remarkable, for wherever you dig, you at once encounter water, pure and not even slightly spoiled by the nearness of the sea. The nearby forests afford an abundant supply of fuel; all other necessities are supplied by the town of Ostia. . . .

Now don't you think I have good reason to dwell and live in and cherish my retreat? You are too citified if you do not have a yearning for it. And I wish you did. Then to the many great gifts of my little villa would be added the supreme recommendation of your companionship. Farewell.

45. A ROMAN GENTLEMAN'S DAILY ROUND

Pliny, *Letters* book IX, no. 36

Gaius Plinius to his dear Fuscus, greeting.

You ask how I arrange my day in summertime at my Tuscan villa. I rise when I please, generally at the first hour, often earlier, but seldom later. The windows remain closed; for I am wonderfully removed by the silence and darkness from the things which distract one, and I am free and left to myself. . . . This is when I do my thinking, if I have any composing on hand; I think in finished phrases, like a person actually writing and correcting. This is the way I compose, now less, now more, depending on whether the subject is easy or difficult and how much my memory can retain. Then I call my amanuensis and, letting in the daylight, I dictate to him what I have composed; he leaves, is presently summoned once again, and is again dismissed. About the fourth or fifth hour (for I do not observe a definite, fixed hour), as the weather permits, I betake myself to the terrace or the covered portico, and there I meditate upon and dictate the rest. Then I enter my carriage, and there also I do the same as I did walking or lying down; by this change my attention is refreshed, and it lasts longer. I sleep a little again, and then I take a walk; and after that I read aloud and with vigor a Greek or Latin oration, not so much for the sake of my voice as of my digestion, though the voice is strengthened also. Then I walk again, am anointed, take my exercise, and bathe. When I sup with my wife or a few persons, a book is read; and after supper there is a dramatic reading from a comedy, or music. Then I walk with my domestics, among whom are some learned men. Thus the evening is lengthened by varied conversation, and however long the day, it is quickly spent.

Sometimes the order of some of the activities is changed. For instance, if I have lain abed longer or walked more than usual, after my siesta and the recitation exercise I take a ride on horseback instead of in a carriage, because it is quicker and takes less time. Friends from the neighboring towns visit and claim for themselves a part of the day; and sometimes, by an opportune interruption, they afford me relaxation when I am fatigued. Occasionally I hunt, but I always have my writing tablets with me, so that even though I should catch nothing I may not come home empty-handed. I do not devote enough time to my tenant farmers, at least so it seems to them; yet I find that their rustic complaints give a fillip to my writing and to these citified activities. Farewell.

46. THE "THREE-CHILDREN PRIVILEGE"

The legislation of Augustus that established privileges for parents of three children and legal disabilities for the unmarried and childless (see vol. 1, § 204) remained on the statute books till the sixth century. The emperors, however, frequently granted the "three-children privilege" to prominent individuals who lacked the requisite number of children. The first to receive the grant in this honorary fashion was Augustus' own wife, Livia. Pliny, who received such a grant himself from the Emperor Trajan, here requests it for the well-known biographer Suetonius; in another letter he mentions having obtained it for another old friend. Constantine exempted the Christian clergy from the operation of these laws; see § 174, third selection.

Pliny, *Letters* book x, nos. 94–95

[Pliny to the Emperor Trajan]

Suetonius Tranquillus, my lord, is a person of the highest honesty, integrity, and learning; in consequence of his character and interests I have long since made him one of my intimate friends, and my affection for him has increased the more I have come to know him. Two reasons make the "three-children privilege" necessary for him: that the bequests of his friends may be fulfilled,[56] and because he has had an unfruitful marriage. What the cruelty of fortune has denied him he hopes to obtain from your kindness through my intercession. I know, my lord, what a great indulgence I am requesting; but I am making the request of one whose kindness I obtain in all my requests. How eagerly I wish to obtain this favor you can gather from the fact that I would not make such a request in my absence[57] if I were only moderately interested.

[Trajan to Pliny]

---

56. Being childless, Suetonius stood to lose half of every legacy, in accordance with the Augustan legislation.

57. Pliny is writing from Bithynia, where he was governor at the time.

You cannot fail to know, my dearest Pliny, how sparingly I grant these benefits, since I am wont to declare even in the senate that I have not exceeded the number which I assured that illustrious body I would be content with. I have, however, granted your request and have directed that there be entered in my records that I have given the "three-children privilege" to Suetonius Tranquillus on my usual conditions.

47. THE STOIC CREED AND THE UPPER CLASSES

Greek Stoicism, adapted to Roman needs from the second century B.C. on, was the only important philosophical system that attained widespread acceptance in the Roman ruling classes. It held a particular appeal for them because of its cosmopolitanism and pantheism, its concept of the brotherhood of all mankind, and its righteous justification of monarchy, Roman imperialism, and *status quo*. They espoused Stoic doctrine as a kind of religious creed to help them face with equanimity and fortitude the upheavals to which their lives were frequently subject at the whim of capricious emperors. Some of its adherents even became a focus of philosophical opposition to such emperors, and the school suffered vigorous persecution at the hands of Nero, Vespasian, and Domitian. But Stoicism made its peace with the "Good Emperors," and in the person of Marcus Aurelius a Stoic philosopher mounted the throne. With the triumph of the mystery religions in the crisis of the third century, Stoicism was eclipsed after five hundred years of existence; Christianity, however, had by then absorbed and thereafter carried forward some of its teachings.

Seneca, *Natural Questions* III. preface. 10–17

What is the principal thing in life? . . . To raise the soul above the threats and promises of fortune; to consider nothing as worth hoping for. For what does fortune possess worth setting your heart upon? . . . What is the principal thing? To be able to endure adversity with a joyful heart; to bear whatever betide just as if it were the very thing you desired to have happen to you. For you would have felt it your duty to desire it, had you known that all things happen by divine decree. Tears, complaints, lamentations are rebellion [against divine order]. What is the principal thing? A heart in the face of calamity resolute and invincible, an adversary, yea a sworn foe to luxury;[58] neither anxious to meet nor

58. The wide divergence between Seneca's high-sounding Stoic principles and the facts of his public and private life cannot escape comment. Tacitus says of him (*Annals* XIII. xlii): "By what

anxious to shun peril; a heart that knows how to fashion fortune to its will without waiting for her; which can go forth to face ill or good dauntless and unembarrassed, paralyzed neither by the tumult of the one nor the glamor of the other. What is the principal thing? Not to admit evil counsel into the heart, and to lift up clean hands to heaven; to seek for no advantage that some one must give and some one lose in order that it may reach you; to pray—a prayer that no one will oppose—for purity of heart; as for other blessings that are highly esteemed by humanity, even should some chance bring them to your home, to regard them as sure to depart by the same door by which they entered. What is the principal thing? To lift one's courage high above all that depends on chance; to remember what man is, so that whether you may be fortunate, you may know that this will not be for long, or whether you may be unfortunate, you may be sure you are not so if you do not think yourself so.

What is the principal thing? To have life on the very lips, ready to issue when summoned.[59] This makes a man free, not by right of Roman citizenship but by right of nature. He is, moreover, the true freeman who has escaped from bondage to self; that slavery is constant and unavoidable—it presses us day and night alike, without pause, without respite. To be a slave to self is the most grievous kind of slavery; yet its fetters may easily be struck off, if you will cease to make large demands upon yourself, if you will cease to seek a personal reward for your services, and if you will set before your eyes your nature and your age, even though it be the bloom of youth; if you will say to yourself, "Why do I rave, and pant, and sweat? Why do I ply the earth? Why do I haunt the Forum? Man needs but little, and that not for long."

---

wisdom, by what principles of philosophy had he acquired 300,000,000 sesterces within four years of [Nero's] royal favor? At Rome the childless and their wills are snared in his nets, as it were; Italy and the provinces are drained by his enormous usury." Cassius Pio (*Roman History* LXII. ii) maintains that he helped to precipitate the rebellion of A.D. 61 in Britain by suddenly recalling 40,000,000 sesterces invested in loans in that province.

59. Seneca alludes to the Stoic solution of personal crises by suicide. Seneca himself was compelled by imperial order to commit suicide for implication in a conspiracy against the life of Nero.

48. FREEDMEN

Freedmen constituted a numerous and important class in the life of the Roman Empire. It became almost customary for a master to free at least part of his slave household in his will, as a means either of flattering his own vanity or of showing his gratitude for faithful service. In addition, even during the master's lifetime slaves were frequently able to purchase their freedom with the savings *(peculium)* they were allowed to accumulate, and many were granted manumission as a free gift. Such slaves usually had domestically useful or commercially profitable skills or business experience. Freedmen were, accordingly, to be found in practically all occupations and enterprises large and small, and many amassed considerable fortunes. Indeed, the "wealth of freedmen" became proverbial.

The relation of the ex-slave to his ex-master, parts of whose name he now as a rule added to his former slave name, was that of client to patron (cf. vol. 1, p. 64–65). The patron was expected to protect his freedman's welfare. The freedman in return was legally obligated to render to his patron *obsequium et officium,* "obedience and services" of various kinds, including support if the patron should fall into need; freedmen who were delinquent in these duties were liable to severe punishment, including beating with rods, exile, forced labor in the mines, and even reduction to slavery again. But generally the tie between patron and freedman was close and friendly. Patrons commonly provided burial places for their freedmen's families in the same tomb with their own, and wealthy freedmen, too, often built such common tombs; and though patrons were legally entitled to share in the estates of their freedmen (excepting those who had three—freedwomen, four—children), they frequently did not exercise this right but, on the contrary, left legacies from their own estates to their freedmen.

The freedmen of Roman citizens normally entered into the Roman citizen body, but they were ineligible for equestrian or senatorial rank, for the highest Roman and municipal magistracies and priesthoods, and for the military echelons reserved for freeborn citizens; and at Rome they were in addition the objects of severe social discrimination, being treated as upstarts. These disabilities generally did not apply, however, to their sons, and their grandsons enjoyed complete equality with other freeborn Romans: the poet Horace and the Emperor Pertinax, for example, were sons of freedmen. Freedmen staffed many of the innumerable menial and clerical posts in the municipal and imperial administrations, and the priesthood of the cult of Augustus *(seviri,* "board of six") was practically reserved to them. This office of *Augustalis,* the discharge of which involved considerable expense for its incumbents, was the pinnacle of a freedman's career, except for those of their own freedmen whom the emperors appointed to the important administrative procuratorships and the imperial secretaryships.

AE, 1972, no. 574; C. A.D. 105

In Latin followed by a Greek translation, this inscription recites the career of one Classicus. Manumitted under Claudius or Nero, he held high office in the imperial household under Titus, saw no service under Domitian (who despised his brother Titus), but was reinstated in the imperial service under Nerva and Trajan, when he held offices that imply that he had been promoted to equestrian rank. For a lengthy commentary see G. Boulvert, *Zeitschrift für Papyrologie und Epigraphik* (1981), 43:31–41.

Dedicated to Tiberius Claudius Classicus, imperial freedman, custodian of the imperial bedchamber and camp procurator of the deified Titus, procurator of revels of the deified Nerva and of the Emperor Nerva TRAJAN Caesar Augustus Germanicus Dacicus, procurator of revels and morning [gladiatorial] combats, and procurator of accounting of Alexandria, by Gaius Julius Photinus Celer, his aide in the procuratorship of Alexandria, for his merits.[60]

WEALTHY FREEDMEN

In the course of his famous banquet, the ex-slave Trimalchio tells the story of his rise from slavery to freedom and wealth. Though fictional and deliberately exaggerated for heightened effect—it is told, for instance, in appropriately plebeian language to emphasize the contrast between Trimalchio's vulgar ostentation and his pretense of upper-class refinement—the story is essentially realistic, affording a brief but precious glimpse into an important segment of Italian society (cf. § 43, last selection).

Petronius, Satyricon lxxv. 8–lxxvii. 6

Come, my friends, make yourselves at home. I too was once just like you, but by my ability I've reached my present position. What makes man is the heart, the rest is all trash. "I buy well, and I sell well"; others have different ideas. I am ready to burst with good luck. . . . My good

---

60. The Greek version has two variants. It begins, "The council and people [of Ephesus] honor Tiberius Claudius Classicus. . . ." At the end of the last three words are "his [Celer's] personal benefactor."

management brought me to my present good fortune. I was only as big as the candlestick here when I came from Asia, in fact I used to measure myself by it every day and I smeared my lips with the lamp oil to get a hairy face quicker. Still for fourteen years I was my master's favorite. And where's the disgrace in doing what one's master tells one? All the same I managed to get into my mistress' good graces, too (you know what I mean: I hold my tongue, as I am not one to boast).

But by heaven's help I became master in the house, and then I took in my fool of a lord. To be brief, he made me co-heir with the emperor to his property, and I got a senator's fortune.[61] But no one is ever satisfied, and I wanted to go into business. To cut it short, I built five ships, I loaded them with a cargo of wine—it was worth its weight in gold at that time—and I sent it to Rome. You would have thought I had ordered my bad luck: every ship was wrecked; it's a fact, no story. In one day Neptune swallowed up 30,000,000 sesterces. Do you think I failed? No, I swear the loss only whetted my appetite as if nothing had happened. I built more ships, larger, better, and luckier ones, and everybody called me a courageous man—you know, a great ship shows great strength. I loaded them with wine again, bacon fat, beans, perfume, and slaves. At this point Fortunata [Trimalchio's wife] did the loyal thing: she sold all her jewelry, all her dresses, and put in my hand 100 gold pieces [10,000 sesterces]. This was the leaven which made my fortunes rise. The gods' wishes are soon fulfilled. On one voyage I cleared a round 10,000,000 sesterces. I immediately bought back all the estates that had belonged to my patron. I built a mansion, I bought up young slaves to sell, and beasts of burden: everything I touched grew like a honeycomb.

Once I was worth more than my whole native town put together, I quit the game: I retired from business and started lending money, financing freedmen. I must admit, just when I was wanting to give up my business, I was urged to do so by an astrologer who had just chanced to come to our town, some kind of Greek named Serapas, a man in the counsels of the gods. This man actually mentioned events that I had forgotten; he told me everything as pat as needle and thread; he seemed to be able to see my very insides, and told me everything but what I'd

---

61. In the first century many wealthy testators resorted to naming the emperor their co-heir as a device for insuring their estates against confiscation (cf. chapter 1, note 44). Millionaires of lowly origin often left this kind of will also as a means of raising their family's social standing. Some of the emperors refused on principle to accept such legacies except from close friends or in other special cases. A senator's fortune was at least a million sesterces.

had for dinner the day before. You'd have thought he'd lived with me always. Habinnas, you were there with us, I believe, when he said: "You used your wealth to get your wife. You are unlucky in your friends. No one is ever as grateful to you as he ought to be. You own vast estates. You are nourishing a snake in your bosom." [62] And, well, I really don't see why I shouldn't tell you, I've still got thirty years, four months, and two days to live. What's more, I shall soon receive a legacy. That's what my fortune tells me. But if I am allowed to extend my estates to Apulia, [63] I'll have done well enough in my lifetime. Meantime, with Mercury watching over me, [64] I built this residence. As you know, it was a cottage; now it's fit for a god. It's got four dining rooms, twenty bedrooms, two marble colonnades, and the upstairs apartments, my own bedroom where I sleep, this viper's [cf. note 62] boudoir, an excellent porter's lodge, and enough guest rooms for all my guests—in fact, when Scaurus [65] came here he didn't want to put up anywhere else, even though he can stay at his father's friend's by the sea. And there are lots of other things, which I'll show you presently. Believe me, have a penny, you're worth a penny; have something, you'll be treated like something. And so your friend, once a mere worm, is now a king.

CIL, vol. XI, no. 5,400 (= Dessau, no. 7,812)

[Assisi]

Publius Decimius Eros Merula, freedman of Publius, clinical doctor, surgeon, oculist, member of the board of six. For his freedom he paid 50,000 sesterces. For his membership on the board of six he contributed to the community 2,000 sesterces. For the erection of statues in the temple of Hercules he gave 30,000 sesterces. For paving streets he contributed to the municipal treasury 37,000 sesterces. On the day before he died he left an estate of . . . sesterces.

---

62. A reference to his wife, Fortunata, with whom Trimalchio has a spat at the banquet shortly before this narrative begins. A few sentences below this he again refers to her as a "viper."

63. Earlier in the story Trimalchio was said to have estates near Tarracina (in Latium) and Tarentum (in Calabria).

64. Mercury was the patron god of businessmen.

65. The cognomen of three of Rome's old noble families.

GRATEFUL FREEDMEN AND PATRONS

A large marble plaque, found in Rome, has the following inscriptions below the heads of a man and a woman in high relief.

CIL, vol. VI, no. 2,170 (= Dessau, no. 5,010)

[Under the man's bust:] Lucius Antistius Sarculo son of Gnaeus, of the Horatian tribe, Salian priest of Alba, and also master of the [college of] Salians.

[Under the woman's bust:] Antistia Plutia, freedwoman of Lucius.[66]

[Under both:] Rufus, freedman, and Anthus, freedman, made [these] busts at their own expense for their patron and patroness in return for their kindnesses.

The following are a few of the hundreds of dedicatory inscriptions on tombs which throw light on patron-freedman relations. Cf. also § 54 and introduction.

CIL, vol. XII, no. 4,490; vol. XI, no. 108; vol. VI, no. 11,027; vol. VI, no. 22,915 (= Dessau, nos. 8,221–22); vol. X, no. 4,142; vol. VI, no. 9,222 (= Dessau, no. 7,695); vol. X, no. 8,192

i

[Narbonne, France]

To the spirits of the departed. To Marcus Ulpius Eutyches, imperial freedman, surveyor[?], his freedmen to their patron most well-deserving.

ii

[Ravenna, Italy]

To the spirits of the departed. Titus Veturius Florus, veteran . . . lived fifty-five years. Erected by Titus Veturius Pothinus, freedman, to his well-deserving patron. Frontage 10 feet, depth 8 feet.

---

66. As his wife's name shows, Lucius Antistius Sarculo, like many middle-class Romans, freed and married one of his female slaves.

iii

[Rome]

Marcus Aemilius Artema built this for Marcus Licinius Successus, his well-deserving brother, and for Caecilia Modesta, his wife, and for himself and his freedmen and freedwomen and their descendants, with the exception of the freedman Hermes, whom, because of his offenses, I forbid access, approach, or any admittance to this tomb.

iv

[Rome]

Sextus Nerianus Romulus built this for himself and Cordia Helpis, his wife most dear, and for their freedmen and freedwomen and their descendants of either sex stemming from us. If anyone alters this inscription in an attempt to bring into this tomb the body, bones, or ashes of another family, he shall not have access and shall have to pay to the treasury of the Roman people the sum of 50,000 sesterces. Let no malice aforethought attend this tomb!

v

[Capua, Italy]

[Ashes of] Flavia Nicê, freedwoman, most sweet in her affection and services and attentions, she loved her patron. Titus Flavius Celadus, imperial freedman, erected this.

vi

[Rome]

To the spirits of the departed. [Remains of] Marcus Canuleius Zosimus; he lived twenty-eight years; his patron erected this to a well-deserving freedman. In his lifetime he spoke ill of no one; he did nothing without his patron's consent; there was always a great weight of gold and silver in his possession, and he never coveted any of it; in his craft, Clodian engraving,[67] he excelled everybody.

67. Pliny (*Natural History* XXXIII. xi. 139) mentions this as one of "the varying fashions in silver plate," without giving any details.

vii

[Puteoli (Pozzuoli), Italy]

To Grania Clara, freedwoman of Aulus, a worthy freedwoman; she lived twenty-three years and never caused me any vexation, save by her death.

49. MANUMISSION

Most common of the forms of manumission was the grant of freedom by the master's last will and testament. However, the master could also in his own lifetime (or after his death through his heir) liberate a slave by the ancient *vindicta* (rod) ceremony, a mock lawsuit before one of the higher magistrates, who affirmed the slave's freedom; the master thereupon gave him a slap, symbolizing, it is thought, his last indignity as a slave and emphasizing his future immunity from such treatment. (This ritual is analogous to, and perhaps the source of, the accolade of medieval knighthood.) There were also the informal methods of manumission, which were popular because of their simplicity: a master could write a letter granting his slave freedom; or he could have the slave sit at table with him; or he could announce the slave's emancipation in the presence of a few friends *(inter amicos)* as witnesses. These different forms of Roman manumission are described by our legal sources; only the testamentary manumission (for which see § 53) and the *inter amicos* type (given below) have thus far appeared in actual documents. The Greek-speaking eastern provinces, where most of the extant manumission documents come from, continued even after Caracalla's general grant of Roman citizenship (see § 106) to use Greek forms and formulas.

Among the indirect imposts of the Roman Empire was a tax of 5 percent of the value of all liberated slaves (for examples see § 53, second selection). With the great increase in manumission under the Empire, this tax became an important source of revenue for the fisc.

MANUMISSION "INTER AMICOS"

This deed of manumission is recorded on a wooden diptych found in Egypt. The text of the deed is in Latin; the signatures are in Greek. Though it dates from the third century, it illustrates a practice prevailing during the entire Principate.

Mitteis, no. 362 (= *FIRA,* vol. III, no. 11); A.D. 221

Marcus Aurelius Ammonio son of Lupercus (son of Sarapio) and Terheuta, of the ancient and illustrious [city of] Hermopolis Major, manumitted in the presence of friends his house-born female slave Helene, about thirty-four years old, and ordered her to be free, and received for her freedom from Aurelius Ales son of Inarous, of the village of Tisichis in the Hermopolite nome, 2,200 imperial drachmas,[68] which the said Ales son of Inarous made a present of to the aforementioned freedwoman Helene.[69]

Done at Hermopolis Major ancient and illustrious, July 25, in the consulship of Gratus and Seleucus, year 4 of the Emperor Caesar Marcus Aurelius Antoninus [ELAGABALUS] Pius Felix Augustus, month of Mesore, 1st day.

[Signatures] I, Marcus Aurelius Ammonio son of Lupercus son of Sarapio, freed in the presence of friends my house-born female slave Helene, about thirty-four years old, and I received for her ransom 2,200 imperial drachmas from Aurelius Ales son of Inarous, as stated above.

I, Aurelius Ales son of Inarous, paid in full the 2,200 drachmas, and I will make no claim on the aforementioned freedwoman Helene. I, Aurelius Ammonius son of Herminus, wrote for him because he is illiterate.

GREEK MANUMISSIONS

The *agoranomi* (market supervisors), officials who regulated buying and selling and kept the records of business transactions, are here instructed to issue a certificate of emancipation to a slave who has purchased his freedom. The writers of this authorization were probably the collectors of taxes and fees on transfers of property. The manumission under the aegis of Zeus, Ge, and Helius, the gods of heaven, earth, and sun, is a survival from the Greek form of emancipation through sale or dedication of the slave to a god.

---

68. Though in most of the eastern half of the Empire the Greek drachma was equated with the Roman *denarius;* in Egypt the equivalent of the *denarius* was the tetradrachm, so that an Egyptian drachma equaled a Roman sesterce. On prices of slaves cf. introduction to § 35.

69. Since marriage between slave and freeman was impossible, slaves of both sexes, but especially women, were frequently liberated for the express purpose of marriage. Perhaps that is why Ales here purchases Helene's freedom.

Oxyrhynchus Papyrus No. 49 (= Mitteis, no. 359); A.D. 100

Theo and Theo to the *agoranomi*, greeting. Grant freedom to Horio, a slave being set free under Heaven, Earth, and Sun by his mistress, Sinthoös daughter of Pecysis (son of Zoilus) and Lucia (daughter of Longinus), of Oxyrhynchus, upon ransom of 600 drachmas and [transfer fee of] 10 drachmas in silver specie. Farewell. Year 4 of the Emperor Caesar Nerva TRAJAN Augustus Germanicus, month of New Augustus [cf. chapter 1, note 16] the 2d.

> Under Roman law the situation involved in the following document could not exist, for if one of the owners of a jointly owned slave renounced his ownership, the manumitted share passed automatically to the remaining owners. Under the Hellenistic law of the eastern provinces, however, such part ownership was a salable commodity.

Oxyrhynchus Papyrus No. 716 (= Mitteis, no. 360); A.D. 186

To Asclepiades also known as Sarapio, gymnasiarch, greeting from Horio son of Panechotes (son of Doras) and Taous, from Apollonius son of Dorio (son of Heras) and Thaësis, and from Abascantus, freedman of Samus son of Heraclides, all three of Oxyrhynchus, guardians of the minor children of Theo also known as Dionysius, namely, Eudaemonis, whose mother is Sintheus, and Dionysius and Thaësis, the mother of both of whom is Tauris, all three of the same city. The said minors have inherited from their father and own, Eudaemonis one-sixth share, Dionysius and Thaësis one-half share, total two-thirds share, of a slave named Sarapio, about thirty years old, the remaining one-third share of whom, belonging to Diogenes their half-brother on their father's side, has been set free by him. We therefore present this petition, requesting that the indicated two-thirds share of the minors be sold at public auction and awarded to the highest bidder. Year 27 of the Emperor Caesar Marcus Aurelius COMMODUS Antoninus Pius Felix Augustus Armeniacus Medicus Parthicus Sarmaticus Germanicus Maximus Britannicus, Thoth. [The signatures of the three guardians follow, with Diogenes writing for the illiterate freedman.]

50. THE CONDITION OF SLAVES

Despite the falling off in the number of war captives during the *Pax Romana,* the slave population of the Roman Empire remained quite large. "On one occasion a proposal was made by the senate," says Seneca (*On Clemency* I. xxiv. 1), "to distinguish slaves from freemen by their dress; it then became apparent how great would be the impending danger if our slaves began to count our number." The lot of many slaves was undoubtedly a life of toil under cruel masters, and the law was pitiless toward any who revolted or who fled and tried to pass themselves off as freemen. But the fact that more and more slaves were now home-bred rather than purchased foreigners, the influence upon the upper classes of Stoicism with its preachment of the brotherhood of man, and the general cosmopolitanism of the age were not without effect. Under such influences the attitude toward and the treatment of slaves, both in practice and in law, grew steadily more humane. We find slaves as well as freemen employed in many of the host of manual, clerical, and administrative posts in agriculture, private business, and government service. In the second century, if not earlier, slaves were admitted to membership in some of the lower-class burial societies along with freemen. But the gradual betterment of the slave's lot is reflected most strikingly perhaps in the law. Between Cato's literal application of Aristotle's definition of a slave as "a living tool" (vol. 1, §§ 94, 166) and the legislation of the Roman emperors, there lies a world of difference. The enactments of Augustus and his successors afforded slaves increasing protection against maltreatment. Thus, though the testimony of slaves could be taken only under torture, this practice was hedged about by a whole series of restrictions, including exemptions for women and children. Repeated legislation was directed also against various kinds of arbitrary abuse of slaves by their masters. A law of the first century provided that only judicially condemned slaves could be sent to fight (and die) in the arena. The Emperor Claudius deprived masters of the power to kill or discard sick slaves arbitrarily. Vespasian forbade selling a slave for use as a prostitute. Domitian forbade, under severe penalty, the castration of slaves for commercial purposes. Hadrian strengthened this and similar bans on abusing slaves' bodies, outlawed private prisons, banished a woman for five years for excessive cruelty to her slave girls and forbade the killing of a slave without judicial sentence. Antoninus Pius gave slaves further protection against cruelty and personal outrage and made the killer of a slave liable for homicide. Thus, toward the end of the second century the jurist Florentinus was able to write, "Slavery is an institution of the law common to all peoples (*ius gentium*[70]), by which, in violation of the law of nature, a person is subjected to the mastery of another" (Justinian, *Digest* I. v. 4). And not many years later the great Ulpian—formulating what, in a sense, the Romans had been recognizing from time immemorial by "freeing" their slaves one day a year on the Saturnalia—penned the classic statement: "As far as Roman law (*ius civile*) is concerned, slaves are regarded as nothing, but not so in natural law as well: because as far as the law of nature is concerned, all men are equal" (Justinian, *Digest* L. xvii. 32).

SLAVES TURN ON THEIR MASTERS

Tacitus, *Annals* XIV. xlii–xlv (abridged)

[In A.D. 61] one of his own slaves murdered the prefect of the city [Rome], Pedanius Secundus, either because he had been refused his freedom after the price had been agreed upon, or because in the passion of an infatuation for a catamite he was unable to brook his master's rivalry. In any case, according to ancient custom the whole slave household which had dwelt under the same roof was to be led to execution, but a sudden massing of the populace, which was bent on protecting so many innocent lives, brought matters to the point of insurrection, and the senate was beseiged. In the senate itself there was a strong feeling on the part of some who were averse to excessive severity, but most held that no change should be made. One of these, Gaius Cassius, in stating his views, argued to the following effect:

". . . An ex-consul has been murdered in his own home by a slave's treachery which no one reported. . . . Certainly, decree impunity! But whom will rank shield, when it did not avail the prefect of the city? Whom will a large number of slaves keep safe, when four hundred did not protect Pedanius Secundus? . . . Many clues precede a crime; if our slaves report these, we may live singly amid numbers, safe amid an insecure throng, and, if perish we must, not unavenged, at least, upon the guilty. To our ancestors the temper of their slaves was always suspect, even when they were born on the same farm or under the same roof, and acquired an affection for their masters forthwith. But now that we have in our households foreigners with customs different from our own, with alien religions or none at all, you will not restrain such a

70. On the meaning of this term and of *ius civile,* mentioned a few lines below, see vol. 1, pp. 39–40.

motley rabble except by fear. But, it will be said, innocent lives will be lost. Well, when every tenth man of a routed army is felled by the club,[71] the lot falls on the brave also. In every wholesale punishment there is some injustice to individuals, which is compensated by the advantage to the state."

While no one member dared to oppose Cassius' view, a din of voices rose in reply from those who pitied the number, age, or sex of the victims, and the undoubted innocence of the great majority. Nevertheless, the side which was for decreeing their execution prevailed. But the decision could not be complied with, because a dense crowd had gathered, threatening to use stones and firebrands. Then the emperor reprimanded the people by edict, and when the condemned were being led to punishment he had the whole route lined with detachments of soldiers.

Pliny, Letters book III, no. 14

Gaius Plinius to his dear Acilius, greeting.

Here is the terrible story, deserving of much more than a letter, of how Larcius Macedo, a man of praetorian rank, was treated by his slaves. To be sure, he was a haughty and cruel master, who remembered too little—or rather, only too well—that his own father was once a slave.

He was bathing at his villa near Formiae. Suddenly slaves surrounded him, one seized him by the throat, another struck him in the face, another pommeled him on the chest, the stomach, and even, shocking to relate, on the private parts; and when they thought he was lifeless they threw him onto the hot floor, to see if he was alive. He, either unconscious or pretending to be, lay stretched out and motionless, giving the impression that death was complete. Then, finally, they carried him out as if he had fainted with the heat. Faithful slaves received him, and his concubines rushed up, wailing and shrieking. So, aroused by their noise and refreshed by the cool air, he opened his eyes and moved his body to show, since it was now safe, that he was alive. Slaves fled in all directions, but most of them were apprehended, and search is going on for the rest. He himself was with difficulty kept alive a few days, and did not die without the consolation of revenge. [The rest of the letter is here omitted.]

---

71. The ancient Roman custom of decimation is described in vol. I, p. 47.

FROM SLAVE BOY TO ADOPTED SON

CIL, vol. III, no. 14,206 (21) (= Dessau, no. 7,479)

[Found near Philippi, Macedonia]

Here lies Vitalis, slave of Gaius Lavius Faustus and also his son, a slave born in his home. He lived sixteen years, [was] a clerk at the Aprian shop [?], popular with the public, but snatched away by the gods. I beg your pardon, wayfarers, if I ever gave short measure to make more profit for my father. I beg you by the gods above and below to take good care of my father and mother. And farewell.

THE STOIC INFLUENCE

Seneca, *Moral Epistles* xlvii (abridged); Adapted from *LCL*

I am glad to learn, through those who come from you, that you live on friendly terms with your slaves. This befits a sensible and well educated man like yourself. "They are slaves," people declare. Nay, rather they are men. "Slaves!" No, companions. "Slaves!" No, they are unpretentious friends. . . .

As a result of [their] high-handed treatment the proverb is current: "As many enemies as you have slaves." They are not enemies when we acquire them; we make them enemies. I shall pass over the other cruel and inhuman conduct toward them; for we maltreat them, not as if they were men, but as if they were beasts of burden. When we recline at a banquet, one slave mops up the disgorged food, another crouches beneath the table and gathers up the leftovers of the tipsy guests. Another carves the priceless game birds; with unerring strokes and skilled hand he cuts choice morsels along the breast and rump. . . . Another, who serves the wine, must dress like a woman and wrestle with his advancing years; he cannot get away from his boyhood, but is dragged back to it; and though he has already acquired a soldier's figure, he is kept beardless by having his hair smoothed away or plucked out by the roots, and he must remain awake throughout the night, dividing his time between his master's drunkenness and his lust—in the bedchamber he must be a man, at the feast a boy. Another, whose duty it is to put a valuation on the guests, must stick to his task, poor fellow, and watch to see whose flattery and whose immodesty, whether of appetite or of language, is to get them an invitation for tomorrow. . . .

Kindly remember that he whom you call your slave sprang from the same stock, is smiled upon by the same skies, and like yourself breathes, lives, and dies. It is just as possible for you to see in him a free-born man as for him to see in you a slave. As a result of the massacres of Marius' day,[72] many a man of most distinguished birth who was taking the first steps of the senatorial career by service in the army was humbled by fortune, one becoming a shepherd, another a caretaker of a country cottage. Despise, then, if you dare, the man to whose estate you may possibly descend even while you are despising him. I do not wish to involve myself in too large a question and discuss the treatment of slaves, toward whom we Romans are excessively haughty, cruel, and insulting. But this is my advice in a nutshell: Treat those below you as you would be treated by those above you.[73] And as often as you reflect how much power you have over a slave, remember that your master has just as much power over you. "But I have no master," you say. You are still young, perhaps you will have one. . . .

"He is a slave." His soul, however, may be that of a freeman. "He is a slave." But is that an objection? Show me a man who is not a slave—one is a slave to lust, another to greed, another to ambition, and all men are slaves to fear. I will name you an ex-consul who is a slave to an old hag, a millionaire who is a slave to a little slave girl. I will show you youths of noblest birth the slaves of mimes. No servitude is more disgraceful than that which is self-imposed.

You should therefore not be deterred by these finicky persons from showing yourself to your slaves as an affable person and not proudly superior to them. They ought to respect you rather than fear you. Because I say slaves ought to respect their masters rather than fear them some may maintain that I am now offering the liberty cap to slaves in general and toppling down masters from their high estate: "This is what he plainly means—slaves are to pay respect as if they were clients, or early-morning callers!" Anyone who says this forgets that what is enough for a god cannot be too little for a master. He who respects also loves, and love and fear do not mix.

72. That is, in the civil war between Marius and Sulla, in the first century B.C.
73. This Stoic formulation of the Golden Rule by a Roman contemporary of Jesus, Peter, and Paul is noteworthy.

LEGISLATION AGAINST THE ABUSE OF SLAVES

Justinian, *Digest* XLVIII. viii. II. 2

Since the passage of the Petronian Law[74] and the decrees of the senate relating thereto, masters have been deprived of the power of turning over slaves at their own discretion to fight with wild beasts. If, however, a slave has been brought before a judge and the complaint of the master should prove to be valid, then such penalty may be imposed.

Suetonius, *Life of Claudius* xxv. 2

When certain men were abandoning their sick and worn-out slaves on the Island of Aesculapius[75] because of the trouble of treating them, Claudius decreed that all slaves thus abandoned, if they recovered, would be free and would not revert to the power of their masters.[76] And if anyone chose to kill such a slave instead of abandoning him, he would be liable to the charge of homicide.

Justinian, *Digest* XXXVII. xiv. 7

The deified Vespasian decreed that a female slave would become free if she were made a prostitute after being sold on condition that she should not be made a prostitute; and that if she were later sold to someone else by the purchaser without such stipulation, she would become free by virtue of such sale and would become the freedwoman of the former seller.

"Historia Augusta," *Life of Hadrian* xviii. 7–11

Hadrian forbade masters to kill their slaves, ordering that any who deserved such punishment must be sentenced by the courts. He forbade anyone to sell a slave or slave girl to a procurer or trainer of gladiators without furnishing a reason. . . . He abolished private prisons for slaves and free. . . . He ordained that if a slave owner were murdered in his home not all the slaves should be subjected to questioning but only those who could have been near enough to notice anything.

74. Since this law is mentioned in an inscription from Pompeii, it must antedate the destruction of that town by the eruption of Vesuvius in A.D. 79. There is some possibility that it dates from A.D. 19.

75. The island in the Tiber River in Rome, where there was a famous sanctuary of Aesculapius, the healer-god.

76. Slaves thus freed received Latin status (see introduction to vol. I, § 205).

Justinian, *Digest* XLVIII. XVIII. I. I

A rescript of the deified Hadrian to Sennius Sabinus . . . reads as follows: "Recourse to torturing of slave should be had only when there is a suspect under indictment and other evidence brings the proof so close that only the confession of slaves appears necessary [to complete it]."

Gaius, *Institutes* I. liii

At the present time neither Roman citizens nor any other persons who are under the rule of the Roman people are permitted to treat their slaves with excessive and baseless cruelty. For, by enactment of the Emperor Antoninus, a man who kills his own slave without cause is ordered to be held just as liable as one who kills another's slave.[77] And even excessive severity of masters is restrained by enactment of the same emperor. For, when consulted by certain governors of provinces about those slaves who seek asylum in temples of the gods or at statues of the emperors, he ordained that if the cruelty of the masters is found to be intolerable they are to be compelled to sell their slaves.

Justinian, *Digest* I. vi. 2 (= *Institutes* I. viii. 2)

A rescript of the deified [Antoninus] Pius to Aelius Marcianus, proconsul of Baetica . . . follows: "The power of masters over their slaves ought to remain unimpaired, nor should any man be deprived of his lawful rights; but it is to the masters' interest that relief against cruelty, hunger, or intolerable wrong should not be denied those who seek it with just cause. Investigate,[78] therefore, complaints of those of Julius Sabinus' slave household who have fled for protection to [my] statue, and if you find that they have been treated more harshly than is just, or subjected to indecent acts, order them to be sold with the stipulation that they may not revert to Sabinus' power. And if the said Sabinus seeks to evade my ordinance, he will learn that I will deal more severely with his offense."

---

77. Further details on this are given by Gaius in III. ccxiii: "The owner of a slave who has been killed has the free choice of prosecuting the killer on a capital charge [cf. chapter 8, note 15] or suing him . . . for damages."

78. At Rome, slaves' pleas for protection against cruel masters came before the prefect of the city.

51. RESTRICTIONS ON ASSOCIATIONS

Restrictions on freedom of association, introduced during the political turmoils of the dying Republic (cf. vol. 1, p. 308), were revived and reinforced by Augustus and his successors. The main lines of imperial policy were laid down by Augustus' Julian Law on Associations (A.D. *c.* 7), which required all societies to be authorized by the emperor or Senate. Throughout the period of the Empire, no association (*collegium*) could legally exist without specific governmental permission, and no organization was authorized that might conceivably serve as a focus of political agitation. Associations that served imperial purposes were actually fostered by the emperors; cf. §§ 40, 56, 116. Others were tolerated, mainly burial societies and purely religious societies. These were permitted to hold meetings not more than once a month for religious observances or payment of dues. For the "by-laws" of such a *collegium*, see § 52, first selection, and for the bearing of the legislation concerning associations on the persecution of the Christians, see §§ 167, 169, 172.

Justinian, *Digest* XLVII. xxii. 1–3

Governors of provinces are directed by imperial mandates not to permit political associations to exist and not to allow soldiers to form societies in camp. The lower classes are, however, permitted to make monthly contributions [to a society], provided, however, they meet only once a month, so that no illegal association may assemble under a pretext of this kind. The deified Severus also stated in a rescript that these provisions applied not only in the city [of Rome] but in Italy and the provinces as well. But they are not forbidden to assemble for religious purposes, provided however that nothing is thereby done contrary to the senate's decree by which illegal associations are enjoined.[79] A person may not, moreover, be a member of more than one legal association, as was ordained by the deified brothers [Marcus Aurelius and Lucius Verus]. If a man is a member of two, it was stated in this rescript, he is to choose the one in which he prefers to remain and is to receive from the association from which he resigns what is due him as his share of the common fund.

Anyone who maintains an illegal society is liable to the same penalty as persons who have been condemned for occupying public places or temples with armed men [i.e., for the crime of treason].

79. Part of this decree is quoted in § 52, first selection.

All illegal societies are dissolved by imperial mandates and enactments and by decrees of the senate; but upon their dissolution the members are permitted to divide any common fund they may have and share the money among themselves. In sum, then, unless an association or any such body assembles under the authorization of a decree of the senate or of the emperor, it meets contrary to the decree of the senate and imperial mandates and enactments. Slaves, too, may be admitted into societies of the lower classes with the consent of their masters. Officers of these bodies should therefore be aware of this and not admit [a slave] into a lower-class association without the consent or knowledge of the master, and they should know that in the future they will be liable to a fine of 100 gold pieces [= 10,000 *denarii*] for each person [so admitted].

Pliny, Letters book x, nos. 33–34

[Pliny to the Emperor Trajan]

While I was making a tour of another part of the province, an enormous fire at Nicomedia [cf. chapter 2, note 46] destroyed many private dwellings and two public structures—the old men's shelter and the temple of Isis—though they stood on opposite sides of the street. It spread so far first owing to the force of the wind, and secondly to the inactivity of the people, who, it is clear, stood idle and motionless spectators of such a terrible calamity; and in any case the city possessed not a single pump or fire bucket or any equipment at all for fighting fires. These will, however, be procured, as I have already ordered. Do you, my lord, consider whether you think it well to organize an association of firemen, not to exceed 150 members. I will see to it that none but firemen are admitted into it, and that the privileges granted shall not be abused for any other purpose; and since they would be so few, it would not be difficult to keep them under surveillance.

[Trajan to Pliny]

You are of course thinking of the examples of a number of other places in suggesting that an association of firemen might be organized in Nicomedia. But we must remember that the peace of your province, and particularly of those cities, has been repeatedly disturbed by organizations of this kind. Whatever name we give them, and for whatever purpose, men who have gathered together will all the same become a political association before long. It is therefore better to provide equipment which can be helpful for controlling fires, advise property owners to use these themselves, and, if the situation warrants it, call on the populace for assistance.

Pliny, Letters book x, nos. 92–93

[Pliny to the Emperor Trajan]

The free allied city [cf. vol. 1, §§ 132–134] of Amisus enjoys, by benefit of your indulgence, the use of its own laws. A petition having been presented to me there concerning mutual-benefit societies, I append it to this letter, that you may consider, my lord, whether and to what extent these are either to be permitted or prohibited.

[Trajan to Pliny]

As to Amisus, whose petition you appended to your letter, if they are permitted by their laws, which they enjoy by virtue of their treaty, to maintain a mutual-benefit society, we cannot prevent them from having one, especially if the contributions are employed not for the purposes of rioting and illicit gatherings but for the support of the indigent. In other cities, however, which are subject to our laws, organizations of this nature are to be prohibited.

52. BENEVOLENT SOCIETIES

Burial societies constituted the most common type of association sanctioned under the Empire. Organized in the name of a patron divinity, these societies met once a month and on their special holidays for collection of dues, religious ceremonies, and festal dinners. Though frequently composed of people engaged in the same trade or occupation, these societies were in no sense comparable to guilds or trade unions; they were organized neither to establish the standards of the trade nor to bargain for higher wages or improved working conditions. They served, rather, the function of a kind of social club, in which considerable numbers of humble folk, slave as well as free, found companionship in life and the assurance of decent burial.

BY-LAWS OF A SOCIETY

CIL, vol. XIV, no. 2,112 (=Dessau, no. 7,212=FIRA, vol. III, no. 35)

[Lanuvium, Italy, A.D. 136]

In the consulship of Lucius Ceionius Commodus and Sextus Vettulenus Civica Pompeianus, May 28. . . .

Clause from the Decree of the Senate of the Roman People

These are permitted to assemble, convene, and maintain a society: those who desire to make monthly contributions for funerals may assemble in such a society, but they may not assemble in the name of such society except once a month for the sake of making contributions to provide burial for the dead.

May this be propitious, happy and salutary to the Emperor Caesar Trajanus HADRIAN Augustus and to the entire imperial house, to us, to ours, and to our society, and may we have made proper and careful arrangements for providing decent obsequies at the departure of the dead! Therefore we must all agree to contribute faithfully, so that our society may be able to continue in existence a long time. You, who desire to enter this society as a new member, first read the by-laws carefully before entering, so as not to find cause for complaint later or bequeath a lawsuit to your heir.

By-laws of the Society

It was voted unanimously that whoever desires to enter this society shall pay an initiation fee of 100 sesterces and an amphora of good wine, and shall pay monthly dues of 5 *asses*. It was voted further that if anyone has not paid his dues for six consecutive months and the common lot of mankind befalls him, his claim to burial shall not be considered, even if he has provided for it in his will.[80] It was voted further that upon the decease of a paid-up member of our body there will be due him from the treasury 300 sesterces, from which sum will be deducted a funeral fee of 50 sesterces, to be distributed at the pyre [among those attending]; the obsequies, furthermore, will be performed on foot.

80. That is, even if he has provided for the payment of the arrears.

It was voted further that if a member dies farther than twenty miles from town and the society is notified, three men chosen from our body will be required to go there to arrange for his funeral; they will be required to render an accounting in good faith to the membership, and if they are found guilty of any fraud they shall pay a quadruple fine; they will be given money for the funeral expenses, and in addition a round-trip travel allowance of 20 sesterces each. . . . If a member dies intestate, the details of his burial will be decided by the *quinquennalis*[81] and the membership.[82]

It was voted further than if a slave member of this society dies, and his master or mistress unreasonably refuses to relinquish his body for burial, and he has not left written instructions,[83] a token funeral ceremony will be held.

It was voted further that if any member takes his own life for any reason whatever, his claim to burial [by the society] shall not be considered.

It was voted further that if any slave member of this society becomes free, he is required to donate an amphora of good wine. . . .

Masters of the dinners in the order of the membership list, appointed four at a time in turn, shall be required to provide an amphora of good wine each, and for as many members as the society has a bread costing 2 *asses,* sardines to the number of four, a setting, and warm water with service. . . .

It was voted further that any member who becomes *quinquennalis* in this society shall be exempt from such obligations[?] for the term when he is *quinquennalis,* and that he shall receive a double share in all distributions. It was voted further that the secretary and the messenger shall be exempt from such obligations[?] and shall receive a share and a half in every distribution.

It was voted further that any member who has administered the office of *quinquennalis* honestly shall [thereafter] receive a share and a half of everything as a mark of honor, so that other *quinquennales* will also hope for the same by properly discharging their duties.

It was voted further that if any member desires to make any com-

---

81. The chief officer of the society, who held office for a five-year period.

82. People often specified in their wills whether they wished to be cremated or interred and how much money from their estate was to be used for funeral expenses. Thus, for example, we read in Berlin Papyrus No. 1,695 (A.D. 157): "I desire that I be interred, and that 200 imperial *denarii* be spent on my body. Let no malice aforethought attend this last will and testament!"

83. A slave could not legally make a will.

plaint or bring up any business, he is to bring it up at a business meeting, so that we may banquet in peace and good cheer on festive days.

It was voted further that any member who moves from one place to another so as to cause a disturbance shall be fined 4 sesterces. Any member, moreover, who speaks abusively of another or causes an uproar shall be fined 12 sesterces. Any member who uses any abusive or insolent language to a *quinquennalis* at a banquet shall be fined 20 sesterces.

It was voted further that on the festive days of his term of office each *quinquennalis* is to conduct worship with incense and wine and is to perform his other functions clothed in white, and that on the birthdays of Diana and Antinoüs[84] he is to provide oil for the society in the public bath before they banquet.

DISSOLUTION OF A SOCIETY

CIL, vol. III, pp. 924–927, no. I (=Dessau, no. 7,215a=*FIRA*, vol. III, no. 41)

[Alburnus Major, Dacia, A.D. 167]

Certified copy made from a notice which was posted at Alburnus Major near the office of Resculum and in which was written the following:

Artemidorus son of Apollonius, master of the Society of Jupiter Cernenus, and Valerius son of Nico and Offas son of Menofilus, treasurers of the said society, by depositing this notice publicly attest that of the fifty-four members that used to constitute the above-mentioned society there now remain at Alburnus no more than seventeen; that even Julius son of Julius, his co-master, has not come to Alburnus or to [a meeting of] the society since the day he took office; that he rendered an accounting to those who were present of what he had of theirs and was returning or had spent on funerals and that he recovered the security he had posted for these sums; that now, moreover, there was not enough for burial expenses and he did not have a single coffin, and no one in all this period has been willing to come to meetings on the days required by the by-laws or to contribute burial money or services; and that they therefore publicly attest by this notice that no member is to think that if he dies he has a burial society, or that any request for burial will be entertained by them.

---

84. The society's patron gods. Antinoüs was a favorite of the Emperor Hadrian, who accorded him divine honors after his death (A.D. 130).

Posted at Alburnus Major, February 9, in the consulship of the Emperor LUCIUS Aurelius VERUS (for the third time) and Quadratus. Done at Alburnus Major.

[The names and seals of seven witnesses—the usual number (cf. note 92)—follow.]

53. ROMAN WILLS

Roman citizens throughout the Empire had to draw their wills in Latin to conform to Roman law. In the third century, after Caracalla's grant had made practically all the inhabitants of the Empire Roman citizens (see § 106), the people of the provinces were given the right to draw Roman wills in Greek.

CIL, vol. XIII, no. 5,708 (= Dessau, no. 8,379 = *FIRA*, vol. III, no. 49)

[Langres, France, early second century]

. . . the chapel which I built to my memory I desire to be completed according to the plan I left, as follows: there is to be an exedra in this place, in which my statue, not less than five feet high and in a sitting position, is to be erected of the finest imported marble or of the best tablet-quality bronze. At the foot of the exedra a couch and a bench on either side are to be made of imported stone. The covering to be spread there on those days on which the chapel to my memory is opened is to consist of two counterpanes and two pairs of pillows such as are used at banquets, as well as two woolen robes and a tunic. Before this building an altar is to be erected of the finest Luna stone[85] with the finest possible sculptured decoration, and in it my bones are to repose. And this building is to be closed with Luna stone, in such a way that it can be easily opened and shut again.

This building and the [aforementioned] orchards and ponds are to be cared for under the supervision of my freedmen Philadelphus and Verus, and money shall be provided for rebuilding and repairing if any of these becomes spoiled or destroyed; they are to be cared for by three landscape gardeners and their apprentices, and if one or more of them die or are removed, another or others are to be substituted in their place; each of the three is to receive sixty *modii* of wheat annually and thirty *denarii* for

---

85. White Carrara marble quarried at Luna in northern Etruria, Italy.

clothing. Furthermore, my nephew Aquila and his heirs must singly and collectively provide these things.

And there shall be inscribed on the outside of the building the names of the magistrates in whose term of office this building was begun, and how many years I lived. If ever any other man or woman is cremated, entombed, buried[?], interred, or deposited[?] in these orchards . . . or closer to these orchards than 1,000[?] feet, or if anyone does anything contrary to what is written above, my heir and his heirs . . . shall be bound to see to it that all this is so done and not otherwise. Further, this regulation is established for this burial place in perpetuity, and no one after me is to have title or right to these burial places except to take proper care, or to plant or complete. Those who come to this building . . . to care for it shall have right of access on foot, by vehicle, or by litter[?]. . . . If anyone is cremated or buried[?], or if a monument is erected, or if bones are brought in . . . in these orchards and burial places and their enclosures as I have written above, then Sextus Julius Aquila son of Sextus Julius Aquilinus, and his heir or heirs, mentioned above, shall—if it is within their power to prevent it from being done or to take opposing action, or if they do not see to it that everything is kept by their heir or heirs as above stipulated—be condemned to pay 100,000 sesterces to the public treasury[?] of the Lingones. This penalty is to apply to all owners of this property in perpetuity.

Further, all my freedmen and freedwomen, both those whom I manumitted while still alive and those whom I manumit by this testament, are to make an annual contribution of . . . each, and my nephew Aquila and his heirs are to provide annually the sum of . . . with which they are to prepare food and drink to be offered in sacrifice below, in front of the chapel, to my memory at Litavicrar;[86] and they are to consume it there and to remain there until they use up the whole sum. For this ceremony they shall name from among themselves, by turns, caretakers who will hold this ceremony each year and who will have the right to demand the said sum of money. I entrust the care of this to Priscus, Phoebus, Philadelphus, and Verus. . . . The caretakers thus named shall perform the sacrifice at the above-mentioned altar annually on the first day of April, May, June, July, August, and October.

Further, I entrust the care of my funeral and obsequies and of all my property, buildings, and monuments to my nephew Sextus Julius Aquila

86. The name is uncertain.

and to Macrinus son of Reginus and to Sabinus son of Dumnedorix[87] and to Priscus my freedman and bailiff, and I request them to take care of all these things, and to pass upon the proper performance of the things I ordered done after my death.

Further, I desire all the equipment which I acquired for hunting and fowling to be cremated with me[88] including lances, swords, hunting knives, nets, snares, toils, lime twigs, tents, scarecrows, bathing utensils, litters, sedan chair, and all medicines and equipment of that science, and the rush-work Liburnian boat—nothing of these is to be omitted; also whatever damasks and embroideries I leave behind, and all the stars from the elk horns. . . . [The rest is lost.]

Berlin Papyrus No. 326 (= *Select Papyri*, vol. I, no. 85 = *FIRA*, vol. III, no. 50);
Adapted from *LCL*

[Caranis, Egypt, A.D. 191][89]

[Greek] translation of will. Gaius Longinus Castor, veteran honorably discharged from the praetorian fleet of Misenum, made this will. I direct that my slave Marcella, over thirty years of age, and my slave Cleopatra, over thirty years of age,[90] shall be freed, and they shall each in equal portion be my heirs. All others shall be disinherited. They shall enter upon the inheritance, each on her own portion, as soon as each thinks proper to attest that she is my heir, and it shall not be lawful to sell or mortgage it. But if the aforesaid Marcella suffers the lot of human kind, then I wish her portion of the inheritance to go to Sarapio and Socrates and Longus. Similarly, in the case of Cleopatra, I wish her portion to go to Nilus. Whoever becomes my heir shall be obligated to give, perform, and provide all that is written in this my will, and I entrust to him the faithful execution thereof. My slave Sarapias, daughter of my freedwoman Cleopatra, shall be freed, and I give and bequeath to her five arouras of grain land which I own in the vicinity of the village of Caranis in a locality called Ostrich, likewise one and one quarter arouras of a ravine, likewise one third portion of my house and the third portion of

87. Macrinus and Sabinus, despite these Romanized names, were apparently Gauls who had not yet attained Roman citizenship.

88. Cf. Caesar's description of the customs of the Gauls in vol. 1, p. 223.

89. This is the date of the original will; the date of a later codicil is not given. The will was opened when the testator died, as we learn near the end of the document, in 194.

90. Slaves under the age of thirty manumitted by will did not acquire full citizenship.

the same which I bought formerly from Prapetheus mother of Thaseus, likewise one third portion of a palm grove which I own close to the canal called the Old Canal. I wish my body to be carried out and dressed for burial through the care and piety of my heirs. If I leave any later provision written by my hand in any manner whatsoever, I wish it to be valid. Let no malice aforethought attend this will!

On the making of this will Julius Petronianus purchased the household and chattels for 1 sesterce; Gaius Lucretius Saturnilus acted as scales-holder (acknowledged); and Marcus Sempronius Heraclianus acted as witness (acknowledged).[91]

This will was made in the village of Caranis in the Arsinoite nome on November 17 in the consulship of the two Silani, in the thirtieth year of the Emperor Caesar Marcus Aurelius COMMODUS Antoninus Pius Felix Augustus Armeniacus Medicus Parthicus Sarmaticus Germanicus, Hathyr 21. If I leave any further document written by my hand, I wish it to be valid.

Opened and read in the Arsinoite metropolis in the Augustan Forum in the office of the five-percent tax on inheritances and manumissions on February 21 in the consulship of the present consuls, in the second year of the Emperor Caesar Lucius SEPTIMIUS SEVERUS Pertinax Augustus, Mecheir 27 [A.D. 194]. The remaining sealers:[92] Gaius Longinus Acylas (acknowledged); Julius Bolyssius; Marcus Antistius Petronianus; Julius Gemellus, veteran.

Translation of the codicillary tablets. I, Gaius Longinus Castor, veteran honorably discharged from the praetorian fleet of Misenum, have made a codicil. I have appointed Marcus Sempronius Heraclianus, my respected friend, trustee to act on his own good faith. To my kinsman Julius Serenus I give and bequeath 4,000 sesterces. Written in my own hand on February 7. Sealed by Longinus Acylas and Valerius Priscus. Sealers: Gaius Longinus Acylas (acknowledged); Julius Philoxenus; Gaius

---

91. This paragraph, a survival from the property conveyance of very early times (cf. vol. 1 chapter 3, note 28), remained even under the Principate the regular legal formula for testamentary disposition. The testator, through a symbolic sale in the presence of witnesses, conveyed his whole estate to a friend for the price of a piece of bronze (hence, one of the witnesses is termed the *scales-holder*). "In olden days," says Gaius, writing in the second century A.D. (*Institutes* II. ciii), "the purchaser of the household . . . held the position of heir, and that is why the testator instructed him on what he wanted to be given to each person after his death. But nowadays one person is instituted as heir by the will and charged with the payment of the legacies, and another person is used as purchaser of the household merely as a matter of form, in imitation of the ancient law."

92. That is, four in addition to the three witnesses mentioned earlier, thus making the requisite seven witnesses.

Lucretius Saturnilus (acknowledged); Gaius Longinus Castor; Julius Gemellus, veteran. Opened and read on the same day on which the will was unsealed.

I, Gaius Lucius Geminianus, expert in Roman law, translated the foregoing copy, and it agrees with the original will.

54. SEPULCHRAL INSCRIPTIONS

Both inhumation and cremation were practiced in the Roman Empire. Burials and funerary monuments were protected by law against disturbance. As we have already seen in §§ 52–53, testators frequently included in their wills specific provisions for their funerals and for the upkeep of their tombs. The stipulations most commonly encountered in connection with sepulchres are (1) the property—tomb and site—is retained in the family in perpetuity by a permanent prohibition against alienation; (2) all persons are forbidden to damage the monument; (3) all persons are forbidden to violate the sepulture or place therein the remains of a stranger; (4) specified persons are allowed or forbidden access to the tomb. Tombstones and other memorials of the dead constitute the most numerous category of extant inscriptions, having been found by the thousands in all parts of the Mediterranean world. They tell their mournful story in an infinite variety of ways, some in trite, conventional phrases and some in genuine personal outpourings of love and grief, ranging in length from "the short and simple annals of the poor" to the long and often very flowery memorials of the well-to-do. A few samples follow; these should be read in association with the funerary inscriptions included in §§ 13–14, 48, and 50.

Dessau, no. 7,663

[Pompeii, Italy]

Laturnia Januaria, lime burner, lived 45 years.

CIL, vol. IX, no. 1,721 (=Dessau, no. 7,668)

[Beneventum, Italy]

Publius Marcius Philodamus, freedman of Publius, plasterer, [built this] for himself and his family. Jucunda, his darling, is buried [here].

CIL, vol. VI, no. 11,602 (=Dessau, no. 8,402)

[Rome]

Here lies Amymone, wife of Marcus, most good and most beautiful, wool spinner, dutiful, modest, careful, chaste, stay-at-home.

CIL, vol. XIV, no. 4,827

[Ostia, Italy]

To the spirits of the departed. Gaius Calpenius Hermes built this for himself and his family, and for his freedmen and freedwomen and their descendants, and for Antistia Coetonis, his wife. This place of burial shall not pass to an heir belonging to another family. He built a chamber on the right of the entrance; [placed] sarcophagi on the pavement outside; and opposite [the entrance] and to the left, in two walls, made niches with [funerary] urns and sarcophagi.

CIL, vol. VI, no. 36,467 (=Dessau, no. 8,184)

[Rome]

To the spirits of the departed. Gaius Tullius Hesper built [this] tomb for himself, where his bones are to be placed. If anyone does violence to them or removes them hence, I wish for him that he may live a long time in bodily pain, and that when he dies the gods below may not receive him.

CIL, vol. V, no. 952 (=Dessau, no. 8,239)

[Aquileia, Italy]

Marcus Vocusius Crescens, freedman of Marcus, built this in his lifetime for himself and Vocusia Veneria, his very good wife, and Petronius Vocusianus, his son, soldier of the Third Praetorian Cohort, aged 18 years, 3 months, 18 days. If anyone tries to sell, buy, or break open this repository, then he shall pay a penalty of 20,000 sesterces to the municipality of Aquileia, and the informer shall receive one fourth.

CIL, vol. XI, no. 137 (=Dessau, no. 1,980)

[Ravenna, Italy]

Gaius Julius Mygdonius, a Parthian by origin, born a freeman, captured when a youth and sold into slavery in Roman territory. When I became a citizen with fate's kind help, I prepared a nest egg [or coffin?] against the day when I reached fifty. Ever since youth I sought to attain my old age; now receive me gladly, O stone; with you I shall be freed from care.

AE, 1947, no. 187, and 1948, p. 90 (=L. Robert, *Hellenica*; [Paris, 1946], 3:119)

[Nicomedia, Bithynia]

You see me a corpse, passers-by. My civilian name[93] was Apollonis, my native town Apamea, but now in [?] the soil of Nicomedia the thread of destiny spun by the Fates holds me fast to the ground. Eight times he won in athletic games, but in the ninth boxing match he met his fated end. Play, laugh, passer-by, knowing that you too must die. His wife Alexandria erected this memorial out of his money as a remembrance. If anyone dares to disturb this monument, he shall pay a fine of 2,500 *denarii* to the fisc.

CIL, vol. VI, no. 35,887 (=Dessau, no. 8,168)

[Rome]

I lived dear to my family, I gave up my life yet a maiden.
Here I lie dead and I am ashes, and these ashes are earth.
But if the earth is a goddess, I am a goddess, I am not dead.
I beg you, stranger, do not desecrate my bones.
Mus, lived thirteen years.

CIL, vol. VI, no. 14,672 (=Dessau, no. 8,156), abridged

[Rome]

To the spirits of the departed. To Cerellia Fortunata, dearest wife, with whom he lived forty years without the slightest cause for complaint,[94] Marcus Antonius Encolpus[95] built this. . . .

93. As opposed to his professional name or nickname.

94. This is a stock phrase in Latin sepulchral inscriptions (cf. also the following text), so much so that it is frequently reducted to its initials, *s.u.q. (sine ulla querela).*

95. Interestingly enough, both Encolpus and Fortunata are the names of characters in Petronius' *Satyricon.*

Do not pass by this epitaph, wayfarer,
But stop, listen, and learn, then go.
There is no boat in Hades, no ferryman Charon,
No caretaker Aeacus, no Cerberus dog.
All we dead below
Have become bones and ashes, nothing more.
I have spoken you true; go now, wayfarer,
Lest even though dead I seem to you garrulous . . .

CIL, vol. XIII, no. 1,983 (=Dessau, no. 8,158)

[Lyons, France]

To the spirits of the departed. To the eternal memory of Blandinia Martiola, most blameless girl, who lived 18 years, 9 months, 5 days, Pompeius Catussa, Sequanian, plasterer, to his wife incomparable and most kind to him, who lived with me 5 years, 6 months, 18 days without any kind of fault, erected this in his lifetime for himself and his wife, and consecrated it while under construction.[96] You who read this, go bathe in the baths of Apollo, as I used to do with my wife—I wish I still could.

CIL, vol. VI, no. 9,663 (=Dessau, no. 7,518)

[Rome]

To the spirits of the departed. In this tomb lies a lifeless body, whose spirit was received among the gods, for thus he deserved, Lucius Statius Onesimus, merchant of the Appian Way for many years, a man most trustworthy above all men, whose reputation is recorded forever, who lived sixty-eight years, more or less, without blemish. Statia Crescentina, his wife, built this for her well-deserving husband most worthy and deserving, with whom she lived in good accord without dissension.[97]

---

96. That is, in order to acquire for it, even while still empty, the religious and legal protection afforded tombs.

97. Literally, "without hurting one another's feelings," "without getting on each other's nerves."

CIL, vol. VI, no. 9,792 (=Dessau, no. 7,674)

[Rome]

To the spirits of the departed. You wanted to precede me, most sainted wife, and you have left me behind in tears. If there is anything good in the regions below—as for me, I lead a worthless life without you—be happy there too, sweetest Thalassia, nurse of a *vir clarissimus* and married to me for forty years. Paprius Vitalis, of the painters' craft, her husband, built this for his incomparable wife, himself, and their family.

CIL, vol. VI, no. 7,579 (=Dessau, no. 8,190)

[Rome]

To the departed spirit of Mevia Sophe. Gaius Maenius Cimber to his most sainted wife and protectress, my heart's desire, who lived with me 18 years, 3 months, 13 days, which I lived with her without cause for complaint. But now I complain to her spirit and demand her back of Dis,[98] or else, [ye gods], give me back to my wife, who lived with me so harmoniously to her dying day. Mevia Sophe, bring it to pass, if the spirits of the departed have any influence, that I need not suffer such a criminal separation any longer. Stranger, so may the earth rest lightly upon you after death as you do no damage here; or if anyone does damage, may the gods above not approve of him and the gods below not receive him, and may the earth rest heavily upon him.

CIL, vol. VI, no. 18,817 (=Dessau, no. 8,006)

[Rome]

[Tomb of] a sainted cherished soul, sacred to the spirits of the departed. Furia Spes, freedwoman, to Sempronius Firmus, husband most dear to me. As boy and girl we were bound by mutual love at first sight. I lived with him but a very short time, and during the time we should have lived [together] we were separated by an evil hand. I beg of you, most holy spirit of the departed, take good care of my dear one, and please be most kind to him in the hours of the night, so that I may see him and he may wish me too to persuade fate to let me come and be with him tenderly and speedily.

98. The Roman god of the underworld, counterpart of the Greek Pluto.

CIL, VOL. VI, no. 18,131 (=Dessau, no. 8,155a)

[Rome]

To the spirits of the departed. Titus Flavius Martialis lies here. What I ate and drank is with me here; what I left behind is gone forever.

CIL, vol. VIII, no. 3,463 (=Dessau, no. 8,162)

[Lambaesis, Africa]

Sacred to the spirits of the departed. To Aurelia Vercella, my wife most sweet, who lived seventeen years, more or less. I was not, I was, I am not, I have no more desires. Anthimus, her husband.

55. EDUCATION: THE CURRICULUM

Though the Roman Empire witnessed a great increase in the number of schools, there was nothing resembling a system of free public education. Formal education was available only to the children of the well-to-do. The initiative for the creation of lower schools was left in the hands of localities and parents able to pay. Institutions of higher learning flourished in leading urban centers, with Athens retaining its traditional place as the "university city" *par excellence.* But the emperors early adopted the royal role of patrons of learning and education, granting material privileges and sometimes even stipends to practitioners of the learned professions. The first such salaried professorship was the chair of literature and rhetoric to which Vespasian appointed Quintilian, the greatest of Roman rhetoricians, among whose pupils were the younger Pliny and probably Tacitus; other such chairs—at Rome, Athens, and elsewhere—were endowed by subsequent emperors. With the passage of time this patronage led the emperors to intervene increasingly in educational matters, and by the end of the third century practically all the schools of the Empire were under imperial control.

The curriculum of the Roman schools continued its traditional emphasis on grammar, rhetoric, literature, and philosophy, with oratory, "the mistress of all the arts," as the capstone (cf. vol. 1, §§ 186–187). But since the importance of political oratory in Roman public life ended with the fall of the Republic, leaving the law courts as almost the only practical outlet for oratorical skill, the training in the schools degenerated into rhetorical exercises divorced from reality. Attention was now fixed on style instead of content, the goal being artificial, superficial, epigrammatic brilliance developed through classroom recitations of several kinds. The most common of these were *declamationes,* or set pieces; *suasoriae,* speeches of deliberation, or self-persuasion, on imaginary, often fantastic, themes; and *controversiae,* debates in fictitious and frequently bizarrely contrived lawsuits. Roman education, it may be noted finally, continued to be bilingual until the end of the third century, when Greek began to disappear from the schools in the West.

INTELLECTUAL CAPACITY THE NATURAL BIRTHRIGHT OF MEN

Quintilian, *Institutes of Oratory* I. i. 1–3; From *LCL*

I would, therefore, have a father conceive the highest hopes of his son from the moment of his birth. If he does so, he will be more careful about the groundwork of his education. For there is absolutely no foundation for the complaint that but few men have the power to take in the knowledge that is imparted to them, and that the majority are so slow of understanding that education is a waste of time and labor. On the contrary, you will find that most are quick to reason and ready to learn. . . . Those who are dull and unteachable are as abnormal as prodigious births and monstrosities and are but few in number. A proof of what I say is to be found in the fact that boys commonly show promise of many accomplishments, and when such promise dies away as they grow up, this is plainly due not to the failure of natural gifts but to lack of requisite attention. But, it will be urged, there are differing degrees of intellectual ability. Undoubtedly, I reply, and there will be a corresponding variation in actual accomplishment; but that there are any who gain nothing from education, I absolutely deny.

EARLY TRAINING

Quintilian, *Institutes of Oratory* I. i. 4–11; Adapted from *LCL*

Above all, see that the child's nurse speaks correctly. . . . No doubt the most important point is that they should be of good character; but they should speak correctly as well. It is the nurse that the child first hears, and her words that he will first attempt to imitate. And we are by nature most tenacious of childhood impressions. . . . Do not therefore allow the boy to become accustomed even in infancy to a style of speech that will have to be unlearned.

As regards parents, I should like to see them as highly educated as possible, and I do not restrict this remark to fathers alone. . . . And even those who have not had the fortune to receive a good education should not devote less care to their children's education but should for that very reason show all the greater diligence in other matters where they can help.

As regards the boys in whose company our budding orator is to be brought up, I would repeat what I have said about nurses. As regards his *paedagogi*,[99] I would urge in addition they they should have had a thorough education. . . . Still, if it should prove impossible to secure the ideal nurse, the ideal companions, or the ideal *paedagogus*, I would insist that there should be one person at any rate attached to the boy who has some knowledge of speaking and who will, if any incorrect expression is used by nurse or *paedagogus* in the presence of their charge, at once correct the error and prevent its becoming a habit.[100]

BILINGUAL EDUCATION

Quintilian, *Institutes of Oratory* I. i. 12–14; From *LCL*

I prefer that a boy should begin with Greek, because Latin, being in general use, will be picked up by him whether we will or no; while the fact that Latin learning is derived from Greek is a further reason for his being first instructed in the latter. I do not, however, desire that this principle should be so rigidly observed that he should for long speak and learn only Greek, as is generally done. Such a course gives rise to many faults of language and accent; the latter tends to acquire a foreign intonation, while the former through force of habit becomes impregnated with Greek idioms, which persist with extreme obstinacy even when we are speaking another tongue. The study of Latin ought therefore to follow at no great distance and in a short time proceed side by side with Greek. The result will be that, as soon as we begin to give equal attention to both languages, neither will prove a hindrance to the other.

---

99. A *paedagogus* was a slave who had charge of children at home and accompanied them to and from school.

100. Tacitus comments on how careless of these precepts most parents were (*Dialogue on Oratory* xxix): "Nowadays we entrust the infant to any little Greek slave girl, with one or another of the male slaves to help her—usually the most worthless of the whole household, utterly unfit for any serious service. Tender and impressionable minds are filled from the very start with these slaves' stories and prejudices, and no one in the whole house cares a whit what he says or does in the presence of his infant master."

LITERARY STUDIES

Quintilian, *Institutes of Oratory* I. iv. 1–5; Adapted from *LCL*

As soon as the boy has learned to read and write without difficulty, it is the turn of the teacher of language and literature. My words apply equally to Greek and Latin teachers, though my preference is to start with a Greek; in either case the method is the same. This subject may be most briefly considered under two heads, the art of speaking correctly and the interpretation of the poets; but there is more beneath the surface than meets the eye. For the art of writing is connected with that of speaking, and faultless reading precedes interpretation, and in all of these criticism has its work to perform. . . . Nor is it sufficient to have read the poets only; every kind of writer must be carefully studied, not merely for the subject matter but for the vocabulary, for words often acquire authority from their use by a particular author. Nor can literary study be regarded as complete if it stops short of music, since meter and rhythm have to be taken up. Nor, if astronomy is omitted, can the poets be understood, since they, to mention nothing else, so frequently use the rising and setting of the constellations to indicate time. Omission of philosophy, too, is a drawback, since there are numerous passages in almost every poem based on the most intricate questions of natural science, and Empedocles among the Greeks and Varro and Lucretius among the Latin authors actually expounded philosophical doctrines in verse. No small powers of eloquence also are required to enable the teacher to speak appropriately and fluently on each and every one of the various subjects just mentioned. For this reason those who criticize this branch of teaching as trivial and jejune deserve less consideration.[101] Unless the foundations of the orator-to-be are well and truly laid by this study of literature, the superstructure will collapse. This study is a necessity for boys and the delight of old age, the sweet companion of our privacy and the sole branch of study which has more solid substance than display.

---

101. These criticisms, however, were directed not so much at the study as at the approach and methods used. Seneca, for example, writes (*Moral Epistles* cvi. 12): "It is clearly more useful to employ literature for the improvement of the mind, but we . . . waste our efforts on the inane. . . . We are educated not for life, but for the schoolroom."

DECLAMATION

Quintilian, *Institutes of Oratory* II. x. 1–4; Adapted from *LCL*

These elementary stages are in themselves no small undertaking, but they are merely members and portions of the greater whole; when therefore the pupil has been thoroughly instructed and exercised in these departments, the time will as a rule have come for him to attempt deliberative and forensic themes [i.e., *suasoriae* and *controversiae;* cf. introduction]. But before I begin to discuss these, I must say a few words on the theory of declamation, which is at once the newest and most useful of rhetorical exercises, for it includes practically all the exercises of which we have been speaking and affords a close imitation of reality. As a result it has acquired such a vogue that many think that it is the sole training necessary to shape oratorical ability, since there is no virtue of ordinary speech which is not also to be found in this type of rhetorical exercise. But the actual practice of declamation has degenerated to such an extent through the fault of its teachers that it has come to be one of the chief causes of the corruption of modern oratory, such is the extravagance and ignorance of our declaimers. But it is possible to make sound use of anything that is naturally sound. The subjects chosen for themes should, therefore, be as true to life as possible, and the declamation should, to the greatest degree possible, be modeled on actual pleadings, as a training for which it was devised.

THE RHETORICIANS' SCHOOLS

Tacitus, *Dialogue on Oratory* XXXV; Adapted from *LCL*

But nowadays our boys are escorted to the schools of those rhetoricians, as we call them—persons who came on the scene just before the time of Cicero but failed to find favor with our forefathers, as is obvious from the fact that the censors Crassus and Domitius ordered them to shut down what Cicero calls their "school of shamelessness." [102] They are escorted, as I was saying, to these schools, of which it would be hard to say what is most prejudicial to their intellectual growth, the place itself, or their fellow students, or the studies they pursue. The place has nothing about it that commands respect—no one enters it who is not as

---

102. Crassus and Domitius were censors in 92 B.C.; for their decree expelling rhetoricians from Rome, see vol. I, p. 527.

ignorant as the rest; there is no profit in the company of the students, since they are all boys or young men together, who are equally devoid of any feeling of responsibility whether they take the floor or make up the audience; and the exercises in which they engage largely defeat their purpose. You are of course aware that there are two kinds of subject matter handled in the rhetoricians' schools, the suasory and the controversial. Now, while the former is entrusted to mere boys, as being obviously of less importance and not making such demands of judgment, the more mature scholars are asked to deal with the latter—but, good heavens! what poor quality is shown in their themes, and how unnaturally they are made up! Then, in addition to a subject matter so remote from real life, there is the bombastic style in which it is presented. And so it comes about that themes such as "The Reward of the Tyrannicide," or "The Ravished Maid's Alternatives," or "A Remedy for the Plague," or "The Incestuous Mother," and all the other topics that are encountered every day in the school but seldom or never in actual legal practice, are set forth in magniloquent phraseology.

CLASSROOM EXERCISES

Seneca the Elder, *Suasories* ii–vii

Each of the speeches in Seneca's handbook of rhetorical exercises is preceded by a brief statement of the subject. A selection from these captions is given here.

Three hundred Spartans sent against Xerxes, when the contingents of three hundred sent from all [the rest of] Greece had fled, deliberate whether they too should flee.

Agamemnon deliberates whether he should sacrifice Iphigenia when Calchas avers that it is sinful to sail otherwise.

Alexander the Great deliberates whether he should enter Babylon after he has been warned of danger by a soothsayer's reply.

The Athenians deliberate whether they should remove their trophies of victory over Persia when Xerxes threatens to return unless they do.

Cicero deliberates whether he should beg Antony for mercy.

Cicero deliberates whether he should burn his writings since Antony promises he will be unharmed if he does.

Seneca the Elder, *Controversies* I. ii, vi; II. vii; III. i; V. i

A priestess must be supremely chaste and pure. A maiden was captured by pirates and sold. She was bought by a procurer and made a prostitute. But she prevailed upon those who came to her to pay her her fee [without intercourse]. When she could not prevail upon a soldier who had come to her, and he struggled with her and attacked her, she killed him. She was indicted, acquitted, and returned to her people. She seeks to become a priestess. The petition is opposed.

. . . .

A man was captured by pirates and wrote to his father for ransom; he was not ransomed. The daughter of the pirate chief made him swear that he would marry her if he were released, and he swore to it. She left her father and eloped with the young man. He returned to his father and married her. A rich widow crosses their path. The father orders him to divorce the daughter of the pirate chief and marry the widow. He refuses and is disinherited.

. . . .

A man who had a beautiful wife went abroad. A foreign merchant settled in the neighborhood of the woman. Three times he offered her money to commit adultery, and she refused. The merchant died, and in his will left the beautiful woman heir to all his property, adding the following words of praise: "I found her chaste." She accepted the inheritance. The husband returns and accuses her of adultery on suspicion.

. . . .

A blind man is entitled to receive 1,000 *denarii* from the public treasury. Ten young men, when they had dissipated their fortunes, drew lots under an agreement that the one whose name was drawn would be blinded and thus get 1,000 *denarii*. The lot of one was drawn, and he was blinded. He applies for the 1,000 *denarii*. The application is denied.

. . . .

Injury of known origin is actionable. A man whose life was wrecked, his three children and wife lost when his house burned, hanged himself. A passer-by cut down the noose. He is prosecuted by the released man for injury.

THE DECLINE OF ORATORY

Quintilian, *Institutes of Oratory* VIII. Preface. 22–26; From *LCL*

The usual result of overattention to the niceties of style is the deterioration of our eloquence. . . . In our passion for words we paraphrase what might be said in plain language, repeat what we have already said at sufficient length, pile up a number of words where one would suffice, and regard allusion as better than directness of speech. So, too, all directness of speech is at a discount, and we think no phrase eloquent that another could conceivably have used. We borrow figures and metaphors from the most decadent poets and regard it as a real sign of genius that it should require a genius to understand our meaning. And yet Cicero long since laid down this rule in the clearest of language, that the worst fault in speaking is to adopt a style inconsistent with the idiom of ordinary speech and contrary to the common feeling of mankind. But nowadays our rhetoricians regard Cicero as lacking both polish and learning; we are far superior, for we look down upon everything that is dictated by nature as beneath our notice and seek not for the true ornaments of speech but for meretricious finery, as though there were any real virtue in words save in their power to represent facts. And if we have to spend our lives in a laborious effort to discover words which will at once be appropriate, lucid, and brilliant, and to arrange them with exact precision, we lose all the fruit of our studies.

Tacitus, *Dialogue on Oratory* xxx–xxxii (abridged)

Only he is an orator who can speak on any topic with beauty and elegance and in a manner that carries conviction, in keeping with the importance of the subject, appropriately to the circumstances, with pleasure to the audience. The men of earlier days were convinced of this. They understood that to accomplish this required, not declaiming in rhetoricians' schools, not exercising merely the tongue and the voice in fictitious debates without any sort of approach to reality, but imbuing the mind with those disciplines that deal with good and evil, honor and dishonor, right and wrong; for this is the orator's subject matter. . . . The accomplished speakers of modern times are so completely unconcerned about this that you can detect in their pleadings the unseemly and shameful defects of modern colloquial speech. And also, they know nothing of legislation, have no grasp of the decrees of the senate, actually

scoff at the civil law, and have a positive horror of the study of philosophy and the teachings of the sages. They have banished oratory, as it
were, from her rightful realm and reduce her to a handful of common-
place and narrow platitudes, so that she who was once mistress of all the
arts and imbued our minds with her noble retinue is now clipped and
docked, without state, without esteem, I almost said without her free
birthright, and is learned like one of the meanest handicrafts. This, then,
is in my opinion the prime and principal reason why we have degenerated to such an extent from the eloquence of the orators of old.

56. Education: Imperial Patronage of the Learned Professions

The opposition of the Roman senatorial conservatives to Greek learning
and its teachers died with the Republic. The Roman emperors adopted the
practice of granting to members of the learned, artistic, and athletic
professions subsidies, stipends, and certain legal privileges and exemptions
(from taxation, from billeting of soldiers, from compulsory public services).

IMPERIAL SUBVENTION TO A PHILOSOPHER

Pliny, *Letters* book x, no. 58. 5

Letter of Domitian to Terentius Maximus[103]

Flavius Archippus the philosopher petitioned me to order an estate to be
purchased for him for 100,000 sesterces[104] in the vicinity of Prusias, his
native city, from the income of which he could support his family. I
desire to grant him this. You will charge the sum expended to my
"Personal Gifts" account.

103. Apparently a procurator of imperial estates in Bithynia.
104. This is the same amount as the salaries paid the holders of imperial professorships. Vespasian,
Suetonius tells us in his biography (xvii–xviii), "greatly encouraged literary talent and the arts. He was
the first to establish annual salaries of 100,000 sesterces from the fisc for Latin and Greek professors of
rhetoric."

EXEMPTION PRIVILEGES

AE, 1936, no. 128 (=*FIRA*, vol. I, nos. 73 and 77)

[Pergamum, A.D. 74 and 93/94]

The Emperor Caesar VESPASIAN Augustus, *pontifex maximus,* holding the tribunician power for the sixth year, acclaimed *imperator* fourteen times, father of his country, consul five times and designate for a sixth, censor, declares:

Whereas professions befitting free men are deemed publicly and privately useful to cities and sacred to the gods, to wit, that of the grammarians and rhetoricians, who, under the aegis of Hermes and the Muses, train the minds of the youth to gentility and civic virtue, and that of the physicians and other practitioners, under the aegis of Apollo and Aesculapius, since the care of bodies has been entrusted solely to them[?];

Because these men are thus regarded as[?] sacred and godlike, I order that there is to be no billeting in their homes, nor are taxes to be exacted from them in any manner. And if any of those living under my rule shall dare to wrong, or demand security from, or bring an action against[?], any physician, teacher, or other practitioner, the offenders shall pay a fine of . . . drachmas to Jupiter Capitolinus; whoever cannot pay this sum shall have his property sold, and the fine imposed by the official in charge of this shall be consecrated to the god forthwith; likewise, if he hides and they find him, they may bring him before any tribunal they choose, without hindrance by anyone. And they are to have the undisturbed right to maintain societies in sacred precincts, sanctuaries, and temples, wherever they choose; if anyone shall eject them by force, he shall be brought to trial by the Roman people for sacrilege to the imperial house.

I, the Emperor Caesar Vespasian, have signed and ordered this to be posted in public.

Posted, year 6 . . . December 27.

The Emperor Caesar Domitian, holding the tribunician power for the thirteenth year, acclaimed *imperator* twenty-two times, censor for life, father of his country, to Aulus Licinius Mucianus and Gavius Priscus.

I have decided that the greed of physicians and teachers—who, not for the sake of culture but for the sake of increasing their gain, are most outrageously selling [instruction in] their art, which ought to be transmitted only to some freeborn youths, to many domestic[?] slaves sent to them for training—must be rigorously curbed. Therefore, whosoever of them takes a fee for teaching slaves is to be deprived of the privileges granted by my deified father. . . . [The rest is fragmentary.]

Justinian, *Digest* xxvii. i. 6. 8–12

In the enactments of the Emperor Commodus there is cited a section of a rescript of Antoninus Pius in which it is made clear that philosophers, too, enjoy exemption from being appointed guardians. The exact wording is as follows: "Likewise my deified father [i.e., Hadrian] immediately upon his accession, confirmed the existing privileges and immunities for all these by an edict declaring that philosophers, rhetoricians, grammarians, and physicians were exempt from the obligation to serve as gymnasiarchs, overseers of markets, or priests, or to provide billets, grain, or oil, and were not to serve on juries or on embassies or be conscripted into the army against their will or be forced into any other provincial or other service."

But this too must be understood, that only a man teaching or practicing in his home town enjoys this exemption. If a Comanite lectures on rhetoric or practices medicine or teaches in Neocaesarea, he does not enjoy exemption in Comana. This was ordained by the deified Severus and Antoninus [i.e., Caracalla]. [The jurist] Paulus, to be sure, stating that the deified Antoninus Pius had thus ordered, writes that learned men, both those above the approved number and those practicing in an alien city, are exempt. It was ordained by the deified Severus and Antoninus that a man lecturing on rhetoric in Rome either with or without salary enjoys release just as if he were teaching in his home town. For this enactment the following reasoning may be adduced: Since the imperial city is the common fatherland and is so regarded, then it is logical that such person should enjoy exemption as being one who makes himself useful in his native place. Teachers of law teaching in a province do not enjoy release, but those teaching in Rome are released.

THE EPICUREAN SCHOOL

This inscription of A.D. 121 records an exchange of correspondence between Plotina, Trajan's widow, and the Emperor Hadrian, her son by imperial adoption, concerning the succession to the headship of the Epicurean philosophical school in Athens. It not only illustrates Hadrian's philhellenism but reveals that even before his reign imperial intervention and control in educational matters had reached the point where the head of the school of Epicurus had to be a Roman citizen.

CIL, vol. III, no. 12,283, lines 2–16 (= Dessau, no. 7,784 = *FIRA,* vol. I, no. 79)

In the Consulship of Marcus Annius Verus (for the second time) and Gnaeus Arrius Augur

AULA PLOTINA AUGUSTA

How greatly I favor the school of Epicurus you know full well, my lord. The succession therein needs your help, for since none but a Roman citizen may be elected head of the school the choice is narrowly limited. I pray therefore on behalf of Popillius Theotimus, who is now the head at Athens, that you will allow him to provide by will in Greek [cf. introduction to § 53] concerning that part of his instructions which pertains to the regulation of the headship, and to name a successor to himself of noncitizen status if he is so persuaded by the attainments of the person; and that future heads of the school may hereafter exercise with the same right the privilege you grant to Theotimus, all the more so because the practice is that whenever the testator errs concerning the choice of a head the best candidate is, by common consent, selected by the students of the school, and this will be easier if he can be chosen from a larger number.

The Emperor Caesar Trajanus HADRIAN Augustus to Popillius Theotimus. I permit him to draw his will in Greek in the matters pertaining to the headship of the Epicurean school. And since he will also choose a successor more easily if he has the privilege of naming even a noncitizen, I grant this also to him and to the others who hold the headship hereafter: this right may be transferred either to a noncitizen or to a Roman citizen.

SCIENCE AND PSEUDOSCIENCE IN
THE ROMAN EMPIRE

It has often been remarked that Rome produced no great creative scientist. In the best of the Romans' scientific and technical knowledge, and in their underlying consideration of science as ancillary to ethics, the debt to Greece is everywhere apparent. Pliny (*Natural History* xxvii. i) boasts that the exchange of knowledge was "ensured to us by the immense majesty of the Roman peace," but he is fully aware of the stagnation of theoretical and technical progress. The same author relates (xxxvi. lxvi. 195)—the story may of course be apocryphal—that, "in the reign of Tiberius . . . when a way of preparing glass was invented to make it flexible, the workshop of the artisan was completely destroyed to prevent the value of bronze, silver, and gold from depreciating." (In the version of Petronius *Satyricon* li, the inventor was put to death by the emperor's order.) The characteristic emphasis placed by the Romans on the practical application of scientific knowledge (especially in engineering and military installations), their suspicion of and contempt for theoretical science, their conviction, fostered by the determinism of Stoicism, of the worthlessness of research, and the basic economic parasitism of the Roman landed ruling class brought scientific advance to a standstill by the end of the second century. The last great scientific minds of antiquity were the mathematician, astronomer, and geographer Ptolemy and the physician and medical writer Galen, both Greeks. With the victory of astrology, irrationalism, and the Eastern mystery religions over the minds of men in the crisis of the third century, the eclipse of ancient science was complete.

57. THE PAUCITY OF RESEARCH

Pliny, *Natural History* ii. xlv. 117–118; From *LCL*

More than twenty Greek authors of the past have published observations about these subjects. This makes me all the more surprised that, although when the world was at variance and split up into kingdoms, that is, sundered limb from limb, so many people devoted themselves to these abstruse researches, especially when wars surrounded them and hosts were untrustworthy, and also when pirates, the foes of all mankind, were holding up the transmission of information—so that nowadays a person may learn some facts about his own region from the notebooks of people who have never been there more truly than from the knowledge of the natives—yet now in these glad times of peace, under an emperor who so delights in the advancement of letters and science,[105] no addition whatever is being made to knowledge by means of original research, and in fact even the discoveries of our predecessors are not being thoroughly studied. The rewards were not greater when those ample successes were being contributed by many students, and in fact the majority of these made the discoveries in question with no other reward at all save the consciousness of benefiting posterity. Age has overtaken the character of mankind, not their revenues, and now that every sea has been opened up and every coast affords a hospitable landing, an immense multitude goes on voyages—but their object is profit not knowledge; and in their blind engrossment with avarice they do not reflect that knowledge is a more reliable means even of making profit.

58. FARMER'S ALMANACS

Columella, *On Agriculture* XI. ii (selections)

JANUARY

13. Windy weather; unsettled conditions.
15. Unsettled weather.
16. Sun enters Aquarius; Leo begins to set in the morning; southwest wind, sometimes south wind with rain.
17. Cancer finishes setting; cold.
18. Aquarius begins to rise; southwest wind forecasts storm.
22. Lyra sets in the evening; rainy day.
24. Setting of Cetus forecasts storm; sometimes actual storms.
27. The bright star on the breast of Leo sets, sometimes forecasts winter half over.
28. South or southwest wind; cold, rainy day.
30. Delphinus begins to set; Lyra also sets.
31. Setting of the above-mentioned constellations brings storm, sometimes only forecasts storm.

[There follow instructions, here omitted, on the farm operations to be performed in the above half month.]

105. For Vespasian's patronage of the learned professions, see § 56, first and second selections.

FEBRUARY

1. Lyra begins to set; east wind, sometimes south wind with hail.
3. Lyra sets completely, Leo half; northwest or north wind, sometimes west wind.
5. Half of Aquarius rises; windy weather.
7. The constellation Callisto sets; west winds begin to blow.
8. Windy weather.
11. East wind.

[There follow the farming operations, here omitted.]

13. Sagittarius sets in the evening; severe cold.
14. Crater rises in the evening; change of wind.
15. Sun enters Pisces; sometimes windy weather.
17, 18. West or south wind, with hail and rain storms.
20. Leo finishes setting; the north winds called the "bird winds" generally blow for thirty days; then the swallow returns.
21. Arcturus rises at dusk; chill day with north or northwest wind, sometimes rainy.
22. Sagittarius begins to rise at twilight; variable weather; [period] called "halcyon days"—great calm observed in Atlantic Ocean.
23. Windy weather; swallows are sighted.

[Agricultural instructions, here omitted.]

·   ·   ·   ·

JUNE

13. Hot weather begins.
19. Sun enters Cancer; forecasts storm.
21. Serpentarius, called Ophiuchus by the Greeks, sets in the morning; forecasts storm.
24, 25, 26. Solstice; west wind and heat.
29. Windy weather.

[Agriculture instructions, here omitted.]

·   ·   ·   ·

SEPTEMBER

13. Cetus sometimes forecasts storm.
17. Arcturus rises; west or southwest wind, sometimes the east wind that some call Vulturnus.
18. The brightest star of Virgo rises; west or northwest wind.

19. Sun enters Libra; Crater appears in the morning.
21. Pisces sets in the morning; likewise Aries begins to set; west or northwest wind, sometimes south wind with rain squalls.
22. The constellation Argo sets; forecasts storm, sometimes rain.
23. Centaurus begins to rise in the morning; forecasts storm, sometimes rain.
24, 25, 26. Autumnal equinox forecasts rain.
27. Capricornus rises; west wind, sometimes south wind with rain.
28. Virgo finishes rising; forecasts storm.

[Agricultural instructions, here omitted.]

CIL, vol. VI, no. 2,305 (=Dessau, no. 8,745)

Month of January. 31 days. The Nones fall on the fifth day. The day has 9¾ hours. The night has 14¼ hours. The sun is in the sign of Capricorn. The month is under the protection of Juno. Stakes are sharpened. Willow and reeds are cut. Sacrifices to the household gods.

Month of February. 28 days. The Nones fall on the fifth day. The day has 10¾ hours. The night has 13¼ hours. The sun is in the sign of Aquarius. The month is under the protection of Neptune. The grain fields are weeded. The part of the vines above ground is tended. Reeds are burned. Parentalia, Lupercalia, Dear Relatives' Day, Terminalia.[106]

Month of March. 31 days. The Nones fall on the seventh day. The day has 12 hours. The night has 12 hours. The equinox falls on the twenty-fifth day. The sun is in the sign of Pisces. The month is under the protection of Minerva. The vines are propped up in trenched ground and pruned. Three-month wheat is sown. The bark of Isis.[107] Sacrifices to Mamurius. Liberalia, Quinquatria, Bathing.[108]

Month of April. 30 days. The Nones fall on the fifth day. The day has 13½ hours. The night has 10½ hours. The sun is in the sign of Aries. The month is under the protection of Venus. The lustration of the sheep is made. Sacrifices to the Isis of Pharus.[109] Also festival of Sarapis.

Month of May. 31 days. The Nones fall on the seventh day. The day has 14½ hours. The night has 9½ hours. The sun is in the sign of

106. For some of the traditional Roman festivals mentioned here and later, see vol. 1, §§ 9 and 180.
107. For this ceremony see § 165, third selection. It is interesting to note in this calendar the fusion of Roman religion with the worship of the Egyptian gods Isis and Osiris.
108. A purification ceremony characteristic of mystery cults; cf. § 165.
109. Pharus was the famous lighthouse in the harbor of Alexandria, Egypt.

Taurus. The month is under the protection of Apollo. The grain fields are cleared of weeds. The sheep are shorn. The wool is washed. Young steers are put under the yoke. The vetch for fodder is cut. The lustration of the grain fields is made. Sacrifices to Mercury and Flora.

Month of June. 30 days. The Nones fall on the fifth day. The day has 15 hours. The night has 9 hours. The solstice falls on the twenty-fourth day. The sun is in the sign of Gemini. The month is under the protection of Mercury. The hay is mown. The vines are cultivated. Sacrifice to Hercules and Fors Fortuna.

Month of July. 31 days. The Nones fall on the seventh day. The day has 14¼ hours. The night has 9¾ hours. The sun is in the sign of Cancer. The month is under the protection of Jupiter. Barley and beans are harvested. Apollinaria, Neptunalia.

Month of August. 31 days. The Nones fall on the fifth day. The day has 13 hours. The night has 11 hours. The sun is in the sign of Leo. The month is under the protection of Ceres. The stakes are prepared. Cereals are harvested, likewise the wheat. The stubble is burned. Sacrifices to Hope, Safety, and Diana. Volcanalia.

Month of September. 30 days. The Nones fall on the fifth day. The day has 12 hours. The night has 12 hours. The equinox falls on the twenty-fourth day. The sun is in the sign of Virgo. The month is under the protection of Vulcan. The casks are smeared with pitch. Fruits are gathered. The earth around the trees is dug up. Feast of Minerva.

Month of October. 31 days. The Nones fall on the seventh day. The day has 10¾ hours. The night has 13¼ hours. The sun is in the sign of Libra. The month is under the protection of Mars. Grape gathering. Sacrifices to Bacchus.

Month of November. 30 days. The Nones fall on the fifth day. The day has 9½ hours. The night has 14½ hours. The sun is in the sign of Scorpion. The month is under the protection of Diana. Sowing of wheat and barley. Digging of trenches for trees. Feast of Jupiter. Discovery [a festival of Osiris].

Month of December. 31 days. The Nones fall on the fifth day. The day has 9 hours. The night has 15 hours. The sun is in the sign of Sagittarius. The month is under the protection of Vesta. Beginning of winter, or winter solstice. The vines are manured. Beans are sown. Wood is cut. Olives are gathered and also sold. Saturnalia.

59. ARCHITECTURE AND ENGINEERING

THE TRAINING OF THE ARCHITECT

Vitruvius, *Architecture* I. i. 1–11 (abridged)

The architect should be equipped with knowledge of many branches of study and varied kinds of learning, for it is by his judgment that all work done by the other arts is put to the test. This service of his is the child of practice and theory. Practice is the continuous and regular exercise of employment where manual work is done with any necessary material according to the design of the drawing. Theory, on the other hand, is the ability to demonstrate and explain things wrought in accordance with technical skill and method. It follows, therefore, that architects who have aimed at acquiring manual skill without theory have not been able to reach a position of authority to correspond to their pains, while those who relied only on theories and learning were obviously hunting the shadow, not the substance. . . .

He should be a man of letters, a skillful draftsman, instructed in geometry, versed in history, and a diligent student of philosophy; he should understand music, have some knowledge of medicine, know the opinions of the jurists, and be acquainted with astronomy and the theory of the heavens. The reasons for all this are as follows. An architect ought to be a man of letters so as to leave a lasting record in his treatises. Secondly, he must have skill in draftsmanship so that he can readily make sketches to show the appearance of the work which he proposes. Geometry, also, is of much assistance in architecture, and in particular it teaches us the use of the rule and compasses, and this facilitates the planning of buildings on their sites, and the truing of them by the use of the square, the level, and the plummet. By means of optics, again, light in buildings can be properly drawn from definite quarters of the sky. It is true that by arithmetic the total cost of buildings is calculated, and measurements are computed, but difficult questions involving symmetry are solved by means of geometrical theories and methods.

A wide knowledge of history is requisite because, among the ornamental parts of an architect's design for a work, there are many the underlying idea of whose employment he should be able to explain to inquirers. . . . As for philosophy, it makes an architect high-minded, so that he may not be self-assuming but rather urbane, just, loyal, and without avariciousness. This is very important, for no work can be rightly done without honesty and incorruptibility. . . . Furthermore, philosophy treats of physics (in Greek, *physiologia*), where a rather careful knowledge is required because the problems which come under this head are numerous and varied; as, for example, in the case of water supply. . . . Music, also, the architect ought to know so that he may have knowledge of canonical and mathematical theory, and besides be able to adjust properly ballistas, catapults, and scorpions. For to the right and left in the beams are the holes of the "half tones" [or possibly, "equal tones"] through which ropes of twisted thongs are stretched by means of windlasses and levers, and these ropes must not be clamped and made fast until they make clear and equal sounds in the ear of the skilled workman. . . . If they are not of equal tone, they will prevent the course of the projectiles from being straight. . . . Water engines, too, and the other instruments which resemble them cannot be made by one who is without the principles of music.

The architect should also have a knowledge of the study of medicine on account of questions of climate . . . air, healthiness and unhealthiness of sites, and water supply. For without these considerations, the healthiness of a dwelling cannot be assured. And as for laws, he should know those which are necessary in the case of buildings having party walls, those with reference to water dripping from the eaves, and also those about drains and windows. The water supply, also, and other things of this sort should be known to architects, so that before they begin building they may be careful not to leave disputes to the proprietors after the work is completed, and so that in drawing up specifications the interests of both employer and contractor may be wisely safeguarded. For if specifications are skillfully drawn, each may obtain a release from the other without captious objections. By astronomy, also, we find the east, west, south, and north, as well as the theory of the heavens, the equinox, solstice, and courses of the stars. If one has no knowledge of these matters he will not be able to have any comprehension of the theory of sundials.

WATER SUPPLY

Vitruvius, *Architecture* VIII. vi

The supply of water is made by three methods: by channels through walled conduits, or by lead pipes, or by earthenware pipes. And they are arranged as follows. In the case of conduits, the structure must be very solid; the bed of the channel must be leveled with a fall of not less than half a foot in 100 feet. The walled conduits are to be arched over so that the minimum amount of sun may strike the water. When it comes to the city walls, a reservoir is to be made. To this reservoir a triple distribution tank is to be joined to receive the water; and three pipes of equal size are to be placed in the reservoir, leading to the adjoining tanks, so that when there is an overflow from the two outer tanks, it may deliver into the middle tank. From the middle tank pipes will be laid to all basins and fountains; from the second tank to the baths, in order to furnish an annual revenue to the treasury; to avoid a deficiency in the public supply, private houses are to be supplied from the third, for private persons will not be able to divert the water, since they have their own limited supply from the distribution sources. Another reason why I have made these divisions is that those who take private supplies into their houses may by their taxes paid through tax farmers contribute to the maintenance of the water supply.

If, however, there are hills between the city and the source, we must proceed as follows: underground channels are to be dug and leveled to the fall mentioned above. If the bed is of tufa or stone, the channel may be cut in it; but if it is of soil or sand, the bed of the channel and the walls with the vaulting must be constructed, and the water should be thus conducted. Air shafts are to be so constructed that they are 120 feet apart.

But if the supply is to be by lead pipes, first of all a reservoir is to be built at the source. Then the opening of the pipe is to be determined in accordance with the amount of water, and these pipes are to be laid from the source reservoir to a reservoir which is inside the city. The pipes are to be cast in lengths of not less than ten feet. If the lead pipes are *hundreds,* they should weigh 1,200 lbs. each; if *eighties,* 960 lbs.; if *fifties,* 600 lbs.; if *forties,* 480 lbs.; if *thirties,* 360 lbs.; if *twenties,* 240 lbs.; if *fifteens,* 180 lbs.; if *tens,* 120 lbs.; if *eights,* 100 lbs.; if *fives,* 60 lbs. The pipes receive their size names from the width in inches of the sheets of lead before they are rolled into pipes; for when a pipe is made of a sheet of lead 50 inches wide, it is called a *fifty,* and similarly the rest.

When an aqueduct is to be made with lead pipes it is to have the following arrangement. If there is a fall from the source to the city and the intervening hills are not high enough to interrupt the supply, then if there are valleys, we must build substructures to bring it up to a level, as in the case of channels and conduits. If the way round the valley is not long, a circuit should be used; but if the valleys are expansive, the course will be directed down the hill, and when it reaches the bottom it is carried on a low substructure so that the level there may continue as far as possible. This will form a "belly," which the Greeks call *koilia*. When the "belly" comes to the hill opposite, and the long distance of the "belly" makes the water slow in welling up, the water is to be forced to the height of the top of the hill. . . .

Again, it is not without advantage to put reservoirs at intervals of 24,000 feet, so that if a break occurs anywhere neither the whole load of water nor the whole structure need be disturbed, and the place where it has occurred may be more easily found. But these reservoirs are to be neither in the descent nor on the level portion of the "belly," nor at risings, nor anywhere in a valley, but on unbroken level ground.

But if we wish to employ a less expensive method, we must proceed as follows. Earthenware pipes are to be made not less than two inches thick, but these pipes should be so tongued at one end that they can fit into and join one another. The joints are to be coated with quicklime mixed with oil. . . . Everything also is to be fixed as for lead pipes. Further, when the water is first let in from the source, ashes are to be put in beforehand, so that if any joints are not sufficiently coated they may be lined with the ashes.

Water supply by earthenware pipes has these advantages. First, in the construction: if a break occurs, anybody can repair it. Again, water is much more wholesome from earthenware pipes than from lead pipes. For it seems to be made injurious by lead, because white lead is produced by it; and this is said to be harmful to the human body. So if what is produced by anything is injurious, there is no doubt that the thing itself is not wholesome. We can take an example from the workers in lead who have complexions affected by pallor. For when lead is smelted in casting, the fumes from it settle on the members of the body and, burning them, rob the limbs of the virtues of the blood. Therefore it seems that water should by no means be brought in lead pipes if we desire to have it wholesome. Everyday life can be used to show that the flavor from earthenware pipes is better, because everybody (even those who load their tables with silver vessels) uses earthenware to preserve the purity of water.

But if we are to create springs from which the water supplies come, we must dig wells. In digging wells we must not make light of science. The methods of nature must be considered closely in the light of intelligence and experience, because the soil contains an abundance of various elements. For, like everything else, it is composed of the four elements.

First, it is itself earthy; and of the moist element, it has springs of water; likewise, it has heat, from which sulphur, alum, and bitumen arise; and mighty currents of air. When these currents are heavy and come through the porous intervals of soil to the wells which are being dug, they affect the excavators in that the nature of the exhalation chokes the animal spirits in their nostrils. Hence those who fail to escape quickly die there. The precautions against this are to be carried out as follows. Let a lighted lamp be lowered. If it remains alight the descent will be accomplished without danger. If, however, the light is extinguished by the power of the exhalation, then air shafts are to be dug right and left adjoining the well. In this way the bad vapors will be dissipated, as the air is through the nostrils. When this has been arranged and we come to the water, then let it be enclosed by walling without blocking up the veins.

But if the soil is hard, or if the veins of water lie too deep, then supplies of water are to be collected from the roofs or higher ground in concrete cisterns. . . . If the cisterns are made double or triple, so that they can be changed by percolation, they will make the supply of water much more wholesome. For when the sediment has a place to settle in, the water will be more limpid and will keep its taste without any smell. If not, salt must be added to purify it.

60. GEOGRAPHY

Great advances were made during the Empire in the practical exploration and mapping of the known world. In the field of geography, as in other branches of learning, most of the theoretical work was done by Greeks.

THE LIMITS OF THE KNOWN WORLD

Pliny, *Natural History* II. lxvii; From *LCL*

Today the whole of the west is navigated from Gades and the Pillars of Hercules [i.e., Cádiz and the Strait of Gibraltar] all around Spain and Gaul. But the larger part of the Northern Ocean was explored under the patronage of the deified Augustus, when a fleet sailed round Germany to the promontory of the Cimbrians [Cape Skagen, Jutland] and thence, seeing a vast sea in front of them or learning of it by report, reached the region of Scythia and localities numb with excessive moisture. On this account it is extremely improbable that there is no sea in those parts, as there is a superabundance of the moist element there. But next, on the eastward side, the whole quarter under the same star stretching from the Indian Ocean to the Caspian Sea was navigated throughout by the Macedonian forces in the reigns of Seleucus and Antiochus.[110] . . . And around the Caspian many coasts of the ocean have been explored, and very nearly the whole of the north has been completely navigated from one side to the other, so that similarly there is now overwhelming proof, leaving no room for conjecture, of the existence of the Maeotic Marsh, whether it be a gulf of that ocean, as I notice many have believed, or an overflow from it from which it is separated by a narrow space. On the other side of Gades, from the same western point, a great part of the Southern Gulf is navigated today in the circuit of Mauretania. Indeed, the greater part of it Alexander the Great's eastern conquests also explored as far as the Arabian Gulf; in which, when Augustus' son Gaius Caesar was operating there, it is said that figureheads of ships from Spanish wrecks were identified. Also, when the power of Carthage flourished, Hanno sailed round from Gades to the extremity of Arabia[111] and published a memoir of his voyage, as did Himilco when despatched at the same date to explore the outer coasts of Europe. Moreover, we have it on the authority of Cornelius Nepos that a certain contemporary of his named Eudoxus when fleeing from King Lathyrus [Ptolemy IX Lathyrus, King of Egypt, 116–81 B.C.] emerged from the Arabian Gulf and sailed right around to Gades;[112] and much before him Coelius Antipater states that he had seen someone who had gone on a trading voyage from Spain to Ethiopia.[113] Nepos also records as to the northern circuit that Quintus Metellus Celer, colleague of Afranius in the consulship but at the time proconsul of Gaul, [i.e., 62 B.C.], received from the king of the Suebians a present of some Indians, who on a trading voyage had been carried off their course by storms to Germany. Thus there are seas encircling the globe on every side and dividing it in two, so robbing us of half the world, since there is no region affording a passage from there to here or from here to there.[114]

---

110. The Caspian Sea was believed to have a narrow outlet into the outer ocean.

111. This is untrue. Hanno was a Carthaginian explorer of the end of the sixth century B.C. who sailed down the west coast of Africa, starting from Gades, and got as far south as Sierra Leone.

112. This is untrue. The Greek navigator Eudoxus, after exploring the east coast of Africa, attempted to circumnavigate Africa, starting from Gades, but disappeared on the voyage.

113. That is, around the southern tip of Africa. There is, however, no reliable evidence that the continent of Africa was ever circumnavigated in ancient times.

114. This ancient theory involved the existence of another land mass in the antipodes, now the Americas. Cf. note 115.

THE SPHERICITY OF THE EARTH

Strabo, *Geography* I. i. 20 (abridged); From *LCL*

Most of all, it seems to me, we need . . . geometry and astronomy for a subject like geography. . . . Just as these sciences prove for us in other treatises all that has to do with the measurement of the earth as a whole, and as I must in this treatise take for granted and accept the propositions proved there, so I must take for granted that the universe is spheroidal, and also that the earth's surface is spheroidal . . .[115] and I need only indicate, in a brief and summary way, whether a proposition comes—if it really does—within the range of sense perception or of intuitive knowledge. Take, for example, the proposition that the earth is spheroidal. Whereas the suggestion of this proposition comes to us mediately from the law that bodies tend toward the center and that each body inclines toward its own center of gravity, the suggestion comes immediately from the phenomena observed at sea and in the heavens; for our sense perception and also our intuition can bear testimony in the latter case. For instance, it is obviously the curvature of the sea that prevents sailors from seeing distant lights that are placed on a level with their eyes. At any rate, if the lights are elevated above the level of the eyes they become visible, even though they be at a greater distance from the eyes; and similarly if the eyes themselves are elevated, they see what was before invisible. . . . So also, when sailors are approaching land, the different parts of the shore become revealed progressively, more and more, and what at first appeared to be low-lying land gradually grows higher and higher.

ON MAP MAKING

"Drawing a map on a sphere," writes Ptolemy[116] (*Geography* I. xx), "gives the likeness of the shape of the earth . . . but it is not easy to make it large enough to provide room for the many details that will need to be indi-

---

115. Strabo (*Geography* I. iv. 1) also commends the deduction of the Hellenistic geographer Eratosthenes "that if the earth is spheroidal, just as the universe is, it is inhabited all the way round." The polymath Posidonius (cf. vol. 1, p. 11, note 7) "conjectures that the length of the inhabited world, about 70,000 stades, is half of the whole circle on which it has been taken, so that, he says, by sailing straight from the west the same distance one would come to India" (Strabo II. iii. 6).

116. Claudius Ptolemy (A.D. c. 90–168), who worked at Alexandria, was the greatest geographer of antiquity. His celebrated work on astronomy is preserved only in the Arabic translation and is

cated, and it is impossible to fix one's sight on the whole shape at one time. . . . Making the map on a plane surface is altogether free from these inconveniences, but requires a certain adjustment to correspond to the spherical form, in order to make the distances . . . on the unfolded surface commensurate with the real distances." He proceeds in the two following chapters to give instructions for making the two types of map.

Ptolemy, *Geography* I. xxi–xxii; From M. R. Cohen and I. E. Drabkin, *A Source Book in Greek Science* (New York, 1948)

Precautions to Be Taken in the Case of a Map Drawn on a Plane

For the aforesaid reasons it would be well to keep the lines which represent meridians straight, and to make those which represent parallels of latitude arcs of circles drawn about one and the same center. Now, from this center, taken at the north pole, the straight meridian lines will have to be drawn in such a way that above all the resemblance, both as to form and appearance, to a spherical surface may be preserved. For the meridian lines cut the parallels of latitude here, too, at right angles and at the same time meet at the same common pole.

Now since it is impossible to preserve the spherical proportions through all the parallels of latitude, it would be sufficient to do so for the parallel through Thule[117] and for the equator. In this way the boundaries which encompass our latitudes may be accurately proportioned, and the parallel through Rhodes on which the most numerous measurements of longitudinal distance have been made may be divided in accordance with the ratio it bears to the meridian circle, that is, in accordance with the ratio of approximately 4 to 5 measured along equal arcs. This is Marinus's method.[118] Thus the length of the better-known part of the inhabited earth would be in proper relation to its breadth. The method of doing this we shall make clear after we have set forth how a map may be made on a sphere.

---

known accordingly by its Arabic title *Almagest*. His equally famous *Geography* is the most scientific ancient work on the subject and is the foundation of all modern cartography.

117. The name used in antiquity to designate the northernmost point of the known world. Ptolemy, for example, held this to be the Shetland Islands.

118. Marinus of Tyre, the leading geographer of the generation preceding Ptolemy's, and the latter's principal source. He made the first attempt to draw a map of the world on the principle now known as projection.

How the Inhabited Earth May Be Represented on a Sphere

The decision as to the size of the sphere will depend on the number of details the mapmaker wishes to include. And this, in turn, will depend on his skill and ambition, for as the sphere is increased the amount of detail and the accuracy of the map will likewise be increased. But whatever the size of the sphere is to be, we determine its poles and then carefully attach to it through the poles a semicircle raised just enough from the spherical surface to keep it from rubbing against the sphere as it rotates. This semicircle should be narrow so that it may not cover up many places. One of its edges should extend exactly between the points which mark the poles so that we may draw the meridian lines with that edge. We shall divide the latter into 180 parts and mark the numbers beginning with the midpoint of the semicircle where it will intersect the equator. Now similarly we shall draw the equator, and divide one of the semicircles comprising it into 180 parts, again setting the numbers opposite these parts, beginning with the boundary through which we are to draw the westernmost meridian line.

Now we shall make our map on the basis of the tables of degrees of longitude and latitude for each of the places to be represented, using the divisions on the semicircles, viz., the equator and the movable meridian. We turn the latter to the degree of longitude indicated, that is, to the division of the equator corresponding to that number, and we measure the latitudinal distance from the equator according to the divisions on the meridian. We place a mark corresponding to the indicated number of degrees just as we make a star map on a solid sphere.

Similarly, it will be possible to draw meridians at intervals of as many degrees of longitude as we wish, using as a ruler the aforesaid divided edge of the semicircular ring. It will also be possible to draw parallels of latitude at as great intervals as we wish, by placing the marker next to that number on the edge which indicates the latitude desired, and turning the marker and the semicircular ring as far as the meridians that indicate the limits of the known portion of the earth.

61. MEDICINE

The status of the medical profession rose greatly during the Empire, the same privileges and immunities being granted to doctors, who were almost exclusively Greeks, slaves, and freedmen, as to members of the other learned professions (see § 56). There was no state certification or supervision of medical practice, and widespread charlatanry and reliance on superstition and the irrational prevailed. Nevertheless, there were advances in empirical knowledge, and great strides were made in the organization of military medicine and in the development of a hospital system.

THE ART OF MEDICINE

Celsus,[119] *On Medicine* I. Preface. 1–5, 12, 74–75; From *LCL*

Just as agriculture promises nourishment to healthy bodies, so does the art of medicine promise health to the sick. Nowhere is this art lacking, for the most uncivilized nations have knowledge of herbs, and other things to hand for the aiding of wounds and diseases. This art, however, has been cultivated among the Greeks much more than in other nations —not, however, even among them from their first beginnings but only for a few generations before ours. . . . Diseases were [in olden times] ascribed to the anger of the immortal gods, and from them help used to be sought; and it is probable that with no aids against bad health, nonetheless health was generally good because of good habits, which neither indolence nor luxury had vitiated; since it is these two which have afflicted the bodies of men, first in Greece and later amongst us. . . .

Of the different divisions of the art of medicine, the one which heals diseases, as it is the most difficult, is also the most famous; hence we must speak about it first. . . . There is a primary difference of opinion, some holding that the sole knowledge necessary is derived from experience, others propounding that practice is not sufficient except after acquiring a reasoned knowledge of human bodies and of nature. . . .

[Celsus then presents the leading arguments of the theorists (or dogmatists) and of the empiricists.]

I am of the opinion that the art of medicine ought to be rational but should also draw instruction from evident causes, all obscure ones being rejected from the practice of the art, although not from the practitioner's study. But to dissect the bodies of men while still alive is as cruel as it is needless;[120] that of the dead is a necessity for learners, who should know

---

119. Aulus Cornelius Celsus (early first century A.D.) was the author of an encyclopedia treating of medicine, agriculture, warfare, rhetoric, philosophy, and jurisprudence. Only the section on medicine is extant. Whether he was a practicing physician is much disputed.

120. Vivisection was practiced on criminals supplied to Hellenistic researchers by the Ptolemaic rulers of Egypt, according to Celsus I. Preface. 23.

positions and relations, which the dead body exhibits better than does a living and wounded man. As for the remainder, which can only be learned from the living, actual practice will demonstrate it in the course of treating the wounded in a somewhat slower yet much milder way.

CLINICAL OBSERVATION THROUGH VIVISECTION

Galen,[121] *On the Natural Faculties* III. iv. 155–57; *From LCL*

Suppose you should fill any animal whatsoever with liquid food—an experiment I have often carried out in pigs, to whom I give a sort of mess of wheaten flour and water, thereafter cutting them open after three or four hours; if you will do this yourself, you will find the food still in the stomach. For it is not chylification[122] which determines the length of its stay here—since this can also be effected outside the stomach; the determining factor is digestion, which is a different thing from chylification, as are blood production and nutrition. For just as . . . these two processes depend upon a change of qualities, similarly also the digestion of food in the stomach involves a transmutation of it into the quality proper to that which is receiving nourishment. Then, when it is completely digested, the lower outlet opens and the food is quickly ejected through it, even if there should be amongst it abundance of stones, bones, grape pips, or other things which cannot be reduced to chyle. And you may observe this yourself in an animal, if you will try to hit upon the time at which the descent of food from the stomach takes place. But even if you should fail to discover the time and nothing was yet passing down and the food was still undergoing digestion in the stomach, still even then you would find dissection not without its uses. You will observe, as we have just said, that the pylorus is accurately closed, and that the whole stomach is in a state of contraction upon the food very much as the womb contracts upon the foetus. . . .

Now, I have personally, on countless occasions, divided the peritoneum of a still living animal and have always found all the intestines

121. The Greek physician Claudius Galen (A.D. c. 130–c. 200), a native of Pergamum, was the most important ancient writer on medicine. He attained a brilliant reputation throughout the Roman world and was for some years consulting physician to the Emperor Marcus Aurelius. His great contribution in his prolific writings consists in the systematization of much of Greek medical theory. In particular, he gave definitive form to the theory of the four humors, which remained the basis of medical practice until the eighteenth century.

122. That is, the mere mechanical breakdown of food, as opposed to the distinctive altering action of digestion.

contracting peristaltically upon their contents. The condition of the stomach, however, is found less simple; as regards the substances freshly swallowed, it had grasped these accurately both above and below, in fact at every point, and was as devoid of movement as though it had grown round and become united with the food. At the same time I found the pylorus persistently closed and accurately shut, like the os uteri on the foetus. In the cases, however, where digestion had been completed the pylorus had opened, and the stomach was undergoing peristaltic movements, similar to those of the intestines.

THE FOUR HUMORS

Galen, *On the Natural Faculties* ii. viii. 116–118; From *LCL*

Aristotle stated and demonstrated [that] our bodies [are] compounded out of the Warm, the Cold, the Dry, and the Moist, that among these qualities the Warm is the most active, and that those animals which are by nature warmest have abundance of blood, whilst those that are colder are entirely lacking in blood, and consequently in winter lie idle and motionless, lurking in holes like corpses. . . . Now I, for my part, as I have already said, did not set before myself the task of stating what has been so well demonstrated by the ancients, since I cannot surpass these men either in my views or in my method of giving them expression. Doctrines, however, which they either stated without demonstration, as being self-evident . . . or else which they omitted to mention at all— these I propose to discover and prove.

Now in reference to the genesis of the humors, I do not know that anyone could add anything wiser than what has been said by Hippo-crates, Aristotle, Praxagoras, Philotimus,[123] and many others among the ancients. These men demonstrated that when the nutriment becomes altered in the veins by the innate heat, blood is produced when it is in moderation, and the other humors [i.e., bile, black bile, and phlegm] when it is not in proper proportion. And all the observed facts agree with this argument. . . . How could it be otherwise? For, seeing that every part functions in its own special way because of the manner in which the four qualities are compounded, it is absolutely necessary that the function [activity] should be either completely destroyed, or at least

123. Praxagoras and Philotimus were successive leaders of the Hippocratic school in the fourth century B.C.

hampered, by any damage to the qualities, and that thus the animal should fall ill, either as a whole or in certain of its parts. Also the diseases which are primary and most generic are four in number, and differ from each other in warmth, cold, dryness, and moisture.

MEDICINE AND QUACKERY

Pliny, *Natural History* XXIX. viii. 17–25 (abridged)

Medicine is the only one of the arts of Greece that serious Romans have not yet begun to practice. Even though it is lucrative, very few Roman citizens have touched it; and those who do at once become deserters to the Greeks. Nay, even more than this, if they treat of it in any other language than Greek, they lose authority even with laymen . . . [who] have less confidence in matters which concern their lives if it is intelligible to them.

And so it happens that this is the only one of all the arts, by heaven, in which trust is at once put in any man who declares himself a doctor, whereas there is no form of deception that entails greater danger. To this, however, we pay no attention, so seductive is the hope [of a cure] which every patient entertains.

Besides, there is no law to punish this ignorance, no instance of capital punishment. It is at the expense of our perils that they learn, and by conducting experiments they put us to death; a physician is the only man that can kill a man with sovereign impunity. . . . I shall not even attempt to denounce their avarice, the rapacious haggling while their patients' fate hangs in the balance, the fees for our ailments, the deposits for our death, and their secret doctrines. . . . Not shame but competition keeps the fees down. It is well-known that Charmis . . . for 200 sesterces turned over a patient who was a provincial to the surgeon Alco, and that the Emperor Claudius removed the patient from him and condemned him to pay a fine of 100,000 sesterces; but the same doctor while in exile in Gaul—and later, when recalled—acquired an equally large sum within a few years.

These are faults, however, of individuals. I shall not expatiate on the dregs of the profession, and the ignorance of this crew, and their lack of restraint. . . . Which of the gods, pray, instructed them in this? Human subtlety could not achieve such heights, so apparent is their vain ostentation of skill and their monstrous display of knowledge.

MATERIA MEDICA

In books xx–xxxii Pliny records hundreds of "remedies" for all sorts of ailments, mental as well as physical. Garlic, for example, figures in sixty-one remedies for a wide range of complaints including dropsy, leprosy, erysipelas, snake and animal bites, running ulcers, toothache, headache, epilepsy, and insanity (xx. xxiii). Medical practice was much given to the use of specifics and panaceas, in the concoction of which superstition and magic frequently played a larger part than empirical knowledge. Thus, although he several times in his work digresses to excoriate magicians and deprecate their popularity, Pliny does not scruple to record their "cures." The examples given here are selected from Pliny's lists of remedies using animal products; he has separate lists of those employing vegetable matter and waters.

Pliny, *Natural History* xxviii. vii. 35, lxiv. 227–lxvii. 230

[Spittle]

But we have shown that the most effective protection against snakes is the spittle of a fasting person; and actual daily experience confirms other effective uses of it. We spit against illnesses like epilepsy, that is, we repel contagion; in similar manner we repel witchcraft and the danger in meeting a person lame in the right leg. We also ask pardon of the gods by spitting in the bosom for entertaining some too presumptuous hope. On the same principle it is the custom in all cases where medicine is employed to spit three times in deprecation, so as to assist its efficacy.

[Remedies for Broken Bones]

For broken bones a quick remedy is the ashes of the jawbone of a boar or swine; likewise boiled lard, tied round the broken bone, knits it with marvellous rapidity. For fractures of the ribs, goat's dung applied in old wine is especially extolled; it has aperient, extractive, and healing properties.

[Remedies for Fevers]

Deer's flesh . . . is a febrifuge. Recurrent fevers are cured, if we are to believe the magicians, by wearing the right eye of a wolf, salted and attached. There is a type of fever called quotidian; one can be cured of this, they say, if the patient takes three drops of blood from the vein of an ass's ear and swallows them in a pint of water. For quartan fever the magicians recommend cat's dung together with the toe of an owl to be attached to the body, and, to prevent a relapse, not to be removed until the seventh spasm. . . . More moderate ones recommend for quartan fever the liver of a cat killed during the waning moon, preserved in salt, to be taken in wine just before the attacks. The magicians also recommend that the toes of the patient should be smeared with the ashes of cow dung sprinkled with boy's urine, and that a hare's heart should be attached to the hands; they give hare's rennet to drink before attacks. Fresh goat's milk cheese is also given with honey, the whey being carefully extracted.

[Remedies for Melancholy, Lethargy, and Phthisis]

For patients afflicted with melancholy, calf's dung boiled in wine is a remedy. Lethargic persons are aroused by applying to the nostrils the calluses from an ass's legs steeped in vinegar, or the fumes of goat's horns or hair, or wild boar's liver. This is also given to drowsy persons.

The cure of phthisis is effected by a wolf's liver taken in thin wine, the lard of a sow that has been fed upon grass, or the flesh of a she-ass taken with broth—this last type is used to cure this illness especially in Achaea. They say, too, that the smoke of dried cow dung inhaled through a reed . . . is good for phthisis.

62. THE RACES OF MAN: CLIMATE AND CULTURE

Vitruvius, *Architecture* VI. i. 9–11; Adapted from *LCL*

Southern peoples, owing to the rarity of the atmosphere, with their minds rendered acute by the heat, are more readily and swiftly inclined to resourcefulness in planning; but northern peoples, steeped in a thick climate amid reluctant air, are chilled by the damp and have sluggish minds. We can observe this in the case of snakes: they move quickest when the heat has drawn away the damp with its chilling effect; but in the cold and wintry seasons they are chilled by the change of climate, and are sluggish and motionless. Hence we need not wonder if warm air renders the human mind more acute, and a cool air impedes.

Now, while the southern peoples are of acute intelligence and infinite resource in planning, they give way when courage is demanded, because their strength is drained away by the sun; but those who are born in colder regions, by their fearless courage are better equipped for the clash of arms, yet by their slowness of mind they rush on without reflection, and through lack of tactics are balked of their purpose. Since, therefore the disposition of the world is such by nature, and all other peoples differ by their unbalanced temperament, it is in the true mean within the space of all the world and the regions of the earth that the Roman people holds its territories. For in Italy the inhabitants are exactly tempered in either direction, both in the structure of the body and by strength of mind corresponding to their courage. For just as the planet Jupiter is tempered by running in the middle between the heat of Mars and the cold of Saturn, in the same manner Italy presents laudable qualities which are tempered by admixture from either side both north and south, and are consequently unsurpassed. And so by its policy it shatters the courage of the barbarians and by its strong hand the plans of the southerners. Thus the divine mind placed the state of the Roman people in an excellent and temperate region in order that it might obtain dominion over the whole world.

4

THE ROMAN PEACE (A.D. 14–192): LIFE IN THE MUNICIPALITIES AND PROVINCES[1]

63. LIMITED LOCAL AUTONOMY

Plutarch, *Precepts of Statecraft* x, xvii, xix, xxxii (abridged); From *LCL*

Nowadays, then, when the affairs of the cities no longer include leadership in wars, nor the overthrowing of tyrannies, nor acts of alliances, what opening for a conspicuous and brilliant public career could one find? There remain the public lawsuits and embassies to the emperor, which demand a man of ardent temperament and one who possesses both courage and intellect. But there are many excellent lines of endeavor that are neglected in our cities, which a man may take up, and also many practices resulting from evil custom that have insinuated themselves to the shame or injury of the city, which a man may remove, and thus turn them to account for himself. . . .

You who hold office are a subject, ruling a state controlled by proconsuls and by the procurators of the emperor. . . . Do not have great pride or confidence in your crown [of office], for you see soldiers' boots just above your head. . . .

Officials in the cities, when they foolishly urge the people to imitate

---

1. The unusual proportion of Egyptian material in this chapter is the result of the fact that papyri provide unique documentation for many facets of provincial life, especially those concerning the agricultural masses in their private and governmental relations. Although Egypt occupied an exceptional position in the Roman provincial system and some of the details revealed by the papyri have only local pertinence, much of the material can be taken as illustrative of Roman provincial life in general. A few of the documents included in this chapter are dated somewhat later than A.D. 192, but they are equally applicable to the earlier imperial period.

the deeds, ideal, and actions of their ancestors,[2] however unsuitable they may be in the present times and conditions, stir up the common folk, and, though what they do is laughable, what is done to them is no laughing matter, except when they are treated with utter contempt. . . .

And not only should the statesman show himself and his native state blameless toward our rulers, but he should always have, as a firm bulwark, so to speak, of his administration, a friend among the men of high station who have the greatest power; for the Romans themselves are most eager to promote the political interests of their friends. . . .

However, the statesman, while making his native state readily obedient to its sovereigns, must not further humble it; nor, when the leg has been fettered, go on and subject the neck to the yoke, as some do who, by referring everything great or small to the emperors, bring the reproach of slavery upon their country, or rather wholly destroy its constitutional government, making it dazed, timid, and powerless in everything. . . . Those who invite the emperor's decision on every decree, meeting of a council, granting of a privilege, or administrative measure, force their emperors to be their masters more than they desire. And the cause of this is chiefly the greed and contentiousness of the foremost citizens; for either, in cases in which they are injuring their inferiors, they force them into exile from the state, or, in matters concerning which they differ among themselves, since they are unwilling to occupy an inferior position among their fellow citizens, they call in those who are mightier; and, as a result, council, popular assembly, courts, and the entire local government lose their authority. . . .[cf. § 69].

Then he [the statesman] will instruct his people both individually and collectively and will call attention to the weak condition of Greek affairs, in which it is best for wise men to accept one advantage—a life of harmony and quiet—since fortune has left us no prize open for competition. For what dominion, what glory is there for those who are victorious? What sort of power is it when a small edict of a proconsul may annul or transfer it to another man and which, even if it last, has nothing in it seriously worth while?

---

2. Plutarch is referring to the autonomous city-states of the heyday of Greek civilization.

64. A MUNICIPAL CHARTER

At its height, the Empire presented the appearance of an aggregate of cities and towns (see § 16), enjoying varying degrees of self-government according to the status granted by the central government. In increasing numbers during the Principate urbanized centers were raised to the status of Roman municipalities; some were granted the more privileged rank of colony. The bronze fragments of the charter of the Spanish town of Malaca (Municipium Flavium Malacitanum), found near Málaga, provide valuable evidence for the spread of traditional Roman municipal institutions (see vol 1, § 162) and their adaptation to changing conditions within the Empire. By edict of Vespasian, confirmed by Titus, these towns, like most Spanish urban communities, were granted *Latinitas* (Latin rights), a half-way station between alien status and full Roman citizenship. The formal charters, patterned on Italian municipal constitutions, were promulgated by Domitian in A.D. 81–84. Noteworthy features are the strong local autonomy, the concentration of power in the hands of the local aristocracy, and the access to full Roman citizenship provided for the aristocracy through the holding of a magistracy. In the second century this latter privilege was granted to all members of municipal councils.

THE CHARTER OF MALACA

CIL, vol. II, no. 1,964 and pp. 876–77 (=Dessau, no. 6,089)

R.[3] *On the Nomination of Candidates*

LI. If, up to the day when declaration of intention [to be a candidate] must be made, declaration is made either in the name of no one or of fewer persons than the number which must be elected, or if, out of those persons in whose name a declaration of intention has been made, those who may properly stand for election in accordance with this charter are fewer than the number which must be elected, then the person responsible for conducting the elections[4] shall post, in a place where they may be plainly read from level ground, the names of as many persons, qualified by this charter to stand for the said offices, as are required to make up the number which must be elected by this

---

3. *R(ubrica):* "title"—so called because it was usually colored red.
4. Usually the duovir who was senior in age.

charter. Each of those whose names are so posted shall, if he so desires, go before the magistrate who is to conduct the said elections, and nominate one [additional] person of his own status; in like manner each of the persons so nominated by the aforesaid shall, if he so desires, go before the same magistrate and nominate one [additional] person of his own status. And the said magistrate, before whom such nomination is made, shall post the names of all the aforesaid persons in a place where they may be plainly read from level ground and shall likewise conduct the elections in respect to all the said persons exactly as though, in accordance with the clause in this charter *On Candidature for Office*,[5] declaration of intention had been made in their names within the prescribed time, and as though they had of their own accord in the first instance stood for the said offices and had not withheld their candidacy.[6]

LII. [On the mechanics of conducting the elections.]
LIII. [On the privilege of voting granted to resident aliens who are Roman or Latin citizens.]

R. On Those Whose Candidature May Properly Be Considered at the Elections

LIV. The person responsible for conducting the elections shall first see to the election of duovirs with judicial power from that category of freeborn persons already specified and set forth in this charter; then in succession he shall see to the election of aediles and likewise of quaestors from that category of freeborn persons already specified and set forth in this charter, provided that, in the case of candidates for the duovirate, he does not allow any person to stand for election who is less than twenty-five years of age or has held that office within five years;[7] likewise, in the case of candidates for the aedileship or the quaestorship, he shall not allow consideration of any person who is less than twenty-five years of age or who is subject to any impediments whereby, if he were a Roman citizen, he could not lawfully become a member of the decurions or *conscripti*.[8]

5. This clause is not extant.
6. This clause involving compulsory nomination of candidates is one of the earliest pieces of evidence we have on the burdensome character of and the tendency to avoid municipal offices. Cf. further § 66.
7. There were similar restrictions at Rome during the Republic (cf. vol. 1, p. 290–91). The decurions were recruited from the ex-aediles and ex-quaestors.
8. Cf. the similar provisions in the "Julian Municipal Law," vol. 1, pp. 449–52.

R. On the Casting of Votes

LV. The person conducting the elections in accordance with this charter shall summon the citizens to cast their votes by *curiae*,[9] issuing a single call to vote to all the *curiae*,[10] in such manner that the said *curiae*, each in a separate voting booth, may severally cast their votes by means of tablets. He shall likewise see to it that three citizens of the said municipality are placed at the ballot box of each *curia* who do not themselves belong to that *curia*, to guard and count the ballots; and that before performing such duty each of them shall take oath that he will handle the counting of the ballots and make report thereon in good faith. Furthermore, he shall not hinder candidates for an office from placing one watcher each at every ballot box. And the said watchers, both those placed by the person conducting the elections and those placed by candidates for office, shall each cast his vote in that *curia* at whose ballot box he is placed as a watcher, and the votes of the said watchers shall be just as lawful and valid as if each had cast his vote in his own *curia*.

R. On the Course to Be Taken in the Case of Those Who Have an Equal Number of Votes

LVI. The person conducting the said elections, according as any candidate has more votes in each *curia* than the others, shall declare the person who is ahead of the rest as chosen and elected with reference to that *curia*, until the number to be elected is made up. If in any *curia* two or more candidates have the same number of votes, he shall prefer a married man or one with the rights of a married man to an unmarried man without children or without the rights of married men, a man with children to a man without children, and a man with more children to a man with fewer children, and shall declare the former [elected]. In such matter, two children lost after the ceremony of naming or one boy lost after puberty or one girl of marriageable age lost shall be counted as equivalent to one surviving child.[11] If two or more candidates have the same number of votes and are of the same qualifications, he shall submit their names to choice by lot and shall declare the person whose name is drawn by lot to be ahead of the rest.

9. Voting units (wards) similar to the tribes at Rome.

10. The *curiae* voted simultaneously, as did the tribes in the Comitia Tributa at Rome (cf. vol. 1, p. 38).

11. These provisions are patterned after the Augustan Papian–Poppaean Laws (see vol. 1, § 204).

LVII–LVIII. [On announcement of candidates elected, and on the fine for obstructing the holding of elections.]

LIX. [On the oath to be taken by successful candidates]

LX. [On security to be given by candidates for the duovirate or quaestorship for public moneys that may be entrusted to their care.][12]

LXI. [On the adoption of a patron of the municipality.][13]

R. No Person to Destroy Buildings Except with a View to Restoration

LXII. No person shall unroof or destroy or cause to be demolished any building in the town of the municipality Flavia Malaca or any buildings in the environs of the said municipality except by resolution of the decurions or *conscripti,* passed when a majority of the same is present, unless he intends to restore the said building within the year. Any person acting in contravention of this shall be condemned to pay to the citizens of the municipality Flavia Malaca a sum of money equivalent to the value of the said property and may be sued or prosecuted for that amount at will by any citizen of the said municipality who has the legal right to do so in accordance with this charter.[14]

LXIII. [On the recording and publication of public contracts by duovirs.]

LXIV–LXV. [On legal obligations of sureties to the municipality, and on penalties for false declaration of securities posted.]

LXVI. [On the imposition of fines by magistrates.]

LXVII. [On the rendering of account within thirty days to the municipality of corporate moneys belonging to it.][15]

LXVIII–LXIX. [On the election of a commission of three to investigate accounts due the municipality, and on the assignment of a court to try cases involving corporate moneys.]

65. ELECTION NOTICES

Hundreds of campaign notices, painted in red on white-washed walls of buildings in Pompeii, testify to the spirited political life of Roman municipalities in the first century of the Empire.

12. Cf. the Charter of Tarentum, vol. 1, p. 447.

13. For the patrons of municipalities see § 72.

14. Cf. the Charter of Tarentum, vol. 1, p. 448; the Charter of Urso, vol. 1, p. 456; and vol. 2, § 33, first selection, and vol. 2, § 69, last selection.

15. In the Charter of Urso 150 days were allowed (vol. 1, p. 456).

CIL, vol. IV, nos. 202, 710, 429, 113, 787, 635, 3,775, 3,294, 768, 6,626, 3,702, 581, 576, 1,147 (=Dessau, nos. 6,411*a*, 6,419*e*, 6,412*e*, 6,412*a*, 6,420*b*, 6,436, 6,409, 6,414, 6,438*d*, 6,422*b*, 6,405, 6,418*d*, 6,418*f*, 6,431*d*), and CIL, vol. IV, no. 1,904

i

The fruit dealers together with Helvius Vestalis unanimously urge the election of Marcus Holconius Priscus as duovir with judicial power.

ii

The goldsmiths unanimously urge the election of Gaius Cuspius Pansa as aedile.

iii

I ask you to elect Gaius Julius Polybius aedile. He gets good bread.

iv

The muleteers urge the election of Gaius Julius Polybius as duovir.

v

The worshippers of Isis unaminously urge the election of Gnaeus Helvius Sabinus as aedile.

vi

Proculus, make Sabinus aedile and he will do as much for you.

vii

His neighbors urge you to elect Lucius Statius Receptus duovir with judicial power; he is worthy. Aemilius Celer, a neighbor, wrote this. May you take sick if you maliciously erase this!

viii

Satia and Petronia support and ask you to elect Marcus Casellius and Lucius Albucius aediles. May we always have such citizens in our colony!

ix

I ask you to elect Epidius Sabinus duovir with judicial power. He is worthy, a defender of the colony, and in the opinion of the respected judge Suedius Clemens and by agreement of the council, because of his services and uprightness, worthy of the municipality. Elect him!

x

If upright living is considered any recommendation, Lucretius Fronto is well worthy of the office.

xi

Genialis urges the election of Bruttius Balbus as duovir. He will protect the treasury.

xii

I ask you to elect Marcus Cerrinius Vatia to the aedileship. All the late drinkers support him. Florus and Fructus wrote this.

xiii

The petty thieves support Vatia for the aedileship.

xiv

I ask you to elect Aulus Vettius Firmus aedile. He is worthy of the municipality. I ask you to elect him, ballplayers. Elect him!

xv

I wonder, O wall, that you have not fallen in ruins from supporting the stupidities of so many scribblers.[16]

---

16. Unlike the others above, this inscription is a *graffito,* scratched on the wall.

66. SELECTION OF MUNICIPAL COUNCILMEN

The expense of office holding and the increasing financial responsibilities of local magistrates and councilmen during the growing economic crisis of the second century made the local rich increasingly reluctant to assume public office. Since the municipalities served as the instrumentality of the central government in the collection of the imperial revenues, and since the personal contributions of the officeholders constituted the mainstay of municipal finances (cf., e.g., §§ 67, 71, 73), the shortage of candidates threatened severe administrative and financial dislocations, causing increasing imperial intervention in local affairs, which in turn further sapped the vitality of local self-rule. On orders from the central government compulsion was resorted to increasingly to fill municipal posts, and by the end of the second century even the formality of popular elections had been dispensed with and the choice of municipal officers left to the local senates. Thus, as at Rome where the elections had long since been transferred from people to senate (cf. chapter 1, note 37), the participation of the people was eliminated in the interest of administrative efficiency, and the councils, whose members held office for life, became the central organ of municipal administration. For further developments in the third and fourth centuries, see §§ 115, 128.

REQUEST FOR ELECTION TO THE CITY COUNCIL

Dittenberger, no. 838

[Ephesus, Asia, A.D. 129]

The Emperor Caesar Trajanus HADRIAN Augustus, son of the deified Trajan Parthicus, grandson of the deified Nerva, *pontifex maximus,* holding the tribunician power for the thirteenth year, three times consul, father of his country, to the chief magistrates and council of Ephesus, greeting. Lucius Erastus states that he is a fellow citizen of yours, that he has many times sailed the sea, making himself as useful as he could thereby to his native city,[17] and that he has always transported the governors of the province. He has already sailed with me twice, first when I was traveling to Rhodes from Ephesus, and now on my journey from Eleusis to you. He desires to become a member of your council. I

---

17. Doubtless by bringing in supplies of food; see § 68.

leave the scrutiny of his qualifications in your hands, and if nothing stands in the way and he is judged worthy of the honor, I shall pay on behalf of his election whatever sum of money the councillors pay.[18]

THE GROWTH OF COMPULSION

Pliny, *Letters* book x, nos. 112–13

[Pliny to the Emperor Trajan]

The Pompeian Law,[19] my lord, which Bithynia and Pontus observe, does not provide for those who are named to a city council by the [local] censors to pay any money. But those whom certain cities are permitted by your indulgence to admit beyond the legal number have contributed 1,000 and 2,000 *denarii* each. Then the proconsul Anicius Maximus ordered also those who are named by the censors, in a few cities at any rate, to contribute a sum varying from place to place. It remains, therefore, for you yourself to consider whether in all cities all who henceforth are chosen councilmen should not be required to pay for their admission. For it is appropriate that what is to endure forever should be established by you, whose every deed and word deserve immortality.

[Trajan to Pliny]

I can establish no general ruling as to whether all who become decurions in every city of Bithynia should be required to pay an entrance fee for the decurionate or not. I think therefore that—as is always the most prudent course—each city should conform to its own law. But as against those who are made decurions against their will. . . .[20]

67. Municipal Revenues

Major sources of municipal revenues were local taxes and tolls, and leases of municipal property and concessions. Collections were by tax farmers or by local officials.

18. That is, the *honorarium* (office money) customarily paid into the local treasury by newly elected magistrates and councilmen on taking office.

19. The law by which the province of Bithynia was organized by Pompey the Great.

20. For the conclusion of this sentence, the text of which is hopelessly corrupt, various conjectures have been made. It suffices to note that the necessity of drafting some members to fill the municipal councils is here treated as a matter of course.

A MUNICIPAL TAX COLLECTOR

In a chest unearthed at Pompeii in 1875 were found 153 waxed diptychs and triptychs (cf. § 34) containing business records of one Lucius Caecilius Jucundus. Many of the tablets were charred or crumbled beyond legibility in the eruption of Vesuvius that buried the town. Most of those that can be read are receipts issued to Jucundus either when he paid the proceeds of sale to persons for whom he had auctioned off property (at a commission of two percent or more) or when he paid over to the municipality tax moneys that he had contracted to collect for a four-year period.

CIL, vol. IV, no. 3,340, xxv and cxli (= *FIRA*, vol. III, nos. 129a and 131b); A.D. 56 and 58

i

11,039 sesterces, which sum, after commission, was realized by Lucius Caecilius Jucundus from Umbricia Januaria's auction: Umbricia Januaria declared that she had been paid in full by Lucius Caecilius Jucundus.

Done at Pompeii on December 12 in the consulship of Lucius Duvius and Publius Clodius.

[Signatures of witnesses] [Seals of] Quintus Appuleius Severus, Marcus Lucretius Lerus, Tiberius Julius Abscantus, Marcus Julius Crescens, Publius Terentius Primus, Marcus Epidius Hymenaeus, Quintus Granius Lesbus, Titus Vesonius Le . . . , Decimus Volcius Thallus.

In the consulship of Lucius Duvius Avitus and Publius Clodius Thrasea, December 12. I, Decimus Volcius Thallus, wrote at the request of Umbricia Januaria, after examination of the witnessed tablets[21] that she had received from Lucius Caecilius Jucundus 11,039 sesterces as the proceeds of her auction less commission. . . . Done at Pompeii.

ii

Holograph [acknowledgment] of Privatus, public slave of the colony of Veneria Cornelia,[22] on receipt of 1,652 sesterces for the fullers' tax of the first year.[23]

21. That is, the preceding formal attestation, which is written on the first two tablets of the triptych; the additional personal acknowledgment of receipt is added on the third tablet.
22. The full official name of Pompeii was Colonia Veneria Cornelia Pompeianorum.
23. That is, of Jucundus' four-year contract; see introduction.

Sextus Pompeius Proculus and Gaius Cornelius Macer being the duovirs with judicial power for the year, February 19. I, Privatus, slave of the colony, hereby declare in writing that I received from Lucius Caecilius Jucundus 1,652 sesterces for the fullers' tax from the balance of the first year.

Done at Pompeii in the consulship of Nero Augustus (for the third time) and Marcus Messalla.

NO ESCAPE FROM THE TAX FARMERS

This inscription preserves the only extant rescript of the Emperor Titus. Munigua, to which the rescript is addressed, was a municipality in Spain. Sempronius Fuscus and Gallicanus were successive governors of the province of Hispania Baetica.

AE, 1962, no. 288; September 7, A.D. 79

The Emperor TITUS Caesar Vespasian Augustus, *pontifex maximus,* holding the tribunician power for the ninth year, acclaimed imperator fourteen times, consul for the seventh time, father of his country, expresses greetings to the four magistrates and the decurions of Munigua.

Since you have appealed [to me] against paying the money which you owed to [the tax farmer] Servilius Pollio pursuant to the judgment of Sempronius Fuscus, you ought to be subjected to the penalty for unjustified appeal, but I have preferred to speak in keeping with my indulgence rather than your temerity, and I have remitted 50,000 sesterces in response to the public financial straits which you allege. However, I have written to my friend Gallicanus, the proconsul, that you are to pay the money which was adjudicated to Pollio but he is to release you from the interest computed from the day when the judgment was pronounced.

It is fair that the income from your rents, for which (as you indicate) Pollio held the tax-farming contract, be taken into account so that nothing may be lacking to the state under this heading.

Given seven days before the Ides of September.

A MUNICIPAL WATER ACCOUNT

This unique document contains an accounting of income and expenditures by the water commissioners of the town of Arsinoë, capital of the Arsinoite nome of Egypt. More than half the operating costs were defrayed by monthly contributions from various municipal magistrates.

British Museum Papyrus No. 1,177, abridged (= Wilcken, no. 193 = *Select Papyri*, no. 406); A.D. 113

To Demetrius, ex-gymnasiarch, auditor, from Crispus, also known as Sarapio; Mysthes, also known as Ptolemaeus, son of Ptolemaeus; Mysthes son of Didymus, acting through his father; and Sotas son of Zoilus—all four superintendents of the water supply for the reservoirs and fountains of the metropolis. Account of receipts and of expenses incurred for the water supply from Pachon of the past sixteenth year of the lord Trajan Caesar to Phaophi 30 of the current seventeenth year.

Receipts

From Pappus and Theo, gymnasiarchs of the sixteenth year of the lord Trajan Caesar, 420 drachmas per month: Pachon, dr. 420; Payni, dr. 420; Epeiph, dr. 400; Mesore, dr. 400; and dr. 40 for Epeiph and Mesore, balance. Total, dr. 1,680.

From Asclepiades, *cosmetes*, 1,000 drachmas per month: Pachon, dr. 1,000; Payni, dr. 1,000; Caesareus,[24] dr. 2,000. Total, dr. 4,000. . . .

For supplying water to the baths of Severianus at 18 obols per day: Pachon, dr. 72 ob. 18; Payni, dr. 72 ob. 18; Epeiph, dr. 72 ob. 18. . . . Total, dr. 424 ob. 93. For the Colonnade[?] fountain, at ob. 9 per day: Pachon, dr. 36 ob. 9; Payni dr. 36 ob. 9; Epeiph, 27 days, the proportional dr. 33 ob. 4; Mesore, dr. 36 ob. 9; the five intercalary days, ob. 45. Total, dr. 141 ob. 76. . . . For the fountain in the Cleopatreum[25] quarter, likewise at ob. 9 per day: Pachon, dr. 36 ob. 9; Payni, dr. 36 ob. 9; . . . four intercalary days, dr. 5; Year 17, Thoth, 29 days, dr. 36 (because none supplied one day). . . . Total, dr. 205 ob. 36. For the brewery in the Serapeum quarter, at ob. 13 per day: Pachon, dr. 52 ob. 13. . . . Total, dr. 313 ob. 70. From the officers of the synagogue of the

---

24. That is, Mesore, the Egyptian month (July 25–August 23), here renamed in honor of the emperor, probably Augustus.

25. A temple to a deified queen Cleopatra of the Ptolemaic dynasty.

Theban Jews, at dr. 128 per month: Pachon, dr. 128; Payni, dr. 128. . . . Total dr. 768. For the house of prayer, likewise: Pachon, dr. 128. . . . Total, dr. 768.

Total receipts from Pachon 10 to Phaophi 30 [of the seventeenth year] of the lord Trajan Caesar: 1 talent 5,900 drachmas 6 obols.

Expenditures

For the reservoir at the Grove with its sixteen *shadufs*,[26] at a man and a half[27] drawing water from morning till evening, Year 16 of the lord Trajan Caesar: Pachon—to Aphrodisius, foreman of the pumpers, wages for himself for Pachon, dr. 40, and for payment to the pumpers from the 1st to the 30th, 797 men at the reservoir and the outlet[?], and likewise 306 night workmen, total 1,103 men at a wage of dr. 40 per 30,[28] dr. 1,470; for payment to the men working the Archimedean screws [cf. chapter 2, note 38], 200 men at ob. 10 each, ob. 2,000, equals dr. 276; cost of oil burned in lamps for the night workmen, dr. 12 ob. 2; cost of earthenware buckets, dr. 1. Total for the month, dr. 1,799 ob. 2. . . .

Wages of ox drivers at the reservoir at the Grove with its two *sakiehs*[29] and six ox drivers: Pachon—to Peteeus son of Patynis, oxherd, dr. 32; to six ox drivers likewise for Pachon, three at dr. 16, dr. 48; two others at dr. 14, dr. 28; the remaining one, dr. 24. Equals for the month dr. 132.

> [The remainder of the account includes expenditures for "water pots for the *sakiehs*," "light twine for fastening pots at the *sakiehs*," and miscellaneous other articles.]

26. A water-lifting device consisting of two uprights supporting a horizontal crossbar, on which is balanced a long pole with a bucket at one end and a weight at the other. *Shaduf* is the modern Arabic name for this primitive machine, still in use in Egypt today.

27. Here and in the remainder of this paragraph *men* corresponds to what we today would call *mandays*.

28. For these workmen employed by the month this averages slightly less than the 10 obols per day recorded in the following entry as the wage of day workers.

29. This is the modern Arabic name for the ox-driven wooden water wheels, which, like the *shadufs* (see note 26 above) are still in use in the Egyptian countryside.

A MUNICIPAL FERRY MONOPOLY

OGIS, no. 572

[Myra, Lycia, second or third century]

May good fortune attend! It was decreed by the council and the people, on motion of the chief magistrates: Since as a result of our inability to obtain an acceptable bid for the ferry rights on the river Limyra the revenues are decreased, no one else[30] is permitted to engage in any ferrying either from the Thicket or from the mouth of the harbor or from Andriace, or he will have to pay to the municipality 1,300 *denarii* for each trip, and the [ferry] concessionaire shall have the right to register an attachment[?] against his boat and gear. Only the registered boats and those to which the concessionaire grants permission shall make the crossing, and he shall receive one fourth of every fare and cargo. And if anyone carries a fare on his own, he shall declare it and pay one fourth of every fare, or he will be liable to the aforementioned fine.

INCOME FROM MUNICIPAL LAND

W. H. Pleket, *Epigraphica* (1964), vol. 1, no. 49

[Gazora, Macedonia, A.D. 158]

May good fortune attend! . . . Alcimus son of Taralas moved with explanations that the municipal lands should be planted with grape vines and fruit trees, and that, moreover, there are persons who intend to cultivate them and retain a portion of the yield. The councilmen in consultation deemed his motion to be sound, and they agreed that persons who have already undertaken such cultivation and those who so intend should receive a portion of the yield, as follows: 50 percent of the vines, the other half to go to the treasury of the city; two-thirds of olives; of figs, the rest of the fruits and the pressed olives, the cultivators shall keep the entire yield and nothing shall go to the treasury of the city. When the vote was taken on this motion, the ballots were unanimous. The people approved by show of hands.

---

30. That is, other than those who purchase the right from the city.

LEASE OF MUNICIPAL PROPERTY

Oxyrhynchus Papyrus No. 2,109 (= *Select Papyri*, no. 356); A.D. 261; Adapted
from *LCL*

[Notice by] Aurelius Dioscurides, also known as Sabinus, ex-gymnasiarch, councilman, and, however I am styled, incumbent chief magistrate of the city of Oxyrhynchus, also director of municipal finances. Of
the offer made by the person specified therein for a location belonging
to the city in the Capitol[31] below the East Colonnade with a view to
opening a tavern, a copy is publicly displayed [below], in order that all
may know and those who wish to make better offers may come forward, without prejudice to any kind of right of the city in the matter.
Signed by me. Year 1 of our lords Macrianus and Quietus, Augusti,
Tybi 30.

To Aurelius Dioscurides, also known as Sabinus, ex-gymnasiarch,
incumbent chief magistrate of the city of Oxyrhynchus, also director of
municipal finances, from Aurelius Horio son of Colluthus and Tereus,
of Oxyrhynchus. I voluntarily engage to lease the shop in the city
Capitol below the East Colonnade, with a view to opening a tavern, for
one year from the first day of the coming month Mecheir of the current
first year at a monthly rent of 8 drachmas. If my tender is confirmed, I
am to use the shop with its entrance and exit for the term without
hindrance, and I will pay the rent monthly on the 30th without delay,
and at the end of the term I will surrender the location free from filth
and all uncleanness, and any doors and keys which I received, or will
forfeit the true value of whatever I fail to surrender, right of execution
duly subsisting. This engagement is valid, and in answer to the formal
question concerning it I gave my consent [cf. chapter 2, note 90]. But if
my offer is not accepted, I shall not be bound by this promise. Year 1 of
the Emperors Caesars Titus Fulvius Junius MACRIANUS Pius Felix Augustus and Titus Fulvius Junius QUIETUS Pius Felix Augustus, Tybi 28.

[Signed] I, Aurelius Horio son of Colluthus, have submitted this
tender to lease, and I will pay the rent as aforesaid. I, Aurelius Didymus,
wrote for him as he is illiterate.

31. The municipalities, in imitation of Rome, established precincts of the Capitoline Triad (cf. vol.
1, chapter 1, note 15).

68. THE FOOD PROBLEM

The specter of hunger and famine hovered like a permanent incubus over the cities and towns of the ancient world. In an attempt to cope with the food problem, cities of the Hellenistic world had instituted a regular magistracy expressly charged with procuring grain and regulating its local sale. The population centers of the Roman Empire continued to feel from time to time the pinch of scarcity and high prices. Sometimes in such crises wealthy townsmen provided money to feed the starving. But often some seized the opportunity for profiteering, cornering and hoarding food supplies, and holding out for famine prices. Food riots frequently ensued, necessitating governmental intervention.

One of the prime causes of the recurrent famines was the earmarking of vast quantities of grain to feed the city of Rome and the armies, while throughout the Empire large areas continued to be diverted from the cultivation of cereals to the more profitable production of wine and olive oil—so much so that before the end of the first century the emperors were taking steps to encourage the production of grains in the provinces (cf. §§ 24–25). A contributory cause was the difficulty of overland transport, so that inland towns frequently suffered dearth while grain was available a relatively short distance away.

PERMISSION TO ESTABLISH A MARKET

To operate a market, or fair, individuals and communities needed the sanction of the Roman senate or the emperor. We are told that the Emperor Claudius held markets on his estates (Suetonius, *Life of Claudius* xii. 4). Pliny mentions in one of his *Letters* (book v, no. 4. 1) that "Sollers, a man of praetorian rank, petitioned the Senate to be allowed to establish a market on his estate. His petition was opposed by envoys from Vicetia" —no doubt because there was a market in that town which stood to lose from Sollers' competition.

CIL, vol. VIII, nos. 11,451 and 23,246 (= *FIRA*, vol. I, no. 47)

[Casae, Africa, A.D. 138]

Decree of the senate concerning the market of the Beguensian estate in the territory of Casae. Certified copy from the record of motions made in the senate in the consulship of Canius Junius Niger and Gaius Pomponius Camerinus, in which were recorded the rights of Africanus and what follows.

October 15, at a meeting in the Julian Senate House. Present at the writing were [seven names follow]. Present in the senate were 250[plus] members. The decree of the senate was passed by a division of the house.[32]

Whereas Publius Cassius Secundus and Publius Delphius Peregrinus Alfius Alennius Maximus Curtius Valerianus Proculus Marcus Nonius Mucianus,[33] the consuls, spoke concerning the petition of the friends of Lucilius Africanus, *vir clarissimus,* requesting that he be permitted to establish and maintain market days at Casae in the province of Africa, Beguensian district, territory of the Musulamians, on November 2 and 20 and every month thereafter on the fourth day before the Nones and the twelfth day before the Kalends, [and the consuls asked the senate] what it was pleased to see done;

Concerning this matter the senate decreed as follows: That Lucilius Africanus, *vir clarissimus,* be permitted to establish and maintain a market at Casae in the province of Africa, Beguensian district, territory of the Musulamians, on November 2 and 20 and every month thereafter on the fourth day before the Nones and the twelfth day before the Kalends, and that people from the neighborhood and from outside the district be permitted to gather and assemble there for the purpose of attending market only,[34] without harm or inconvenience to anyone.

Done on October 15 in the consulship of Publius Cassius Secundus and Marcus Nonius Mucianus. [The rest is here omitted.]

A BREAD RIOT

The riot described here may be compared with Dio Chrysostom's account (in his *Discourse* xlvi) of how he and another rich landowner of Prusa (in Bithynia) were nearly lynched by a mob that suspected them of manipulating the grain market to raise prices.

---

32. Cf. vol. 1, § 156. It is interesting to note that the Senate still adhered to its traditional forms of parliamentary procedure.

33. These two sets of names belong to one person, not two. Beginning in the second century it became customary to add to one's own (father-derived) names those of such persons as maternal grandfathers, great-grandfathers, and adoptive fathers.

34. Similar restrictions on assembly of frontier peoples were enforced along the Danube; cf. § 11.

Philostratus, *Life of Apollonius of Tyana*[35] I. xv (abridged); Adapted from *LCL*

When he came to Aspendus in Pamphylia . . . he found nothing but vetch on sale in the market, and the citizens were feeding upon this and on anything else they could get; for the rich men had locked up all the grain and were holding it for export from the country. Consequently an excited crowd of all ages had set upon the chief magistrate and was lighting a fire to burn him alive even though he was clinging to the statues of the emperor, which were at the time more dreaded and a more inviolable sanctuary than that of Zeus in Olympia [cf. § 162, last selection]. . . . Apollonius turned to the bystanders and beckoned to them that they must listen; and they not only held their tongues from wonderment at him, but they placed their fire on the altars that were there. The chief magistrate then plucked up courage and said, "So-and-so and So-and-so," naming several, "are to blame for the famine which has arisen, for they have taken away the grain and are keeping it in different parts of the country." A hue and cry thereupon rose among the Aspendians to make for these men's estates, but Apollonius shook his head to tell them not to do that but rather to summon those who were to blame and obtain the grain from them with their consent. And when they arrived, he very nearly broke out in speech against them, so affected was he by the tears of the crowd—for the children and women had all flocked together, and the old men were groaning as if they were on the point of dying of hunger. However, he respected his vow of silence and wrote his indictment on a writing board, and handed it to the chief magistrate to read aloud; and his indictment ran as follows: "Apollonius to the grain dealers of Aspendus. The earth is the mother of us all, for she is just; but you, because you are unjust, have made her the mother of yourselves alone, and if you do not stop I will not permit you to remain upon her." They were so terrified by these words that they filled the market place with grain, and the city revived.

EMERGENCY MEASURES

In the first of the following edicts the governor of the province of Galatia orders the sale of surplus grain in a famine area and fixes a ceiling price. In the second, the proconsul of Asia steps in to end a bakers' strike with

35. For Philostratus see note 59. Apollonius was a first-century Pythagorean ascetic who carried out a five-year vow of silence and became famous as a holy man.

which the city authorities were unable to cope after, apparently, provoking it by their exacting demands. To assure the steady production of "the staff of life" some towns operated municipal bakeries.

AE, 1925, no. 162*b*

[Antioch, Pisidia, A.D. *c. 93]*

Lucius Antistius Rusticus, legate with rank of praetor of the Emperor Caesar DOMITIAN Augustus Germanicus, declares:

Whereas the duovirs and decurions of the most illustrious colony of Antioch have written to me that on account of the severity of the winter the price of grain has soared, and they have petitioned that the populace be given an opportunity to buy;

Therefore—may good fortune attend!—all who are either citizens or residents of the colony of Antioch shall declare before the duovirs of the colony of Antioch, within thirty days after this edict of mine is posted in public, how much grain each has and in what place, and how much he deducts for seed or for the year's supply of food for his household; and he shall make all the remaining grain available to purchasers of the colony of Antioch. Furthermore, I fix next August 1 as the date of the sale. And if anyone fails to comply, let him know that I shall claim for confiscation whatever is withheld contrary to my edict, reserving a one-eighth share as a reward for informers.

Whereas, furthermore, I am assured that before this prolonged severe winter a *modius* of grain in the colony cost eight or nine *asses,* and it is most unjust for anyone to profiteer from the hunger of his fellow citizens, I forbid the price of grain to exceed one *denarius* per *modius.*[36]

SEG, vol. IV, no. 512

[Ephesus, Asia, second century]

. . . Thus it happens at times that the populace is plunged into disorder and riots by the inexcusable audacity[?] of the bakers' agitation in the market place. Under these circumstances they should by now have been haled into court and have paid the penalty. But since it is necessary to prefer the welfare of the city to the punishment of these individuals, I

---

36. At that, the governor is permitting a maximum price of about twice the prefamine normal price. It is probable that there is a reference to this famine in the New Testament (*Revelation* 6:6): "And I heard a voice, as it were, in the midst of the four animals saying, 'A *choenix* of grain for a *denarius,* and three *choenices* of barley for a *denarius;* and cheat not on the oil and wine.' "

thought it best to bring them to their senses by an edict. Wherefore, I forbid the bakers to assemble in association[37] and their officers to make inflammatory speeches, and I order them to give complete obedience to those in charge of the community's welfare and to provide the city fully with the necessary production of bread. If any of them is caught from this time on either meeting contrary to my orders or leading any riot or agitation, he shall be haled into court and suffer the appropriate punishment; and if anyone dares to hide and continue disrupting the city, he shall in addition be branded on the foot with the word *decuria*,[38] and anyone who harbors any such person shall thereby become liable to the same punishment. [The rest is here omitted.]

69. IMPERIAL INTERVENTION

Dependent in considerable part on the contributions of the wealthy and on other unstable sources of income, and freely disbursed by municipal administrations on nonproductive public works and services such as theaters, baths, festivals, and banquets, many civic treasuries were in a state of chronic insolvency by the second century. To overcome the chaotic effect of such conditions upon the imperial revenues, the central government took, increasingly, a direct hand in local affairs. This development was, it may be noted, in keeping with the growing centralization of administration in general in the hands of the emperors. Beginning with Nerva or Trajan, the emperors frequently appointed their own representatives *(correctores* or *curatores)* to direct the finances of municipalities in difficulties. One of the principal tasks with which Pliny the Younger was charged when sent to govern Bithynia was a systematic reorganization of municipal finances. Three of his letters on this subject are given in the second selection here. Among his other letters, one reported to the emperor that the town of Apamea refused to open its books for his inspection on the ground that it was guaranteed local autonomy in its treaty of alliance with Rome (cf. vol. 1, §§ 132, 134), but Trajan ordered the investigation to be made "at my personal wish without prejudice to their privileges." In another, Pliny suggested a plan whereby members of the municipal council would be compelled to pledge their own property as a means of solving the town's financial problem; though the emperor disapproved this proposal as "inconsistent with the justice of our times," it is in fact entirely in keeping with the already established principle and con-

37. The governor by this act suspends the right of association that the bakers had apparently enjoyed (cf. §§ 51–52).
38. "City council," indicating presumably that he was branded by its order.

ditions of compulsory public services and a harbinger of the more wide-spread compulsion of the third and fourth centuries. It is one of the ironies of Roman history that the municipal status within the Roman body politic, for which Rome's "allies" once fought a war in order to gain citizenship and independence (cf. vol. 1, § 103), ended by placing the cities in even more complete subjection to the authority of Rome.

VESPASIAN'S GRANT TO SABORA

CIL, vol. II, no. 1,423 (=Dessau, no. 6,092=*FIRA*, vol. I, no. 74)

[Sabora, Spain, A.D. *78]*

The Emperor Caesar VESPASIAN Augustus, *pontifex maximus,* holding the tribunician power for the ninth year, acclaimed *imperator* eighteen times, eight times consul, father of his country, sends greetings to the *quattuorviri* [cf. vol. 1, chapter 7, note 34] and decurions of Sabora. Since you inform me that you are impoverished and beset by many difficulties, I permit you to build the town under my name in the plain, as you wish. The revenues which you say you were granted by the deified Augustus I reaffirm; if you desire to add any new ones, you must apply to the proconsul therefor, since I can make no decision if there is no appeal. I received your decree on July 25 and dismissed your envoys on the 29th of the same.[39] Farewell.

The duovirs, Gaius Cornelius Severus and Marcus Septimius Severus, had this inscribed on bronze at public expense.

PLINY IN BITHYNIA

Pliny, *Letters* book x, nos. 17a, 37, 43

[Pliny to the Emperor Trajan]

. . . I am at present examining the expenditures, income, and outstanding debts of the municipality of Prusa, and the more I investigate the more necessary I perceive the examination to be. Many sums of money are detained in private hands for a variety of reasons, and in addition some are disbursed for quite illegitimate expenditures. This, my lord, I write to you immediately upon my arrival.

·   ·   ·   ·

39. This sentence is added to impress the provincials with the promptness with which their petitions are answered by the emperor.

The town of Nicomedia, my lord, has expended 3,329,000 sesterces on an aqueduct, which has been abandoned still unfinished and has even been torn down. Again they disbursed 200,000 sesterces for another aqueduct, but this, too, has been abandoned. So now, after throwing away all that money, they must make a new expenditure in order to have water. I have personally visited a very pure spring from which in my opinion the water ought to be brought on arches, as was tried in the first place, so that it will reach not alone the level and low parts of the city. A very few arches are still standing, and some can also be erected with the hewn stone which has been torn down from the previous structure; some part, I think, will have to be carried out in brick, since that is easier and cheaper. But first of all it is necessary for you to send here an inspector of aqueducts or an engineer, so that what happened may not occur again. This one thing I am certain of, that the usefulness and beauty of the structure will be entirely worthy of your age.

[Trajan in reply approves completing the aqueduct, but wants Pliny to determine and report to him "whose fault it is that Nicomedia has squandered so much money up to now."]

. . . .

On looking into the very great expenditures which the municipality of Byzantium has made, I discovered, my lord, that an envoy is sent to you every year with a decree of greetings, and 12,000 sesterces are allocated for him. Therefore, mindful of your purpose,[40] I judged it proper that the decree should be sent but the envoy kept at home, so that the expense would be lightened and the public duty would at the same time be fulfilled. The same city is charged with 3,000 sesterces as the annual travel allowance for an envoy to go and bring official greetings to the governor of Moesia.[41] This expense, too, I deemed it right to elminiate in the future. I beg you, my lord, to write in reply what you think and deign either to confirm my counsel or correct my error.

[Trajan's reply is a terse approval of Pliny's actions.]

40. To force municipalities to retrench unessential expenditures.
41. Probably because of the trade to Byzantium with the towns and armies in Moesia and as a token of gratitude for protection.

HADRIAN'S GRANT TO STRATONICEA

Dittenberger, no. 837 (= *FIRA*, vol. I, no. 80)

[Stratonicea, Asia, A.D. 127]

The Emperor Caesar Trajanus HADRIAN Augustus, son of the deified Trajan Parthicus, grandson of the deified Nerva, *pontifex maximus,* holding the tribunician power for the eleventh year, three times consul, to the chief magistrates, council, and people of Stratonicea-Hadrianopolis, greeting. You appear to me to be requesting what is just and necessary for your recently constituted city.[42] Therefore, I grant you the revenues derived from your territory; and as for the house of Tiberius Claudius Socrates which is in the city, Socrates shall either repair it or give it up to one of the inhabitants, so that it may not become dilapidated through age and neglect [cf. § 33, first selection]. I have sent these orders also to the proconsul Stertinius Quartus, *vir clarissimus,* and to my procurator Pompeius Severus. Claudius Candidus came [to me] as [your] envoy, and he is to be paid his travel allowance, unless he undertook it at his own expense. Farewell. March 1, from Rome. I, Claudius Candidus, delivered this letter to Lollius Rusticus, the chief magistrate, on May 14 in the assembly.

A TOWN IN MACEDONIA

This Greek inscription from the province of Macedonia contains a reply from the Emperor Antoninus Pius to an embassy regarding matters of municipal finance and administration. The lost beginning of the inscription contained the name of the town, which some scholars have suggested was Parthicopolis, a name presumably commemorating Trajan's successful invasion of the powerful kingdom on Rome's eastern frontier. The small municipal council and its small entry fee bespeak a town of no great size. The year is that of the era dating from the Battle of Actium in 31 B.C.

---

42. The city of Stratonicea was amalgamed with its surrounding territory by Hadrian. This emperor pursued an active policy of urbanization, evidenced by numerous city foundations, especially in the already highly urbanized eastern provinces. Donations of public works, enlargement of city territories, and grants of revenue rights were some of the methods by which he attempted to resuscitate municipal treasuries and stem the fiscal deterioration of towns.

SEG, vol. XIV, no. 479; A.D. 158/159

. . . I grant you permission to impose an additional denarius apiece on free personnel who regularly pay poll tax, so that you may have this too as a ready resource for your needs. Your town councilors shall be eighty [in number] and [upon election] each one shall pay in five hundred Attic drachmas, so that thus you may derive honor from the size of the council and revenue from the moneys they will pay in. Property owners among you, when plaintiffs or defendants, shall come under the jurisdiction of your magistrates [for sums] up to 250 denarii.[43] Your envoys were Demeas son of Paramonus and Crispus son of Tuscus, whose travel expenses you will pay unless they undertook to act gratis.

[The appropriate local ordinance] was drafted and ratified when Valerius Pyrrhus and colleagues were politarchs, year 189.

70. THE IMPERIAL CHILD-ASSISTANCE SYSTEM (ALIMENTA)[44]

In keeping with Augustus' policy of fostering the survival of the Italian stock, the Emperor Nerva in his short reign devised a scheme "for girls and boys born of needy parents to be supported at public expense throughout the towns of Italy" (Aurelius Victor,[45] *Epitome* xii. 4). Implemented by Trajan and extended by succeeding emperors (eventually even to the provinces), this program of child assistance continued in existence for nearly two hundred years, though increasingly impaired by the economic crisis and monetary inflation of the third century. With the establishment of the Dominate the program was terminated, but it was later revived under Church auspices.

The imperial *alimenta* system operated as follows. In each town participating in the program the emperor's privy purse (the fisc) made loans to farm owners, which, to avoid the creation of an excessive burden of debt, were limited to very small fractions of the value of the farms registered as security. The interest on these loans, at 5 percent, was then paid into a special municipal fund earmarked for the support of a predetermined

---

43. Lawsuits involving larger amounts would bypass the local magistrates and go directly to the courts of the Roman provincial administration.

44. See also § 71.

45. Sextus Aurelius Victor wrote, about the middle of the fourth century, a short history of the emperors from Augustus to Constantine. A slightly later work purporting to be an epitome of his *Caesars* actually derives from it only slightly.

number of poor children. Thus, working capital was made available to farmers at less than the normal interest rate, the payment of the interest was virtually assured by the low ratio of the loan to the value of the security, and the income from the loans provided a steady source of funds to help poor farmers raise their families and assure the necessary agricultural labor force. Though it is not specifically stated in the extant sources, these subsidies were presumably paid until boys came of age, at fourteen; for girls the payments may have ceased two years earlier (cf. p. 268). The program entailed a huge outlay of fiscal funds for the loans and for administrative expenses, but there is no evidence that it had more than a palliative effect.

Two extant inscriptions, both on large bronze tablets, contain the records of the loans making up the *alimenta* programs of the town of Veleia (near Parma) in northern Italy and an area near Beneventum in southern Italy.[46] Portions of both of these documents follow. In the first, that of Veleia, the amount of the loan is uniformly about one twelfth, or 8 percent, of the stated value of the land offered as security; in the second the ratio of loan to valuation varies, but does not exceed approximately 12 percent. Apart from the *alimenta,* these inscriptions provide rare and vivid evidence of how small and medium-sized farms, though they had by no means disappeared completely in these parts of Italy, were here too being combined or incorporated into larger estates; in the Veleia register, for example, the names of more than three hundred different farms occur, but they belong to only forty-eight owners (one of them the town of Lucca).

CIL, vol. XI, no. 1,147 (=Dessau, no. 6,675 = *FIRA,* vol. III, no. 116)

[Veleia, A.D. *109–112]*

Liens on properties to the amount of 1,044,000 sesterces, so that through the indulgence of the best and greatest *princeps,* the Emperor Caesar Nerva Trajan Augustus Germanicus Dacicus, boys and girls may receive support [as follows]: legitimate boys, 245 in number, at 16 sesterces each [per month], equals 47,040 sesterces; legitimate girls, 34 in number, at 12 sesterces each [per month], equals 4,896 sesterces; illegitimate boy, 1, 144 sesterces [per year]; illegitimate girl, 1, 120 sesterces [per year]; total, 52,200 sesterces, which equals 5 percent interest on the aforementioned principal.

Gaius Volumnius Memor and Volumnia Alce, through Volumnius Diadumenus their freedman, registered the Quintiac-Aurelian farm and

---

46. A group of happy parents and *alimenta*-supported children is depicted in one of the reliefs decorating a triumphal arch of Trajan erected in A.D. 114 and still standing at Benevento.

Muletas Hill with its woods, which is in the territory of Veleia, Ambitrebian district, bounded by Marcus Mommeius Persicus, Satrius Severus, and the community,[47] worth 108,000 sesterces; he is to receive 8,692 sesterces and put up the aforementioned farm as security.

Marcus Virius Nepos registered country properties worth 310,545 sesterces, deducting rentals.[48] He is to receive 25,353 sesterces and to put up as security the Planian farm, which is in the territory of Veleia, Junonian district, bounded by Priscus Palamenus, Velleius Severus, and the community, and which he registered at 14,000 sesterces; the Suigian farm with three cabins, aforementioned district, bounded by Gaius Calidius, Velleius Proculus, and the community, which he registered at 20,000 sesterces; the Petronian farm, district and boundaries aforementioned, which he registered at 4,000 sesterces; [there follow the names of many more farms, to make up the total valuation of 310,545 sesterces]. . . .

Gaius Coelius Verus, through Onesimus his slave, registered country properties in the territories of Placentia, Veleia, and Libarna worth 843,879 sesterces, deducting rentals and the properties which Cornelius Gallicanus and Pomponius Bassus[49] placed under lien. He is to receive 67,850 sesteres and put up as security one half of the Collacteran farm . . . [the names of many other farms follow] . . . also one third of the Bitinian-Albitemian estate,[50] which is in the territory of Veleia and Luca, Albensian, Minervian, and Statiellian districts, bounded by the town of Luca, the Annius brothers, and the community, and which he registered at 350,000 sesterces for [a loan of] 30,000 sesterces; [and many more farms]. . . .

Likewise the liens on properties taken by Cornelius Gallicanus to the amount of 72,000 sesterces, so that through the indulgence of the best and greatest *princeps,* the Emperor Caesar Nerva TRAJAN Augustus Germanicus,[51] boys and girls may receive support [as follows]: legitimate

47. This is generally interpreted as meaning a public road.

48. That is, lands held on lease are registered, for *alimenta*-loan purposes, at their valuation less the annual rental.

49. These were agents of the emperor in the establishment of smaller child-assistance funds some years earlier; see the next paragraph.

50. The Latin word here is *saltus,* which is the term used to designate the imperial estates of North Africa (see § 25). However, it may be that the word is used here in its earlier meaning of "pasture land."

51. Since Trajan's epithet Dacicus is here omitted, the date of this smaller *alimenta* undertaking must be earlier than A.D. 102.

boys, 18 in number, at 16 sesterces [per month], equals 3,456 sesterces; legitimate girl, 12 sesterces [per month]; total of both 3,600 sesterces, which equals 5 percent interest on the aforementioned amount.

[There follows a list of properties like the preceding, but much shorter, in keeping with the much smaller sum of money involved.]

CIL, vol. IX, no. 1,455 (=Dessau, no. 6,509 = *FIRA*, vol. III, no. 117)

[Vicinity of Benevento, A.D. 101]

In the consulship of the Emperor Caesar Nerva Trajan Augustus Germanicus (for the fourth time) and Quintus Articuleius Paetus . . . in accordance with the ordinance of the best and greatest *princeps,* the following[?] Baebian Ligurians[52] offered properties as security . . . so that through his indulgence boys and girls may receive support. . . .

By Crispia Restituta: the Pomponian farms, in the territory assigned to Beneventum, Aequan district in the Ligurian area, adjoining Nasidius Vitalis, valued at 50,000 sesterces for [a loan of] 3,520 sesterces

88 sesterces[53]

By Lucius Naeratius Diadumenus: the Rubrian farms, in the Beneventan territory, Ligurian district, valued at 34,000 sesterces for [a loan of] 1,000 sesterces   25 sesterces

.   .   .   .   .

By Neratius Corellius: the Paccian farms and cabins of Aurelianus, adjoining Julius Saturninus, valued at 22,000 sesterces for [a loan of] 2,000 sesterces   50 sesterces

.   .   .   .   .

By Gnaeus Marcius Rufinus: the Marcian and Satrian farms, valued at 130,000 sesterces; also the Julian farms, valued at 14,000 sesterces; also the Avillian farms, valued at 42,000 sesterces; also the Vitellian, Nasennian, and Marcellian farms, adjoining Suellius Flaccus, valued at 120,000 sesterces for [a loan of] 10,000 sesterces; also the Curian and Satrian farms, Herculanean district, adjoining Tettius Etruscus, valued at 35,000 sesterces for [a loan of] 3,000 sesterces; also the Albian farms with cabins, Meflan district, adjoining Nonius Restitutus, valued at 110,000

52. In 180 B.C. the Apuan Ligurians on the Riviera were subjugated by the consuls Publius Cornelius and Marcus Baebius, and 40,000 of them were deported to Samnium, where they were known thereafter as Cornelian or Baebian Ligurians.

53. The figure placed alongside each entry, being 2.5 percent of the amount of the loan, is presumably the interest for a half year (cf. the introduction to this section).

sesterces for [a loan of] 10,000 sesterces; also—put up as security for the ninth time—the Caesian farms, in the Beneventan territory, Tucian district, adjoining Messius Aper, valued at 50,000 sesterces for [a loan of] 3,000 sesterces. Equals 466,000 sesterces[54] for [a loan of] 42,440 sesterces   1,061 sesterces

By Lucius Tettius Etruscianus: the Albian, Amarantian, Surian, and Annian farms, in the Beneventan territory, Saeculan district, adjoining Marius Restitutus, valued at 150,000 sesterces for [a loan of] 12,000 sesterces   300 sesterces

By Publius Titius Ajax: the Veiaean farms, in the Beneventan territory, Roman district in the Ligurian area, adjoining our emperor, valued at 14,000 sesterces for [a loan of] 1,000 sesterces   25 sesterces

.   .   .   .   .

By Clodius Conveniens: the Primigenian, Albian, Sutorian, and Suellian farms, Salutarian district, adjoining Suellius Flaccus and Rufus, purchased at 109,000 sesterces for [a loan of] 9,000 sesterces   225 sesterces

[The remaining entries follow the same pattern.]

71. PRIVATE PHILANTHROPY

In addition to the expenses that they incurred on the assumption and in the discharge of municipal offices and priesthoods, the wealthy frequently regaled their fellow townspeople with banquets, entertainments, and largess to celebrate festive occasions such as births, weddings, and holidays, and they even left bequests for such celebrations to be held annually in memory of themselves. Very common too, under imperial encouragement and example, were donations or bequests to native towns or other places with which the donor had ties of property, family, or sentiment, for public works and embellishments. In the second century many of these local philanthropists followed the emperors' lead and established *alimenta* foundations for the support of poor children in their home towns. These public benefactors were frequently honored with the title of "patron" of the community. Inscribed plaques and bases of statues erected to them by the towns have been found by the hundreds throughout the Roman Empire. See further §§ 72–73.

54. The total should be 501,000 sesterces; obviously the item of 35,000 sesterces was overlooked in the addition.

CIL, vol. II, no. 3,270

[Cazlona (Castulo), Spain, first century (?)]

To Quintus Toreus Culleo son of Quintus, imperial procurator of the province of Baetica—because he at his own expense repaired the town walls dilapidated through old age; gave a plot of ground to build baths; paved the road leading through the mountain passes of Castulo to Sisapo,[55] which had been washed out by incessant rains; erected statues of Venus Genetrix[56] and Cupid at the theater; remitted the sum of 10,000,000 sesterces which was owed him by the municipality and even gave a banquet to the public in addition—the municipality of Castulo held circus games for two days and dedicated this in gratitude.

CIL, vol. II, no. 4,514 (=Dessau, no. 6,957)

[Barcelona (Barcino), Spain, second century]

Lucius Caecilius Optatus son of Lucius, of the Papirian tribe, centurion of Legion VII Gemina Felix and centurion of Legion XV Apollinaris, honorably discharged by the Emperors MARCUS AURELIUS Antoninus [Augustus] and [LUCIUS] Aurelius VERUS Augustus, included by the town of Barcino among those exempted from public charges, attained the offices of aedile, duovir three times, flamen of Rome and the deified emperors. He left a legacy to the municipality of Barcino as follows: I give, bequeath, and desire to have given 7,500 *denarii*, with the six-percent interest on which I desire a boxing contest to be held each year on June 10 at a cost of up to 250 *denarii*, and on the same day 200 *denarii* worth of oil to be supplied to the public in the public baths. I desire these bequests to be carried out on condition that my freedmen, and also the freedmen of my freedmen and freedwomen, who attain the honor of the board of six[57] be excused from all the obligations of the office. But if any of them is assigned such burdens, then I order the said 7,500 *denarii* to be transferred to the municipality of Tarraco [modern Tarragona], with the same program of shows as aforementioned to be held at Tarraco.

---

55. Modern Almadén. The road was important for the transportation of mine products (see § 23).
56. "Venus the Procreatress" of the Julian imperial line.
57. These were the Augustales, on whom see introduction to § 48. Their number in most municipalities was six.

Pliny, *Letters* book vi, no. 34

Gaius Plinius to his dear Maximus, greeting.

You were right to promise a combat of gladiators to our good friends of the people of Verona, by whom you have so long been loved, admired, and honored. It was from there, too, that you took your wife most dear and lovely, to whose memory some public monument or show was due, preferably this exhibition, which is especially appropriate for commemorating the dead. Besides, you were so unanimously pressed to do so, that to refuse would have seemed not constancy but obstinacy. It was a distinguished gesture, too, that you were so ready, so generous in providing them; for these, too, are the marks of a noble spirit. I am sorry the many African panthers you had purchased did not arrive in time; but even though they were delayed by bad weather and failed to appear, it was nevertheless understood, as you deserved, that it was not your fault that you did not exhibit them. Farewell.

Dittenberger, no. 850

[Ephesus, Asia, A.D. 145]

The Emperor Caesar Titus Aelius Hadrianus ANTONINUS Augustus, son of the deified Hadrian, grandson of the deified Trajan Parthicus, descendant of the deified Nerva, *pontifex maximus,* holding the tribunician power for the eighth year, twice acclaimed *imperator,* four times consul, father of his country, to the chief magistrates, council, and people of Ephesus, greeting. The munificence which Vedius Antoninus lavishes upon you I learned of not so much from your letter as from his own. For, desiring to obtain assistance from me for the embellishment of the public works which he offered you, he made known to me how many and what great buildings he is adding to the city,[58] but you do not properly appreciate him. I granted him all he requested, and I welcomed the fact that he prefers, not the usual method of those participating in public affairs, who for the sake of immediate popularity expend their munificence on shows and doles and prizes for games, but means whereby he hopes to make the city more stately in the future. Documents transmitted by Claudius Julianus, *vir clarissimus,* proconsul. Farewell.

58. Among these buildings was an Odeum (music hall), in the ruins of which this inscription was found.

PHILANTHROPY IN THE GRAND MANNER

One of the most noted philanthropists of all time was the fabulously wealthy Athenian Herodes Atticus, who lived under the "Good Emperors" of the second century, held the consulship twice, and was a competent sophist in addition. The munificence of this man and his family extended to numerous Greek cities besides their native Athens, notably the famous sanctuaries at Delphi, Eleusis, and Olympia, where several of their statue bases have been found.

Philostratus,[59] *Lives of the Sophists* II. i (abridged); Adapted from *LCL*

No man used his wealth to better purpose. . . . The sources of his wealth were many and derived from several families, but the greatest were the fortunes that came from his father [Atticus] and his mother. . . . This Atticus [the father], was also distinguished for his lordly spirit. As an instance, at a time when his son Herodes was overseer of the free cities of Asia,[60] he observed that Troy was ill supplied with baths and that the inhabitants drew muddy water from their wells and had to dig cisterns to catch rain water. Accordingly, he wrote to the Emperor Hadrian to ask him not to allow an ancient city, conveniently near the sea, to perish from lack of water, but to bestow 3,000,000 drachmas upon them for a water supply, since he had already bestowed on mere villages many times that sum. The emperor approved of his advice in the letter as being in accordance with his own disposition and appointed Herodes himself to take charge of the water project. But when the outlay had reached the sum of 7,000,000 drachmas and the officials who governed Asia kept writing to the emperor that it was a scandal that the tribute of five hundred cities should be spent on the fountain of one city, the emperor expressed his disapproval of this to Atticus; whereupon Atticus replied in the most lordly fashion in the world, "Do not, O Emperor, allow yourself to be irritated over such trifles. The amount spent in excess of 3,000,000 I am presenting to my son, and my son will present it to the city." His will, moreover, in which he bequeathed to

---

59. Flavius Philostratus (A.D. c. 170–c. 250), one of a family of sophists and a favorite of the Empress Julia Domna (wife of Septimius Severus), wrote several works, the most important of which are the *Life of Apollonius of Tyana* and the *Lives of the* [second-century] *Sophists.*

60. This office, to which he was appointed by the emperor, is an example of the increasing imperial supervision of municipal affairs (cf. § 69).

the people of Athens 100 drachmas annually for every citizen, proclaims the man's magnanimity, which he exercised also in other ways. He would often sacrifice a hundred oxen to the goddess [Athena] in a single day and entertain at the sacrificial feast the whole population of Athens by tribes and families. And whenever the festival of Dionysus came around . . . he would furnish wine to drink for citizens and strangers alike as they lay in the Ceramicus on couches of ivy leaves. . . .

Herodes held the office of eponymous archon[61] at Athens, and the charge of the Panhellenic festival; and when he was offered the crowning honor of the charge of the Panathenaic festival he made this announcement: "I shall welcome you, O Athenians, and those Hellenes that shall attend, and the athletes that are to compete, in a stadium of pure white marble." In accordance with this promise he completed within four years the stadium on the other side of the Ilissus, a monument beyond all other marvels, for there is no theater that can rival it. . . . Herodes also erected for the Athenians the theater in memory of Regilla,[62] roofing it with cedar, though this wood is considered costly even for making statues. These two monuments, then, are at Athens, and they are such as exist nowhere else in the Roman Empire. Worthy of mention also are the roofed theater which he built for the Corinthians, far inferior indeed to the one at Athens but still among the few noteworthy ones anywhere, and the statues at the Isthmus—the colossus of the Isthmian god, that of Amphitrite, and the others—with which he filled the sanctuary; nor must I pass over the dolphin sacred to Melicertes. He also dedicated the stadium at Delphi to the Pythian god, and the aqueduct at Olympia to Zeus, and, for the Thessalians and Greeks around the Maliac Gulf, the swimming pools at Thermopylae that heal the sick. Further, he colonized Oricum in Epirus, which by this time had fallen into decay, and also Canusium in Italy, which he made habitable by giving it a much-needed water supply. And he benefited the cities of Euboea and the Peloponnesus and Boeotia in various ways.

---

61. The chief archon, by whose name the year was designated at Athens.

62. His wife. The theater was the Odeum (music hall), considerable remains of which may still be seen in Athens.

IG, vol. XIV, no. 1,392 (=Dittenberger, No. 858)

[Rome, after A.D. 161]

. . . Herodes erected this also to be a memorial of his misfortune and of his wife's virtue. But it is not her tomb. Her body is in Greece and now with her husband. His son by her was proposed to the senate by the Emperor Antoninus, called Pius by his fatherland and by all, and by decree of the senate was enrolled in Rome among the patricians.

.　　　.　　　.　　　.

This Greek inscription of 117 very long lines of text recites the past benefactions bestowed by Gaius Julius Demosthenes upon his native city of Termessus in Asia Minor and memorializes the three-week-long festival of cultural events that he now endows. The terms of his gift are specified in great detail, including the amount and use to be made of the endowment funds, the ceremonies to be performed, and the precise dates and money prizes of each contest. An abridged translation of this long inscription follows.

Vestigia (1988), 39; A.D. 125

i

The Emperor Caesar, son of the deified Trajanus Parthicus grandson of the deified Nerva Germanicus, Trajanus HADRIAN Augustus, *pontifex maximus,* holding the tribunician power for the eighth year, thrice consul, to the magistrates, council and people of Termessus, greeting. I approve Gaius Julius Demosthenes for his generosity towards you, and I confirm the cultural competition which he promised you. He himself will pay the costs from his own resources. And the penalties which he has fixed for those violating the provisions of his bounty are to be valid. . . . Farewell. Four days before the Kalends of September, [sent] from Ephesus.

ii

[Date.] I, Gaius Julius Demosthenes son of Apollonius, of the Fabian tribe, *prytanis* and secretary of the council of Oenoanda, having loved my native city most dear from earliest childhood; and having not only maintained but even exceeded the high-mindedness of my ancestors toward her both in lowering food prices in the annual sales which I arrange . . . and in having built a food market and three stoas in front of it (two at street level and one with an upper storey), having spent, including the purchase of the houses [whose razing] made way for the work, over 15,000 *denarii;* and wishing to leave behind for my native city, like these works, also a permanent endowment fund, I [now] announce a theatrical festival to be called the Demosthenia, which will be mounted beginning three years from now . . . for which festival I or my heirs will donate 1,000 *denarii* in the month of Dius beginning with the coming year . . . which *denarii* are to be lent out at interest every three years. . . . As the total, including the interest of the triennium . . . will amount to 4,450 *denarii,* as prizes of the contests there shall be given to the victors [various amounts from 150 to 1,900 *denarii* are specified, with any surplus] to be given as honoraria to the councilmen and to others honored with allotments of public grain . . . chosen by lot to a total of 500 in number, so that each of them receives 3 *den.;* and the remaining 300 *den.* and any additional sum accruing from set-asides shall be divided among the citizens outside the council, and the freedmen, and the resident aliens.

In the election of magistrates of the year before the festival it will be necessary to choose from among the councilmen a festival director, who will expend none of his own money. . . .[63]

[The following schedule is then detailed for the month of Artemisios.]

DAYS	EVENTS	WINNER'S PRIZES (*denarii*)
1	trumpeters and heralds	50 each
2–4	none: days of council and assembly meetings	
5	writers of prose panegyrics	75
6	none: market day	
7	poets	75
8, 9	flute accompanists (of choruses)	1st pl.: 125 2d pl.: 75

63. In many places the office was a liturgy, which required the incumbent to defray the expenses out of his own pocket.

DAYS	EVENTS	WINNER'S PRIZES (*denarii*)
10, 11	writers of comedy	1st pl.: 200 2d pl.: 100
12	none: "sacrifice to our ancestral Apollo"	
13, 14	writers of tragedy	1st pl.: 250 2d pl.: 125
15	none: "second sacrifice to our ancestral Apollo"	
16, 17	citharists	1st pl.: 300 2d pl.: 150
18	"open to all"	1st pl.: 300 2d pl.: 150[a]
19, 20, 21	hired performances, incl. mimes, recitals, and spectacles	budget: 600
22	"naked contests of citizens"	budget: 150 per contestant

[a] Plus 25 *denarii* to the scenery handler.

iii

[Date.] . . . regarding the matters pertaining to the festival of the Demosthenia established to be held in our midst and regarding the arrangements for all matters relating to it, there came forward our most eminent citizen who ordained the festival, Julius Demosthenes, a most high-minded man foremost in worth, family and character, not only in his native city but also in the province; in addition to all the other benefits which he, its founder[64] and incessant benefactor, showered upon the city, for the quinquennial cultural festival which he himself has established from his private funds for all eternity he has announced that he has had made from his private funds and has dedicated to the city both a gold crown with the faces in relief of the Emperor Nerva Trajanus HADRIAN Caesar Augustus and of our ancestral god Apollo our guide — which crown the festival director shall wear — and a silver-clad altar bearing an inscription of the dedicator himself;

[Therefore,] the council commends the abovementioned (?) man for

64. An honorific title.

his outstanding good will to his native city and his current generosity and his unsurpassed high-mindedness and his piety toward the emperors, and honors him with every honor, and in order that the festival be adorned in every way and that the piety toward the Emperor who has proclaimed it be most complete, [the council] votes the following:

[The] festival director shall wear the abovementioned gold crown and a purple robe, and at the beginning of the New Year he shall perform the first step by carrying out the reverences toward the Emperor and the ancestral gods on the 1st of the month of Dius and marching in procession with the other magistrates. . . ,

and in [the ensuing] year the festival director shall choose from among the councilmen three festival officials who shall see to the market during the festival, having the power to inscribe prices for the purchasables of the food supply and approve them and dispose of the commodities bought for the food supply and penalize those disobeying,

and likewise he shall choose also ten imperial-cult attendants who, wearing white clothing and crowns of celery,[65] shall lift up and bring forward and parade the imperial effigies and that of our ancestral Apollo and the aforementioned sacred altar, and likewise he shall choose also twenty whipbearers, who in white garments and with shields and whips . . . will see to good deportment in the theater as they are assigned by the festival director, the choice of all these to be made from the citizens. . . .

[Next, sacrifices of oxen are specified, to be contributed on festival days by the festival director, the several city officials (civic and religious), and some two dozen dependent villages. Failure to carry out this obligation is subject to a penalty of 300 drachmas.]

. . . There shall be a suspension of taxation during all the days of the festival on all things for sale and sacrifice and purchasables entering, imported or exported. . . . Regarding the suspension of taxation during the festival and the [five-year] immunity of the festival director [from holding other offices or liturgies], it was voted that a petition [requesting approval] be presented to his Excellency the governor Flavius Aper. . . .[66]

[The governor's reply:] The festival director designated for this competition may have a five-year immunity, and there may be a suspension of taxation for the days of the competition, provided you see to it that

65. Such crowns were worn by victors in the Nemean and Isthmian Games in Greece.
66. Marcus Flavius Aper went on to become consul in A.D. 130.

the revenues of the city are nothing diminished. [The names of the envoys are recorded.]

CHILD ASSISTANCE FUNDS (ALIMENTA)

Alimenta funds established by private philanthropy are attested in inscriptions from several places in Italy and from Spain and North Africa. Representative examples of these will be found under this and the following caption. An interesting forerunner of these child-assistance foundations is the grant of Helvius Basila to his native town of Atina in Latium, recorded in the inscription immediately following.

CIL, vol X, no. 5,056 (=Dessau, no. 977)

[Atina, Italy, middle of first century]

To Titus Helvius Basila son of Titus, aedile, praetor, proconsul, imperial legate, who bequeathed to the people of Atina 400,000 sesterces; out of the income from this bequest their children are to be given grain until they reach maturity, and thereafter 1,000 sesterces each. Procula, his daughter, set this up.

CIL, vol. X, no. 6,328 (=Dessau, no. 6, 278)

[Tarracina, Italy, second century]

Caelia Macrina daughter of Gaius left 300,000 sesterces in her will for the construction of this monument, and . . . thousand sesterces for its decoration and upkeep. She also left 1,000,000 sesterces to the town of Tarracina in memory of her son Macer, so that out of the income from this money child-assistance subsides might be paid to one hundred boys and one hundred girls — to each citizen boy 5 *denarii* each month, to each citizen girl 4 *denarii* each month, the boys up to sixteen years, the girls up to fourteen years — in such a way that the payments should always be received by groups of a hundred boys and a hundred girls.[67]

---

67. In this inscription and the next, interest at 5 percent on the principal of the fund exceeds the total of the *alimenta* payments stipulated by roughly one sixth. This difference, which some scholars have sought to explain and others to eliminate by emendation of the text, was perhaps intended to allow for the cost of administering the program and to provide some leeway in case the fund did not produce the full amount of anticipated income in any given year. It is interesting to note too that in both inscriptions the payments to the girls terminate two years sooner than the payments to the boys.

CIL, vol. VIII, no. 1,641 (=Dessau, no. 6,818)

[Sicca, Numidia, A.D. 169–180]

To Publius Licinius Papirianus son of Marcus, of the Quirine tribe, imperial procurator of revenues of the Emperors Caesar MARCUS AURE-LIUS Antoninus Augustus Germanicus Sarmaticus Maximus, father of his country, and of the deified [Lucius] Verus, to whom the most illustrious senate of Sicca because of his services. . . .

"To my fellow townsmen of Cirta Sicca, most dear to me, I desire to give 1,300,000 sesterces. I commit this to your trust, my dearest fellow townsmen, so that out of the five-percent interest on this sum three hundred boys and two hundred girls may be supported each year, the boys from the age of three to the age of fifteen, each boy to receive 2½ *denarii* per month, the girls from the age of three to the age of thirteen, 2 *denarii*. Moreover, residents as well as townspeople are to be chosen, provided they are residents who remain domiciled within the confines of our colony. It will be best, if you approve, for them to be chosen by the duovirs of each year; and care should be taken to fill the place of each grown-up or deceased child promptly, so that the full number may always be supported.

THE YOUNGER PLINY'S PHILANTHROPIES

CIL, vol. V, no. 5,262 (=Dessau, no. 2,927)

[Como, Italy, early second century]

This inscription reciting Pliny's career and philanthropies was placed by his hometown of Comum on the baths built with Pliny's bequest.

Gaius Plinius Caecilius Secundus [born Publius Caecilius Secundus but adopted by his uncle, the Elder Pliny] son of Lucius, of the Oufentine tribe; consul; augur; legate with rank of praetor in the province of Pontus and Bithynia sent to that province with consular power in accordance with a decree of the senate by the Emperor Caesar Nerva TRAJAN Augustus Germanicus Dacicus, father of his country; commissioner of the bed and banks of the Tiber and of the sewers of the city; prefect of the treasury of Saturn; prefect of the soldiers' bonus fund; praetor; tribune of the plebs; quaestor of the emperor; member of the board of six of the Roman *equites;* military tribune of Legion III Gallica; member of the board of fifteen for judging lawsuits. He left . . . sesterces in his will for the construction of baths, with an additional

300,000[plus?] sesterces for decoration, and in addition to that 200,000 sesterces for upkeep; and for the support of his freedmen, a hundred persons, he likewise bequeathed to the municipality 1,866,666 sesterces, the income from which he desired to have applied thereafter [i.e., after the freedmen have died] to an annual banquet for the public. In his lifetime he also gave 500,000 sesterces for the support of the boys and girls of the lower class,[68] and also a library and 100,000 sesterces for the upkeep of the library.

Pliny, *Letters* book IV, no. 13 (abridged)

Gaius Plinius to his dear Cornelius Tacitus, greeting. . . .

When I was in my native town recently, a young lad, the son of one of my fellow townsmen, came to pay his respects to me. "Do you go to school?" I asked. "Certainly," he replied. "Where?" "At Milan" [about eighty miles away]. "Why not here?" "Because," rejoined his father, who was with him and had in fact brought the boy, "we have no teachers here." "Why no teachers?" I asked. "Surely it would be tremendously to the interest of you who are fathers" (and quite opportunely several fathers were listening) "that your sons should by all means have their schooling here. For where could they live more happily than in their native town, or be kept under better control than under the eyes of their parents, or at less expense than at home? It is no greater task, certainly, to collect the money to hire teachers, and you can apply toward their salaries what you now spend for [the boys'] lodgings, travel, and the things that have to be paid for when one is away from home (and away from home everything costs money). Indeed I, who do not yet have children, am ready to give for the benefit of the municipality, as if for a daughter or parent, one third of any sum it will please you to assemble. I would even promise the whole if I were not afraid that such an endowment might one day be tampered with through political corruption, as I see happen in many places where teachers are hired by the municipality. This danger can be met by only one remedy, namely, if the right of hiring is left to the parents alone and scrupulous care for choosing is instilled in them by the necessity of contributing. . . . Then

68. Pliny tells in one of his *Letters* (book VII, no. 18) how he set up this *alimenta* fund: "In lieu of 500,000 sesterces, which I had promised for the support of freeborn boys and girls, I deeded some land of mine worth far more to the public administrator and took it back on a rental basis to pay 30,000 sesterces a year. By this means the municipality's principal is secure and the income assured, and the land itself, inasmuch as [the income it produces] far exceeds the rent, will always find a master to work it." In this way Pliny retained the use of his land during his lifetime and Como received annually the equivalent of 6 percent interest on 500,000 sesterces.

agree among yourselves, unite, and draw increased spirit from mine, for I am desirous that what I shall have to contribute shall be as large as possible. . . ."

I thought it necessary to repeat all this in detail and from the very beginning, as it were, so that you might the better understand how glad I should be if you would undertake what I request. Now then, I request, and in keeping with the importance of the matter I beg, that you look around, among the great number of students who come to you out of admiration of your genius, for teachers whom we can solicit — on this condition, however, that I do not make a binding contract with anyone, for I leave complete freedom of choice to the parents. They shall judge, they shall select. For myself I claim only the trouble and the expense.

Pliny, Letters book IV, no. 1 (abridged)

Gaius Plinius to Fabatus, his dear grandfather-in-law, greeting.

There is a town near my estate called Tifernum-on-Tiber [cf. § 24, fifth selection] which, with more good will than good sense, chose me as its patron when I was still practically a boy. They celebrate my arrivals, express sadness at my departures, rejoice in my honors. To express my thanks — for nothing is more shameful than to be outdone in affection — I have built a temple in this place at my own expense; and since it is completed, it is really irreligious to delay the dedication of it any longer. We shall therefore be there on the day of the dedication, which I have decided to celebrate with a public banquet.

A PRINCELY BENEFACTOR

In these two inscriptions the city of Apamea in Syria honors, for his many benefactions, a local Roman citizen descended from the client kings who used to rule the area prior to its annexation by Rome.

AE, 1976, nos. 677 and 678; c. A.D. 110

i

For the health of the Emperor Nerva TRAJAN Caesar Augustus Germanicus Dacicus, Lucius Julius Agrippa son of Gaius of the Fabian tribe, who has royal honors and ancestors inscribed in bronze on the Capitol as allies of Rome, who also, while enjoying exemption from liturgy, has voluntarily displayed every generosity, at his own expense buying the plot and founding the baths and the basilica thereon and the portico in front of those [buildings] with all their decoration and works of bronze, dedicated them to his native city in the governorship of Julius Bassus, propraetorian legate of the Emperor.

ii

[The beginning is lost.] . . . [who while enjoying] the rights derived from his ancestors and his own abovementioned exemption from liturgy among the other honors inscribed in bronze tablets on the Capitol in Rome, [nevertheless] performed magistracies and liturgies and [other] generosities for his native city: he was priest; he was a generous markets commissioner, providing grain for six months at an expenditure of _____ silver *denarii;* he provided oil [for the gymnasium]; he built several miles of the _____ aqueduct; he was an exceptional city secretary, himself requesting the post for a year and choosing his colleagues, and in the same year he took charge of policing and grain distribution, founded the baths and the portico on the square in front of them and the adjacent basilica, bought at his own expense the entire plot of land required, and erected in the said baths bronze works of art, viz. a Theseus and the Minotaur, and an Apollo with Olympus and Scythes and Marsyas; he often went, at no expense to the city, on embassies to the emperors at Rome and the governors of the province.

Both on his father's and on his mother's side he had many esteemed and generous ancestors, including tetrarchs invested with royal honors, most notably Dexander, the first priest [of the imperial cult] in the province, his great-grandfather, who by the deified Augustus on account of his friendship and loyalty to the Roman people was by decree inscribed as friend and ally in bronze tablets on the Capitol, in which tablets are mentioned also the other exceptional honors granted to him and his family, of which tablets a copy was deposited in the archives here on Xandicus 28 of year _____, and he [Dexander] was honored by our city in a decree of the council and people on Peritios 27, in which decree. . . . [The rest is lost.]

72. PATRONS OF MUNICIPALITIES

From the beginning of the Empire it was very common for local councils to adopt prominent personages as patrons to protect the interests of the municipality. It was possible for such an individual to be patron of several municipalities and for a community to have a number of patrons. Numerous bronze patronage tablets, presented to patrons in recognition of their acceptance of the relationship, have survived.

CIL, vol. V, no. 4,919 (=Dessau, no. 6,100)

[Vicinity of Brescia, Italy, A.D. 27]

In the consulship of Marcus Crassus Frugi and Lucius Calpurnius Piso, February 11, the municipality of Themetra in Africa contracted a patronage relationship with Gaius Silius Aviola son of Gaius, of the Fabian tribe, and chose him, his children, and their descendants as patrons for themselves, their children, and descendants. Gaius Silius Aviola son of Gaius, of the Fabian tribe, accepted the people of the municipality of Themetra, their children, and descendants for himself, and his children, and their descendants under his protection and patronage. Done by Banno son of Himilo, *sufes,*[69] and by Azdrubal son of Baisillex and Iddibal son of Bosthar, envoys.

CIL, vol. VIII, no. 8,837 (=Dessau, no. 6,103)

[North Africa, A.D. 55]

In the consulship of Nero Claudius Caesar Augustus Germanicus and Lucius Antistius Vetus, August 1, Quintus Julius Secundus son of Quintus, of the Quirine tribe, legate with rank of praetor, contracted a patronage relationship with the decurions and citizens of the colony Julia Augusta Tupusuctu, [composed of veterans] of Legion VII, and received them under his protection and patronage for himself, his children, and their descendants. Done by the envoys Quintus Caecilius Firmanus son of Quintus, of the Palatine tribe, and Marcus Pomponius Vindex son of Marcus, of the Quirine tribe.

CIL, vol. XI, no. 4,815 (=Dessau, No. 6,638)

[Spoleto, Italy]

Gaius Torasius Severus son of Gaius, of the Horatian tribe, *quattuorvir* with judicial power [cf. vol. 1, chapter 7, note 32], augur, built this

---

69. It is interesting to note the survival of the Punic title for the chief magistrate, as well as of Punic personal names.

[probably the public baths] in his own name and in the name of his son, Publius Meclonius Proculus Torasianus, pontiff, on his own land and at his own expense. He likewise gave to the community for celebrating the birthday of his son 250,000 sesterces, out of the income from which on August 30 annually the decurions are to hold a public banquet and the townspeople who are present receive eight sesterces apiece. Likewise he gave to the board of six priests of Augustus and the priests of the Lares of Augustus and the block captains[70] 120,000 sesterces, so that out of the income from this sum they might have a public repast on the same day. Because of his services to the municipality the council of decurions adopted him as patron of the municipality.

73. The Municipal Aristocracy

See Introduction to § 71.

CIL, vol. XIV, no. 3,014 (=Dessau, no. 6,252)

[Praeneste, Italy]

To Gnaeus Voesius Aper son of Gnaeus, quaestor, aedile, duovir, flamen of the deified Augustus, member of the board of six priests of Augustus, commissioner of the grain supply for three years in succession, commissioner of the public gladiatorial exhibition three times — because during the time of his public offices and commissionerships he made very great contributions with fullest zeal and munificence to the enjoyment and welfare of the people and also presented a public gladiatorial exhibition and a *spoliarium*[71] constructed on land purchased at his own expense. Because of his services, at the request of the people it was decreed to erect a statue to him at public expense. By decree of the decurions.

CIL, vol. VIII, no. 22,737 (=Dessau, no. 6,780)

[Gigthis, North Africa]

To Marcus Servilius Draco Albucianus son of Publius, of the Quirine tribe, duovir, lifetime flamen — because, in addition to his many services to the town and his most generous acts of munificence, he undertook at his own expense two embassies to Rome to secure the greater

70. All these were freedmen associated with the cult of the emperors; cf. introduction to § 48.
71. A place where the bodies of slain gladiators were stripped of clothing and equipment.

Latin rights and finally brought back favorable news — the council decreed that [this statue] be erected with public funds. And when he, content with the honor, turned the money back to the town, the people erected it as their own expense.

IGRR, vol. III, no. 739, col. 10, lines 1–45, and col. 11, lines 1–31 [72]

[Rhodiapolis, Lycia, A.D. 124–153]

Decreed by the league of the people of Lycia at a legal meeting. Whereas Opramoas son of Apollonius (son and grandson of Calliades), president of the league, scion of the leading families in the province, in addition to his other kindnesses to the people and the improvements he made during the offices he held, singularly displayed his magnanimity in all things by giving an additional 55,000 *denarii* [73] — may good fortune attend! — it was decreed to honor him now also in the present year, as the people voted, and to record this decree.

Cornelius Proculus, imperial legate with rank of praetor, to Julius Capitolinus[?], secretary of the city of Myra, greeting. As for the terms in which the council and people honored Opramoas, son of Apollonius (son and grandson of Calliades), I permit and authorize him to be so addressed, unless this is contrary to either your laws or your customs. [74] I bid you farewell. Recorded in the high-priesthood of Polycharmus. . . .

The Emperor Caesar Titus Aelius Hadrianus ANTONINUS Augustus, son of the deified Hadrian, grandson of the deified Trajan Parthicus, great-grandson of the deified Nerva, *pontifex maximus,* holding the tribunician power for the seventh year, hailed *imperator* twice, three times consul, father of his country, to the league of the Lycians. If Opramoas son of Apollonius had been so exceedingly zealous toward one city, he naturally would have obtained testimonials from the city. But since many cities, as you write, have received some contribution for the restoration of the places which suffered from the earthquake [cf. chapter 1, note 38], it was proper for the [entire] province to bear testimonial to

72. From an enormous inscription, in twenty columns of writing, covering the walls of the mausoleum of Opramoas, president of the league of Greek cities of Lycia. The inscription contains over 150 honorary decrees passed by the league assembly and by towns in Lycia testifying to his benefactions.

73. In honor of his election to the presidency of the Lycian League.

74. The more important acts of municipal legislation were subject to approval by the governor of the province or by the emperor; cf. § 63.

him. Eupolemus son of Eupolemus was the envoy. Farewell. September 22, from Rome.

74. THE HUMBLE TOWNSPEOPLE: FROM THE WALLS OF POMPEII

The house walls of Pompeii facing the streets were usurped not only for election appeals (see vol. 1, p. 463; vol. 2, § 66) but for messages and jottings of every kind, from notices of entertainments, market days, properties to let, boldly painted in bright red, to the scribblings and scratchings (*graffiti*) of shoppers, drunkards, lovelorn swains — in short, a kaleidoscope as varied as the pulsating life of the community itself. A few examples are given here to illustrate this vast body of material.

CIL, vol. IV, nos. 3,884, 5,380 1,679, 64, 1,824, 1,928, 5,372 (= E. Diehl, *Pompeianische Wandinschriften* (Bonn, 1910), nos. 242, 390, 34, 432, 27, 1, 463), and H. Geist, *Pompeianische Wandinschriften* (Munich, 1936), pp. 98, 58, 74)

i

Twenty pairs of gladiators[75] of Decimus Lucretius Satrius Valens, lifetime flamen of Nero son of Caesar Augustus, and ten pairs of gladiators of Decimus Lucretius Valens, his son, will fight at Pompeii on April 8, 9, 10, 11, 12. There will be a full card of wild beast combats, and awnings [for the spectators]. Aemilius Celer [painted this sign], all alone in the moonlight.

ii

Market days: Saturday in Pompeii, Sunday in Nuceria, Monday in Atella, Tuesday in Nola, Wednesday in Cumae, Thursday in Puteoli, Friday in Rome.[76]

iii

6th: cheese 1, bread 8, oil 3, wine 3[77]
7th: bread 8, oil 5, onions 5, bowl 1, bread for the slave[?] 2,
     wine 2

75. Another, similar notice speaks of "twenty pairs of gladiators and their replacements."

76. In Latin the days of the week are called those of Saturn, Sun, Moon, Mars, Mercury, Jupiter, Venus; cf. their names in the Romance languages.

77. The initial number is the day of the months, the numbers following the items of food indicate expenditures in *asses*, except where *denarii* are specified.

8th: bread 8, bread for the slave[?] 4, grits 3

9th: wine for the winner 1 *denarius,* bread 8, wine 2, cheese 2

10th: . . . 1 *denarius,* bread 2, for women 8, wheat 1 *denarius,* cucumber 1, dates 1, incense 1, cheese 2, sausage 1, soft cheese 4, oil 7

iv

Pleasure says: "You can get a drink here for an *as,* a better drink for two, Falernian[78] for four.

v

A copper pot is missing from this shop. 65 sesterces reward if anybody brings it back, 20 sesterces if he reveals the thief so we can get our property back.

vi

The weaver Successus loves the innkeeper's slave girl, Iris by name. She doesn't care for him, but he begs her to take pity on him. Written by his rival. So long.

[Answer by the rival:] Just because you're bursting with envy, don't pick on a handsomer man, a lady–killer and a gallant.

[Answer by the first writer:] There's nothing more to say or write. You love Iris, who doesn't care for you.

vii

Take your lewd looks and flirting eyes off another man's wife, and show some decency on your face!

viii

Anybody in love, come here. I want to break Venus' ribs with a club and cripple the goddess' loins. If she can pierce my tender breast, why can't I break her head with a club?

---

78. One of the prized wines of the Italian countryside (named after a district in Campania), best known from the poems of Horace that sing its praises.

ix

I write at Love's dictation and Cupid's instruction;
But damn it! I don't want to be a god without you.

x

[A prostitute's sign:] I am yours for 2 *asses* cash.

75. PROVINCIAL ADMINISTRATION

TECHNIQUES OF ROMAN RULE

Tacitus, *Agricola* xix–xxi

Agricola fully understood the temperament of the province [Britain], and he was aware from the experience of others that little is gained by conquest if it is followed by injustices. He therefore determined to root out the causes of war. Starting with himself and his retinue, he kept his household in check—a thing as difficult for many as governing a province. He transacted no official business through his freedmen or slaves. No personal feelings, no recommendations, no pleas induced him to take centurions or soldiers on his staff; in each case he regarded the best man as the most reliable. . . .

He made the exaction of grain and tributes less onerous by removing inequities in these obligations, eradicating schemes for profit which were more intolerable than the tribute itself. For example, people used to be compelled to go through the farce of waiting around [with their grain] while the granaries were kept closed, and of having to pay for grain [already stored] in order to quit themselves of their obligations in money.[79] In addition, devious routes and remote districts used to be assigned, so that some tribes, with an army camp nearby, had to carry their grain to remote and inaccessible places. . . .

By suppressing these abuses in the very first year [A.D. 78] of his administration, Agricola restored the popularity of peace, whereas under his predecessors—thanks to their indifference or arrogance—peace had been dreaded no less than war. Furthermore, when summer came, the

---

79. This and other corrupt practices mentioned just below are suspiciously reminiscent of the operations of Verres, the rapacious governor of Sicily in the last century of the Republic (see vol. 1, § 144), and are probably typical Tacitean rhetorical embellishments.

army was assembled, and he took an active part in maneuvers, praising good discipline and checking stragglers. He would personally choose the site of the camp and personally explore the estuaries and forests. Meanwhile, he allowed the enemy no rest, making sudden raids and devastating their lands. And when he had sufficiently cowed them, he would in turn by his clemency hold out to them the attractions of peace. In consequence, many tribes which up to that time had lived in independence gave hostages and abandoned their hostility, and they were so skillfully and carefully ringed with garrisons and forts that they were annexed with less incident than any part of Britain had previously been.

The following winter was employed in salutary measures. For, in order that people who were scattered, uncivilized, and hence prone to war might be accustomed to peace and quiet through comforts, Agricola gave personal encouragement and public assistance to the building of temples, forums, and houses. By praising the energetic and reproving the indolent, he replaced compulsion with competition for honor. He likewise provided a liberal education for the sons of the chiefs, and, preferring the native ability of the Britons to the industriousness of the Gauls, he so encouraged them that though they had lately disdained the Roman language they now eagerly aspired to rhetoric.[80] Hence, too, our style of dress came to be esteemed, and the toga became fashionable. Step by step they turned aside to alluring vices, porticoes, baths, elegant banquets. This in their inexperience they called "culture," whereas it was but an aspect of their enslavement.

THE SPANISH PROVINCES

Strabo, *Geography* iii. iv. 20; Adapted from *LCL*

At the present time, now that some of the provinces have been declared the property of the people and senate and the others that of the emperor [cf. vol. 1, § 201], Baetica belongs to the people; and to govern it they send a praetor, who has under him both a quaestor and a legate. . . . But all the rest [of Iberia] is Caesar's; and he sends thither two legates, a praetorian and a consular—the praetorian legate, who has with him a legate of his own, being sent to administer justice to those of the Lusitanians whose country is situated alongside Baetica and extends as far as the Douro river and its outlets. . . . The remainder of Caesar's territory (and this is most of Iberia) is under the consular governor, who

---

80. Cf. Juvenal, *Satires* xv. 112: "Even Thule speaks of hiring a professor of oratory."

has under him not only a noteworthy army of three legions but also three legates. One of the three, with two legions, guards the frontier of the whole country beyond the Douro to the north. . . . The part beyond, along the mountains as far as the Pyrenees, is guarded by the second of the three legates and the other legion. The third legate oversees the interior and also protects the interests of the peoples who are already called "toga'd" (which is to say, "peaceably inclined"), and have become transformed, clad in their togas, to their present gentleness of disposition and their Italian mode of life; these latter are the Celtiberians and the peoples that live near them on both sides of the Ebro as far as the regions next to the sea. As for the governor himself, he passes his winters administering justice in the regions by the sea, and especially in New Carthage and Tarragona, while in the summertime he goes the rounds of his province, always making an inspection of some of the things that require rectification. There are also imperial procurators there, of equestrian rank, who distribute among the soldiers the things that are necessary for the maintenance of their lives.

THE IMPORTANCE OF ACCURATE RECORDS

This decree was issued by the first governor of Lycia, which was made a Roman province in A.D. 44.

AE, 1976, no. 673; A.D. c. 44

Decree of Quintus Veranius, propraetorian legate of Tiberius CLAUDIUS Caesar Augustus. Trypho, a public slave of the city of Tlos, having failed to learn from my edicts and threats—and not even from the punishment of public slaves guilty of similar faults—that he must not accept [for the archives] transactional documents having interpolations or erasures, I have led him to recognize my displeasure at the likes of him by having him thrashed with whips, and I demonstrated to him with such proof that if he is again unmindful of the edict regarding documents [to record], I will, by subjecting him not only to blows but to the supreme penalty, compel the rest of the public slaves to forget [about continuing] their past indifference. Apollonius son of Diopithes, of Patara, who exposed Trypho, is to receive from the city of Tlos through the incumbent treasurers three hundred drachmas, which is the sum I have fixed by way of reward for those exposing [the malfeasance of] public slaves.

And, so that persons transacting business—on account of whom my diligence has ordered the investigation(?) regarding these matters—may cease acting contrary to their own security, I [now] make known that every transaction of every kind will be invalid from today's day on if it is written in palimpsest or has interpolations or erasures, whether it be a contract or a bond or an agreement or an order or a notice-and-accounting or an offer or a deposition for a trial or dowry details or a decision of arbiters or judges. And if through some such document a delay is sought with a view to [later] interpolation of [the results of] the delay, anyone failing to observe the orders will render the document invalid. . . .

The incumbent magistrates of the month of Artemisios shall by inscriptions publish this decree throughout the whole province entrusted to me.

THE ADMINISTRATION OF EGYPT

The province of Egypt possessed an exceptional status and a correspondingly unique administrative system. The existing Hellenistic administrative apparatus was preserved by Augustus and adapted to the function assigned to Egypt by him—to serve as a granary of Rome and as a copious source of a multiplicity of revenues for the imperial fisc. It was autocratically ruled under a virtual viceroy assisted by an elaborate bureaucracy, was deliberately kept unurbanized (except for four cities such as Alexandria), and was systematically exploited and drained of its wealth.

Strabo, *Geography* XVII. i. 12; Adapted from *LCL*

Egypt is now a province. It pays considerable tribute and is governed by prudent men, the different prefects sent there. This official has the rank of the [former] king; and subordinate to him is the administrator of justice, who has authority over most of the lawsuits;[81] and another is the official called the *idiologus,* who inquires into all properties that are without owners and that ought to fall to Caesar [cf. pp. 297–98 and § 79]; and these [officials] are attended by imperial freedmen and also by procurators who are entrusted with affairs of greater or lesser importance. There are also three legions of soldiers,[82] one of which is stationed

81. The *juridicus,* an equestrian official who served as vice-prefect and to whom some of the prefect's judicial powers were delegated.
82. Reduced to two legions by Tiberius and to one by Trajan.

in the city [of Alexandria] and the others in the country; and apart from these there are nine Roman cohorts, three in the city, three on the borders of Ethiopia in Syene, as a guard for that region, and three in the rest of the country. And there are also three cavalry units, which are likewise assigned to the various critical points. Of the native officials in the city, one is the *exegetes,* who is clad in purple, has hereditary prerogatives, and has charge of the interests of the city; another is the recorder; another the chief judge;[83] and a fourth the commander of the night watch.

CONTROL OF MOVEMENT IN EGYPT

As the successor of three millennia of absolute monarchs in Egypt, the Roman emperor was the lord of the land and of all it contained, and the movement of goods and persons into and out of this imperial preserve was rigidly controlled.

Strabo, *Geography* II. iii. 5

[In Ptolemaic times it was] not permitted to sail from Alexandria without a pass. . . . Nor could one have sailed out secretly, since the harbor and other exits were kept closed by as strong a guard as I (who have lived in Alexandria a long time) personally know still exists at this time [the first decades of the first century], though now, under Roman possession, it is much relaxed.

Oxyrhynchus Papyrus No. 1,271 (= *Select Papyri,* no. 304); A.D. 246

To Valerius Firmus, prefect of Egypt, from Aurelia Maeciana of Side [a town in Pamphylia, Asia Minor]. I wish, my lord, to sail out via Pharus;[84] I request you to write to the procurator of Pharus to grant me clearance according to the usual practice. Pachon 1. Farewell.

The reason for the following injunction is not stated in the extant portion of this document, but presumably the petitioners had a claim or lawsuit pending against the man denied exit.

83. Despite his high-sounding title this local offical had jurisdiction over only minor civil suits; he was, in other words, the chief judge of the local, as opposed to the imperial, administration.

84. The island in the harbor of Alexandria, on which stood the famous lighthouse of the same name, one of the Seven Wonders of the World in antiquity.

Oxyrhynchus Papyrus No. 3,118; third century

Corellius Galba to Chrestio, procurator of Pharus, greeting. I have ordered to be appended hereto the petition addressed to me by Claudia Philoromaea (through her daughter Claudia Isidora) and Claudia Erotilla also known as Apolinaria. Do you take cognizance thereof and see to preventing the departure of the man they mention, Septimius Ammonius, and give orders to the others who keep watch over such matters so that. . . [The rest is lost.]

THE ASSIZES OF THE PREFECT OF EGYPT

Roman governors made an annual circuit of their provinces, holding assizes in designated cities. The first of the following papyri preserves part of the itinerary of a prefect of Egypt on such a tour some time in the first century. The second, pieced together from two fragments, one in the Library at Strasbourg and the other in a private collection in Trieste, records the membership of a prefect's advisory council.

Oxyrhynchus Papyrus No. 709 (= Wilcken, no. 32)

. . . the prefect on his journey will stop first at Pelusium, where he will hold the assizes for the Tanite, Sethroite, Arabian, and Avian nomes; then at Memphis similarly for the Thebaid, the Heptanomia, and the Arsinoite nome; and for the remaining nomes of the Lower Country . . . in Alexandria. . . . [The rest is fragmentary.]

Strasbourg Papyrus No. 179 + *Aegyptus* (1983), 63:124–125; A.D. 170

Extract from the second volume of minutes of hearings before Pactumeius Magnus, prefect, at his assizes of the Arsinoite nome. Year 10 of Aurelii Antoninus [Marcus Aurelius] and Commodus the lords Emperors in [the capital?] of the Arsinoite nome, before the tribunal, present in the [prefect's] council being: Julius Crispinus, chief financial officer [of the province]; Flavius Valens, *epistrategus;* Bal[. .]urius Lucullinus, navy prefect; Julius Crispinus, military tribune; Junius Gilo, public prosecutor; Messius Bassus, imperial secretary for Greek correspondence.

CRIMINAL JURISDICTION

The introductory paragraph of this edict, issued by the prefect of Egypt, is illegible except for the opening sentence. The legible part lists the types of cases that will be heard by the prefect sitting as the court of first instance. All other disputes would normally reach a Roman provincial governor only on appeal. As the offenses here listed were usually tried in local courts, and as Roman citizens everywhere in the Empire enjoyed an automatic right of appeal from local courts to Roman jurisdiction as high as the emperor himself, it seems likely that the present memorandum applied only to Roman citizens.

Yale Papyrus inv. 1,606 (= *SB*, no. 10,929); A.D. 133–137

MARCUS PETRONIUS MAMERTINUS DECLARES: . . .
the prefect will take cognizance:

concerning murder
concerning robberies
concerning poisonings
concerning kidnapping
concerning cattle rustling
concerning armed violence
concerning forgery
concerning negligence
concerning annulled wills

concerning excessive abuse
concerning complaints of manu-
    mitters against freedmen or par-
    ents against children
All others will be heard by me only
    on appeal, the appellants to post
    as bond one-quarter of the esti-
    mated value of the subject of
    the suit.

PREPARATIONS FOR A PREFECT'S VISIT

An impending visit by the governor, even if only for an overnight halt, was a busy time for the inhabitants of the locality, who were required to provide lodgings, food, and often transport for the governor and his retinue (cf. vol. 1, p. 397).

British Museum Papyrus No. 1,159 (= Wilcken, no. 415); A.D. 145–147

From the village scribes. In accordance with your [probably the nome strategus'] request for a list of persons to provide the necessities being made ready for the beneficent visit of Valerius Proculus, most glorious prefect, we submit, omitting those excused in accordance with official memoranda, [a list of persons] in place of those transferred to other public services and of those deceased.[85]

[There follows a long list of names of individuals who will be responsible for the different provisions; among the latter are listed bread (pure), lamb, wine, vinegar, hay, chaff, barley, wood, charcoal, torches, lamps, geese, oil, relishes, cheeses, vegetables, fish, and pack asses.]

76. LETTER OF CLAUDIUS TO THE ALEXANDRIANS

On the accession of Claudius in A.D. 41 an embassy was sent by the Alexandrians to the new emperor to bestow various honors on him and to request favors and the solution of a number of problems. Among the latter was the explosive relationship between Greeks and Jews, which had erupted into riots and massacres at the news of the death of Caligula, whose aggressive claim to divine worship the Jews had resisted. One of the principal causes of the friction was the jealously guarded Alexandrian citizenship, which the Jews, who were juridically and politically inferior to the Greeks, were desirous of obtaining because of its political and economic advantages and because it provided an avenue to Roman citizenship.

British Museum Papyrus No. 1,912 (= *Select Papyri*, no. 212); Adapted from *LCL*

Lucius Aemilius Rectus [prefect of Egypt] declares: Since the whole of the city, owing to its numbers, was unable to be present at the reading of the most sacred and most beneficent letter to the city, I have deemed it necessary to display the letter publicly in order that reading it individually you may admire the majesty of our god Caesar and feel gratitude for his good will toward the city. Year 2 of the Emperor Tiberius CLAUDIUS Caesar Augustus Germanicus, 14th of New Augustus.

The Emperor Tiberius CLAUDIUS Caesar Augustus Germanicus, *pontifex maximus,* holder of the tribunician power, consul designate, to the city of Alexandria, greeting. Tiberius Claudius Barbillus, Apollonius son of Artemidorus, Chaeremo son of Leonidas, Marcus Julius Asclepiades, Gaius Julius Dionysius, Tiberius Claudius Phanias, Pasio son of Potamo, Dionysius son of Sabbio, Tiberius Claudius Archibius, Apol-

---

85. Since the last such visit. The list of provisioners was obviously in the official files, and the present report was intended to bring it up to date.

lonius son of Aristo, Gaius Julius Apollonius, Hermaiscus son of Apollonius, your envoys, delivered your resolution to me and discoursed at length concerning the city, directing my attention to your good will toward us, which from long ago, you may be sure, had been stored up to your advantage in my memory; for you are by nature reverent toward the emperors, as I have come to know well from many evidences, and in particular you have taken a warm interest—warmly reciprocated—in my house, of which fact (to mention the latest instance, passing over the others) the supreme witness is my brother Germanicus Caesar when he addressed you in franker tones [by word of mouth].

Wherefore I gladly accepted the honors given to me by you, though I am not partial to such things. And first I permit you to keep my birthday as an Augustan day in the manner you have yourselves proposed, and I agree to the erection by you in their several places of the statues of myself and my family; for I see that you were zealous to establish on every side memorials of your reverence for my house. Of the two golden statues, the one made to represent the Claudian Augustan Peace, as my most honored Barbillus suggested and persisted in when I wished to refuse for fear of being thought too offensive, shall be erected at Rome, and the other according to your request shall be carried in procession on my name days in your city; and it shall be accompanied in the procession by a throne, adorned with whatever trappings you wish. It would perhaps be foolish, while accepting such great honors, to refuse the institution of a Claudian tribe and the establishment of sacred groves after the manner of Egypt; wherefore I grant you these requests as well, and if you wish you may also erect the equestrian statues given by Vitrasius Pollio my procurator. As for the erection of the statues in four-horse chariots which you wish to set up to me at the entrances to the country, I consent to let one be placed at the town called Taposiris, in Libya, another at Pharus in Alexandria, and a third at Pelusium in Egypt. But I deprecate the appointment of a high priest for me and the building of temples, for I do not wish to be offensive to my contemporaries, and my opinion is that temples and the like have by all ages been granted as special honors to the gods alone.[86]

Concerning the requests which you have been eager to obtain from me, I decide as follows. All those who have become ephebes[87] up to the time of my principate I confirm and maintain in possession of the

---

86. On the policies of the emperors toward emperor worship, see vol. 1, § 207, and vol. 2, § 162.
87. In the Greek cities youths of eighteen eligible for citizenship were termed ephebes.

Alexandrian citizenship with all the privileges and indulgences enjoyed by the city, excepting those who by fraud have contrived to become ephebes though born of slaves. And it is equally my will that all the other privileges shall be confirmed which were granted to you by the emperors before me, and by the kings and by the prefects, as the deified Augustus also confirmed them. It is my will that the overseers of the temples of the deified Augustus in Alexandria shall be chosen by lot in the same way as those of the same deified Augustus in Canopus are chosen by lot. With regard to the municipal magistrates being made triennial, your proposal seems to me to be very good; for through fear of being called to account for any misrule your magistrates will behave with greater circumspection during their term of office. Concerning the city council, what your custom may have been under the ancient kings I have no means of saying, but that you had no council under the former emperors you are well aware. As this is the first broaching of a novel project, whose utility to the city and to my interests is not evident, I have written to Aemilius Rectus to hold an inquiry and inform me whether in the first place it is right that the body should be constituted, and, if it should be right to create one, in what manner this is to be done.

As for which party was responsible for the riot and feud (or rather, if the truth must be told, the war) with the Jews, although your envoys, particularly Dionysius son of Theo, confronting [your opponents] put your case with great zeal, nevertheless I was unwilling to make a strict inquiry, though guarding within me a store of immutable indignation against any who renewed the conflict; and I tell you once for all that unless you put a stop to this ruinous and obstinate enmity against each other, I shall be driven to show what a benevolent emperor can be when turned to righteous indignation. Wherefore once again I conjure you that, on the one hand, the Alexandrians show themselves forbearing and kindly toward the Jews, who for many years have dwelt in the same city, and dishonor none of the rights observed by them in the worship of their god but allow them to observe their customs as in the time of the deified Augustus [cf. § 83, second selection], which customs I also, after hearing both sides, have confirmed. And, on the other hand, I explicitly order the Jews not to agitate for more privileges than they formerly possessed, and in the future not to send out a separate embassy as if they lived in two separate cities—a thing unprecedented—and not to force their way into gymnasiarchic or cosmetic games,[88] while enjoy-

88. That is, games presented under the supervision of the gymnasiarchs and the *cosmetae* of Alexandria, who were in charge of the municipal gymnasia.

ing their own privileges and sharing a great abundance of advantages in a city not their own, and not to bring in or admit Jews from Syria or those who sail down from Egypt, a proceeding which will compel me to conceive serious suspicions; otherwise I will by all means proceed against them as fomenters of what is a general plague of the whole world.[89] If, desisting from these courses, you both consent to live with mutual forbearance and kindliness, I on my side will exercise a solicitude of very long standing for the city, as one bound to us by ancestral friendship. I bear witness to my friend Barbillus of the solicitude which he has always shown for you in my presence and of the extreme zeal with which he has now advocated your cause, and likewise to my friend Tiberius Claudius Archibius. Farewell.

77. Growth of Compulsory Public Services

Conscription of manual labor for public works and services was a general practice of the ancient Orient and the city-states of Greece. The assignment of compulsory public offices (liturgies) to financially able citizens was especially developed among the Greeks. It was left for the Roman Empire to organize such services into an elaborate system of municipal and provincial administration. Our fullest and most detailed information on this subject comes from Egypt, where the system doubtless attained its most extensive development. To guarantee the steady flow of local and imperial revenues the emperors at first relied on a salaried bureaucracy and on the keen competition for municipal offices, whose expenses were defrayed by the incumbents. But increasing economic difficulties forced the abandonment of this policy. The change is clearly apparent, though not yet fully developed, by the end of the first century. Thereafter, the emperors found it increasingly necessary to intervene, directly or through their provincial governors, in the local affairs (especially financial) of the cities and towns (§ 69), and it became increasingly necessary to draft unwilling candidates to fill municipal offices (cf. §§ 64, 66). By the middle of the second century the liturgical system had been extended to embrace practically all local administrative functions, and the principle of compulsory service in these functions was as firmly established for possessors of stated property (serving as security for proper performance of the assigned

---

89. Some commentators, remembering the similar expression of Tacitus (see p. 140), have taken this phrase to be the earliest known allusion to Christianity. But it is much more likely that it refers to the agitation for special privileges by the Jews of the Diaspora, who had settled in many cities of the Empire; cf. § 90.

duties), as was the assignment of imperial and public lands for compulsory cultivation when no voluntary lessees appeared. Furthermore, municipal magistrates and councilmen and all other liturgists were made collectively responsible for the expenses and revenues of their offices, so that any default by one automatically became an obligation of the remaining members of the group. "The main object of the system was to get public work done at private expense; in effect it was a heavy tax on the moneyed classes and eventually brought them to ruin" (*Select Papyri*, 2, xx–xxi). Not infrequently, propertied liturgists—like penniless peasants—resorted to flight from home and to other measures of desperation in an attempt to escape from their crushing fiscal burdens. Only certain privileged groups and persons already performing essential services for the state or army in their regular capacities were exempted from liturgic service. Among these were soldiers and veterans, professional athletes, priests, members of learned professions, village clerks, women, and men over sixty-five or fathers of five children; and the exemptions of even some of these were occasionally canceled. See further §§ 115 and 128 for the continued spread and increasing rigor of the liturgic system in the third and fourth centuries.

TAX FARMERS BY COMPULSION

This papyrus of the latter part of the first century is particularly interesting in the light of the prefect's edict of A.D. 68 (§ 78) assailing the use of compulsion in the leasing of public contracts.

Oxyrhynchus Papyrus No. 44; (= *Select Papyri*, no. 420)

Paniscus . . . *strategus* of the Oxyrhynchite nome, to Asclepiades, royal secretary of the same nome, greeting. At the last auction of tax contracts held by myself and you in the presence of the customary officials, since the farmers in charge of the tax on transfers of real property and of the *agoranomus*[90] office refused to bid on the ground that they were incurring substantial losses and may even withdraw, I wrote our opinion to His Excellency the Prefect concerning the matter. He replied to the effect that I should examine the former leases and as far as possible lighten the burden of the tax farmers, so as not to have persons engaged against their will become fugitives. I previously sent you a copy of the letter for your information and [told you] that in your absence, as the contracts

---

90. This tax on sales of real and certain other forms of property apparently remained fixed at 10 percent under the Principate. On the function of the *agoranomus* see earlier p. 174.

had not been accepted by the tax farmers and no other persons were coming forward for them in spite of repeated announcements, I took affidavits from those in charge of the tax on sales of real property and the record office. . . .[91] [The rest is lost.]

PERSONAL RESPONSIBILITY

The poll-tax collectors in this document have a fixed monthly quota to pay to the government, irrespective of the amount actually collected by them. Under the circumstances it is not surprising to find them employing an armed guard, no doubt both to provide them with physical protection and to help them enforce collections.

Tebtynis Papyrus No. 391; A.D. 100

We, Heracles, Athenodorus, Hero, and Zoilus, all four collectors of the poll tax of the village of Tebtynis, agree voluntarily and of our own free will that we have made a division [of our duties], from the 15th of the month Hathyr, the receipts of which are credited to Phaophi, of the third year of the lord Trajan Caesar for the current third year only of the Emperor Caesar Nerva TRAJAN Augustus Germanicus; and that Athenodorus and Heracles have been allotted the inhabitants of and settlers in the village, while Hero and Zoilus have for their part been allotted all the inhabitants and settlers [of Tebtynis] at other villages or in the metropolis, with the stipulation that those who have been allotted the external district shall pay each month 1,100 silver drachmas, while those who have been allotted the village shall make up the balance of the monthly quota for the poll tax, the wages of the armed guard being chargeable to those who have been allotted the village. If any one of us four violates any of the aforesaid provisions, he shall pay to the party abiding by them 500 drachmas and to the public treasury an equal sum. This bond shall be valid, as if it had been publicly registered. The coming extra levy of the current third year shall be collected by each of them from persons allotted to him. Year 3 of the Emperor Caesar Nerva TRAJAN Augustus Germanicus, Hathyr. . . .

91. Despite the implication in this letter that tax farmers were not to be compelled to renew their contracts, the practice continued. It is again deprecated in a rescript of the Emperor Hadrian (Justinian, *Digest* XLIX. xiv. 3. 6): "It is a most inhuman practice to compel lessees of public revenues and land to continue when the contracts cannot be let at the same price. Indeed, lessees will come forward even more readily if they can be sure that they will not be compelled to continue should they wish to withdraw when the five-year [contract] period is completed."

NOMINATION TO LITURGIC SERVICE

Berlin Papyrus No. 18 (= Wilcken, no. 398 = *Select Papyri*, no. 342); A.D. 169; Adapted from *LCL*

Copy of announcement. Serenus, royal secretary of the Arsinoite nome, division of Heraclides, and acting *strategus*. To be assessors of unsold [state] lands—in place of Gaius Julius Ptollis, Amarantus son of Hestiaeus, Hero surnamed Eudaemo, and Diodorus son of Theogito, who have all four completed the prescribed period, and of Anubio son of Hero and Demetrius son of Suchammo, both stated to be deceased— the persons named below have been nominated by the city secretaries as well-to-do and suitable for compulsory public services. They are ordered to take up the task entrusted to them honestly and faithfully, so as not to incur blame in any respect. Signed. Year 9 of the lord [Marcus] Aurelius Antoninus Caesar Armeniacus Medicus Parthicus Maximus, Mesore 17. They are:

Gaius Julius Apollinaris, owning land at Caranis, having property worth 4,000 drachmas; Mysthes son of Cornelius, owning land at New Ptolemais, having property worth one talent; Antonius Heraclianus, owning land at the hamlet of Nestus, likewise 4,000 drachmas; Gaius Julius Saturnilus, owning land at Tanis, having property worth 4,000 drachmas; Ptolemaeus, or however he is styled, public secretary of Pharbaetha, worth 4,000 drachmas; Pasio son of Petermuthis (son of Petermuthis), of the Hellenium quarter [of Arsinoë], having property worth 4,000 drachmas.

Registered by me, Hero, special assistant, Mesore 20.

SB, no. 9,060; first to second century

From the orders of Mettius Rufus [Prefect of Egypt A.D. 89–91; cf. § 82] sent to the *strategi*. If any persons discharging compulsory public services appear to you to be unsuitable either because they do not have the requisite wealth or because of physical disability or because they seem unworthy for any other reason, you will send me three names in place of each one, after investigating that all are suitable not only in property but also in age [i.e., under sixty-five; cf. introduction] and in the conduct of life which those who are performing the emperor's business ought to have. Accordingly, you will add their wealth, their ages, whether they are literate, and what public offices they previously held.

And be careful that the three are not from one household or from the same locality, that they have not previously been in the same offices or been found guilty of improper conduct in other offices, and that the officials for the same locality are not relatives.

. . . .

Year 15 of the deified Trajan, Phamenoth 25, in Naucratis. Dioscorus son of Dionysius appeared and said, "We are two brothers in compulsory public services, and I request that one of us be released in order to have the time to attend to our farming." Sulpicius Similis[92] asked, "Have you a father [living]?" When he replied, "No," Sulpicius Similis ordered, "One is to be released."

EXEMPTION FROM LITURGIES

Petitions for release from compulsory public services are frequent. In the extant documents of this type the petitioners repeatedly plead illegal nomination, lack of means, and impoverishment caused by previous performance of liturgies. For further examples see § 115.

Philadelphia Papyrus No. 1, lines 18–34; early second century

Section from an edict of Vibius Maximus, prefect of Egypt [in A.D. 103–107]. Even among the categories listed below those will perform compulsory public service who own private land and whose wealth is established to exceed one talent, not by unofficial declaration but by their true value. As for priests, they will be compelled [to perform liturgies] only if they cultivate private land.

Those exempt from public services are: priests of important temples . . . cattle raisers . . . over-age and feeble, officially certified . . . physicians . . . merchants, potters[?], oil workers . . . fullers . . . carpenters . . . goldsmiths and . . . tax on trades. . . . [The rest is lost.]

Philadelphia Papyrus No. 10; A.D. 139

To Dio, *strategus* of the Arsinoite nome, division of Heraclides, from the weavers of the village of Philadelphia. There was recently sent us from the public treasury a sum of money with orders for us to make clothing for the state [probably intended for the army; cf. § 147]; and our group of artisans, reduced as it is to a small number, considered it an answer to

92. Prefect of Egypt, A.D. 107–112. The date of this hearing during his assizes at Naucratis is 112.

its prayer to be able to execute the orders received. But now four among us have been assigned to escort duty [on the grain boats]. They have been taken from us to perform compulsory public service and have departed for Alexandria; thus our number has been still further reduced. We are therefore compelled to appeal to you and to beg you, if you deem it proper, to give orders that we, who have hitherto been left to our trade, be left alone and undisturbed by other public service, so that we may make and deliver the clothing ordered (especially as we expect a further order to fill for the state), and so that we may thus be the beneficiaries of your benevolence. We were twelve men in number, of whom four have been removed, so that we now remain only eight. Year 3 of the Emperor Caesar Titus Aelius Hadrianus ANTONINUS Augustus PIUS, month of Hadrianus, the 20th.

Fayum Papyrus No. 106, lines 6–25 (= *Select Papyri*, no. 283); A.D. c. 140; From *LCL*

To Gaius Avidius Heliodorus, prefect of Egypt, from Marcus Valerius Gemellus, physician. Contrary to the prohibitions I have been impressed as a superintendent of confiscated property within the villages of Bacchias and Hephaestias in the Heraclides division of the Arsinoite nome, and through laboring on this task for the last four years I have become quite impoverished, my lord. Wherefore I entreat you, my preserver, to have pity on me and order me now to be released from my task, in order that I may be able to recover from the effects of my labors. I have at the same time appended precedents by which complete exemption from compulsory public services is granted to persons practicing the profession of medicine, especially to those who have been certified,[93] like myself, so that I may experience your benevolence. Farewell.

The following document is published here in its 1964 revision.

Oxyrhynchus Papyrus No. 2,340; March 13, A.D. 192

Year 32 of Lucius Aelius Aurelius COMMODUS Caesar our lord, Phamenoth 17. In re the petition of Isidorus, Eudaemo his lawyer said: "Epimachus son of Gaius, assistant *strategus* of the fourth district [of Alexan-

---

93. Cf. Oxyrhynchus Papyrus No. 40 (=*Select Papyri*, no. 245); A.D. 141–142: "Copy of memorandum of Valerius Eudaemo, then prefect of Egypt. . . . Claim of Psasnis. Psasnis appeared and said, 'I am a physician by profession and I have treated these very persons who have nominated me for a compulsory public service.' Eudaemo said, 'Perhaps you have treated them unskilfully. If you are a state-salaried physician for mummification, apply to the strategus and you shall have exemption from compulsory public service.' "

dria], has nominated my client to succeed him. My client is a foreman weaver who has many workmen in his factory. Such men have been exempted [from liturgy] because it is in the interest of the imperial treasury, and I appeal to you to order Epimachus to nominate someone else as his replacement, and I shall read a minute of Macrinus [Decimus Veturius Macrinus, prefect of Egypt, A.D. 181–183] dated in the 22d year, Pharmouthi."

Hippias [the opposing] lawyer said: "Epimachus submits that Isidorus is not a weaver but a perfume merchant and a well-to-do man."

Julianus [the hearing officer] said: "According to decisions in similar cases, if he is a foreman weaver he can benefit from the said precedent and ask that someone else be nominated instead of him."

FLIGHT FROM LITURGY

Berlin Papyrus No. 372 (= Wilcken; no. 19); A.D. 154

Marcus Sempronius Liberalis, prefect of Egypt, declares: I learn that some persons have left their homes because of the recent disturbance[94] . . . and that others, who fled from certain liturgies because of the poverty about them at the time,[95] are still living away from home in fear of the proscriptions that were immediately declared. I therefore urge all to return to their own places of abode and reap the first and greatest fruit of prosperity and of the solicitude of our lord the emperor for all men, and not to wander abroad without hearth or home. That they may comply more readily and gladly, let them know that anyone . . . who is still held back for this reason will perceive the good will and kindness of our greatest emperor in his order that there shall be no judicial inquiry against them, or even against others proscribed by the *strategi* for any cause whatever. . . . [About one fourth of the text is lost here.]

. . . and they associate with fugitives who have chosen a life of criminals and brigands. That they may understand that I advise and do

94. In the preceding year there had been a revolt in Egypt in which the then prefect was killed by the rebels and which seems to have required the personal intervention of the emperor before it was suppressed.

95. Cf. § 85, second selection. Since the people could not pay their taxes, the collectors could not deliver to the government the tax quotas for which they were personally financially responsible; faced with ruin, they fled. Several other papyri give us further details on this desperate recourse to flight to avoid ruinous officeholding. One (British Museum Papyrus No. 342; A.D. 185) concerns two men who fled, fearing nomination to a liturgy. In another (Geneva Papyrus No. 37 [=Wilcken, no. 400]; A.D. 186) mention is made of four men who disappeared while their names were still on the list of possible nominees, even before the selection was made.

this not only for them but also for the others, let them know that their excellencies the *epistrategi,* the *strategi,* and the soldiers dispatched by me for the safety and security of the country districts have been given orders to nip incipient raids in the bud by provident and timely measures, to give immediate chase when raids are committed, and to call troublemakers caught in the act to account as fully as those engaged in actual brigandage but not to annoy others of those once proscribed who are living quietly and attending to their farming at home. Let them return, therefore, without fear, and let their period of grace be three months from the time when this edict of mine is posted in each nome. But if anyone is found wandering abroad after such great benefaction of mine, such person shall be arrested and sent to me no longer as a suspected but as a confessed malefactor. Year 18 of the lord Antoninus, Thoth 1.

78. EDICT OF THE PREFECT TIBERIUS JULIUS ALEXANDER

Considerable light on the internal administration of Egypt is afforded by this edict, issued in A.D. 68 by the prefect Tiberius Julius Alexander. The edict orders an end to a number of abuses which administrative personnel, especially fiscal officials, had introduced during the reign of Nero, perhaps under pressure of increased exactions demanded by that emperor.

H. G. Evelyn-White and J. H. Oliver; *The Temple of Hibis* (New York, 1938), no. 4
(abridged)

Tiberius Julius Alexander declares: Since I am exercising every solicitude for the city [of Alexandria] to maintain its proper political status in the enjoyment of the benefactions which it has from the emperors, and for Egypt to continue in prosperity and cheerfully contribute to the grain supply and to the very great felicity of the present times unoppressed by novel and unlawful exactions; and since practically from the moment I entered the city I have been assailed by clamors of petitioners, both in small groups and in throngs, both from the most respectable people here and from the country farmers, complaining about the recent abuses, I have lost no time in righting pressing matters to the extent of my authority. And that you may the more cheerfully expect everything for your salvation and happiness from our benefactor, the Emperor Galba Augustus, who has brought light to us for the salvation of the whole human race, and that you may know that I have been concerned with the matters relating to your relief, I have perforce set forth the decisions and actions that are in my power concerning each of the requests, and the weightier matters requiring the authority and majesty of the emperor I shall report to him in all truth, for the gods have preserved to this most sacred age the security of the inhabited world.

First of all, I recognize the complete reasonableness of your petition that persons not be forced against their will, contrary to the general practice of the provinces, into tax farming or other leases of imperial estate; no little harm has been done by the compulsion of many persons inexperienced in such duties, when [the collection of] the taxes was imposed upon them. Wherefore I myself have not forced and shall not force anyone into tax farming or lease, for I know that it is to the advantage of the imperial revenues, too, to have competent men administer these willingly and zealously. I am confident that in the future no [official] will force tax farmers or lessees against their will, but, observing the invariable practice of the former prefects instead of imitating someone's temporary wrongdoing, will lease to persons willing to come forward voluntarily.[96]

Whereas some [officials] have also had loans of others assigned to themselves under pretense of public obligations and have then proceeded to consign some persons to the debtor prison or to other jails which I know have been abolished for this very reason, that loans may be executed out of the properties and not out of the persons [of the debtors]; in keeping with the wish of the deified Augustus I order that no one shall, under pretense of public obligations, have loans assigned from others which he did not originally make, and that no free persons shall ever be locked up in any jail whatsoever, except a criminal, or in the debtor prison, except those indebted to the fisc.

> [The next section, here omitted, concerns prior liens of the state on the private property of persons who have entered into public contracts.]

I have also received petitions concerning tax exemptions and reductions . . . from persons requesting that these privileges be reaffirmed in accordance with the rescript of the deified Claudius to Postumus[97]

---

96. By the beginning of the second century, however, practically all tax collectors in Egypt, at least on the local level, were assigned to their postions as compulsory public services (cf. § 77).

97. Gaius Julius Postumus, prefect of Egypt A.D. 45–47. The prefects mentioned later and the known dates of their tenure of office are Tiberius Claudius Balbillus, 55–59, and Lucius Julius Vestinus, 59–62.

granting such release. . . . Since, therefore, Balbillus and Vestinus granted these releases, I reaffirm the decisions of both prefects, especially as they are in accord with the grant of the deified Claudius; hence they have been released from the charges not yet exacted from them, and in the future certainly the tax exemption and reduction will remain in force for them.

> [The next section, here omitted, guarantees purchasers of confiscated properties sold by the state against having to pay fiscal rents in addition to normal taxes.]

It is in keeping with the grants of the emperors that native Alexandrians residing in the country for business reasons are not to be forced into any rural compulsory public service. You have often requested this and I confirm it, so that no one of the native Alexandrians shall be forced into rural public services. . . .

In general I order that whenever a prefect has already decided to dismiss a case brought before him, it is not to be brought again before the [prefect's] assizes. And if two prefects have been of the same mind, a state accountant who brings up the same matters before the assizes is also to be punished [in addition to having the case thrown out], seeing that he does nothing else than reserve for himself and the other civil officials a pretext for enrichment. Many persons, in fact, have decided rather to abandon their private possessions, because they have expended more than their value through the same matters being brought to judgment at each assize.

I also establish the same rule for matters brought up under the "Special Account" [see § 79], so that if any matter has been judged and dismissed, or shall be dismissed, by the [procurator] appointed for the "Special Account," the [accuser] shall not again be permitted to submit [the same charge] to a prosecutor or to bring it to trial, or else the person so doing will be punished mercilessly; for there will be no end of vexatious denunciations if dismissed matters are brought up till someone decides to condemn. Since already the city has become practically uninhabitable because of the multitude of informers and every household is thrown into confusion, I perforce order that if any of the prosecutors attached to the "Special Account" introduces a suit as spokesman for another, he shall produce the real accuser in court, so that the latter, too, may not be free from risk;[98] and if he brings three suits on his own

---

98. Informers whose denunciations proved to be false were penalized.

responsibility and does not prove them, he shall not again be permitted to prosecute, but half his estate shall be confiscated; for it is most unjust that a person who brings upon many the dangers of [loss of] property and penalty should himself be completely free from liability. In general I shall order that the code of regulations of the "Special Account" remain in force, since I have amended the innovations introduced contrary to the grants of the emperors. And I shall openly publicize how I have meted out condign punishment to convicted informers.

79. Rules for Administering the "Special Account" of Egypt

This unique papyrus, "the most important document yet discovered in Roman Egypt" (*ESAR*, 2:711), contains a digest of the code of regulations that guided the administration of the *idiologus*. This high official—like the governor, he was of equestrian rank—had charge of the special account *(idios logos)* in which were collected the revenues of the imperial fisc from sources other than taxation, such as fines and confiscated or unclaimed property. The code, which has aptly been termed "a finished instrument of fiscal oppression," affords a striking illustration of the thoroughness and efficiency of the Roman exploitation of Egypt, revealing in particular detail the rigid class system maintained by the Roman rulers of that ancient land. A selection from the 115 clauses in this long document is given here.

Berlin Papyrus No. 1,210 (= *Select Papyri*, no. 206 = *FIRA*, vol. I, no. 99); A.D. 150–161; Adapted from *LCL* and *ESAR*

I[99] have appended for you a copy of the code of regulations which the deified Augustus established for the administration of the Special Account and of additions made to it from time to time either by the emperors or the senate or the various prefects or *idiologi*, summarizing the sections in current use, so that by applying your memory to the condensed form of the exposition you may readily master the topics.

4. The estates of those who die intestate and who have no legal heirs fall to the fisc.

5. Property bequeathed by Alexandrians to persons not qualified is given to those who can legally inherit from them, if such there be and if they claim it at law.

99. Perhaps an *idiologus* who prepared this digest as a memorandum to his staff.

6. An Alexandrian may not bequeath to his wife, if he has no off-spring by her, more than a fourth part of his estate; and if he has children by her, he may not allot to his wife a larger share than what he bequeathes to each of his sons.

7. All wills which are not in the form of public instruments are invalid.

8. If to a Roman will is added a clause saying, "Whatever bequests I make in Greek codicils shall be valid," it is not admissible, for a Roman is not permitted to write a Greek will.

16. All property which is bequeathed to freedmen of Romans with the stipulation that it is to descend to their offspring is confiscated on the decease of the recipients if it be proved that no offspring had yet been born when the bequest was written.

17. Property left to provide sacrifices to the departed is confiscated when there are no longer any persons to take charge of these.

18. Inheritances left in trust by Greeks to Romans or by Romans to Greeks were confiscated by the divine Vespasian; nevertheless those acknowledging their trust have received half.

19. Bequests made to freedmen who have not yet acquired legal emancipation are confiscated. It is legal emancipation if the person freed is over thirty years of age.[100]

20. Bequests made to one who as a slave was put in chains and afterwards freed or who was freed when not yet thirty years old are confiscated.

22. The property of deceased Latins[101] is given to their patrons and to the sons and daughters and heirs of these; and bequests made by those who have not yet acquired legal Roman freedom are confiscated.

23. Romans are not permitted to marry their sisters or their aunts, but marriage with their brothers' daughters has been conceded. Pardalas [an *idiologus*], indeed, when a brother married a sister, confiscated the property.

24. The dowry brought by a Roman woman over fifty years of age to a Roman husband under sixty years of age is after death confiscated by the fisc.[102]

---

100. This and the next clauses reveal the influence of the legislation of Augustus on freedmen (see vol. 1, § 205).

101. That is, Junian Latins, on whom see introduction to vol. 1 § 205.

102. This and the following clauses reveal the influence of the Papian–Poppaean legislation of Augustus (see vol. 1, § 204).

25. That likewise is confiscated which is brought by a woman under fifty years of age to a husband over sixty.

27. Whatever property is inherited by a Roman sixty years old who has neither wife nor child is confiscated. If he has a wife but no children and declares his position, he is allowed to take half.

28. If a woman is fifty years old, she does not inherit; if she is younger and has three children, she inherits, but in the case of a freedwoman, if she has four children.

29. A freeborn Roman woman having a property of 20,000 sesterces pays 1 percent annually as long as she is unmarried, and a freedwoman possessing 20,000 sesterces pays the same until she marries.

30. Inheritances left to Roman women possessing 50,000 sesterces are confiscated if they are unmarried and childless.

31. A Roman woman is permitted to leave to her husband the tenth part of what she possesses; anything more is confiscated.

32. Romans possessing more than 100,000 sesterces, if unmarried and childless, do not inherit, but those who have less inherit.

34. Soldiers in service and after leaving service have been allowed to dispose of their property both by Roman and Greek wills and to use what words they choose; but in every case they must leave it to fellow nationals and to those to whom it is permitted.

35. Children and kinsmen of soldiers in active service who die intestate are permitted to inherit from them, if the claimants are of the same nationality.

36. The estates of persons convicted of murder or major crimes, and of those who go into voluntary exile on such charges are confiscated; but a tenth is allowed to their children, and the dowries consisting of money are restored to their wives. The lord Antoninus Caesar allowed them a twelfth.

37. Those who acted in any way contrary to edicts of the kings or prefects were fined, some a fourth of their estates, some a half, and others their entire estates.

41. If an Egyptian rears a child exposed on a dung heap and adopts him, a fourth of his estate is confiscated at death.

42. Those who style themselves improperly [in public and private documents] and those who knowingly concur therein are fined a fourth of their estates.

43. A fourth of the estate has been confiscated in the case of any Egyptian who after the death of his father has declared him as a Roman.

49. Freedmen of Alexandrians may not marry Egyptian women.

52. Marriage between Romans and Egyptians is [not]¹⁰³ permitted.

53. Egyptian women married to discharged soldiers are, if they formally style themselves Romans, subject to the article on nonconformity of status.

56. Soldiers who have not received a legal discharge, if they style themselves Romans, are fined a fourth of their property.

58. Persons who do not register themselves and those whom they ought in the house-by-house census [see § 82] are fined a fourth of their property, and if they are reported not to have registered on two occasions, they are sentenced to the same fine doubled.

60. Those who fail to register slaves suffer confiscation of the slaves only.

62. Soldiers in active service are not held responsible if unregistered, but their wives and children are called to account.

64. Cases of persons departing by sea without a pass are now under the jurisdiction of the prefect [cf. § 75, fourth and fifth selections].

66. Persons permitted to depart by sea who sail without a pass are fined a third of their property, and if they export slaves of their own without a pass they suffer confiscation of the whole.

70. Persons engaged in public services and members of their families are not permitted to engage in buying or moneylending in the districts in which they function, nor [acquire] land registered as unproductive or sold at public auction in the entire nome. Dummies put up for them are equally accountable, and such purchases were sometimes confiscated. The penalties are as follows: if a purchase from a private citizen, an amount equal to the purchase price; if a loan, an amount equal to the principal; if a sale, the *bona fide* price received; and dummies the same, at the risk of their principals.

76. A priest wearing a woolen garment and long hair suffers a penalty of 1,000 drachmas.

92. A child who has been exposed on a dung heap may not become a priest.

100. Notaries are allowed sixty days to register documents from the Thebaid in the city [of Alexandria]; from other districts, thirty days; from the city itself, fifteen days. The penalty for nonregistration is 100 drachmas; . . . to register before the fifth of the following month.

---

103. Scholars are divided as to whether the word *not* belongs here and was omitted from the text through error.

101. A fine of fifty drachmas is assessed on anyone writing a contract of mortgage or sale without registry thereof.

104. It is forbidden to sell crops before harvest, nor may anyone export[?] a crop that has not been registered.

105. If money is loaned at more than 1 drachma [per mina per month; cf. introduction to § 34], half the estate is confiscated, and a fourth of the estate of the borrowers.

106. It is not permitted to exchange money at more than the value [fixed by law].

108. Members of [unauthorized] associations were fined 500 drachmas; sometimes only the presiding officers have been fined [on restrictions on association see § 51].

109. *Caesariani*[104] are not permitted to purchase [confiscated] property sold at public auction.

110. *Vicarii* are forbidden to acquire ownership of property or to marry freedwomen.

111. Soldiers on active duty were forbidden to acquire property in the province wherein they were stationed.

80. Egyptian Agriculture

Egypt, the "gift of the Nile," was the agricultural country par excellence of the Empire, one of the principal granaries of Rome and Italy. The annual rise of the Nile, with its fertilizing silt, and the proper irrigation of the land were of paramount importance for Egypt's agricultural economy. At a number of places from Elephantine, near where the Nile enters Egypt, to Memphis, where the delta begins, there were stone flood gauges called Nilometers, some of them still visible today. By taking the reading of each year's flood crest the administration was able, on the basis of experience going back to pharaonic times, to calculate the expected crop and to impose taxes accordingly. To keep the country's elaborate network of irrigation canals and dikes in repair, every male native, either in person or through a substitute, was required to perform five days of dike corvée each year, and received a certificate attesting his performance of this compulsory service. When this work was neglected during crises, the canals became choked with silt, embankments collapsed, and the country faced economic catastrophe. Twice after such deterioration Roman emperors—Augustus in 30 B.C. and Probus in A.D. 275—put their armies to

104. *Caesariani* and *vicarii* (in the next clause) were minor functionaries in charge of confiscated property.

work cleaning out the canals. Most of the land of Egypt was imperial or state domain, leased out to tenant farmers, the backbone of the economy of Egypt.

THE NILOMETERS

Pliny, *Natural History* v. x. 58

A rise of sixteen cubits [at Memphis] is just right. Smaller rises of water do not irrigate all places; larger ones delay operations by receding too slowly. In the latter case the time for sowing is used up, because the soil is soaked; in the former case no time for sowing is afforded, because the soil is parched. The province is concerned over either extreme. In a rise of twelve cubits it senses famine; in a rise of thirteen cubits it still feels hungry; but fourteen cubits brings rejoicing, sixteen security, and eighteen luxury.

Strabo, *Geography* xvii. i. 48

The Nilometer [at Elephantine] is a well on the bank of the Nile constructed of ashlar masonry on which are indicated the greatest, least, and mean rises of the Nile; for the water in the well rises and drops with the river. Accordingly, there are marks on the wall of the well, measures of the full rises and of the others. Now, watchers inspect these and give out word to the rest of the people for their information; for long beforehand they know from such signs and the dates what the coming rise will be, and they predict it. This is useful both to the farmers with regard to water control, embankments, canals, and other such matters, and also to the prefects with regard to the revenues; for the greater rises mean also greater revenues.

IGRR, vol. I, no. 1,290, col. D

The following is a portion of the record inscribed on the walls of one of the Nilometers at Elephantine

Year 14 of Trajan Caesar . . . 25 cubits . . .
Year . . . of Tiberius Caesar, 24 cubits, 3 palms . . .
Year . . . of the lord . . . Caesar, 24 cubits, 5 palms, 2 digits
Year . . . of . . . Caesar, 24 cubits, 5 palms . . .
Year 7 of Nero Caesar . . .

Year 10 of Domitian Caesar, 24 cubits, 4 palms . . .
Year 25 of Augustus Caesar, 24 cubits, 4 palms, 1 digit
Year 13 of Nero Caesar, 24 cubits, 6 palms, 1 digit

CERTIFICATE FOR DIKE CORVÉE

Rylands Papyrus No. 210 (= *Select Papryi,* no. 389); A.D. 131

Year 16 of the Emperor Caesar Trajanus HADRIAN Augustus. Has worked
on embankment operations of the said year 16 from Phaophi 4 through
8 at the canal of Patsontis in Bacchias: Zoilus son of Petesuchus (son of
Elites), his mother being Taorsenuphis. I, Dioscorus signed [this certifi-
cate].

DECLARATION OF UNINUNDATED LAND

Michigan Papyrus No. 368; A.D. 170

To Sarapio, *strategus,* and to Serenus, royal secretary of the Arsinoite
nome, division of Heraclides, and to the village secretary of Perseae,
from Harpocratio son of Heracle ____ of the metropolis. I declare[105] the
five and five-eighths arouras of catoecic land [cf. note 110] belonging to
me near the village of Perseae, entered for taxation in the name of Suchas
son of Mysthes,[106] as unwatered for the current tenth year. I therefore
present this declaration.[107]

[Signed] I, Phaseis, village clerk, have received a copy for verifica-
tion. Phamenoth 1.

CROP DAMAGE

> This edict issued by the governor of Egypt deals with a chronic problem,
> keeping grazing animals from breaking into sown fields and destroying
> the crops there.

105. This is usually preceded in such declarations of unindated land by the phrase "in accordance
with the orders issued by the prefect."
106. Presumably, Suchas was farming the land on lease from Harpocratio; such arrangements were
quite common (cf. § 24).
107. That is, with a view to tax abatement, since the productivity of this land would be abnormal
because the fecundating Nile waters had not reached it during the annual flood. Cf. further § 78 and 84,
third selection.

Oxyrhynchus Papyrus No. 2,704; February, A.D. 292

Titus Honoratus, *vir perfectissimus,* prefect of Egypt, declares: There would be no profit at all from farming and its labors unless those who are in the habit of damaging crops were to take care not to do that. I learn, in fact, that the time of year has produced the greatest possible crops but the said herdsmen are damaging them. Therefore I order [all] to take care not to allow the animals into the crops; anyone who disobeys this shall be prosecuted before me, so that he shall be deprived of the animals themselves and shall himself be punished with severity.

Post in public. [Date.]

81. TAXATION: PROPERTY RECORDS

Upon the acquisition of taxable property, movable or immovable, owners were required to make a report thereof to the record office.

EDICT OF THE PREFECT OF EGYPT

Oxyrhynchus Papyrus No. 237, col. 8, lines 27–43 (= *Select Papyri,* no. 219); A.D. 89; From *LCL*

Marcus Mettius Rufus, prefect of Egypt, declares: Claudius Arius the *strategus* of the Oxyrhynchite nome has informed me that neither private nor public business is receiving proper treatment owing to the fact that for many years the abstracts in the property record office have not been kept in the manner required, although the prefects before me have often ordered that they should undergo the necessary revision, which is not really practicable unless copies are made from the beginning. Therefore I command all owners to register their property at the property record office within six months, and all lenders the mortgages which they hold, and all other persons the claims which they possess. In making the return they shall declare the source from which in each case the possession of the property devolved upon them. Wives also, if on the strength of some native law they have a lien on the property, shall add an annotation to the property statements of their husbands, and likewise children to those of their parents, if the enjoyment of the property has been secured to the latter by public instruments and the possession of it after their death has been settled on their children, in order that those who make agreements with them may not be defrauded through ignorance. I also command the scribes and recorders of contracts to execute no deed without an authorization of the record office, being warned that such a transaction has no validity and that they themselves will suffer the due penalty for disregarding orders. If the record office contains any property returns of earlier date, let them be preserved with the utmost care, and likewise the abstracts[108] of them, in order that if afterwards an inquiry should be held concerning persons who have made false returns they may be convicted therefrom. In order, then, that the use of the abstracts may become secure and permanent, so that another [general] registration shall not be required, I command the keepers of the record office to revise the abstracts every five years, transferring to the new lists the most recent property statement of each person, arranged under villages and kinds. Year 9 of Domitian, Domitianus[109] the 4th.

PROPERTY DECLARATIONS

Oxyrhynchus Papyrus No. 715 (= Mitteis, no. 212); A.D. 131

To Heras and Origenes, ex-gymnasiarchs, keepers of property records of the Heracleopolite nome, from Gorgias and Galestus, both sons of Polemo (son of Gorgias) and Dionysia (daughter of Galestus), of the village of Toëmisis. In accordance with orders we register at our own risk [i.e., for fraudulent or erroneous statement] jointly and equally for the current fifteenth year of the lord Hadrian Caesar the property which has come to us from that belonging to our deceased father Polemo son of Gorgias and Tapontos of the said Toëmisis, namely: his one-third share of a house in the said Toëmisis, and his share of a bare plot of ground, and—previously the property of his sister Helene daughter of Gorgias and the said Tapontos, in accordance with a will opened in the twelfth year of the lord Hadrian Caesar—near the village of Ibio Pachnubis one and seven-eighths arouras of catoecic land[110] from the allot-

---

108. Brief summaries of the real estate transactions reported in the returns were drawn in the property office and kept in a continuous file.

109. The month of Phaophi (September 28–October 27), so renamed in honor of the reigning emperor.

110. Land originally granted by the Ptolemies to Greek and Macedonian military settlers *(catoeci)*. It is interesting to observe that these lands continued for hundreds of years embracing a change of regime (from Ptolemaic to Roman) to be designated not only as "catoecic" but even by the names of the original grantees.

ment of Zoilus and Numenius, and near Pselmach. . . one-fourth aroura of catoecic land from the allotment of Menippus and Artemidorus. And we swear by the fortune of the Emperor Caesar Trajanus HADRIAN Augustus and by our ancestral gods that we have submitted the foregoing return honestly and truthfully and have made no false statement, or else may we be liable under the oath.[111] Year 15 of the Emperor Caesar Trajanus HADRIAN Augustus, month of Caesareus [see note 24], the 5th.

[Signatures] I, Gorgias the aforementioned, have submitted this. I, Heras, ex-gymnasiarch, through Hippod ____, my appointed secretary, have entered it in the records at the joint risk of the registrants without injury to any public or private interest. Intercalary day 5.

Oxyrhynchus Papyrus No. 246 (=Wilcken, no. 247); A.D. 66

To Papiscus, ex-*cosmetes* of the city and *strategus* of the Oxyrhynchite nome, Ptolmaeus, royal secretary, and the nome secretaries, from Harmiusis son of Petosiris (son of Petosiris) and Didyme (daughter of Diogenes), of the village of Phthochis in the eastern toparchy. I registered in the current twelfth year of the Emperor NERO Claudius Caesar Augustus Germanicus twelve lambs born from the sheep which I have near the said Phthochis, and I now register in this second return seven additional lambs born from the same sheep (=seven lambs). And I swear by the Emperor NERO Claudius Caesar Augustus Germanicus that I have kept nothing back. Farewell.

[Signatures] I, Apollonius, clerk of Papiscus, *strategus,* have recorded seven lambs. Year 12 of the lord Nero, Epeiph 30. I, Horio, clerk of Ptolemaeus, royal secretary, have recorded seven lambs. Year 12 of the lord Nero Caesar, Epeiph 30. I, Zeno, clerk of the nome secretaries, have recorded seven lambs. Year 12 of the lord Nero Caesar, Epeiph 30.

82. TAXATION: CENSUS AND POLL TAX

The assessment of provincial taxes and tribute, which in some provinces at least included a head tax on the subject population, was based on census as well as property records. The periodicity and procedures of the census varied with the historical background of the province. Here again the

---

111. The oath by the reigning emperor or his fortune appears in some but not all property and census declarations. There does not seem to have been a fixed prescription in the matter, but the penalties of fraud applied whether the oath was written or not.

papyri provide uniquely detailed information. In Egypt the census was instituted by Augustus in 10/9 B.C. and taken at fourteen-year intervals thereafter. For each census all heads of households had to submit in their *idia,* or place of origin, declarations registering themselves and all those living with them. The poll tax rolls were compiled on the basis of these declarations and the personal appearance at the registration office of the persons named therein. Except for Roman citizens and perhaps Alexandrians, who were exempt, all male inhabitants of Egypt between the ages of fourteen and (at different times) sixty or sixty-five were subject to the poll tax. The rate of the tax varied—townspeople, for example, paying less than villagers. Slaves were included in the declarations and paid for by their owners at the same rate as they paid for themselves.

THE CENSUS IN JUDAEA

Gospel According to Luke 2:1–5

It happened that in those days an edict went forth from Caesar Augustus for the whole world to register in the census. This first census was taken when Quirinius was governor of Syria.[112] And all journeyed forth to register, each to his own [native] town. And Joseph too went up from Galilee from the town of Nazareth to Judaea to the city of David which is called Bethlehem, since he was of the house and family of David, to register with Mary his betrothed, who was with child.

EDICT OF THE PREFECT OF EGYPT

British Museum Papyrus No. 904, lines 18–38 (= *Select Papryi,* no. 220), and *Aegyptus* (1951), 31:153; A.D. 104

Gaius Vibius Maximus, prefect of Egypt, declares: The house-by-house census having begun, it is essential that all persons who for any reason at all are absent from their nomes be notified to return to their own hearths in order that they may fulfill the customary procedure of registration and apply themselves to the farming incumbent upon them.[113] Knowing, however, that our city [Alexandria] has need of some of the people from the country, I desire all who think they have a satisfactory

112. Publius Sulpicius Quirinius conducted the first Roman assessment of Judaea while governor of Syria in A.D. 6. Efforts to assign another date for his governorship in order to reconcile it with the Gospels have proved unsuccessful.

113. The prefect here profits by the occasion of the census to order the fugitive peasants back to their land; cf. §§ 85, and 77, last selection.

reason for remaining here to register their reasons with Bul ____ Festus, squadron prefect, whom I have appointed for this purpose. Those showing their presence to be necessary will receive signed permits from him in accordance with this edict before the 30th of the present month of Epeiph, and all others shall return home within . . . days. Anyone found without a permit thereafter[?] will be severely punished; for I know well . . . [The rest of this final sentence is mutilated.]

A CENSUS DECLARATION

Michigan Papyrus No. 176; A.D. 91

To Horus son of Haryotes, census officer of Bacchias, and Apunchis son of Onnophris and the other elders [of the village], from Peteuris son of Horus, of the village of Bacchias. There belongs to me in the village one fourth of a house in which I dwell, and I register both myself and those of my household for the census of the past ninth year of the Emperor Caesar DOMITIAN Augustus Germanicus: myself, Peteuris son of Horus (son of Horus) and Herieus (daughter of Menches), cultivator of state land, about thirty years old, without identifying marks,[114] also my wife Tapeine daughter of Apkois, twenty-five years old, and my full[115] brothers Horus, about twenty years old, and Horio, about seven years old. And my brothers also own one fourth of the aforementioned house and courtyard in which we live.

[Signatures] I, the aforementioned Peteuris, have submitted this, and I swear by the Emperor Caesar DOMITIAN Augustus Germanicus that the foregoing is true and that I have made no false statement [cf. note 111]. Aphrodisius, village secretary, wrote for him since he is illiterate. Year 10 of the Emperor Caesar DOMITIAN Augustus Germanicus, Pachon 15.

83. TAXATION: RECEIPTS AND REPORTS

In addition to the poll tax the inhabitants of Egypt paid an enormous number and variety of taxes on agriculture, on trades and business activities, and for the maintenance of administrative and public services. Except

---

114. Identifying scars, moles, and such, though not always specified in these returns, were carefully recorded in the census rolls when the registrants made their personal appearance at the census office.

115. Literally, "born of the same father and of the same mother."

for the basic agricultural tribute and army supplies, which were delivered in kind, most levies were paid in money. In the collection, tax farmers were gradually replaced by liturgic local officials (cf. § 77). Collectors sent reports of receipts to the *strategus* of the nome every five days and every month, and in some if not all cases they had to file annual reports as well. Since the taxpayer had to furnish the material on which the tax receipt was written, *ostraca* (potsherds) became a favorite material for the purpose, since a ready supply of sherds could always be had in any household, whereas papyrus had to be purchased; this fact also helps to explain why, when papyrus was used, a whole series of tax payments was often recorded on a single piece. The following is a brief selection from the thousands of extant receipts for taxes of all kinds.

MISCELLANEOUS TAX RECEIPTS

Michigan Papyrus No. 393

[Caranis, A.D 158]

Year 21 of the Emperor Caesar Titus Aelius Hadrianus ANTONINUS Augustus PIUS, Mesore 16. We, Ptolemaeus son of Teus and associate collectors of grain taxes of the village of Philopator, or Theogenes, have received at the granary of the aforesaid village from the produce of the same year by level public wheat measure for rent of state land in Allotment 63 [cf. note 110] of Caranis to the account of Amatius Marcianus three artabs of wheat.

I, Sarapio[?], grain collector, have received the aforesaid three artabs.

Michigan Papyrus No. 383 (abridged)

[Caranis, A.D. 106–109]

Tenth year of the Emperor Caesar Nerva TRAJAN Augustus Germanicus Dacicus, Hathyr 30: paid to the collector Ptolemaeus[?] by Petheus son of Phaëis (son of Sarapio) and Taseus, for poll tax of the tenth year in Caranis, sixteen drachmas one half obol two *chalci* (dr. 16 ob. ¾); for police tax, dr. 1 ob. 2½. Tybi 23: eight drachmas (dr. 8). Pharmuthi 30: twelve drachmas (dr. 12) for half the bath tax, and for other taxes ob. 7, and for poll tax four drachmas (dr. 4). And in Year 11, month of Augustus [cf. chapter 2, note 31] for head tax[?] and prison-guard tax, two drachmas four obols (dr. 2 ob. 4). . . .

Twelfth year of the Emperor Caesar Nerva TRAJAN Augustus Germanicus Dacicus, Pachon 23: to the account of the eleventh year, paid to Socr . . . , collector's clerk [?], by Petheus son of Phaësis, for the one-sixth on gardens for the eleventh year in Psenarpsenesis, two drachmas four obols (dr. 2 ob. 4); for oil-delivery tax, ob. 2 *chal.* 2; for *naubium*,[116] ob. 1½ *chal.* 2; supplement, ob. 4; aroura tax, dr. 1 ob. 4½ *chal.* 2; supplement, ob. 11; for exchange,[117] ob. ½ *chal.* 2; fee for issuing receipt . . . for land survey tax, six drachmas four obols (dr. 6 ob. 4); supplement, ob. 2½; fee for issuing receipt. . . .

Strasbourg Ostracon No. 54

[Thebes, A.D. 15]

Paid into the public bank at Diospolis Magna by Maieuris son of Horus, for the tax on builders for the second year, twenty-two drachmas (dr. 22), and a supplement at the rate of ob. 1½ on the *stater*.[118] Year 2 of TIBERIUS Caesar Augustus, the Augustan day of New Augustus.[119]

Wilbour Ostracon No. 33

[Elephantine, A.D. 188]

Antonius Julius, farmer of the monthly tax on trades and the tax on prostitutes. Papremithes son of Pachnubis, weaver[?], has paid for Thoth and Phaophi of the current twenty-ninth year four drachmas (dr. 4). Year 29, Hathyr 10.

Wilbour Ostracon No. 14

[Thebes, A.D. 33]

Psenmonthes son of Phaëris has paid for the dike tax[120] of the nineteenth year six drachmas four obols, and for the bath tax ob. 4½; total dr. 7 ob. 2½, and supplement at the rate of ob. 1½. [cf. note 118] Year 20 of TIBERIUS Caesar Augustus, month of Augustus [cf. chapter 2, note 31] the 30th. [Signed] Petemenophis son of Picos.

116. The *naubium*, a cubic measure, was used as the unit of labor of the dike corvée (cf. § 80). Landholders frequently paid a tax in money in lieu of digging the required number of *naubia*.

117. Of copper money to silver. The supplementary charges mentioned in this receipt are also connected with the discount in copper coinage.

118. A *stater* was a 4-drachma piece. The rate of the supplementary payment (cf. note 117) is thus ¹⁄₁₆, or 6.25 percent.

119. Cf. chapter 1, note 16. The date is September 28. The designation "Augustan" or "Julian Augustan" was applied to a number of days in the calendar to commemorate birthdays or other notable events in the life of the imperial family.

120. This per-capita money tax for the maintenance of the irrigation canals was apparently paid in addition to, not in lieu of, the five days' corvée on the dikes, for which see § 80.

Grenfell Papyrus, vol. II, no. 50c; (= *Select Papyri,* no. 382); A.D. 147

Paid at the toll house of Philadelphia, the desert-guard tax by Diogenes outward bound with one donkey-load of fresh dates and one donkey-load of wheat. Eleventh year of the lord Antoninus Caesar, Thoth eighteenth (18).

TAX COLLECTORS' REPORTS

Oslo Papyrus No. 90; A.D. 138

To Aelius Numisianus, *strategus* of the Arsinoite nome divisions of Themistes and Polemo, from Ptolemaeus son of Eudaemo, Gaius Longus son of Dioscorus, Didymus son of Didymus, Sarapio son of Patermuthis, Didymus son of Heraclides, and associate superintendents of the pastures and marshes of Theadelphia and Polydeucia. The account of revenues from fishing from the 26th to the 30th of the month of Phaophi of the current second year of the lord Antoninus Caesar: 26th, dr. 48 ob. 5; 27th, dr. 36 ob.3; 28th, dr. 44 ob. 11; 29th, dr. 48 ob. 24; 30th, dr. 32 ob. 1; total, dr. 215. Submitted by Ptolemaeus son of Diodorus. Year 2 of the lord Antoninus Caesar, Hathyr 1. [Signed] I, Apollonius, keeper of records, have received a copy of this.

Berlin Papyrus No. 25 (= Wilcken, no. 270); A.D. 200

To Demetrius, *strategus* of the Arsinoite nome division of Heraclides, from Harpalus and associate collectors of money taxes of the village of Socnopaei Nesus. We paid into the public bank to the account of the month of Payni of the current eighth year for the tax on altars[?] four hundred drachmas (dr. 400). Year 8 of Lucius SEPTIMIUS SEVERUS Pius Pertinax Augustus and Marcus Aurelius Antoninus Augustus [CARACALLA], Epeiph 1.

Likewise, [Epeiph?] 4, for the tax on art wares one hundred drachmas (dr. 100). Total, 500 dr.

84. TAXATION: PRIVILEGES AND ABATEMENTS

The emperors frequently granted temporary or permanent tax privileges and exemptions from liturgies to favored groups. A few examples follow; for others, see §§ 29, 40, 56, 77, 151.

NERO "LIBERATES" GREECE

In A.D. 66–67 Nero toured Greece, competing in lyric and dramatic contests and chariot races in all the famous Greek games. "To make this possible, he gave orders that even those games which were widely separated in time should be brought together in a single year, so that some had to be given twice" (Suetonius, *Life of Nero* xxiii. 1). Everywhere he went he was greeted with flattering enthusiasm, and of course he was awarded every prize for which he competed. This did not stop him from plundering the art treasures of Athens, like Sulla and Caligula before him. But "on his departure he presented the entire province with freedom and gave the judges [of the contests] Roman citizenship and a large sum of money" (Suetonius, *Life of Nero* xxiv. 2). At a special convocation of the Isthmian Games, where in 196 B.C. Flamininus had proclaimed through a herald the liberation of Greece (cf. vol. 1, §§ 68, 122), Nero in person proclaimed a second liberation and granted all Greece exemption from tribute. The privilege of autonomy was withdrawn soon after by Vespasian, but most of the cities of Greece continued to enjoy freedom from imperial taxation. An inscription erected by the little town of Acraephiae (modern Karditza) in Boeotia preserves the text of Nero's edict summoning the Greeks to the Isthmus and of his "liberation" speech.

IG, vol. VII, no. 2,713 (=Dessau, no. 8,794=Dittenberger, no. 814); A.D. 67

The Emperor Caesar declares: Desiring to reward most noble Hellas for its good will and loyalty to me, I bid as many as possible from this province to assemble at Corinth on November 28.

When the crowds had gathered in assembly, he proclaimed the following: "It is an unexpected gift, Hellenes—though there is nothing that may not be hoped for from my magnanimity—which I grant you, one so great that you were incapable of requesting it. All Hellenes who inhabit Achaea and the land until now called[121] the Peloponnesus receive liberty and exemption from tribute, which not even in your most fortunate days did you all enjoy, for you were subjects either of foreigners or of one another. Would that I were making this gift while Hellas was still at its height, so that more people might enjoy this boon; for this, indeed, I have a grudge against time, for squandering in advance the fullness of

---

121. This suggests that Nero planned to change its name to Neronesus. Cf. Suetonius, *Life of Nero* lv: "He had an unreasoning passion for perpetuating his name forever, and so he removed the old names from many things and places and assigned them new ones after his own name, and also he renamed the month of April Neroneus; he had even intended to call Rome Neropolis."

my boon. Yet even now it is not out of pity but out of good will that I bestow this benefaction upon you, requiting your gods, whose care for me both on land and on sea I have never found to fail, for affording me an opportunity to bestow so great a benefaction; for to cities other rulers too have granted freedom, but Nero alone to an entire province."

[There follows a decree of the town of Acraephiae, here omitted, which repeats with adulatory embellishment some of Nero's language concerning "the restoration of our ancient state of autonomy and liberty," and orders the town's gratitude to be shown by the dedication of an altar inscribed "To Zeus the Liberator Nero forever" next to that of Zeus the Savior, and the dedication of "statues of Nero Zeus Liberator and the goddess Augusta Messalina alongside our ancestral gods in the sanctuary of Apollo."]

PRIVILEGES OF THE JEWS

Julius Caesar and the Roman emperors after him down to Claudius continued the privileges granted to the Jews of the Diaspora (cf. vol. 1, § 206) because of their religious obligations, by earlier Persian and Seleucid kings. After the Jewish rebellion of A.D. 66–70, however, Vespasian canceled the tax privileges of the Jews throughout the Empire and established a special "Jewish Account" of the imperial fisc, in which the annual contribution of two drachmas per capita previously made, with the emperors' permission, to the Temple at Jerusalem was henceforth collected for the benefit of the Temple of Jupiter on the Capitoline Hill in Rome.

Philo, Embassy to Gaius xl. 314–317

"Gaius Norbanus Flaccus, proconsul, to the magistrates of Ephesus, greeting. Caesar [Augustus] has written to me saying that it is a special ancestral custom of the Jews, wherever they live, to meet and contribute money which they send to Jerusalem. He does not wish them to be prevented from doing this. I am therefore writing to you, for your information, that these are his instructions."

Is this [letter of Norbanus Flaccus] not clear proof, Emperor [Gaius], of the policy of Caesar [Augustus] with regard to the respect due to our Temple? He did not want the assemblies [i.e., synagogues] of the Jews which are held for the collection of the first fruits and for other cultic purposes to be abolished in the same way as the common type of clubs were. There is another equally conclusive proof of Augustus' intentions.

He gave orders for regular sacrifices or holocausts to be offered daily at his own expense to the Most High God. These sacrifices continue to this very day. Two lambs and a bull are the offerings with which Caesar [Augustus] gave glory to the altar, knowing quite well that there was no image, visible or concealed.

TAX MORATORIA

In addition to the general cancellations of tax arrears in the second century (see § 20), the emperors on occasion granted remissions or moratoria to distressed areas. In the following edict Hadrian proclaims such a moratorium in Egypt, which had suffered a series of low Niles and sharply reduced crops.

Oslo Papyrus No. 78 (= *FIRA*, vol. I, no. 81); A.D. 135/136

The Emperor Caesar Trajanus HADRIAN Augustus, son of the deified Trajan Parthicus, grandson of the deified Nerva, *pontifex maximus,* holding the tribunician power for the twentieth year, twice acclaimed *imperator,* three times consul, father of his country, declares:

Since I have been informed that this year again, just as it did last year, the Nile has risen rather insufficiently and incompletely—even considering the fact that during the preceding years it produced successive rises that were not only full but even almost higher than at any time before, and that, flooding the entire country, it caused the production of most abundant and beautiful crops—nevertheless I have deemed it necessary to bestow a benefaction on the farmers, although I hope—may this be said with divine favor!—that any present deficiencies will be restored in the coming years by the Nile itself and the earth; [for such is (?)] the nature of things, changing from productivity and abundance to scarcity, and from scarcity to plenty.

May good fortune attend! Know that the money tax due for this year shall be distributed, as concerns inhabitants of the Thebaid, who have probably been most heavily injured by the scarcity, over five annual payments; as concerns those in the Heptanomia [cf. chapter 1, note 18] over four, and those in the Delta over three. The mode of paying semiannually is allowed those wishing to do so, the time limits granted remaining for those in the Thebaid five years, those in the Heptanomia four years, those in the Delta three years. Issued at Alexandria in the twenty-first year, Payni 16.

·   ·   ·   ·

This edict of the governor of Egypt dates from a decade when other documents tell us of widespread abandonment of farms and villages.

SB, no. 11,374; A.D. 168

Baienus Blassianus to Phocio, *strategus* of the Arsinoite nome, Themistes and Polemo divisions, greeting. The capitation taxes of the propertyless fugitives, customarily collected through a special assessment, I allow to be suspended for the present in order that persons in flight may return home and those who are at home may be able to remain there; and that all may know this, a copy of my letter is to be posted in the nome capital and in every village. It also behooves you not only to attend to the reports of the tax collectors and other functionaries, but also to ascertain carefully who really are fugitives, also displaying the list publicly in the villages from which they severally fled; for if a suspension of the collection has become necessary for now, [then surely] provision should be made to assure that also hereafter the country dwellers are not burdened with the tax payments of the non-fugitives.

85. Flight from Fiscal Oppression

In a list of standard questions addressed to oracles (see § 89, last selection), along with inquiries concerning other personal fortunes and misfortunes, appears, "Shall I become a fugitive?" When the regular and irregular demands of the imperial regime and its implacable representatives became intolerable, the last resort of the peasant or the liturgist was to take to flight (cf. § 77). The fugitive Egyptian might make for Alexandria or one of the other cities, hoping to be swallowed up amid the motley population, or he might hide in the desert and live, with others like himself, by brigandage. When a man left home in this way "for parts unknown," his family was required to notify the authorities. In the second century the "Good Emperors" imposed a compensating tax that distributed the tax defaults of these fugitives per capita upon the remaining population of a village or district.

NOTICE OF FLIGHT

Oxyrhynchus Papyrus No. 252 (= Wilcken, no. 215); A.D. 19/20

To Theo and Eutychides, local and village secretaries, from Thoönis daughter of Ammonius. My brother Ammonius son of Ammonius, weaver, registered [cf. § 82] in the part of a house formerly belonging to him in Tcumenuthis Street . . . fled abroad possessed of no other taxable estate. I therefore submit this memorandum, requesting that he be entered in the list of fugitive paupers from the current sixth year of TIBERIUS Caesar Augustus. [The signature and date are fragmentary.]

FROM A PETITION TO THE PREFECT OF EGYPT

Graux Papyrus No. 2, lines 1–13 (= *SB*, no. 7,462 = *Select Papyri*, no. 281); A.D. 55–59

To Tiberius Claudius Balbillus from . . . six collectors of poll tax of the aforesaid villages. . . . The formerly numerous inhabitants in the aforesaid villages have now been reduced to a few, some having fled in poverty, others having died without leaving heirs-at-law, and for this reason we are in danger, because of [the general] impoverishment, of having to abandon the collectorship.

OFFICIAL RECORD OF FUGITIVE PAUPERS

Rylands Papyrus No. 595; A.D. 57

[Report] from Nemesio, collector of poll tax of Philadelphia. Owed up to the month of New Augustus [cf. chapter 1, note 16] of the fourth year of the Emperor NERO Claudius Caesar Augustus Germanicus for poll tax, pig tax, and dike tax [122] of the said year:

Poll tax	dr. 4,728 ob. 3
Pig tax	dr. 121 ob. 1 [123]
Dike tax	dr. 1,100

---

122. For the dike tax, see note 120. The pig tax, anachronistically retaining its original name, was also levied by the Romans as a per-capita tax on the entire population of Egypt.

123. This amount is crossed out on the papyrus, presumably an inaccurate total.

Breakdown. Fugitive paupers in the list from the first year: [There follow forty-three names with amounts owed.][124]

Others who have fled since Payni of the aforesaid year to parts unknown: [Fifty-five names follow, with amounts owed.]

Defaulters in the . . . year, month of Augustus [cf. chapter 2, note 31] . . . : [Seven names, with amounts, follow.][125]

Others who have fled since Payni of the first year owing only the dike tax, who have [returned], paid the poll tax, and thereafter been excused [from the dike tax] by the royal secretary: [Forty-seven names follow, with the amount of the dike tax.]:

86. ABUSIVE CONDUCT OF OFFICIALS
AND SOLDIERS

One of the boons of the Principate to the provinces was its check upon the almost limitless orgy of corruption, brutality, and extortion into which Roman provincial administration in the last century of the Republic had degenerated (see vol. 1, §§ 141–146). Despite the good intentions of some of the emperors to regularize the financial and personal obligations of provincials—"to have my sheep shorn, not skinned alive," in the classic phrase of Tiberius (Suetonius, *Life of Tiberius* xxxii. 2)—the vastness of the Empire and its bureaucracy made it impossible for the central government to protect the population from the venality and arrogance of local officials and soldiers. From these it was subjected to a whole series of abuses, harbingers of the Roman holiday of violence and looting during the anarchy of the third century and of the pervasive corruption on all levels of officialdom during the fourth and fifth centuries.

Wilcken, no. 413, lines 1–30 (= *Select Papyri,* no. 211); A.D. 19

The proconsul Germanicus Caesar, son of Augustus, grandson of the deified Augustus, declares:[126]

[Inasmuch as I have heard that in view of my visit] requisitions . . . of boats and animals are being made and that quarters for lodgings are

124. A papyrus in the collection of Cornell University (no. 24) lists forty-four paupers missing from this village in July A.D. 56. Of these forty-four, thirty-four are here recorded as still missing fifteen months later; the other ten presumably returned and paid their arrears, at least in part (cf. below).

125. The total of 105 missing persons is estimated by the editors of the papyrus to equal 10 percent or more of the male inhabitants of Philadelphia.

126. For other records of Germanicus' visit to Egypt, see § 162, third selection.

being occupied by force and private persons intimidated, I have deemed
it necessary to make known that I wish neither boat nor beast of burden
to be seized nor quarters to be occupied by anyone except on the order
of my friend and secretary Baebius. For if it is necessary Baebius himself
will allot the quarters fairly and justly; and for requisitioned boats or
animals I order that hire be paid in accordance with my schedule. Those
who oppose [my orders] I desire to be brought before my secretary,
who will either himself prevent private persons from being injured or
will report the case to me. And I forbid any who meet beasts of burden
passing through the city [of Alexandria] to appropriate them by force;
for this is but an act of confessed robbery.

Philo, *Special Laws* II. xix. 92–94, III. xxx 159–62; From the translation of M.
Rostovtzeff, *Journal of Economic and Business History* (1928/29), 1:353–55

The rulers of the cities must stop breaking the necks of the cities by
continuous and heavy taxes and imposts. In doing so they fill their own
treasuries, hoarding in them alongside the money the ignoble vices
which defile their whole life. They choose on purpose the most merci-
less tax collectors full of inhumanity, giving them by this a starting
point for illicit gain. These men add to their natural brutality the free
hand granted to them by the orders of their masters, and since they have
set their mind on doing everything which pleases their masters they
indulge in the most wicked deeds, while justice and gentleness never
appear to them even in their dreams. Consequently they throw all things
into confusion and disorder in collecting the taxes, to the extent of
levying not only on the property but also on the person, with outrages
and violence, and the invention of new and unprecedented torture. . . .[127]

Recently a man was appointed tax collector among us. When some
of those who were supposed to owe taxes fled because of poverty and in
fear of unbearable punishment [cf. § 85], he carried off by force their
wives, their children, their parents, and the rest of their families, striking
them, and insulting them, and visiting all manner of outrages upon
them in an effort to force them either to inform against the fugitive or
else to make payment in his stead. But they could satisfy neither of these
requirements, for they knew nothing of the whereabouts of the fugitive

127. Tax collectors were frequently accompanied on their rounds by armed guards or soldiers (cf.
§ 77, second selection), whom they needed for protection but whom they often used to intimidate and
maltreat the taxpayers. Cf. also § 78 and note 131.

and they were themselves no less poverty-stricken than the man who had run away. Nevertheless the tax collector did not release them until he had tortured their bodies with racks and wheels and had killed them with newly invented devices of death. . . . [Others, fearing the same fate,] took their own lives by sword, or poison, or hanging, deeming it great good fortune, in view of their evil plight, to be able to die without torture. But those who did not hasten to kill themselves but were seized before they could do so were led away in a row, according to their nearness of kin, as in the case of actions for inheritance, the closest relatives first, then those next to them in succession, in the second or third place, till they came to the last. When there were no relatives left, the cruelty was visited upon the friends and neighbors of the fugitives. At times it was carried even into the cities and villages, which soon became desolate, being emptied of all their inhabitants, who left their homes and scattered to places where they hoped to escape detection.

British Museum Papyrus No. 1,171; (=Wilcken, no. 439); A.D. 42

Lucius Aemilius Rectus [prefect of Egypt] declares:

No one shall be permitted to requisition transportation facilities from the people in the country districts nor demand viatica or anything else gratis without a permit from me; and each of those possessing such permit may take sufficient supplies on payment of the price therefor. But if any of the soldiers or police or anyone at all among the aides in the public services is reported to have acted in violation of my edict or to have used force against anyone of the country people or to have exacted money, I shall visit the utmost penalty upon him.[128] Year 2 of the Emperor Tiberius CLAUDIUS Caesar Augustus, Germaniceus[129] the 4th.

AE, 1979, no. 565; A.D. c. 70

Lucius Vinuleius Pataicus, procurator of the Emperor Caesar Vespasian Augustus, to the magistrates, council and people of Thasos, greeting. I have ruled in your favor in the matter of your colony and you have received the money due you, and for the future I release you from the obligation to provide transport beyond your own territory. As for the

128. Cf. "Historia Augusta," *Life of Avidius Cassius* iv. 2: "Soldiers who had forcibly carried off anything from provincials he crucified in the very places in which they had transgressed."

129. The Egyptian month Pachon (April 26–May 25), so renamed probably in honor of the Emperor Claudius.

past decisions of Lucius Antonius, most eminent [imperial legate], I am unable to reverse them, but I have assigned you a soldier for the [disputes over?] boundaries, and I will fix those on the spot when I am there in person and you will have no cause for complaint; for I have a most intense desire to benefit everyone in Thrace, and you most especially. [The rest is lost.]

Inscr. Gr. Lat. Syriae, vol. V, no. 1,998; A.D. 81–96

From the orders of the Emperor Domitian Caesar Augustus, son of Augustus. To the procurator Claudius Athenodorus: Among the select matters demanding great pains I am aware that the attention of my divine father Vespasian Caesar was directed to the cities' privileges, intent upon which he commanded that the provincial territories be oppressed by neither [forced] rentals of beasts of burden nor importunate demands for lodgings. Nevertheless, wittingly or not modification has taken place and that [order] has not been enforced; there subsists to this day an old and persistent custom which would gradually develop into law if it were not forcibly prevented from prevailing. Therefore I order you also to see to it that no one requisition a beast of burden unless he has a permit from me; for it is most unjust that the influence or rank of any persons should occasion requisitions which no one but me is permitted to authorize. Let nothing, then, occur which will annul my order and thwart my purpose most useful to the cities (for it is just to come to the aid of exhausted provinces which with difficulty provide for their daily necessities), let no one oppress them contrary to my wish, and let no one requisition a guide unless he has a permit from me; for if the farmers are snatched away, the lands will remain uncultivated. And you, whether leasing beasts or using your own, will do best. . . . [The rest is lost.]

Italian Society Papyrus No. 446 (= *Select Papyri,* no. 221); A.D. 133–137; Adapted
from *LCL*

Marcus Petronius Mamertinus, prefect of Egypt, declares:

I am informed that without having a permit many of the soldiers when traveling through the country requisition boats and animals and persons improperly, in some cases seizing them by force, in others obtaining them from the *strategi* through favor or obsequiousness, the result of which is that private persons are subjected to insults and abuses and the army is reproached for greed and injustice. I therefore command the *strategi* and the royal secretaries in any case not to furnish to any person whatsoever, whether traveling by river or by land, any contribution for the journey without a permit, understanding that I will vigorously punish anyone who after this edict is discovered receiving or giving any of the aforesaid things. Year . . . of the lord Hadrian Caesar, Thoth 8.

SB, no. 9,207; A.D. *c.* 140?

[PRIVATE ACCOUNT OF PAYMENTS]

To the *stationarius*[a]	2 drachmas 1 obol
Gift	240 drachmas
Suckling pig	24 drachmas
To the guard	20 drachmas
For extortion[b]	2,200 drachmas
To the two police agents	100 drachmas
To Hermias, police agent	100 drachmas
To the . . .	2,574 drachmas 3 obols

[a] On the *stationarii* (military police) see chapter 2, note 35.

[b] The Greek term here is exactly translated by our American slang expression "shakedown." The artlessness with which this item is entered in the account is indicative of how completely routine the natives had come to regard such recurrent shakedowns. This account, with its frequent payments to soldiers, is an apt footnote to the *Gospel according to Luke* 3:12–14: "And even tax farmers came to be baptized; and they said to him, 'Master, what shall we do?' He said to them, 'Exact no more than what has been assigned to you.' And even soldiers would ask him, 'And what shall we do?' He said to them, 'Do not extort money by intimidation, or make false accusations against anyone, but be content with your pay.' "

OGIS, no. 609; A.D. C. 185

Julius Saturninus [governor of Syria] to Phaenae, chief village of the district of Tracho, greeting. If anyone billets himself by force in your houses, whether soldier or civilian, send word to me and you will receive satisfaction. For neither do you owe any contribution to visitors, nor, since you have a public hospice, can you be compelled to receive visitors in your homes. Post this letter of mine in a conspicuous place of your chief village, so that no one may plead ignorance.

IG, vol. XII, part 5, no. 132

[Island of Paros, A.D. 204]

Imperial letter.[130] You appear to us to be unaware of the decree of the senate, but if you consult persons who are informed you will learn that a senator of the Roman people is not required to receive guests in his house against his will. Issued on May 31, at Rome, in the consulship of Fabius Cilo (for the second time) and Annius Libo.

87. EXPOSURE OF CHILDREN

Among the Greeks and Romans unwanted infants were commonly cast out to die or to be picked up by a chance passerby. By the Hellenistic tradition of the eastern provinces such children could be raised slave or free, at the option of the finder. In Roman law, however, the status of a child was determined by its parentage, so that foundlings who were freeborn could not be reduced to slavery. Trajan's extension of the Roman practice to the East, which made it possible for freeborn children reared as slaves to reclaim their freedom without the obligation of reimbursing the rearer for the expenses of upbringing, must have served as a deterrent to the rearing of exposed children of uncertain parentage. The practice of exposure was condemned by Jews and Christians, and it was perhaps under such influence as well as because of the sharp rise in exposure produced by critical economic conditions that the first Christian emperor, Constantine, instituted various measures to alleviate the situation (see § 131), including public assistance to all needy and legalization throughout the Empire of the Hellenistic principle of finder's option. It was not until A.D. 374 that exposure was ruled a capital offense, and finally Justinian, in A.D. 529, reversing Constantine, enacted that exposure per se was to be regarded as evidence of freeborn status.

Oxyrhynchus Papyrus No. 744 (= *Select Papyri*, no. 105); I B.C.

Hilario to Alis, his sister,[131] many greetings, and to my lady Berous and Apollonarion. Know that we are still in Alexandria. Do not worry if they really go home and I remain in Alexandria. I ask and entreat you to

130. This text, written in Greek and Latin, was posted on the wall of the house whose exemption it confirmed. A bronze tablet of the second century (*SB*, no. 4,226) reads: "Immunity from taxation and from requisitions for the estate of Agrippina and Rutilia, now belonging to our lord the emperor."

131. The word *sister* may be here merely a term of endearment, but it is just as possible that Hilario married his sister, a common practice in Roman Egypt.

take care of the child, and as soon as we receive our pay I will send it up to you. If you chance to bear a child and it is a boy, let it be; if it is a girl, expose it. You have said to Aphrodisias that I should not forget you. How can I forget you? I ask you, then, not to worry. Year 29 of [Augustus] Caesar, Payni 23.

Pliny, *Letters* book x, nos.65–66

[Pliny to the Emperor Trajan]

There is an important question, one that affects the whole province, namely, concerning the status and maintenance of those whom they call foundlings. I have had read to me the enactments of the emperors on this matter, but since I found nothing either specific or general referring to the Bithynians I thought it necessary to consult you as to what you desire to be observed. For I did not think that I could be content with precedent in a matter that demands your authoritative decision. A purported edict of the deified Augustus was read to me concerning Asia; also a letter of the deified Vespasian to Sparta, and another of Titus to the same . . . and others of Domitian to the proconsuls Avidius Nigrinus and Armenius Brocchus, and likewise to Sparta. The reason I have not transmitted them to you is that they seem poorly copied and some are of doubtful authenticity, and that I suppose genuine and perfect versions are in your archives.

[Trajan to Pliny]

The question relating to freeborn persons who have been exposed and subsequently picked up by certain persons and reared in slavery has often been treated. But no enactment for all the provinces is found in the records of the emperors who preceded me. It is true that there are letters of Domitian to Avidius Nigrinus and Armenius Brocchus which ought perhaps to be observed, but only in those provinces concerning which he wrote; and Bithynia is not among these. My view therefore is that those who desire to be emancipated for such reason should not be denied the right to make a public declaration of their status, and they are not required to purchase their freedom by repaying the cost of their maintenance.

88. COMPLAINTS TO THE POLICE

The following two papyri are representative of numerous extant complaints of arson, assault and battery, theft, trespass, and other offenses addressed to police or judicial authorities.

Rylands Papyrus No. 125 (= *Select Papyri,* no. 278); A.D. 28; Adapted from *LCL*

To Serapio, chief of police, from Orsenuphis son of Harpaësis, notable of the village of Euhemeria in the division of Themistes. In the month of Mesore of the past fourteenth year of TIBERIUS Caesar Augustus I was having some old walls on my premises demolished by the builder Petesuchus son of Petesuchus, and while I was absent from home to gain my living, Petesuchus in the process of demolition discovered a hoard which had been secreted by my mother in a little box as long ago as the sixteenth year of [Augustus] Caesar, consisting of a pair of gold earrings weighing four quarters, a gold crescent weighing three quarters, a pair of silver armlets of the weight of twelve drachmas of uncoined metal, a necklace with silver ornaments worth eighty drachmas, and sixty silver drachmas. Diverting the attention of his assistants and my people, he had them conveyed to his own home by his unmarried daughter, and after emptying out the aforesaid objects he threw away the box empty in my house, and he even admitted finding the box, though he pretends that it was empty. Wherefore I request, if you approve, that the accused be brought before you for the due consequences. Farewell.

Orsenuphis, aged fifty, scar on left forearm.

Michigan Papyrus No. 423; A.D. 197; From the translation of H. C. Youtie and O. M. Pearl (Ann Arbor, 1944)

To Hierax also called Nemesio, *strategus* of the division of Heraclides of the Arsinoite nome, from Gemellus also called Horio, son of Gaius Apolinarius, Antinoite. I appealed, my lord, by petition to the most illustrious prefect, Aemilius Saturninus, informing him of the attack upon me by a certain Sotas, who held me in contempt because of my weak vision and wished himself to get possession of my property with violence and arrogance, and I received his sacred subscription authorizing me to appeal to his excellency the *epistrategus*. Then Sotas died and his brother Julius, also acting with the violence characteristic of them, entered the fields that I had sown and carried away a substantial quantity of hay; not only that, but he also cut dried olive shoots and heath plants from my olive grove near the village of Cercesucha. When I came there at the time of the harvest, I learned that he had committed these transgressions. In addition, not content, he again trespassed with his wife and a certain Zenas, having with them an infant,[132] intending to hem in my cultivator with black magic so that he should abandon his labor after having harvested part of another allotment of mine, and they themselves gathered in the crops. When this happened, I went to Julius in the company of officials, in order that these matters might be witnessed. Again, in the same manner, they threw the same infant toward me, intending to hem me in also with black magic, in the presence of Petesuchus and Ptollas, elders of the village of Caranis who are exercising also the functions of the village secretary, and of Socras their assistant, and while the officials were there, Julius, after he had gathered in the remaining crops from the fields, took the infant away to his house. These acts I made matters of public record through the same officials and the collectors of grain taxes of the same village. Wherefore of necessity I submit this petition and request that it be kept on file so that I may retain the right to plead against them before his excellency the *epistrategus* concerning the outrages perpetrated by them and the public rents due to the imperial fisc from the fields, because they wrongfully did the harvesting.

Gemellus also called Horio, about twenty-six years of age, whose vision is impaired.

Year 5 of Lucius Septimius Severus Pius Pertinax Augustus. Pachon 27.

89. Private Life in a Roman Province

Thousands of inscriptions, papyri, and ostraca, of which the following documents are the merest sampling, reveal the multiform activities in the lives of the inhabitants of the Roman Empire from the cradle to the grave.

---

132. Embryos and newborn infants (live as well as stillborn) were believed to have magical powers for evil.

INVITATION TO A FEAST

Fuad Papyrus No. 76; second century

Sarapous invites you to dine at his house on the occasion of the offering to our lady Isis, tomorrow, namely the 29th, beginning at the 9th hour.

ENGAGEMENT OF CASTANET DANCERS

Cornell Papyrus No. 9 (= *Select Papyri,* no. 20); A.D. 206; Adapted from *LCL*

To Isidora, castanet dancer, from Artemisia, of the village of Philadelphia. I wish to engage you with two other castanet dancers to perform at my house for six days from the 24th of the month of Payni according to the old reckoning;[133] you will receive among you for wages 36 drachmas for each day and for the whole six days four artabs of barley and twenty pairs of loaves; and whatever garments or gold ornaments you bring we will safely guard; and we will provide two donkeys for you when you come down and the same when you return. The fourteenth year of Lucius SEPTIMIUS SEVERUS Pius Pertinax Augustus and Marcus Aurelius Antoninus [CARACALLA] Pius Augustus and Publius Septimius GETA Caesar Augustus, Payni 16.

DEATH IN CHILDBIRTH

Fuad Papyrus No. 75; A.D. 64

Thaubas to his father Pompeius, greeting. You will do well to come immediately upon receipt of my letter, because your unfortunate daughter Herennia, ever blessed, died on Phaophi 9 of premature childbirth. She gave birth to an eight-month child stillborn, lived for four days after that, and then died and was given a fitting burial by us and her husband. She was taken to Alabanthis so that, if you come and wish to, you can see her. Alexander sends regards to you and the children. Farewell. Year II of the Emperor NERO Claudius Caesar Augustus Germanicus, Phaophi 18.

---

133. The old Egyptian year was still in common use despite the introduction of the Julian calendar.

A PRODIGAL SON

Berlin Papyrus No. 846 (= *Select Papyri,* no. 120); second century; From *LCL*

Antonius Longus to Nilous his mother, very many greetings. I pray always for your health; every day I make supplication for you before the lord Serapis. I would have you know that I did not expect that you were going to the metropolis; for that reason I did not come to the city myself. I was ashamed to come to Caranis, because I go about in filth. I wrote to you that I am naked. I beg you, mother, be reconciled to me. Well, I know what I brought on myself. I have received a fitting lesson. I know that I have sinned. I heard from . . . who found you in the Arsinoite nome, and he has told you everything correctly. Do you not know that I would rather be maimed than feel that I still owe a man an obol? . . . [The rest is lost.]

HOROSCOPE

Oslo Papyrus No. 6 (= *Select Papyri,* no. 199); A.D. 150; From *LCL*

The birth of Philoë. Year 10 of the lord ANTONINUS Caesar, Phamenoth 15 to 16, first hour of the night. Sun in Pisces, Jupiter and Mercury in Aries, Saturn in Cancer, Mars in Leo, Venus and Moon in Aquarius, horoscope[134] Capricorn.

QUESTIONS TO ORACLES

Wilcken, no. 122; A.D. 6

To the most great, powerful god Socnopaeus from Asclepiades son of Areus. Is it not granted me that I marry Tapetheus daughter of Marrieus and that she not become the wife of another? Reveal it to me and fulfill this that I have written. Tapetheus was formerly the wife of Horio. Year 35 of [Augustus] Caesar, Pachon 1.

Oxyrhynchus Papyrus No. 1,477 (= *Select Papyri,* no. 195); A.D. c. 300; From *LCL*

The following is a fragment of a list of standard questions addressed by visitors to an oracle.

134. That is, the point on the zodiac that was just rising above the horizon at the time of birth.

72. Shall I receive the allowance? 73. Shall I remain where I am going? 74. Am I to be sold? 75. Am I to obtain benefit from my friend? 76. Has it been granted me to make a contract with another person? 77. Am I to be reconciled with my offspring[?]? 78. Am I to get a furlough? 79. Shall I get the money? 80. Is he who is away from home alive? 81. Am I to profit by the transaction? 82. Is my property to be put up at auction? 83. Shall I find a means of selling? 84. Am I able to carry off what I have in mind? 85. Am I to become a beggar[?]? 86. Shall I become a fugitive? 87. Shall I be an ambassador[?]? 88. Am I to become a senator? 89. Is my flight to be stopped? 90. Am I to be divorced from my wife? 91. Have I been poisoned? 92. Am I to get my own?

90. Pro-Roman and Anti-Roman Sentiments

The attitude of the subject peoples toward their Roman rulers under the Republic is described in vol. I (see § 147). The masses hated their foreign conquerors and exploiters; the propertied minority in general acquiesced in and supported the foreign regime of "law and order" that protected their vested economic and political interests. This situation continued without essential change under the rule of the emperors, except for the increase in the size of the privileged classes throughout the Empire. The literature of the first two centuries, the imposing array of public works and philanthropies whose proud inscribed testimonials have come down to us—these, products of the upper strata of Roman and provincial society, echo faithfully the official imperial propaganda celebrating the enlightened, beneficent government of the Principate (cf. § 7). The major theme is that liberty has been exchanged for peace, protection, and prosperity; a secondary theme is that in any case revolt against the worldwide dominion and unprecedented might of Rome is futile. But underneath the surface calm of the *Pax Romana,* the hatred of the Roman regime and its visible symbols—the inexorable tax collector and the wealthy landholder or merchant, the arrogant government official and the bullying soldiery— smoldered among the masses and erupted in recurrent local riots and occasionally in sizable revolts.

THE BLESSINGS OF ROMAN IMPERIAL RULE

Tacitus, *Histories* IV. lxxiv

The following is an excerpt from a speech put by Tacitus, in the conventional practice of ancient historiography, into the mouth of the

Roman general Petilius Cerialis addressing the Gauls after suppressing their revolt of A.D. 70.

"Gaul always had its kingdoms and wars till you submitted to our authority. We, though so often provoked, have used the right of conquest to burden you only with the cost of maintaining peace. For the tranquillity of peoples cannot be had without armies, nor armies without pay, nor pay without tribute. All else is common between us. You often command our legions. You govern these and other provinces. There is no privilege, no exclusion. From praiseworthy emperors you derive equal advantage though you dwell far away, while the cruel ones are most formidable to those near them. Endure the extravagance and rapacity of your masters just as you bear barren seasons and excessive rains and other natural disasters. There will be vices as long as there are men. But they are not everlasting, and they are compensated by the intervals of better times. Perhaps you expect a milder rule under Tutor and Classicus,[135] and imagine that armies to repel the Germans and the Britons will be provided for less tribute than you now pay. Should the Romans be driven out—which the gods forbid!—what will result but wars among all these peoples? The good fortune and order of eight centuries has consolidated this mighty fabric of empire, and it cannot be pulled asunder without destroying those who sunder it. And yours will be the greatest peril, for you have gold and wealth, which are the chief causes of war. Therefore love and cherish peace and the city in which we enjoy an equal right, conquered and conquerors alike. Let the lessons of fortune in both its forms [i.e., good and bad] warn you not to prefer contumacy and ruin to obedience and security."

Aelius Aristides,[136] *To Rome* xxxvi–xxxix; Adapted from the translation of S. Levin
(Glencoe, Illinois, 1950)

[The emperor] governs the whole world as if it were a single city. . . . Just as cases are appealed from a district court to a [provincial] jury, imperial officials have to answer to an appellate tribunal where they are no safer from an adverse verdict than the appellants. . . . Is not this better than any democracy? Under democracy, once a man's case is decided in his town, he cannot take it elsewhere or to other judges. . . . Under the Roman Empire, neither the plaintiff nor the defendant need

135. Leaders of the Trevirans in the unsuccessful revolt against Roman rule.
136. Cf. chapter 1, note 45.

submit to an unjust decision.[137] Another great judge remains from whom justice is never hidden. At that bar there is profound and impressive equity between small and great, obscure and eminent, poor and rich, nobleman and commoner.

THE FUTILITY OF REVOLT

The following is part of a long, conventionally rhetorical harangue in which King Herod Agrippa of the Jews attempts, on the eve of the revolt of A.D. 66–70, to dissuade his people from taking up arms against Rome. See further the introduction to the following selection.

Josephus, *The Jewish War* II. xvi. 4. 348–361 (abridged); From *LCL*

"Now I know that there are many who wax eloquent on the insolence of the procurators and pronounce pompous panegyrics on liberty. . . . Granted that the Roman ministers are intolerably harsh, it does not follow that all Romans are unjust to you, and surely not Caesar; yet it is against them that you are going to war. It is not by their orders that an oppressive official comes from them to us. . . . How absurd it were because of one man to make war on a whole people, for trifling grievances to take arms against so mighty a power! . . .

"Will you, I say, defy the whole Roman Empire? Look at the Athenians, the men who, to maintain the liberty of Greece, once even consigned their city to flames. . . . Those men today are subjects of the Romans, and the city that was the queen of Greece is governed by order from Italy. Look at the Spartans . . . content to serve the same masters. Look at the Macedonians who . . . with Alexander scattered broadcast . . . the seeds of world empire; yet they submit to endure such a reversal of fate and bow before those to whom Fortune has transferred her favors. Myriads of other peoples, swelling with greater pride in the assertion of their liberty, have yielded. And will you alone disdain to submit to those to whom the whole world is subject?"

137. This sentence is corrupt in the original. The translation gives the general sense, which seems clear.

THE RAVAGES OF REVOLT

Among the most serious disturbances of the *Pax Romana* were the three Jewish revolts. Like the other peoples of the provinces, the Jews were divided by and large into pro-Roman rich and anti-Roman poor. There were additional stimulants to Jewish unrest, however, in their religious opposition to emperor worship and in other peoples' (especially Greeks') resentment of the privileges enjoyed by the Jews (§§ 76, 84). In fact, this anti-Semitism itself erupted at times in massacres of the Jews in cities, such as Alexandria and Cyrene, having sizable Jewish communities. The first revolt—of which Josephus has left us a long and detailed account in his *The Jewish War*—centered in Judaea and was put down after four years (A.D. 66–70), despite fanatic resistance. (Josephus' description of the triumph celebrated by Titus in Rome for this victory is given in § 5.) In reprisal, the Temple at Jerusalem was destroyed and the Jews' annual contributions for its upkeep were confiscated; this marked the end of Judaea as a Jewish religious and political center until recent times. The second revolt, kindled by reports that Trajan's armies were bogged down in Mesopotamia, erupted in A.D. 115 in a Greek–Jewish clash in Cyrene and spread eastward, sowing destruction of lasting effect in many places; it was not completely suppressed until A.D. 117, after Trajan's death. The two inscriptions that follow attest to the damage wrought by this desperate struggle in Cyrene. The city, theretofore one of the most prosperous in the Mediterranean, and the province never recovered from these ravages. These inscriptions are followed by a brief selection on the outbreak and devastation of the final revolt (A.D. 132–135), led by Simon, called *Bar Kochba* (Son of the Star), when Hadrian ordered a Roman colony founded on the site of Jerusalem.

AE, 1928, nos. 1–2

[Cyrene, A.D. 119]

The emperor Caesar Trajanus HADRIAN Augustus, son of the deified Trajan Parthicus, grandson of the deified Nerva, *pontifex maximus,* holding the tribunician power for the [third] time, three times consul, restored through the agency of Quintus . . . the road which had been ripped up and ruined in the Jewish revolt.

The Emperor Caesar Trajanus HADRIAN Augustus, son of the deified Trajan Parthicus, grandson of the deified Nerva, *pontifex maximus,* holding the tribunician power for the third time, three times consul, ordered the restoration for the city of Cyrene of the baths together with their porticoes and ball courts and other appurtenances, which had been torn down and burned in the Jewish revolt.

Cassius Dio, *Roman History* LXIX. xii. 1–xiv. 1; From *LCL*

At Jerusalem Hadrian founded a city in place of the one which had been razed to the ground, naming it Aelia Capitolina, and on the site of the temple of the god he raised a new temple to Jupiter. This brought on a war of no slight importance nor of brief duration, for the Jews deemed it intolerable that foreign peoples should be settled in their city and foreign rites planted there. . . .

At first the Romans took no account of them. Soon, however, all Judaea had been stirred up, and the Jews everywhere were showing signs of disturbance, were gathering together, and giving evidence of great hostility to the Romans, partly by secret and partly by overt acts; many outside peoples, too, were joining them through eagerness for gain, and the whole world, one might almost say, was being stirred up over the matter. Then, indeed, Hadrian sent his best generals against them. Foremost among these was Julius Severus, who was dispatched against the Jews from Britain, where he was governor. . . . He was able, rather slowly . . . but with comparatively little danger, to crush, exhaust, and exterminate them. Very few of them in fact survived. Fifty of their most important strongholds and 985 of their most famous villages were razed to the ground; 580,000 men were slain in the various raids and battles, and the number of those that perished by famine, disease, and fire was past finding out.[138]

HATRED OF ROME THE OPPRESSOR

Babylonian Talmud, *Sabbath* 33b; From the translation of M. Hadas, *Philological Quarterly* (1929), 8:373

Why did they call [Rabbi Judah ben Ilia] the first of the speakers? For once Rabbi Judah and Rabbi Jose and Rabbi Simeon were sitting, and Judah son of proselytes was sitting with them. Rabbi Judah began and said: "How excellent are the deeds of this nation. They have instituted

---

138. These figures, even if exaggerated, are sufficiently indicative of vast destruction. According to Eusebius (*Ecclesiastical History* IV. vi. 5), "Since then, by decree and enactments of Hadrian, the entire people is strictly forbidden to set foot even upon the land around Jerusalem; it was his order that not even from afar should they view their ancestral soil."

market places, they have instituted bridges, they have instituted baths."
Rabbi Jose was silent. Rabbi Simeon ben Yohai answered and said: "All
that they have instituted they have instituted only for their own needs.
They have instituted market places to place harlots in them; baths, for
their own pleasure; bridges, to collect toll." Judah son of proselytes
went and reported their words and they were heard by the government.
They said: "Judah who exalted shall be exalted; Jose who remained silent
shall be banished to Sopphoris; Simeon who reproached shall be put to
death."[139]

Cassius Dio, *Roman History* LXII. iii. 1–iv. 2 (abridged); From *LCL*

The following is part of a rhetorical speech put into the mouth of Budicca
(Boadicea), queen of East Anglia, addressing the Britons after the initial
success of their revolt under her leadership (A.D. 61).

"You have learned by actual experience how different freedom is from
slavery. Hence, even if anyone of you had previously, through ignorance of which was better, been deceived by the alluring promises of the
Romans, yet now that you have tried both, you have learned how great
a mistake you made in preferring an imported despotism to your ancestral mode of life, and you have come to realize how much better is
poverty with no master than wealth with slavery. For what treatment is
there of the most shameful or grievous sort that we have not suffered
since these men made their appearance in Britain? Have we not been
robbed entirely of most of our greatest possessions, while for those that
remain we pay taxes? Besides pasturing and tilling for them all our other
possessions, do we not pay a yearly tribute for our very bodies? How
much better it would be to have been sold to masters once and for all
than, possessing empty titles to freedom, to have to ransom ourselves
every year! How much better to have been slain and to have perished
than to go about with a tax on our heads! Yet why do I mention death?
For even dying is not free of cost with them; nay, you know what fees
we pay even for our dead. Among the rest of mankind death frees even
those who are in slavery to others; only in the case of the Romans do
the very dead remain alive for their profit. . . . We have . . . been
despised and trampled underfoot by men who know nothing else than
how to secure gain."

139. He is said to have escaped and to have spent the next fourteen years hiding in a cave. The
episode here reported took place in A.D. c. 135, about the time of the third Jewish revolt (see the
preceding selection).

Tacitus, *Life of Agricola* xxix–xxx

The following is a speech put into the mouth of Calgacus, a Caledonian chieftain, during the attempt of Agricola, governor of the Roman province of Britain, to subdue Caledonia to the north (A.D. 83–84).

Taught at last that a common danger must be repelled by union, the Britons had, by embassies and treaties, called forth the forces of all their states. Already more than 30,000 armed men were to be seen, and still there poured in all the youth and those whose old age was yet hale and vigorous, men renowned in war, each the bearer of decorations of his own. Preeminent among the many chieftains in valor and in birth was one named Calgacus, who is reported to have addressed in the following vein the multitude gathered round him and clamoring for battle.

"Whenever I consider the causes of this war and our present straits, my heart beats high that this very day and this unity of yours will be the beginning of liberty for all Britain. . . . Now they have access to the farthest limits of Britain; there are no more tribes beyond, nothing but waves and rocks, and more deadly than these, the Romans, whose oppression you have sought in vain to escape by obedience and submissiveness. Plunderers of the world, now that there are no more lands for their all-devastating hands, they search even into the sea. If the enemy is rich, they are rapacious, if poor, they lust for dominion. Not East, not West has sated them; alone of all mankind they covet riches and poverty with equal passion. They rob, butcher, plunder, and call it "empire"; and where they make a desolation, they call it "peace."[140]

APOCALYPTIC VISIONS OF VENGEANCE

Sibylline Oracles[141] VIII. 1–3, 31–42, 91–95, 121–129; From the translation of M. S. Terry (New York, 1890)

God's revelation of great wrath to come
In the last time upon a faithless world,
I make known, prophesying to all men.

·   ·   ·   ·

They waste the poor, that they themselves more land
Procuring may enslave them by deceit.

---

140. This sentence is one of the most famous quotations in all Latin literature.

141. Cf. vol. 1, introduction to § 147. Book VIII, which dates from the end of the second century, is clearly of Judaeo-Christian origin.

And if the huge earth from the starry heaven
Held not her throne afar, even light to men
Had not been equal, but, being bought with gold,
Had by the rich been owned, and for the poor
God must have then prepared another world.
On thee some day shall come, O haughty Rome,
A fitting stroke from heaven, and thou the first
Shalt bend the neck, be leveled to the earth,
And fire shall utterly consume thee, bent
Upon thy pavements, thy wealth shall perish,
And on thy site shall wolves and foxes dwell.
And then shalt thou become all desolate
As though thou hadst not been.

.   .   .   .

Near at hand
Is the end of the world, and the last day
And judgment of immortal God for such
As are both called and chosen. First of all
Inexorable wrath shall fall on Rome;
A time of blood and wretched life shall come.
Woe, woe to thee, O land of Italy,
Great, barbarous nation.

.   .   .   .

With images of gold and silver and stone
Be ready, that unto the bitter day
Ye may come, thy first punishment, O Rome,
Even a gnashing anguish to behold.
And no more under slavish yoke to thee
Will either Greek or Syrian put his neck,
Barbarian or any other nation,
Thou shalt be plundered and shalt be destroyed
For what thou didst, and wailing aloud in fear
Thou shalt give until thou shalt all repay.

The Revelation of John[142] 18:1–20

After this I saw another angel coming down out of heaven, having great
authority; and the earth was lighted up with his glory. And he cried out
in a mighty voice, saying: "Fallen, fallen is Babylon the great, and is

142. This work, in the tradition of Jewish apocalyptic literature, was written A.D. c. 95 in the
province of Asia to console Christians there for the persecutions of Domitian.

become a habitation of demons, and a hold of every unclean spirit and a hold of every foul and loathsome bird. For from the wine of the passion of her fornication[143] all the heathen are fallen, and the kings of the earth committed fornication with her, and the merchants of the earth waxed rich from the power of her wantonness. . . .

"How much soever she glorified herself and waxed wanton, so much give her of torment and mourning. . . . And the kings of the earth, who committed fornication and lived wantonly with her, shall weep and wail over her, when they look upon the smoke of her burning, standing afar off for fear of her torment, saying, 'Woe, woe, the great city, Babylon, the mighty city! for in one hour is thy judgment come.' And the merchants of the earth weep and mourn over her, for no man buyeth their cargoes any more—cargoes of gold, and silver, and precious stone, and pearls, and fine linen, and purple, and silk, and scarlet, and all thyine wood, and every vessel of ivory, and every vessel made of most precious wood, and of bronze and iron and marble, and cinnamon, and spice, and incense, and ointment, and frankincense, and wine, and oil, and fine flour, and wheat, and cattle, and sheep, and horses, and carriages, and slaves, and souls of men.

"And the fruit of thy soul's desire is gone from thee, and all luxury and splendor are perished from thee, and men shall find them no more at all. The merchants of these things, who waxed rich from her, shall stand afar off for fear of her torment, weeping and mourning, saying, 'Woe, woe, the great city, she that was arrayed in fine linen and purple and scarlet, and decked with gold and precious stone and pearl! for in one hour such great wealth is made desolate.' And every steersman, and everyone that saileth anywhither, sailors and all seafaring men, stood afar off, and cried out as they looked upon the smoke of her burning, saying, 'What city was like the great city?' And they cast dust on their heads, and cried out, weeping and mourning, saying, 'Woe, woe, the great city, wherein all that had their ships in the sea waxed rich from her extravagance! for in one hour is she made desolate.' Rejoice over her, heaven, and ye saints and apostles and prophets, for God hath judged your judgment upon her."

---

143. In the Septuagint this word is used in the metaphorical sense of *idolatry,* and some scholars take it in this sense in this passage.

5

WOMEN IN THE ROMAN WORLD

The status, expectations, and lives of most women in the Roman Empire persisted essentially as they had been from time immemorial in the Greek East and in Roman patriarchal society (see vol. 1, § 191). The traditional Roman woman was devoted to housekeeping, child bearing, chastity, submissiveness, and the ideal of being all her life *univira* (one-man woman). In practice, lower-class women—slave as well as free—had more freedom than those in the upper strata because they participated in work outside the home; also, prostitution was widespread in Rome, Italy (Pompeii, for example, had seven brothels), and the cities of the provinces. As for upper-class women, most led the respected life of the Roman *matrona,* but some broke out of the traditional restraints and followed in the pattern of the liberated women at the end of the Republic (see vol. 1, § 191). Without access to political power and the professions, they exercised their influence behind the scenes; they also emulated the activities and vices of men, a pattern deplored by the Roman poet Horace at the beginning of the imperial period (vol. 1, § 204, second selection). Augustus sought to curb these tendencies by stringent legislation on marriage and adultery (vol. 1, § 204).

91. GUARDIANSHIP OF WOMEN

Cicero, *In Defense of Murena* xii. 27

Our ancestors established the rule that all women, because of their weakness of intellect, should be under the power of guardians.

Ulpian, *Rules* xi. 1, 18, 25, 27

Guardians are appointed for males as well as for females: for males only when under age, on account of their tender age; but for females, when under and of age, on account of the weakness of their sex and their ignorance of business matters.

The Atilian Law orders that, for women and for wards who have none, guardians be granted by the praetor and a majority of the tribunes of the plebs, and these we call Atilian guardians. But, because the Atilian Law is in force only at Rome, it is provided by the Julian-Titian Law that guardians of such persons be similarly granted in the provinces also by the governors.[1]

The guardians of male and female wards transact their business and give their authorization; the guardians of women merely give their authorization.

The authority of a guardian is necessary for women in the following transactions: if they take legal action in accordance with statute or judgment, if they undertake an obligation, if they transact any civil business, if they permit a freedwoman of theirs to cohabit with the slave of another, if they alienate salable property.

APPOINTMENT OF A GUARDIAN

Oxythynchus Papyrus No. 1,466; A.D. 245

To Valerius Firmus, prefect of Egypt, from Aurelia Arsinoë. I beg, my lord, that you assign Aurelius Herminus to me as guardian in accordance with the Julian and Titian Laws. Year 2, Pachon 26. Page 94, Volume I.[2]

Translation of the [preceding] Latin. To Valerius Firmus, prefect of Egypt, from Aurelia Arsinoë. I beg, my lord, that you assign Aurelius Herminus to me as guardian in accordance with the Julian and Titian Laws. Submitted on May 21 in the consulship of the Emperor Philip Augustus and Titianus. I, Aurelia Arsinoë, daughter of Sarapio, have submitted the petition requesting that Aurelius Herminus be appointed my guardian. I, Aurelius Timagenes[?] son of . . . wrote for her since

---

1. The Atilian Law is known to have been in effect by 186 B.C.; how much earlier than that it was passed is unknown. The Julian and Titian Laws (they were probably separate though related measures) belong to the principate of Augustus.

2. This notation gives the file number of the petition in the prefect's office.

she is illiterate. I, Aurelius Herminus son of Dionysius, consent to the petition. Year 2, Pachon 26.

[The prefect's subscription] Unless you are under the control of another guardian, I grant you the guardian you request.

WOMEN INDEPENDENT OF GUARDIANSHIP: THE "THREE-CHILDREN PRIVILEGE"

Gaius, *Institutes* I. cxlv, cxciv

If anyone by will assigns a guardian to his son and daughter and both reach puberty, the son ceases to have a guardian but the daughter nonetheless remains under guardianship; for, in accordance with the Julian and Papian-Poppaean Laws, it is only by the right of children that women are freed from guardianship.

Moreover, freeborn women are freed from guardianship by the right of three children; freedwomen, if they are under the legal guardianship of their patron or of his children, by that of four.

REQUEST FOR RELEASE FROM GUARDIANSHIP

Oxyrhynchus Papyrus No. 1,467 (= *Select Papyri*, no. 305); A.D. 263

. . . [laws have been made], Most Eminent Prefect, which empower women who are honored with the right of three children to be independent and act without a guardian in whatever business they transact, especially those who know how to write.[3] Accordingly, as I have been fortunate in being blessed with goodly offspring and am literate and able to write with a high degree of ease, it is with complete assurance that I address your Highness through this petition of mine with the object of being empowered to accomplish without hindrance whatever business I henceforth transact. I beg you to place it without prejudice to my rights in your Eminence's file, in order that I may obtain your aid and acknowledge my eternal appropriate[?] gratitude. Farewell.

[Signed] I, Aurelia Thaïsous, also called Lolliana, transmitted this for submission. Year 10, Epeiph 21.

[Subscription] Your petition shall be kept in the file.

---

3. Literacy was not a necessary condition for the "three-children privilege." This superfluous detail was doubtless added as another evidence of the petitioner's qualifications for independence.

MALE CONTROL

Justinian, *Institutes* I. ix

Children whom we have begotten in lawful wedlock are in our power. Matrimony is the union of male and female, involving the habitual intercourse of daily life. The power we have over our children is peculiar to Roman citizenship and is found in no other nation. The offspring of you and your wife are in your power, as well as that of your son and his wife, that is, your grandson and granddaughter, and so on. But the offspring of your daughter are not in your power, but in that of their own father.

Not only our natural children are under our authority but those whom we adopt as well. . . . Women also cannot adopt because they have no control even over their own children. . . .

When a guardian violates the chastity of his female ward, he shall be sentenced to deportation, and all his property shall be confiscated to the treasury. . . .

A man who contracts marriage with his own female ward in violation of the decree of the senate is not legally married. And he who was her guardian or curator can be prosecuted for adultery if he marries a girl under twenty-six years of age who has not been betrothed to him, or destined for him, or mentioned for this purpose in a will.

Ulpian,[4] *Rules* v. 8–9

When legal marriage takes place, the children always follow the father; but if it does not take place, they follow the condition of the mother, except where a child is born of an alien father and a mother who is a Roman citizen, as the Minician law directed that where a child is born of parents one of whom is an alien it follows the condition of the inferior parent.

A child born of a father who is a Roman citizen and a Latin mother is a Latin, one born of a freeman and a female slave is a slave, since the child follows the mother as in cases where there is no legal marriage.

---

4. Domitius Ulpianus, one of Rome's most famous jurists, was the author of numerous legal works. He was active in the early third century.

92. Marriage by Arrangement

This letter gives us a vivid picture of how marriages were arranged in the upper classes, and reveals also some of the criteria used in these circles for judging the suitability of a match.

Pliny, Letters book 1, no. 14

Gaius Plinius to his dear Junius Mauricus, greeting.

You request me to look for a husband for your niece; and it is fitting for you to give me this commission rather than anyone else. For you know how much I esteemed and loved that great man, her father, and with what encouragement he helped me in my youth, and how he caused me to appear to deserve the praises he used to bestow upon me. You could not give me a more important or more pleasant commission, nor could I undertake a more honorable task than to choose a young man worthy of begetting the grandchildren of Rusticus Arulenus.

Such a person would take a long time to find, were not Minicius Acilianus ready to hand, almost as if by prearrangement. While he loves me very warmly with the affection usual between young men (for he is just a few years younger), he reveres me as he would an old man; for he is as desirous of modeling himself on me and of being instructed by me as I was by you and your brother.

He is a native of Brixia,[5] a city of that Italy of ours, the Italy which still retains and preserves much of the modesty, the frugality, and even the rustic simplicity of the olden days. His father is Minicius Macrinus, one of the leading men of the equestrian order, who desired no higher status; for though elevated to praetorian rank by the deified Vespasian, he very steadfastly preferred an honorable repose to this display—or shall I call it rank—of ours. His maternal grandmother is Serrana Procula, of the municipality of Padua. You are acquainted with the manners of the place; yet Serrana is even to the Paduans a model of strictness. He is fortunate in having also Publius Acilius as his uncle, a man of almost unequaled gravity, wisdom, and integrity. In short, there is nothing in his entire family which would not please you as if it were in your own. As for Acilius himself, he has great energy as well as great application, joined with a high degree of modesty. He has already passed with the greatest credit through the offices of quaestor, tribune, and praetor, so

---

5. Modern Brescia, in northern Italy, the region where Pliny was born.

that he has already spared you the necessity of canvassing for him. He has the look of a gentleman, fresh-colored and blooming, and a natural handsomeness in his whole build together with a certain senatorial grace. I think that these factors should not be slighted in the least, for this is a kind of reward that should be given to the chastity of maidens.

I don't know whether to add that his father is very rich. For when I consider the kind of person you are, for whose niece I am seeking a husband, I feel it is unnecessary to mention wealth. But when I look at the public morality and even the laws of the state, according to which a person's wealth claims paramount attention, it certainly merits some notice. And, indeed, where children—in fact, a goodly number of them —are to be thought of, this consideration too is to be weighed in arranging matches. You may perhaps think that I have indulged my affection and exaggerated beyond the merits of the case. But I stake my integrity that you will find everything far greater than what I am telling you in advance. I do love the young man very warmly, as he deserves; but it is one of the characteristics of a lover not to overburden the object of one's affection with praises. Farewell.

93. CONTRACTUAL AGREEMENTS

MARRIAGE CONTRACT

Berlin Papyrus No. 1,052 (= *Select Papyri*, no. 3); 13 B.C.; From *LCL*

To Protarchus[6] from Thermion daughter of Apio, with her guardian Apollonius son of Chaereas, and from Apollonius son of Ptolemaeus. Thermion and Apollonius son of Ptolemaeus agree that they have come together to share a common life, and the said Apollonius son of Ptolemaeus acknowledges that he has received from Thermion by hand from the house a dowry of a pair of gold earrings weighing three quarters and . . . silver drachmas; and from now on Apollonius son of Ptolemaeus shall furnish to Thermion as his wedded wife all necessaries and clothing in proportion to his means and shall not ill-treat her nor cast her out nor insult her nor bring in another wife, or else he shall straightway forfeit the dowry increased by half, with right of execution both upon the person of Apollonius son of Ptolemaeus and upon all his property as if

6. Chief of a tribunal at Alexandria, to whom contractual agreements had to be submitted for official validation.

by legal decision; and Thermion shall fulfill her duties toward her husband and the common life and shall not absent herself from the house for a night or a day without the consent of Apollonius son of Ptolemaeus, nor dishonor nor injure their common home nor consort with another man, or she, if guilty of any of these actions, shall, after trial, be deprived of the dowry; and in addition the transgressing party shall be liable to the prescribed fine. Year 17 of [Augustus] Caesar, Pharmuthi 20.

DEED OF DIVORCE

Berlin Papyrus No. 1,103 (= *Select Papyri*, no. 6); 13 B.C.; From *LCL*

To Protarchus from Zois daughter of Heraclides, with her guardian— her brother Irenaeus son of Heraclides—and from Antipater son of Zeno. Zois and Antipater agree that they have separated from each other, severing the union which they had formed on the basis of an agreement made through the same tribunal in Hathyr of the current seventeenth year of [Augustus] Caesar, and Zois acknowledges that she has received from Antipater by hand from his house the material which he received for dowry, namely clothes to the value of 120 drachmas and a pair of gold earrings. The agreement of marriage shall henceforth be null, and neither Zois nor any other person acting for her shall take proceedings against Antipater for restitution of the dowry, nor shall either party take proceedings against the other about cohabitation or any other matter whatsoever up to the present day, and hereafter it shall be lawful both for Zois to marry another man and for Antipater to marry another woman without either of them being answerable. In addition to this agreement being valid, the one who transgresses it shall moreover be liable both to damages and to the prescribed fine. Year 17 of [Augustus] Caesar, Pharmuthi 2.

94. WOMEN'S ROLE IN MARRIAGE

Plutarch, *Marriage Advice (Moralia)* 138A–146A (abridged); From *LCL*

Muses may lend their presence and co-operation to Aphrodite, and may feel that it is no more fitting for them to provide a lyre or lute well attuned than it is to provide that the harmony which concerns marriage and the household shall be well attuned through reason, concord, and philosophy. Indeed, the ancients gave Hermes a place at the side of Aphrodite, in the conviction that the pleasure in marriage stands especially in need of reason; and they also assigned a place there to Persuasion and the Graces, so that married people should succeed in attaining their mutual desires by persuasion and not by fighting and quarrelling. . . .

The bride will provide for him who does not run away or feel annoyed at her first display of peevishness and unpleasantness a docile and sweet life together. Those who do not patiently put up with the early girlish disagreements are on a par with those who on account of the sourness of green grapes abandon the ripe clusters to others. Again, many of the newly married women because of their first experiences get annoyed at their husbands, and find themselves in like predicament with those who patiently submit to the bees' stings, but abandon the honeycomb. . . .

Fishing with poison is a quick way to catch fish and an easy method of taking them, but it makes the fish inedible and bad. In the same way women who artfully employ love-potions and magic spells upon their husbands, and gain the mastery over them through pleasure, find themselves consorts of dull-witted, degenerate fools. . . .

Whenever the moon is at a distance from the sun we see her conspicuous and brilliant, but she disappears and hides herself when she comes near him. Contrariwise a virtuous woman ought to be most visible in her husband's company, and to stay in the house and hide herself when he is away.

Herodotus was not right in saying that a woman lays aside her modesty along with her undergarment. On the contrary, a virtuous woman puts on modesty in its stead, and husband and wife bring into their mutual relations the greatest modesty as a token of the greatest love.

Whenever two notes are sounded in accord the tune is carried by the bass; and in like manner every activity in a virtuous household is carried on by both parties in agreement, but discloses the husband's leadership and preferences. . . .

Cato expelled from the Senate a man who kissed his own wife in the presence of his daughter. This perhaps was a little severe. But if it is a disgrace (as it is) for man and wife to caress and kiss and embrace in the presence of others, is it not more of a disgrace to air their recriminations and disagreements before others, and, granting that his intimacies and pleasures with his wife should be carried on in secret, to indulge in admonition, fault-finding, and plain speaking in the open and without reserve?

Just as a mirror, although embellished with gold and precious stones, is good for nothing unless it shows a true likeness, so there is no advantage in a rich wife unless she makes her life true to her husband's and her character in accord with his. . . .

A wife ought not to make friends of her own, but to enjoy her husband's friends in common with him. The gods are the first and most important friends. Wherefore it is becoming for a wife to worship and to know only the gods that her husband believes in, and to shut the front door tight upon all queer rituals and outlandish superstitions. For with no god do stealthy and secret rites performed by a woman find any favor. . . .

Nature unites us through the commingling of our bodies, in order that, by taking and blending together a portion derived from each member of a pair, the offspring which she produces may be common to both, so that neither can define or distinguish his own or the other's part therein. Such a copartnership in property as well is especially befitting married people, who should pour all their resources into a common fund, and combine them, and each should not regard one part as his own and another part as the other's, but all as his own and nothing as the other's. . . .

The marriage of a couple in love with each other is an intimate union; that of those who marry for dowry or children is of persons joined together; and that of those who merely sleep in the same bed is of separate persons who may be regarded as cohabiting, but not really living together. As the mixing of liquids, according to what men of science say, extends throughout their entire content, so also in the case of married people there ought to be a mutual amalgamation of their bodies, property, friends and relations. . . .

From the outset the bride should realize the stepmother's attitude in her mother-in-law, and, in the event of some harsher incident later on, may not feel indignant or resentful. A wife ought to take cognizance of this hostility, and try to cure the cause of it, which is the mother's jealousy of the bride as the object of her son's affection. The one way to cure this trouble is to create an affection for herself personally on the part of her husband, and at the same time not to divert or lessen his affection for his mother. . . .

For your wife you must collect from every source what is useful, as do the bees, and carrying it within your own self impart it to her, and then discuss it with her, and make the best of these doctrines her favourite and familiar themes. For to her "Thou art a father and precious-loved mother, Yea, and a brother as well."[7] No less ennobling is it for a man to hear his wife say, "My dear husband, Nay, but thou art to me guide, philosopher, and teacher in all that is most lovely and divine."[8] Studies of this sort, in the first place, divert women from all untoward conduct; for a woman studying geometry will be ashamed to be a dancer, and she will not swallow any beliefs in magic charms while she is under the charm of Plato's or Xenophon's words. And if anybody professes power to pull down the moon from the sky, she will laugh at the ignorance and stupidity of women who believe such things.

95. WOMEN OF AUGUSTUS' FAMILY

The women of the imperial court enjoyed extraordinary opportunities for reflected power and for luxury living. Augustus' wife Livia, Rome's first lady for about sixty years, and his half-sister Octavia were exemplars of traditional Roman womanhood. The former, devoted mother of Augustus' successor Tiberius, was the butt of malicious gossip. But Augustus died with her name on his lips: "Livia, live mindful of our marriage, and farewell" (Suetonius, *Life of Augustus* lxxxix. 1). Octavia was a retiring figure, devoted to her own children and those of Antony, her "only husband." To Augustus' shame and frustration, his only child, Julia, from her youth the pawn of his dynastic plans, in a mature display of independence turned out to be one of the most dissolute women of the time, as was her daughter Julia (II).

LIVIA

Tacitus, *Annals* v. 1

She was a woman of most eminent nobility through her birth in the Claudian family and by virtue of her adoption among the Livii and Julii. She had children by her first marriage to Tiberius Nero, who was an exile from the Perusine War but returned to the city when peace had been reached between Sextus Pompey and the triumvirs [39 B.C.]. Shortly after, Caesar [the later Augustus], attracted by her beauty, took her

7. Adapted from Homer, *Iliad* vi. 429.
8. Adapted from *ibid*.

from her husband (no one knows if she was unwilling) and was so hasty that he brought her pregnant into his home with no decent interval allowed for her labor. After this she produced no other offspring, but her connection with the Augustan blood-line increased with the marriage of Agrippina and Germanicus, by which she shared [with Augustus] great-grandchildren. In the purity of her household she used the ancient model, but she was more sophisticated than approved by women of old. Headstrong as a mother and gracious as a wife, she complemented well the political skills of her husband.

Cassius Dio, *Roman History* LVII. xii. 2–6

Livia was honored very greatly, far above all women of the past, so that she could at any time receive the Senate and those individuals of the people who desired to greet her at home. And this was entered in the public record. The rescripts of Tiberius for some time included her name also, and communications were addressed to both alike. She never ventured to enter the Senate House or the camps or the assemblies, but she undertook to administer everything as if she were the empress. For during Augustus's lifetime she had enormous influence, and she often claimed that she had made Tiberius the emperor. . . . Many expressed the opinion that she should be addressed as "Mother of her Country," while many others proposed that she be called "Parent."

OCTAVIA

Plutarch, *Life of Antony* xxxi. 1–3; lix. 1–2

Augustus loved his sister very much, a wondrous thing of a woman, as the saying goes. . . . All encouraged this marriage [with Antony], hoping that Octavia, who had dignity and intelligence in addition to such great beauty, as soon as she became his and the object of his love—as is natural with such a woman—would be the source of agreement and complete salvation for them. Therefore, when both men [Antony and Octavian] came to an agreement, they went to Rome and there they celebrated the marriage of Octavia, although remarriage was not permitted by law until ten months after the death of the husband. However, by a special decree of the Senate the time restriction was remitted for them. . . .

Octavia was deemed to have been insulted [by Antony's affair with Cleopatra], and so Caesar ordered her, when she returned from Athens, to live in her own house. However she refused to leave her husband's home, and indeed she begged Octavian, unless for other reasons he had decided to declare war on Antony, to ignore her situation, declaring that it was an ugly thing to hear that the two greatest generals, one out of love for a woman, the other because of jealous rivalry, immersed the Romans in civil war. The things she said were confirmed by her deeds. For she lived in her husband's house as if he were present, and splendidly and magnificently raised his children, not only those born from her but also those born from Fulvia. Receiving friends of Antony's who were sent [to Rome] to seek political offices or on business, she helped them in their requests to Caesar [later Augustus]. Through this she unintentionally hurt Antony, for he was hated because of his mistreatment of such a woman.

JULIA

Suetonius, *Life of Augustus* lxiv. 2

In bringing up his daughter and granddaughters Augustus even had them trained in weaving, and he forbade them to say or do anything except openly and what might be recorded in the household diary. Indeed, he forbade contact with outsiders to such an extent that he once wrote Lucius Vinicius, a distinguished and proper youth, that he had not behaved with propriety because he had come to Baiae to pay his respects to his daughter [without permission].

Macrobius, *Saturnalia* II. v. 2–3

Julia was thirty-eight years old, a period in life, if she had kept any good sense, verging on old age. But she often abused her good fortune and the indulgence of her father. On the other hand, she had a sincere love for literature and great learning, which were easy to obtain in that household. In addition to these qualities, a gentle regard for humanity and a disposition not in the least cruel gained great respect for the woman from those who were aware of her vices and yet marveled as well at the great diversity in her.

Again and again, in language balanced between gentle indulgence and severity, her father admonished her to restrain her extravagant lifestyle and her notorious companions. At the same time, whenever he looked at his numerous grandchildren and noticed their resemblance to Agrippa, he was ashamed to have doubted his daughter's virtue.

Velleius Paterculus, *Roman History* II. c. 2–5

In the city in the very same year [2 B.C.] . . . in Augustus' own house-hold a storm broke loose, indecent even to mention and horrible to recall. For his daughter Julia, completely unmindful of her distinguished father and husband [Tiberius], left unperformed not a single act tainted by excess and sexual passion which a woman could do or disgracefully experience. She was in the habit of measuring the magnitude of her fortune by the grossness of her offense, championing as licit anything that was her desire. . . . [Many men of the senatorial and equestrian orders] debauched the daughter of Caesar and wife of Nero [Tiberius], and they paid the penalty which they would have suffered if they had violated the wife of any man. Julia was relegated to an island [Pandateria] and removed from the sight of her fatherland and parents, although her natural mother Scribonia voluntarily accompanied her and remained a constant companion in her exile.

96. ESTEEMED WOMEN OF THE AUGUSTAN AGE

MURDIA

CIL, vol. VI, no. 10,230 (=Dessau, no. 8,394)

Murdia, daughter of Lucius, mother. [The next part of this inscription is lost.] She made all her sons equal heirs after giving a share to her daughter. Her maternal love is apparent from her affection for her children and the equality of the shares. She bequeathed to her [second] husband a fixed sum of money so that his dowry right might be increased by the honor of her judgment. Recalling the memory of my father into consultation, and in accordance with her agreement and planning in her will that she prepared, she bequeathed definite legacies, not with the thought of giving any offense by preferring me to my stepbrothers. But remembering my father's generosity, she decided that there be given to me what in the judgment of her husband she had received from my father's estate, so that these things, kept in custody by her orders, might be restored to my ownership.

And so she herself was determined in this to preserve with obedience and integrity her marriages to worthy men, and as a bride to become more pleasing by her merits, to be held dearer because of good faith, to be left more adorned by her judgment, and after her death to be praised by the consensus of the citizens, inasmuch as the division of the shares contains a pleasing and faithful attitude toward her husbands, equality to her children, and to justice and truth.

For these reasons, since the praise of all good women is simple and similar, for the natural and proper good trust they have preserved does not demand a variety of words, it is enough to say that they have all done the same things worthy of a fine reputation. And because it is difficult for a woman to acquire new praises, since their lives are less subject to change, of necessity their common virtues should be celebrated, because if anything is lost of just precepts it might harm the rest.

Therefore, my dearest mother deserved greater praise than all because with her modesty, integrity, chastity, obedience, making of wool, diligence, trust, she was equal and similar to the other upright women. Nor in the midst of any dangers did she give up her virtue, work, wisdom. [The rest is lost.]

CORNELIA

Cornelia, wife of Lucius Aemilius Paullus (consul 34 B.C.; censor 22 B.C.), was half-sister of Augustus' daughter Julia, the mother of both being Scribonia. Cornelia is depicted here as speaking from the tomb.

Propertius, *Elegies* book IV, no. 11

Cease, Paullus, importuning my tomb with tears; the gate of darkness is not opened to any prayers. . . .

What help was there in my marriage to Paullus, in the triumphs of my ancestors, in such illustrious offspring that are witnesses to my fame? The Fates were no less cruel to Cornelia, and I am but a handful of dust. . . .

If ancestral trophies have ever brought fame and glory to anyone, our statues bespeak [famous ancestors on both sides]. Later when my girl's attire gave way to marriage, another kind of ribbon caught up and bound my hair. I was joined to your bed, Paullus, destined to leave it thus. On this stone the inscription will read that I was married to one man only. I call to witness the ashes of my ancestors, revered by you, O Rome. . . .

Cornelia never tarnished such spoils of war. Nay, even in that great house hers was a role to be emulated. My life was never altered, it is wholly without censure. I have lived with distinction between the torch of marriage and the torch of death. Nature gave me laws derived from blood, not to be virtuous through pressure of fear or criticism. . . . Nor have I shamed you, my sweet mother Scribonia. What would you have wished changed in me except my fate? I am praised by my mother's tears and the laments of the city, and my ashes are covered also by the grief of Caesar [Augustus]. He is saddened because I lived as worthy half-sister to his daughter, and we saw tears come from a god [Augustus].

And yet I deserved the dress of honor that is the mark of a fertile woman, nor was I snatched away from a sterile house. You, Lepidus, and you, Paullus [her sons], are my solace after death. . . .

And you, my daughter . . . be sure you imitate me and have but one husband. And, my children, support the house with a line. I am ready for the boat of death to sail, now that I have so many who will prolong my deeds. This is the highest reward of a woman, her triumph, that common talk praises her in death after a life well lived.

And now to you, Paullus, I commend our children, our mutual pledges. This concern of mine still breathes, burned into my ashes. Father, play the role of a mother. The throng of all my children must be the burden of your shoulders. When you kiss them as they weep, add the kisses of their mother. . . .

OVID'S DEVOTED WIFE

From his place of exile at Tomi on the Black Sea, Ovid pours out his heart to his loyal wife who remained at home.

Ovid, *Laments* i. vi

Not so beloved was Lyde by the poet of Claros [Antimachus] nor Bittis by the poet of Cos [Philetas], as you, my wife, are fixed in my heart, worthy you of a less wretched husband, not a better one. My ruin is propped up by you as by a supporting pillar. If I am still anything, it is all your gift. It is all your doing that I have not been plundered or stripped bare by those who have attacked the timbers of my shipwreck. . . . Someone, unfaithful in my bitter circumstances, would have come into my property if you had allowed it. Your virtue, with the aid of courageous friends, drove him off, friends to whom it is not possible to render proper thanks. . . .

If you had been fated to have Homer as your poet, the fame of

Penelope would be second to yours. I don't know whether you owe this to yourself, made into a devoted woman without a teacher, or whether such character was bestowed on you at birth, or whether the first lady [i.e., Livia], revered by you through all the years, teaches you to be the exemplar of a good wife and by long training has made you like herself. . . .

You will hold first place among the saintly heroines, you will be the first in reputation for the goodness of your heart. Through whatever power my praises will have, you will live on in my songs forever.

97. SULPICIA IN LOVE

Daughter of Servius Sulpicius Rufus (consul 51 B.C.), Sulpicia was the niece and ward of Marcus Valerius Messalla Corvinus, a leading senator of the Augustan age, and a member of his literary circle. Of her poetry only 140 lines survive, the only extant remains of a Roman woman poet. These poems—"The Garland of Sulpicia"—are preserved among the elegies attributed to another member of the circle, Tibullus.

"Tibullus," *Elegies* xiii, xiv, xviii

i

At last love has come and such a love that I would be more ashamed of a rumor that I concealed it than that I bared it to someone. Venus in answer to my songs brought him to me and put him into my arms; Venus fulfilled her promises. Let anyone tell of my joys who does not have his own. I resent having to entrust anything to sealed letters, so that no one may read it before my darling. Indeed, I glory in my indiscretion, and I loathe having to put on appearances for the sake of reputation. Let people say of me that I was worthy of him as he was of me.

ii

The dreaded birthday is here which in sadness I must observe, bored in the country and without my Cerinthus. What is sweeter than the city? Is a country villa the right place for a girl? or some chilly brook in a field near Arretium [modern Arezzo, in Tuscany]. Messalla, you are too fond of me. Now relax; journeys, my kinsman, are often untimely. Secluded, I leave here my heart and my feelings; compulsion does not allow me my own judgment.

iii

My sweetheart, I hope I may not be again such a burning concern to you as I seemed to have been a few days ago, if in my entire life I did anything foolishly for which I would confess more regret than the fact that I left you alone last night, wishing to conceal my passion.

98. AT THE COURT OF THE EMPEROR CLAUDIUS

Exploiting their positions at the apex of power and society Valeria Messalina, granddaughter of Augustus's sister Octavia, and Agrippina the Younger, granddaughter of Augustus himself, became exemplars of promiscuity and the destructive use of power. Messalina, Claudius's third wife, was executed for promiscuity and adultery in A.D. 48. Agrippina, his niece and fourth wife, wielded immense power and succeeded in eliminating him to make way for her son Nero, who in turn murdered her.

MESSALINA

Tacitus, *Annals* XI. xii, xxxvii–xxviii

The affection of the people carried over from their memory of Germanicus, whose only male survivor was Nero. Moreover, the compassion for his mother Agrippina was increased because of the cruelty of Messalina, who was always hostile and at the time more aggressive in stirring up accusations and accusers. But she was diverted by a new amour close to frenzy. For she was so inflamed by Gaius Silius, the handsomest of the Roman youth, that she caused him to end his marriage to Junia Silana, a noble woman, and took complete possession of the adulterer. Silius was not unaware of the scandal or the danger. But he was certain that he would be destroyed if he refused, and he harbored some hope of deceiving Claudius. At the same time he had great rewards, and consoled himself by closing his eyes to the future and enjoying the present. As for Messalina, she did not act furtively, but came to his house with a large retinue, clung to his steps, and lavished riches and honors on him.

Finally, as if the imperial power had already passed to another, the slaves and freedmen of Claudius, the splendor of the *princeps* were seen at the house of the adulterer. . . .

Meanwhile, Messalina in the gardens of Lucullus was prolonging her life, fashioning pleas, not without hope and at times with anger. Such pride did she exhibit in her extremity. And if Narcissus had not hastened her death, she might have turned destruction upon her accuser. Now Claudius, having returned home and soothed by a prolonged meal, ordered that she be visited and that they inform the *wretch* (this was the very word they said he used) that she was to present herself to plead her case the next day. At these words it was feared that his anger was abating and her attraction for him returning, and if he delayed, the coming night and the memory of the conjugal bed would intervene. So Narcissus burst forth and enjoined one of the centurions and a tribune [of the Praetoran Guard] to carry out the murder. Such was the order of the emperor, he said. One of the freedmen, Euodus, was assigned to watch over and carry out the execution. Hastening to the gardens speedily, he found her stretched on the ground, with her mother Lepida present. She had not been on good terms with her daughter during her success, but was now moved to pity at her supreme trouble, and was trying to persuade her not to wait for the executioner, telling her that her life was over, and that nothing else remained but to render her death honorable. But in such a mind corrupted by debauchery not a shred of honor was left. Messalina was pouring out tears and useless plaints when the doors were beaten in by the rush of those entering. The tribune stood there in silence, while the freedman inveighed against her with many insults worthy of a slave. Then for the first time clearly realizing her fate, she took a dagger and moved it in fear to her throat and breast. She was stabbed by a blow of the tribune. Her body was granted to her mother, and it was announced to Claudius at dinner that Messalina was dead.

AGRIPPINA

Suetonius, *Life of Claudius* xliii–xliv

Near the end of his life Claudius openly gave some indication that he regretted his marriage with Agrippina and his adoption of Nero. When some of his freedmen noted with approval his condemnation of a woman accused of adultery the day before, he said, "It has been my misfortune to have wives who have been unfaithful to my bed. But they did not escape punishment."

Soon after, he made his will, and had it witnessed by all the magistrates. But he was prevented from proceeding further by Agrippina, who was accused of a variety of crimes by her own guilty conscience as well as by informers. It is agreed that he was killed by poison, but it remains uncertain where and by whom it was administered. Some authors say that as he was dining with the priests in the Capitolium it was given to him by his taster, the eunuch Halotus. Others say it was done by Agrippina at his own table, with mushrooms, a dish of which he was very fond.

99. Satire on Women

Juvenal, *Satires* vi [9] (abridged)

If you are lucky to find a wife of modest character, you should prostrate yourself before the Tarpeian threshold and sacrifice to Juno a heifer with gilded horns. Few indeed are the wives worthy of touching the fillets of Ceres, few whose kisses a father would not fear. Weave a garland for your doorposts and a wreath thick with ivy berries for your lintel. Is Hibernia satisfied with one man? You will sooner extort from her that she would be content with one eye. . . .

Can any one be shown worthy of your vows? . . . Do shows in all parts of the theaters have one woman you may love with confidence, one you could pick out among them? When the effeminate Bathyllus dances the role of the pantomining Leda, Tuccia has no control over her bladder, Apulia screams as if she were in a sudden embrace. . . .

Listen to what Claudius endured. When his wife saw that her husband was asleep, the imperial whore had the nerve to prefer a mat to the royal bed, putting on a hood at night and leaving attended by no more than one maid. Hiding her black hair with a yellow cap, she entered the brothel reeking with an old patchwork covering, to an empty cubicle all her own. Then, naked with gilded nipples, she prostituted herself under the fake name of Lycisca, and exposed her belly that bore you, O noble Britannicus. She seductively received those who entered, and demanded money, and all night long took the thrusts of all who came. Then, when

9. This is Juvenal's justly famous but highly exaggerated and rhetorical denunciation of Roman women in all walks of life.

the pimp sent off all his girls, she left sadly, the last to close her cubicle, still passionate with the lust of her stiff vagina. She left tired out by the men yet not satisfied, her cheeks dirty and bruised, grimy with lamp smoke, she brought back to her bed the smell of the brothel.

Should I talk of love charms and brewed poison administered to a stepson? Women commit more serious crimes through the power of sex, and their sins of lust are the least of these. . . .

Is no worthy woman, in your view, to be found among all these crowds? Let her be beautiful, charming, rich, fertile, let her display in her halls the images of old ancestors, let her be more chaste than all the Sabine women who stopped the war with dishevelled hair, a rare bird on the earth, very like a black swan. Who could endure a wife who has all these virtues? I very much prefer a woman of Venusia than you, Cornelia, mother of the Gracchi, if with your great virtues you bring a haughty snobbery and count triumphs as part of your dowry. . . .

Some faults are small, yet intolerable to husbands. What is more offensive than that no one thinks herself beautiful unless she, a Tuscan woman, has become a Greekling. . . . Everything is in Greek, although it is more disgraceful for our people not to know Latin. In this language they show their fears, anger, joys, troubles. What's more, they make love in Greek. You might grant this to girls. But you, on the verge of eighty-six, still in Greek? That tongue is not decent in an old woman. . . .

If your mother-in-law is alive, give up all peace. She is the one who teaches her daughter to rejoice when her husband is despoiled. She teaches her to respond to a seducer's letters. She deceives the guards or bribes them. It is she who calls in a doctor though her daughter is well, and throws off the heavy blankets. The adulterer meanwhile lies hidden in secret, silent though impatient at the delay, and he masturbates. Do you really expect the mother to teach honest ways different from her own? Indeed, it is profitable for the immoral old woman to bring up an immoral daughter.

There is hardly a law case in which a woman has not started the litigation. Manilia is the plaintiff if she is not the defendant. They compose and frame the pleadings all by themselves. . . .

Who does not know of the purple cloaks and the ointment of women wrestlers? Who has not seen the wound on the dummy which she strikes with frequent stabbings and her shield, and goes through all the routine, a matron more worthy of blowing the trumpet at the Floralia unless she nurses something more in her breast and is actually preparing for the gladiatorial arena. What modesty can you expect of a woman with a helmet, who denies her sex and likes manly strength? But she wouldn't want to become a man for the pleasure of men is so small. . . .

We are now suffering from the evils of a long peace. Luxury, more deadly than weapons, has descended on us, and avenges the conquered world. From the time that poverty perished in Rome, no crime, no deed of lust is absent from us. . . . Filthy lucre first brought in foreign ways, and enervating wealth has corrupted the ages with foul indulgence. What does drunken Venus care? She does not know the difference between the groin and the head. . . .

But even worse is the woman who when she sits down to dinner praises Vergil and sympathizes with Dido about to commit suicide. She matches and compares poets, weighing Vergil in one part of the scale and Homer in the other. Schoolmasters yield, teachers of rhetoric are defeated, the whole group is silent, neither a lawyer nor an auctioneer will speak, not even another woman. . . . As a philosopher she sets down definitions also on moral matters. . . . Let not your wife know all history; let there be some things in books she does not understand. . . .

There is nothing a woman will not allow herself, nothing she deems base, when she puts green gems on her neck and fastens huge pearls to her distended ears. Nothing is more intolerable than a rich woman.

100. A Gallery of Praiseworthy Women

ARRIA

Arria's husband was condemned to death for participation in a conspiracy against the Emperor Claudius.

Cassius Dio, *Roman History* LX. xvi. 5–6

Arria, the wife of Caecina Paetus did not want to live after the execution of her husband, although she could have been in a position of some honor (for she was quite intimate with Messalina). Indeed, she fortified her husband when he was faint-hearted. For taking the sword, she stabbed herself and handed it to him, saying, "See, Paetus, it doesn't hurt."

HELVIA

Seneca, To Helvia, On Consolation xvi. 1–4

Don't resort to the excuse of being a woman. It is almost a right accorded to women to weep to excess, but within limits. And so our ancestors gave a space of nine months to widows grieving over their husbands, a public law providing that they should cease persistence in womanly grief. They did not prohibit mourning, but limited it. . . . There is no reason to look at certain women whose sadness once begun did not end until death. You have known some women who from the time of the loss of children have never taken off their mourning garments. Your life, being more courageous, demands more of you. Feminine excuse cannot touch a person from whom all feminine faults are absent.

Lack of chastity, the greatest evil of the century, does not count you in the number of many. Neither gems nor pearls have seduced you. Riches have not glittered for you as the greatest good of the human race. Well brought up in an old and austere home, you have not been turned aside by imitation of worse people, dangers even to the upright. Never have you been ashamed of your fertility, as if this might be a reproach to your time. Never, like others, have you concealed your pregnancies, as if they were indecent burdens, nor have you aborted your hope of children conceived in your womb. Never have you stained your face with cosmetics and artificial adornments. Never has a garment pleased you which when taken off would bare your nakedness. For you the unique ornament, supremely beautiful and beholden to no age, is modesty.

CALPURNIA, PLINY'S THIRD WIFE

Pliny, Letters book IV, no. 19; From LCL

She is incomparably discerning, incomparably thrifty; while her love for her husband betokens a chaste nature. Her affection to me has given her a turn to books; and my compositions, which she takes a pleasure in reading, and even getting by heart, are continually in her hands. How full of solicitude is she when I am entering upon any cause! How kindly does she rejoice with me when it is over! When I am pleading, she stations messengers to inform her from time to time how I am heard, what applauses I receive, and what success attends the cause. When at any time I recite my works, she sits close at hand, concealed behind a curtain, and greedily overhears my praises. She sings my verses and sets them to her lyre, with no other master but Love, the best instructor.

From these circumstances I draw my most assured hopes, that the harmony between us will increase with our days, and be as lasting as our lives. For it is not my youth or my person, which time gradually impairs; it is my glory of which she is enamoured. But what else could be expected from one who was trained by your hands, and formed by your [Calpurnia's mother] instructions; who was surrounded under your roof with all that is pious and moral, and had learned to love me from your account of my character? For while you honoured my mother as if she were your own, so you formed and encouraged me from infancy, presaging that I should become all that my wife now thinks I am. Accept therefore of our mutual thanks, that you have given us to each other, and, as it were, chosen the one for the other. Farewell.

MINICIA MARCELLA

Pliny, *Letters* book v, no. 16; From *LCL*

I write this to you[10] under the utmost oppression of sorrow: the younger daughter of our friend Fundanus is dead! Never surely was there a more agreeable or amiable young person, or one who better deserved to have enjoyed a long, I had almost said, an immortal life! She was scarce thirteen, and already had all the wisdom of age and sedateness of a matron, though joined with youthful sweetness and virgin modesty. With what an engaging fondness would she hang upon her father! How affectionately and respectfully embrace us who were his friends! How warm her regard for the nurses, conductors to school, and teachers, who, in their respective offices, had the care and education of her! How studious, how intelligent, at her book, how sparingly and discreetly she indulged in play! With what forbearance, patience, nay courage, did she endure her last illness! She complied with all the directions of her physicians; she encouraged her sister and her father; and when all her strength of body was exhausted, supported herself by the single vigour of her

10. Aefulanus Marcellinus, not otherwise known. Fundanus mentioned in the next line, was consul in A.D. 107.

mind. *That,* indeed, continued even to her last moments, unbroken by the pain of a long illness, or the terrors of approaching death; and it is a reflection which makes the loss of her so much the more to be lamented.

ALLIA POTESTAS

CIL, vol. VI, no. 37,965

To the spirits of the dead of Allia Potestas, freedwoman of Aulus.

Here lies a woman of Perusia. No other woman among many, scarcely one or two were more precious. Industrious in a big way, you are held in a small urn. O cruel arbiter of fate and stern Proserpina, what good you deprive us of, and what woes have prevailed? She is missed by all. I am weary of answering questions. They shed tears, the kindly tokens of their thoughts.

She was brave, chaste, resolute, innocent, a most faithful guardian, neat at home, very neat in public, very well known to the people. She alone could confront all things. She was brief in her talk, and so remained irreproachable. She was the first to get out of bed, likewise the last to retire, when everything had been put in order. Her yarn never left her hands without cause. No one was before her in obedience and in wholesome habits. She did not think of her own pleasure, and seemed never to take liberties. Her skin was white, her eyes beautiful, golden her hair, and an ivory glow remained on her face, such as they say no mortal ever had. And on her snow white bosom the shape of her breast was small. What shall I say of her legs? . . .

She was never troubled, but beautiful with a kindly body. She had smooth limbs; every hair was removed. Perhaps one might find fault that her hands were rough. Nothing pleased her unless she had done things by herself. There was no pursuit she knew enough of. She remained unblemished because she never committed any wrong. . . .

These verses her patron offers weeping endlessly. . . .

Whoever dares to harm this tomb dares also to harm the gods. This tomb distinguished by its inscription, believe me, has divine power.

101. Benefactress

H. Pleket, *Epigraphica* II (Leiden, 1969), no. 8; A.D. 43

The people of Patara [in Lycia] decreed: Whereas Junia Theodora, a Roman living in Corinth, a woman held in the highest esteem . . . who with full measure and generosity aided many of our citizens from her own means, and welcomed them in her home, and in particular never ceased benefiting our citizens regarding any favor asked, the majority of the citizens have met in assembly to give testimonial on her behalf. In gratitude our people agreed to vote to commend Junia and to give testimonial of her generosity to our native city and her good will, and declares that it urges her to increase her generosity to our city, knowing that our people too will not cease in their good will and gratitude to her, and will do everything for the excellence and glory she deserves. For this reason—may good fortune attend—it was decreed to commend her for all that she has done. [Cf. also p. 268.]

102. Professions and Occupations

A PHILOSOPHER

Hypatia, distinguished astronomer, mathematician, follower of Platonism in Alexandria, was murdered in A.D. 415, at age forty-five, during a fanatical antipagan riot.

Synesius,[11] *Letters* 124

"If they forget the dead in Hades, even there will I remember dear Hypatia."[12] I am overwhelmed and distressed at the sufferings of my native city [Cyrene], for daily I see weapons of war and men being slaughtered like sacrificial victims, and I breathe air corrupted by the putrefaction of their bodies. Even though I expect to endure other pains of this kind (for what hope is there for one to whom the atmosphere is most distressful, covered by the shadows of vultures eating flesh?), even so I am fond of the place. For what indeed can I suffer, being a native of

11. Synesius of Cyrene (*c.* A.D. 370–413), a Christian Neoplatonist, was a pupil of Hypatia.

12. Adapted from Homer, *Iliad* xxii. 389–390, where Achilles vows he will never forget his friend Patroclus.

Libya, born there and seeing the tombs of my ancestors not dishonored. Because of you alone I think I will despise my native land, and I might be induced to deviate from my school of thought.

Greek Anthology book IX, no. 400; From *LCL*

Revered Hypatia, ornament of learning, stainless star of wise teaching, when I see you and your discourse I worship you, looking on the starry house of the Virgin [the constellation Virgo]; for your business is in heaven.

PAINTERS

Pliny, *Natural History* book XXXV. xl. cxlvii–cxlviii

There have also been women painters. . . . When Marcus Varro was a youth, Iaia of Cyzicus, who remained unmarried, painted at Rome with the brush, also drew on ivory with the graver, chiefly portraits of women. At Naples she did a portrait of an old woman on a large tablet. And she also did a self-portrait with a mirror. She excelled all in the swiftness of her hand in painting, and her talent was so great that in the prices she received she surpassed the most famous portrait painters of the same period, Sopolis and Dionysius, whose paintings fill the galleries. A certain Olympias also painted, but about her only this is recorded, that Autobolus was her pupil.

MIDWIVES

Soranus,[13] *Gynaecology* book I (excerpts); Translated by O. Temkin (Baltimore, 1956)

A suitable person . . . must be literate in order to be able to comprehend the art through theory too: she must have her wits about her so that she may easily follow what is said and what is happening: she must have a good memory to retain the imparted instructions (for knowledge arises from memory of what has been grasped). She must love work in order to persevere through all vicissitudes (for a woman who wishes to acquire such vast knowledge needs manly patience). She must be respectable since people will have to trust their household and the secrets of their lives to her and because to women of bad character the semblance of

---

13. Famed Greek physician of the time of the emperors Trajan and Hadrian, author of numerous works on medicine.

medical instruction is a cover for evil scheming. She must not be handicapped as regards her senses since there are things which she must see, answers which she must hear when questioning, and objects which she must grasp by her sense of touch. She needs sound limbs so as not to be handicapped in the performances of her work and she must be robust, for she takes a double task upon herself during the hardship of her professional visits. Long and slim fingers and short nails are necessary to touch a deep lying inflammation without causing too much pain. This skill, however, can also be acquired through zealous endeavour and practice in her work. . . .

We call a person the best midwife if she is trained in all branches of therapy (for some cases must be treated by diet, others by surgery, while still others must be cured by drugs); if she is moreover able to prescribe hygienic regulations for her patients, to observe the general and the individual features of the case, and from this to find out what is expedient, not from the causes or from the repeated observations of what usually occurs or something of the kind. Now to go into detail: she will not change her methods when the symptoms change, but will give her advice in accordance with the course of the disease: she will be unperturbed, unafraid in danger, able to state clearly the reasons for her measures, she will bring reassurance to her patients, and be sympathetic. And it is not absolutely essential for her to have borne children, as some people contend, in order that she may sympathize with the mother, because of her experience with pain; for [to have sympathy] is not more characteristic of a person who has given birth to a child. She must be robust on account of her duties but not necessarily young as some people maintain, for sometimes young persons are weak whereas on the contrary older persons may be robust. She will be well disciplined and always sober, since it is uncertain when she may be summoned to those in danger. She will have a quiet disposition, for she will have to share many secrets of life. She must not be greedy for money, lest she give an abortive wickedly for payment; she will be free from superstition so as not to overlook salutary measures on account of a dream or omen or some customary rite or vulgar superstition. She must also keep her hands soft, abstaining from such wool-working as may make them hard, and she must acquire softness by means of ointments if it is not present naturally. Such persons will be the best midwives.

WET-NURSES

Soranus, *Gynaecology* book I. xix–xx; Translated by O. Temkin (Baltimore, 1956)

To be sure, other things being equal, it is better to feed the child with maternal milk, for this is more suited to it, and the mothers become more sympathetic towards the offspring, and it is more natural to be fed from the mother after parturition. But if anything prevents it one must choose the best wet-nurse, lest the mother grow prematurely old, having spent herself through the daily sucking.

One should choose a wet-nurse not younger than twenty nor older than forty years, who has already given birth twice or thrice, who is healthy, of good constitution, of large frame, and of a good colour. Her breasts should be of medium size, lax, soft and unwrinkled, the nipples neither big nor too small and neither too compact nor too porous and discharging milk overabundantly. She should be self-controlled, sympathetic and not ill-tempered, a Greek, and tidy. And for each of these points the reasons are as follows:

She should be in her prime because younger women are ignorant in the rearing of children and their minds are still somewhat careless and childish; while older ones yield a more watery milk because of the atony of the body. In women in their prime, however, every natural function is at its highest. She should already have given birth twice or thrice, because women with their first child are as yet unpractised in the rearing of children and have breasts whose structure is still infantile, small and too compact; while those who have delivered often have nursed children often and, being wrinkled, produce thick milk which is not at its best. [She should be healthy because healthful] and nourishing milk comes from a healthy body, unwholesome and worthless milk from a sickly one; just as water which flows through worthless soil is itself rendered worthless, spoiled by the qualities of its basin. And she should be of good constitution, that is, fleshy and strong, not only for the same reason, but also lest she easily become too weak for hard work and nightly duties with the result that the milk also deteriorates. Of large frame: for everything else being equal, milk from large bodies is more nourishing. Of a good colour: for in such women bigger vessels carry the material up to the breasts so that there is more milk. And her breasts should be of medium size: for small ones have little milk, whereas excessively large ones have more than is necessary so that if after nursing the surplus is retained it will be drawn out by the newborn when no longer fresh, and in some way already spoiled. If, on the other hand, it is all sucked out by other children or even other animals, the wet-nurse will be completely exhausted. . . .

The wet-nurse should be self-controlled so as to abstain from coitus, drinking, lewdness, and any other such pleasure and incontinence. For coitus cools the affection towards the nursling by the diversion of sexual pleasure and moreover spoils and diminishes the milk or suppresses it entirely by stimulating menstrual catharsis through the uterus or by bringing about conception. In regard to drinking, first the wet-nurse is harmed in soul as well as in body and for this reason the milk also is spoiled. Secondly, seized by a sleep from which she is hard to awaken, she leaves the newborn untended or even falls down upon it in a dangerous way. Thirdly, too much wine passes its quality to the milk and therefore the nursling becomes sluggish and comatose and sometimes even afflicted with tremor, apoplexy, and convulsions, just as suckling pigs become comatose and stupefied when the sow has eaten drugs. [She should be] sympathetic and affectionate, that she may fulfill her duties without hesitation and without murmuring. For some wet-nurses are so lacking in sympathy towards the nursling that they not only pay no heed when it cries for a long time, but do not even arrange its position when it lies still; rather, they leave it in one position so that often because of the pressure the sinewy parts suffer and consequently become numb and bad. Not ill-tempered: since by nature the nursling becomes similar to the nurse and accordingly grows sullen if the nurse is ill-tempered, but of mild disposition if she is even-tempered. Besides, angry women are like maniacs, and sometimes when the newborn cries from fear and they are unable to restrain it, they let it drop from their hands or overturn it dangerously. For the same reason the wet-nurse should not be superstitious or prone to ecstatic states, so that she may not expose the infant to danger when led astray by fallacious reasoning, sometimes even trembling like mad. And the wet-nurse should be tidy-minded lest the odor of the swaddling clothes cause the child's stomach to become weak and it lie awake on account of itching or suffer some ulceration subsequently. And she should be a Greek so that the infant nursed by her may become accustomed to the best speech.

Berlin Papyrus No. 1,107; 13 B.C.; From *LCL*

To Protarchus from Isidora daughter of . . . , having as her guardian her brother Eutychides son of . . . , and from Didyma daughter of Apollonius . . . having with her as guardian her brother Ischyrio son of Apollonius. . . . Didyma agrees to nurse and suckle, outside her home in the city, with her own milk pure and untainted, for a period of sixteen months from Pharmuthi of the current 17th year of Caesar [Augustus], the foundling infant slave child . . . called . . . which Isidora has given out to her, receiving from her, Isidora, as wages for milk and nursing ten silver drachmas and two measures of oil every month. So long as she is duly paid she shall take proper care both of herself and of the child, not injuring her milk nor sleeping with a man nor becoming pregnant nor suckling another child, and whatever things of the child she receives or is entrusted with she shall keep safe. . . . Didyma has forthwith received from Isidora by hand from the house oil for the first three months, Pharmuthi, Pachon, and Payni. She shall not cease nursing before the end of the time, and if she breaks the agreement in any way she shall forfeit the wages which she has already received and those which she may have received besides, increased by one half, plus damages and expenses, and shall moreover pay 500 drachmas and the prescribed fine. . . . Didyma shall visit Isidora every month regularly on four separate days bringing the child to be inspected by her. . . . I, Eutychides, have professed myself guardian of my sister and have written for her as she is illiterate. I, Didyma, agree on the above terms. I, Ischyrio, have professed myself guardian of my sister and have written for her, as she is illiterate. . . . The seventeenth year of Caesar.

IN THE THEATER

G. Kaibel, *Epigrammata Graeca* (Berlin, 1878), no. 609; third century

In days gone by she had won acclaim among many peoples and many cities, performing on the stage in all sorts of shows, in mimes, choruses, frequently in dances. But even so, she did not die, this tenth Muse, for whom the skilled speaker and eminent biographer Heraclides set up this inscription. Though departed, she has attained the same honor as she did in life, when she caused her body to die on the floor of the stage. Her fellow actors say to you: Farewell, Bassilla. No one is immortal.

ATHLETES

H. Pleket, *Epigraphica* II (Leiden, 1969), no. 9

Hermesianax, son of Dionysius, of Caesarea in Tralles and of Corinth, for his daughters, who also have the same citizenships. Tryphosa each time was first in the girls' single-course race at the Pythian Games with Antigonus and Cleomachus as judges, and at the Isthmian Games with Juventius Proclus as president. Hedea won the race in armor and the chariot race at the Isthmian Games with Cornelius Pulcher as judge; she won the single-course race at the Nemean Games with Antigonus as president, likewise in Sicyon with Menoites as president. She also won the children's lyre contest at the Augustan Games in Athens with Nuvius son of Philinus as president. She was first in her age group. . . . Dionysia won . . . the single-course race at the Asclepian Games at the sanctuary of Epidaurus with Nicoteles as president.

103. Priestesses

VESTAL VIRGINS

Aulus Gellius, *Attic Nights* I. xii; From *LCL*

It is unlawful for a girl to be chosen who is less than six, or more than ten years old; she must also have both father and mother living; she must be free from any impediment in her speech, must not have impaired hearing, or be marked by any other bodily defect; she must not herself have been freed from paternal control, nor her father before her, even if her father is still living and she is under the control of her grandfather; neither one nor both of her parents may have been slaves or engaged in mean occupations. But they say that one whose sister has been chosen to that priesthood acquired exemption, as well as one whose father is a flamen or an augur, one of the Fifteen in charge of the Sibylline Books, one of the Seven who oversee the banquets of the gods, or a [Salian] dancing priest of Mars. Exemption from that priesthood is regularly allowed also to the betrothed of a pontiff and to the daughter of a priest of the festival of the sacred trumpets. Furthermore the writings of Ateius Capito inform us that the daughter of a man without residence in Italy must not be chosen, and that the daughter of one who has three children must be excused.

Now, as soon as the Vestal virgin is chosen, escorted to the House of Vesta and delivered to the pontiffs, she immediately passes from the control of her father without the ceremony of emancipation or loss of civil rights, and she acquires the right to make a will.

Now the Vestal is said to be "taken," it appears, because she is grasped by the hand of the chief pontiff and led away from the parent under whose control she is, as if she had been taken in war. In the first book of Fabius Pictor's *History* the formula is given which the chief pontiff should use in choosing a Vestal. It is this: "I take thee, Amata, as one who has fulfilled all the legal requirements, to be priestess of Vesta, to perform the rites which it is lawful for a Vestal to perform for the Roman people."

OTHER CULTS

Zeitschrift für Papyrologie und Epigraphik (1978) 29:213–228
Cyzicus, first century A.D.

The people and the Roman businessmen in the city honor Apollonis daughter of Procles because of the virtue of her parents and her husband, and because of her own moderation. . . . [Provisions for her funeral are outlined.] There is to be set up a base for a statue of her in the Temple of the Graces on the right of those entering from the Sacred Agora, in which there stands another statue of her. And since she also was priestess of Artemis among the Pythaistrides, in testimony of her piety concerning religious rites, on the seventh of the month Artemisium annually, when the priestesses and the Pythaistrides and temple overseers assemble in the Temple of the Graces, they shall crown her statue. [Provisions for other statues of Apollonis to be set up.] Beneath the statues the following inscription is to be written: "The people and the Roman businessmen in the city honored Apollonis daughter of Procles because of the virtue of her parents and her husband, and because of her own moderation."

CIL, vol. X, no. 810; Pompeii, first century A.D.

Eumachia daughter of Lucius, public priestess, in her own name and that of her son Marcus Numistrius Fronto, built the porch, covered passage and colonnade with her own funds, and dedicated them to Concordia Augusta and to Pietas.

H. Pleket, *Epigraphica* II (Leiden, 1969), no. 13; Arneae, Lycia; first century A.D.

The people of Arneae and the vicinity, to Lalla daughter of Timarchus son of Diotimus, fellow citizen, wife of Diotimus son of Vassus. Priestess of the emperor's cult, gymasiarch out of her own funds, five times honored, chaste, educated, devoted to her husband, a paragon of all virtue, outstanding in every respect. She has glorified the virtues of her ancestors with the example of her own character. In recognition of her virtue and good will.

H. Pleket, *Epigraphica* II (Leiden, 1969), no. 18; Aphrodisias, second century A.D.

The council, the people and the senate honor with first-class honors Tata daughter of Diodorus son of Diodorus son of Leo, reverend priestess of Hera for life, mother of the city. She became and remained the wife of Attalus son of Pytheas the "crown wearer," herself a member of an illustrious family of the highest rank. As priestess of the imperial cult for a second time, she twice provided oil for athletes in bottles, filled most plentifully from basins most of the night as well [as the day]. She became a "crown wearer," offered sacrifices all year long for the health of the imperial family. She provided banquets for the people many times and provided banqueting couches for the public. For dances and plays she herself brought in the leading performers in Asia, and displayed them in her native city. . . . She was a woman who spared no expense, and loved honor, and was glorious in her virtue and chastity.

CIL, vol. VI, no. 1,779 (= Dessau, no. 1,259); Rome, A.D. 384

Aconia Fabia Paulina, a priestess of mystery cults, and her husband Vettius Agorius Praetextatus, a senator, were married for forty years. She is here commemorated in verse inscriptions.

Vettius Agorius Praetextatus to his wife Paulina.

Paulina, handmaiden of truth and chastity, devoted to temples and friend of divine powers, preferring her husband to herself, Rome to her husband, modest, faithful, of pure mind and body, kindly to all, devoted to our household gods. . . .

Paulina, partner of my heart, source of modesty, the bond of chastity and pure love and trust born in heaven, to whom I have entrusted the secrets enclosed in my mind; a gift of the gods, who join the marital bed with loving and chaste bonds; with the devotion of a mother, conjugal grace, the ties of a sister, the modesty of a daughter; with the great trust by which we are joined to friends; by the experience of years, agreement in religious devotion with faithful yoke and simple harmony, helper of her husband, industrious, honoring, cherishing him.

[Paulina now is made to speak.] The luster of my parents gave me nothing greater than that I seemed even then worthy of my husband. But the name of my husband, Agorius, is all splendor and distinction, who born of proud stock has adorned country, senate and wife with the integrity of his mind, his character and industry, and has attained the supreme pinnacle of virtue.

6

THE CRISIS OF THE THIRD CENTURY
AND THE EMERGENCE OF THE
BYZANTINE STATE, A.D. 193–337

"Our history," proclaims Cassius Dio (*Roman History* LXXI. xxxvi. 4) as
he records the death of Marcus Aurelius, "now plunges from a kingdom
of gold to one of iron and rust." With foreign peoples exerting steadily
increasing pressures on the frontiers and internal economic troubles reaching the proportions of an empire-wide crisis (see §§ 110–112), the might
of the indispensable legions stood ever more clearly revealed as the underlying foundation of the Principate. In the social revolution of the third
century, the soldiery, enriched by legal emoluments and illegal extortions,
became the new privileged class, supplanting the civilian, propertied class.
Henceforth, this former privileged class had to shoulder the costs of
government in increasing measure (see §§ 107, 115), while the actual
power of their governmental bodies—the local councils, the provincial
assemblies, and even the Roman Senate—declined. The Senate, indeed,
ceased after A.D. 282 to share in the formalization of the emperor's powers
(cf. § 4), ceased to legislate (its last known decree is dated A.D. *c.* 280), and
emerged at the end of the century as little more than the city council of
Rome. Soldiers from the ranks now rose in increasing numbers into the
equestrian order, and members of this class, which had already begun to
encroach upon the prerogatives of the senatorial career in the middle of
the second century, now replaced men of senatorial rank as provincial
governors, legionary commanders, and even emperors. Marcus Aurelius
had once "refused his soldiers' demand for a donative, saying that anything they received above and beyond the established practice would have
to be wrung from the blood of their parents and relatives." In sharp
contrast, Severus "before he died is reported to have said to his sons . . .
'Live in harmony, enrich the soldiers, and scorn all others' " (Cassius Dio
LXXL iii. 3 and LXXVI. xv. 2); cf. also pp. 381–82.

Under these conditions there took place in the third century a rapid polarization of society into two classes, officially recognized in law (cf. §§ 159–60). Those in the upper stratum of society were known as *honestiores,* or *potentiores;* among them were men (usually of military background) who were able, in connivance with or in open defiance of government functionaries, to build up positions of great power and estates of vast extent—the forerunners of feudal barons on medieval manors. The rest of the population—the poor and the *déclassés*—were known as *humiliores;* and these, helpless under the grinding oppression of fiscal demands compounded by the illegal extortions of soldiery and officialdom, sought refuge by placing themselves, in increasing numbers, under the protection of the local great, the *potentiores.*

The changes are clearly reflected also in the language of the period. For example, as the Principate drifted toward absolutism, the ruling house took on the attributes and terminology of divine-right monarchy. In the West as well as in the East the imperial family became the "divine" house, and everything connected with it was spoken of as sacred. By the fourth century the political, social, and cultural pattern of the Middle Ages was already clearly emerging.

104. THE MILITARY MONARCHY

THE POWER OF THE PRAETORIAN GUARD: AN EMPIRE FOR SALE

Cassius Dio, *Roman History* LXXIV. xi. 2–6; From *LCL.*

Didius Julianus, at once an insatiate money getter and a wanton spendthrift, who was always eager for revolution, and hence had been exiled by Commodus to his native city of Milan, now, when he heard of the death of Pertinax[1] hastily made his way to the [Praetorian] camp and, standing at the gates of the enclosure, made bids to the soldiers for the rule over the Romans. Then ensued a most disgraceful business and one unworthy of Rome. For, just as if it had been in some market or auction room, both the city and its entire Empire were auctioned off. The sellers were the ones who had slain their emperor, and the would-be buyers were Sulpicianus[2] and Julianus, who vied to outbid each other, one from the inside, the other from outside. They gradually raised their bids up to

---

1. The successor of Commodus, whose reign lasted for only eighty-seven days. For a proclamation in Egypt of his accession, see § 3, last selection.
2. The father-in-law of Pertinax and prefect of the city.

20,000 sesterces per soldier. Some of the soldiers would carry word to Julianus, "Sulpicianus offers so much; how much more do you bid?" And to Sulpicianus in turn, "Julianus promises so much; how much do you raise him?" Sulpicianus would have won the day, being inside and being prefect of the city and also the first to name the figure of 20,000, had not Julianus raised his bid no longer by a small amount but by 5,000 at one time, shouting it in a loud voice and also indicating the amount with his fingers. So the soldiers, captivated by this extravagant bid and at the same time fearing that Sulpicianus might avenge Pertinax (an idea Julianus put into their heads), received Julianus inside and declared him emperor.[3]

NEW PRIVILEGES FOR SOLDIERS

Herodian, *History* III. viii. 4–5

[In A.D. 197, after defeating the pretender Albinus at Lugdunum (Lyons), Septimius Severus returned to Rome.] After going up to the sanctuary of Jupiter and performing the rest of the religious ceremonies, Severus returned to the palace and in honor of his victories distributed very great largess to the populace. He bestowed large donatives on the soldiers, granted them many privileges which they did not previously have: he was the first to increase their grain ration, and permitted them to wear gold rings[4] and to live with their wives in wedlock—all of which used to be considered incompatible with military discipline and with preparedness and readiness for war. He was the first to undermine their famous vigor, the austerity of their mode of life, their acquiescence in hard work, and their well-disciplined respect for their officers, teaching them to covet money and turning them aside to luxurious living.[5]

3. Shortly afterward (see second selection following), Septimius Severus dismissed this Praetorian Guard and, in accordance with his policy of democratizing the army, reconstituted it with non-Italian provincials from the frontier legions.

4. Until this time the exclusive insignia of the equestrian order.

5. This is an exaggeration by Herodian. There is no reliable evidence that the discipline and training of the army were relaxed by Severus. The increases in pay were probably necessary because of inflation.

PROVINCIALIZATION OF THE PRAETORIAN GUARD

Cassius Dio, *Roman History* LXXV. ii. 3–6; From *LCL*

There were many things Severus did that were not to our liking:[6] he was blamed for making the city turbulent through the presence of so many troops and for burdening the state by his excessive expenditures of money and, most of all, for placing his hope of safety in the strength of his army rather than in the good will of his associates [in the government]. But some found fault with him particularly because he abolished the practice of selecting the bodyguard exclusively from Italy, Spain, Macedonia, and Noricum—a plan that furnished men of more respectable appearance and of simpler habits—and ordered that any vacancies should be filled from all the legions alike. Now, he did this with the idea that he should thus have guards with a better knowledge of the soldier's duties, and should also be offering a kind of prize for those who proved brave in war; but, as a matter of fact, it became only too apparent that he had incidentally ruined the youth of Italy, who turned to brigandage[7] and gladiatorial fighting in place of their former service in the army, and had filled the city with a throng of motley soldiers most savage in appearance, most terrifying in speech, and most boorish in conversation.

INCREASING DEMANDS OF THE SOLDIERS

Cassius Dio, *Roman History* LXXVIII. xxxvi. 1–3

Macrinus[8] wrote a letter also to Maximus, prefect of the city, in which, after mentioning various matters of a routine nature, he stated that the soldiers, and even the recruits, were insisting on receiving everything they had previously gotten, and that those who had not been deprived of anything were making common cause with them over what was not being granted them. And, to pass over, he said, all the other means devised by Severus and his son [Caracalla] for the destruction of military discipline, it was impossible to give them their pay in full in addition to the donatives they were receiving (for the increase in their pay granted by Caracalla amounted to 280,000,000 sesterces annually), and [equally] impossible not to give it.

6. Cassius Dio was a member of the senatorial order.
7. On the spread of brigandage in the third century, see § 109.
8. Marcus Opellius Macrinus, a native of Mauretania, who ruled for about a year (217–218), the first equestrian to become emperor without first attaining senatorial rank.

"EVERYONE IS IN THE ARMY"

Berlin Papyrus No. 1,680 (= *Select Papyri,* no. 134); third century; From *LCL*

Isis to Termuthion her mother, very many greetings. I make supplication for you every day before the lord Sarapis and his fellow gods. I wish you to know that I arrived in Alexandria safe and sound in four days. I send salutations to my sister and the children, and Eluath and his wife, and Dioscorous and her husband and children, and Tamalis and her husband and son, and Hero and Ammonarion and her children and husband, and Sanpat and her children. And if Aio wishes to join the army, let him come; for everyone is in the army. I pray for the health of all your household.

THE PROBLEM OF MILITARY DISCIPLINE

"Historia Augusta," *Life of Aurelian* vii; Adapted from *LCL*

Aurelian was so feared by the soldiers that, under him, after offenses had once been punished by him in the camp with the utmost severity, no one offended again. . . . There is a letter of his, truly that of a soldier, written to his deputy as follows: "If you wish to be a tribune, or rather if you wish to remain alive, restrain the hands of your soldiers. None shall steal another's fowl or touch his sheep. None shall carry off grapes, or thresh out grain, or exact oil, salt, or firewood, and each shall be content with his own allowance. Let them have these things from the booty taken from the enemy and not from the tears of the provincials. Their arms shall be kept burnished, their implements bright, their boots stout. Let old uniforms be replaced by new. Let them keep their pay in their belts and not spend it in public houses. Let them wear their collars, arm rings, and finger rings [cf. note 4]. Let each man curry his own horse and baggage animal, let no one sell the fodder allowed him for his beast, and let them take care in common of the mule belonging to the century. Let one yield obedience to another as to a master, and no one as a slave, let them be attended by physicians without charge, let them give no fees to soothsayers, let them conduct themselves in their lodgings with propriety, and let anyone who begins a brawl be thrashed." [9]

9. On the authenticity of documents quoted in the "Historia Augusta," see vol. 1, pp. 31–32.

105. ANARCHY: THE LEGIONS BECOME EMPEROR MAKERS

The specious stability of the Empire under the Severan dynasty was shattered by the rebellion of Maximinus in A.D. 235, which touched off a half century of civil war and internal chaos, attended by devastating epidemics, depopulation, runaway inflation, invasions of northern barbarians, and incursions by the resurgent Persian Empire of the Sassanids in the East. Armies became a law unto themselves, terrorizing the population, elevating and liquidating emperors at will. From the assassination of Severus Alexander in 235 to the accession of Diocletian in 284, twenty-six soldier-emperors were proclaimed, all but one of whom died a violent death, usually at the hands of their own soldiers. A number of them exercised their ephemeral reigns only in that part of the Empire that their armies controlled; other pretenders "ruled" simultaneously elsewhere. Political separatism emerged as Gaul was temporarily detached from the Empire. When political unity was finally restored, the death blow had been given not only to the Principate but to the foundations of Graeco-Roman culture.

Aurelius Victor,[10] *Lives of the Emperors* xxiv–xxvii (abridged)

Aurelius Alexander . . . although only a young man, with an ability beyond his age made great preparations at once for the war against Xerxes [Ardashir], king of the Persians. After conquering and routing him, he came with great speed to Gaul, which the Germans were trying to invade. When he arrived there, he discharged with great firmness several mutinous legions. This act, which at the time won him great glory, was not long afterwards the cause of his destruction: the soldiers, offended by such great severity (whence he had acquired the surname Severus),[11] killed him in Vicus Britannicus,[12] where he chanced to be staying with a small escort. . . . Although he had reigned only thirteen years, he left the state strengthened on every side. From Romulus to Septimius [Severus] the state rose steadily in power, but it came to a halt

10. Author of an epitome of imperial history in the form of biographies of the emperors, published A.D. 360; cf. chapter 4, note 45.

11. Actually, Alexander, a cousin of Elagabalus, his predecessor, assumed the name Severus to associate himself with the founder of the dynasty. Officially he was styled the son of Caracalla and grandson of Septimius Severus.

12. Bretzenheim near Mainz. It is more probable that Alexander Severus was killed because of his inadequacy as a soldier and because the armies on the Rhine objected to his efforts to secure a peace with the Germans through the payment of cash subsidies.

at its peak, as it were, because of Caracalla's designs. It was Alexander's accomplishment to retard its rapid decline. The emperors after him, more concerned with tyrannizing their subjects than subduing foreign peoples, and with warring among themselves, precipitated the Roman state into a steep decline. Then good men and bad, nobles and low-born, and even many barbarians,[13] were indiscriminately elevated to the purple. . . .

After a month or two of unstable rule, Florian was killed by his troops near Tarsus. After him they accepted Probus, who had been elevated in Illyria.[14] Probus was a man highly skilled in military science, and almost another Hannibal in the art of exercising troops in various ways and of hardening young men. Indeed, just as Hannibal had employed his soldiers in planting olive trees in several places in Africa, fearing that their idleness might be dangerous to the state and its leaders, so Probus filled Gaul, Pannonia, and the hills of Moesia with vine-yards,[15] after he had worn down the barbarian tribes which had made incursions when our emperors had been slain through their crimes, and after he had killed Saturninus in the East and Bonosus with his army at Cologne. Both had attempted, employing the troops which they commanded as generals, to seize the imperial power. For this reason, when all territory had been recovered and pacified, he is reported to have said that in a short time there would be no need of soldiers. Provoked by this, the troops, when he compelled them to dig openings and ditches in order to drain the land which the winter rains turn into marshes in the vicinity of Sirmium, his native city, murdered him near that city in the sixth year of his reign [A.D. 282]. Thenceforth the military power regained the ascendant, and the senate has remained until our time[16] deprived of the power and right of choosing the emperor. It is uncertain whether this took place through default, with the consent of the senate, or through fear, or dislike of discord. Yet it is certain that . . . military discipline could have been reestablished in consequence of the moderate conduct of the legions during Tacitus' reign; that Florian would then

13. An exaggeration. Many of the emperors of the third century were of provincial origin, hailing from such provinces as Africa, Syria, Illyria, Thrace, Arabia, Pannonia; cf. note 36.

14. Florian was the half-brother of the Emperor Tacitus. Actually, Probus was proclaimed emperor in 276 by the armies in the East, where he was governor of Syria and Egypt.

15. Probus employed his troops on many projects in Egypt, including the cleaning of the irrigation canals (cf. introduction to § 80). On the assignment of soldiers to nonmilitary labor as part of their normal routine, see introduction to § 143.

16. That is, A.D. 360, when Aurelius Victor's work was published.

not have been so bold as to seize power; that, finally, if the members of an order so distinguished and important had spent their lives in military camps, the imperial power would not be bestowed on anyone, even a good man, by the decision of the soldiery. But, by giving themselves up to the delights of leisure and fearing for their riches, whose enjoyment and abundance they thought would last longer than eternity, they paved the way for the soldiery, and almost the barbarians, to dominate them and posterity.

106. The Extension of Citizenship

The centuries-long process of enfranchisement and Romanization (see §§ 15, 64) reached its culmination in A.D. 212, when inhabitants of the Empire were admitted to Roman citizenship *en masse* by a sweeping edict of the Emperor Caracalla, the famous *Constitutio Antoniniana*. "It is true that by approximating the Empire formally to the politico-philosophical ideal of a universal community of equal men the edict impressed the imagination of later ages, but even in the political sphere it merely marked the end of a process." (*Cambridge Ancient History*, 12:47). The immediate motives behind Caracalla's grant as well as its precise effects are still imperfectly understood. Cassius Dio's statement (§ 107, first selection) that its principal object was to effect an increase in imperial revenues is superficial and biased. It did, among its effects, sweep away many administrative anomalies, simplify financial and judicial administration, and equalize municipal obligations throughout the Empire, and it may have been to achieve this simplification that the military-minded emperor issued his edict.[17]

The prime piece of evidence on Caracalla's measure is a papyrus from Egypt, unfortunately much mutilated, containing a Greek version of the edict. Despite an enormous literature of frequently heated controversy over attempted restoration and interpretation since the papyrus was first published in 1910, it is still not entirely clear which categories of the population were excluded from the grant of citizenship. It is certain, however, that after the *Constitutio Antoniniana* there remained many noncitizens in the Roman Empire, despite the classic statement of Ulpian, presumably incompletely quoted in Justinian's *Digest* (I. v. 17), that "all living in the Roman world were made Roman citizens by a constitution of the Emperor Caracalla." The newly enfranchised citizens and their

17. Such was the general administrative tendency of the military emperors of the third and fourth centuries; cf. §§ 115–116, 120–125, 128–130.

descendants bore the name of Aurelius, just as citizens earlier enfranchised had taken the family names of the emperors from whom they had received their citizenship (cf. introduction to § 15).

Giessen Papyrus No. 40, col. I (= *FIRA*, vol. I, no. 88); A.D. 212

The Emperor Caesar Marcus Aurelius Severus Antoninus Augustus [Caracalla] declares: . . . I may show my gratitude to the immortal gods for preserving me in such. . . .[18] Therefore I consider that in this way I can . . . render proper service to their majesty . . . by bringing with me to the worship[?] of the gods all who enter into the number of my people. Accordingly, I grant Roman citizenship to all aliens[19] throughout the world except the *dediticii*,[20] local citizenship remaining intact.[21] For it is proper that the multitude should not only help carry[?] all the burdens but should also now be included in my victory. This edict shall . . .[22] the majesty of the Roman people. . . . [The rest is fragmentary.]

107. Increased Financial Burden on the Civilian Population

The civil wars of the third century and the increased military budget, necessitated by the demands of imperial defense and the upkeep of the privileged armies, brought widespread misery and opened the door to all manner of abuses of authority by civil and military officials far exceeding those of the preceding centuries (cf. §§ 78, 86). The vast confiscations by Septimius Severus and by other emperors of the estates of their political enemies, the sharp increases in taxes, requisitions and special contributions, and widespread looting by the soldiery convulsed economic life and ultimately brought on mass impoverishment. "The chief evil, however, was the enormous number of government agents, mostly soldiers per-

18. The reference here is to the alleged plot against his life by his brother and coruler Geta, whom he had put to death earlier that year.

19. This word is supplied in a lacuna; it may of course have been another similar term, for example, "my subjects."

20. There is uncertainty and controversy, too, on the category of persons designated by this term. The word means, literally, "people who surrendered [to the Romans]," but its meaning and scope underwent considerable evolution in the course of the first two centuries.

21. Or, "without detriment to the rights of their communities." This clause, so vital to the interpretation of the text, has to be restored because of a lacuna in the papyrus. Of several reasonable restorations proposed over the years by different scholars, that given in our text appears now to be confirmed by the parallel clause in the last selection of § 15.

22. The missing word is presumably something like *increase, extend, consolidate,* or *show*.

forming the duties of policemen—the *frumentarii, stationarii* and *colletiones*
—who in their pursuit of political 'criminals' penetrated into all the cities
and villages and searched private houses, and who were, of course, accessible to bribes. Still more serious were the exactions of these same agents
in connexion with the frequent military expeditions of the emperor. In
time of civil war no one cared a straw for the people" (M. Rostovtzeff,
Social and Economic History of the Roman Empire, 2d ed., p. 412).

Cassius Dio, *Roman History* LXXVII. ix–x (abridged)

Antoninus [i.e., Caracalla; cf. note 36] was prodigal toward the soldiers,
whom he kept in great numbers about him, alleging one excuse after
another and one war after another; but he took pains to strip, despoil,
and grind down all the rest of mankind, and not the least the senators.
In addition to the gold crowns he frequently demanded, on the constant
pretext that he had conquered some enemy (and I am not speaking of
the actual making of the crowns—for what does that amount to?—but
of the large quantity of money customarily given under that name by
the cities for the "crowning" of the emperors) [cf. § 113, second selec-
tion], there were the provisions that were exacted of us in great quantities and from every side, sometimes without payment, sometimes at
additional cost to ourselves—all of which he either bestowed upon the
soldiers or sold at retail; and there were the gifts which he kept demanding from wealthy private persons and from communities; and the taxes,
both the new ones he promulgated and the ten-percent tax that he
instituted in place of the five-percent tax on manumissions and bequests
and legacies left to anyone, for he abolished the right of succession and
tax exemption which had been granted in such cases to those who were
closely related to the deceased. For this reason also he declared all the
people in his empire Roman citizens; nominally he was honoring them,
but his real purpose was to increase his revenues thereby, inasmuch as
aliens did not have to pay most of these taxes [cf. introduction to § 106].
But apart from all these burdens, we were also compelled to build at our
own expense all sorts of houses for him whenever he set out from
Rome, and costly lodgings in the middle of even the very shortest
journeys; yet he not only never lived in these but was not destined even
to see some of them. In addition, we constructed amphitheaters and race
courses wherever he spent the winter or expected to spend it, all without
receiving any remuneration from him; and they were all promptly demolished, the sole reason for their construction being, apparently, that
we might be ruined. . . .

Indeed, Caracalla often used to say, "Nobody in the world should have money but I, so that I may bestow it upon the soldiers." And once, when Julia [Domna, his mother] censured him for his great expenditures for them and said, "There is no longer any revenue, either just or unjust, left to us," he answered, exhibiting his sword, "Be of good cheer, mother, for as long as we have this, we shall not run short of money."

Herodian, *History* VII. iii. 1–iv. 6

What was the use of destroying the barbarians, when the killing in Rome itself and in the provinces subject to her was on a larger scale? What was the use of seizing booty from the enemy, only to be stripped naked oneself and see one's relatives deprived of their property? An invitation has been given to informers to do their dastardly work with complete license, including attempts to rake up matters concerning one's ancestors — matters which one knows nothing about and therefore cannot refute. Any person merely summoned to court by an informer was immediately found guilty, and went away from the proceedings stripped of his entire property. Every day one could see the very wealthy of yesterday reduced to beggary for the future—so great was the love of money of the tyrannical government [of Maximinus]. The pretext was the constant need of supplies for the soldiers. . . .

So long as these things happened to individuals . . . it did not make any difference at all to the peoples of the cities or the provinces. The masses were not interested in the misfortunes of those believed to be well-off or rich. Indeed, some of the malicious and common type, in their envy of the more powerful and the well-to-do, are even delighted by such occurrences. But then Maximinus, after reducing most of the notable houses to poverty, and finding the income obtained thereby small and insufficient for his purpose, began to lay hands on the public treasuries. He expropriated whatever public moneys there were—funds which had been collected for the grain supply or for distribution to the people, or ear-marked for shows or festivals. Dedications in temples, statues of gods, honors to heroes, and whatever embellishment there was of a public nature, or adornment of a city, or material out of which money could be made—he melted all of it. . . . In the cities and provinces the hearts of the masses were inflamed. Now that exactions were being made upon themselves, they resented the soldiers; and relatives and friends reproached them with hate in their hearts, believing that Maximinus was doing these things on behalf of the soldiers.

For these reasons, not unjustifiable ones, the masses were being inflamed to hatred and revolt. . . . After three years of his reign, for a small and insignificant reason—the usual stumbling block of tyranny— the Africans were the first to take up arms, and resolutely raised the standard of revolt.

[The insurrection was touched off when the procurator of Africa moved to collect heavy fines imposed on a number of wealthy landowners, who would have been compelled to sell their property to pay the fines.]

The young men, though outraged at this, promised to pay the money to him but requested a delay of three days. Forming a conspiracy, and winning over all those who they knew had been ill-treated or feared they would be, they ordered their tenants to come down from their fields and to arm themselves with staves and axes. And, in obedience to the orders of their masters, they assembled in the city before dawn, concealing under their clothes the weapons which they had brought for a hand-to-hand battle. Quite a large number gathered, for Africa with its large population has many persons farming the land. As soon as dawn came, the young men came forward and bade the band made up of their tenants to follow them as if they were part of the mass of people. And they ordered them to conceal the weapons they were carrying and to make a brave stand if any of the soldiers or the people should set upon them to avenge the deed they had planned. They themselves, grasping daggers concealed under their garments, approached the procurator as if to discuss the payment of the money. Then, falling upon him suddenly and unexpectedly, they struck and slew him. When the soldiers in his guard drew their swords to avenge the assassination, the men who had come down from the fields brought out their staves and axes, came to the defense of their masters, and easily routed their opponents. . . .[23]

23. This is interesting evidence of the growing reliance of many humble folk in the Empire on rich and powerful landowners because of the rapacity and corruption of officialdom and their own inability to obtain justice through an appeal to the emperor; cf. § 117.

108. Reform Program for the Crisis
of the Third Century

The fictitious speech that Cassius Dio put into the mouth of Maecenas, one of Augustus's most trusted advisers of the early Principate, actually reflects Cassius Dio's own political, economic, social, and religious thought. It embodies the contemporary concerns of a distinguished senator of the first third of the century during the political crisis of the Severan Age. Written from the viewpoint of a Roman senator at the highest level of the Roman social system (he served under seven emperors), the speech is the only comprehensive political and economic program of the third century known to us. The following excerpts contain Dio's approval of the upward mobility of the equestrian order and use of imperial freedmen in the governance of the Empire; recommendation for a garrison frontier army instead of the traditional mobile army; economic reforms to reinvigorate agriculture; warnings against unproductive expenditures in the Empire; criticism of emperor worship and call for respect for the ideal king in the Stoic tradition; and advice on the maintenance of Roman religious traditions.

Cassius Dio, *Roman History* LII. xxv. 6–xxxvi. 3 (excerpted); From *LCL*

If any of the knights, after passing through many branches of the service, distinguishes himself enough to become a senator, his age ought not to hinder him at all from being enrolled in the senate. Indeed, some knights should be received into the senate, even if they have seen service only as company commanders in the citizen legions, except such as have served in the rank and file.

A standing army also should be supported, drawn from the citizens, the subject nations, and the allies, its size in the several provinces being greater or less according as the necessities of the case demand; and these troops ought always to be under arms and to engage in the practice of warfare continually. They should have winter quarters constructed for them at the most advantageous points, and should serve for a stated period, so that a portion of life may still be left for them between their retirement from service and old age. The reason for such a standing army is this: far removed as we are from the frontiers of the empire, with enemies living near our borders on every side, we are no longer able at critical times to depend upon expeditionary forces; and if, on the other hand, we permit all the men of military age to have arms and to practise warfare, they will always be the source of seditions and civil wars.

.   .   .   .

From what source, then, is the money to be provided for these soldiers and for the other expenses that will of necessity be incurred? I shall explain this point also, prefacing it with a brief reminder that even if we have a democracy we shall in any case, of course, need money. For we cannot survive without soldiers, and men will not serve as soldiers without pay. Therefore let us not be oppressed by the idea that the necessity of raising money belongs only to a monarchy, and let us not be led by that consideration to turn our backs upon this form of government, but let us assume in our deliberations that, under whatever form of government we shall live, we shall certainly be constrained to secure funds. My proposal, therefore, is that you shall first of all sell the property that belongs to the state—and I observe that this has become vast on account of the wars—reserving only a little that is distinctly useful or necessary to you; and that you lend out all the money thus realized at a moderate rate of interest. In this way not only will the land be put under cultivation, being sold to owners who will cultivate it themselves, but also the latter will acquire a capital and become more prosperous, while the treasury will gain a permanent revenue that will suffice for its needs. In the second place, I advise you to make an estimate of the revenues from this source and of all the other revenues which can with certainty be derived from the mines or any other source, and then to make and balance against this a second estimate of all the expenses, not only those of the army, but also of all those which contribute to the well-being of a state, and furthermore of those which will necessarily be incurred for unexpected campaigns and the other needs which are wont to arise in an emergency. The next step is to provide for any deficiency by levying an assessment upon absolutely all property which produces any profit for its possessors, and by establishing a system of taxes among all the people we rule. For it is but just and proper that no individual or district be exempt from these taxes, inasmuch as they are to enjoy the benefits from the taxation as much as the rest. . . .

I am not unaware that some will object if this system of assessments and taxes is established. But I know this, too—that if they are subjected to no further abuses and are indeed convinced that all these contributions of theirs will make for their own security and for their fearless enjoyment of the rest of their property, and that, again, the larger part of their contributions will be received by none but themselves, as governors, procurators, or soldiers, they will be exceedingly grateful to you, since they will be giving but a slight portion of the abundance from which they derive the benefit without having to submit to abuses. Especially will this be true if they see that you live temperately and spend nothing foolishly. For who, if he saw that you were quite frugal in your expenditures for yourself and quite lavish in those for the commonwealth, would not willingly contribute, believing that your wealth meant his own security and prosperity? . . .

In the second place, the cities should not indulge in public buildings unnecessarily numerous or large, nor waste their resources on expenditures for a large number and variety of public games, lest they exhaust themselves in futile exertions and be led by unreasonable rivalries to quarrel among themselves. They ought, indeed, to have their festivals and spectacles—to say nothing of the Circensian games held here in Rome—but not to such an extent that the public treasury or the estates of private citizens shall be ruined thereby, or that any stranger resident there shall be compelled to contribute to their expense, or that maintenance for life shall be granted to every one without exception who has won a victory in a contest. For it is unreasonable that the well-to-do should be put under compulsion to spend their money outside their own countries; and as for the competitors in the games, the prizes which are offered in each event are enough, unless a man wins in the Olympian or Pythian games or in some contest here in Rome. For these are the only victors who ought to receive their maintenance, and then the cities will not be wearing themselves out to no purpose nor will any athlete go into training except those who have a chance of winning; the rest will be able to follow some occupations that will be more profitable both to themselves and to the commonwealth. This is my opinion about these matters. But as to the horseraces in connection with which there are no gymnastic contests, I think that no city but Rome should be permitted to have them, the object being to prevent the wanton dissipation of vast sums of money and to keep the populace from becoming deplorably crazed over such a sport, and, above all, to give those who are serving in the army an abundant supply of the best horses. It is for these reasons, therefore, that I would altogether forbid the holding of such races anywhere else than here in Rome; as to the other games, I have proposed to keep them within bounds, in order that each community, by putting upon an inexpensive basis its entertainments for both eye and ear, may live with greater moderation and less factious strife. . . .

None of the cities should be allowed to have its own separate coinage or system of weights and measures; they should all be required to use ours. They should send no embassy to you, unless its business is one that involves a judicial decision; they should rather make what representations they will to their governor and through him bring to your attention such of their petitions as he shall approve. In this way they will be spared expense and be prevented from resorting to crooked practices to gain their object; and the answers they receive will be uncontaminated by their agents and will involve no expense or red tape. . . .

As regards your subjects, then, you should so conduct yourself, in my opinion. So far as you yourself are concerned, permit no exceptional or prodigal distinction to be given you, through word or deed, either by the senate or by any one else. For whereas the honor which you confer upon others lends glory to them, yet nothing can be given to you that is greater than what you already possess, and, besides, no little suspicion of insincerity would attach to its giving. No subject, you see, is ever supposed to vote any such distinction to his ruler of his own free will, and since all such honours as a ruler receives he must receive from himself, he not only wins no commendation for the honor but becomes a laughing-stock besides. You must therefore depend upon your good deeds to provide for you any additional splendor. And you should never permit gold or silver images of yourself to be made, for they are not only costly but also invite destruction and last only a brief time; but rather by your benefactions fashion other images in the hearts of your people, images which will never tarnish or perish. Neither should you ever permit the raising of a temple to you; for the expenditure of vast sums of money on such objects is sheer waste. This money would better be used for necessary objects; for wealth which is really wealth is gathered, not so much by getting largely, as by saving largely. Then, again, from temples comes no enhancement of one's glory. For it is virtue that raises many men to the level of gods, and no man ever became a god by popular vote. . . .

Therefore, if you desire to become in very truth immortal, act as I advise; and, furthermore, do you not only yourself worship the Divine Power everywhere and in every way in accordance with the traditions of our fathers, but compel all others to honor it. Those who attempt to distort our religion with strange rites you should abhor and punish, not merely for the sake of the gods (since if a man despises these he will not pay honor to any other being), but because such men, by bringing in new divinities in place of the old, persuade many to adopt foreign practices, from which spring up conspiracies, factions, and cabals, which are far from profitable to a monarchy. Do not, therefore, permit anybody to be an atheist or a sorcerer. Soothsaying, to be sure, is a necessary art, and you should by all means appoint some men to be diviners and augurs, to whom those will resort who wish to consult them on any matter; but there ought to be no workers in magic at all. For such men, by speaking the truth sometimes, but generally falsehood, often encourage a great many to attempt revolutions.

109. THE RISE OF BRIGANDAGE

The late second and third centuries saw a marked increase in robber bands in many parts of the Empire. To these bands flocked ruined people, war refugees, army deserters, and many persons who had fled from the land and the cities to escape onerous fiscal demands and compulsory public services.

AE, 1979, no. 624; A.D. 190

The Emperor Caesar . . . Marcus Aurelius COMMODUS Antoninus Pius Felix Augustus Sarmaticus Germanicus Maximus Britannicus, *pontifex maximus,* holding his fifteenth tribunician power, acclaimed imperator eight times, consul for the sixth time, father of his country, to the magistrates, council and people of Bubo, greeting. I praise you for your zeal and bravery and I approve the joint decision of the province of Lycia. You with such great zeal rushed to arrest the brigands, overcoming them, killing some and taking some alive. For this the league of Lycian cities did right in according you the fitting honor, giving you an additional vote, whereby you were destined to become more esteemed, and it encouraged the others to such brave deeds. Indeed I myself confirm the intent of the joint resolution and I [hereby] bestow upon you [the right] to be counted in future among the cities having three votes [in the Lycian league]. Your envoy was Meleager son of Meleager son of Artemo. Farewell.

Cassius Dio, *Roman History* LXXVI. x. 1–5; From *LCL*

At this period one Bulla, an Italian, got together a robber band of about six hundred men, and for two years [A.D. 206–207] continued to plunder Italy under the very noses of the emperors and of a multitude of soldiers. For though he was pursued by many men, and though Severus eagerly followed his trail, he was never really seen when seen, never found when found, never caught when caught, thanks to his great bribes and his cleverness. For he learned about everybody that was setting out from Rome and everybody that was putting into port at Brundisium, and knew both who and how many there were, and what and how much they had with them. In the case of most persons he would take a part of what they had and let them go at once, but he detained artisans for a time and made use of their skill, then dismissed them with a present. Once when two of his robber band had been captured and were about to be given to wild beasts, he paid a visit to the prison keeper, pretending that he was a magistrate of his native district and needed some men of this kind, and in this way he secured and saved the men. And he approached the centurion who was trying to exterminate the band and accused himself, pretending to be someone else, and promised, if the centurion would accompany him, to deliver the robber to him. So, on the pretext that he was leading him to Felix (this was another name by which he was called), he led him into a defile beset with thickets, and easily seized him. Later, he assumed the dress of a magistrate, ascended the tribunal, and having summoned the centurion caused part of his head to be shaved, and then said, "Carry this message to your masters: 'Feed your slaves, so that they may not turn to brigandage.' " Bulla had with him, in fact, a very large number of imperial freedmen, some of whom had been poorly paid, while others had received absolutely no pay at all.

Oxyrhynchus Papyrus no. 1,408, lines 11–21 (= *Select Papyri*, no. 224); A.D. 210–214; Adapted from *LCL*

Baebius Juncinus [prefect of Egypt] to the *strategi* of the Heptanomia and the Arsinoite nome, greeting. I have already ordered you in a previous letter to make careful search for the brigands, warning you of peril if you neglect this, and now I wish to add weight to my resolve by an edict, in order that all the inhabitants of Egypt may know that I am not treating this duty as an affair of secondary importance, but I am offering rewards to those of you who cooperate and threaten with peril those who choose to disobey. This edict I desire to be publicly displayed in both the metropolises and the most conspicuous places of the nomes, penalties and peril awaiting you if in the future any evil-doer is able to use violence without being detected. I wish you good health. Year . . ., Phaophi 28.[24]

110. BARBARIAN INVASIONS

Internal political, social, and economic chaos so loosened the imperial defenses that hordes of barbarian peoples were enabled to pierce the laboriously erected *limites* of the Empire (see introduction to § 8) at many points, and to devastate parts of Gaul, the Danubian provinces, Macedonia, Greece, Asia Minor, Egypt, Africa, Spain, and even Italy (where a German tribe advanced up to the gates of Rome during the reign of Gallienus). The emperors of the third century—as a glance at their honorific military titles shows—were almost without interruption occupied in wars with various German, Dacian, and Gothic tribes, and with Parthia and its successor, Sassanid Persia. One of the results of the fluidity of the Danube frontier was that Dacia, having lost its strategic importance, was permanently evacuated in A.D. 275 under Aurelian, after 150 years of Roman rule. The destruction of wealth and the depopulation caused by the incursions were so great that the emperors were forced to grant regular subsidies to peoples beyond the frontiers in return for pledges of non-aggression—the final debasement of the diplomatic policy introduced by earlier emperors of giving cash payments to client states (see § 9). Under Caracalla the amount of money thus paid to the barbarian peoples is said to have equaled the pay of the Roman armies, and in the East Macrinus paid the king of Parthia 200,000,000 sesterces to terminate hostilities. Even more important was the enormous extension of the earlier policy of settling barbarians inside the frontiers (see § 11). In the third century large numbers were granted lands near the borders and entrusted with defending them against barbarians beyond. In addition, sizable numbers of for-

---

24. A contemporary petition (*SB*, no. 4, 284; A.D. 207) reveals that the emperors, in an edict issued presumably in connection with the census of A.D. 201/202 had also taken cognizance of the prevalence of brigandage: "Our lords the most divine and invincible Emperors Severus and Antoninus, when they appeared in their Egypt [A.D. 199–201] desired, among the very many boons they bestowed, also that those living away from home should all return to their own places of abode [cf. introduction to § 82], breaking with their violent and lawless life; and in accordance with their sacred urgings we returned." Cf. also the language of § 77, last selection.

eign troops were incorporated into the auxiliary corps of the Roman armies. This barbarization of the Roman army is one of the prime causes of the crumbling of the Roman Empire in the subsequent two centuries.

Cassius Dio, *Roman History* LXXVII. xiv; From *LCL*

Caracalla waged war also against the Cennians, a German tribe. These warriors are said to have assailed the Romans with the utmost fierceness, even using their teeth to pull out from their flesh the missiles with which the Osroenians[25] wounded them, so that they might have their hands free for slaying without interruption. Nevertheless, even they accepted a defeat in name for a large sum of money and allowed Caracalla to make his escape back into the province of Germany. Some of their women who were captured by the Romans, upon being asked by Caracalla whether they wished to be sold or slain, chose the latter fate; then, upon being sold, they all killed themselves and some slew their children as well.

Many also of the people living close to the ocean itself near the mouths of the Elbe sent envoys to him asking for his friendship, although their real purpose was to get money. This was made clear by the fact that, when he had done as they desired, many attacked him, threatening to make war, and yet he came to terms with all of them. For even though the terms proposed were contrary to their wishes, yet when they saw the gold pieces they were captivated. The gold he gave them was of course genuine, whereas the silver and gold currency that he furnished to the Romans was debased; for he manufactured the one kind out of lead plated with silver and the other out of copper plated with gold.[26]

"Historia Augusta," *Life of Severus Alexander* lviii. 3–5; From *LCL*

The captives taken from the various peoples, if their childhood or youth permitted it, were given to the emperor's friends, but those who were of royal blood or noble rank were enrolled for warfare, though not for any of great importance. The lands taken from the enemy were presented to the leaders and soldiers of the frontier armies, with the provision that they should continue to be theirs only if their heirs entered military service, and that they should never belong to civilians, for, he

---

25. A people from the Roman province of Osroëne in northwestern Mesopotamia.
26. For the debasement of Roman coinage in the third century, see §§ 112, 123.

said, men serve with greater zeal if they are defending their own lands.[27]
He added to these lands, indeed, both draft animals and slaves, in order
that they might be able to till what they had received and that it might
not come to pass that, through a lack of inhabitants or the old age of the
owners, the lands bordering on the country of the barbarians should be
left uninhabited; for this, he thought, would be most reprehensible.

"Historia Augusta," *Life of Probus* xiv. 7, xviii. 1–2; From *LCL*

He took 16,000 [German] recruits, all of whom he scattered through the
various provinces, incorporating bodies of fifty or sixty in the detachments or among the soldiers along the frontier, for he said that the aid
that the Romans received from barbarian auxiliaries must be felt but not
seen. . . . Having made peace, then, with the Persians, he returned to
Thrace, where he settled 100,000 Bastarnians on Roman soil, all of
whom remained loyal. But when he had likewise brought over many
from other tribes—that is, Gepedians, Greuthungians,[28] and Vandals—
they all broke faith, and when Probus was busied with wars against the
pretenders they roamed over well-nigh the entire world on foot or in
ships and did no little damage to the glory of Rome.

NEGOTIATIONS WITH THE JUTHUNGIANS

Dexippus,[29] *Fragment* 6 (abridged)

When Aurelian had inflicted a smashing defeat upon the Scythian Juthungians,[30] and had slaughtered many of them as they withdrew to
their refuge across the Danube, the survivors sent an embassy to make a

27. During the Principate, military service tended to become an occupation in which sons followed
fathers, and with the Severan dynasty the military became a veritable caste. This is, however, the
earliest known case where military service was formally made hereditary (cf. introduction to § 150).
With similar grants of borderlands by subsequent emperors, the entire frontier defense by the end of
the fourth century had been reorganized on this principle. Along the Empire's frontiers was strung a
chain of fortresses (*castella*), around which these hereditary military settlers (*limitanei*) were concentrated.

28. These two were Gothic tribes. With this selection may be compared Zosimus' report (*New
History* I. lxviii. 3) that Probus, after defeating Burgundians and Vandals, "sent to Great Britain the
prisoners he had taken in the war, and gave them lands in that island to inhabit. They were subsequently
very serviceable to him whenever the older inhabitants of the island undertook to revolt."

29. Publius Herennius Dexippus, an Athenian, one of the last important historians in antiquity,
wrote in the second half of the third century three major works, including a history of Rome's Scythian
wars, from which this fragment and the next come.

30. A Suebian tribe settled on the Lower Danube, east of Dacia. Elements of this people had
advanced as far as Rome during the reign of Aurelian's predecessor, Gallienus.

truce. But they gave the appearance of making their plea for peace without the extreme fear and panic of defeat, in an attempt to obtain also the restoration of the regular subsidy previously paid them by the Romans.

[Aurelian drew up his army in full battle array in order to overawe the Juthungian envoys. The latter, speaking through an interpreter, delivered a long, rhetorical address, which ended as follows:]

"It would be best for you to make peace and obtain the advantages accruing from harmony, and to come to a settlement with us over the issues of the war and thus, strengthened by our alliance, to have greater resources against your attackers. If you should decide to do this, it is just that we should get what we used to receive from you regularly in gifts of coined and uncoined gold and silver to guarantee friendship. If we are denied this, we will defend ourselves against you as enemies and fight with all our might."

To this the king of the Romans replied as follows: ". . . If you bring an honest offer of peace, what need is there to mention a demand of money? . . . If you think that signing a treaty will weaken your position with respect to the profit and gains derived from the war and you therefore come here, though defeated, to demand tribute from us, thinking that we are eager at any cost for the pleasures of indolence which peace affords—why, then, try an attack like your previous one. . . . Although treaty-bound, you launched hostilities against us without a declaration of war. . . . Your horde is far from strong either in body or in spirit. It has been cut off inside . . . our territory; it is afflicted with scarcity of food and other hardship; some sufferings are now upon it, and still others await it; and, worn out in constant hardship, it will become more demoralized, and we shall be able without fighting to do whatever we please with it. . . ."

At these words of the king the Juthungians were panic-stricken, and as none of the results they had hoped for was being achieved, faced completely as they were with despair about the truce, they returned to their people.

TREATY WITH THE VANDALS, A.D. 271

Dexippus,[31] *Fragment 7*

In the reign of Aurelian the Vandals, after suffering a smashing defeat at the hands of the Romans, sent an embassy to the Romans to negotiate an armistice and a treaty. . . . The Roman soldiers were . . . assembled, and were asked by the king what they thought the better course in the existing circumstances. Deciding wisely . . . to preserve their present good fortune, they all voted for an end to the war, indicating their desire with a shout. . . .

The kings and chieftains of the barbarians came and, as they had been ordered, gave hostages not inferior to themselves in rank or station (their kings each give their sons as hostages without hesitation). . . . Thus they came to an agreement, and the treaty was drawn up. Thereafter two thousand Vandal cavalrymen would serve with the Romans, part of them drafted from the ranks and enrolled in this allied force, the rest volunteers undertaking military service of their own accord. The rest of the Vandal horde would return home, and the Roman governor would provide them with a market hard by the Danube.

III. DEPOPULATION OF CITY AND COUNTRYSIDE

CITIES RAVAGED BY CIVIL WAR: THE CASE OF AQUILEIA

Herodian, *History* VIII. ii. 3–iv. 8 (abridged)

Aquileia was even in earlier times a very big city with a large population of its own. Situated on the sea like an emporium of Italy and fronting all the Illyrian peoples, she provided the merchants sailing there with the products received from the interior by land or river, and she shipped into the hinterland the products from overseas needed by the inhabitants, which their land did not readily produce because of its cold climate; and also, as they did not cultivate the vine and her territory was especially productive of wine, she furnished them with an abundance of drink. Accordingly, a large population lived there, consisting not only of citizens but also of foreigners and merchants. At this time [A.D. 238],

31. See note 29.

however, the population was even further increased by all the crowds streaming thither from the countryside, leaving the neighboring towns and villages to seek safety inside the great city and its surrounding wall. The ancient wall had for the most part been demolished earlier, since after the advent of Roman rule the cities of Italy no longer needed walls or weapons, for they enjoyed, in place of wars, profound peace and association in Roman citizenship. But now necessity drove them to restore the wall, rebuild its ruins, and raise towers and battlements. . . .

The army [of Maximinus] crossed over and marched upon the city. Finding the houses of the suburbs deserted, they cut down all the vines and trees, set some on fire, and made a shambles of the once-thriving countryside. . . . After destroying all this to the root, the army pressed on to the walls . . . and strove to demolish at least some part of the wall, so that they might break in and sack everything, razing the city and leaving the land a deserted pasturage.

THE "PURGING" OF ALEXANDRIA

In A.D. 215 Caracalla turned his soldiery loose on the population of Alexandria, which had demonstrated against him on his arrival. After the massacre he sent to the prefect of Egypt a letter, from which this papyrus preserves two extracts, instructing him to expel from the city all persons who had no business there. On the floating population of Alexandria, cf. §§ 82, 85.

Giessen Papyrus no. 40, col. 2, lines 16–29 (= *Select Papyri,* no. 215); A.D. 215; Adapted from *LCL*

All Egyptians who are in Alexandria, and especially countryfolk who have fled from other parts and can easily be detected, are by all means to be expelled, with the exception, however, of pig dealers and riverboatmen and the men who bring down reeds for heating the baths. But expel all others, as by the numbers of their kind and their uselessness they are disturbing the city. I am informed that on the festival of Sarapis and on certain other festal days Egyptians are accustomed to bring down bulls and other animals for sacrifice, and even on other days; for this they are not to be stopped. The persons who ought to be stopped are those who flee from their places of origin[32] to escape rustic toil, not

32. Cf. introduction to § 82. A.D. 215/216 was a census year.

those, however, who congregate here with the object of viewing the glorious city of Alexandria or come down for the sake of enjoying a more civilized life or for incidental business.

And farther along [in the letter]: For true Egyptians can easily be recognized among the linen weavers by their speech, which proves them to have assumed the appearance and dress of another class;[33] moreover, their mode of life, their far-from-civilized manners, reveal them to be Egyptian countryfolk.

THE PETITION OF SCAPTOPARA

In this petition to the emperor we encounter again a picture already familiar in the two preceding centuries (§§ 85, 86): villagers fleeing from their homes to escape the abuses of officials and soldiers. Further examples for the third century will be found in § 104, last selection; in § 117; and in note 24 above.

CIL vol. III, no. 12,336, col. 2 (= Dittenberger, no. 888)

[Scaptopara, Thrace, A.D. 238]

To the Emperor Caesar Marcus Antonius GORDIAN Pius Felix Augustus, petition from the villagers of Scaptopara and Gresa[?]. During the most fortunate and eternal time of your reign you have often stated in rescripts that the villages should be inhabited and improved instead of having the inhabitants driven from their homes. Such a policy is conducive to the security of your subjects and the advantage of your most sacred treasury. Wherefore we too convey a just supplication to your divinity, praying that you may graciously grant our petition to this effect.

We dwell in and are property owners in the afore-mentioned village, which is exposed to wanton damage because it possesses the advantage of hot springs and is situated between two of the army camps that are in your Thrace. And in the past, as long as the inhabitants remained undisturbed and unharmed, they paid their tribute and other levies unexceptionably. But when certain parties began at times to proceed to insolence and employ violence, then indeed the village began to decline. A famous festival is celebrated two miles from our village, and those

---

33. On the rigid class barriers in Roman Egypt and the severe penalties for passing one's self off as a member of a higher class see § 79.

who visit there for fifteen days for the festival do not remain at the site of the festival but leave it and descend upon our village, forcing us to provide them with hospitality and furnish many other things for their entertainment without payment. In addition to these, soldiers too, when sent elsewhere, leave their proper routes and come to us, and likewise compel us to provide them with hospitality and supplies and pay us no money. And the governors of the province and even your procurators for the most part visit here for the benefit of the waters. We are continually entertaining the authorities, as we needs must; but, unable to bear the burden of the others, we appealed repeatedly to the governors of Thrace, who in accordance with the divine [i.e., imperial] ordinances gave orders that we be left undisturbed. For we pointed out that we could no longer abide it, but actually had a mind to abandon even our ancestral hearths on account of the violence of those who descend upon us — and in truth we have declined from many home owners to a very few.

For some time the edicts of the governors prevailed, and no one disturbed us with a demand either for hospitality or for provision of supplies; but as time went on, the whole throng who are contemptuous of our defenselessness again dared to foist themselves upon us. Since, therefore, we can no longer endure the oppression, and since in truth we, too, like the rest, are in danger of having to abandon the abode of our forefathers, on this account we beg you, O invincible Augustus, that by your sacred rescript you give orders that everyone proceed by his proper route, and that they not leave the other villages to come to us and force us to furnish them with supplies free of charge, or even to provide hospitality to those to whom we are not obliged to — for the governors have more than once issued orders that hospitality is not to be provided for any but those sent by the governors and procurators on government service. And if we are oppressed, we will flee from our homes, and the treasury will be involved in very great loss. But pitied through your divine foresight, we will remain in our places of origin and be able to provide the sacred tribute and the other taxes.[34] And this will come about for us in the most fortunate times of your reign, if you give orders for your divine letter to be inscribed on a stele and set up in public, so that we shall be able, if we obtain this, to acknowledge our thanks to your fortune. . . .[35]

34. The plea of this sentence and the preceding is encountered also in the papyri from Egypt (cf. § 86).

35. The final clause of this sentence is not clear and is here omitted.

112. MONETARY CRISIS

Debasement of the Roman coinage had begun as early as the reign of Nero. But in the third century, with mounting inflation, widespread hoarding of specie, and sharply reduced revenues, the emperors resorted to reckless adulteration of the imperial coinage to meet their military and administrative costs. As a result, distrust of new currency was widely manifested, by individuals as well as by banks. Ultimately the government refused to accept its own coinage for many taxes and insisted on payment in kind (cf. § 122).

BLACK MARKET IN MONEY

The city of Mylasa in Caria, which leased its exchange monopoly to a private banker, was forced to take action to halt illegal exchange between local and imperial currencies in order to protect the city's revenues and the interests of the lessee. This local monetary problem was probably precipitated by a debasement of the imperial silver coinage by Septimius Severus.

OGIS, no. 515, lines 15–53; A.D. 209–211

It has been decreed by the council and the people: If anyone, in any manner whatever, whether freeman or slave, other than the lessee and operator of the bank, is caught exchanging or buying currency, such person shall be brought to face the banker on information laid before the council by any citizen who so desires. Upon conviction before the magistrates and council, if he did it without agio, the banker and the informer who obtained his conviction shall have the right to recover the money, with the banker having also the right of legal execution against him as he has been guaranteed; but if at an agio, a freeman shall pay a penalty of 500 *denarii* to the most sacred fisc of our most divine lords the emperors, 250 *denarii* to the municipality, and 100 *denarii* to the informer who obtained his conviction, and the money discovered to be involved shall be forfeit to the banker, and a slave convicted as aforestated shall be handed over by his master to the magistrates in the presence of the council, given fifty[?] stripes, cast into prison, and assigned to confinement for six months; if the master wishes the slave not to be so treated, he shall owe the aforestated fines to the most sacred fisc, the municipality, and the informer who obtained his conviction. Informations of this character shall be received by the secretary of the magistrates, and after an information is presented public notice shall be given for three successive days in sacred and public places, the notice expressly stating that the council is being convened for this purpose. If the magistrates or the secretary neglect to do any of the things decreed, or if the councilmen fail to assemble, though able to do so and present in town, the magistrates and the secretary shall each pay a fine to the most sacred fisc of the emperors at the rate of 300 *denarii,* and the councilmen at the rate of. . . .

This decree shall be inscribed on a stele which is also to be erected in the agora in the most conspicuous place, as a law to be established for all time. In truth, the safety of the city is in dire straits as a result of the evil-doing and wickedness of some few who raid and embezzle the public moneys and by whose power a kind of currency exchange has invaded the market place which prevents the city from having the necessities of life, since many are in need and the community is in want. And for this reason the flow of the revenues to our lords the emperors is delayed. . . . [The rest is fragmentary.]

DISTRUST OF IMPERIAL COINAGE

Because of the ephemeral character of some reigns in this period, banks were understandably hesitant to accept the coinage issued by the usurpers, as is shown by this official letter ordering them to accept the coins bearing the imprint of Macrianus and Quietus.

Oxyrhynchus Papyrus No. 1,411 (= *Select Papyri,* no. 230); A.D. 260; Adapted from *LCL*

From Aurelius Ptolemaeus, also called Nemesianus, *strategus* of the Oxyrhynchite nome. Whereas the public officials have assembled and have accused the bankers of the exchange banks of having closed them because of their unwillingness to accept the divine coin of the emperors, it has become necessary to issue an order to all the owners of the banks to open them and to accept and exchange all coin except the absolutely spurious and counterfeit—and not alone to them but to those who engage in business transactions of any kind whatever—knowing full well that if they disobey this order they will experience the penalties already ordained for them in the past by his Highness the Prefect. Signed by me. Year 1, Hathyr 28.

113. REMISSION OF TAXES

Faced with sharply curtailed revenues, the emperors of the third century
—in the absence of the concept of a national debt in antiquity—resorted
to increased demands for taxes and personal services from the reduced
population of the Empire. At the same time, acutely aware of the unrest
due to the inability of the population to pay, they occasionally afforded
relief through sweeping remissions of taxes, as had the emperors of the
second century under less critical conditions (see § 20).

CANCELLATION OF TAXES IN AFRICA

This edict was issued by Caracalla for the benefit of the African provinces
in A.D. 216, when he was engaged in a military campaign in the East and
needed men and supplies.

AE, 1948, no. 109

The Emperor Caesar Marcus Aurelius Antoninus Pius Augustus Parthicus Maximus Britannicus Maximus Germanicus Maximus Ponticus
Maximus, son of the deified Severus Pius Arabicus Adiabenicus Parthicus Maximus Britannicus Maximus, grandson of the deified Marcus
Antoninus Germanicus Sarmaticus, great-grandson of the deified Antoninus Pius, great-great-grandson of the deified Hadrian, descendant of
the deified Trajan Parthicus and the deified Nerva,[36] holding the tribunician power for the nineteenth year, acclaimed *imperator* three times,
consul four times, father of his country, proconsul, declares:

In reward for your allegiance and fidelity, I remit to you all debts
whatsoever owed to the fisc, whether of grain or of money, even if suits
therefor are pending, but not in cases where judgment has been rendered
and no appeal has followed. What is more, I do hereby declare that my
benefaction extends also to those cases where an appeal is proved to

36. The Severan dynasty, of Punic–Syrian stock, was legitimized by its founder, Septimius Severus, who shortly after his accession adopted himself into the family of the Antonines. The biographers
of the "Historia Augusta" recount with evident gusto details illustrative of their non-Roman origin.
Septimius Severus' voice "was clear, but retained an African accent even to his old age"; and a visit
from his sister made him blush, "since she could scarcely speak Latin." Severus Alexander spoke Greek
better than Latin, which he did not care for. Similarly, Maximinus, who succeeded the Severan
dynasty, is described as "half barbarian and scarcely yet master of the Latin tongue, speaking almost
pure Thracian."

have been interposed, even if it has not yet been accepted. I am sure that you will repay my dispensation by loyally placing at my disposition all the resources of your villages and provinces, which serve the state well not only with brave men eminently distinguished in every rank of military and civilian office[37] but also with the very forests teeming with animals of a celestial species.[38] I anticipate that in return for my benefaction you will henceforth pay your annual assessments, whether in grain or in money, all the more readily when you recall that I did not wait but offered you of my own accord, without your petitioning or even hoping for them, new measures of relief and my magnanimous remission.

Lucius Antoninus Sosibianus and Aulus Pompeius Cassianus, duovirs, saw to [setting this up].

REMISSION OF CROWN TAX

"Crown gold" *(aurum coronarium)* was for centuries an important source of revenue for the fisc. The custom of communities offering golden crowns to rulers was of Hellenistic origin; eventually it became a tax imposed by these monarchs. Roman generals of the Republic operating in the East were accustomed to receive such crowns from various communities. During the Empire the payment of "crown gold" became a tax on all communities of the Empire, imposed annually and on various special occasions (cf. p. 381).

Fayum Papyrus No. 20 (= *Select Papyri,* no. 216; rev. ed. in *Archiv für Papyrusforschung* [1941], 14:44–59); A.D. 222

The Emperor Caesar Marcus Aurelius SEVERUS ALEXANDER Pius Felix Augustus, son of the deified Magnus Antoninus Pius, grandson of the deified Septimius Severus Pius, *pontifex maximus,* holder of the tribunician power, consul, father of his country, declares:

. . . lest through making a manifestation of their joy, which they experience at my accession to rule, they be compelled to pay[?] more than they are able. Wherefore I have formed this resolution, not wanting in precedents, among which I sought to imitate my ancestors Trajan and Marcus [Aurelius], emperors most assuredly worthy of admiration; and,

37. Macrinus, the later emperor, whom Caracalla had recently appointed prefect of the Praetorian Guard, was a Moor (cf. note 8).

38. Elephants are meant. They are called "celestial" because of their association with Caracalla, whose chariot they drew in processions, or from contemporary religious symbolism and mythological associations.

in order to emulate their policy, I make the present decision—indeed, if the fact of the poverty of the state in these times had not stood in the way, I should have shown a much more conspicuous proof of my magnanimity and should not have hesitated to remit also any arrears still owing from the past for contributions of this sort and whatever sums had previously been voted under the title of crowns for my proclamation as Caesar[39] or might yet be voted by the cities for the same cause. These, however, I do not believe [I can remit], for the reasons which I have stated just above, but I have not overlooked the fact that these, as I see from present circumstances, are all that the cities can put up.

Therefore, let all persons in all the cities, those in Italy and those in the other provinces, know that, on the occasion of my rule as emperor, to which I have acceded to the wishes and prayers of all, in lieu of the golden crowns it behooves me to remit to them the sums called for; and that I do this not because of a surplus of wealth but because it is my policy to strive[?], even though hard pressed, to retrieve the decline, not by searching for limits[40] but by economy, even though expenses all but reach the privy purse. For this will be my earnest endeavor, to increase the Empire not by exaction of money but rather by liberality and benefactions, so that my Fortune may counsel the governors and the men dispatched by me to procuratorships, whom I tested and selected by the most rigid standards before dispatching, to behave with the utmost moderation. For the governors of the provinces will learn more and more how zealously it behooves them to care for and look to the provinces to which they have been appointed, when they can all see the emperor also conducting the business of the realm with such propriety, economy, and self-restraint.

The chief magistrates in each city shall make it their business to post copies of this decree of mine in public where they will be most clearly visible to readers. Year I, Payni 30.

---

39. That is, emperor designate; cf. chapter 1, note 10.

40. At this point some scholars have emended the Greek text to read "not by quests for revenues," but this seems supererogatory; the phrase as it stands means "not by trying to squeeze out the last ounce of revenue," and its indirection is entirely in keeping with the high-flown language of the edict.

114. Decline of Provincial Assemblies

THE INSCRIPTION OF THORIGNY

The base of a statue erected to Titus Sennius Sollemnis in his native village is inscribed on the front with the record of his career; on one side with a letter from Claudius Paulinus, governor of Britain and previously governor of Lyonese Gaul, who heaps presents upon him for his "services and good will"; and on the other side with the following text, which shows by what kind of services to the Roman governors he had earned such rich rewards. The action of Sollemnis here recorded illustrates how, in the disorders of the third century, the assemblies of the provincial leagues lost what little power and initiative they had once been allowed and fell completely under the thumb of the governors of the provinces. The inscription was cut when the statue was erected, in A.D. 238, but the following letter was originally written in 223.

CIL, vol. XIII, no. 3,162

[Araegenuae (Vieux), Gaul]

Copy of a letter of Aedinius Julianus, prefect of the Praetorian Guard, to Badius Comnianus, procurator and acting governor. Aedinius Julianus to Badius Comnianus, greeting. When I was acting governor in the province of Lugdunensis, I observed that most [of the assembly delegates] were good men, particularly this Sollemnis, a native of the municipality of the Viducassians and the priest,[41] to whom, on account of the worth of his principles and his upright conduct, I took a great liking. In addition to this, when an attempt was made in the Gallic Assembly, at the instigation of certain members who considered themselves slighted by him in view of their services, to draft an indictment as if it were the unanimous sense of the province, against Claudius Paulinus, my predecessor,[42] this good friend of mine, Sollemnis, blocked their intention by interposing a challenge to the effect that his native town, when it had made him among others a delegate, had given him no instructions concerning any legal action but had on the contrary praised [Paulinus]. The consequence of this argument was that all abandoned the indict-

41. Of the cult of Rome and Augustus at the provincial altar erected at the confluence of the Rhone and Saône rivers at Lyons. The holder of this office, elected by the Gallic Assembly, was at once the chief priest of Gaul and the president of the assembly.
42. As governor of Lyonese Gaul *(Gallia Lugdunensis)*.

ment. And so my fondness and liking for him grew more and more. Confident of my regard for him, he has come to see me in the capital [Rome], and, being now about to depart, he asks me to commend him to you. You will be doing the right thing if you accede to his request, etc.[43]

115. Compulsory Services of Municipal Officers

The interference of the imperial government in municipal administration, on the increase since the time of Trajan (see § 69), was sharply stepped up in the third century. One of the solutions of the central government for the shrinkage of taxable resources was to impose a form of capital levy on the rich through the regimentation of the propertied classes into a hereditary caste obligated, as members of the municipal councils (*decuriones,* or *curiales*), to discharge various local offices. The most important of these— and by the time of Constantine practically the only important function of the *curiales*—was the collection of the imperial revenues, and personal liability for the collection was placed upon the *decaproti,* a committee of the municipal council consisting of the ten (sometimes twenty) wealthiest decurions. Caught between the hammer of inexorable governmental demands and the anvil of limited means, the *curiales* sought with increasing desperation, which frequently erupted in physical violence, to avoid these ruinous duties, only to have one loophole after another closed as the rules governing their compulsory services were systematized by the jurists of the third and fourth centuries, from whose works the first selection following is drawn.

Justinian, *Digest* L. ii. 1 and 2.8, iv. 1.2, iv. 3.15–16, iv. 4

The governor of the province shall see to it that decurions who are proved to have left the area of the municipality to which they belong and to have moved to other places are recalled to their native soil and perform the appropriate public services. . . .

Persons over fifty-five are forbidden by imperial enactments to be called to the position of decurion against their will, but if they do consent to this they ought to perform the duties, although if they are over seventy they are not compelled to assume compulsory municipal services. . . .

43. The *etc.* indicates the omission of the stereotype close of letters of recommendation.

Municipal duties of a personal character are: representation of a municipality, that is, becoming a public advocate; assignment to taking the census or registering property; secretaryships; camel transport; commissioner of food supply and the like, of public lands, of grain procurement, of water supply; horse races in the circus; paving of public streets; grain storehouse; heating of public baths; distribution of food supply; and other duties similar to these. From the above-mentioned, other duties can be deduced in accordance with the laws and long-established custom of each municipality. . . .

The governor of the province shall see to it that the compulsory public services and offices in the municipalities are imposed fairly and in rotation according to age and rank, in accordance with the gradation of public services and offices long ago established, so that the men and resources of municipalities are not inconsiderately ruined by frequent oppression of the same persons. If two sons are under parental power the father is not compelled to support their public services at the same time. . . .

The care of constructing or rebuilding a public work in a municipality is a compulsory public service from which a father of five living children is excused;[44] and if this service is forcibly imposed, this fact does not deprive him of the exemption that he has from other public services. The excusing of those with insufficient resources who are nominated to public services or offices is not permanent but temporary. For if a hoped-for increase comes to one's property by honorable means, when his turn comes an evaluation is to be made to determine whether he is suitable for the services for which he was chosen. . . . A person who is responsible for public services to his municipality and submits his name for military service for the purpose of avoiding the municipal burden cannot make the condition of his community worse.[45]

Oxyrhynchus Papyrus No. 705, lines 54–79 (= Wilcken, no. 407); A.D. 200

The Emperor Caesar Lucius SEPTIMIUS SEVERUS Pius Pertinax Augustus Arabicus Adiabenicus Parthicus Maximus and the Emperor Caesar Marcus Aurelius Antoninus Pius Augustus [CARACALLA] to Aurelius Horio, greeting. We commend you also for this endowment which you see fit to bestow upon the villages of the Oxyrhynchite nome by presenting the wherewithal for acquisition of property. The established rule shall

44. For other benefits enjoyed by parents of large families, cf. § 91.
45. That is, he is obligated to fulfill his duties to the community.

be observed in this case also, so that your grant shall be expended as you desired and not be diverted to any other purpose.

The request is as follows: "To the most gracious emperors Severus and Antoninus, the saviors and benefactors of all mankind, Aurelius Horio, former *strategus* and former chief judge of the most illustrious city of Alexandria, greeting. Certain villages of the Oxyrhynchite nome, O most benevolent emperors, in which I and my sons possess lands, have been utterly exhausted by the burdens of the annual liturgies of the fisc and of policing their districts, and there is danger that they will be ruined as far as the fisc is concerned and that your land will be left uncultivated.[46] Accordingly, in an endeavor to be both philanthropic and useful, I desire in the interest of their recovery to make to each village some small endowment for the purchase of land, the revenue from which shall be earmarked for the maintenance and expenses of those who perform the annual liturgies for the. . . ." [The rest is lost.]

Oxyrhynchus Papyrus No. 1,406 (= *FIRA*, vol. I, no. 89); A.D. 215/216

The Emperor Caesar Marcus Aurelius Severus Antoninus Parthicus Maximus Britannicus Maximus Germanicus Maximus Pius Augustus [CARACALLA] declares: If a councilman strikes or reviles the council president or a councilman, such councilman shall be removed from council membership and reduced to common rank.

Posted in . . . in the public colonnade, in the magistracy of Aurelius Alexander son of . . . of Heliopolis.[47]

Oxyrhynchus Papyrus No. 1,405; A.D. 200

. . . you ceded [your property][48] . . . it is perfectly clear that the cession was made not to our fisc but to the person who nominated you for the liturgy. He will take possession of your property, furnish the [security?] and perform the liturgy; our fisc is not concerned with such cessions. Your citizenship, however, will be not at all impaired as a result of this, nor will you be subjected to physical violence. Posted in Alexandria, year 8, Pharmuthi.

46. The propertied class was understandably concerned for the normal functioning of the economy, because persons assigned to tax collection were personally liable for revenues due the fisc; cf. §§ 77, 85.

47. In contrast to the traditional absence of city councils in Egypt (see p. 287). Septimius Severus had established such bodies in Alexandria and in the nome capitals, partly in order to extend and unify the system of municipal liturgies.

48. Persons nominated to municipal office were permitted to surrender their property in a form of voluntary bankruptcy rather than serve (cf. the following document).

To Aurelius Leonides, *strategus* of the Oxyrhynchite nome, from Aemilius Stephanus son of Hatres and Tasorapis, of the village of Sinkepha. This present day I learned that I have been nominated by Aurelius Amois son of Patas and Demetrous, of the same village, as a person of means and qualified to succeed him in the office of collector of the village money revenues of the said Sinkepha for the current third year. This is unreasonable and not in keeping with the principle of sharing the liturgy. I therefore resign my property to him in accordance with the divine [i.e., imperial] decree cited above, and I declare that I have property at. . . . [The rest is lost.]

Rainer Papyrus No. 20, col. 1 (= Wilcken, no. 402); A.D. 250

Aurelius Hermophilus son of Horio, former *cosmetes* of the great, ancient, illustrious, and most august city of Hermopolis, to the right honorable Aurelius Eudaemo, also known as Theodotus, former gymnasiarch, former high priest, councilman, acting council president of the said city, greeting. The other day I submitted to the most excellent council through you the answer of our most illustrious prefect, Appius Sabinus, contained in the letter of the nome *strategus*, Aurelius Hiero, sent to me by his clerk Aurelius Hermes, in reply to my petition to him to relinquish all that I own to those who nominated my son, Aurelius Horio, also known as Hermaeus, for *cosmetes* of the said city, since my means had been exhausted by my own recent discharge of that office in my own name.

The prefect in his reply ruled that the nominators bear the risk involved in proposing names,[49] and he ordered the nome *strategus* to prevent the use of force if it should arise[50] contrary to his benign orders, which were delivered on the 21st of the present month Epeiph, according to the receipt issued to me by the clerk in charge of this. Yesterday, namely Epeiph 22, there was sent to me through a council clerk a letter from you, Eudaemo, also known as Theodotus, in which you give your personal answer concerning the said office even after my [offer of] surrender of property, and you invidiously cite some passages from the laws . . . taken [out of context] to suit your need. Now I write to you again, since a man surrendering his property and relinquishing his pos-

---

49. Local officials who nominated inhabitants for compulsory public office did so at the risk of having to take on the office themselves if they nominated someone financially or otherwise ineligible.

50. That this fear was not groundless is confirmed by a letter in column 2 of this papyrus, addressed by Hermophilus on the same day to the prefect, in which he reports: "I have been kept under arrest since the 20th by a council attendant and the council president's guard."

sessions is entitled in accordance with the laws and the divine [i.e., imperial] enactments to . . . protection against any violence, in keeping with which the most illustrious and devoted prefect desired the *strategus* to prevent the use of force, adding that the risk of nomination rested with the nominators. If you are so minded, take all my property yourself, returning the customary one third; then you can discharge all the duties of the office, and not impair [the smooth functioning of] either the city or the most excellent council. Such a reply [from you] will satisfy me in my principal claim. I, Aurelius Hermophilus son of Horio, ex-*cosmetes,* bid you farewell, most dear sir. Year 1 of the Emperor Caesar Gaius Messius Quintus Trajanus DECIUS Pius Felix Augustus, Epeiph 23.

116. INCREASING REGIMENTATION OF MERCHANT AND ARTISAN GUILDS

Paralleling its intensified constraints upon the decurial class, the military monarchy relied more and more upon merchant and artisan guilds *(collegia, corpora)* to assure the vital economic needs of the Empire and exerted ever-tighter control over these associations, especially over those that helped supply the city of Rome and the armies. To obtain their ready cooperation, their previously granted privileges (cf. § 29) were generally maintained and even somewhat extended. In the end, however, these functions, too, became obligatory and hereditary (cf. § 129).

"Historia Augusta," *Life of Severus Alexander* xxxiii. 2; *From LCL*

He also formed guilds of all the wine dealers, the greengrocers, the bootmakers, and, in short, of all the trades, and he granted them advocates chosen from their own number and designated the judge to whose jurisdiction each should belong.

THE SHIPOWNERS' ASSOCIATIONS OF ARLES

The river port of Arelate (Arles) in Narbonese Gaul was one of the principal grain export centers of the West. Its shipowners' associations had a central office at Ostia (cf. § 27, fourth selection), an office in Berytus (Beirut) for the provisioning of the army in Syria (as attested by the following inscription), and presumably also branch offices in other important ports of the Empire. This inscription, containing a letter from the prefect of the grain supply, illustrates the close government supervision of their activity and shows that they, like other elements of the population, had cause to complain of their treatment at the hands of corrupt government functionaries.

CIL, vol. III, no. 14,165 (8) (=*ESAR,* 3:478)

[Berytus, Syria, A.D. *201]*

Claudius Julianus to the marine shipowners of the five associations of Arles, greeting. I have ordered appended what, after reading your resolution, I have written to Gaius Valerius Severus, imperial procurator, *vir eminens.* I send you my best wishes for your prosperity and health.

Copy of the Letter

I have appended a copy of the resolution of the marine shipowners of the five associations of Arles, together with the measures taken on my part. And since the same complaint is spreading more widely, with others also imploring the aid of justice and making it clear that they will bring their loyal services to a halt shortly if the injustice continues, I request that attention be given both to the payment of the account and to the security of the persons who are in the service of the *annona.* Give orders under your authority that the iron fastenings [of the cargoes] be stamped with a mark, and that escorts be attached to deliver in the city [of Rome] the weight which they have taken on board.[51]

117. Conditions of the Tenant Farmers (Coloni)

The turbulent conditions of the third century resulted in the devastation of large areas of land and wholesale abandonment of cultivation. To encourage settlers and revive production Septimius Severus and Caracalla issued a rescript reaffirming the established custom whereby occupants of untilled land received a prescriptive right against eviction (cf. § 25). Another development was the spread of the imperial estates, brought about by the sweeping confiscations of the period, and the continued growth of the estates that remained in private ownership. The conditions of tenant

---

51. On the sealing and military escort of *annona* cargoes, cf. § 17, fifth selection.

farmers *(coloni)* in the general upheaval of the times are vividly illuminated by a number of extant petitions against illegal exactions and oppression by imperial officials, soldiers, and local magnates. It is noteworthy, moreover, that despite these abuses large numbers of people fled to country estates to escape municipal obligations and the general insecurity of city life. Agricultural tenants still possessed freedom of movement, but we can see a first step in the direction of serfdom in an administrative order of A.D. 247 by which *coloni* who had fallen in arrears to the fisc were bound to their tenancies till they discharged their tax debts. This order was for many tantamount to binding them, and their children who succeeded to their tenancies, to the soil forever. This *de facto* situation was eventually formalized by Constantine and by later emperors (see § 129).

"SQUATTER RIGHTS"

Berlin Papyrus No. 267 (= *Select Papyri*, no. 214 = *FIRA*, vol. I, no. 84); A.D. 199

The Emperor Caesar Lucius SEPTIMUS SEVERUS Pertinax Augustus Arabicus Adiabenicus Parthicus Maximus and the Emperor Marcus Aurelius Antoninus Augustus [CARACALLA] to Juliana daughter of Sosthenianus, through her husband Sosthenes. To those who had a legal ground[52] and who remained in undisputed possession, the prescriptive right of long possession is secured by the space of twenty years as against persons dwelling in another city and ten years as against persons in the same city. Posted in Alexandria, Year 8, Tybi 3.

COMPLAINT OF IMPERIAL TENANTS

CIL, vol. III, no. 14,191 (= *IGRR*, vol. IV, no. 598)

[Aragua, Phrygia, A.D. 244–247]

May good fortune attend!

The Emperor Caesar Marcus Julius PHILIP Augustus and Marcus Julius Philip, most noble Caesar, to Marcus Aurelius Eclectus. . . . The proconsul, *vir clarissimus,* will look into the truth of the facts you allege and will make it his care that no injustice is perpetrated.[53]

52. For entering into possession. The importance of the legal origin of a right is emphasized also in another rescript of Septimius Severus and Caracalla (*CIL*, vol. III, no. 781 =*FIRA*, vol. I, no. 86), lines 9–12): "The city of Tyra does not show the origin of the privilege granted, and it is not easy for anything that was acquired by error or at will to be confirmed by the prescriptive right of time."

53. This reply from the emperors and the sentence quoted below from a rescript are inscribed in Latin. The petition that follows is in Greek.

To the Emperor Caesar Marcus Julius PHILIP Pius Felix Augustus and to Marcus Julius Philip, most noble Caesar, petition from Aurelius Eclectus on behalf of the community of Aragua, your *coloni* and farmers. . . . While all men in your most blessed times, most pious and faultless among kings that have ever been, live calm and peaceful lives and all wrongdoing and extortion [cf. chapter 4, note 131] have ceased, we alone suffer treatment alien to these most fortunate times and come to you with this supplication, secure in the justice of the petition herein. We who flee as suppliants to the refuge of your divinity are the entire population of your most sacred estate. We are suffering extortion and illegal exactions beyond all reason at the hands of those who ought to preserve the public welfare.[54] Although we happen to be inlanders and not . . . we are suffering treatment alien to your most blessed times. For those passing through the Appian region abandon the highways—military commanders[?], soldiers, and powerful and influential men in the city and your officials abandon the highways, swoop down upon us, take us away from our work, requisition our plow oxen, and illegally exact what is not due them. As a result we are suffering extraordinary injustice by this extortion. We wrote about all this to your majesty, Augustus, when you held the prefecture of the Praetorian Guard . . . and how your divinity was moved the rescript quoted herewith makes clear: "We have transmitted the content of your petition to the governor, who will see to it that there is no further cause for complaint." But inasmuch as this rescript has brought us no aid, it has resulted that we are still suffering throughout the countryside illegal exactions of what is not owing, as certain parties assault us and trample upon us unjustly, and we are still suffering extraordinary extortion at the hands of the officials, and our resources[?] have been exhausted and the estates deserted. . . . [The rest is lost.]

RESTRICTION ON FREEDOM OF MOVEMENT OF COLONI

Berlin Papyrus No. 7; A.D. 247

Septimius Ammonius, also called Dionysius, *strategus* of the Arsinoite nome divisions of Themistes and Polemo. Orders are issued[55] to all those definitely reported to me by the *decaproti* [cf. introduction to §

---

54. The last five words of this sentence are supplied to fill a lacuna. Another proposed restoration would read, "least to wrong their neighbors." In any case, the general sense is clear enough.

55. No doubt by the prefect of Egypt, possibly acting on instructions from the emperors.

115] as being cultivators of the section called Little Phrôu that they are unequivocally bound by their tenancy, in order that what is owed the most sacred fisc may be discharged[?] without hindrance . . . in accordance with the requests in the petitions which they submitted to me. . . . Year 5 of the Emperors Caesar Marcus Julius PHILIP Pii Felices Augusti, Hathyr 29. [There follows a list of persons, with the size of the holding of each.]

118. ROME'S THOUSANDTH BIRTHDAY

In A.D. 248, in the midst of civil war, anarchy, and unprecedented economic crisis, the Secular Games and other spectacles were held in celebration of the thousandth anniversary of the founding of Rome. The following passage gives a glimpse of the prodigal expenditure that must have gone into the making of that Roman holiday.

"Historia Augustus," *Lives of the Three Gordians* xxxiii. 1–2

There were at Rome in the time of Gordian thirty-two elephants (of which Gordian himself had sent twelve and [Severus] Alexander ten), ten elk, ten tigers, sixty tame lions, thirty tame leopards, ten *belbi,* or hyenas, 1,000 pairs of gladiators belonging to the imperial fisc, six hippopotamuses, one rhinoceros, ten wild lions, ten giraffes, twenty wild asses, forty wild horses, and various other animals of this nature without number. All of these [the Emperor] Philip presented or slaughtered at the Secular Games. All these animals, wild, tame, and savage, Gordian intended for a Persian triumph; but his public vow[56] proved of no avail, for Philip exhibited them all at the Secular Games and at the gladiatorial and circus spectacles when he celebrated Rome's thousandth anniversary in his own and his son's consulship.

56. That is, to present the spectacle if victorious; cf. vol. 1, p. 155.

The Reforms of Diocletian

119. THE EMERGENCE OF ABSOLUTE MONARCHY (DOMINATE)

In the century from the death of Marcus Aurelius to the accession of Diocletian the regime established by Augustus completed its evolution from Principate to undisguised absolutism, complete with Oriental royal trappings and court ceremonial. It is true that premature and abortive attempts had been made in the first two centuries of the Empire by such rulers as Caligula, Domitian, and Commodus to introduce the concept of the emperor as a god on earth (cf. § 162). But with the Punic–Syrian Severan dynasty the forms of Oriental autocracy came more commonly into use. Obeisance in the presence of the emperor came into vogue, and the appellation *dominus noster* (our lord and master) replaced the concept of *primus inter pares* attached to the earlier emperors. In conformity with these absolutist tendencies the great jurist Ulpian in the early third century formulated the principle that "the emperor is above the laws" (Justinian, *Digest* I. iii. 31). With the reign of Diocletian [A.D. 285–305] all these developments, including the rite of adoration of the emperor, were standardized and made official.

"Historia Augusta," *Lives of the Two Gallieni* xvi. 3–6

Gallienus always spread his tables with golden table cloths. He had jeweled vessels made, and likewise golden ones. He sprinkled gold dust on his hair. He often came into public with the radiate crown.[57] At Rome, where the emperors always used to appear in the toga, he appeared in a purple cloak with jeweled and golden clasps. He wore a man's sleeved tunic of purple and gold. He used a jeweled sword belt. . . . He invited matrons into his council, and to those of them who kissed his hand he gave four gold pieces bearing his name.

Aurelius Victor,[58] *Lives of the Emperors* xxxix. 1–8 (abridged)

By decision of the generals and [military] tribunes, Valerius Diocletian, commander of the palace guards, was chosen emperor because of his wisdom. A mighty man he was, and the following were characteristics

---

57. The radiate crown had been the emblem of only a deified emperor, until the emperors of the third century began to adopt it as part of their insignia.

58. See chapter 4, note 45.

of his: he was the first to wear a cloak embroidered in gold and to covet shoes of silk and purple decorated with a great number of gems. Though this went beyond what befitted a citizen and was characteristic of an arrogant and lavish spirit, it was nevertheless of small consequence in comparison with the rest. Indeed, he was the first after Caligula and Domitian to allow himself to be publicly called "lord," and to be named "god," and to be rendered homage as such. . . . But Diocletian's faults were counterbalanced by good qualities; for even if he took the title of "lord," he did act [toward the Romans] as a father.

120. Diocletian and the Tetrarchy

To divide the administrative responsibilities of the vast Empire, prevent a recurrence of the military anarchy of the preceding half century, and guarantee orderly succession to the throne, Diocletian in A.D. 293 established a four-man rule, the tetrarchy. In 305 Diocletian and Maximian, the two senior members, abdicated, but their provisions for the continuation of the system by a new tetrarchy proved short-lived (cf. introduction to § 125).

Aurelius Victor, *Lives of the Emperors* xxxix. 17–48 (abridged)

Forthwith he proclaimed as coemperor Maximian[59] a faithful friend, a semi-rustic with, however, great military talent and native ability. Afterward he acquired the surname Herculius, from the cult of Hercules, his favorite divinity, while Valerius [Diocletian] took the surname of Jovius; and these surnames were assigned to those military units which excelled the rest of the army. . . . [The rise of usurpers and foreign attacks decided the two emperors] to select as Caesar Julius Constantius and Galerius Maximianus, surnamed Armentarius, and to associate them with themselves in marriage. The former received Herculius' stepdaughter, the latter Diocletian's daughter, the previous marriage of each being dissolved, just as Augustus had once done in the case of Tiberius Nero and his daughter Julia. All these men were, indeed, natives of Illyria; but although little cultured, they were of great service to the state, because they were inured to the hardships of rural life and of war. . . . The harmony which prevailed among them proved above all that their native

59. Diocletian became emperor in A.D. 285 and made Maximian coregent the following year. Constantius and Galerius were named Caesars (emperors designate: cf. chapter 1, note 10) in 293.

ability and their skill in military science, which they had acquired from Aurelian and Probus, almost sufficed to compensate for lack of high character. Finally, they looked up to Valerius [Diocletian] as to a father or as one would to a mighty god. . . .

As the burden of the wars mentioned above became heavier, a sort of division of the Empire was made: all the countries beyond the Gallic Alps were entrusted to Constantius; Herculius had Africa and Italy [and Spain]; Galerius, Illyria as far as the Black Sea; and Diocletian retained all the rest. After this, part of Italy was subjected to the heavy burden of paying tribute. . . . A new law for regular tax payments was introduced. At that time it was still endurable, because not excessive, but it has grown in our age[60] into a scourge. . . .

With no less zeal [than in their military exploits] did the emperors take up the administration of civil affairs, in which connection their laws were eminently just. They suppressed the *frumentarii,* a group that was a veritable scourge and whom now the *agentes in rebus* closely resemble.[61] These men, who appear to have been established to investigate and report possible seditious movements that might exist in the provinces, trumped up false accusations, and under the universal terror they inspired, especially in persons in very remote areas, they practiced shameful rapine everywhere. The emperors showed no less concern and solicitude for the provisioning of the city and the welfare of those who paid tribute. . . . The ancient cults were maintained in all their purity. Rome and other cities, especially Carthage, Milan, and Nicomedia, were extraordinarily embellished with new structures of great splendor. . . .[62]

Diocletian kept his eyes on threatening dangers, and when he saw that the Roman state, in the course of destiny, was going to become a prey to civil wars and was approaching its breakup, so to speak, he celebrated the twentieth anniversary of his reign and abdicated the government of the state, although he was in good health. Herculius, who had held power one year less, he induced to follow his example, though he did so with great reluctance. Although there exists a variety of explanations [for Diocletian's abdication], and the truth has been per-

60. Middle of the fourth century. On Italy's being made tributary, cf. introduction of § 122.

61. *Frumentarii* were imperial secret service agents who replaced the *speculatores* in that activity toward the end of the first century and quickly became notorious for abusing their positions for personal gain (cf. pp. 318, 380–81). By A.D. 319, and perhaps as early as Diocletian's reign, they were replaced with a more comprehensive organization of *agentes in rebus,* who ultimately achieved the same evil reputation.

62. The most famous of these are the Baths of Diocletian at Rome and his palace at Salonae (modern Split in Yugoslavia, the older part of which is contained within the palace walls).

verted, it is my view that it was out of the excellence of his character that, scorning ambition for power, he descended to the life of an ordinary citizen.

121. DIOCLETIAN'S ADMINISTRATIVE REORGANIZATION

Diocletian, the reorganizer of the Empire after the military anarchy, completed and systematized the political, social, and economic changes brought about by the revolution of the third century. The pattern of society he established, brought to completion by Constantine, remained the basis of the regimented life of the people in the Roman Empire for centuries to come. The following evaluation by a Christian writer of Diocletian's reorganization is colored by the severe persecution of the Christians during his reign.

Lactantius, *On the Deaths of the Persecutors* vii

While Diocletian, who was the inventor of wicked deeds and the contriver of evils, was ruining everything, he could not keep his hands even from God. This man, through both avarice and cowardice, overturned the whole world. For he made three men sharers of his rule; the world was divided into four parts, and armies were multiplied, each of the rulers striving to have a far larger number of soldiers than former emperors had had when the state was ruled by single emperors.[63] The number of those receiving [pay from the state] was so much larger than the number of those paying [taxes] that, because of the enormous size of the assessments, the resources of the tenant farmers were exhausted, fields were abandoned, and cultivated areas were transformed into wilderness. And to fill everything with fear, the provinces also were cut into bits;[64] many governors and more minor offices lay like incubi over each region and almost on every municipality, likewise many procurators of revenues, administrators, and deputy prefects.[65] Very few civil cases came before all of these, but only condemnations and frequent confiscations, and there were not merely frequent but perpetual exac-

---

63. Lactantius exaggerated the size of Diocletian's military establishment. It was increased from the long-established army of 300,000 to 400,000.

64. For Diocletian's provincial reorganization see § 124.

65. The *vicarii*, deputies to the Praetorian prefects, were purely civil officials; there was one for each of the twelve new dioceses of the Empire; cf. § 124.

tions of innumerable things, and in the process of exaction intolerable wrongs.

Whatever was imposed with a view to the maintenance of the soldiery might have been endured; but Diocletian, with insatiable avarice, would never permit the treasury to be diminished. He was constantly accumulating extraordinary resources and funds so as to preserve what he had stored away untouched and inviolate. Likewise, when by various iniquities he brought about enormously high prices, he attempted to legislate the prices of commodities.[66] Then much blood was spilled . . . nothing appeared on the market because of fear, and prices soared much higher. In the end, after many people had lost their lives, it became absolutely necessary to repeal the law.

In addition, he had a certain endless passion for building, and made no small exactions from the provinces for maintaining laborers and artisans and for supplying wagons and whatever else was necessary for the construction of public works. Here basilicas, there a circus, here a mint, there a shop for making weapons, here a house for his wife, there one for his daughter. Suddenly a great part of the city [of Nicomedia] was demolished. All went elsewhere with their wives and children, as from a city taken by enemies. And when those structures were completed, to the ruin of the provinces, he said, "They are not properly made; let them be done on another plan." Then they had to be pulled down, and remodeled, to undergo perhaps another demolition. By such constant folly did he endeavor to make Nicomedia the equal of Rome.

I omit mentioning, indeed, how many perished on account of their possessions or wealth; for this was a common thing and became almost lawful as people grew accustomed to these evils. But this was peculiar to him, that wherever he saw a rather well-cultivated field, or an uncommonly elegant house, a false accusation and capital punishment were ready against the owner, so that it seemed as if he could not seize someone else's property without bloodshed.

PROLIFERATION OF BUREAUCRACY

Occasional attempts were made under Diocletian to curtail the growth of bureaucracy. But these attempts were foredoomed to failure since it was the governmental system itself which engendered the bureaucracy and rendered it powerful.

66. For Diocletian's edict on maximum prices, see § 123.

Oxyrhynchus Papyrus No. 58 (= *Select Papyri,* no. 226); A.D. 288; Adapted from *LCL*

Serbaeus Africanus to the *strategi* of the *epistrategia* of Heptanomia and the Arsinoite nome, greeting.[67] It is apparent from the accounts alone that many persons wishing to batten on the estates of the treasury have devised titles for themselves, such as administrators, secretaries, or superintendents, whereby they procure no advantage for the treasury but eat up the revenues. It has therefore become necessary to send you instructions to have one competent superintendent chosen for each estate on the responsibility of the municipal council concerned, [cf. §§ 66, 115], and to put an end to the other offices, although the superintendent chosen shall have the power to choose two or at most three others to assist him in the superintendence. In this way the wasteful expenses will stop, and the estates of the treasury will receive proper attention. You will, of course make sure that only such persons are chosen to assist the superintendents as will be able to pass the test. Farewell. Year 5, also year 4, Thoth 16.

122. THE NEW TAXATION SYSTEM

After the establishment and consolidation of the Tetrarchy Diocletian turned his attention to economic reorganization, in order to stabilize and assure the vast revenues that the imperial government required. Just as he had ended the political anarchy, so he sought to end the profound economic crisis that had ravaged the Empire for a century through measures of regimentation characteristic of his military background. In A.D. 296 he wiped out the by then anarchic accretion of local practices that had characterized the Roman taxation system and, regularizing the special requisitions to which the government had had to resort increasingly in recent years, he decreed a new, unified system of land tax and poll tax for the whole Empire, including Italy, which thus lost, at least in part, its tax-free status. Land and manpower together constituted the foundation of the new tax structure. The unit on which the basic tax in kind *(annona)* was calculated was an area of cultivable land *(iugum)* that could in theory be worked by one man *(caput)* and provide him with the means of subsistence. Many details of this new system are still not clear, but the taxpayer was evidently required to pay according to the number of *iuga* and *capita* he was assessed. Reassessment took place at first every five years, but

67. The writer of this letter was probably the *epistrategus* of the district formed by the Heptanomia (cf. chapter 1, note 18) and the Arsinoite nome.

beginning with A.D. 312 every fifteen years. Areas equivalent to a *iugum* were established by fiat for several different classes of land according to location and productivity; the host of other local variations were simply ignored. Thus, there was substituted for the previous system of quotas and revenues varying from year to year a system of fixed returns. But the fixed return could be guaranteed only if the manpower to produce it were guaranteed. It was thus but a logical corollary of the new system that occupations should be made hereditary and people tied to them with increasing rigidity. The final result was the well-known economic "sclerosis" of the Byzantine state.

PROMULGATION OF THE NEW TAX SYSTEM IN EGYPT

Cairo Isidorus Papyrus No. 1; A.D. 297

Aristius Optatus, *vir perfectissimus,* prefect of Egypt, declares: Our most provident Emperors, the eternal[?] Diocletian and Maximian, Augusti, and Constantius and Maximian, most noble Caesars, having learned that it has come about that the levies of the public taxes are being made haphazardly, so that some persons are let off lightly and others overburdened, have decided to root out this most evil and baneful practice for the benefit of their provincials and to issue a deliverance-bringing rule to which the taxes shall conform. Accordingly, the levy on each aroura[68] according to the classification of the land, and the levy on each head of the peasantry, and from which age to which, may be accurately[?] known to all from the [recently] issued divine [i.e., imperial] edict and the schedule annexed thereto, copies of which I have prefaced for promulgation with this edict of mine. Accordingly, seeing that in this, too, they have received the greatest benefaction, the provincials should make it their business in conformity with the divinely issued regulations to pay their taxes with all speed and by no means wait for the compulsion of the collector; for it is proper to fulfill most zealously and scrupulously all the loyal obligations, and if anyone should be revealed to have done otherwise after such bounty, he will risk punishment. The magistrates and council presidents of every city have been ordered to send out to every village and even locality a copy of the divine edict together with the schedule, and also of this [edict] as well, in the interest of having the munificence of our Emperors and Caesars come speedily to the knowledge of all. And also the collectors of each revenue are reminded to

---

68. *Aroura* is here probably a Greek rendering of *iugum.*

uphold [the regulations] with all their might; for if any should be revealed to have transgressed, he will risk the death penalty.

Year 13 and 12 and 5 of our lords Diocletian and Maximian, Augusti, and Constantius and Maximian, most noble Caesars, Phamenoth 20.[69]

INTRODUCTION OF THE IUGUM UNIT

"Syro-Roman Law Book"[70] cxxi

The *iugum* measure was decreed in the days of the Emperor Diocletian and made law. Five *iugera,* which equal 10 *plethra,* of vineyard were established as 1 *iugum;* 20 *iugera* of grain land, which equal 40 *plethra,* pay the tax in kind of 1 *iugum;* 220 *perticae* of mature olive grove pay the tax in kind of 1 *iugum;* 450 *perticae* in the mountains pay 1 *iugum.* So, too, land which is of poorer quality and is reckoned just like mountainous land: 40 *iugera,* which equal 80 *plethra,* pay 1 *iugum;* if, however, it is reckoned or assessed as third quality, 60 *iugera,* equaling 120 *plethra,* pay 1 *iugum.*

Mountainous land is assessed as follows. At the time of the assessment there were certain men who were given the authority by the government; they summoned other mountain dwellers from other regions and bade them assess how much land, by their estimate, produces a *modius* of wheat or barley in the mountains. In this way they also assessed unsown land, the pasture land for cattle, as to how much tax it should yield to the fisc. And for the pasture land the prescription was that it pay annually to the fisc one *denarius;* but there is also such land which pays two and three *denarii.*

123. DIOCLETIAN'S EDICT ON MAXIMUM PRICES

In A.D. 296, in conjunction with his revision of the taxation system, Diocletian introduced a new coinage to replace the wildly inflated and depreciated currency of the preceding decades (see § 112). But the huge

---

69. The years are those of the reigns of Diocletian, of Maximian, and of the two Caesars, respectively: cf. note 59. The date Phamenoth 20, corresponding to March 16, shows that the new tax system was inaugurated in Egypt early in the year following its promulgation.

70. A schoolbook of Roman civil law written orginally in Greek in the late fifth century but now extant only in Syriac and various other Oriental-language versions made some centuries later. Our translation is based on a modern version, in Latin, in *FIRA*, vol. II, no. 791.

governmental expenditures for war, for the maintenance of the increased army, court, and bureaucracy, and for building operations in large part nonproductive—further aggravated possibly by widespread distrust of the new coinage, understandable after a century of repeated currency devaluations—brought on a new wave of inflation. At last, in an attempt to curb runaway prices and stabilize the economy, especially in the interest of assuring the needs of the army and bureaucracy, Diocletian took the drastic step—unprecedented in Roman history—of decreeing fixed ceilings on prices and wages throughout the Empire. Death or exile were prescribed as punishment for charging or paying above-ceiling prices or for attempting to circumvent the regulation by hoarding. The edict on maximum prices was published early in A.D. 301, but because of business opposition and the difficulty of enforcement it was finally revoked. (For Lactantius' biased account see § 121.) Numerous fragments of the official Latin text and of Greek copies of the edict are extant, all (except for one found in Italy) coming from the eastern provinces. Together they form the longest extant document in the economic history of the ancient world. Most of the preamble and a few selections from the extensive price lists are given below.

INFLATION

This text is eloquent testimony both of the monetary troubles of the Empire and of the prevalence and impunity of official skulduggery shortly before the issuance of the edict on maximum prices. The writer, a government official, is here seen taking advantage of his inside knowledge of a forthcoming currency devaluation to have his agent convert all his available cash into goods.

Rylands Papyrus No. 607; A.D. *c.* 300

Dionysius to Apio, greeting. The divine fortune of our masters has given orders that the Italian coinage be reduced to half a *nummus* [a synonym for sesterce]. Make haste therefore to spend all the Italian money you have and purchase for me all kinds of goods at whatever price you find them. . . . But I tell you in advance that if you try any shenanigans[71] I won't let you get away with it. I pray you may continue long in health, my brother.[72]

---

71. Such as pretending he paid more for things than he did and pocketing the difference.
72. This is still a form of polite salutation in the Near East.

THE EDICT ON MAXIMUM PRICES

CIL, vol. III, pp. 801–841, 1055–1058, 1909–1953, 2208–2211, 2328 (=*ESAR*, 5:307–421) and *Transactions of the American Philological Association* (1940) 71:157–74; Adapted in part from the translation of E. Graser[73]

[Diocletian, Maximian, Constantius, and Galerius] declare:

As we recall the wars which we have successfully fought, we must be grateful to the fortune of our state, second only to the immortal gods, for a tranquil world that reclines in the embrace of the most profound calm, and for the blessings of a peace that was won with great effort. That this fortune of our state be stabilized and suitably adorned is demanded by the law-abiding public and by the dignity and majesty of Rome. Therefore we, who by the gracious favor of the gods previously stemmed the tide of the ravages of barbarian nations by destroying them, must surround the peace which we established for eternity with the necessary defenses of justice.

If the excesses perpetrated by persons of unlimited and frenzied avarice could be checked by some self-restraint—this avarice which rushes for gain and profit with no thought for mankind . . . ; or if the general welfare could endure without harm this riotous license by which, in its unfortunate state, it is being very seriously injured every day, the situation could perhaps be faced with dissembling and silence, with the hope that human forbearance might alleviate the cruel and pitiable situation. But the only desire of these uncontrolled madmen is to have no thought for the common need. Among the unscrupulous, the immoderate, and the avaricious it is considered almost a creed . . . to desist from plundering the wealth of all only when necessity compels them. Through their extreme need, moreover, some persons have become acutely aware of their most unfortunate situation, and can no longer close their eyes to it. Therefore we, who are the protectors of the human race, are agreed, as we view the situation, that decisive legislation is necessary, so that the long-hoped-for solutions which mankind itself could not provide may, by the remedies provided by our foresight, be vouchsafed for the general betterment of all. . . .

We hasten, therefore, to apply the remedies long demanded by the situation, satisfied that no one can complain that our intervention with regulations is untimely or unnecessary, trivial or unimportant. These

73. In *ESAR* and *Transactions of the American Philological Association,* as cited above.

measures are directed against the unscrupulous, who have perceived in our silence of so many years a lesson in restraint but have been unwilling to imitate it. For who is so insensitive and so devoid of human feeling that he can be unaware or has not perceived that uncontrolled prices are widespread in the sales taking place in the markets and in the daily life of the cities? Nor is the uncurbed passion for profiteering lessened either by abundant supplies or by fruitful years. . . .

It is our pleasure, therefore, that the prices listed in the subjoined schedule be held in observance in the whole of our Empire. . . .

It is our pleasure that anyone who resists the measures of this statute shall be subject to a capital penalty for daring to do so. And let no one consider the statute harsh, since there is at hand a ready protection from danger in the observance of moderation. . . . We therefore exhort the loyalty of all, so that a regulation instituted for the public good may be observed with willing obedience and due scruple, especially as it is seen that by a statute of this kind provision has been made, not for single municipalities and peoples and provinces but for the whole world. . . .

The prices for the sale of individual items which no one may exceed are listed below.

			Denarii
I.	Wheat	1 army *modius*[a]	100
	Barley	1 army *modius*	60
	Rye	1 army *modius*	60
	Millet, ground	1 army *modius*	100
	Millet, whole	1 army *modius*	50
	Panic grass	1 army *modius*	50
	Spelt, hulled	1 army *modius*	100
	Beans, crushed	1 army *modius*	100
	Beans, not ground	1 army *modius*	60
	Lentils	1 army *modius*	100
	Pulse	1 army *modius*	80
	Peas, split	1 army *modius*	100
	Peas, not split	1 army *modius*	60
	Rice, cleaned	1 army *modius*	200
	Barley grits, cleaned	1 *modius*	100
	Spelt grits, cleaned	1 *modius*	200
	Sesame	1 army *modius*	200

Denarii

II. Likewise, for wines:
    Picene   1 Italian *sextarius*   30
    Tiburtine   1 Italian *sextarius*   30
    Sabine   1 Italian *sextarius*   30

    Falernian   1 Italian *sextarius*   30
    Likewise, aged wine, first
       quality   1 Italian *sextarius*   24
    Aged wine, second quality   1 Italian *sextarius*   16
    Ordinary   1 Italian *sextarius*   8
    Beer, Gallic or Pannonian   1 Italian *sextarius*   4
    Beer, Egyptian   1 Italian *sextarius*   2

III. Likewise, for oil:
    From unripe olives   1 Italian *sextarius*   40
    Second quality   1 Italian *sextarius*   24

    Salt   1 army *modius*   100
    Spiced salt   1 Italian *sextarius*   8
    Honey, best quality   1 Italian *sextarius*   40
    Honey, second quality   1 Italian *sextarius*   24

IV. Likewise, for meat:
    Pork   1 Italian pound   12
    Beef   1 Italian pound   8

    Leg of pork, Menapic or
       Cerritane, best   1 Italian pound   20

    Pork mincemeat   1 ounce   2
    Beef mincemeat   1 Italian pound   10
    Pheasant, fattened   250
    Pheasant, wild   125

    Chickens   1 brace   60

    Venison   1 Italian pound   12

    Butter   1 Italian pound   16

V. Likewise, for fish:
    Sea fish with rough scales   1 Italian pound   24

		Denarii
Fish, second quality	1 Italian pound	16
River fish, best quality	1 Italian pound	12
River fish, second quality	1 Italian pound	8
Salt fish	1 Italian pound	6
Oysters	100	100

VII. For wages:

Farm laborer, with maintenance	daily	25
Carpenter, as above	daily	50
Wall painter, as above	daily	75
Picture painter, as above	daily	150
Baker, as above	daily	50
Shipwright working on a seagoing ship, as above	daily	60
Shipwright working on a river boat, as above	daily	50
Muleteer, with maintenance	daily	25
Veterinary, for clipping and preparing hoofs	per animal	6
Veterinary, for bleeding and cleaning the head	per animal	20
Barber	per man	2
Sewer cleaner, working a full day, with maintenance	daily	25
Scribe, for the best writing	100 lines	25
Scribe, for second-quality writing	100 lines	20
Notary, for writing a petition or legal document	100 lines	10
Elementary teacher,[b] per boy	monthly	50
Teacher of arithmetic, per boy	monthly	75
Teacher of shorthand, per boy	monthly	75

		Denarii
Teacher of Greek or Latin language and literature, and teacher of geometry, per pupil	monthly	200
Teacher of rhetoric or public speaking, per pupil	monthly	250
Advocate or jurist, fee for a complaint		250
Advocate or jurist, fee for pleading		1,000
Teacher of architecture, per boy	monthly	100
Check room attendant, per bather		2

ª Castrensis modius, literally "the modius of the army camps."
ᵇ On the teachers here listed in ascending order in the educational sequence, see § 55.

A DECLARATION OF PRICE CONFORMITY

When the edict on maximum prices was promulgated in Egypt, the artisan guilds were apparently ordered to file sworn schedules of the prices at which they sold their products, as proof that they did not exceed the ceilings fixed by the edict. It is possible that this procedure was followed in all provinces by imperial order.

Antinoöpolis Papyrus No. 38; April 13, A.D. 301

To the superintendent[?] of . . . of Antinoöpolis the most illustrious . . . from the silversmiths' guild of the said city. . . . We swear by the fortune of our lords Diocletian and Maximian, Augusti, and Constantius [and Maximian, the most noble] Caesars, that we report for your information, in accordance with the governor's order, the price of a pound of worked silver to be 62 *denarii* and of a pound of cast silver, 31 *denarii;* and that we have made no false statement, or else may we be liable under the imperial oath. In response to the formal question we gave our assent [cf. chapter 2, note 90].

Year 16 and year 15 of our lords Diocletian and Maximian, Augusti, and year 8 of our lords Constantius and Maximian, the most noble Caesars, Pharmuthi 17. I, Aurelius Sarapammo, councilman of Antinoöpolis, swore the oath as aforesaid. I, Aurelius Ammonis son of Besario, swore the oath as aforesaid. I, Aurelius Isidorus, swore the oath as aforesaid.

124. THE PROVINCIAL REORGANIZATION

In the latter years of his reign (A.D. 297–305), Diocletian effected a complete provincial reorganization, the first such since that of Augustus. The separation into imperial and senatorial provinces was ended, as was also the privileged treatment of Italy. The whole Empire was divided into twelve dioceses, six in the East and six in the West, and it is striking to observe how those of the West, at least, foreshadow national entities of modern Europe. To reduce the power concentrated in the hands of any governor, the dioceses were subdivided into a total of about a hundred provinces, and the civil and military administrations were divided and placed under separate chief officers. One result was, of course, a multiplication of the already swollen bureaucracy. Although some provinces were further subdivided by later emperors, and although some other organizational changes were made (e.g., the city of Rome was made a separate diocese), Diocletian's scheme remained the fundamental administrative structure of the Empire for centuries to come. The roster of dioceses and provinces, with a few later interpolations but substantially as set up by Diocletian, is preserved in a seventh-century manuscript of an unknown fourth-century source. The "Verona List," as the manuscript is called, after the place where it was discovered, lists the provinces in a generally geographical sequence for the Eastern dioceses, and according to the rank of the governors for the Western.

Theodor Mommsen, *Gesammelte Schriften* (Berlin, 1908) 5:563–564 (= O. Seeck, *Notitia Dignitatum* [Berlin, 1876], pp. 247–251)

The Names of All the Provinces

The Diocese of the Orient has provinces to the number of eighteen: Libya Superior, Lybia Inferior, Thebais, Aegyptus Jovia, Aegyptus Herculia,[74] Arabia, Arabia Augusta Libanensis, Palaestina, Phoenice, Syria Coele, Augusta Euphratensis, Cilicia, Isauria, Cyprus, Mesopotamia, Osroena.[75]

The Diocese of Pontus has provinces to the number of seven: Bithynia, Cappadocia, Galatia, Paphlagonia . . . , Diospontus, Pontus Polemiacus, Armenia Minor. . . .

The Diocese of Asia has provinces to the number of mine: Pamphylia,

74. On the epithets Jovia and Herculia cf. p. 414.
75. The discrepancy between the stated total and the number of provinces actually listed in this and other dioceses presumably reflects to some extent the changes introduced between the provincial reorganization of Diocletian and the time when this roster was compiled, some decades later.

Phrygia Prima, Phrygia Secunda, Asia, Lydia, Caria, The Islands, Pisidia, Hellespontus.

The Diocese of Thrace has provinces to the number of six: Europa, Rhodope, Thracia, Haemimontus, Scythia, Moesia Inferior.

The Diocese of the Moesias has provinces to the number of eleven: Dacia, Moesia Superior Margensis, Dardania, Macedonia, Thessalia, Achaea, Praevalentia, Epirus Nova, Epirus Vetus, Creta.

The Diocese of the Pannonias has provinces to the number of seven: Pannonia Inferior, Savensis, Dalmatia, Valeria, Pannonia Superior, Noricus Ripariensis, Noricus Mediterranea.

The Diocese of the Britains has provinces to the number of six: Britannia Prima, Britannia Secunda, Britannia Maxima Caesariensis, Britannia Flavia Caesariensis.

The Diocese of the Gauls has provinces to the number of eight: Belgica Prima, Belgica Secunda, Germania Prima, Germania Secunda, Sequania, Lugdunensis Prima, Lugdunensis Secunda, Alpes Graiae et Poeninae.

The Diocese of Vienne has provinces to the number of seven: Viennensis, Narbonensis Prima, Narbonensis Secunda, Nine Peoples, Aquitanica Prima, Aquitanica Secunda, Alpes Maritimae.

The Diocese of Italy has provinces to the number of sixteen: Venetia Histria, Flaminia, Picenum, Tuscia Umbrena, Apulia, Calabria, Lucania, Corsica, Alpes Cottiae, Raetia. . . .[76]

The Diocese of the Spains has provinces to the number of seven: Baetica, Lusitania, Carthaginiensis, Gallaecia, Tarraconensis, Mauretania Tingitania.

The Diocese of Africa has provinces to the number of seven: Proconsularis Zeugitana, Byzacena, Numidia Cirtensis, Numidia Militiana, Mauretania Caesariensis, Mauretania Zabia Insidiana.[77]

76. There is a lacuna here. The other provinces of Italy at this time were perhaps Aemilia, Ligura, Samnium, Campania, Sicilia, Sardinia, Valeria.

77. The text is corrupt here. At the time of Diocletian's reorganization this province may have been called Mauretania Tripolitania; by A.D. 315 it was named Mauretania Sitifensis.

The Age of Constantine

125. CONSTANTINE'S ADMINISTRATIVE AND MILITARY REORGANIZATION

The system of the tetrarchy established by Diocletian did not long survive his abdication in A.D. 305. Out of the rivalries among his successors there emerged in 313 two joint emperors, Licinius and Constantine, and in 324 the latter, after defeating his colleague, became sole ruler. Constantine brought to completion the imperial reorganization initiated by Diocletian. The essence of his administrative reforms was the fractioning of the power of his chief functionaries and the almost universal separation of civil and military functions. These remained the fundamental principles of the imperial administation for the next three centuries, during which the size and power of the Byzantine bureaucracy increased steadily. Constantine also transformed the Roman military system. Reducing the importance and strength of the frontier garrisons, which became local border militias *(limitanei, riparienses)* commanded by *duces* (dukes) and *comites* (counts), he based the imperial defenses primarily on mobile field armies *(comitatenses)*, under the direct command of himself and his deputies. In a further break with tradition, Constantine made the cavalry, instead of the infantry, his basic military arm, thus introducing the type of military organization which prevailed throughout the Middle Ages.

Zosimus, *New History* II. xxxii–xxxv (abridged)

Constantine drastically reorganized the long-established offices. There had been two Praetorian prefects, who administered the office jointly and controlled by their supervision and power not only the Praetorian cohorts but also those which were entrusted with the guarding of the city and those which were stationed in the outskirts.[78] The office of Praetorian prefect had been considered second to that of the emperor; he made the distributions of grain and redressed all offenses against military discipline by appropriate punishments. Constantine, altering this good institution, divided the single office into four. To one prefect he assigned all Egypt, together with the Pentapolis in Libya, and the East as far as Mesopotamia, and, in addition, Cilicia, Cappadocia, Armenia, the entire coast from Pamphylia to Trapezus, and the forts along the Phasis river; to the same person were entrusted Thrace, and Moesia as far as the

---

78. Septimius Severus, who abolished the privileged position of Italy in this respect, had stationed a legionary garrison at Albanum near Rome.

Haemus and Rhodope mountains, and the territory of the town of Doberus, and likewise Cyprus and the Cyclades Islands except Lemnos, Imbros, and Samothrace. To another he assigned Macedonia, Thessaly, Crete, Greece together with the nearby islands, both Epiruses, and in addition the Illyrians, the Dacians, the Triballians, the Pannonians as far as Valeria, and Upper Moesia besides. To the third prefect he entrusted all Italy and Sicily with the neighboring islands, and also Sardinia and Corsica, and Africa from the Syrtes to Cyrene; to the fourth, the Transalpine Gauls and Iberia, and in addition the island of Britain. Having thus divided the office of these prefects, he strove to reduce their power in other ways. For though there were not only centurions and tribunes in command of the soldiers everywhere but also those called *duces,* who in each district held the rank of commanders, he established masters of the soldiers, some for the cavalry, some for the infantry, and by transferring to these the power of marshaling the soldiers and punishing offenders, he diminished in this respect the authority of the prefects. . . .

Constantine likewise took another measure, which gave the barbarians unhindered access into the lands subject to the Romans. For the Roman Empire was, by the foresight of Diocletian, everywhere protected on its frontiers . . . by towns and fortresses and towers, in which the entire army was stationed; it was thus impossible for the barbarians to cross over, there being everywhere a sufficient opposing force to repel their inroads. But Constantine destroyed that security by removing the greater part of the soldiers from the frontiers and stationing them in cities that did not require protection; thus he stripped those of protection who were harassed by the barbarians and brought ruin to peaceful cities at the hands of the soldiers, with the result that most have become deserted. He likewise softened the soldiers by exposing them to shows and luxuries. To speak plainly, he was the first to sow the seeds of the ruinous state of affairs that has lasted up to the present time.

126. LEGISLATION ON TAXATION

Theodosian Code XI. vii. 3; A.D. 320[79]

In connection with the payment of taxes due, no person shall fear that he will suffer, at the hands of perverse and enraged judges, imprisonment, lashes of leaded whips, weights, or any other tortures devised by

---

79. Selections from the *Theodosian Code* in chapters 6–10 are mostly based on or adapted from the translation of C. Pharr (Princeton, 1952). These laws are all in the form of imperial rescripts addressed to various high officials.

the arrogance of judges.[80] Prisons are for criminals. . . . In accordance with this law, taxpayers shall proceed in security; or indeed, if a man is so alien to human feeling that he contumaciously abuses this indulgence, he shall be detained in the free and open military custody established for ordinary use. If he persists in his stubborn wickedness, his fellow citizens shall be given access to his property and all his substance, and with the ownership of his substance they shall undertake the performance of his obligations [to the state] [cf. § 115, fourth and fifth selections]. Since we grant such an opportunity, we believe that all men will be the more inclined to pay that which is demanded for the use of our army in behalf of the common safety.

Theodosian Code XI. xvi. 3; A.D. 324/325

Whenever it is necessary for a tax assessment to be made, the assessment of each municipality shall be made in accordance with the plans and direction of the governor, so that the mass of the lower classes may not be subjected to the wantonness and subordinated to the interests of the more powerful and thus suffer the infliction of grave and iniquitous outrages.

Theodosian Code XI. iii. 2; A.D. 327

Slaves assessed in the census rolls shall be sold within the boundaries of the province, and any persons who obtain ownership by purchase shall know that they must look into this. It is reasonable that the same rule should be observed also in the case of landholding . . . [where] the burdens and public payments shall pertain to the duty of those to whose ownership the said holdings have passed.

127. ECONOMIC DISTRESS: REMISSION OF TAXES[81]

Latin Panegyrics[82] v. v–xiv (abridged)

I have told, O Emperor [Constantine], how much the Aeduans deserved the aid you brought them; it follows that I should tell how serious was their distress. . . . Our community lay prostrate, not so much because

---

80. Maltreatment of taxpayers by officials and collectors was a common and long-standing abuse of Roman rule; cf. vol. 1, §§ 140, 144, 146; vol. 2, §§ 86, 111, 117.

81. Cf. §§ 84, 113.

82. These are a collection of eleven anonymous orations from the late third and fourth centuries,

of the destruction of our walls as from exhaustion of resources, ever since the severity of the new tax assessment had drained our very life. We could not, however, rightly complain, since we had the lands which had been assigned to us, and we were comprised in the common formula of the Gallic assessment, we who can be compared to none in our good fortune. Wherefore, O Emperor, all the more do we give thanks to your clemency for granting remedies of your own accord and making us appear to have obtained justly what we could not rightfully request. . . .

And yet anyone would deservedly forgive these tillers of the soil, who are grieved by labor that brings no return. Indeed a field which never meets expenses is of necessity deserted; likewise the poor country folk, staggering beneath debts, were not permitted to bring in water or cut down forests, so that whatever usable soil there was has been ruined by swamps and choked with briers. . . . Why should I speak of other districts of that community, over which you admitted that you yourself wept? For whereas throughout the fields of other cities you saw almost all parts under cultivation, cleared and flowering, and accessible roads, and rivers under navigation washing the very gates of the towns, here directly from the bend which leads the highway back toward Belgica, you saw everything waste, uncultivated, neglected, silent, shadowy— even military roads so broken . . . that scarcely half-filled, sometimes empty wagons cross them. As a result it often happens that our taxes are late, since our little produce is more difficult for us to transport than a great abundance for others.

You gave us our whole life. . . . To relieve the tax assessment you restricted the total; to remit our arrears you asked how much we owed. . . . You remitted 7,000 *capita* [cf. § 122], more than a fifth of our assessment, and yet you inquired often whether this would be enough for us. . . . By your remission of 7,000 *capita* you gave strength to 25,000 [persons]. . . . You remitted our arrears for five years. . . . Therefore the immortal gods created you emperor for us especially; for each of us this felicity was born when you began to rule. . . . How many, Emperor Augustus, whom poverty had compelled to lie in hiding on the estates, or even to go into exile, are coming forth to the light, returning to their native land, as a result of this remission of arrears!

---

preserved together with Pliny's *Panegyric of Trajan* (§ 7), on which they are patterned. When their fulsomeness is discounted, these works become valuable sources for the history of the Dominate.

128. COMPULSORY PUBLIC SERVICES

Under the fiscal system of the Dominate, compulsory public services became an all-pervading institution of rigidly controlled, hereditary classes. Those who suffered the heaviest economic burdens were the town decurions, who were liable with their own property for imperial taxes due from the local population. They constantly sought to evade their burdensome responsibilities by flight into the army, bureaucracy, or clergy.

Theodosian Code XI. xiv. 4; A.D. 328

The assessment of extraordinary public services shall not be entrusted to chief decurions, and therefore governors of the provinces shall be admonished to perform this assessment themselves and with their own hand write out and in ink annex the names. The following general rule shall be observed, namely, that the services to be given shall be rendered first by the more powerful and then by those of middle and lowest station. A farmer urgently occupied in planting or in gathering his harvest shall never be dragged off to extraordinary burdens, since it is a matter of prudence to satisfy such necessities at the opportune season. The neglect of these regulations affects the honorable status of your vicars,[83] and shall entail capital punishment for the office staffs of governors. Moreover, governors must write with their own hand what is needed and in what obligation for each *caput* [cf. introduction to § 122] —how much public post service or how much personal service, or what and in what measure it must be furnished. Thus they shall write that they have certified it, and the aforesaid order of exaction among the richer, the middling, and the lowest shall be observed.

Theodosian Code XV. ii, 1; A.D. 330

It is our will that the landholders over whose lands the courses of aqueducts pass shall be exempt from extraordinary burdens, so that by their work the aqueducts may be cleansed when they are choked with dirt. The said landholders shall not be subject to any other burden of a superindiction [i.e., special tax levies], lest they be occupied in other matters and not be present to clean the aqueducts. If they neglect this

83. This constitution is addressed to a praetorian prefect; on vicars see note 65.

duty, they shall be punished by the forfeiture of their landholdings; for the fisc will take possession of the landed estate of any man whose negligence contributes to the damage of the aqueducts. Furthermore, persons through whose landed estates the aqueducts pass should know that they may have trees to the right and left at a distance of fifteen feet from the aqueducts, and your[84] office shall see to it that these trees are cut out if they grow too luxuriantly at any time, so that their roots may not injure the structure of the aqueduct.

BURDENS OF DECURIONS

Theodosian Code XII. i. 1; A.D. 313–326

No judge shall attempt to grant exemption from compulsory municipal services to any decurion, nor shall he free anyone from the municipal council at his own discretion. For if anyone is impoverished by a misfortune of such kind that he needs to be relieved, his name should be referred to our wisdom, so that an exemption from compulsory municipal services may be extended to him for a limited space of time.

Theodosian Code XII. i. 10; A.D. 325

Since we have granted to different persons the privilege of being assigned to the legions or cohorts or of being restored to the military service, if any person should produce a grant of this kind, inquiry shall be made as to whether he is of a family of decurions or whether he has been previously nominated to the municipal council, so that, if any such thing is proved, he may be returned to his own municipal council and municipality. It will be appropriate to observe this general rule with reference to all who have already been approved and are serving in military offices, or who have already been restored and are protected by the oath of military service, or who shall be approved hereafter by official decisions.

Theodosian Code XII. i. 11; A.D. 325

Since some men desert the municipal councils and flee for refuge to the protection of the military service, we command that all persons who are found to be not yet under the authority of the chief centurion shall be discharged from the military service and shall be returned to the same

84. This rescript was addressed to the administrator of the water supply.

municipal council. Only those persons shall remain in the military service who, in accordance with their position and rank, are already in the commissary service.

Theodosian Code XII. i. 12; A.D. 325

If anyone derives his origin from a greater or lesser municipality, and if in an effort to avoid [the duties of] the said origin he betakes himself to another municipality for the purpose of establishing residence there and attempts to submit a plea [to the emperor] about this or to depend on any fraud whatsoever in order to escape the origin of his own municipality, he shall sustain the burdens of the decurionate of both municipalities, in the one because of his personal desire, in the other because of his origin.

Theodosian Code XII. i. 13; A.D. 326

Since we have learned that the municipal councils are being left deserted by persons who, though subject to them through origin, are requesting military service for themselves through supplications [to the emperor] and are running away to the legions and the various government offices, we order all municipal councils to be advised that if they catch any persons in government service less than twenty years who have either fled from [the duties of] their origin or, rejecting nomination [to municipal office], have enrolled themselves in the military service, they shall drag such persons back to the municipal councils. . . .

Theodosian Code XIII. v. 2; A.D. 314/315

An enactment was issued which directs that henceforth no decurion or descendant of a decurion or even any person provided with adequate resources and suitable for undertaking compulsory public services shall take refuge in the name and service of the clergy [of the Christian Church], but that in the future only such persons shall be chosen in place of deceased clerics as have slender fortunes and are not held bound to such compulsory municipal services. But we have learned that those persons also are being disturbed who joined in the fellowship of the clergy before the promulgation of the law. We therefore command that such persons be freed from all annoyance, but that those who after the issuance of the law took refuge in the number of the clergy in evasion of public duties shall be completely separated from that body, shall be restored to their municipal councils and [social] orders, and shall perform their municipal duties.

129. Occupations Become Hereditary

The crisis of the third century had led to steadily tighter imperial control over the numerous trade associations or "guilds" *(collegia, corpora, consortia)* of the Empire, especially those engaged in activities essential to the provisioning of urban centers and of the military or to the protection of life and property (cf. § 116). With the increase in taxes collected in kind under the Dominate, regimentation of persons concerned with the shipment, storage, and processing of such revenues was deemed essential by the state. Like the decurions, persons bound to such services sought to escape their obligations by entry into the army or civil service, or by becoming tenant farmers. By the time of Constantine many occupations (including military service: cf. note 27 above) had been transformed into compulsory hereditary obligations to the state.

Theodosian Code VII. xxii. i; A.D. 313 or 319

Of the veterans' sons who are fit for military service, some indolently object to the performance of their compulsory military duties and others are so cowardly that they desire to evade the necessity of military service by mutilation of their bodies. If they should be judged useless for military service because of amputated fingers, we order them to be assigned to the compulsory services and duties of decurions with no ambiguity.

Theodosian Code XIII. v. i; A.D. 314

If any shipmaster by birth becomes captain of a lighter, he shall nonetheless continue right along to remain in the same group in which his parents appear to have been.

Theodosian Code XIII. v 2; A.D. 314/315

Shipmasters nominated to the guild of city breadmakers but not subject to these breadmakers by any succession of inheritance must be released from this compulsory public service. But if they should chance to be bound to the breadmakers by hereditary right, they shall have the opportunity, if they perchance prefer, to relinquish the adventitious inheritance of breadmakers to the said guild or yield it to any next of kin of the deceased, in order to free themselves from the guild of breadmakers. But if they embrace the inheritance, it is necessary for them to undertake association in the compulsory public service of breadmaking by reason of the inheritance, and to sustain from their own resources the burdens of shipmasters. Evidently the prefect of the city, *vir clarissimus,* will make decisions concerning such matter.

130. THE COLONATE: TENANT FARMERS BOUND TO THE SOIL

The crisis in Roman agriculture during the third and early fourth centuries was partly due to the decline in the rural population and to flight from the land because of heavy fiscal burdens. For some time, barbarians had been settled inside the Empire as state tenants bound to their tenancies (cf. § 110), and the *coloni* of imperial and private estates had tended all through the Principate to become hereditary tenants (see § 117). Now, in keeping with the tendency toward making all occupations hereditary, a long series of laws formally transformed the *coloni* into hereditary serfs permanently bound to the soil of the estates they tilled. The earliest datable enactment of this series is the following rescript of Constantine.

Theodosian Code v. xvii. 1; A.D. 332

Any person whatsoever in whose possession a *colonus* belonging to another is found not only shall restore the said *colonus* to his place of origin but shall also assume the capitation tax on him for the time [that he had him]. And as for *coloni* themselves, it will be proper for such as contemplate flight to be bound with chains to a servile status, so that by virtue of such condemnation to servitude they may be compelled to fulfill the duties that befit free men.

131. CHILD ASSISTANCE

Cf. the introduction to § 87.

Theodosian Code XI. xxvii. 1; A.D. 315 or 329

A law shall be written on bronze or waxed tablets or on linen cloth, and posted throughout all the municipalities of Italy, to restrain the hands of parents from infanticide and turn their hopes to the better. Your office shall administer this regulation, so that, if any parent should report that he has offspring which on account of poverty he is unable to rear, there shall be no delay in issuing food and clothing, since the rearing of a new born infant can not tolerate delay. For this matter we order that both our fisc and our privy purse shall furnish their services without distinction.

Theodosian Code XI. xxvii. 2; A.D. 322

We have learned that provincials suffering from scarcity of food and lack of sustenance are selling or pledging their children. Therefore, if any such person is found who is sustained by no substance of family possessions and is supporting his children with hardship and difficulty, he shall be assisted through our fisc before he becomes a prey to calamity. The proconsuls, governors, and procurators of accounts throughout all Africa shall have the power and shall distribute the necessary support to all persons whom they observe to be placed in dire need, and they shall immediately assign adequate substance from the [state] storehouses. For it is repugnant to our customs to allow any person to be destroyed by hunger or rush forth to the commission of a shameful deed.

132. Efforts to Suppress Official Corruption

The ever-present corruption practiced by the huge bureaucracy of the Empire during earlier centuries reached unprecedented proportions in the enlarged officialdom of the autocratic state. The difficulty that the imperial government experienced in trying to stem the extortions of tax collectors —a chronic abuse—is strikingly illustrated by the fact that the first of the following selections was the third edict that the Emperors Septimius Severus and Caracalla had to issue on the subject within the space of a few months. A century later Constantine promulgated a series of orders against official corruption; and his fulminations were followed by a long series of similar enactments by the emperors of succeeding centuries in a continuing but largely futile attempt to control the rapacity of their functionaries (cf. also § 126).

Michigan Papyrus No. 529 verso; January–February A.D. 200

The Emperors Caesar Lucius SEPTIMIUS SEVERUS Pius Pertinax Augustus Arabicus Adiabenicus Parthicus Maximus and the Emperor Caesar Marcus Aurelius Antoninus [CARACALLA] Pius Augustus declare: Since many still petition to be freed from being forced, contrary to prior edicts, to pay levies of others as if on mutual security, we deem it necessary to reaffirm our previously proclaimed edict on this matter, viz. that no one is to be forced to pay levies of another—neither a father for a son, nor a son for a father, nor anyone for anyone else—nor substituted(?) for another under the claim of any such collection. If anyone is revealed contemptuously collecting levies of another from anyone, he will suffer no ordinary danger.

Posted in Alexandria [date].

Theodosian Code I. xii. 2; A.D. 319

It is to the interest of public discipline, and it likewise befits the proconsular dignity, that you should bring under your power the administration and cognizance of public-revenue collection and all other matters. You shall not be content with the prepared reports and fraudulent statements of the functionaries, but you shall study the administration of the very judges and the statement of the prefect of the grain supply and of the procurators of accounts [to determine] whether the aforesaid prepared reports are trustworthy. For thus it will be possible to afford relief to the provincials against unjust exactions.

Theodosian Code I. xvi. 7; A.D. 331

The rapacious hands of the functionaries shall immediately stop, they shall stop, I say; for, if after due warning they do not stop, they shall be cut off with the sword. The curtain of the judge['s chamber] shall not be venal;[85] entrance shall not be purchased; his private chamber shall not be notorious for its bids;[86] the very sight of the governor shall not be at

---

85. A curtain shut off the private council chamber of the judge from the public. Court attendants demanded bribes to conduct litigants before the judge in chambers.

86. By litigants who desired priority in having cases heard.

a price. The ears of the judge shall be open equally to the poorest as well as to the rich. The introduction of persons inside shall be free from depredation by the one who is called the office head; the assistants of the said office heads shall employ no extortion on litigants; the intolerable onslaught of the centurions and other officials who demand small and large sums shall be crushed; and the unsated greed of those who deliver records to litigants shall be restrained. The ever-watchful diligence of the governor shall see that nothing is taken from a litigant by the aforesaid classes of men. And if they imagine they have to demand something in connection with civil cases, armed punishment will be at hand to cut off the heads and necks of the scoundrels, for all persons who have suffered extortion will be given an opportunity to provide information for an investigation by the governors. And if they dissemble, we open to all persons the right of complaint thereon before the *comites*[87] of the provinces—or before the Praetorian prefects, if they are closer at hand—so that we may be informed by their referrals and may produce punishments for such villainy.

Theodosian Code I. xxxii. I; A.D. 333

Through the fault of the procurators of the privy purse, of dyeworks, and of weaving establishments, our private substance is being diminished, the products manufactured in the weaving establishments are being ruined, and in the dyeworks the fraudulent admixture of impure dye produces blemishes. Such procurators shall abstain from the patronage whereby they obtain the aforementioned administrative positions, or, if they contravene this order, they shall be removed from the number of Roman citizens and beheaded.

Theodosian Code X. iv. I; A.D. 313 or 326

If any person is harassed by an agent or procurator of our privy purse, he shall not hesitate to lodge a complaint concerning his chicanery and depredations. When such charge is proved, we sanction that such person as dares to contrive anything against a provincial shall be publicly burned, since graver punishment should be fixed against those who are under our jurisdiction and ought to observe our mandates.

---

87. Officers of the court ("counts"), created by Constantine as part of his administrative fragmentation (cf. § 124) and entrusted by him with a variety of functions in the central government and in the provinces.

133. LEGISLATION ON SLAVES

The institution of slavery survived for centuries after the triumph of Christianity. Under Christian influence, however, the growing tendency of the preceding centuries toward more humane treatment of slaves (cf. § 50) received fresh impetus. The following is a directive of Constantine on the subject.

Theodosian Code II. xxv. 1; A.D. 325 or 334

When . . . estates in Sardinia were recently distributed among the various present proprietors, the division of holdings ought to have been made in such a way that a whole family of slaves would remain with one individual landholder. For who could tolerate that children should be separated from parents, sisters from brothers, and wives from husbands? Therefore, any persons who have separated slaves and dragged them off to serve under different ownerships shall be forced to restore such to single ownership; and anyone who loses slaves through the reuniting of families shall be given slaves in exchange by the person who receives the aforesaid. And take pains that throughout the province no complaint shall hereafter persist over the separation of the loved ones of slaves.

134. THE GRANDEUR OF ROME

With the construction of the new imperial capital of the East, Constantinople, the New Rome, ceremonially inaugurated in A.D. 330 on the site of the ancient Greek city of Byzantium, old Rome receded in importance, except as the center of the Catholic Church. The following anonymous document, known by the titles *Curiosum Urbis Romae* or *Notitia,* was composed about the middle of the fourth century but is derived from earlier sources, probably official documents. The fourteen districts of the city—the administrative division instituted by Augustus—are treated in numerical order. The four districts given here indicate the pattern of the whole catalogue. Suspension points, except in the summary at the end, indicate our omission of unidentified or uncertain items.

District III, Isis and Serapis, contains:

Mint; amphitheater, which has 87,000 *loca*,[88] great training school for gladiators; house of Bruttius Praesens; central theatrical storehouse;

88. The Colosseum, whose seating capacity could not have exceeded 45,000. The term *loca* is now generally interpreted to mean running feet of sitting space; the number of spectators accommodated

Shepherds' Fountain; . . . Baths of Titus and Trajan; Portico of Livia; camp of the sailors of the Misenum fleet; wards—12; crossroad shrines —12; block captains—48; commissioners—2; blocks of tenements— 2,757; private houses—60; storehouses—18; baths—80; fountains—65; bakeries—16; area—12,350 feet.

District VIII, Great Roman Forum, contains:
Three rostra; [shrine of the] Genius of the Roman People; Senate House; Atrium of Minerva; Forums of Caesar, of Augustus, of Nerva, of Trajan; Temple of Trajan, and the spiral column 128½ feet high, with 185 steps and 45 windows inside;[89] Cohort VI of the night patrol; bank basilica; Temples of Concord, of Saturn, of Vespasian and Titus; Capitolium; Golden Milestone;[90] Vicus Jugarius [a main street leading from the Forum]; . . . Julian Basilica; Temple of Castor and Pollux; [Temple of] Vesta; storehouses of Agrippa; . . . Atrium of Cacus; Portico of the Pearl Dealers; [statue of the] elephant eating grass[?]; wards—34; crossroad shrines—34; block captains—48; commissioners—2; blocks of tenements—3,480; private houses—130; storehouses—18; baths—86; fountains—120; bakeries—20; area—14,067 feet.

District IX, Circus Flaminius, contains;
Six stables of the four circus factions; Portico of Philip; the Minucian porticoes—the old one and the one for the grain dole; Grotto of Balbus; three theaters: Balbus', which has 11,510 *loca,* Pompey's, with 17,580 *loca,* Marcellus', with 20,000 *loca;* Odeum [for musical performances], with 10,600 *loca;* Stadium with 30,088 *loca;* Campus Martius; Trigarium [an open space for exercising horses]; Kneeling Storks [statue]; Pantheon; Basilicas of Neptune, of Matidia, of Marcianus; Temple of Antoninus and the spiral column 175½ feet high, with 203 steps and 56 windows inside;[91] Baths of Alexander and of Agrippa; Portico of the

---

must be calculated here and in other places in this catalogue at slightly more than half the number of *loca.*

89. This column was erected to commemorate Trajan's Dacian victory (see § 10, third selection). The height given here includes the pedestal. The actual number of "windows"—narrow slits lighting the spiral stair in the interior—is forty-three.

90. A column of gilt bronze, erected under Augustus and regarded as the point of convergence of all the great roads radiating from the city. On it were engraved the names of the principal cities of the empire and their distances from the gates of Rome.

91. The temple of Marcus Aurelius and the column were erected to commemorate the victories over the Marcomannians and Sarmatians (see chapter 1, note 65). The true height of the column is 106½ English feet (about 116 Roman feet), the number of steps only 200.

Argonauts and Meleager; [Temple of] Isis and Serapis; . . . [Temple of the] Deified Emperors; Felicles tenement [famous for its height]; wards —35; crossroad shrines—35; block captains—48; commissioners—2; blocks of tenements—2,777; private houses—140; storehouses—25; baths— 63; fountains—120; bakeries—20; area—32,500 feet.

[Summary]

Libraries—28; obelisks—6: two in the Circus Maximus (the smaller 87½ feet high, the taller 122½), one on the Vatican (75 feet high), one in the Campus Martius (72½ feet high), two at the Mausoleum of Augustus (each 42½ feet high);[92] bridges—8 . . . ; hills—7 . . . ; fields—8 . . . ; forums—11 . . . ; basilicas—10 . . . ; baths—11[93] . . . ; aqueducts—19 . . . ; roads—29. . . .

92. More complete descriptions of these obelisks are given by Pliny (*Natural History* XXXVI. xiv–xv), who gives slightly different heights for some of them.

93. Only the great public baths are included in this figure.

7

THE ROMAN ARMY

135. DISPOSITION OF THE ARMED FORCES

The "Roman Peace," which the Principate held forth as its gift to the peoples of the Empire, was assured by strong military concentrations guarding the frontiers and by smaller garrisons policing the interior. Throughout the Principate, this professional army remained, as established by Augustus, a force consisting of about thirty legions of Roman citizens (c. 150,000 men) complemented by an equal number of conscripted provincial auxiliaries. Under the conditions of the first two centuries the army tended to become provincialized and transformed into a sedentary garrison army. These tendencies were formalized by Hadrian, who began the practice of recruiting the frontier garrisons from the provinces in which they were stationed, and by Septimius Severus, who completed this evolution by barbarizing and democratizing the Roman armies. The strategic disposition of the armed forces of the Empire underwent such occasional modifications as were necessitated by the annexation of additional provinces on the periphery and by increasing pressures on the northern and eastern frontiers.

Tacitus, *Annals* IV. iv. 4–v. 6

[The Emperor Tiberius in a speech stated that] the number of army volunteers was inadequate,[1] and that even if there were a sufficient number, they did not conduct themselves with the traditional bravery and discipline, as it was principally the needy and the vagrants who adopted military service of their own choice. He rapidly reviewed the

---

1. Voluntary enlistments usually sufficed to keep the military forces at maximum strength. It has been estimated that the legions required about 7,000 recruits annually.

number of the legions and the provinces they had to protect. I think that I ought to do the same here, showing what forces Rome then had under arms, what client kings there were, and how much smaller our empire was.

Italy was guarded on both seas by two fleets, [based] at Misenum and at Ravenna; the nearby coast of Gaul was protected by warships captured in the victory at Actium and sent by Augustus, powerfully manned, to the town of Forum Julium [present-day Fréjus, near Marseilles]. But our chief strength was along the Rhine, serving as a defense against Germans and Gauls alike; this force numbered eight legions. The Spanish provinces, recently subjugated,[2] were held by three legions. Mauretania had been received by King Juba as a gift of the Roman people; the rest of Africa was garrisoned by two legions, and Egypt by the same number. Next, from the borders of Syria to the Euphrates river, all the territory that is encompassed in this vast sweep was controlled by four legions, flanked by the Iberian, Albanian, and other kings, who are protected by our greatness against foreign powers. Thrace was held by Rhoemetalces and the children of Cotys; the bank of the Danube, by two legions in Pannonia and two in Moesia. The same number were stationed in Dalmatia, where, because of the situation of the region, they served as a rear guard for the Danubian legions and could be summoned from a short distance should Italy suddenly require aid. But the capital was garrisoned by its own special soldiery, three urban and nine Praetorian cohorts, levied for the most part in Etruria and Umbria, or ancient Latium and the old Roman colonies. There were besides, in appropriate places in the provinces, allied fleets, cavalry forces, and auxiliary cohorts, whose strength was about the same [as that of the legions]. But it is difficult to recount them in detail since they moved from place to place as circumstances required, and they were sometimes increased in number and sometimes decreased.

THE ROSTER OF THE LEGIONS

This inscription, dating probably from the reign of Antoninus Pius, lists the legions in territorial order proceeding clockwise from Britain along the frontiers. It is known that at that time three of the legions were in

---

2. Though Spain was annexed in the third century B.C., some parts of the Iberian peninsula were not completely subjected to Roman rule until the campaigns of Agrippa in 19 B.C..

Britain, four along the Rhine, eleven on the Danube, nine in the East, one each in Egypt, Numidia, and Spain, and the remainder directly north of Italy.

CIL, vol. VI, no. 3,492 (=Dessau, no. 2,288)

Names of the Legions

II Augusta	I Parthica
VI Victrix	II Adiutrix
XX Victrix	IV Flavia
VIII Augusta	VI Claudia
XXXII Primigenia	I Italica
I Minervia	V Macedonica
XXX Ulpia	XI Claudia
I Adiutrix	XIII Gemina
X Gemina	XII Fulminata
XIV Gemina	XV Apollinaris
III Gallica	II Traiana
II Parthica	III Augusta
IV Scythica	VII Gemina
XVI Flavia	II Italica
VI Ferrata	III Italica
X Fretensis	III Parthica
III Cyrenaica	

136. THE IMPERIAL ARMY

Josephus, *The Jewish War* III. v. 71–107; Adapted from *LCL*

If one goes on to study the organization of their army as a whole,[3] it will be seen that this vast empire of theirs has come to them as the prize of valor, and not as a gift of fortune. For they do not wait for the outbreak of war, nor do they sit with folded hands in peacetime only to put them in motion in the hour of need. On the contrary, as though they had been born with weapons in hand, they never have a truce from training, never wait for the emergencies to arise. Moreover, their peace-time maneuvers are no less strenuous than veritable warfare; each soldier

---

3. On this subject cf. Polybius' description of the Roman army in the second century B.C. (vol. 1, § 164).

daily throws all his energy into his drill, as though he were in action. Hence that perfect ease with which they sustain the shock of battle. . . .

The Romans never lay themselves open to a surprise attack; for, whatever hostile territory they may invade, they engage in no battle until they have fortified their camp. [The traditional Roman encampment arrangements are next described in detail. For the structure of a Roman camp, see vol. I, pp. 468–70.] Thus an improvised city, as it were, springs up, with its market place, its artisan quarter, its judgment seats, where officers [it is not clear which officers are meant] adjudicate any differences which may arise. The outer wall and all the installations within are completed more quickly than thought, so numerous and skilled are the workmen. . . .

Once entrenched, the soldiers take up their quarters in their tents by companies, quietly and in good order. All their fatigue duties are performed with the same discipline, the same regard for security: the procuring of wood, of food supplies, and water, as required—each company having its allotted task. The hour for supper and breakfast is not left to individual discretion; all take their meals together. The hours for sleep, sentinel duty, and rising are announced by the sound of trumpets; nothing is done without a word of command. At daybreak the rank and file report to their respective centurions, the centurions go to salute the tribunes, the tribunes with all the officers then wait on the commander-in-chief, and he gives them according to custom the watchword and other orders to be communicated to the lower ranks. The same precision is maintained on the battlefield; the troops wheel smartly round in the requisite direction, and, whether advancing to the attack or retreating, all move as a unit.

When the camp is to be broken up, the trumpet sounds a first call; at that none remain idle; instantly, at this signal, they strike the tents and make all ready for departure. The trumpets sound a second call to prepare the march; at once they pile their baggage on the mules and other beasts of burden, and stand ready to start. . . . They then set fire to the encampment, both because they can easily construct another . . . and to prevent the enemy from ever making use of it. A third time the trumpets give a similar signal for departure, to hasten the movements of stragglers, whatever the reason for their delay, and to ensure that none is out of his place in the ranks. Then the herald, standing on the right of the commander, inquires in their native tongue whether they are ready for war. Three times they loudly and lustily shout in reply, "We are ready," some even anticipating the question; and worked up to a kind of martial frenzy, they raise their right arms in the air along with the shout. . . .

The infantry are armed with cuirasses and helmets and carry a sword on either side; that on the left is far the longer of the two, the dagger on the right being no longer than a span. The picked infantry, forming the general's guard, carry a spear and round shield, the regiments of the line a javelin and oblong shield; the equipment of the latter includes, further, a saw, a basket, a pick, and an axe, not to mention a strap, a bill-hook, a chain, and three days' rations, so that an infantry man is almost as heavily laden as a pack mule.

The cavalry carry a large sword on their right side, a long pike in the hand, a buckler resting obliquely on the horse's flank, and in a quiver slung beside them three or more darts with broad points and as long as spears; their helmets and cuirasses are the same as those worn by all the infantry. The select cavalry, forming the general's escort, are armed in precisely the same manner as the ordinary troopers. The legion which is to lead the column is always selected by lot. . . .

By their military exercises the Romans instill into their soldiers fortitude not only of body but also of soul; fear, too, plays its part in their training. For they have laws which punish with death not merely desertion but even a slight neglect of duty; and their generals are held in even greater awe than the laws. For the high honors with which they reward the brave prevent the offenders whom they punish from regarding themselves as treated cruelly.

This perfect discipline with regard to their generals make the army an ornament of peacetime, and in battle welds the whole into a single body; so compact are their ranks, so alert their movements in wheeling, so quick their ears for orders, their eyes for signals, their hands for tasks. Prompt as they consequently ever are in action, none are slower than they in succumbing to suffering, and never have they been known in any predicament to be beaten by numbers, by ruses, by difficulties of terrain, or even by fortune; for victory is more certain for them than fortune. When counsel thus precedes active operation, where the leaders' plan of campaign is followed up by so efficient an army, no wonder that the Empire has extended its boundaries on the east to the Euphrates, on the west to the Ocean, on the south to the most fertile tracts of Africa, and on the north to the Danube and the Rhine.

THE ARMY ON THE MARCH

Josephus, *The Jewish War* III. vi. 115–126; Adapted from *LCL*

But Vespasian, impatient to invade Galilee himself, now set out from Ptolemais, after drawing up his army for the march in the customary Roman order. The auxiliary light-armed troops and archers were sent in advance, to repel any sudden incursions of the enemy and to explore suspected woodland suited for the concealment of ambushes. Next came a contingent of heavy-armed Roman soldiers, infantry and cavalry. They were followed by a detachment composed of ten men from each century, carrying their own equipment and the instruments for marking out the camp; after these came the road makers to straighten the curves on the road, to level the rough places and to cut down obstructing woods, in order to spare the army the fatigues of a toilsome march. Behind these Vespasian posted his personal baggage and that of his legates, with a strong escort of cavalry to protect them. He himself rode behind with the pick of the infantry and cavalry and his guard of lancers. Then came the cavalry units of the legions; for to each legion are attached 120 horse. These were followed by the mules carrying the siege towers and the other machines. Then came the legates, the prefects of the cohorts, and the tribunes, with an escort of picked troops. Next the standards surrounding the eagle, which in the Roman army precedes every legion. . . . These sacred emblems were followed by the trumpeters, and behind them came the solid column, marching six abreast. A centurion, according to custom, accompanied them to superintend the order of the ranks. Behind the infantry the servants attached to each legion followed in a body, conducting the mules and other beasts of burden which carried the soldiers' baggage. At the end of the column came the crowd of mercenaries, and last of all for security a rearguard composed of light and heavy infantry and a considerable body of cavalry.

137. RECRUITMENT

Chronique d'Egypte (1949), 24:296–301; A.D. 92

Titus Flavius Longus, subaltern of Legion III Cyrenaica, of the century of Arellius[?], attested . . . and declared on oath[?] . . . that he was freeborn and a Roman citizen, and had the right to serve in a legion.

Hereupon his guarantors[?] . . . declared on oath by Jupiter Best and Greatest and by the *genius* of the Emperor Caesar DOMITIAN Augustus Germanicus . . . that the said Titus Flavius Longus was freeborn and a Roman citizen, and had the right to serve in a legion.

Done in the Augustan camp in the winter quarters of Legion III. [Month and day], year 17 of the Emperor Caesar DOMITIAN Augustus Germanicus, consulship of Quintus Volusius Saturninus and Lucius Venuleius Montanus Apronianus.

Pliny, *Letters* book x, nos. 29–30

[Pliny to the Emperor Trajan]

Sempronius Caelianus, an outstanding young man, sent two slaves to me who were discovered among the recruits. I have deferred punishing them so as to consult you, the founder and strengthener of military discipline, on the proper penalty. For I am especially in doubt about this, because though they have already taken the oath, yet they have not yet been assigned to the ranks. I beg you therefore, my lord, to write me what course I should follow, especially since precedent is involved.

[Trajan to Pliny]

Sempronius Caelianus acted in accordance with my instructions in sending to you these persons, concerning whom an investigation will be necessary to determine whether they seem deserving of capital punishment. It is material whether they enlisted voluntarily, or were levied, or offered as proxies. If they were levied, the examination was at fault; if they were offered as proxies, the guilt lies with those who offered them; but if they themselves, although they were fully aware of their status, enlisted, then they are the ones to be punished. It does not make much difference that they have not yet been assigned to the ranks; for on the very day on which they were approved they were required to give a true statement of their birth status.

Oxyrhynchus Papyrus No. 1,022 (= *Select Papyri,* no. 421); A.D. 103

Gaius Minucius Italus [prefect of Egypt] to his Celsianus, greeting. Give instructions that the six recruits approved by me for the cohort you command be included in the rolls as of February 19. I append their names and descriptions to this letter. Farewell, dearest brother.

Gaius Veturius Gemellus, aged 21, without distinguishing mark
Gaius Longinus Priscus, aged 22, scar on left eyebrow
Gaius Julius Maximus, aged 25, without distinguishing mark
. . . Lucius Secundus, aged 20, without distinguishing mark
Gaius Julius Saturninus, aged 23, scar on left hand
Marcus Antonius Valens, aged 22, scar on right side of forehead

[Docket] Received February 24, year 6 of our Emperor Trajan, through Priscus, orderly. I, Avidius Arrianus, adjutant of the Third Cohort of Ituraeans [see note 22], hereby declare that the original letter is in the archives of the cohort.

138. MILITARY TRAINING

Vegetius,[4] *Military Science* I. i, ix, x, xix, xxvii; II. xxiii, xxv

In every battle victory is granted not by mere numbers and innate courage but by skill and training. For we see that the Roman people owed the conquest of the world to no other cause than military training, discipline in their camps, and practice in warfare. . . .

At the very beginning of their training, recruits should be taught the military step. For there is nothing to be maintained more, on the march and in the line, than the keeping of their ranks by all the soldiers. This cannot be attained in any other way than by learning through training to march quickly and together. For a separated and disorderly army exposes itself to the gravest danger at the hands of the enemy. Now, twenty miles with the military step should be done in five hours, in the summer only; with the full step, which is quicker, twenty-four miles should be completed in the same number of hours. . . .

The soldier is to be trained in leaping also, to enable him to leap across ditches or overcome some impeding height, so that when difficulties of this nature arise he can cross without effort. Moreover, in actual combat the soldier, advancing with running and leaping, dulls the eyesight of his adversary, strikes terror into his mind, and inflicts a blow before the latter makes definite preparations to avoid it or resist. . . .

4. Flavius Vegetius Renatus, a writer of the fourth to fifth centuries A.D.. His manual on military affairs, in four books, based on secondary sources, describes the Roman military establishment of earlier centuries. This work has exerted great influence in modern times: From the Renaissance on, military men have regarded it as the classic handbook on military organization and have trained their armies according to its precepts.

Every recruit, without exception should in the summer months learn to swim; for it is not always possible to cross rivers on bridges, but a retreating and pursuing army is frequently compelled to swim. Sudden rains or snowfalls often cause torrents to overflow their banks, and risk is increased by ignorance not only of the enemy but of water. The ancient Romans, therefore, perfected in every branch of military science by so many wars and perpetual dangers, chose the Field of Mars next to the Tiber in which the young might wash off the sweat and dust after military exercise, and by swimming gain relaxation from their weariness in marching. It is opportune for not only the infantry but also the cavalry, the horses, and the sutlers, whom they call "helmeters," to be trained to swim, lest they be inexperienced when necessity arises and faces them. . . .

Recruits should be obliged frequently to carry burdens weighing up to sixty pounds, and to march with the military step. For on arduous expeditions they find themselves under the necessity of carrying their provisions as well as their arms. . . .

It was a survival of ancient custom, confirmed by enactments of the deified Augustus and Hadrian, to exercise both cavalry and infantry three times a month by marches. . . . The infantry was instructed to march ten miles with the military step, wearing armor and equipped with all weapons, and return to camp; and to take part of the journey at the quicker pace. The cavalry, likewise, separated in squadrons and similarly armed, performed the same march, practicing cavalry exercises, sometimes pursuing, sometimes retreating, and then returning to the attack. They did not make these marches in plains; rather, both branches were compelled to ascend and descend sloping and steep places. . . .

The younger soldiers and recruits used to be drilled morning and afternoon in every type of weapon; the older and experienced ones were drilled in weapons once a day. . . . For length of service or age alone does not bestow the science of war, but after any number of years of service an undisciplined soldier is always a recruit. . . . It is very desirable to drill them also at the post with wooden stakes, as they learn to attack the sides or feet or head both with the point and the edge [of the sword]. They should be accustomed also to leap and strike blows at the same time, to rise up with a bound and sink down again below the shield, now eagerly rushing forward with a leap, now leaping back to the rear. They must also practice throwing their javelins at the posts from a distance in order to increase their skill in aiming and the strength of the arm. . . .

The legion in practice is victorious because of the number of soldiers and the type of machines. First of all, it is equipped with hurling machines which no cuirass, no shield can withstand. For the practice is to have a ballista mounted on a carriage for each century, to each of which are assigned mules and a detail of eleven men for loading and firing. The larger these are, the farther and more powerfully do they hurl missiles. Not only do they defend the camps, but they are placed in the field in the rear of the heavy-armed infantry. Before their fire power neither enemy cavalrymen with cuirasses nor infantry men with shields can hold their ground. It is customary to have fifty-five such mounted ballistas in each legion. Likewise, there are ten *onagri*,[5] one for each cohort; they are drawn ready-armed on carriages by oxen, so that in case of an enemy attack on the rampart the camp can be defended with arrows and stones.

The legion also carries with it small boats, each hollowed out of a single piece of timber, with very long cables and sometimes iron chains. When these "single plankers," as they are called, are joined together and covered with boards, rivers which cannot be forded are crossed without bridges by the infantry and cavalry without danger. The legion is provided with grappling hooks, called "wolves," and with iron scythes fixed to the ends of long poles; likewise mattocks, hoes, spades, shovels, buckets, and baskets to carry earth in ditch-digging operations; also hatchets, axes, and saws for hewing and sawing timber. Besides these, it has workmen equipped with all tools, who make various kinds of wooden sheds, battering rams, and movable towers for besieging cities. To avoid the enumeration of more of these, I shall add that the legion ought to carry with it everywhere everything which is believed necessary to every kind of warfare, so that whenever it pitches its camp it forms an armed city.[6]

---

5. Literally, "wild asses"; they were catapults for discharging stones.

6. In II. xi Vegetius gives the following details about the corps of engineers: "The legion has, moreover, carpenters, masons, wagon makers, smiths, painters, and other artisans on hand for the construction of the barracks and the winter quarters, for making or repairing damaged machines, wooden towers, and other equipment with which cities of the enemy are besieged or our own defended, also arms, carriages, and various kinds of shooting instruments. They had also workshops for shields, cuirasses, and bows, in which arrows, missiles, nets, and all types of weapons were made. For it was their special concern that whatever seemed necessary for an army should never be lacking in camp. . . . The officer in charge of these was the prefect of the workmen."

139. MILITARY OPERATIONS

The strategy and tactics of the imperial army remained for two centuries based on the principles developed by the great generals of the last century of the Republic, familiar to readers of Caesar's *Gallic War* and *Civil War*. During the third century, with the growing provincialization and barbarization of the army and the importance of a mobile army for wars of movement, native tactics came to the fore, and by the time of Constantine the famous legionary tactics, encampment, and weapons had become virtually obsolete (cf. introduction to § 125).

THE TESTUDO

Cassius Dio, *Roman History* XLIX. xxx; From *LCL*

This *testudo* ("tortoise shell") and the way in which it is formed are as follows. The baggage animals, the light-armed troops, and the cavalry are placed in the center of the army. The heavy-armed troops who use the oblong, curved, and cylindrical shields are drawn up around the outside, making a rectangular figure; and, facing outward and holding their arms at the ready, they enclose the rest. The others, who have flat shields, form a compact body in the center and raise their shields over their own heads and the heads of all the others, so that nothing but shields can be seen in every part of the phalanx alike, and all the men by the density of the formation are under shelter from missiles. Indeed, it is so marvelously strong that men can walk upon it, and whenever they come to a narrow ravine, even horses and vehicles can be driven over it. Such is the plan of this formation, and for this reason it has received the name *testudo,* with reference both to its strength and to the excellent shelter it affords. They use it in two ways: either they approach some fort to assault it, often even enabling men to scale the very walls, or sometimes, when they are surrounded by archers, they all crouch together—even the horses being taught to kneel or lie down—and thereby cause the foe to think that they are exhausted; then, when the enemy draws near, they suddenly rise and throw him into consternation.[7]

---

7. The effectiveness of this formation impressed all the peoples with whom the Romans fought in combat. Knowledge of it penetrated, it seems, indirectly to China; cf. H. H. Dubs, *American Journal of Philology* (1941), 62:322–330.

A PONTOON BRIDGE

Cassius Dio, *Roman History* LXXI. iii. 1; Adapted from *LCL*

River channels are bridged by the Romans with very great ease, since the soldiers are always practicing this operation, like any other military exercise, on the Danube, the Rhine, and the Euphrates. Now the method, which is not familiar to everybody, is as follows. The boats by means of which the river is to be bridged are flat bottomed, and these are anchored a little way upstream from the spot where the bridge is to be constructed. When the signal is given, they first let one ship drift downstream close to the bank that they are holding; and when it has come opposite to the spot that is to be bridged, they throw into the stream a wicker basket filled with stones and fastened by a cable, which serves as an anchor. Made fast in this way, the ship remains in position near the bank, and by means of plank and clamps, which the vessel carries in large quantity, a floor is at once laid to the landing place. Then they send down another ship at a little distance from the first, another one beyond that, until they have extended the bridge to the opposite bank. The ship that is nearest the enemy's bank carries towers upon it and a gate and archers and catapults.

THE SIEGE

"There is nothing of which barbarians are so ignorant," writes Tacitus (*Annals* XII. xlv. 4), "as military engines and skill in siege operations, while that is a branch of military science in which we are especially skilled." Construction details and measurements of the principal siege mechanisms and of machines for defense against sieges (many of Greek origin) are given in Vitruvius, *Architecture* X. xiii–xvi. Among other features of Roman siege operations was the use of carrier birds to transmit messages across siege lines (Frontinus, *Strategems* III. xiii. 8). A typical Roman siege operation, described below, is the famous investment and storming of Marseilles by Caesar's army in 49 B.C.

Caesar, *Civil War* II. i–ii, viii–xi (abridged); In part adapted from *LCL*

Gaius Trebonius, Caesar's lieutenant, who had been left for the siege of Marseilles, began to build a mound, breaching huts, and towers near the city. . . . To complete these works Trebonius called for a great number of draught animals and men from the entire province; he ordered twigs and lumber to be gathered. When these were procured, he constructed a mound eighty feet high. But there was so much war equipment of all kinds in the town from older times, and such a quantity of hurling engines, that none of the huts woven with twigs could stand up against their power. For poles twelve feet long with pointed ends, shot from enormous ballistas, pierced four layers of wickerwork and lodged in the earth. Consequently, galleries were covered over by joining one-foot-thick beams, and thereby the mound was carried forward by a hand-to-hand operation. In advance of this was a sixty-foot shed for leveling the area, constructed likewise of very strong beams and enveloped in everything that could protect it against the firebrands and stones being hurled. But the size of the works, the height of the wall and towers, and the mass of engines slowed up the whole operation. . . .

In consequence of the frequent sorties of the enemy, the legionaries who were conducting operations on the right noticed that they could provide a great protection to themselves if they constructed there a tower of brick hard by the wall, to serve as a stronghold and a place of retreat. This they constructed at first of low elevation and small size to meet sudden sallies. To this they used to retire; from this shelter they fought if a strong assault pressed them; from this they issued forth to repel and pursue the foe. Its dimensions were thirty feet each way, and the thickness of the walls was five feet. But afterwards, as experience is the guide in all human conduct, by applying their wits they discovered that this tower could be of greater service to them if it were raised in height. This was accomplished in the following manner.

[Under complete protection, the soldiers laboriously raised the tower to a height of six stories.]

When they were sure that from the tower they could protect all the surrounding works, they set about making out of timber two feet square a shed sixty feet long, to be carried from the brick tower to the enemy's tower and wall. . . . They completed this construction, entirely protected by breaching huts, up to the tower itself, and suddenly, when the enemy was off guard, they put rollers under it . . . and pushed it forward to the enemy's tower, so as to join it onto that structure.

Dismayed at this sudden calamity, the townsmen brought forward with cranes the largest possible stones, and rolled them headlong from the wall onto the shed. The strength of the timber bore the blow, and everything that fell on it slipped off owing to the sloping roof of the shed. Observing this, they changed their plan and set on fire barrels filled with pine wood and pitch, and rolled them down from the wall onto the shed. When, however, they had rolled onto it they slipped off and, having fallen from the tiles, were removed from the work with poles and forks. Meanwhile some soldiers under the shed pried out with crowbars the lowest stones of the enemy's tower which served to hold the foundations together. The shed was defended by our men on the brick tower with missiles and catapults; the enemy were dislodged from their wall and towers; and no easy opportunity of defending their wall was allowed them. When now a number of stones had been withdrawn from the tower next to the shed, a part of it suddenly collapsed and fell. The rest was beginning to follow it and fall forward, when the enemy, terrified at [the prospect of] the sacking of their city, flung themselves, without their arms and wearing fillets, in a mass outside the gate and stretched out their hands as suppliants to the lieutenants and the army.

140. Mutiny in the Ranks

"The principal glory and the mainstay of the Roman Empire, maintained with salutary perseverence sound and unimpaired to the present time, is the unrelaxing bond of military discipline, in the embrace and protection of which reposes our serene and tranquil state of blessed peace," wrote Valerius Maximus (*Memorable Deeds and Sayings* ii. vii. Introd.). Nevertheless, the conditions of the *Pax Romana* tended to relax the traditional rigors of Roman military discipline (cf. § 145), and the history of the Principate was marked by a number of serious military mutinies. The first of these, a harbinger of the evolution that was ultimately to raise the military to the ruling class in the third century (see §§ 104–105), was the rebellion of the legions in Pannonia and on the Rhine that greeted the news of the death of Augustus in A.D. 14.

Tacitus, *Annals* i. xvii, xxxi, xxxv

[A leader of the mutineers in Pannonia harangues the soldiers.]

Why should they obey like slaves a few centurions and fewer tribunes? When would they dare to claim redress if they did not approach with petitions or weapons the new and still unstable emperor? Mistakes enough had been made in all the years by inaction, when old men, and many who had lost limbs from wounds, were serving thirty and forty years. Even after discharge their service was not over; but in the reserve they endured the same labors under another name.[8] And suppose that a man survived this multitude of hazards: he was dragged again to the ends of the earth to receive under the name of a "farm" some swampy morass or a barren mountain side. In fact, military service itself was burdensome and profitless. Ten *asses* a day was the value set on body and soul; with that they had to buy clothes, weapons and tents, bribe the cruel centurion, and purchase exemptions from duties. But lashings and wounds, hard winters and severe summers, terrible war or barren peace—these, by heaven, were everlasting. There would be no relief until military service was entered under precise regulations—the pay to be a *denarius* a day, the sixteenth year to end the term of service, no further detention in the reserve to be required, but the bonus to be paid in cash right in the camp. Did the Praetorian cohorts, who received two *denarii* a day—and who were restored to their homes after sixteen years —face more dangers? They did not disparage sentinel duty at Rome; still, they were among savage clans, with the enemy visible from their very tents. . . .

On almost the same days and for the same reasons the legions of Germany mutinied, with more violence because of their greater numbers and with high hopes that Germanicus Caesar would be unable to endure the sovereignty of [Tiberius] and would offer himself to the legions, whose force could carry everything before it. There were two armies along the bank of the Rhine. The upper army was under the legate Gaius Silius, and Aulus Caecina was in charge of the lower one. The supreme command was in the hands of Germanicus, then occupied with taking the census of the Gallic provinces. . . . The soldiery of the lower army flared up in a frenzy, beginning with the twenty-first and fifth legions. Then the first and twentieth legions also were dragged into it; for they were quartered in the same summer camp in the territory of the Ubians, idle or on light duties. Thus, when they heard of the death of Augustus, the multitude of city-bred men from the recent levy held at Rome, accustomed to license, chafing at hardships, filled the simple minds of the rest [with talk such as this]: The time had come for veterans to demand timely discharge, for the younger men to ask for higher pay, and for all to obtain a limit to their suffering and to take vengeance for the cruelty of the centurions. . . . The Roman state lay in their hands; by their victories the state was extended. . . .

---

8. Veterans remained in camp in this period for five additional years as a privileged elite corps, technically exempt from onerous camp duties.

When Germanicus [in a speech to the army] touched on the sedition, asking where their military restraint was, where their famous former discipline, where they had driven the tribunes, where the centurions, all bared their bodies, complaining of the scars from wounds and marks of lashes. Next, in a confusion of voices they complained of the fees for exemption from duties, the smallness of the pay, the strenuousness of the work, mentioning specifically the rampart, trenches, the gathering of fodder, timber, and firewood, and the other duties which were imposed by necessity or devised to prevent idleness in camp. The fiercest outcry arose from the veterans, who, enumerating their thirty or more years of service, begged him to give relief to weary men and not leave them to die in the same labors, but to fix a limit for such trying service and not abandon them to a poverty-stricken retirement. There were some also who demanded of him the money bequeathed by the deified Augustus. They suggested favorable omens for Germanicus—if he wished the imperial power, they showed that they were ready. Then indeed, as if defiled by their crime, he leaped straight from the tribunal. They opposed his withdrawal with their weapons and threatened him unless he returned. But, shouting that he would rather die than break his oath, he drew the sword from his side, raised it and would have plunged it into his side had not those nearby seized his arm and forceably restrained it. . . . But a soldier by the name of Calusidius drew his own sword and offered it to him, adding that it was sharper.

141. HADRIAN'S TOUR OF INSPECTION

After abandoning most of Trajan's conquests because the economic resources and manpower of the Empire could not support the strain of further territorial expansion, Hadrian reconstituted the Roman military establishment as a garrison army. For about half of his twenty-one-year reign he toured the provinces of the Empire, principally to inspect its military forces and installations. His efforts were concentrated on strengthening frontier fortifications and reforming military discipline to raise it to the highest level of efficiency.

Cassius Dio, *Roman History* LXIX. ix. 1–5; From *LCL*

Hadrian traveled through one province after another, visiting the various regions and cities and inspecting all the garrisons and forts. Some of these he removed to more desirable places, some he abolished, and he also established new ones. He personally viewed and investigated absolutely everything, not merely the usual installations of the camps, such as weapons, engines, trenches, ramparts, and palisades, but also the private affairs of everyone, both of the men serving in the ranks and of the officers themselves—their lives, their quarters and their habits—and he reformed and corrected in many cases practices and arrangements for living that had become too luxurious. He drilled the men for every kind of battle, honoring some and reproving others, and he taught them all what should be done. And in order that they should be benefited by observing him, he everywhere led a rigorous life and either walked or rode on horseback on all occasions, never once at this period setting foot in either a chariot or a four-wheeled vehicle. He covered his head neither in hot weather nor in cold, but alike amid German snows and under scorching Egyptian suns he went about with his head bare. In short, both by his example and by his precepts he so trained and disciplined the whole military force throughout the entire Empire that even today the regulations then introduced by him are the code of the army. This best explains why he lived for the most part at peace with foreign nations; for as they saw his state of preparation and were themselves not only free from [Roman] aggression but received money besides,[9] they made no uprising.

HADRIAN REVIEWS THE GARRISON OF AFRICA

In A.D. 128 Hadrian inspected the frontier defenses of North Africa and reviewed the garrison army of the province of Numidia, the Legion III Augusta and its auxiliary contingents, at its headquarters at Lambaesis (modern Lambèse, the site of the best-preserved Roman fortified camp). To commemorate the emperor's review, the garrison set up a column on the base of which were inscribed excerpts from his five addresses to the troops following maneuvers.

CIL, vol. VIII, nos. 2,532 and 18,042 (=Dessau, nos. 2,487 and 9,133–9,135)

The Emperor Caesar Trajanus HADRIAN Augustus addressed his Legion III Augusta after inspecting their exercises, as recorded below, in the consulship of Torquatus (for the second time) and of Libo, July 1.

9. For cash subsidies paid to foreign peoples, see §§ 9, 110.

To the Chief Centurions

. . . [Your commander] himself has on your behalf told me in detail the circumstances which should excuse you in my eyes, to wit: that one cohort is absent, because one is detailed annually in rotation to the service of the proconsul; that two years ago you gave up a cohort and four men from each of the centuries as reinforcements for your comrades of the Third Legion;[10] that many widely scattered posts keep you separated. In my own recollection you have not only changed camp twice, but actually built new ones. For these reasons I would have excused you if the legion had been remiss in its exercise for any length of time. But you were not at all remiss. . . . The chief centurions and the other centurions were quick and brave as usual.

To the Cavalry of the Legion

Military exercises have, I may say, their own rules, and if anything is added to or taken away from these rules, the exercise becomes either of little value or too difficult. The more elaborateness is added, the poorer a show it makes. But you performed the most difficult of all exercises, namely, javelin throwing, clad in cuirass. . . . In addition, I congratulate you on your spirit. . . .

[To a Cavalry Cohort]

. . . Entrenchments which others take several days to construct you have completed in a single day. You have built a wall entailing long labor, such as is customarily made for permanent winter quarters, in a time not much longer than that required to build one of sod. In this kind the turf is cut to standard size and is easy to carry and to handle, and the laying is not troublesome, as the turf is naturally soft and level. But yours was built of large heavy stones of all sizes; and no one can carry or lift or lay these without their irregularities making themselves felt. You have cut a trench straight through hard coarse gravel and have made it even by smoothing it. When this task was approved, you entered the camp speedily, got your rations and your arms, following the cavalry that had been sent out, and with a loud shout as it returned. . . .

I compliment [my legate] for having introduced this maneuver among

10. That is, Legion III Gallica or III Cyrenaica, both of which were stationed in the East.

you, which assumed the appearance of real combat; and it trains you [so well that] I am able to praise you. Cornelianus too, your prefect, has handled his duties satisfactorily. . . . The cavalryman should ride out from cover and use caution in pursuit. For unless he sees where he is going and is able to check his horse whenever he wants to, he will surely be exposed to pitfalls. . . .

On July . . . to the First Company of Pannonians

You did everything in orderly fashion. You filled the field with maneuvers. Your javelin hurling was not without grace, although you used javelins which are short and stiff. Several of you hurled your lances equally well. And your mounting was smart just now and lively yesterday. If there were anything lacking I should notice it; if there were anything conspicuously bad, I should point it out. But you pleased me uniformly throughout the whole exercise. My legate Catullinus,[11] *vir clarissimus,* devotes equal care to all the branches he commands. . . . Your prefect evidently looks after you carefully. I bestow upon you a largess. . . .

To the Cavalry of the Sixth Cohort of Commagenians

It is difficult for the cavalry of the cohorts to make a good impression even by themselves, and still harder for them not to give dissatisfaction after the exercise of the auxiliary cavalry. They have a larger ground coverage, a larger number of men throwing javelins; their right wheeling is in close array, their Cantabrian maneuver closely knit; the beauty of their horses and the elegance of their equipment is in keeping with their level of pay. Nevertheless, and despite the heat, you avoided being tedious by doing promptly what had to be done. In addition you hurled stones from slings and fought with missiles. Your mounting was everywhere brisk. That the care taken by my legate Catullinus, *vir clarissimus,* has been outstanding is apparent from the fact that such men as you under his command. . . . [The rest is lost.]

142. MOVEMENTS AND TRANSFERS OF TROOPS

For further examples of troop movements see the military careers of § 152.

11. Quintus Fabius Catullinus, who was rewarded with the consulship in A.D. 130.

Berlin Papyrus No. 2,492; second century

. . . You should know that Gemellus has come to serve in the fleet, and he told me, "Your mother is going to court with your father in Memphis, before the chief justice." Please, mother, as soon as you receive this letter send Germanus to me [in Alexandria], because the word is out that our cohort is leaving for Mauretania. Up to today the [cavalry] Wing of Moors and the Cohort of Africans [see note 22] have left. That cohort is brought up to full strength [by men] from our cohort; men from three [enrollment] years are leaving.

Berlin Papyrus No. 423 (= *Select Papyri*, no. 112); second century; Adapted from *LCL*

Apio to Epimachus, his father and lord, very many greetings. Before all else I pray for your health and that you may always be well and prosperous, together with my sister and her daughter and my brother. I thank the lord Serapis that when I was in danger at sea he straightway saved me. On arriving at Misenum I received from Caesar three gold pieces for traveling expenses. And it is well with me. Now I ask you, my lord and father, write me a letter, telling me first of your welfare, secondly of my brother's and sister's, and enabling me thirdly to make obeisance before your handwriting, because you educated me well and I hope thereby to have quick advancement, the gods willing. Give many salutations to Capito and my brother and sister and Serenilla and my friends. I have sent you by Euctemo a portrait of myself. My name is now Antonius Maximus, my century the Athenonica. I pray for your health.

[P.S.] Serenus son of Agathodaemo salutes you, as does . . . and Turbo son of Gallonius. . . .

[Address, on back] To Philadelphia, to Epimachus from Apio his son.

[Additional notation] Deliver at [the camp of] the First Cohort of Apamenians to Julianus, vice-secretary, this letter from Apio to be forwarded to his father Epimachus.

143. DUTIES AND OCCUPATIONS OF THE GARRISON ARMY

The Roman armies were an important factor in the administrative and economic life of the provinces where they were stationed. In addition to their prime function of guarding the frontiers, the soldiers were regularly detailed to police and patrol duties, especially in connection with the grain supply, tax collection and the exploitation of natural resources. Moreover, the labor of the army was frequently employed for the construction and maintenance of public works, such as roads, bridges, canals, and temples and other public buildings.

TOURS OF DUTY

Geneva Latin Papyrus No 1, col 3

[From the records of a legion stationed near Alexandria, Egypt, A.D. c. 80–90]

MARCUS PAPIRIUS RUFUS C. . . .

Assigned to granary at Neapolis[12] as secretary[?] . . . to Titus Suedius Clemens, prefect of the camp, year 3 of the Emperor Titus. . . . Returned, same year, January 21. Assigned to granary at Mercurium, year 1 of the Emperor Domitian. . . . Returned, same year, July 13. Assigned with . . . year 4 of Domitian, April 21. Returned, same year. . . . Assigned to granary at Neapolis, year. . . . Returned, same year, July 7.

TITUS FLAVIUS SATURNINUS

Assigned to harbor dredging, year . . . January 14. Returned, same year. . . . Assigned with Timinius, prefect[?] . . . Returned, same year, November 28. Assigned with Maximus Liberalis. . . .

TITUS FLAVIUS VALENS

Assigned to papyrus manufacture, year . . . January 15. Returned, same year. . . . Assigned to mint, year. . . . Returned, same year, January 17. Assigned to . . . year . . . of the Emperor Domitian, A[pril?] 13. . . . Assigned to granary at Mercurium. . . . Returned, same year, July 14. Assigned to . . . year 7 of Domitian, September 19. . . .

TITUS FLAVIUS CELER

Assigned to granary at Neapolis, year . . . February 11. Returned, same year. . . . Assigned with river patrol boat. . . . Returned, same year, May 24. . . . [The rest is fragmentary.]

---

12. Neapolis and Mercurium were the names of districts of the city of Alexandria.

LIFE OF A MILITARY GARRISON

Following is a small sampling of some 80 papyrus documents that survive from the files of one Flavius Abinnaeus, who was in the mid-fourth century the prefect (i.e., commandant) of an auxiliary unit stationed in a fortress at the village of Dionysias in the Arsinoite nome of Egypt. All of the following date from A.D. C. 346.

Abinnaeus Papyrus No. 3

Flavius Macarius, most illustrious superintendent of imperial domains, to Flavius Abinnaeus, prefect of the camp of Dionysias, greeting. His lordship my lord Flavius Felicissimus the most illustrious count and duke, exercising care about the imperial revenues, has ordered my office that a military detachment be furnished from the troops under your command for the collection of the imperial taxes. See to it, therefore, in accordance with the instructions issued to you by my said lord the most illustrious duke, that you promptly send soldiers for the said collection by the official sent by my said lord the most illustrious duke as well as by my lord the most illustrious chief of revenues, knowing that if you should decline to send them it will be brought to the attention of my said lord the duke that you have impeded the collection of the imperial revenues. I pray, my lord and brother, that you remain in health for many years.

Abinnaeus Papyrus No. 28

To my master and patron Abinnaeus [from] Demetrius, assistant of Isio, very many greetings. I want you to know, my lord patron, that when I was about the collection of taxes in grain a soldier named Athenodorus, who is under your command, came up to me and wreaked no small violence upon me, and not only upon me but also he repeatedly goes out drunk into the fields and makes the village his prey. I have therefore written to your excellency because I know that you will call him to account in the camp and will do me justice in all things. I was intending to go up to the nome capital and complain to my landlord and to the commandant of the soldiers [there], Castinus, for them to do me justice, but first of all I have written to you, my master, to do me justice. May the divine providence preserve you in health with all your household.

To my master and beloved brother Abinnaeus, commandant, [from] Kaor [Christian] priest of Hermopolis, greeting. I send many greetings to your children. I want you to know, my lord, about the soldier Paul, about his absence without leave, allow it him this once. [I write] because I am not free to come to you these days. And afterwards, if he does not stop, he falls into your hands another time. I pray that you remain in health for many years, my lord brother.

To my master Abinnaeus [from] Clematius. We always pray that our friends prosper in affairs of importance, so that we too may be seen to take pleasure in their success. This then is my one reason for appealing by letter to your excellency, and lest you think I am doing this for some personal profit, I shall explain the matter to your nobility. A certain Isio, a petty officer of the troops under your command, is related to me and is related also to my lord and brother Paul, the adjutant of the camp. He is also, as it happens, the son-in-law of Timotheus, a veteran and landowner at Par . . ton, who is own brother to the aforementioned Paul. . . . I appeal to you to grant him leave to look after our affairs, since you can, in case of pressing need, summon him back, and right after that again allow him, as I have said, to look after our affairs. That we may know that you have assented to our request, be so kind, when you have received my letter, my lord, to reply to me about this. I pray that you remain in health for many years, my lord.

LIFE OF A GUARD DETAIL

The following are from a group of several dozen Latin and Greek ostraca found at the site of an ancient quarry and gold mine on the desert road from Coptus to the Red Sea (cf. § 30, third selection). These ostraca, which date from the late first to the middle of the second century, show that a military garrison was stationed there in that period for the double purpose, no doubt, of guarding both the trade route and the diggings.

Bulletin de l'Institut français d'archéologie orientale (1941), 40:141–196, nos. 1 and 13

i

Rustius Barbarus to his brother Pompeius, greeting. How come you haven't answered me if you received the loaves of bread? I sent you fifteen loaves by Popillius and Dutuporis, then fifteen more and a vase[?] by the carter Draco; you've used up four *matia* [= ⅓ artab] of wheat. I sent you six loaves by the cavalryman Thiadices, who said he could take them with him. Please, brother, have some . . . made for my personal use, as beautiful as possible, and write me so that in payment for them I can make you bread or send you money, whichever you wish. I want you to know, now, that I'm getting married. As soon as I have, I'll write you at once to come. Goodbye. Regards to . . . lius.

ii

. . . to Terentius and . . . and Atticus, his . . . , hearticst greeting. First of all I pray that you are in good health; my dearest wish . . . is for you and the children to stay well.[13] I received from Ca . . . the bunch of radishes[?] that you sent. You are getting [from me] gourds and citron; divide it with your brothers as you yourselves wish. Regards to the soldiers. Isidorus sends regards. I pray that you are well.

144. RECEIVING A FOREIGN ENVOY

Dura Papyrus No. 60B; A.D. *c.* 208

Marius Maximus [governor of Syria] to tribunes, prefects and heads of units, greeting. For your information I have appended what I have written to Minicius Martialis, procurator of our emperors. I hope you are well.

Copy

See to it that Goces, the envoy sent by Parthia to our lords the most mighty emperors, is offered the customary hospitality by the quartermasters of the units through which he passes. And of course write me

---

13. Even in this remote military outpost many of the soldiers lived with their "wives" and children (cf. § 149).

what you spend in each unit. [Units at:] Gazica, Appadana, Dura,
Eddana, Biblada.

145. RELAXATION OF DISCIPLINE

The natural tendency toward relaxation of strict discipline in a garrison
army was aggravated by Hadrian's reform of military recruitment, whereby
soldiers were assigned to service in units stationed in their native provinces
(cf. § 135). The purpose of this measure was undoubtedly to make the
professional military career more attractive to provincials and to make the
soldiers the defenders of their own homes, but it also had the adverse
effect of fostering a centrifugal provincial consciousness as well as a breakdown in discipline. The selections below reveal the unmilitary behavior of
the army in Syria about the middle of the second century. For the third
century see § 104.

Fronto, Letter to Lucius Verus xix; From LCL

The army you took over was demoralized by luxury and immorality
and prolonged idleness. The soldiers at Antioch were wont to spend
their time applauding actors and were more often found in the nearest
tavern garden than in the ranks. Horses shaggy from neglect, but every
hair plucked from their riders; a rare sight was a soldier with arm or leg
hairy. Withal the men were better clothed than armed, so much so that
Pontius Laelianus, a man of character and a disciplinarian of the old
school, in some cases ripped up their cuirasses with his finger tips; he
found horses saddled with cushions, and by his orders the little pommels
on them were slit open and the down plucked from the saddles of the
cavalry as from geese. Few of the soldiers could vault upon their steeds,
the rest scrambled clumsily up by dint of heel or knee or ham; not many
could make their spears hurtle, most tossed them like toy lances without
verve and vigor. Gambling was rife in camp, sleep night-long, or, if a
watch was kept, it was over the wine cups.

Fronto, Elements of History xi–xii; From LCL

So by long unfamiliarity with fighting the Roman soldier was reduced
to a cowardly condition. For as to all the arts of life, so especially to the
business of war is sloth fatal. It is of the greatest importance also for
soldiers to experience the ups and downs of fortune, and to take strenuous exercise in the open.

The most demoralized of all, however, were the Syrian soldiers, mutinous, disobedient, seldom with their units, straying in front of their prescribed posts, roving about like scouts, tipsy from one noon to the next, unused even to carry their arms, and, as one man after another from dislike of toil laid them aside, like skirmishers and slingers half naked. Apart from scandals of this kind, they had been so cowed by unsuccessful battles as to turn their backs at the first sight of the Parthians and to listen for the trumpet as the signal for flight.

146. MILITARY PAY AND EXPENSES

The pay of the rank-and-file legionnaire, which had been one third of a *denarius* a day (minus deductions) in the second century B.C. (cf. vol. 1, p. 471), was fixed by Augustus at 225 *denarii* annually (minus deductions for equipment and maintenance). Legionary soldiers' pay rose, with inflation and increased privileges to the army, to 300 *denarii* under Domitian, to 500 under Septimius Severus, to 800 under Caracalla, and to 1,800 later in the third century. It has been estimated that a soldier could live fairly comfortably on about five sevenths of his pay.

COMPULSORY SOLDIERS' DEPOSITS

Vegetius, *Military Science* II. xx

It was indeed an admirable institution of the ancients that one half of the donatives which the soldiers obtained was sequestered in the soldiers' depository and kept there for the soldiers, lest it be squandered by them in luxuries and the purchase of useless things. For very many men, particularly poorer ones, spend whatever they can get. This laying aside of money, moreover, is, in the first place, evidently for the welfare of the soldiers themselves; since they are maintained at the public expense, their personal camp funds increase proportionately with every donative. Secondly, the soldier who knows that his money is kept in the soldiers' depository entertains no thoughts of desertion, cherishes the standards more, and fights for them in the line with greater bravery. . . . One bag was placed in each of the ten cohorts, and in it these funds were kept. There was, in addition, an eleventh bag in which the entire legion made a small contribution for a burial fund, so that if any of the soldiers died, the expenses for his burial were taken from this eleventh bag; this fund was kept in a basket in the custody of the standard bearers. . . . And therefore standard bearers are chosen not only for their integrity but also for their education, so that they will know how to protect the deposits and render accounts to each man.

MILITARY PAYROLL ACCOUNT

Geneva Latin Papyrus No. 1, col. 1 (abridged)

[Account for A.D. 81 of a cavalryman of a legion stationed outside Alexandria]

Year 3 of the Emperor TITUS Vespasianus Augustus, consulship of Lucius Flavius and Lucius Asinius.

QUINTUS JULIUS PROCULUS, FROM DAMASCUS

	drachmas
Received first salary payment for our lord's third year	248
Deductions	
Hay	10
Toward rations	80
Boots, leggings	12
Camp Saturnalia	20
Toward clothing	60
[Total] expenses	182
Remainder deposited to his account	66
Previous balance	136
Total balance	202

	drachmas
Received second salary payment for same year	248
Deductions	
Hay	10
Toward rations	80
Boots, leggings	12
To "the standards"[a]	4
[Total] expenses	106
Remainder deposited to his account	142
Previous balance	202
Total balance	344

Received third salary payment for same year	248
Deductions	
Hay	10
Toward rations	80
Boots, leggings	12
Toward clothing	146
[Total] expenses	248
On deposit to his account	344

[Verified by] Rennius Innocens

ᵃThis was probably an assessment for a burial fund for deceased soldiers; such military funds were kept by the standard bearers: see the preceding selection.

AN ADVANCE OF RATIONS AND PAY

This receipt is written on an ostracon found at the site of one of the quarries between the Nile and the Red Sea, where a military garrison guarded the convict labor, the road, and the vital water store (cf. § 143, last selection). Archaeological excavation has revealed the characteristic rectangular enclosure of the Roman military camp (cf. vol. 1, pp. 468–470), wells, water conduits, baths, houses, and a temple.

SB, no. 9,457; A.D. 136/137(?)

Ptolemaeus son of Irenaeus to Adrastus, commissary officer, greeting. I acknowledge that I have been advanced my ration and one *denarius*[?] of my allowance for clothing and beans for the month of Choiak, which I will repay to Gaio, imperial agent[?]. Year 21[?] of the lord Hadrian[?] Caesar.

[Signed] I have received in accordance with the above-written. Ptolemaeus son of Irenaeus.

A LOAN TILL PAYDAY

This loan agreement—written in Latin, the official language of the Roman army, but signed in Greek, the *lingua franca* of the eastern provinces—is notable both for the items pledged as security and for its brief term of seven days (from August 25 to the borrower's next payday, September 1). The interest on the loan is calculated at the legal maximum of 1 percent for each month or part thereof.

SB, no. 12,609, A.D. 27

Lucius Caecilius Secundus, cavalryman in the wing of Paullinus, squadron of Dicacus, to Gaius Pompeius, soldier in the cohort of A____
Habetus under centurion Betitus, greeting. I acknowledge that I owe
you two hundred Imperial and Ptolemaic drachmas, which I will repay
to you out of my next pay, and the interest thereon at the rate of 1
drachma per 100 drachmas 3 *asses* per month, without any dispute, [this]
aside from the other 400 Imperial and Ptolemaic drachmas, on security
of a helmet with silver decoration and an emblem with silver decoration
and a dagger scabbard inlaid with ivory.

Done at Alexandria-at-Egypt, eight days before the Kalends of September in the consulship of Gaius Sallustius Crispus and Lucius Lentulus
Scipio. I,   , wrote for them because they are illiterate.
[2d hand, Greek] I, Lucius Caecilius Secundus, the aforementioned cavalryman, have received as aforestated. Year 13 of Tiberius Caesar Augustus, intercalary day 2.

147. PROVISIONS FOR THE ARMY

Food and equipment were supplied to the armies from the production of
provincial agriculture and industry. Considerable quantities of most supplies were delivered from provincial tribute; additional requirements were
supplied by purchase or requisition from farmers and artisans in the
regions where the units were stationed. For large-scale military operations, requisitions were made upon other provinces as well.

PROCUREMENT OF GARMENTS AND BLANKETS

Berlin Papyrus No. 1,564; A.D. 138

Copy of authorization. Ammonius son of Polydeuces and Syrio son of
Heras and Heraclides son of Heraclides, all three collectors of [requisi-
tioned] clothing, and Hermas, *ex-agoranomus,*[14] to the banker Heraclides,
greeting. Pay out to Heraclides son of Horigas, to Hero, freedman of
Publius Mevius, and to Dioscorus, freedman of the great god Sarapis,[15]
weavers of the village of Philadelphia, for themselves and all[?] the other

14. On the office of *agoranomus,* see introduction to § 49, second selection.
15. On the survival of Greek sacral manumission, see § 49.

weavers of the same village, on their mutual responsibility, [the following sums] as advance payment for the price of the clothing which the prefect [of Egypt], Avidius Heliodorus, *vir egregius,* ordered manufactured for the requirements of the armies in Cappadocia: for one belted tunic, white, length 3½ cubits, width 3 cubits 4 digits, weight 3¾ minas —24 drachmas on account; and for four Syrian cloaks, white, length 6 cubits each, width 4 cubits, weight 3¾ minas—24 drachmas each on account, equals 96 drachmas; total, 120 drachmas; and for the requirements of the infirmary in the imperial camp,[16] for one blanket, plain white, length 6 cubits, width 4 cubits, weight 4 minas—28 drachmas on account, making a total for this authorization of 148 drachmas of silver, less 6½ percent deducted for the imperial fisc from the 28 drachmas advanced for the blanket; on condition that they will use for the clothing only fine, soft, pure white wool, free of all dirt, and will produce the clothing well-woven, firm-textured, with finished hems, meeting specifications, flawless, and full value for the advance payment made them for these items. If at [the time of] delivery any of these items is missing or is appraised as inferior, they shall, on their mutual responsibility, pay the price of the missing items (together with dues and expenses) and the difference on the inferior items, delivering these promptly in the aforesaid sizes and weights and entirely apart from other public clothing requisitions which they owe. Year 2 of the Emperor Caesar Titus Aelius Hadrianus ANTONINUS PIUS, Thoth 12.

DELIVERIES OF GRAIN

Amherst Papyrus No. 107 (= Wilcken, no. 417); A.D. 185

To Damario, *strategus* of the Hermopolite nome, from Antonius Justinus, *duplicarius* [see note 18], dispatched by Valerius Frontinus, prefect of the Heraclian Company stationed at Coptus. Of the 20,000 artabs of barley ordered by the prefect [of Egypt], Longaeus Rufus, *vir clarissimus,* to be purchased from the harvest of the past twenty-fourth year for the requirements of the aforesaid company, I have received, in accordance with the assessment made by the nome officials, from the elders of the village of Terton Epa in the Upper Patemite district the quota imposed upon their village, viz., one hundred artabs of barley (100 art. barley) by the public receiving measure for the stipulated delivery. I have issued

16. It is uncertain whether this means the camp of the emperor himself, or merely the camp of imperial troops.

this receipt in quadruplicate. Year 25 of the Emperor Caesar Marcus Aurelius COMMODUS Antoninus Augustus Pius Armeniacus Medicus Parthicus Sarmaticus Germanicus Britannicus Maximus, Payni. . . .

[Signed] I, Antonius Justinus, *duplicarius,* have received the one hundred artabs (100 art.) of barley, as stated above.

> The Emperor Caracalla entered Syria with his army in A.D. 215. This papyrus gives us a rare glimpse of one of the measures taken to feed his army. The service here described was a liturgy (§ 77), the distance from Oxyrhynchus to Alexandria, about 250 miles.

Oxyrhynchus Papyrus No. 3,091; A.D. c. 216

To Aurelius Anubio, *strategus* of the Oxyrhynchite nome, [from] Aurelius Mousis . . . landowner in the village of Sinary. Having been named by the village clerk of these parts to convey to Alexandria barley being sent to Syria for the imperial army of our lord the Emperor Severus Antoninus Felix Pius Augustus, I swear by the fortune of our lord the Emperor Marcus Aurelius Severus Antoninus Caesar that I will at once undertake the service entrusted to me, or else may I be liable to the consequences of my oath. I have provided as my surety Aurelius Serenus . . . landowner in the said Sinary, here present and consenting. [Date, incompletely preserved.]

ACKNOWLEDGMENT OF PURCHASE FOR THE ARMY

> This waxed tablet, found in Frisia (northern Netherlands), records the purchase of a cow from a German farmer by a Roman, probably an army provisioner. The document is unique, and the text at points extremely abbreviated; the translation must therefore be based in part on conjecture. Especially noteworthy is the waiver of Roman legal formalities such as might lead to needless controversy or litigation.

FIRA, vol. III, no. 137; A.D. 29 or 116

I, Gargilius Secundus, duly and in lawful manner purchased a cow for 115 pieces[17] from Stelus son of Reperius, Beosian, of the estate of Lopetius, with Cesdius, first[?] centurion of Legion V, and Mutus Admetus, first[?] centurion of Legion I, as witnesses. Right to cancel[?] and formalities of Roman civil law are waived. Bought in the consulship of

17. Probably *denarii.*

Gaius Fufius and Gnaeus Minicius, September 9. Proper delivery vouched for by Lilus Duerretus, veteran.

[Witnesses] Titus Cesdius son of Titus, of Legion V; Numerius Junnius son of Marcus; Tiberius Lieuus Erepus son of Numerius, of Legion V; Gaius Seceduus son of Tiberius. [Seal] of the seller himself.

148. PERSONNEL RECORDS

The sheer bulk of the detailed records kept by each military unit was enormous. In addition to the listing of duties and assignments of individual soldiers (§ 143), there were voluminous daily records of the variations caused in a unit's strength by temporary assignments and permanent transfers and an annual or semiannual summary of the same. Examples of such records follow. All are, of course, in Latin, the official language of the army.

Brooklyn Museum Papyrus No. 24 (=*Journal of Roman Studies* [1977], 67:51–52);

A.D. c. 215

An Annual (or Semi-Annual) Summary from the Files of an Auxiliary Cohort of Infantry and Cavalry

Additions to the strength.

Transferred: from *cohors I Apamenorum Antoniniana*	
by Aurelius Septimius Heraclitus, prefect of Egypt	1 centurion
from the soldiers of *legio II Traiana Antoniniana Fortis*	
by the same prefect of Egypt	1 centurion
from the soldiers of *legio II Traiana Antoniniana Fortis*	
by the same prefect of Egypt	1 soldier
from *cohors I Apamenorum Antoniniana* by the same	
prefect of Egypt	2(?) soldiers
from the same cohort's cavalry unit by the same	
prefect of Egypt	1 soldier

. . . . .

[Deductions from the strength (several lines of text lost).]

posted to the fleet at Alexandria(?) by the same prefect of Egypt	1 soldier
invalided out by the same prefect of Egypt	1 soldier

died, among them 1 cavalryman, 1 camel–rider   7 soldiers
Total of those who have permanently left the strength,
   among them 2 centurions, 11 cavalrymen, 1 camel-
   rider   30 soldiers
Net remaining number, among them 6 centurions, 4
   decurions, 100 cavalrymen, 13 camel-riders   457 soldiers
Absent on assignments in the countryside   126 soldiers

[There follows a fragmentary list of temporary assignments off the base.]

Dura Papyrus No. 82; A.D. c. 233

March 27: net number of enlisted men 914, including 9 centurions, 8 *duplicarii*, 1 *sesquiplicarius*, 34 camel-riders (including 1 *sesquiplicarius*), 223 cavalry (including 5 decurions, 7 *duplicarii*, 4 *sesquiplicarii*), Twentieth Palmyrene Cohort of Severus Alexander.[18]

> Julius Rufianus tribune [gave the] watchword: . . . from the seven planets.
>
> Sent on missions 5 soldiers including 2(?) camel-riders: from the century of Marianus, Aurelius Licinnius; from the century of Pudens, Aurelius Demetrius; from the century of Nigrinus, Aurelius Romanus and Aurelius Rufus; from the squadron of Antoninus, Iarhaboles son of Odeatus.
>
> Returned: those previously dispatched with . . . from the squadron of Tiberinus. . . .
>
> Timinius Paulinus, decurion, announced the orders which had been sent. . . . "We will do what is ordered, and at every command we will be ready." Standing watch at the insignia of our lord Alexander Augustus were: decurion Timinius Paulinus, sacristan Aurelius Silvanus, ____ son of Vabalathus, overseer Aurelius Rubathis, ____ Iarhaeus son of Malchus, second overseer Claudius Agrippa, cavalryman. . . .
>
> March 29: net number of enlisted men 914 . . . Twentieth Palmyrene Cohort of Severus Alexander. . . .
>
> Sent to collect barley __ soldiers including __ cavalrymen.
>
> Sent as escort for the barley collectors __ soldiers from the century of Marianus. . . .

18. A *duplicarius* received double, a *sesquiplicarius* one and a half times, the base pay; see further below, note 47.

Returned: those previously dispatched to Atha, 2 soldiers from the century of Nigrinus, Julius Zabdibolus and. . . .

Returned: those previously dispatched to the governor's headquarters with letters, __ soldiers. . . .

Sent to procure wood for the bath: 1 soldier from the century of Nigrinus, Zebidas son of Barneus.

Timinius Paulinus, decurion, announced the order which had been sent. . . . [The rest is fragmentary.]

Of 146 Latin ostraca recently discovered in Tripolitania 117 turned out to contain records from the office of a military unit stationed there in the early to mid-third century. At full strength the unit would have numbered 80 men. Of the three ostraca published to date, only the following two are well preserved.

AE, 1979, nos. 643 and 644

December 24, unit strength	58
of them:	
bookkeeper	1
adjutant	1
guide for transients	1[19]
cavalry	8
market(?) duty	22
on watchtower	1
at the gate	1
at commanding officer's	1
doing construction work(?)	1
sick:	3
Sulpicius Donatus	
Titus Buzuris	
Aurelius Rufus	
at flogging	1
the rest, all told(?):	17
[with] Furnus	15
[at the] bath	2

19. This line was crossed out.

To Octavius Festus, decurion, my commanding officer, [from] Aemilius Aemilianus, soldier, greeting. I have sent you, my lord, with Macargus two *siddipia* of rice-wheat, which make twenty-four *modii*. Under the consuls to be after the consuls Tuscus and Bassus. Received January 21.[20]

R. O. Fink, *Roman Military Records on Papyrus* (Cleveland, 1971), no. 64; A.D. 156

Register of the month of August[21] in the consulship of Silvanus and Augurinus of the First Augustan Praetorian Mounted Cohort of Lusitanians,[22] which has been encamped opposite Apollinopolis Major in the Thebaid since July 8 in the consulship of Pontianus and Rufinus. [A.D. 131].

Prefect: Marcus Julius Silvanus son of Marcus, of the Quirine tribe, native of Thubursicum [in Numidia] began his duties on April 23 in the consulship of Commodus and Lateranus [A.D. 154], replacing Allius Pudentillus.

August 31.

Total number of men on January 1:   505
(includes 6 centurions, 3 decurions, 114 cavalry, 19 dromedary riders, 363 infantry).

Added since January 1

Appointed from civilian[23] by Sempronius Liberalis, prefect of Egypt: Sextus Sempronius Candidus (of the consulship of Silvanus and Augurinus),[24] April 27

Transferred back from the First Mauretanian Company of Thracians to office in the cohort: Aulus Flavius Vespasianus (of the consulship of Vibius and Varus) [A.D. 134]   1 centurion
March 2.   1 decurion

20. The consuls who had taken office in Rome on 1 January A.D. were not yet known in this location in North Africa, hence the dating as the year after the consuls of the preceding year.

21. The year in the Egyptian calendar ended in late August.

22. Units of the auxiliaries were named for the region where they were first recruited, and they retained their original names even after Hadrian instituted the policy of recruiting replacements in the regions where the units were stationed. Thus in this Lusitanian Cohort stationed in Egypt the new recruits mentioned below are clearly Egyptians, as may be seen from their names.

23. An appointment to officer rank directly from civilian status was rare, and was usually awarded to persons with "connections."

24. This is the year of enlistment, a necessary part of every soldier's identification.

Recruits, voluntary, approved by Sempronius Liberalis, prefect of Egypt, including 1 cavalryman, 1
dromedary rider: 9
In the century of Herculanus, Philo Isiognis[?] (of the
consulship of Silvanus and Augurinus), May 2[?] . . .
In the century of Marcus, Anubas Ammo (same consulship), May 2[?]
In the century of Gaianus, Gaius Sigillius Valens (same
consulship) . . .
In the century of Sempronianus, Ammonius . . . (same
consulship). . . .

149. THE FAMILIES OF SOLDIERS

All classes of soldiers through the grade of centurion were forbidden to
marry while in military service, and even legal marriages contracted before admission to the army were dissolved by entry into service. Despite
the official ban, most soldiers did "marry" and beget children during their
period of military service (cf. note 13). The practice was so common that
by the second century the emperors, without altering the illegitimate
status of such "wives" (legally, concubines) and children, allowed a soldier the privilege of drawing a will to provide for his family in the event
of his death during military service (cf. § 53 and p. 300). The ban on
soldier marriages was lifted in A.D. 197 by Septimius Severus.

RULINGS OF PREFECTS

Mitteis, no. 372 (in part); A.D. 114–42

Year 20 of the deified Trajan, Tybi 10 [January 5, A.D. 117]. Lucia
Macrina, represented by the advocate Fannius, stated that she claimed a
deposit from the property of the deceased soldier Antonius Germanus.
Lupus[25] declared: "We assume that such deposits are dowries. I do not
grant a trial for such causes, since a soldier is not permitted to marry;
and if you claim a dowry and I do grant a trial, I shall give the appearance of believing that the marriage is legal." . . .

Year 18 of Trajan, Phaophi 27 [October 24, A.D. 114]. Longinus Hy
. . . declared that he, a Roman citizen, had served in the First Cohort of

25. Marcus Rutilius Lupus, prefect of Egypt A.D. 113–117.

Thebans under Severus and had during military service cohabited with a Roman woman by whom he had begotten Longinus Apollinarius and Longinus Pomponius, and he requested that these sons be certified [as Roman citizens]. Lupus discussed it with his legal experts and declared: "The children will be so certified, as being born of a Roman woman. You desire also to make them [legitimate on the basis of this certification?], but I cannot make you their legal father."

Year 18 of Trajan, Payni 10 [June 4, A.D. 115]. Chrotis, represented by the advocate Philoxenus, stated that she, an Alexandrian, had married Isidorus, an Alexandrian; that thereafter, while he was serving in a cohort, she bore him a son, Theodorus, concerning whom she now petitioned, requesting that his inheritance tax be remitted if it had been neglected; and that it was clear from the will he had drawn that this was his son since he had made him heir to his property. The will of Julius Martialius,[26] soldier of the First Cohort of Thebans, was read. Lupus then discussed it with his advisers and declared: "Martialius could not while in military service have a legal son, but he made him his heir legally."

INHERITANCE RIGHTS OF SOLDIERS' CHILDREN

Berlin Papyrus No. 140 (= *Select Papyri*, no. 213 = *FIRA*, vol. I, no. 78); A.D. 119

Copy of a letter, translated from the Latin, of the Emperor Trajanus HADRIAN Augustus, posted, in the consulship of Publius Aelius[27] (for the third time) and Rusticus, in . . . at the headquarters of the winter camp of Legion III Cyrenaica and Legion XXII Deioteriana on August 4, which equals Mesore 11:

I am aware, my dear Rammius,[28] that those whom their parents acknowledged as their offspring during their period of military service have been debarred from succession to their paternal property, and this was not considered harsh, since the parents had acted contrary to military discipline. But for my own part I am very glad to introduce a precedent for interpreting more liberally the quite stern rule established by the emperors before me. Therefore, whereas offspring acknowledged

---

26. The Roman name acquired by Isidorus on entering the cohort.

27. The Emperor Hadrian. The text of this prescript is given according to the revision in A. Stein, *Die Präfekten von Ägypten* (Bern, 1950), p. 207, note 212.

28. Quintus Rammius Martialis, prefect of Egypt A.D. 117–119.

during the period of military service are not legal heirs of their fathers, nevertheless I rule that they, too, can claim possession of property in accordance with that part of the edict by which this right is given also to blood relatives. This grant of mine it will be your duty to make clearly known to both my soldiers and my veterans, not for the sake of seeming to exalt me to them, but in order that they may avail themselves of this privilege if they are unaware of it.

DECLARATIONS OF BIRTH OF SOLDIERS' CHILDREN

By the Aelian-Sentian and Papian-Poppaean laws of Augustus (see vol. 1, §§ 204–205), for every child born of lawful wedlock of two Roman citizens, the father (or his representative) was required to file a declaration with the appropriate official within thirty days after the birth. These declarations were recorded in a public register, and official notices were posted in a central place in Rome or in the provincial capitals, from which families might have certified copies made. Illegitimate children were until the reign of Marcus Aurelius excluded from the public register. Therefore, parents of children born during the father's military service frequently drew up unofficial attestations of birth, signed by witnesses, to provide *prima facie* evidence for establishing the child's civic status after the father's discharge and enfranchisement.

AE, 1937, no. 112; A.D. 127

Marcus Lucretius Clemens, cavalryman in the squadron of Silvanus in the First Cohort of Thracians, called the undersigned to witness and swore by Jupiter Best and Greatest and by the divinity of the deified emperors and by the *genius* of the Emperor Caesar Trajanus HADRIAN Augustus that while in military service he had become the father, by Octavia Tamustha, of a natural son, named Serenus, on April 25 in the year 11 of the Emperor Caesar Trajanus HADRIAN Augustus; and he stated that he made this attestation on account of the restriction imposed by military service, so as to be able to have proof at his certification of [citizen] status after his honorable discharge that he [Serenus] is his natural son.

Done in the winter camp of the First Cohort of Thracians opposite Apollinopolis Magna in the Thebaid, on May 1 in the year above-stated.

[Witnesses] Gaius Antonius Maximus, keeper of arms in the squadron[?] of Lucius Farsuleius; Marrius Antoninus, of the squadron of

Rufus; Gaius Barga, soldier in the squadron[?] of Lucius Farsuleius; Gaius Julius Marcellus, adjutant in . . . ; Titus Marsias Bammogalis[?] . . . ; Numerius Alexa son of Longus; Marcus Lucretius Clemens. . . .

Michigan Papyrus No. 169 (= FIRA, vol. III, no. 4); A.D. 145

Sempronia Gemella, acting with the approval of her guardian [see § 91], Gaius Julius Saturninus, called the undersigned to witness that on March 21 last she had borne twin sons of uncertain father, and that these are named Marcus Sempronius Sarapio and Marcus Sempronius Socratio, sons of Spurius: [i.e., "father unknown"]; and she stated that she interposed this attestation for the reason that the Aelian-Sentian and Papian-Poppaean Laws forbid illegitimate sons and daughters to be entered in the public register. . . .

Done at Alexandria on the coast of Egypt on April 29 in the consulship of the Emperor Caesar Titus Aelius Hadrianus ANTONINUS Augustus PIUS (for the fourth time) and MARCUS AURELIUS Caesar (for the second time), in year 8 of the Emperor Caesar Titus Aelius Hadrianus ANTONINUS Augustus PIUS, on the 4th day of the month Pachon.

I, Sempronia Gemella, with my guardian Gaius Julius Satornilus, called witnesses to attest that twin sons had been born of uncertain father and that these have been named Marcus Sempronius Sarapio and Marcus Sempronius Socratio, sons of Spurius, as stated above. I, Gaius Julius Satornilus, was designated her guardian, and I wrote for her since she is illiterate.[29]

[Witnesses] Marcus Vibius Pollio; Marcus Octavius Serenus; Lucius Aemilius Maximus; Lucius Caponius Saturninus; Gaius Aebutius Saturninus; Gaius Vibievius Crassus; Marcus Holconius Ampissus.

150. PRIVILEGES OF VETERANS: CITIZENSHIP AND LEGAL MARRIAGE

The length of military service was fixed by Augustus at twenty years in the legions. Before the end of his reign, veterans were kept in service an additional five years as active reservists assigned to light duties (cf. note 8). By the second century, the enlistment period was uniformly twenty-five years for all branches (including legions and infantry and cavalry

29. This summary paragraph is written in Greek, the *lingua franca* of the eastern part of the Roman Empire; the rest of the document is in Latin, the official language used in military circles.

auxiliaries), except for the fleets, where the term was one year longer, and the Praetorian and urban cohorts, who served sixteen years. The legions and elite Praetorian and urban cohorts were composed exclusively of Roman citizens. The provincials who served in the cavalry and infantry auxiliaries and in the fleets were granted Roman citizenship upon discharge. But in the second and third centuries the distinction in status between legions and auxiliaries tended to disappear. All classes of soldiers received upon discharge the right to contract a legal Roman marriage *(conubium)*, forbidden during military service; for many, however, this grant meant the legitimization of a long-established conjugal relation and the enfranchisement of offspring begotten during service. The grant of citizenship to veteran auxiliaries was until A.D. 140 uniformly made to the veteran, his children, and descendants; by then provincials were being admitted to the legions, and the grant was made thereafter to the veteran alone, and children born during military service did not receive the franchise until they enlisted in the legions—a regulation which gave new impetus to the tendency for military service to become a hereditary profession (cf. chapter 6, note 27).

Grants of honorable discharge were made by the emperor or, in the frontier provinces, by the provincial governor acting on orders from the emperor. These were not issued to each veteran as he completed his period of service, but from time to time to all eligibles in a military unit; as a result many veterans were obliged to remain in service beyond their time. The emperor's edict granting official discharge and citizen status was inscribed on bronze and posted in Rome; the veteran received a small bronze diptych, inscribed in his name and containing a copy of the emperor's edict, to serve him in civilian life as proof of his privileges. About two hundred of these military "diplomas" have been found in various parts of the Empire, especially in the frontier provinces. A perusal of this body of documents reads like a cross section of the peoples of the Empire and reveals how widely the manpower of the Empire was recruited to guard the frontiers.

CERTIFICATE OF DISCHARGE

A wooden tablet containing temporary certification of discharge to serve the veteran until the official bronze "diploma" became available.

Wilcken, no. 457 (=Dessau, no. 9,060); A.D. 122

Consulship of Marcus Acilius Aviola and Pansa, January 4. Titus Haterius Nepos, prefect of Egypt, granted honorable discharge to Lucius Valerius

Noster, cavalryman in the Gavian Squadron of the Vocontian Company, who had completed his service.

[Signature of prefect] I perused the foregoing statement and granted the honorable discharge. [January] 4.

MILITARY DIPLOMAS

CIL, vol. XVI, no. 12; A.D. 71

The Emperor Caesar VESPASIAN Augustus, *pontifex maximus,* holding the tribunician power for the second year, acclaimed *imperator* six times, father of his country, three times consul, has granted to the veterans whose names appear below, who served in the fleet of Misenum under Sextus Lucilius Bassus, completing twenty-six or more years, and who have been settled in a colony at Paestum,[30] to themselves, their children and descendants, citizenship and right of marriage with the wives they had when citizenship was granted them, or, if any were single, with those they might later take, limited to one wife for each man.

Done on February 9 in the consulship of the Emperor Caesar VESPASIAN Augustus (for the third time) and Marcus Cocceius Nerva.

Centurion Hezbenus Son of Dulazenus, Sappaean,[31] and His Son Doles[32]

Certified copy taken from bronze tablet posted at Rome in the Capitol at the altar of the Julian family, on the outer side at the foot, Tablet I.

[Witnesses] Decimus Liburnius Rufus, from Philippi; Gaius Sallustius Crescens, soldier in the century of Augurinus [?] in the Fourth Praetorian Cohort, from Philippi; Publius Popillius Rufus, from Philippi; Lucius Betuedius Valens, from Philippi; Lucius Betuedius Primigenius, from Philippi; Gnaeus Cornelius Florus, from Philippi; Gaius Herennuleius Chryseros, from Philippi.

30. Such specific mention in diplomas of settlement in a veterans' colony is found only in a group issued to men discharged from the fleets in A.D. 71. The veterans of the Misenum fleet were settled in that year at Paestum in southern Italy, those of the Ravenna fleet in Pannonia. Since this diploma was found in Thrace, it is evident that Hezbenus returned to his native land (cf. note 31). Cf. Tacitus, *Annals* XIV. xxvii (A.D. 60): "A further enrollment of veterans in Tarentum and Antium did but little to arrest the depopulation of these places, for most scattered themselves in the provinces where they had completed their military service."

31. The Sappaeans were a Thracian people.

32. Inclusion of wife or children by name is rare in these documents.

CIL, vol XVI, no. 21 (=Dessau, no. 1,993); A.D. 76

The Emperor Caesar VESPASIAN Augustus, *pontifex maximus,* holding the tribunician power for the eighth year, acclaimed *imperator* for the eighteenth time, father of his country, censor, seven times consul, consul designate for an eighth time. I have appended the names of the members of my personal bodyguard who have served in my Praetorian guard, likewise of the soldiers who have served in the nine Praetorian cohorts and the four urban cohorts. To these, who have bravely and dutifully completed their service, I grant the right of marriage, with one woman only and with first wives, so that even if they join to themselves in matrimony women of foreign legal status they may raise up children just as if they were born of two Roman citizens.

December 2 in the consulship of Galeo Tettienus Petronianus and Marcus Fulvius Gillo.

Sixth Praetorian Cohort: Lucius Ennius Ferox Son of Lucius, of The Tromentine Tribe, of Aquae Statellae[33]

Certified copy taken from bronze tablet posted at Rome in the Capitol on the base of the statue of the African Jupiter.

CIL, vol. XVI, no. 35; A.D. 88

The Emperor Caesar DOMITIAN Augustus Germanicus, son of the deified Vespasian, *pontifex maximus,* holding the tribunican power for the eighth year, acclaimed *imperator* seventeen times, fourteen times consul, censor for life, father of his country, has granted to the cavalrymen and infantrymen whose names appear below, who completed twenty-five or more years of service in three companies and seventeen cohorts stationed in Syria under Publius Valerius Patruinus—namely, the Second Pannonian, the Third Thracian Augustan, and the Veteran Gallic [Companies], and the First Flavian composed of Roman citizens, the First Thousand-Man, the First Lucan, the First Ascalonian, the First Sebastene, the First Ituraean, the First Numidian, the Second Italic composed of Roman citizens, the Second Thracian composed of Roman citizens, the Second Marine, the Third Thracian Augustan, the Third

---

33. In Liguria, northern Italy, modern Acqui. His diploma, however, was found near Constanta, Romania; cf. note 30.

Thracian Syrian, the Fourth Bracaraugustan, the Fourth Syrian, the Fourth Galician Lucan, the Pannonian Augustan, and the Musulamian [Cohorts][34]—to themselves, their children and descendants, citizenship and right of marriage with the wives they had when citizenship was granted them, or, if any were single, with those they might later take, limited to one wife for each man.

November 7 in the consulship of Marcus Otacilius Catulus and Sextus Julius Sparsus.

To Infantryman Bithus Son of Seuthus, Bessian,[35] of The Musulamian Cohort, Whose Commanding Officer is Marcus Caecilius September

Certified copy taken from bronze tablet posted at Rome in the Capitol on the left side of the Public Archives.

[Witnesses] Quintus Mucius Augustalis; Marcus Calpurnius Justus; Gaius Lucretius Modestus; Gaius Claudius Sementivus; Gaius Pompeius Eutrapelus; Gaius Julius Helenus; Lucius Pullius Verecundus.

GRANT OF CITIZENSHIP BEFORE DISCHARGE

Soldiers were sometimes discharged and granted citizenship before the completion of the regular term of service for bravery or physical disability.

AE, 1944, no. 57; A.D. 106

The Emperor Caesar Nerva TRAJAN Augustus Germanicus Dacicus, son of the deified Nerva, *pontifex maximus,* holding the tribunician power for the fourteenth year,[36] acclaimed *imperator* six times, five times consul, father of his country, has granted Roman citizenship before completion of military service to the infantrymen and cavalrymen whose names appear below, serving in the First British Thousand-Man Ulpian Decorated Loyal Fortunate Cohort composed of Roman citizens, which

34. The places or peoples after which these cohorts were named (cf. note 22) are as follows (only less familiar ones are listed): Lucan—probably Dalmatia (or Galicia); Ascalonian—southern Palestine; Sebastene—Samaria in Palestine [?]; Ituraean—Lebanon; Bracaraugustan—Tarragonese Spain; Galician—Spain-Portugal; Musulamian—Tripolitania.

35. The Bessians were a Thracian people; since his diploma was found in Thrace, Bithus obviously returned to his native land after his discharge; cf. note 30.

36. This is an error for *tenth.*

is on duty in Dacia under Decimus Terentius Scaurianus, for having dutifully and faithfully discharged the Dacian campaign.

August 11, at Darnithithium[?], in the consulship of Lucius Minicius Natalis and Quintus Silvanus Granianus.

To Infantryman Marcus Ulpius Novantico Son of Adcobrovatus, Rataean[37]

Certified copy taken from bronze tablet posted at Rome on the wall behind the temple of the deified Augustus, near [the statue of] Minerva.

[Witnesses] Publius Cornelius Alexander; Lucius Pullius Verecundus; Publius Atinius Amerimus; Gaius Tuticanius Saturninus; Lucius Pullius Trophimus; Gaius Julius Paratus; Marcus Junius Eutychus.

REQUEST FOR DISCHARGE CERTIFICATES

Italian Society Papyrus No. 1,026; A.D. 150

Certified copy taken from a petition posted together with others in the portico of Junia . . . containing the text which follows:

To Villius Cadus, legate of the emperor with rank of praetor, from twenty-two veterans of Legion X Fretensis who began their military service in the consulship of Glabrio and Torquatus or of Paulinus and Aquilinus [A.D. 125 and 126], and whose names are subjoined. Since we served, my lord, in the Praetorian Fleet of Misenum and, after transfer to the Fretensis Legion through the indulgence of the deified Hadrian, we maintained an unbroken record as good soldiers for over twenty years, now we have in most auspicious times been released from our military oaths and seek to go home to Alexandria on the coast of Egypt, and we ask that you deign to confirm in writing that we have been discharged by you, so that it may be plain from your confirmation that we have been discharged [from the said legion], not from the fleet, so that your subscript may be able to serve us as credentials in case of necessity and we may render thanks forever to your kindness.

[There follow the names of the twenty-two veterans, each with indication of the century in which he had served.]

37. That is, from Ratae in Brittany; but the diploma was found in Dacia (Romania), where the veteran presumably settled; cf. note 33.

I, Lucius Petronius Saturninus, submitted this petition on behalf of myself and my fellow veterans. I, Pomponius, wrote it.

Subscript: It is not customary for veterans from the legions to receive a written document, but you want the prefect of Egypt to be informed that you have been released from your military oaths by me under orders from our emperor. I shall give you such a document in addition to your bonus.[38] Post [this]. Done at the First Flavian Augustan Colony of Caesarea [in Palestine], January 22 in the consulship of Squilla Gallicanus and Carminius Vetus.

CERTIFICATION OF STATUS OF VETERAN

Hamburg Papyrus No. 31; A.D. 103

Extract from the register of certifications of status by the then prefect, Vibius Maximus, headed "Certifications of status by Vibius Maximus, with the tribune . . . son of Proclus [as adjutant], in year 7 of the deified Trajan, month Hathyr."

Reference—Page 27: Lucius Cornelius Antas, desiring to make his home in the Arsinoite nome with his wife and children, Heraclides aged __, Crispina aged __, and Ammonarion aged __.[39] The aforesaid Antas exhibited a bronze table (copy herewith), showing that he has been enrolled as a citizen together with his children and wife, viz.: "Lucius Cornelius Antas son of Heraclides, soldier "born in camp"[40] and *duplicarius*[41] of the Augustan Company, whose prefect is Messius Junianus, his wife Antonia daughter of Crispus, his son Heraclides, his daughter Crispina, his daughter Ammonarion." He has produced also a copy from the archives [in the temple] of Castor and Pollux containing the statement that he has served in the armed forces twenty-six years and has been honorably discharged; and he furnished three witnesses of his identity, Claudius . . . , Ignatius Niger, and Julius. . . . [The rest is lost.]

---

38. Since soldiers in the legions were normally Roman citizens, they needed no discharge document to attest that fact. The case of these veterans was, however, slightly anomalous because they had begun their service as noncitizens in the fleet before being transferred to a legion.

39. The blank spaces left for the ages of the children were never filled in.

40. That is, born while his father was in military service. Sons of ex-soldiers formed a specially privileged group in the legions.

41. A soldier receiving double pay as a reward for bravery. A soldier who received pay and a half was known as a *sesquiplicarius*.

151. PRIVILEGES OF VETERANS: IMMUNITIES AND EXEMPTIONS

In addition to Roman citizenship and legal wedlock (see § 150), honorably discharged veterans enjoyed various legal and economic privileges, including exemption from taxes, billeting, and other compulsory public services. During the second century, probably because of the growing economic crisis, their economic privileges were reduced; they were required to pay various taxes, and—in Egypt, at least—their general exemption from public services seems to have been limited to the first five years after discharge. Under the military monarchy of the third and fourth centuries these privileges were again increased.

EDICT OF DOMITIAN ON PRIVILEGES OF VETERANS

With this document should be compared the similar edict of Octavian (vol. 1, § 153).

Wilcken, no. 463, col. 2, lines 10–20 (=Dessau, no. 9,059=*FIRA*, vol. 1, no. 76); A.D. 88/89

The Emperor Caesar DOMITIAN Augustus Germanicus, son of the deified Vespasian, *pontifex maximus,* holding the tribunician power for the eighth year, acclaimed *imperator* sixteen times, censor for life, father of his country, declares: It has seemed appropriate to me to make known by edict that veteran soldiers among all of you are to be freed and exempt from all state taxes and customs tolls; that they, their wives, children, and parents . . . are to be Roman citizens with fullest legal right; that they are freed and released with total exemption, and their above-mentioned parents and children have total exemption by the same right and condition; and that the lands, homes, and shops of honorably discharged[?] veterans are not to be entered against their will. . . .[42] [The rest is lost.]

---

42. The last clause is garbled and mutilated. Our translation gives an approximation of the sense.

A VETERAN'S TAX EXEMPTION

SB, no. 12,508; A.D. 149

Aurelius Petronius [title lost] to Diophantus, royal scribe of the Arsinoite nome, Heraclides division, greeting. Achillas son of Harpocrates, cavalryman of the Vocontian wing—before his military service his name was Oronnous son of Rapaliōs(?) and Tamestremphi—residing in the village of Syngna, is recorded as having served in the army for more than twenty-five years. It is appropriate therefore to write [you] that in accordance with the grant of our Emperor most great he has been released from the payment of capitation taxes. [Hand of Aurelius Petronius] I bid you farewell. [3d hand, date.]

COMPLAINT OF A VETERAN

Berlin Papyrus No. 180 (= *Select Papyri,* no. 285); A.D. 172

To . . . from Gaius Julius Apollinarius, a veteran owning land in the village of Caranis. It has been decreed, my lord, that veterans are to have a five-year period of respite after their discharge. Yet despite this regulation I was molested two years after my discharge and was arbitrarily nominated for a compulsory public service, and from then until now I have been on duty without a break. Since there is a rigid ban on treating the natives in such a way, it ought much more to be observed in the case of myself who have served such a long time in the army. Wherefore I have been compelled to have recourse to you with a righteous request, and I ask you to secure for me an equivalent period of respite, in accordance with the decree on this subject, in order that I may be able to tend to my own property, now that I am elderly and alone, and may be forever grateful to your fortune. Farewell.

I, Gaius Julius Apollinarius, have submitted [this petition]. Year 12, Mecheir 29.

[Subscript] Submit your case to the *strategus,* and he will take suitable action.

PRIVILEGES GRANTED SOLDIERS BY CONSTANTINE

This bronze tablet, discovered in Hungary in 1930 on the site of the camp of the Legion I Adiutrix at Brigetio on the Danube, contains a letter from the Emperors Constantine and Licinius to the military commander in Illyricum decreeing improved tax privileges and discharge procedures for soldiers. The purpose of this ordinance was obviously to win and consolidate the loyal support of the troops after the recent civil wars by reaffirming and extending existing privileges.

AE, 1937, no. 232 (=*FIRA*, vol. 1, no. 93); A.D. 311

The Emperor Caesar Flavius Valerius CONSTANTINE Pius Felix Invictus Augustus, *pontifex maximus,* holding the tribunician power for the seventh year, acclaimed *imperator* six times, consul, father of his country, proconsul, and the Emperor Caesar Valerius Licinianus LICINIUS Pius Felix Invictus Augustus, *pontifex maximus,* holding the tribunician power for the fourth year, acclaimed *imperator* three times, consul, father of his country, proconsul.[43]

Copy of Sacred[44] Letter

Greeting, our dearest Dalmatius. Since we are ever desirous that due provision be made in all matters for the welfare and advantages of our soldiers in keeping with their devotion and labors, so also in this matter, dearest Dalmatius, we believe that provision must be made for our said soldiers through the foresight of our arrangements. Wherefore, observing the labors which our said soldiers in their incessant movements undergo for the stability and welfare of the state, we believe that provision and arrangement should be made so that during the period of their military service they may happily enjoy as a result of our foresight the pleasant fruits of their labors, and that after their military service they may obtain peaceful retirement and fitting security. Accordingly, we believe Your Devotion[45] should be notified that our said soldiers even in the period of their military service are to enjoy in consequence of our

43. The date of this prescript is about ten years later than the date placed at the end of the letter. Actually, the prescript was, it seems, omitted through inadvertence when the letter was inscribed on the tablet and was added in the upper margin years later.

44. That is, "imperial"; cf. p. 373.

45. This is one of the many honorific abstractions used, with the advent of the Dominate, in addressing officials.

decision an exemption of five *capita* [cf introduction to § 122] on property rating and on the customary deliveries of taxes in kind, and that
they are to have the same privileges also when they obtain honorable
discharge after completing the legal period of service [probably twenty-
four years at this time]; those, however, who have likewise obtained
honorable discharge although after only twenty years of service are to
enjoy an exemption from taxes in kind of two *capita,* that is both their
own and their wives'; anyone who happens to become disabled as a
result of a battle wound, even if he obtains release from his duties for
that reason before twenty years of service, is to share in the benefaction
of this same indulgence of ours so as to enjoy an exemption of his own
and his wife's *capita;* so that the said soldiers may rejoice that thanks to
our foresight provision has been made in every way both for the security
of their retirement and also for their welfare. It has hitherto been the
custom that a large number of men were issued their honorable discharge simultaneously by the general, with each man receiving a copy
for himself while the original of the discharge document remained in the
adjutant's office; we, however, desire that when soldiers obtain a discharge, either honorable or for disability as stated above, each shall
receive from the general a separate discharge addressed to him in person,
so that with this authentic and reliable proof in their own possession
they may enjoy undisturbed and lasting security. Of course, Your
Consecration [cf. note 45] realizes that those who are discharged for
offense cannot share in the benefaction of this same law, since both
things ought to be taken into account—the habits of a commendable life
and honorable discharge. Moreover, since it is only right that they
should know the fitting rewards decreed by us for meritorious military
service, so that the said soldiers may enjoy forever the perpetual benefaction of the said indulgence of ours and that the everlasting foresight of
our arrangements may acquire force, we desire the content of this indulgence of ours to be transcribed onto a bronze tablet and dedicated amid
the military standards[46] in each and every camp, so that alike the legionary soldiers of Illyricum and also the cavalrymen there organized in
detachments may enjoy equal benefits from our foresight, even as they
undergo equal labors in military service.

Added in the divine [cf. note 44] hand: Farewell dearest Dalmatius.

---

46. That is, posted in the camp sanctuary, where the military standards were kept.

In the consulship of the deified Maximianus, consul for the eighth time, and of our lord Maximinus Augustus, consul for the second time, June 10, at Serdica [modern Sofia].

Theodosian Code VII. xx. 2; A.D. 320 or 326

When he had entered the army headquarters and had been saluted by the prefects and tribunes and most eminent men, the acclamation arose, "Augustus Constantine! May the gods preserve you for us! Your salvation is our salvation. In truth we speak, on our oath we speak."

The assembled veterans cried out, "Constantine Augustus! To what purpose have we been made veterans if we have no special privilege?"

Constantine Augustus said, "I should more and more increase rather than diminish the happiness of my fellow veterans."

Victorinus, a veteran, said, "Do not allow us to be liable for compulsory public services and burdens in all places."

Constantine Augustus said, "Indicate more plainly. Which in particular are the compulsory public services that insistently oppress you?"

All the veterans said, "Surely, you yourself understand."

Constantine Augustus said, "Now be it manifest that this has been granted to all veterans by my munificence: that no one of them shall be liable for any compulsory municipal service, any public works, or any contribution. . . . In whatsoever public markets they participate, they shall not have to pay any imposts; the tax collectors also, as they are accustomed to collect more than is due . . . shall keep away from such veterans. After their labors the veterans shall forever enjoy tranquillity. By this same letter we have also prohibited our fisc from disturbing any one at all of these [veterans], but they shall be allowed to buy and sell [freely], so that they may enjoy their benefits unimpaired under the repose and peace of our era, and their old age may enjoy tranquillity after labors. . . ."

Theodosian Code VII. xx. 3; A.D. 320 or 326

Pursuant to our order, veterans shall receive vacant lands, and they shall hold them tax-free in perpetuity. They shall receive 25,000 *folles* in cash for the purchase of equipment necessary for farm life and also a pair of oxen and 100 *modii* of assorted grains. If, however, any veteran desires to engage in business, we permit him to have the sum of 100 *folles* tax-free. Except those veterans, therefore, who are established in homesteads or in businesses, all you who are unemployed and are engaged in no occupation should have recourse to this relief that you may not suffer want.

152. DISTINGUISHED MILITARY CAREERS

THE "CAPTOR" OF DECEBALUS

This Latin inscription is cut on a large stele that was found near ancient Philippi in Macedonia. In its present state with the bottom missing the stele stands almost 9 feet high. Under its corniced top is a relief showing a Roman cavalryman charging a fallen barbarian. Actually, the Dacian king Decebalus committed suicide to avoid being captured alive. Presumably the Maximus of this inscription seized the dying Decebalus. A second relief, below the capture scene, depicts two torques and two arm rings, which were some of Maximus' military "gifts," or decorations. Despite his voluntary prolongation of his enlistment to a total of thirty or more years, and despite his repeated decorations for bravery, Maximus' advancement in his career, in striking contrast to that of Maximianus below, was very slow. This inscription is the subject of an exhaustive commentary by M. Speidel in *Journal of Roman Studies* (1970), 60:142–153.

AE, 1969–1970, no. 583; A.D. c. 115

Tiberius Claudius Maximus, veteran, had this [tombstone] prepared while he was still alive. He served as cavalryman in *Legio VII Claudia Pia Fidelis,* was made quaestor of cavalry, an aide of the commander of the said legion and standard-bearer of cavalry, when also he was presented with [military] gifts by the Emperor Domitian for his valor in the Dacian war, made *duplicarius*[47] in the Second Wing of Pannonians by the deified Trajan, by whom he was also made a commander of scouts in the Dacian war and was twice presented with [military] gifts for his valor in the Dacian war and the Parthian, and by the same made centurion in the said Wing because he had captured Decebalus and had brought his head to the Emperor at Ranisstorum.[48] Discharged as *voluntarius*[49] with an honorable discharge by Terentius Scaurianus, consular [commander] of the army of the new province [Dacia]. . . . [The rest is lost.]

47. Literally "a recipient of double rations"; this term here designates one of the lower officers in an auxiliary unit.

48. Not hitherto known, this was presumably Trajan's most advanced camp in the Dacian war.

49. Presumably denoting a soldier who continued his service voluntarily after the expiration of the normal term of service, this term occurs here for the first time in this technical sense.

A BRILLIANT CAREER

AE, 1979, no. 601; A.D. c. 168

[The council and people of Ephesus honor] Junius Maximus, laticlave,[50] tribune of *Legio III Gallica;* recipient, from the best and greatest Emperors Antoninus [Marcus Aurelius] and Verus Augusti Armeniaci Medici Parthici Maximi for their most successful Parthian expedition, of military gifts, the mural and rampart crown,[51] the spear of valor and a banner, and likewise of an extraordinary donative; quaestor appointed without a vote of the senate; charged with the mission of [bringing] the laureate dispatch of the Parthian victory [to Rome]; propraetorian quaestor of the province of Asia.

WIDE-RANGING MILITARY SERVICE

The career of this man is notable not only for having taken him to far-flung reaches of the Empire, but also for the rapidity of his advancement, especially in the last ten years. Other extant inscriptions, filling the information gap where this one breaks off, tell us that he went on to become governor of the province of Numidia and then consul. This inscription was found in Libya, at the site of ancient Diana Veteranorum in the province of Africa.

AE, 1956, no. 124; A.D. c. 185

To Marcus Valerius Maximianus son of Marcus Valerius Maximianus, member of the Board of Five for Performing Sacrifices and priest of the colony of Poetovio, of the equestrian order; prefect of the First Cohort of Thracians; tribune of the First Cohort of Hamians made up of Roman citizens; commanding officer on the coast of Pontus Polemoniacus; presented with military gifts for the Parthia war; chosen by the Emperor Marcus [Aurelius] Antoninus Augustus and sent to the front during his German expedition with the mission of bringing food down the Danube to supply both armies in Pannonia; commanding officer of detachments of the praetorian fleets of Misenum, Ravenna and Britain, and likewise

---

50. The broad purple stripe worn by senators and by military tribunes of the equestrian order.
51. For these honors see chapter 1, note 75.

[commanding officer] of African and Moorish cavalry chosen for scout service; prefect in Pannonia of the First [Cavalry] Wing of Aravacans; at the German front praised in person by the Emperor [Marcus Aurelius] Antoninus and given the horse, military decoration and arms [of Valao] because with his own hand he slew Valao, the chieftain of the Naristians; in the same Wing recipient of the honor of his fourth campaign; as prefect of a wing of lancers presented with military gifts for the German and Sarmatian campaigns; commanding officer of cavalry of the Marcoman, Naristian and Quadian peoples for punishing those conducting the uprising in the East,[52] honored with centenarian rank; invested at that increased salary with the procuratorship of Lower Moesia and at the same time commanding officer, sent by the Emperor as procurator of Upper Moesia, of detachments to get rid of a band of Brisean brigands on the borders of Macedonia and Thrace; procurator of the province of Dacia; chosen by our most sacred Emperors [Marcus Aurelius and Commodus] for the senatorial order among the praetorians; soon after, commander of *Legio I Adiutrix;* likewise commander of *Legio II Adiutrix* in command of detachments wintering at Laugaricio;[53] likewise commander of *Legio V Macedonica;* likewise commander of *Legio I Italica;* likewise commander of *Legio XIII Gemina;* likewise as propraetor commander of *Legio III Augusta;* presented by our most noble *princeps* Marcus Aurelius Commodus Augustus with gifts during his second Germanic expedition; [dedicated] by the most honorable order [i.e., Senate] of Diana Veteranorum with money raised. . . . [The rest is lost.]

> A cavalry veteran living at Cotiaeum near the river Tembris in Asia Minor erected this tombstone for his wife. The Greek inscription suffered considerable damage when the stone was reused in house building. Still, we can discern that this cavalryman served in twenty-three provinces and dioceses, four cities, and five regions beyond the imperial frontiers. What is more, this inscription provides us with an example of a veteran who, before Constantine's conversion, was an openly declared Christian.

AE, 1981, no. 777; A.D. *c.* 300

Aurelius Gaius II, who served in *Legio I Italica* in [Lower] Moesia, was selected for *Legio VIII Augusta* in Germany . . . who as recruit served as apprentice cavalryman, then lancer, adjutant of a third-rank centurion,

52. The reference is to the revolt of Avidius Cassius in A.D. 175. It began in Syria and spread to Cilicia, Judaea and Egypt.
53. An outpost about 80 miles north of the Danube frontier.

adjutant of a staff centurion, adjutant of a chief centurion, adjutant of imperial aides . . . *Legio I Iovia Scythica,* who traveled around the empire, to Caria . . . Lydia, Lycaonia, Cilicia . . . Phoenicia, Syria, Arabia, Palestine, Egypt, Alexandria, India . . . Mesopotamia, Cappadocia . . . Galatia, Bithynia, Thrace . . . Moesia, the Carpians' territory . . . Sarmatia four times, Viminacium[54] . . . the Goths' territory twice, Germany . . . Dardania, Dalmatia, Pannonia . . . Gaul, Spain, Mauretania . . . then advancing and after much toil(?) I came to my native place Pessinus,[55] where I was brought up, [and am now] dwelling in Cotiaeum . . . in tribute to Julia Arescusa my own wife most dear I have erected this stele from [the fruits of] my own labors as a memorial till the Resurrection. Farewell all.

54. The town on the site of present-day Vienna.
55. A town in Galatia, on the border with Phrygia, famous as the site of the worship of Cybele.

8

ROMAN LAW

This chapter illustrates some of the general principles and basic concepts of the Roman legal system, whose continuing influence is apparent from the striking resemblance to legal principles and practices of the present day. Because of limitations of space no attempt has been made to sample the minutiae of cases and actions that constitute the bulk of the voluminous source materials for Roman law.

The jurists of the Republic and the Principate were concerned essentially with the meaning and application of legal rules; related matters, whether incidental (e.g., procedural, formulaic) or causal they disregarded almost completely. "The politico-economic conditions underlying the establishment of a legal rule are nowhere described or even mentioned,"[1] yet they are everywhere apparent to the modern reader. The growing and repeated insistence, for example, that the spirit or intent should prevail over the letter or wording of a statute or document, the increasing emphasis on the claim of equity, on the benevolent interpretation, on the benefit of the doubt, are all evidences of the progressive humanization of the law under the influence of social forces. (cf. § 50) The maxim "Letter of law is height of injustice" was already trite in Cicero's day.[2]

The Roman legal writers, however, showed a marked disinclination for abstract formulation of legal rules, preferring instead to make a point by citing one or more illustrative cases. Cicero, impressed by Greek systematization, complained that "jurisconsults split up into endless cases what can be stated in a single formulation."[3] In addition, the Roman jurists distinguished public law very carefully from private law, concentrating on the latter. In the provinces, where it was carried by Roman citizens and armies, the law of Rome was influenced by contact with native legal institutions, especially those of the Hellenistic law in the eastern provinces. Caracalla's Empire-wide grant of citizenship (see § 106)

1. F. Schulz, *Principles of Roman Law* (Oxford, 1936), p. 24.
2. Cicero, *On Duties* I. x. 33.
3. Cicero, *Laws* II. xix. 47.

accelerated the interaction of these and other forces, under whose influence the law of the city of Rome developed ultimately into the ecumenical legal system of Justinian's codification.

On the legal sources included in this chapter, see vol. 1, pp. 37–44. The specific topics and texts of §§ 155–159 should be compared with the relevant parts of §§ 153–154.

153. DEFINITIONS AND DIVISIONS OF THE LAW

Gaius, Institutes 1. i–xi, xlviii–xlix; From the translation of F. de Zulueta, *The Institutes of Gaius* (Oxford, 1946)

Every people that is governed by statutes and customs observes partly its own peculiar law and partly the common law of all mankind. That law which a people establishes for itself is peculiar to it, and is called civil law *(ius civile)* as being the law peculiar to that particular state *(civitas)*, while the law which natural reason establishes throughout all mankind is followed by all peoples alike and is called the law of nations *(ius gentium)*, as being the law observed by all peoples *(gentes)*. Thus the Roman people observes partly its own peculiar law and partly the common law of mankind. This distinction we shall apply in detail at the proper places.

The laws of the Roman people consist of statutes, plebiscites, decrees of the senate, imperial constitutions, edicts of those possessing the right to issue them, and responses of the learned. . . . An imperial constitution is what the emperor by decree, edict, or letter ordains; it has never been doubted that this has the force of statute, seeing that the emperor himself receives his *imperium* through a statute. The right of issuing edicts is possessed by magistrates of the Roman people. Very extensive law is contained in the edicts of the two praetors, the urban and the peregrine, whose jurisdiction is possessed in the provinces by the provincial governors; also in the edicts of the curule aediles, whose jurisdiction is possessed in the provinces of the Roman people by quaestors; no quaestors are sent to the provinces of Caesar, and consequently the aedilician edict is not published there. The responses of the learned are the decisions and opinions of those who are authorized to lay down the law. If the decisions of all of them agree, what they so hold has the force of statute, but if they disagree the judge is at liberty to follow whichever decision he pleases. This is declared by a rescript of the deified Hadrian.

The whole of the law observed by us relates either to persons or to things or to legal actions. Let us first consider persons.

The principal distinction in the law of persons is this, that all men are either free or slaves. Next, free men are either freeborn or freedmen. Freeborn are those born free, freedmen those manumitted from lawful slavery. . . .

Next comes another division in the law of persons. For some persons are independent and others are dependent upon another. Again, of dependent persons some are in the power of parents, others of husbands, and others of masters.

> [There follow illustrative cases of each category. After the law of persons Gaius takes up the law of things (books II–III), and then the law of legal actions (book IV).]

Justinian, Digest I. i, iii–iv[4]

(Ulpian, *Institutes* I)[5] Manumissions are also comprised in the law of nations. Manumission is the dismissal from hand *(manus)*, that is, the giving of freedom. For as long as anyone is in a state of slavery, he is subject to hand and control; when manumitted, he is freed from control. This had its origin in the law of nations, seeing that by natural law all were born free and manumission was not known since slavery was unknown; but after slavery made its appearance under the law of nations, the benefaction of manumission followed. And whereas we used to be called by the one natural name of men, under the law of nations there came to be three classes: freemen; in contradistinction to these, slaves; and a third class, freedmen, that is those who had ceased to be slaves.

(Hermogenianus, *Epitomes of Law* I) Under this same law of nations, wars were begun, peoples distinguished, kingdoms founded, ownerships marked off, boundary stones placed for fields, buildings erected, commercial relations, sale, hire, and obligations instituted, with the exception of a few which were introduced under civil law.

(Ulpian, *Institutes* I) Civil law is that which neither wholly departs from natural law or the law of nations nor is altogether subordinate thereto; thus, when we add to or subtract from universal law, we bring

---

4. Part of Title ii appears in vol. 1, § 25.

5. For illustrative purposes we include here and in § 154 the source citation (jurist and work) that precedes every *Digest* text. The names encountered in this references are those of eminent jurists from the late first to the mid-third or early fourth centuries.

about our own peculiar law, that is, civil law. Now, this law of ours exists either in writing or without writing . . . .

(Papinian, *Definitions* II) The civil law is that which is derived from statutes, plebiscites, decrees of the senate, enactments of the emperors, and the authority of the learned [in the law]. Praetorian law is that which was introduced by the praetors in order to clarify, supplement, or amend the civil law with a view to the public advantage. This is also called honorary law, so named after the public office *(honor)* of the praetors.

(Marcianus, *Institutes* I) Indeed, this very honorary law is the living voice of the civil law.

(Gaius, *Institutes* I) [Gaius' two opening sentences—see first selection, above—are quoted here.]

(Ulpian, *Rules* I) Justice is a constant, unfailing disposition to give everyone his legal due. The principles of law are these: to live uprightly, not to injure another man, to give every man his due. To be learned in the law *(jurisprudentia)* is the knowledge of things divine and human, the science of the just and the unjust. . . .

Statutes, Decrees of the Senate, and Long Usage

(Papinian, *Definitions* I) A statute is a rule of general application, a decision of prudent men, a restraint upon offenses committed voluntarily or in ignorance, a general covenant of the state.

(Marcianus, *Institutes* I) The orator Demosthenes defines it thus: "A law is that which all men ought properly to obey for many reasons, and chiefly because every law is an invention and gift of God,[6] a decision of prudent men, a means of correcting offenses intentional and unintentional, a general covenant of the city in accordance with which all in the city ought properly to live." And Chrysippus, the philosopher of the highest wisdom of the Stoics, begins his book *On Law* thus: "Law is the king of all things, both divine and human. It should be an indicator, ruler, and guide of both the good and the base, and accordingly a standard of just and unjust and of beings political by nature,[7] enjoining what ought to be done and forbidding what ought not to be done."

(Pomponius, *On Sabinus* XXV) Laws ought to be laid down, as Theophrastus said, in matters which happen "for the most part," not which happen "against reasonable expectation." . . .

6. Demosthenes actually wrote, "of the gods."
7. The phrase is the famous Aristotelian definition of man (*Politics* I. ii. 9).

(Modestinus, *Rules* I) The essence of a statute is this: to order, to forbid, to permit, to punish.

(Ulpian, *On Sabinus* III) Laws are not laid down with reference to particular individuals but for general application.

(Celsus, *Digest* XXVI, XXIX, XXXIII) To know the statutes means to grasp, not their wording, but their force and scope. Statutes ought to be interpreted rather liberally, so as to preserve their intent. . . .

(Ulpian, *On the Julian–Papian Law* XIII) The emperor is not bound by statutes.[8] The empress to be sure is bound by statutes, but the [reigning] emperor grants her the same privileges that he himself enjoys.

(Julianus, *Digest* LXXXIV) In cases where we have no written statutes to observe, that rule ought to be followed which has been established by custom and usage; and if such should be lacking in any matter, then that which is nearest and consequent thereto; and if even this cannot be found, then we ought to go by the law which is observed in the city of Rome. Long-standing usage is not unreasonably followed in place of a statute; and this is what is called the law established by custom. . . .

(Ulpian, *On the Office of Proconsul* I) It is the practice for usage of long standing to be observed in place of law and statute in such matters as do not come under a written rule. . . .

(Callistratus, *Questions* I) In fact our Emperor Severus ruled in a rescript that in ambiguities proceeding from statutes, usage or the authority of matters constantly decided in similar manner ought to acquire the force of a statute. . . .

Imperial Constitutions

(Ulpian, *Institutes* I) What the emperor has determined has the force of a statute; seeing that by a royal law which was passed concerning his authority the people transfers to him and upon him the whole of its own authority and power. Accordingly, whatever the emperor has laid down by letter with his signature, or has decreed upon judicial investigation, or has pronounced extrajudicially, or ordained by edict, amounts beyond question to a statute. Clearly, some of these are of individual application and are not extended into a precedent; for whatever an

---

8. On the emergence of this principle, see introduction to § 119.

emperor grants to anyone for his merits, or if he imposes any penalty or provides someone with unprecedented aid, it applies only to the individual. . . .

(Modestinus, *Excuses* II) Later enactments have more force than those which precede them.

154. GENERAL RULES OF LAW

Justinian, *Digest* L. xvii[9]

(Paulus, *On Sabinus* VIII) [cf. note 5] That which is faulty in the beginning cannot become valid with the passage of time.

(Ulpian, *On Sabinus* XXXVI) Not cohabitation but consent makes a marriage.

(Ulpian, *On Sabinus* LI) No one who has the power to condemn lacks the power to acquit.

(Ulpian, *On the Edict* XXVI) Anything not permitted the defendant ought not be allowed the plaintiff.

(Ulpian, *On the Edict* XXX) Advice not fraudulent entails no obligation; but if calculated deceit is involved, an action for fraud is in order.

(Paulus, *On the Edict* XXXIX) He who has knowledge [of a crime] but is unable to prevent it is free of blame.

(Ulpian, *On the Edict* XLVI) No one can transfer to another more legal right than he himself may possess.

(Gaius, *On the Urban Edict, Concerning Legacies* III) In cases of doubt, the more liberal interpretations should always be preferred.

(Papinian, *Questions* VI) Whenever the principle of natural desire or doubt as to the law blocks equity, the matter should be tempered by just decisions.

(Paulus, *Questions* XV) In all matters certainly, but especially in the case of law, equity should be given due regard.

(Scaevola, *Responses* V) If a copyist commits an error in transcribing the text of a stipulation, it in no way impairs the liability of the debtor and the surety.

(Ulpian, *Trusts* II) Superfluous matter ordinarily does not vitiate a document.

---

9. This, the final title of the *Digest,* contains 211 entries; only a selection is given here.

(Maecianus, *Trusts* XII) In ambiguous language the intention of the party who produced it should be given chief consideration.

(Paulus, *On Judicial Investigations*) When a statute makes mention of two months, a party who appears on the sixty-first day should be heard; for thus the Emperor Antoninus together with his deified father ruled in a rescript.

(Paulus, *On the Edict* I) No one may be forcibly removed from his own house.

(Paulus, *On the Edict* II) Liberty is a possession on which no evaluation can be placed.

(Paulus, *On the Edict* IX) In cases of obscurity it is customary to consider what is more likely or what the general practice is.

(Ulpian, *On the Edict* XI) Nothing is so contrary to consent . . . as force and fear, to approve which is contrary to morality.

(Gaius, *On the Provincial Edict* V) Freedom is beloved above all things.

(Paulus, *On the Edict* XIX) In case of equal [conflicting] claims, the party in possession ought to be considered in the stronger position.

(Paulus, *On the Edict* XXVII) The gravity of a past offense never increases *ex post facto*.

(Ulpian, *On the Edict* LXX) No one is compelled to defend a cause against his will.

(Paulus, *On Plautius* II) He inflicts an injury who orders it to be inflicted; but no guilt attaches to him who is obliged to obey.

(Paulus, *On Plautius* III) An act of a judge which does not pertain to his office is not valid.

(Paulus, *On Plautius* VI) When judgment is rendered against persons to the extent of their ability, their entire possessions are not to be taken away, but consideration is to be shown them so that they are not reduced to want.

(Paulus, *On Plautius* XVI) When the intent of a person granting manumission is obscure, a decision should be rendered in favor of freedom.

(Marcellus, *Digest* III) Although no change should be made lightly in legal formalities, still relief should be granted where equity clearly demands it.

(Celsus, *Digest* VIII) An obligation to do the impossible is null and void.

(Javolenus, *Epistles* VII) Whenever a judicial investigation cannot be made without injury, the course should be adopted which is productive of the least unfairness.

(Pomponius, *From Various Texts* IX) It is right under natural law that no one should increase his wealth through harm or injury to another.

(Ulpian, *On the Julian–Papian Law* I) An adjudicated matter is accepted as truth.[10]

(Paulus, *On the Julian–Papian Law* III) He who never had cannot be considered to have ceased to have.

Justinian, *Digest* XLVIII. xix. 18, 42

(Ulpian, *On the Edict* III) No one suffers a penalty for what he thinks.

(Hermogenianus, *Epitomes* I) By the interpretation of statutes penalties should be mitigated rather than increased in severity.

155. EQUITY AND CUSTOM

Cicero, *Classification of Oratory* xxxvii. 130; Adapted from *LCL*

"Equity" has a twofold meaning, one of which rests on the straightforward principle of truth and justice—of the "fair and good," as the phrase is[11]—while the other concerns requital, which in the case of a kindness is called gratitude and in the case of an injury retaliation. These things belong in common to nature and to law; but peculiar to law are the written and unwritten rules preserved by the law of nations or by ancestral custom. Of the written code, part is private and part public; the public code consists of laws, decrees of the senate, and treaties, while the private code includes compacts, covenants, and contracts. The unwritten rules are maintained either by custom or by the conventions and virtual consensus of men. And also—a point of primary importance—it is, in a way, prescribed by natural law that we shall preserve our own customs and laws.

---

10. An interesting instance of the application of this principle of *res adjudicata* is preserved in *CIL,* vol. VI, no. 266 (=*FIRA,* vol. III, no. 165). This inscription concerns a lawsuit brought in A.D. 226 before the prefect of the night patrol (probably in his capacity as superintendent of public thoroughfares), and twice appealed to subsequent holders of that office, one of them being the celebrated jurist Herennius Modestinus. Both these later prefects dismissed the case as already adjudicated, Modestus ruling, "Any matter which has been duly judged possesses its own authority."

11. This traditional definition of law continued in use for centuries and was included in the first citation of Justinian's *Digest.*

Justinian, *Code* VIII. lii. 2

The Emperor Constantine to Proculus.[12] The authority of custom and long-continued usage should not be treated lightly, but it should not of its own weight prevail to the extent of overcoming either reason or statute.

156. No Ex Post Facto Laws

Cicero, *Second Speech Against Verres*[13] I. xli. 106–xlii. 109; Adapted from *LCL*

Read please [from Verres' praetorian edict]: *"Any man who, since the censorship of Aulus Postumius and Quintus Fulvius or any following year . . . has done or shall do so."*

"Has done or shall do!" Did ever such an expression occur in an edict before? Did an edict ever before attach illegality, or liability to punishment, to an act that . . . there was no reason to avoid before it was issued? . . . It appears the Voconian Law enjoyed your approval. You might well have followed the example of Quintus Voconius himself, then. For his statute did not deprive any girl or woman of her position of heiress if she had it already; it merely enjoined that no one registered in the census after the year of the censors named should make a girl or woman his heiress in the future. In the Voconian Law we do not find "has done or shall do"; nor in any statute is a past action made subject to censure, except such as of their own nature are criminal and vile, so that they ought to have been avoided at all costs even if no statute forbade them. And even so we often find that a statute prohibiting such actions precludes prosecution of those who have already committed them. The Cornelian Laws on wills, for instance, and coinage, and a number of others, set up no new legal principle for the community but provide that what has always been in fact an immoral action shall become subject to criminal proceedings before the community after a fixed date. Surely, then, where a man introduces some innovation in *civil* law, he must allow all acts previously committed to be legally valid. Look at the Atinian Law, the Furian, the Fusian, the Voconian Law

---

12. The date of this imperial constitution is A.D. 319.
13. For Cicero's prosecution of Verres, see vol. 1, §§ 143, 144, 158, 188.

itself, as I have said, in fact all that are concerned with civil law: in all of them you will find the same thing, law that is to be binding on the community *after* the statute comes into force.

157. THE SPIRIT VS. THE LETTER OF THE LAW

Cicero, *In Defense of Caecina* xviii. 51–53; Adapted from *LCL*

Can it indeed be doubted that neither our own language, which is said to be deficient, nor even any other contains so large a store of words to distinguish every matter by a definite and peculiar term; or indeed, that words are superfluous when the matter is clear? . . . What statute, what senatorial decree, what magisterial edict, what treaty or agreement, or (to speak once more of our private concerns) what testament, what rules of law or undertakings or formal pacts and agreements can not be invalidated and nullified if we choose to sacrifice the meaning to the words without taking into account the plan, the purpose, and the intention of the writer? Why, the familiar speech of every day will not have a consistent meaning if we set verbal traps for one another. Even our authority at home will cease to exist if we allow our slave boys to obey our orders to the letter only, without paying any attention to the meaning implied in our words. And now I suppose I must produce examples of all these points . . . to support my plea that law does not depend on words, but that words are subservient to the purpose and intentions of men. This opinion was supported by the great orator Lucius Crassus . . . who proved to everyone, and with ease, that Manius Curius, who was named heir "in the event of the death of a posthumous son,"[14] was entitled to be the heir although the son not only was not dead, but had not even been born. Well, did the wording of the will provide adequately for this situation? Far from it. Then what was the deciding consideration? Intent. And if this could be made clear without our speaking, we should not use words at all; but because it cannot, words have been invented, not to conceal but to reveal intent.

14. *Posthumous* here has the sense of one born after the father's will was drawn, and not necessarily after his death.

Justinian, *Digest* L. xvi. 6, 219

The expression "in accordance with statutes" is to be taken to mean in accordance with the spirit of the statutes as well as in accordance with the words.

It has been held that in agreements the intent of the contracting parties is to be taken into consideration rather than the words.

158. Bona Fides

Cicero, *On Duties* III. xvii. 70–72; Adapted from *LCL*

It was Quintus Scaevola, the *pontifex maximus,* who used to attach the greatest importance to all questions of arbitration to which the formula "as good faith requires" was appended; and he held that the expression "good faith" had a very extensive application, for it was employed in guardianships and partnerships, in trusts and commissions, in buying and selling, in hiring and letting—in a word, in all the transactions on which the social relations of daily life depend; in these, he said, it required a judge of great ability to decide the extent of each individual's obligation to the other, especially as there were counterclaims in most cases. . . .

It is not only in the case of real-estate transactions that the civil law, based upon a natural feeling for the right, punishes trickery and deception; but also in the sale of slaves every form of deception on the vendor's part is disallowed. For by the aediles' edict, [the vendor], who ought to know if a slave is unhealthy, a runaway, or a thief, is responsible therefor [cf. chapter 2, note 94].

From this we come to realize that since nature is the source of right, it is in accord with nature that no one should so act as to profit by his neighbor's ignorance.

159. CRIMINAL LAW

CAPITAL PUNISHMENT

Justinian, *Institutes* IV. xviii. 1–2

Public trials are so called because generally any citizen at all has the right to institute their prosecution. Of public prosecutions some are capital, some are not capital. We call those capital which inflict the supreme penalty, or interdiction from fire and water, or deportation, or condemnation to the mines;[15] the others, if they impose public disgrace[16] and money fine, are public also but not capital.

BENEFIT OF THE DOUBT; INTENT

Justinian, *Digest* XLVIII; XIX. 5

. . . The deified Trajan ruled in a rescript to Assidius Severus that no one was to be convicted on suspicion alone, saying that it was better for the crime of a guilty person to be left unpunished than for an innocent person to be condemned. . . . In the case of major offenses it makes a difference whether something is committed purposely or accidentally. And, indeed, in all crimes this distinction ought either to elicit a strict penalty or to permit moderation.

INDIVIDUAL GUILT, NOT COLLECTIVE

Justinian, *Digest* XLVIII. xix. 26; L. xviii. III, 164

The guilt or punishment of a father can impose no stigma upon the son; for every individual is subjected to treatment in accordance with his own action and no one is made the inheritor of the guilt of another, as the deified brothers stated in a rescript addressed to the city of Hierapolis.[17]

15. The "supreme penalty" means death; "interdiction from fire and water," exile. Deportation was usually to an island. A citizen's *caput* was either his head or, politically speaking, his civic status (cf. vol. 1, p. 392); hence, those penalties that entailed the impairment of *caput* in one sense or the other were all forms of "capital punishment."

16. *Infamia*, or public disgrace, was visited upon Roman citizens for any of a variety of criminal or moral offenses, such as dishonorable discharge from the army, engagement in a dishonorable occupation (such as acting or procuring), conviction on a charge of violation of a trust, slander, theft, and the like.

17. "The deified brothers" refers to the Emperors Marcus Aurelius and Lucius Verus. The em-

Legal actions which are penal as a result of such infractions as theft, damage, armed robbery, or injuries do not carry over to an heir.

Penal cases once accepted [by the court] can be carried over to heirs.

EXTENUATING CIRCUMSTANCES

Justinian, *Digest* L. xvii. 108 and 155. 2

In inflicting penalties, the age and inexperience of the guilty party must be taken into account.

In penal cases the most benevolent construction should be adopted.

CAPITAL CRIMES

Paulus, *Opinions* v. xxii–xxiv (abridged)

Concerning Seditious Persons[18]

Instigators of sedition and riot or rousers of the people are, according to the nature of their rank, either crucified, thrown to wild beasts, or deported to an island. As for those who dig up or plow up boundary stones or destroy boundary trees, if slaves do it of their own volition, they are condemned to the mines; if humble persons, to [labor on] public works; if of superior rank, they are deprived of one third of their property and relegated to an island or driven into exile. Roman citizens who permit themselves or their slaves to be circumcised under the Jewish rite are deprived of their property and relegated to an island for life; the physicians [who perform the operation] suffer capital punishment. . . .

On the Cornelian Law Concerning Assassins and Poisoners[19]

The Cornelian Law inflicts the penalty of deportation on a person who kills a man, or carries a weapon for that purpose or to commit robbery, or has in his possession, sells, or prepares poison for the purpose of killing a man, or gives false testimony so that some one may lose his life, or causes a death. For all these crimes it has been decreed that capital

---

perors, especially in the first century, did not always abide by this precept, as, for example, when Nero punished the children of the men involved in the conspiracy of Piso by banishment, death, or deprivation of livelihood (Suetonius, *Life of Nero* xxxvi).

18. Cf. also § 6.

19. A law passed c. 81 B.C., in the dictatorship of Lucius Cornelius Sulla.

punishment shall be meted out to persons of superior rank; humble persons, however, are either crucified or thrown to wild beasts.

One who kills a man is sometimes acquitted, and one who does not kill is condemned as a homicide, for an individual's purpose and not his act is punished. Therefore, one who intended to kill but was unable to accomplish the crime through some accidental circumstance is punished as a homicide, and a person who accidentally and inadvertently kills a man by throwing a weapon is acquitted. . . .

A judge who takes money [for a decision] against the life or property of a man is deprived of his property and deported to an island.

Instigators of murder are punished in the same way as homicides. . . .

Persons who administer abortion potions or love philtres—even if they do not do so with evil intent, nevertheless, as it is an evil practice —are, if humble, deported to the mines; if of superior rank, deprived of part of their property and relegated to an island. But if the man or the woman perishes as a result, they are visited with the supreme penalty.

Persons who perform, or cause to be performed, impious or nocturnal rites in order to enchant, bewitch, or bind, are crucified or thrown to wild beasts. . . . It has been decreed that persons who are privy to the art of magic shall be visited with the supreme penalty, that is, be thrown to wild beasts or crucified. The magicians themselves are burned alive. No one is permitted to have books on the art of magic in his possession; those in whose possession they are found (the books are burned in public) are deprived of their property and deported to an island if of superior rank, and suffer capital punishment if humble. Not only the profession but even the knowledge of this art is prohibited. . . .

On the Pompeian Law Concerning Parricides[20]

Persons who kill father or mother, grandfather or grandmother, brother or sister, patron or patroness, although formerly they were sewn up in a sack and hurled into the sea,[21] are nowadays burned alive or offered to wild beasts.

---

20. This law was passed in one of the consulships of Pompey the Great (70, 55, or 52 B.C.).

21. Cf. Justinian, *Institutes* IV. xviii. 6: "The Pompeian Law on parricides provides that if anyone hastens the death of a parent or any relation comprehended in the term of 'parricide' . . . he will be subjected neither to sword nor to fire nor to any other ordinary punishment, but he is to be sewn up in a sack with a dog, a cock, a snake, and an ape, and . . . cast into the nearby sea or river, so that he may begin while still alive to be deprived of all enjoyment of the elements and may be denied the light of heaven while living and the earth when dead."

160. Rules of Evidence

Acts of the Apostles 25: 16

It is not the Roman custom to condemn any man before the accused meets his accusers face to face and has an opportunity to defend himself against the charge.

Justinian, *Digest* xxii. iii. 2

The burden of proof is upon the party affirming, not on the party denying.

Justinian, *Digest* xxii. v. (abridged)

The credibility of witnesses should be carefully weighed. Therefore, in investigating their persons attention should be paid first of all to the rank of each, whether a man is a decurion or a plebeian; and whether his life is honorable and blameless or on the contrary he is a man branded with public disgrace [see note 16] and is reprehensible; whether he is rich or poor, so that he may readily do something for the purpose of gain;[22] whether he is hostile to the party against whom he bears testimony, or friendly to the party for whom he gives testimony. For if his testimony is free from suspicion either in view of the person by whom it is borne (because he is honorable), or in view of his motives (because he is motivated neither by gain, nor by favor, nor by hostility), he is to be admitted. Therefore the deified Hadrian stated in a rescript to Vivius Varus, governor of the province of Cilicia, that the person sitting in judgment is better able to know how much credence should be placed in witnesses. The wording of the letter is as follows: "You are better able to know how much credence should be placed in the witnesses; who they are and of what rank and reputation; which among them have apparently spoken frankly; whether they have offered one and the same premeditated story or have without preparation made true-sounding answers to the questions you put to them."

There is extant also a rescript of the same emperor to Valerius Verus on ascertaining the credibility of witnesses, in the following terms: "No adequate ruling can be laid down with any fixed precision as to what

---

22. Juvenal in his famous Third Satire remarks bitterly on how the credibility of witnesses varied with their wealth: see p. 52.

manner of evidence is sufficient to constitute proof of a given matter. Though not always, yet often the truth of a given matter is discovered without public records. In some cases, the number of the witnesses, in others their rank and authority, in still others, for example, their unanimous reputation, confirms the credibility of the matter under investigation. Therefore, I can write you only this in brief, that a judicial investigation certainly ought not to be confined exclusively to one kind of proof, but you have to determine what in your best judgment you are to believe or what you think has not been proved to your satisfaction." . . .

The Julian Law Concerning Violence [enacted probably in the principate of Augustus] provides that the following are not permitted to give testimony under this statute against a defendant: a person who has obtained freedom from him or his father, or persons who are under age, or anyone who has been condemned in a public trial and has not been completely reinstated, or who is in chains or in a public prison, or who has hired himself out to fight with wild beasts, or any woman who is or has been a prostitute, or anyone who has been sentenced or convicted for having taken money for giving or withholding testimony. For some persons should not be admitted to credibility of testimony because of deference to persons, others because of the unreliability of their judgment, and still others because of the stigma and public disgrace of their lives.

Witnesses should not be summoned rashly from great distances, and much less should soldiers be called away from their units or duties for the purpose of presenting testimony, as the deified Hadrian ruled in a rescript. . . .

The deposition of a slave is to be believed when there is no other proof for getting at the truth.

A father is not a competent witness for a son, nor a son for a father.

It is understood that no one is a competent witness in his own case. . . .

If the circumstances of a case are such that we are compelled to admit a gladiator or similar person [i.e., a slave; cf. introduction to § 50] as a witness, his testimony is not to be believed unless taken under torture. . . . If some of the witnesses contradict the others, even though they are a minority [they may] be believed . . . for it is not to numbers that one must look, but to the sincere credibility of the witnesses and to the testimony in which the light of truth most probably resides.

9

THE CONFLICT OF RELIGIONS AND THE TRIUMPH OF CHRISTIANITY

161. ROMAN STATE RELIGION

During the first two centuries of the Empire the official state religion was an amalgam of the traditional native ritual as rehabilitated by Augustus and of the ruler cult instituted by him. The formal ceremonials of the native religion were almost exclusively the domain of the senatorial aristocracy, who conservatively preserved its legalistic formulas and antiquated priesthoods. In its domestic counterpart the native cult survived longest among the country folk *(pagani)*. But all through the Principate the older gods of the state cult—with the exception of the Capitoline Triad of Jupiter, Juno, and Minerva (cf. vol. 1, chapter 1, note 15)— declined steadily in importance and became, in fact, adjuncts of the increasingly dominant cult of the imperial house (§ 162).

RELIGIOUS FORMALISM

Pliny, *Natural History* XXVIII. iii. 10–12, iv. 18

To slaughter a sacrificial victim without a prayer does not seem to be of any avail or to constitute due consultation of the gods. In addition, there is one formula for obtaining favorable omens, another for averting evil, another for praising the gods. And we see that the highest magistrates employ definite formulas in their prayers, that not a single word may be omitted or said out of its proper place, that someone dictates from writing [the formula to the magistrate], and another is assigned as watcher to listen carefully, and a third is placed in charge of ordering that ceremonial silence be maintained, while a flutist plays to prevent any other words from being heard. There are memorable instances on record of the times when unlucky portents impeded and spoiled [the ceremony], and when there was a mistake in the prayer. . . . There still exists an outstanding example in the formula by which the Decii, father and son, devoted themselves [see vol. 1, § 55]; there is also preserved the prayer which the Vestal Tuccia employed to ward off violation of chastity as she carried water in a sieve, in the 609th year of the city [145 B.C.]. Indeed, even our own age has seen a Greek man and woman, or persons of some other people with whom we had difficulties then, buried alive in the cattle market [cf. vol. 1, p. 509–10]. If anyone should read the prayer used for this ritual, which is customarily dictated by the master of the College of Fifteen [cf. vol. 1, p. 612–16; vol. 2, pp. 519–20], he would assuredly admit the potency of the formulas, all of which are confirmed by the experience of 830 years. . . .[1] Verrius Flaccus [a scholar and teacher of the Augustan period] cites authors whom he considers reliable to show that in sieges it was the practice of the Roman priests before all else to summon forth the tutelary divinity of the town and to promise him the same or more splendid rites among the Romans [see vol. 1, pp. 152–54], and this ritual still exists in the discipline of the pontiffs.

THE REBUILDING OF THE CAPITOL

In A.D. 70, Vespasian restored the temple of Jupiter Best and Greatest on the Capitoline Hill, the center of the state cult, which had been razed by fire the previous year. After another fire in 80, it was rebuilt by Domitian, and survived until 455.

Tacitus, *Histories* IV. liii

The supervision of the rebuilding of the Capitol was entrusted by Vespasian to Lucius Vestinus [see § 15, third selection], a man of the equestrian order, in influence and reputation on a par with the nobility. The soothsayers assembled by him directed that what was left of the old shrine should be carried away to the marshes, and a new temple should be erected on the original site, declaring that the gods were unwilling that the old plan be altered. On June 21, beneath a cloudless sky, the entire space devoted to the sacred precinct was encircled with fillets and garlands. Soldiers who had auspicious names entered with boughs of

1. That is, from the traditional date of the founding of Rome, 753 B.C., to the time when Pliny was writing.

good-omened trees. Next, the Vestal Virgins, together with boys and girls both of whose parents were alive, sprinkled it with water drawn from springs and rivers. Then the praetor Helvidius Priscus, in terms dictated by the pontiff Plautius Aelianus, having first purified the area with pig-sheep-bull sacrifices and placed the entrails on an altar of turf, prayed to Jupiter, Juno, and Minerva, and to the tutelary gods of the Empire, to prosper the undertaking and by their divine help to raise up their abodes begun by human piety. He then touched the fillets which were wound around the foundation stone and entwined around the ropes. At the same time the other magistrates, the priests, senators, *equites,* and a great part of the people, uniting their efforts with zeal and joy, dragged the huge stone. Everywhere there were thrown into the foundations contributions of silver and gold, and of virgin metals never smelted in furnaces but in their natural state; the soothsayers had previously declared that the work should not be defiled by stone or gold intended for any other purpose. The height of the temple was increased; this was the only variation which religious scruple permitted, and the one feature which had been thought wanting in the magnificence of the old temple.

RITUAL OF THE ARVAL PRIESTS

The Arval Brotherhood, devoted to the worship of the agricultural deity Dea Dia, had its origin in the time of the early Roman kingdom (see vol. 1, § 11, where the primitive hymn still sung in the third century is given). Reestablished by Augustus, this priestly college, which included the emperor, continued its traditional activities until the collapse of the native religion in the late third or early fourth century. It is noteworthy that the priesthood devoted most of its activity to expressions of loyalty to the ruling house. The twelve members of the college met in a sacred grove near Rome, where extensive remains of the inscribed record of their proceedings, dating from 21 B.C. to A.D. 241, have been found. Only a brief selection from these lengthy archives of the Arval priests is given here.

CIL, vol. VI, no. 2,041 (=Dessau, no. 229); A.D. 58–59

In the same consulship, on October 13, Lucius Salvius Otho Titianus, master of the college, performed the following sacrifices in the name of the Arval Brethren in the Capitol in behalf of the rule of NERO Claudius

Caesar Augustus Germanicus: to Jupiter, an ox; to Juno, a cow; to Minerva, a cow; to Public Felicity, a cow; to the *genius* of the emperor, a bull; to the deified Augustus, an ox; to the deified Augusta, a cow; to the deified Claudius, an ox. Present in the college: Lucius Salvius Otho Titianus, master of the college, Gaius Piso, Gaius Vipstanus Apronianus, Marcus Valerius Messalla Corvinus, Aulus Vitellius, Sulpicius Camerinus, Publius Memmius Regulus, Titus Sextius Africanus.

In the same consulship, on November 6, Lucius Salvius Otho Titianus, master of the college, in the name of the Arval Brethren performed the following sacrifices in the Capitol for the birthday of Agrippina, mother of the emperor: to Jupiter, an ox; to Juno, a cow; to Minerva, a cow; to Public Safety, a cow; to the Concord of the Emperor, a cow. Present in the college: [Three members are listed.]

In the same consulship, on December 4, Lucius Salvius Otho Titianus, master of the college, in the name of the Arval Brethren performed the following sacrifices in the Capitol for the tribunician power of NERO Claudius Caesar Augustus Germanicus: to Jupiter, an ox; to Juno, a cow; to Minerva, a cow. Present in the college: [Six members are listed.]

In the consulship of Gaius Vipstanus Apronianus and Gaius Fonteius Capito, on January 3 [see introduction to § 3], Lucius Piso son of Lucius, master of the college, in the name of the Arval Brethren pronounced vows for the safety of NERO Claudius Caesar Augustus Germanicus, son of the deified Claudius, grandson of Germanicus Caesar, great-grandson of Tiberius Caesar Augustus, great-great-grandson of the deified Augustus, *pontifex maximus,* holding the tribunician power for the fifth year, acclaimed *imperator* six times, three times consul, consul designate for a fourth time, and of his wife Octavia, sacrificing victims in the Capitol in fulfilment of the vows which the master of the preceding year had made, and he pronounced the vows for the next year, in terms dictated by the consul Gaius Vipstanus Apronianus, as recorded below: to Jupiter, two oxen; to Juno, two cows; to Minerva, two cows; to Public Safety, two cows; in the new temple to the deified Augustus, two oxen; to the deified Augusta, two cows; to the deified Claudius, two oxen. Present in the college: [Five members are listed.]

In the same year, on January 12, in the Pantheon, Lucius Calpurnius Piso son of Lucius, master, with Gaius Vipstanus Apronianus, consul, Lucius Salvius Otho Titianus, Marcus Aponius Saturninus, Marcus Valerius Messalla Corvinus, Sulpicius Camerinus, and Titus Sextius Africanus, Arval Brethren, being present, Lucius Calpurnius son of

Lucius, master, proclaimed a sacrifice to Dea Dia, in terms dictated by Lucius Salvius Otho Titianus, on May 27 at his home, on May 29 in the grove and at his home, and on May 30 at his home. Present in the college: the same as recorded above.

CIL, vol. VI, no. 2,065, lines 15–40 (=Dessau, no. 5,037); A.D. 87

In the consulship of Gaius Bellicus Natalis Tebanianus and Gaius Ducenius Proculus, May 19, in the grove of Dea Dia, during the mastership of Gaius Julius Silanus, under the supervision of Gaius Nonius Bassus Salvius Liberalis, the Arval Brethren made a sacrifice to Dea Dia. Gaius Salvius Liberalis, acting master in place of Gaius Julius Silanus, before the grove sacrificed on the altar two expiatory sows for the pruning and the work done in the grove;[2] then he sacrificed a white honorary cow to Dea Dia. Gaius Salvius Liberalis Nonius Bassus, Lucius Maecius Postumus, Aulus Julius Quadratus, Publius Sallustius Blaesus, Quintus Tillius Sassius sat down in the tetrastyle and dined from the sacrifice, and assuming their purple-bordered robes and wreaths with ears of grain and fillets, they ascended the grove of Dea Dia to the retreat, and through Salvius Liberalis Nonius Bassus, acting master, and Quintus Tillius Sassius, acting flamen, they sacrificed a fat lamb to Dea Dia, and when they had completed the sacrifice they all offered incense and wine. Then, after the wreaths were brought in and the images were anointed, they made Quintus Tillius Sassius annual master from the coming Saturnalia to the next, likewise Tiberius Julius Celsus Marius Candidus flamen; then they descended to the tetrastyle and there, reclining on couches, they dined in honor of[?] the master Gaius Julius Silanus. After the banquet, veiled and wearing sandals and a wreath plaited with roses, he ascended to the retreat above the starting point and sent a signal to the charioteers and acrobats, who were supervised by Lucius Maecius Postumus; he honored the victors with palms and silver wreaths. On the same day in Rome at the home of Gaius Julius Silanus the same persons dined as had dined in the grove.

---

2. That is, to expiate the work done to keep the grove in good condition. It was forbidden, for example, to bring iron into the grove.

CIL, vol VI, no. 2,074, lines 22–33 (=Dessau, no. 5,035); A.D. 101

In the consulship of Quintus Articuleius Paetus and Sextus Attius Suburanus, on March 25, in the Capitol, the Arval Brethren proclaimed vows for the safety, return, and victory of the Emperor Caesar Nerva TRAJAN Augustus Germanicus, in the words recorded below:

"O Jupiter Best and Greatest, we pray, beseech, and supplicate that you will cause the Emperor Caesar Nerva TRAJAN Augustus Germanicus, son of the deified Nerva, our *princeps* and father, *pontifex maximus,* holding the tribunician power, father of his country, of whom we deem that we are speaking, prosperously and happily to return safe and victorious from those places and provinces to which he is going, and grant him a felicitous issue of those affairs which he is now conducting and will conduct, and preserve him in his present condition or better, and convey him back safe and victorious to the city of Rome at the earliest possible time—and may you so do these things!—then we vow that you shall have, in the name of the Arval Brethren, a gilded ox." [This is followed by similar vows to Juno the Queen, Minerva, Jupiter Victor, Public Safety, Father Mars, Mars Victor, Victory, Fortune the Home-bringer, Mother Vesta, Father Neptune, Hercules Victor. The occasion of these vows was the opening of Trajan's first Dacian campaign.]

THE SECULAR GAMES

The 110-year cycle adopted by Augustus for the solemn Secular Games (see vol. 1, § 206) was followed by Domitian and by Septimius Severus and Caracalla, who celebrated the famous "centennial" event in A.D. 88 and 204. The Emperors Claudius, Antoninus Pius, and Philip the Arab, adhering to the tradition of the 100-year cycle, conducted the games in A.D. 47, 147, and 248, the last time the games were celebrated, on the occasion of Rome's thousandth birthday (see § 118).

CIL, vol. VI, no. 32,327 (=Dessau, no. 5,050a) and Accademia Nazionale dei Lincei, *Notizie degli Scavi,* 1931, pp. 322–345; (=AE, 1932, no. 70); A.D. 204.

. . . [Geta Caesar] sacrificed to Mother Earth a pregnant sow as a whole burnt offering according to the Greek-Achaean rite, with the following prayer: "O Mother Earth! As it has been prescribed for thee in those books—and by virtue of this may every good fortune come to the Roman people, the Quirites—let sacrifice be made to thee with a perfect pregnant sow as a whole burnt offering. I beseech and pray thee, just as thou hast increased the empire and majesty of the Roman people, the Quirites, in war and in peace, so may the Latins ever be obedient," the rest as above. He followed the order of sacrifice in the same manner as on the first night to the Fates, and having completed the sacrifice, placed aside his fringed tunic . . . with the other members of the College of Fifteen, were present at the night games. Julia Augusta, mother of the camps [honorary title of Julia Domna, wife of Septimius Severus], and the 109 matrons held *sellisternia* for Juno and Diana.

On June 3 the Emperors Severus and Antoninus Augusti, together with Geta Caesar, the Praetorian prefects, and the other members of the College of Fifteen . . . proceeded to the Temple of Apollo on the Palatine garbed in the purple-bordered toga and wearing wreaths, and there Severus Augustus at the temporary wooden altar . . . in the precinct of Apollo before the tetrastyle . . . in terms dictated by his son Antoninus Augustus, assisted by Geta Caesar, the Praetorian prefects and the other members of the College of Fifteen, made it sacred with incense and honorary wine; then Severus Augustus made a sacrifice to Apollo and Diana of nine sacrificial cakes, nine *popana,* and nine *phthoes,* with the following prayer which he himself read: "O Apollo! As it has been prescribed for thee in those books—and by virtue of this may every good fortune come to the Roman people, the Quirites—let sacrifice be made to thee with nine sacrificial cakes, nine *popana,* and nine *phthoes.* I beseech and pray thee, just as thou hast increased the empire and majesty of the Roman people, the Quirites, in war and in peace, so may the Latins ever be obedient," the rest as above. . . .[3]

162. THE IMPERIAL CULT

Emperor worship in the first two centuries followed in the main the lines laid down by Augustus—divine honors to the *genius* of the living emperor and deification after death (the latter honor being often accorded to other members of the imperial family as well). Despite official deprecation, the worship of the living emperor was widely practiced throughout the Empire, especially in the eastern provinces. The attempts by Caligula and Domitian in the first century to institute such worship at Rome were premature aberrations. Cf. Cassius Dio, *Roman History* LXVII. v. 7: "Domitian even

---

3. On details of this text, cf. the Augustan Secular Games in vol. 1, § 206. The conservatism of the ritual and formulas is noteworthy.

insisted upon being considered a god and was exceedingly proud of being called 'master' (*dominus*) and 'god' (*deus*). These titles were used not merely orally but also in written documents." But with the passage of time the transition to divinization of the living emperor was not a difficult one. In the first place, the emperor was usually the natural or adoptive "son of a god," his deified predecessor. Further, with the increasing centralization of administration in the hands of the emperor, the Eastern concept of the divine ruler gradually spread to the West. By the third century the divine nature of the imperial house was firmly established, and in the reorganization of Diocletian the emperor assumed officially the character of a god-king.

TIBERIUS DEPRECATES DIVINE HONORS

The following inscriptions of A.D. 14/15 contain a decree of the Greek city of Gythium and the emperor's reply thereto.

AE, 1929, nos. 99–100 (= E-J, no. 102)

i

. . . he [probably a public official of Gythium] shall place . . . on the first [pedestal, the statue] of the deified Augustus Caesar, his father; on the second, to the right, that of Julia Augusta;[4] and on the third, [to the left], that of the Emperor TIBERIUS Caesar Augustus, the city providing him with the statues. And a table shall be set out by him in the middle of the theater and a censer placed upon it, and the councilmen and all the magistrates shall offer sacrifice for the preservation of our rulers, but not before the performers enter. On the first day the performance shall honor the son of the deified [Julius] Caesar, the deified AUGUSTUS our savior and deliverer; on the second day, the Emperor TIBERIUS Caesar Augustus, father of his country; on the third day, Julia Augusta, the Good Fortune of our province and city; on the fourth, the Victory of Germanicus Caesar; on the fifth, the Venus of Drusus Caesar; and on the sixth, Titus Quinctius Flamininus;[5] and he shall see to the orderly behavior of the contestants. . . . And when the procession reaches the Temple of Caesar, the superintendents shall sacrifice a bull for the preservation of our rulers and for the deified ones and for the eternal duration of their rule. . . .

4. That is, Livia, wife of Augustus and mother of Tiberius. The term *our rulers,* below, refers to Tiberius and Livia.

5. The conqueror of Philip V of Macedon and "liberator" of Greece; see vol. 1, § 68.

ii

TIBERIUS Caesar Augustus, son of Augustus, *pontifex maximus,* holding the tribunician power for the . . . year . . . to the superintendents and city of Gythium, greeting. Decimus Turranius Nicanor, the envoy sent by you to me and to my mother, transmitted to me your letter to which were appended the measures passed by you in reverence to my father and in my honor. I commend you for this, and consider it fitting that all men in general and your city in particular should reserve special honors befitting the gods in keeping with the greatness of my father's services to the whole world; but I myself am content with the more modest honors appropriate to men. My mother, however, will answer you herself when she learns from you your decision about honors to her.

Tacitus, *Annals* IV. xxxvii–xxxviii

About the same time [A.D. 25] Farther Spain through envoys sent to the senate requested permission to erect a shrine to Tiberius and his mother, following the example of Asia. On this occasion the emperor, vigorously scornful of honors in any case, and considering that an answer was due those who in their gossip charged him with having descended to vainglory, began a speech of the following tenor:

"I know, Senators, that in the eyes of a good many of you I was lacking in consistency inasmuch as recently when the cities of Asia made this same request, I offered no opposition. I shall therefore disclose both a defense for my previous silence and what I have determined for the future. Since the deified Augustus had not forbidden the erection of a temple at Pergamum to himself and the city of Rome [cf. introduction to vol. I, § 207], observing as I do his every action and word as law, I followed the precedent already approved by him all the more readily as reverence for the senate was associated with worship of myself. To have accepted once is pardonable; but to be consecrated in the image of deity through all the provinces would be pretentious and arrogant, and the honor paid to Augustus will become empty if it is vulgarized by indiscriminate acts of flattery.

"As for myself, Conscript Fathers, that I am mortal, that my functions are those of human beings, and that I hold it enough if I occupy the foremost place—this I call upon you to witness, and I desire posterity to remember. For they will do justice, and more, to my memory if they believe me worthy of my ancestors, solicitous of your interests, firm in danger, not fearful of offense for the sake of the public welfare. These are my temples in your heart, these my fairest and abiding statues. For those that are erected of stone, if the judgment of posterity should turn to hatred, are scorned as sepulchers. Accordingly, my prayers to allies, citizens, and the gods themselves are these: to the gods, that to the end of my life they may endow me with an unperturbed mind, gifted with understanding of human and divine law; and to the others that, whenever I depart, they may escort my deeds and fair name to the tomb with praise and kindly remembrances."

And henceforth, even in private conversations he persisted in spurning this worship of himself.[6]

EDICT OF GERMANICUS

Germanicus Caesar, nephew and adopted son of the Emperor Tiberius, while on a special mission to settle affairs in the eastern part of the Empire, journeyed to Alexandria in A.D. 19 to alleviate a food shortage there. His benefactions occasioned such enthusiastic public demonstrations that he judged it politic to issue the following edict.

Wilcken, no. 413, lines 31–45 (= *Select Papyri*, no. 211)

Germanicus Caesar, son of Augustus and grandson of the deified Augustus, proconsul, declares: Your good will, which you always display when you see me, I acknowledge, but your acclamations, which are odious to me and such as are accorded to the gods, I altogether deprecate. For they are appropriate only to him who is really the savior and benefactor of the whole human race, my father, and to his mother, my grandmother. But my position is [but a reflection?] of their divinity, so that if you do not obey me, you will compel me not to show myself to you often.

---

6. Cf. Suetonius, *Life of Tiberius* xxvi: "He forbade the decreeing of temples, flamens, and priests in his honor, and even the setting up of statues and busts without his permission; and these latter he permitted only on the following condition, that they were not to be placed among the statues of the gods but among the adornments of temples. He was opposed to an oath being taken in support of his acts, and to changing the name of the month of September to Tiberius and of October to Livius [in honor of his mother Livia]."

HONORS TO THE DEAD GERMANICUS

Upon the death of Germanicus October 10, A.D. 19, there ensued an outpouring of mourning and honors in Rome and throughout the Empire. The following bronze inscription, set up at the municipality Fortunales Siarenses in Spain contains decrees of the Roman Senate similar to those in the bronze inscription found at the town of Heba in Italy, for which see *American Journal of Philology* (1954), 75:225–249 (= E. J. no. 365).

AE, 1984, no. 508

. . . to preserve the memory of Germanicus Caesar, who ought never to have died. . . . The Senate decided that a decree of the Senate should be made concerning the deserved honors of Germanicus Caesar. . . . It was voted that the matter be conducted in consultation with Tiberius Caesar Augustus, our *princeps,* and that a memorandum be made for him of our opinions, so that he, with his usual foresight should select out of all the honors which the Senate deemed should be bestowed those which Tiberius Caesar Augustus, our *princeps,* and Augusta his mother, and Drusus Caesar, and the mother of Germanius Caesar, and Agrippina his wife in consultation with him considered the most sufficiently suitable to be held. Concerning this matter the Senate passed the following decree:

It was its pleasure that a marble archway be erected, with public funds, in the Circus Flaminius next to the place where the statues of the deified Augustus and the House of Augustus have already been dedicated by Gaius Norbanus Flaccus, with gilded representations of the conquered peoples, and an inscription on the front of that gateway stating that the Senate and the Roman people dedicated this marble monument to the memory of Germanicus Caesar, and recording that he, after conquering those Germans in war, removed them from Gaul and recovered the military standards, and, having avenged the deceitful destruction of an army of the Roman people, and having reestablished the condition of the Gauls, he was sent as proconsul to the transmarine provinces. There, while engaged in those provinces and the client kingdoms of that region in accordance with the instructions of Tiberius Caesar Augustus, including installing a king in Armenia, and not sparing his efforts, until by decree of the Senate an ovation was bestowed on him, he met his death giving his all to the Roman state.

And atop this archway a statue of Germanicus Caesar is to be placed in a triumphal chariot. And about him statues of Drusus Germanicus, the latter's natural brother Tiberius Caesar Germanicus, and Antonia his mother, and Agrippina his wife, and Livia his sister, and Tiberius Germanicus his brother, and his sons and daughters.

[A second archway is proposed, to be set up on Mt. Amanus in the Province of Syria.]

A third archway or monument is to be set up at the bank of the Rhine near that burial mound which the army of the Roman people hastily raised up for Drusus the brother of Tiberius Caesar Augustus, our *princeps;* it later was completed by permission of the deified Augustus. In like manner a burial mound in honor of Germanicus Caesar is to be set up portraying him accepting those supplications from the Germans, and especially from the Gauls and Germans on the other side of the Rhine, whose communities were ordered by the deified Augustus to make a sacrifice at the burial mound of Drusus and to give to his memory customary ritual sacrifice, annually making offerings to the dead on that day on which Germanicus Caesar died. . . .

Likewise it was voted that a marble tomb to the memory of Germanicus Caesar should be erected at Antioch in the forum [where the body of Germanicus was cremated?], and also at Epidaphna where Germanicus Caesar passed away a tribunal is to be erected. . . .

And that on that day it shall not be permitted to conduct any official public business by magistrates in charge of legal matters in a municipality or colony of Roman citizens or Latins, nor public banquets be held, nor marriages of Roman citizens take place, nor betrothals, nor receipt of money owed by someone, nor payment to anyone, nor shows to be held or viewed, or anything brought in for shows. . . .

Likewise, it was decreed by the Senate that the urban plebs should officially place the statues of Germanicus with his triumphal regalia in those temples and on those public altars which the deified Augustus and Augusta had authorized for Drusus Germanicus his father . . . with an inscription of the poem which Tiberius Caesar Augustus had presented in that body on December 16 praising the dead Germanicus. . . .

[There follow provisions for setting up a bronze inscription of these decrees on the Palatine in Rome, and authorizing dissemination of the decrees for posting in municipalities and colonies in Italy and the provinces.]

Passed. Present in the Senate 285 members. . . .
And that on the Palatine in the portico adjoining the temple of Apollo

in which the Senate is accustomed to meet among the statues of men of distinguished ability Germanicus Caesar and Drusus Germanicus his natural father and brother of Tiberius Caesar Augustus. . . .

And that the Salian priests shall incorporate in their hymns the name of Germanicus Caesar in honor of his memory, an honor which was accorded to Gaius and Lucius Caesar, the brothers of Tiberius Caesar Augustus. . . . [The rest is lost.]

EXCESSES OF CALIGULA

Suetonius, *Life of Caligula* xxii

Caligula came close to assuming the diadem at once and changing the semblance of a principate into the form of a monarchy. On being reminded once that he had surpassed the heights both of princes and of kings, he began from that time on to lay claim to divine majesty for himself. He made it his business to have statues of the gods which were famous for the reverence attached to them or for their artistic merit, including the Olympian Zeus [by the famous Greek sculptor Phidias], brought from Greece, so as to remove their heads and replace them with his own. He extended a part of the palace as far as the Forum, and, transforming the Temple of Castor and Pollux into its vestibule, he often took his stand between the brother gods and exhibited himself in their midst to be worshiped by those who approached; and some hailed him as Jupiter of Latium. He also set up a separate temple to his own godhead, with priests and with sacrificial victims of the choicest kind. In this temple stood a golden life-size statue [of Caligula], and it was dressed each day in clothing such as he himself wore. Very rich persons obtained in turn the office of master of the priesthood through influence and by offering the highest bids. The sacrificial victims were flamingoes, peacocks, woodcocks, guinea hens, and pheasants, one kind being sacrificed each day.

IG, vol. VII, no. 2,711, lines 21–43 (=Dessau, no. 8,792)

[Acraephiae, Greece, A.D. 37]

The Emperor Augustus Caesar [CALIGULA], great-grandson of the deified Augustus, grandson of Tiberius Caesar, *pontifex maximus,* holder of the tribunician power, consul, to the League of Achaeans, Boeotians, Locrians, Phocians, and Euboeans, greeting. I have read the decree given me by your envoys and perceive that you have omitted no extreme of zeal and reverence for me. You have offered sacrifice each individually and have held a common festival for my safety, and you have voted me the greatest honors you could. For all these I commend you, and I accept them, and mindful of the age-old fame of each of the Greek states, I permit you to convene your league. As for the statues you voted me, dispense with the greater part, if it be your pleasure, and confine yourselves to those to be set up at Olympia, Nemea, Delphi, and the Isthmus [the sites of the four great Panhellenic games], so as . . . not to burden yourselves more heavily with expenses. Your decree was transmitted to me by the envoys whose names are recorded below. Farewell.

[There follow, fragmentarily preserved, the names of some seventeen envoys.]

Done on August 19, at Rome.

APOTHEOSIS OF AN EMPEROR

Herodian, *History* IV. ii

It is the custom among the Romans to deify those of their emperors who die with sons to succeed them.[7] This rite is called apotheosis. The whole city takes on the air of a religious festival mingled with mourning. They bury the body of the departed in the customary manner of mortals, giving it a sumptuous funeral, and they fashion a wax image like the deceased in every respect and let it lie in state on a huge ivory couch spread with coverlets interwoven with gold and raised up high at the entrance to the palace. . . . During most of the daytime a watch is kept on both sides of the couch: on the left by the entire senate wearing black garments, on the right by all the matrons on whom the rank of their husbands or fathers confers honored status; all the latter appear unadorned by gold or necklaces but, clothed in plain white garb, present the appearance of mourners. This is done for seven days, during which physicians make daily visits; they approach the couch, actually examine the "invalid," and issue daily bulletins announcing that his condition is more serious. When he is reported to have died, the noblest of the equestrian order and chosen youths of the senatorial order raise up the couch and convey it along the Sacred Way and place it in state in the ancient Forum, where the Roman magistrates lay down their offices.

7. This is an error. In fact, emperors (e.g., Pertinax) were sometimes deified even when their successor was not a son (natural or adopted).

On either side are some steps like a staircase, and on the one side stands a chorus of noble and patrician children, on the opposite a chorus of matrons of high reputation, singing both hymns and paeans to the departed, intoned in solemn, mournful measure.

After this they lift up the couch again and bear it out of the city to the so-called Field of Mars. There, at the widest part of the field a square structure has been erected, constructed exclusively of very large-sized logs, in the form of a chamber. The whole structure is filled inside with firewood and adorned on the outside with coverlets interwoven with gold, ivory statues, and colorful paintings. Above this is another chamber, similar in shape and decoration but smaller, with its little gates and doors open. A third and fourth, each smaller than the one below, lead to the last and narrowest. . . . They carry the couch up into the second chamber and place therein all the spices and incense that the earth produces, and they gather also any fruits, herbs, or juices that produce fragrance, and they bring it up and pour it out in profusion. There is no province, no city, no man of reputation or rank, that does not vie in sending these last gifts in honor of the emperor. When there is a huge mound of spices and the whole space is filled, there is a cavalry procession around this structure, and the entire equestrian order rides in a circle around it, in a regular order and wheeling movement, in the Pyrrhic course and rhythm.[8] Chariots are driven around in the same ordered array, bearing the officials in charge [of the ceremony], who are garbed in the purple-bordered toga and wear masks in the likenesses of all the outstanding Roman generals and emperors.

When this ritual has been completed, he who has succeeded to the throne takes a torch and applies it to the chamber. Then the others apply fire on all sides; with the mass of firewood and incense piled there, all is most readily and easily kindled by the fire. Then from the last and narrowest chamber, as from a battlement, an eagle is released to rise up into the upper air with the fire; the bird is believed by the Romans to carry the soul of the emperor from earth to heaven. And from then on the emperor is worshiped along with the other gods.[9]

8. The Pyrrhic dance was a war dance of Greek origin.

9. The tradition of consecrating the dead emperor survived even in the early Christian period. But the rites accorded to Constantine and a few of his successors could hardly have been more than a traditional honor.

MILITARY CALENDAR OF RELIGIOUS FESTIVALS

This unique document is contained in a papyrus roll found in the 1931–1932 excavation of the Roman town of Europus (Dura) on the Euphrates river. A calendar of the official religious holidays celebrated by the garrison stationed at that military base on the Empire's eastern frontier during the third century, it affords striking evidence of the focal role the worship of the imperial house played in the religion of the Empire.

Dura Papyrus No. 54; A.D. 225–227

January 1. . . .

January 3. Vows fulfilled and offered for the preservation of our lord Marcus Aurelius SEVERUS ALEXANDER Augustus and for the eternity of the Empire of the Roman people [see introduction to § 24]. To Jupiter Best and Greatest, an ox; to Juno, a cow; to Minerva, a cow; to Jupiter Victor, an ox . . . to Father Mars, a bull; to Mars Victor, a bull; to Victory, a cow. . . .

January 7. Honorable discharge and enjoyment of privileges granted, and salary installment paid to soldiers. To Jupiter Best and Greatest, an ox; to Juno, a cow; to Minerva, a cow; to Safety, a cow; to Father Mars, a bull. . . .

January 11[?]. Birthday of Lucius Seius Caesar, father-in-law of the emperor. . . .

January 24. Birthday of the deified Hadrian. To the deified Hadrian, an ox.

January 28. The Arabian, Adiabenic and very great Parthian victories of the deified Severus, and accession of the deified Trajan. To the Parthian Victory, a cow; to the deified Trajan, an ox.

February 4. Accession of the deified Antoninus Magnus [i.e., Caracalla]. . . . To the deified Antoninus Magnus, an ox.

March 1. Birthday rites of Father Mars Victor. To Father Mars, a bull. . . .

March 6. Accession of the deified Marcus [Aurelius] Antoninus and the deified Lucius Verus. To the deified Marcus, an ox; to the deified Lucius, an ox. . . .

March 13. The Emperor Caesar Marcus Aurelius SEVERUS ALEXANDER acclaimed emperor. To Jupiter, an ox; to Juno, a cow . . . to Mars, an ox. Also, the Emperor Caesar Marcus Aurelius SEVERUS ALEXANDER Augustus first acclaimed *imperator* by the soldiers. Pubic prayer[?].

March 14. Our Emperor Alexander acclaimed Augustus and Father of his Country and *pontifex maximus*. Public prayer. . . .

March 19. Day of the Quinquatria.[10] Public prayers continuing to the 23d. . . .

April 21. Birthday of the city of Eternal Rome. To the city of Eternal Rome, a cow.

April 26. Birthday of the deified Marcus [Aurelius] Antoninus. To the deified Marcus Antoninus, an ox.

May 7. Birthday of the deified Julia Maesa.[11] Public prayer to the deified Julia Maesa.

May 10. Crowning of the military standards.[12] Public prayer. . . .

May 24. Birthday of Germanicus Caesar. Public prayer to the memory of Germanicus Caesar. . . .

June 9. Vestalia. Public prayer to Mother Vesta. . . .

June 26. Our lord Marcus Aurelius Severus Alexander named Caesar and clad in the toga of manhood. To the *genius* of Alexander Augustus, a bull. . . .

July 12. Birthday of the deified Julius [Caesar]. To the deified Julius, an ox.

July 23. Day of the Neptunalia. Public prayer; sacrifice.

August 1. Birthday of the deified Claudius and the deified Pertinax. To the deified Claudius, an ox; to the deified Pertinax, an ox. . . .

September. . . . Birthday of the deified Faustina.[13] To the deified Faustina, public prayer.

September 23. Birthday of the deified Augustus. To the deified Augustus, an ox. . . .

December 17. [Day of the Saturnalia; cf. § 41.] Public prayers continuing to the 23d. . . . [The rest is lost.]

163. THE SPREAD OF IRRATIONALISM

Under the societal conditions of the Roman Empire the rational spirit underwent a complete collapse, and in its place came widespread superstition and a conviction of fatalism in human affairs. In this milieu astrology

---

10. A festival of Minerva, originally in honor of Mars: cf. vol. 1, chapter 1, note 27.

11. The sister-in-law of Septimius Severus and grandmother of the Emperors Elagabalus and Severus Alexander.

12. In this ceremony the standards were grouped by the camp altar and decorated with crowns of roses.

13. The wives of Antoninus Pius and Marcus Aurelius bore this name.

attained its greatest vogue in history, dominating all levels of society, even the best minds, with supreme authority. Side by side with the spread of Oriental mystery religions, magical practices penetrated the life of the Roman world; despite recurrent police action against practitioners of the occult, they maintained a flourishing existence throughout the Empire.

CURIOSITIES OF NATURE

In contrast to the heights of rationalism reached by the finest products of Greek genius, the Roman mind, in high places and in low, and the uneducated masses throughout the Empire, were increasingly responsive to the irrational. Symptomatic of this tendency is the collection of marvels by Phlegon, a freedman of the Emperor Hadrian, which catered to the popular taste in such matters.

Phlegon, *Amazing Stories* x xxviii (selections)

There was born in Rome a hermaphrodite, in the year when Jason was archon at Athens and Marcus Plautius Hypsaeus and Marcus Fulvius Flaccus were consuls at Rome [125 B.C.] On this account the senate bade the pontiffs consult the Sibylline Oracles, and they interpreted the oracular responses.

. . . . .

Not a few cities of Sicily and the area about Regium suffered from the earthquake, and not a few of the peoples in Pontus were also shaken. In the fissures in the earth were revealed bodies of quite large size. The natives were astounded and shrank from moving them, but they sent a tooth of one to Rome as a sample. The tooth was not just a foot long but actually exceeded that size. The envoys showed it to [the Emperor] Tiberius and asked whether he wanted the heroic figure brought to him. The emperor made a wise decision about this, by which he both did not deprive himself of learning its size and at the same time avoided the impiety of stealing corpses. He summoned a renowned geometer, Pulcher by name, whom he prized for his skill, and bade him reconstruct the face in scale to the size of the tooth. Pulcher calculated what the proportions of the whole body and the face would be by the size of the tooth, and quickly fashioned it and brought it to the emperor. The latter declared that he was satisfied with this viewing of it, and sent the tooth back whence it had been brought. . . . One should not mistrust these stories, reflecting that in early times nature in its prime bred everything close to the gods, but that as time wasted away the size of creatures wasted with it.

.   .   .   .

There was brought to Nero a child having four heads and its other members corresponding, in the year when Thrasyllus was archon at Athens and Publius Petronius Turpilianus and Lucius Caesennius Paetus were consuls at Rome [A.D. 61]. And another child was born with its head growing out of its left shoulder.

.   .   .   .

There happened an incredible wonder in Rome, in the year when Demophilus was archon at Athens and Quintus Veranius and Gaius Pompeius Gallus were consuls at Rome [A.D. 49]. One of the most esteemed serving women of the wife of Raecius Taurus, a man of praetorian rank, gave birth to an ape.

.   .   .   .

Antigonus tells that in Alexandria one woman bore twenty offspring in four births, and that most of them survived.

MAGIC CHARMS

This document, characteristic of the numerous magical texts in the papyri and inscriptions, contains a variety of spells which derive from traditional formulas.

British Museum Papyrus no. 46, col. 1, lines 1–52, col. 3, lines 172–201 and 293–303;
fourth century

A Sarapian Divination

[To be wrought by the help] of a boy, with a lamp, a bowl, and a stand. I invoke thee, O Zeus, Helius, Mithra, Sarapis, unconquerable, possessor of honey, Melicertes, father of honey, abraalbabachambechi, baibeizoth, ebaibeboth, seriabeboth, amelchipsithiouthipithoio, pnoutenin, thereterou, iueueoo, aieia, eeoia, eeai, eueie, ooooo, eueoiao, ai, bakaxichuch, bosepseteth, phobe, biboth, the great, great Sarapis; samasphreth, odargazas, odarmagas, odaphar, ykiaboth, ephia, zelearthar, methomeo, lamarmera, optebi, ptebi, marianou, appear and give heed to him who has manifested before fire and snow, bainphoooch, for thou art he who didst manifest light and snow, terrible-eyed-thundering-and-lightning-swift-footed one, pintouche, etomthoout, opsianaeak, arou-rongoa, paphtha, enosade, iae, iaoai, aoiao, oeu. . . .

Tell what I inquire of thee. Say as follows: Let the throne of the god enter, zatera kyma, kyma, luageu, apsitadrus, ge moliandron, bonbli-lon, peuchre. Let the throne be brought in. Then, if it be borne by four men, inquire what they are crowned with and what precedes the throne. If he says, "They are crowned with olive, and a censer precedes," the boy speaks true. The dismissal: Depart, lord, to thine own world, and to thine own thrones, to thine own orbits, and guard me and this boy unhurt, in the name of the most high god Samasphreth. Perform [this divination] when the moon is in a firm sign of the zodiac in conjunction with beneficent stars, or when she is in favorable limits, not when she is at the full, for thus it is better, and thus is the divination performed in orderly fashion. But in other versions it has been recorded that it should be performed when the moon is full.

To Catch a Thief

I call thee, Hermes, immortal god, who cuttest a furrow down Olympus, and who [presidest over] the sacred boat, O light-bringer Iao, the great ever-living, terrible to behold and terrible to hear, give up the thief whom I seek. Aberamentho oulerthe xenax sonelueothnemareba. This spell is to be said twice at the purification. The spell of bread and cheese. Come to me, lisson maternamau, erte, preptektioun, intiki, ous, oloko-tous, periklusai, bring to me that which is lost, and make the thief manifest on this very day. And I invoke Hermes, the discoverer of thieves, and the sun and the eye-pupils of the sun, the two bringers-to-light of unlawful deeds, and Justice, and Errinys, and Ammon, and Parammon, to seize the throat of the thief and to manifest him this very day, at the present hour. The ceremony: the same spell [as that] pro-nounced at the purification. Take a flush-green vessel and put water in it and myrrh, and the herb cynocephalium, and dipping in it a branch of laurel, sprinkling each person with the water, take a tripod and place it upon an altar of earth. . . . Offer myrrh and frankincense and a frog's tongue, and taking some unsalted winter wheat and goat's cheese, give these to each, pronouncing the spell at length. And write this name, and glue it beneath the tripod: "Lord Iao, light-bearer, give up the thief whom I seek." And if any of them does not swallow what was given him, that one is the thief.

CURSES

On "binding" curses, inscribed on thin lead tablets, see vol. 1, § 179.

IGRR, vol. I, no. 117; Rome

I conjure you up, holy beings and holy names; join in aiding this spell, and bind, enchant, thwart, strike, overturn, conspire against, destroy, kill break Eucherius, the charioteer, and all his horses tomorrow in the circus at Rome. May he not leave the barriers well; may he not be quick in the contest; may he not outstrip anyone; may he not make the turns well; may he not win any prizes; and if he has pressed someone hard, may he not come off the victor; and if he follows someone from behind, may he not overtake him; but may he meet with an accident; may he be bound; may he be broken; may he be dragged along by your power, in the morning and afternoon races. Now! Now! Quickly! Quickly!

CIL, vol. VI, no. 20,905; Rome

To the spirits of the dead, the tomb of Junia Procula daughter of Marcus. She lived eight years, eleven months, five days. Marcus Junius Euphrosynus put up this altar for himself and _____ [name deleted].

May the bones of your daughter and of your parents rest together without you. What you have done to us, may you suffer the same yourself. Believe me, you will witness yours. Inscribed here are the signs of the eternal shame of the freedwoman Acta, a treacherous, deceptive, cruel poisoner. For her a nail and a rope to fasten around her neck, and hot pitch to burn her evil heart. Manumitted gratis, she absconded with an adulterer, deceived her patron, and stole his slaves, a girl and a boy, as he lay in bed, leaving him a lonely, robbed, broken-hearted man. The same curse on Hymus and those who went off with Zosimus.

.   .   .   .

This inscription on a lead tablet was found in a vase with a clay image of a woman kneeling, hands bound behind her back, pierced with needles.

SEG, vol. XXVII, no. 1,717

I entrust this binding charm to you gods of the underworld, Pluto and Kore-Persephone, Ereschigal, Adonis also named Barbaritha, and Hermes of the Underworld Thoth, *phokeusepseu erektathou misonktaik,* the mighty, *pseriphtha,* who has the keys to Hades, and divine demons of the underworld, those who died before their time, youths and maidens, year by year, month by month, day by day, hour by hour, night by night. I conjure up all the demons in this place to assist this demon Antinoüs. Stir yourself for me and go to every place, to every district, to every house, and bind Ptolemaïs whom Aias bore, the daughter of Horigenes, so that she may not have intercourse or be buggered, and give no pleasure to any man companion except only me, Sarapammon, whom Area bore. And let her not eat, nor drink, nor be happy, nor go out, nor sleep with anyone but me Sarapammon, whom Area bore. I conjure you Antinoüs demon of the dead, by your name of Terrible and Fearful, hearing whose name the earth will open up, and at whose name the demons are frightened with fear, and hearing it the rivers and rocks will be shattered. I conjure you up, Antinoüs, demon of the dead, by Barbaratham *cheloumbra barouch* Adonai and by Abrasax, and by Iao *pakephtoth pakebraoth sabarbaraei* and by Marmardououth and by Marmachtha *mamazagar.* Do not be deaf to me, demon of the dead Antinoüs but rouse yourself for me, and go to every place, to every district, to every house, and lead to me Ptolemaïs whom Aias bore, the daughter of Horigenes. Restrain her from eating and drinking until she comes to me, Sarapammon whom Area bore, and do not permit her to experience another man except me alone, Sarapammon whom Area bore. Drag her by the hair and her entrails until she does not reject me, Sarapammon, whom Area bore, and I have Ptolemaïs herself, whom Aias bore, the daughter of Horigenes, submissive for her entire life, loving me, desiring me, telling me what she has in her mind. If you do this, I will release you.

MIRACULOUS CURES

IGRR, vol. I, no. 41; Rome

In these very days [Aesculapius][14] gave a response to a certain Gaius, a blind person, to go to the sacred platform and make obeisance, then to go from right to left and place his five fingers on the platform and lift up his hand and place it on his own eyes; and he recovered his sight, in the presence of the populace, who rejoiced that the active divine powers manifested themselves during the reign of our Augustus, Antoninus.

14. The Graeco-Roman god of medicine (see vol. 1, § 53). With these cures also see those described in § 61.

[Aesculapius] gave a response to Lucius, who was suffering from pleurisy and was given up in despair by everyone, to go and lift up the ashes from the altar and mix well with wine and apply it to his side; and he was saved, and he gave thanks to the god publicly, and the populace rejoiced with him.

[Aesculapius] gave a response to Julianus, who was spitting up blood and had been given up in despair by everyone, to go and lift up from the altar pine-cone seeds and eat them with honey for three days; and he was cured, and he came and gave thanks publicly before the populace.

The god gave a response to the blind soldier Valerius Aper that he should go and take blood from a white cock and mix an eye salve with honey, and smear it on his eyes for three days; and he recovered his sight, and he came and gave thanks publicly to the god.

MAGICAL PRACTICES OUTLAWED

This order by the prefect of Egypt is a striking testimony to the spread of irrationalism.

Yale Papyrus inv. 299 (= *SB*, 12,144); A.D. 199

Cognizant of [the complaints of] many thinking that they were being duped by the ways of the diviners' craft, I deemed it absolutely(?) necessary, with a view to no one's being at risk through following them, hereby clearly to enjoin all persons to desist from that dangerous prying. Accordingly, neither through [spoken] oracles or inscribed messages issued ostensibly under divine guidance, nor through parade of images and suchlike mummery(?), is anyone to pretend to know the superhuman and discover the obscure shape of things to come, and no one is to devote himself to those who inquire into this, or else he will answer for it. If anyone is found violating(?) this proclamation [of mine], let him be assured that he will be handed over to the extreme penalty.

Each of you [nome *strategi*] is to see to displaying in public, on a whitened board in characters that are clear and easily legible, a copy of this letter in the nome capitals and in each village, and upon finding anyone acting in violation of my interdiction he is to send him in fetters for my judgment. Nor will it be without risk to you if I should learn of such ones being overlooked in the nomes under you, but you will undergo the same punishment as those being shielded. For each of them, even though he dares to act in defiance of my interdiction, is but one person, but he who does not stay them in every way has ipso facto become the cause of danger to many.

164. ASTROLOGY

The vogue of astrology, an age-old Near Eastern system of beliefs, entered the Greek world in the fourth century B.C. and burgeoned in the Hellenistic period. "From this time it became an increasingly important factor in the civilisation of Greece and Rome, reaching its apogee in imperial times, and affecting every level of society. . . . At its height it commanded the ardent allegiance of the best minds of the ancient world" (*Oxford Classical Dictionary,* 2d ed., p. 134). Astrologers were expelled from Rome and Italy many times, yet their practice remained legal. Under Christian emperors, beginning with Constantius in 357, divination was declared a capital crime (see § 179).

Manilius,[15] *Astronomica* I. 46–65

Then the priests who offered worship in temples all their lives and who were chosen to express the prayers of the people obtained by their service the favor of the gods. The very presence of the divine power kindles their pure minds, and the god himself brought god into their hearts and revealed himself to his servants.

These were the men who established our noble science. They were the first to see, through their art, how fate depends on the wandering stars. Over the course of many centuries they assigned with persistent care to each period of time the events connected with it: the day on which someone is born, the kind of life he shall lead, the influence of every hour on the laws of destiny, and the enormous differences made by small motions. They explored every aspect of the sky as the stars returned to their original positions. They assigned to the unchangeable sequences of the fates the specific influence of certain configurations. As a result, experience, applied in different ways, produced an art; examples pointed the way; from long observation it was discovered that the stars control the whole world by mysterious laws, that the world itself moves by an eternal principle, and that we can, by reliable signs, recognize the ups and downs of fate.

The case against astrology is presented in this model speech by Arellius Fuscus, professor of rhetoric in the Augustan age.

---

15. Manilius wrote in the age of Augustus and Tiberius a didactic poem on astrology in five books. An advocate of the practice, he sought to convert readers to belief in astrology.

Seneca the Elder, *Suasoriae* III. vii. 4

Who is this man who claims for himself knowledge of the future. . . .
Great and above the human condition is the man who can frighten
Alexander. Let him place his ancestors among the stars and derive his
origin from heaven. Let the god acknowledge the prophet as his own.
. . . If all these things are true, why does not every area pursue this
study? Why do we not from infancy consort with nature and the gods
as far as possible, since the stars are accessible to us and we can mingle
with the gods? Why do we sweat so in useless eloquence? Why are our
hands calloused with dangerous weapons? Can talent thrive by a better
guarantee than by knowledge of the future? But those who, as they
declare, have thrown themselves into the midst of the guarantees of fate,
ask for the birthdays, and hold the first hour of life as predictive of one's
entire life. They calculate the movement of the stars then, in what
directions they scattered, whether the sun stood adversely in a contrary
position or shone brightly, whether the moon was full or at the beginning of her waxing, or had hidden her head in dark night. Did Saturn
welcome the newborn child to become a farmer, or Mars as soldier in
war, or Mercury as businessman for profit, or charming Venus nod on
the newborn child, or did Jupiter raise it from humble to the sublime?
So many bustling gods around one head! They announce the future.
Many, they say, will live long, but their final day overwhelmed them
while they feared nothing. To others they had assigned an imminent
end, but they have survived, leading useless lives. They have promised
happy years to the newborn, but Fortune has hurried them off to every
harm. For our lives are of uncertain lot. These are contrived for each
person with cleverness but without belief. Will there be any place in the
whole world which has not seen you victorious?

Ptolemy,[16] *Tetrabiblos* I. ii. 5: III. ii, xiii; From G. Luck, *Arcana Mundi* (Baltimore, 1985)

It would be wrong to dismiss this type of [astrological] prediction
completely only because it sometimes can be wrong. After all, we do
not discredit the art of navigation as such simply because it is often
imperfect.

When we deal with any art, but especially when we deal with a divine
art, we must accept what is possible and be happy with it. It would be

16. Claudius Ptolemaeus (first half of second century), the famed astronomer, map maker, geographer, and mathematician, sought in this work to provide a "scientific" basis for astrology.

wrong to demand—in a typically human, haphazard manner—every-thing from it and to expect final answers, which it cannot give, instead of quietly appreciating its beauty. We do not blame physicians who talk about the disease in general and about the patient's "idiosyncrasy" when they examine him. Why should we object to astrologers when they include in their diagnosis the native's nationality, country of origin, manner of upbringing, and other given circumstances? . . .

Often there is a problem about the foremost and principal fact, the fraction of the hour of birth. In general, only observation by a "horo-scopic" [i.e., hour-watching] astrolabe at the very moment of birth can, for a trained observer, give the exact time. Almost all other "horo-scopic" instruments that most serious astrologers use are in many ways capable of errors: sundials, because of their incorrect position or the incorrect angle of the "gnomon" [i.e., a pin or triangular plate that casts a shadow]; water clocks, because of the stoppage and irregular flow of the water for various reasons, or just by accident. Thus it seems neces-sary to explain first how to find by a natural, logical method the degree of the zodiac which would be rising, using as a premise the. . . , given the degree of the hour known nearest to [the time of] birth, which is determined by the method of "ascensions." We must take the syzygy [i.e., conjunction or opposition] of two heavenly bodies immediately preceding the birth—it may be a new moon or a full moon—and when we have determined the exact degree of both luminaries [i.e., sun and moon] if it is a new moon, or, if it is a full moon, the exact degree of the one that is above the earth, we must see what stars control it at the time of birth. . . .

Saturn associated with Mars in honorable positions produces people who are neither good nor bad: they are hard-working, outspoken busy-bodies, boastful cowards, austere in their conduct, pitiless, contemp-tuous, rough, quarrelsome, foolhardy troublemakers, schemers, hijack-ers, stubborn in their anger, inexorable demagogues, tyrants, greedy, and they hate their fellow citizens. . . .

In the opposite positions [Mars and Saturn make]: robbers, pirates, counterfeiters, wretches, profiteers, atheists . . . thieves, perjurers, mur-derers, eaters of unlawful food, criminals, killers, poisoners, robbers of temples and graves, and, in general, men who are totally evil.

Firmicus Maternus,[17] *Mathesis* II. xxiv–xxvi
From the translation of J. R. Bram (Park Ridge, N.J., 1975)

We must explain what parts of the body the twelve signs control, for this is very useful for forecasting from the stars, especially when you wish to find the house of health or of defects. The head of man is in the sign of Aries, the neck in Taurus, the shoulders in Gemini, the heart in Cancer, the breast and stomach in Leo, the belly in Virgo, the kidneys and vertebrae in Libra, the sex organs in Scorpio, the thighs in Sagittarius, the knees in Capricorn, the legs in Aquarius, and the feet in Pisces. In this way all parts of the human body are divided among the signs.

Now we must explain the following subject: which stars portend how many hours, months, years of life—more if the stars are well located, fewer if badly situated.

When you look carefully at the Giver of Life, that is, the ruler of the chart, and you see in what house it is located, and in what kind of a sign, and in what degrees, and you also consider the ruler of the sign in which the Life-Giver is situated, in what sign and in what house and in what degree it is, and to what extent the Giver of Life and the benefic planets are aspected to the Sun and Moon, you will easily be able to delineate the whole character of this life. For, if the Life-Giver is situated in a good house, in a good sign and in good degrees, a healthy number of years is portended, especially if Jupiter in a diurnal nativity, or Venus in a nocturnal nativity, is in favorable aspect to the Giver of Life.

If Saturn is the Giver of Life and is favorable, he decrees 57 years; but if he portends evil he decrees 30 years, or 30 months and 12 hours.

If Jupiter is the Giver of Life and is favorable, he decrees 79 years, but if unfavorable 12 years, or 12 months and 12 days and 12 hours.

If Mars is the Life-Giver and is favorable, he portends 63 years; if unfavorable 15 years, or 15 months, 15 days, and 12 hours.

If the Sun is favorable he decrees 120 years; if unfavorable 18 years; if moderate 45 years.

Venus, if she decrees favorably, 84 years; if unfavorably 8 years, 8 days, 12 hours.

Mercury, if he decrees favorably, 108 years; if moderately 79 years; if unfavorably 20 years, or 29 months, 20 days, 20 hours.

If the Moon decrees favorably, 84 years; if unfavorably 25 years.

17. Firmicus Maternus of Syracuse (first third of fourth century) was a convert to Christianity and a Christian polemicist. He is the author of *On the Error of the Profane Religions* and also *Mathesis,* a handbook on astrology.

If the Ruler of Life or the Giver of Life, that is the ruler of the nativity, is in his own house or in his own exaltation or in his own terms, and if planets in his own condition exert a favorable influence on him, that is, are favorably aspected to his position, and those stars themselves which influence him are well placed, then a larger number of years is portended. But they indicate an average age if the Giver of Life is in his own terms or in his sign or in his rising while the ascendant is in Libra.

165. DIFFUSION OF ORIENTAL RELIGIONS

"The propagation of the Oriental religions, with the development of Neo-Platonism, is the leading fact in the moral history of the pagan empire" (F. Cumont, *Oriental Religions in Roman Paganism,* p. xv). Despite the efforts of various emperors to strengthen the Hellenized state religion and the native family cult (cf. vol. 1, §§ 52–53), and despite the official policy of exclusion of Oriental gods from the Roman pantheon, the vitality of the ancestral religion steadily diminished. The West was with constantly mounting intensity penetrated by a variety of Oriental cults, especially mystery religions, of which Christianity was one. This religious ferment was facilitated by numerous factors: the tolerance by the Roman government of private religious activity entailing no political dangers or threats to law and order; the political unity of the Empire; the movement of merchants, slaves, and armies; the appeal of cosmopolitanism and individualism to the masses of the Empire; the breakdown of rationalism and the scientific spirit. By the third century, Oriental cults began to be adopted into the state religion, and for a time sun worship, tending toward solar monotheism, was a powerful rival (especially in military circles) of the traditional religion and of the mystery cults. This religion, with its great temple of the sun god, its new college of pontiffs, and its great festival on December 25, the birthday celebration of the sun at the winter solstice, was thereafter the principal official imperial cult until the triumph of Christianity. But it was the eschatological mystery cults, among which Persian Mithraism (mostly known from monumental and a mass of brief inscriptional evidence) and Christianity were the most powerful rivals, that won the greatest number of adherents. Banded in private religious brotherhoods, the worshipers were attracted by the pageantry of the mysteries, the elaborate rituals often culminating in orgiastic frenzy (including initiation, often by baptism, and other purification rites), the esoteric doctrines, and above all by the intense emotional appeals and the promise of personal immortality.

INVASION OF ORIENTAL CULTS

Minucius Felix, *Octavius* vi, xxiii. 1–4; From *LCL*

Hence it is that throughout wide empires, provinces, and towns, we see each people having its own individual rites and worshiping the local gods—the Eleusinians Ceres, the Phrygians the Great Mother, the Epidaurians Aesculapius, the Chaldaeans Baal, the Syrians Astarte, the Taurians Diana, the Gauls Mercury, the Romans one and all. Thus it is that their power and authority have embraced the circuit of the whole world, and have advanced the bounds of the Empire beyond the paths of the sun and the confines of ocean; while they practise in the field god-fearing valor, make strong their city with awe of sacred rites, with chaste virgins, with many a priestly dignity and title. . . . In captured fortresses, even in the first flush of victory, they reverence the conquered deities [see vol. 1, pp. 152–54]. Everywhere they entertain the gods and adopt them as their own; they raise altars even to the unknown deities, and to the spirits of the dead. Thus is it that they adopt the sacred rites of all nations, and withal have earned dominion. . . .

Consider the sacred rites of the mysteries; you will find tragic deaths, dooms, funerals, mourning and lamentations of woebegone gods. Isis, with her Dog-head and shaven priests, mourning, bewailing, and searching for her lost son; her miserable votaries beating their breasts and mimicking the sorrows of the unhappy mother; then, when the stripling is found, Isis rejoices, her priests jump for joy, the Dog-head glories in his discovery; and, year by year, they cease not to lose what they find or to find what they lose. Is it not absurd either to mourn your object of worship, or to worship your object of mourning? Yet these old Egyptian rites have now found their way to Rome, so that you may play the fool to the swallow and sistrum of Isis, the scattered limbs and the empty tomb of your Serapis or Osiris.

Ceres, with lighted torches, serpent-girt, with anxious, troubled footsteps follows the trail of her decoyed and ravished Proserpina—such are the Eleusinian mysteries. . . . Of Cybele and Dindyma it is a shame to speak: unable to satisfy the affections of her luckless paramour—for mothering of many gods had made her plain and old—she could not allure him to lust and castrated him, so as to make a god, no less, a eunuch; and in deference to this fable her *galli* priests worship her by inflicting the same mutilation on their own bodies. Such practices are not sacred rites but tortures.

Tertullian, *Apology* vi. 7–10; From *LCL*

To come next to your gods themselves, the decrees which your fathers prudently enacted you, the most law-abiding of men, have repealed. Father Bacchus and his mysteries—the consuls with the approval of the senate turned him not only out of the city but out of the whole of Italy [see vol. 1, § 176]. Serapis and Isis and Harpocrates [i.e., the Egyptian God Horus, son of Isis and Serapis] with his Dog-head were forbidden the Capitol—in other words, expelled from the assembly of the gods; and Piso and Gabinius [in 58 B.C.]—consuls, not Christians, you know —actually overturned their altars and banished them, in the endeavor to restrain the vices that go with foul and idle superstition. You have restored them and bestowed on them supreme majesty. Where is the religious awe, where is the veneration owed by you to your ancestors? In dress, habit of life, furniture, feeling, yes! and speech, you have renounced your great-grandfathers! You are forever praising antiquity, and every day you improvise some new way of life. All of which goes to prove that while you abandon the good usages of your ancestors you keep and maintain the practices you should not have, and what you should have kept you have not maintained. In fact, as to that very point of ancestral tradition, which you think you most faithfully guard, which above all else you have used to mark down the Christians as lawbreakers —I mean the passion for worshiping the gods (and that is where antiquity made its worst mistake)—though you may have rebuilt his altars for Serapis Romanized, though you make an offering of your frenzy to Bacchus Italianate, I will show in its proper place that you despise, neglect, and destroy that tradition, straight against the authority of your ancestors.

WORSHIP OF ISIS

The Hellenized Egyptian cult of Isis and Serapis had reached Italy through the Greek cities in the south as early as the third century B.C. After a long period of official persecution, it was granted public recognition by Caligula. Thereafter it spread throughout the Empire, reaching its height in the third century. The following is a famous description of one of the festivals of the cult, the "Bark of Isis," symbolizing the spring opening of the navigation season.

Apuleius, *The Golden Ass (Metamorphoses)* xi. ix–xi, xvi–xvii

Now the special procession of the savior goddess was moving by. Women resplendent in white garments, rejoicing in varied ornaments and wearing wreaths of spring flowers, strewed with blossoms from their bosoms the path along which the sacred procession was passing. Others turned shining mirrors, held behind their backs, toward the goddess as she came, to demonstrate their reverence on the way. Others, carrying ivory combs, with the gestures of their arms and the movements of their fingers went through the motions of combing and adorning the queenly hair. Others also sprinkled the streets with various ointments, including delightful balsam scattered drop by drop. In addition, there came a great number, of both sexes, with lamps, torches, wax tapers and other lights, propitiating with light the offspring of the celestial stars. Then pleasant harmonies sounded, pipes and flutes in the sweetest tones. These were followed by a delightful chorus of very select young men, resplendent in white garments and festal array, repeating a charming song. . . . There came, too, the trumpeters devoted to great Serapis, who with slanting reeds stretched to the right ear repeated the familiar melody of the temple and god. And there were many who called for free room for the sacred rites. Then poured in masses of initiates in the divine rites, men and women of every rank and every age, who glistened in their pure white linen garb. The women had their hair anointed and decked with a bright covering, but the men, their hair completely shaven, had glistening pates . . . and with timbrels of bronze, silver, aye and gold, they made a loud shrill jingling. But the principal priests, overseers of the sacred rites, who were appareled in surplices tightly girt round with white linen cloth and hanging down to the ground, carried the splendid trappings of the most powerful gods. . . .

Presently the gods came forth, deigning to walk on human feet. Here was Anubis, the awful messenger of the gods above and below, his face partly black and partly golden, lofty, raising up on high his dog's head, and bearing in his left hand his wand, and in his right hand shaking the green palm. Directly after followed, raised to an upright position, the image of the goddess, that is, the fruitful mother of all. . . . Another carried a spacious box of secrets concealing within the mysteries of the glorious religion. Another bore in his happy bosom the venerable image of the godhead, not like any beast, bird, wild animal or even human being, but made by a clever discovery, and therefore to be revered, an emblem ineffable of a somehow higher religion, one to be guarded with great silence. . . .

Meanwhile, amid the hubbub of the festive prayers, proceeding little by little we reached the sea. . . . There, after the images were duly arranged, we saw a boat skillfully wrought and variegated round about with the marvelous paintings of the Egyptians. This boat, most scrupulously purified, the high priest named after and dedicated to the goddess, intoning the most solemn prayers from his holy lips and purifying it with a glowing torch, an egg, and sulphur. A gleaming sail of this blessed bark bore the words of a vow woven into it; these words renewed the vow concerning the prosperous navigation of the new sailing season. The mast rose up high, made of pine, round and splendid, conspicuous for its remarkable masthead; the poop, fashioned in the shape of a goose's neck, gleamed with its covering of gold plate; and the whole ship, finished with bright citron wood, was magnificent. Then all the people, both priestly and lay, vied in heaping winnowing fans loaded with spices and such like offerings, and poured over the waves libations of these offerings mixed with milk, until the ship was filled with abundant devotions and propitious prayers; then it was loosened from its cables and given to the sea with a special serene breeze. And when we had lost sight of it because of the distance it had gone, each of them that bore the holy objects took up again and carried what he had brought, and eagerly took his way back to the shrine, maintaining the same order of procession.

When we came to the temple itself, the high priest, those who carried the divine images, and especially those who had long been initiated in the venerable secrets went into the chamber of the goddess and arranged in due fashion the lifelike images. Then one of these, whom all call the secretary, taking his place before the doors, summoned to a kind of meeting the company of the *pastophori* [literally, "shrine bearers," priests of Isis], which is the name of the holy college. From a raised platform he read forth from a book, offering propitious vows for the great emperor, the senate, the *equites,* the entire Roman people, and for the sailors and ships under the control and sovereignty of our world. Then he pronounced in the Greek tongue and manner, *"Ploiaphesia"* [i.e., release of the ship]. The ensuing shout of the people indicated that this word brings good luck to all. And then, gleaming with joy, the populace, carrying leafy boughs, twigs, and garlands, kissed the places on the steps where the silver statue of the goddess had rested, and departed to their homes.

RELIGIOUS SYNCRETISM

Apuleius, *The Golden Ass (Metamorphoses)* XI. v

I am she that is the mother of the nature of things, mistress of all the elements, the initial progeny of the ages, highest of the divine powers, queen of the departed spirits, the first of the heavenly deities, the uniform manifestation of the gods and goddesses. The luminous summits of the sky, the wholesome breezes of the sea, and the lamented silences of the dead below I control at my will. My sole divine power is adored throughout all the world in manifold guise, with varied rites, and by varied names. Hence the Phrygians, first born of mankind, call me Mother of the Gods at Pessinus; the autochthonous Athenians, Cecropian Minerva; the Cyprians, sea-girt, Paphian Venus; the arrow-bearing Cretans, Dictynnian Diana; the trilingual Sicilians, Stygian Proserpina; the Eleusinians, their ancient goddess Ceres; some Juno, others Bellona, others Hecate, others Rhamnusia; and both types of Ethiopians, whose land is lighted by the first rays of the rising god of the sun, and the Egyptians, who are preeminent in ancient lore and worship me with special ceremonies, call me by my true name, Queen Isis.

ORGIASTIC FRENZY

Widespread over the Mediterranean was the worship of the Syrian fish-goddess of Hierapolis, Atargatis, and her spouse Hadad. The Syrian cults, though not as popular in the West as those of Asia Minor and Egypt, were spread by Syrian slaves, merchants, and soldiers, who also brought with them the worship of various local baals. The following passage describes the devotees of Atargatis; similar ritual orgies characterized several of the mystery cults.

Apuleius, *The Golden Ass (Metamorphoses)* VIII. xxvii–xxviii

They appeared garbed in various colors, misshapen, their faces smeared with foul paint and their eyes painted with oil, wearing turbans, saffron-colored vestments, and garments of fine linen and silk; and some wore white tunics painted with purple stripes in all directions like little spears, girt with belts, their feet shod with yellow shoes. . . . Then with their arms naked up to their shoulders, holding up huge swords and axes, they shout and dance a frenzied dance, aroused by the sound of the pipe. After we had passed not a few cottages, we came to the villa of a certain rich property owner, where as soon as they entered they let forth with discordant howlings and darted about in a frenzied way. And for a long time they would bend their heads down, twist their necks with supple movements, and whirl their hanging hair in a circle. And sometimes they would take to biting their own flesh, and finally each one cut his arms with the two-edged sword he was carrying, while one of them, who was more frenzied, panting rapidly from the depths of his heart, as though he were filled with the divine spirit of deity, feigned he was smitten with madness. . . . He began to speak with a noisy prophecy, inventing a lie, assailing and accusing himself, alleging that he had perpetrated some wrong against the rules of the holy religion, and demanding just punishment at his own hands for the noxious crime. And finally, seizing a whip, a special accoutrement of these effeminate men . . . he scourged himself. . . . You might see the ground wet and defiled with the effeminate blood from the cutting of the swords and the blows of the scourges. . . . But when at length they were weary, or at least satisfied with lacerating themselves, they put a stop to this bloody business; and they received in the wide folds of their garments contributions of bronze coins—aye, silver too—many vying to offer these, and also a cask of wine, cheese, and some meal and winter-wheat.

THE WORSHIP OF CYBELE

For six centuries, from its importation in 205/204 B.C. (see vol. 1, § 177) to the triumph of Christianity, the cult of the Phrygian mother-goddess Cybele (*Magna Mater*) remained one of the important mystery religions of the Roman Empire. The center of the cult was Rome itself. Though it was kept under close surveillance until the end of the Republic, and though participation in its priesthoods and rituals was forbidden to Roman citizens, all such restrictions were rescinded by the Emperor Claudius, and the worship of Cybele and her lover Attis became part of the state religion. One of the important rites of this cult, later taken over into Mithraism, was the *taurobolium*, baptism with a shower of the blood of a freshly slain bull.

Lucretius,[18] *On the Nature of Things* ii. 600–628; From *LCL*

She it is of whom the ancient and learned poets of the Greeks have sung, [how that from her sanctuary she rides in state] on a chariot driving a pair of lions. . . . And they have surrounded the top of her head with a

18. Titus Lucretius Carus (*c*. 99–*c*. 55 B.C.), author of the Latin poem *De rerum natura* (On the Nature of Things), which expounds aspects of Epicureanism.

mural crown, because embattled in excellent positions she sustains cities; which emblem now adorns the divine mother's image as she is carried over the earth in awesome state. She it is whom different nations in their ancient ritual acclaim as the Idaean Mother, and give her troops of Phrygians to escort her, because men declare that first from that realm came the wheat, which then spread over the world. They gave her eunuch priests, as wishing to indicate that those who have violated the majesty of the Mother, and have been found ungrateful to their parents, should be thought unworthy to bring living offspring into the regions of light. The taut tomtoms thunder under the open palm, the hollow cymbals sound around, horns with hoarse-echoing blare affright, hollow flutes prick up the spirits with their Phrygian cadences, martial arms show a front of violent fury, that they may amaze the ungrateful minds and impious hearts of the vulgar with fear of the goddess's majesty. Therefore as soon as she rides through mighty cities, silently blessing mankind with unspoken benediction, they bestrew the whole of her progress with silver and bronze, enriching it with bounteous largess, and snow down rose flowers in a shower, overshadowing the Mother and her escorting troops.

EDICT AGAINST MANICHAEISM

The ascetic Persian cult founded by the Babylonian prophet Mani in the middle of the third century began to penetrate the Roman Empire *c.* A.D. 270. This cult, which is regarded by some scholars as a Christian heresy, was persecuted by both the Persian and the Roman governments. It was destined, nevertheless, to become one of the great universal religions. The following edict against the Manichaeans was issued by Diocletian, probably in A.D. 296, as part of his policy of strengthening the traditional native cults.

Comparison of Mosaic and Roman Law[19] xv. 3

The Emperors Diocletian and Maximian, Augusti, and Constantius and Maximian, most noble Caesars, to Julianus, proconsul of Africa. Excessive idleness, my dear Julianus, sometimes drives people to join with

---

19. Composed between A.D. 390 and 438 by an unknown Christian writer. The text appears in *FIRA*, vol. II, pp. 544–589; there is an edition with English translation by M. Hyamson (Oxford, 1913).

others in devising certain superstitious doctrines of the most worthless and depraved kind. In so doing, they overstep the bounds imposed on humans. Moreover, they lure on many others to accept the authority of their erroneous doctrine.

But the immortal gods in their providence have deigned to dispose and arrange matters so that good and true principles should be approved and fixed by the wisdom and constant deliberation of many good, eminent, and very wise men. These principles it is not right to oppose or resist, nor ought the age-old religion be disparaged by a new one. For it is the height of criminality to reexamine doctrines once and for all settled and fixed by the ancients, doctrines which hold and possess their recognized place and course. Wherefore it is our vigorous determination to punish the stubborn depraved minds of these most worthless people.

We take note that those men concerning whom Your Sagacity has reported to Our Serenity,[20] namely the Manichaeans, have set up new and unheard-of sects in opposition to the older creeds, with the intent of driving out to the benefit of their depraved doctrine what was formerly granted to us by divine favor. We have heard that these men have but recently sprung up and advanced, like strange and unexpected portents, from the Persian people, our enemy, to this part of the world, where they are perpetrating many outrages, disturbing the tranquillity of the peoples and also introducing the gravest harm to the communities. And it is to be feared that peradventure, as usually happens, they may try, with the accursed customs and perverse laws of the Persians, to infect men of a more innocent nature, namely the temperate and tranquil Roman people, as well as our entire Empire with what one might call their malevolent poisons. And since, as Your Sagacity has set forth in your report on their religion, all types of offenses against the statutes have very plainly been devised and falsehoods contrived, we have accordingly established for these people afflictions and deserving and condign penalties.

Now, therefore, we order that the founders and heads be subjected to severe punishment: together with their abominable writings they are to be burned in the flames. We instruct that their followers, and particularly the fanatics, shall suffer a capital penalty, and we ordain that their property be confiscated for our fisc. But if indeed any office holders or

20. For such appellations see chapter 7, note 45.

persons of any rank or distinction have gone over to a hitherto unheard-
of, disgraceful, and wholly infamous sect, particularly to the creed of
the Persians, you shall cause their estates to be added to our fisc, and the
persons themselves to be sent to the Phaenensian or Proconnesian mines.[21]

In order, then, that this plague of iniquity may be extirpated by the
roots from this most happy age of ours, Your Devotion shall carry out
with despatch the orders and enactments of Our Tranquillity.

Given on March 31, at Alexandria.

166. Dedication to a Germanic Goddess

The following inscription was found in the Netherlands, an area that was
part of the Roman province of Lower Germany. Its dedication by a
Roman is another example of the religious outreachings of the third
century.

AE, 1981, no. 657; A.D. 222–235

To the goddess Seneucaga(?) Ulfenus son of Publius, tribune of the
Thirteenth Ulpian Victorious A̶l̶e̶x̶a̶n̶d̶r̶i̶a̶n̶ Legion, made the altar with
the temple from the ground up, discharging a vow gladly and deservedly, under the Emperor our lord Severus A̶l̶e̶x̶a̶n̶d̶e̶r̶-̶A̶u̶g̶u̶s̶t̶u̶s̶.[22]

167. Imperial Policy Toward the Christians

This famous correspondence between Trajan and Pliny (governor of Bi-
thynia-Pontus in A.D. *c.* 111–113) is a prime source for the spread of
Christianity in Asia Minor and for the official policy toward the Christians
in the two centuries from Nero to Decius, in whose brief reign (A.D. 249–
251) the organized imperial persecution of Christianity was begun [see §
172]. Before that the Roman state did not proscribe the religion *per se* but
treated the Christians with a hostility based on political considerations.
Christians were constantly exposed to prosecution for such overt acts as
obstinate disobedience of imperial officials, violation of the statutes on
illegal associations, disloyalty and treason (evidenced by their refusal to

21. Phaena is modern el-Musmieh, about 25 miles south of Damascus; Proconnesus is the large
island (modern Marmora) in the Sea of Marmora.

22. These words were defaced, presumably under one of Severus Alexander's successors.

participate in the state religion and the imperial cult), and other specific offenses. In addition, there was persistent popular agitation against Christians locally, so that provincial governors often employed their police powers for summary repression of the growing religion in the interest of maintaining civil order; cf. § 170.

Pliny, Letters book x, nos. 96–97

[Pliny to the Emperor Trajan]

It is my practice, my lord, to refer to you all matters concerning which I am in doubt. For who can better give guidance to my hesitation or inform my ignorance? I have never participated in trials of Christians. I therefore do not know what offenses it is the practice to punish or investigate, and to what extent. And I have been not a little hesitant as to whether there should be any distinction on account of age or no difference between the very young and the more mature; whether pardon is to be granted for repentance, or, if a man has once been a Christian, it does him no good to have ceased to be one; whether the name itself, even without offenses, or only the offenses associated with the name are to be punished.

Meanwhile, in the case of those who were denounced to me as Christians, I have observed the following procedure: I interrogated these as to whether they were Christians; those who confessed I interrogated a second and a third time, threatening them with punishment; those who persisted I ordered executed. For I had no doubt that, whatever the nature of their creed, stubbornness and inflexible obstinacy surely deserve to be punished. There were others possessed of the same folly; but because they were Roman citizens, I signed an order for them to be transferred to Rome.

Soon accusations spread, as usually happens, because of the proceedings going on, and several incidents occurred. An anonymous document was published containing the names of many persons. Those who denied that they were or had been Christians, when they invoked the gods in words dictated by me, offered prayer with incense and wine to your image, which I had ordered to be brought for this purpose together with statues of the gods, and moreover cursed Christ—none of which those who are really Christians, it is said, can be forced to do—these I thought should be discharged. Others named by the informer declared that they were Christians, but then denied it, asserting that they had been but had ceased to be, some three years before, others many years, some as much as twenty-five years. They all worshiped your image and the statues of the gods, and cursed Christ.

They asserted, however, that the sum and substance of their fault or error had been that they were accustomed to meet on a fixed day before dawn and sing responsively a hymn to Christ as to a god, and to bind themselves by oath, not to some crime, but not to commit fraud, theft, or adultery, not to falsify their trust, nor to refuse to return a trust when called upon to do so [apparently a reference to the Ten Commandments]. When this was over, it was their custom to depart and to assemble again to partake of food—but ordinary and innocent food [see § 168]. Even this, they affirmed, they had ceased to do after my edict by which, in accordance with your instructions, I had forbidden political associations. Accordingly, I judged it all the more necessary to find out what the truth was by torturing two female slaves who were called attendants. But I discovered nothing else but depraved, excessive superstition.

I therefore postponed the investigation and hastened to consult you. For the matter seemed to me to warrant consulting you, especially because of the number involved. For many persons of every age, every rank, and also of both sexes are and will be endangered. For the contagion of this superstition has spread not only to the cities but also to the villages and farms. But it seems possible to check and cure it. It is certainly quite clear that the temples, which had been almost deserted, have begun to be frequented, that the established religious rites, long neglected, are being resumed, and that from everywhere sacrificial animals are coming, for which until now very few purchasers could be found. Hence it is easy to imagine what a multitude of people can be reformed if an opportunity for repentance is afforded.

[Trajan to Pliny]

You observed proper procedure, my dear Pliny, in sifting the cases of those who had been denounced to you as Christians. For it is not possible to lay down any general rule to serve as a kind of fixed standard. They are not to be sought out; if they are denounced and proved guilty, they are to be punished, with this reservation, that whoever denies that he is a Christian and really proves it—that is, by worshiping our gods—even though he was under suspicion in the past, shall obtain pardon through repentance. But anonymously posted accusations ought to have no place in any prosecution. For this is both a dangerous kind of precedent and out of keeping with [the spirit of] our age.

168. PROPAGANDA AGAINST CHRISTIANITY

During the second and third centuries the spread of Christianity was rapid, especially among the lowest social strata in the urban centers of Asia and Africa. It gradually penetrated the highest circles of the provinces and of Italy, gaining adherents even in the Senate, the court, and the imperial family. The contemporary Christian apologists are given to rhetorical overstatements of the extension of their religion (it has been estimated that by the time of Constantine's conversion in A.D. 312 about one tenth of the inhabitants of the Empire were Christians). As the new religion began to gain sizable strength, it was called upon to defend itself from fantastic charges, the most persistent of which were atheism, eating of babies, sexual orgies, and incest.

SPREAD OF CHRISTIANITY

Tertullian, *Apology* xxxvii. 4

We are but of yesterday, and we have filled everything of yours—cities, islands, forts, towns, *conciliabula* [see vol. 1, chapter 7, note 38], even the camps, tribes, courts, palace, senate, Forum. We have left you only the temples.

CALUMNIES AGAINST THE CHRISTIANS

Minucius Felix, *Octavius* viii. 3–xii. 6 (abridged)

Is it not deplorable that a faction . . . of abandoned, hopeless outlaws makes attacks against the gods? They gather together ignorant persons from the lowest dregs, and credulous women, easily deceived as their sex is, and organize a rabble of unholy conspirators, leagued together in nocturnal associations and by ritual fasts and barbarous foods, not for the purpose of some sacred rite but for the sake of sacrilege—a secret tribe that shuns the light, silent in public but talkative in secret places. They despise the temples as if they were tombs, they spit upon the gods, they ridicule our sacred rites. Pitiable themselves, they pity . . . our priests; half-naked themselves, they despise offices and official robes. What amazing folly! What incredible arrogance! They despise present tortures yet dread uncertain future ones; while they fear to die after death, they have no fear of it in the meantime; deceptive hope soothes away their terror with the solace of a life to come.

Already . . . decay of morals spreads from day to day throughout the entire world, and the loathsome shrines of this impious conspiracy multiply. This plot must be completely rooted out and execrated. They recognize one another by secret signs and tokens; they love one another almost before they are acquainted. Everywhere a kind of religion of lust is also associated with them, and they call themselves promiscuously brothers and sisters, so that ordinary fornication, through the medium of a sacred name, becomes incest. And thus their vain and mad superstition glories in crimes. And for themselves, if there were not a basis of truth, knowing rumor would not tell of gross and unspeakable abominations. I hear that in some absurd conviction or other they consecrate and worship the head of an ass,[23] the most repulsive of beasts—a religion worthy of the morals that begot it. Others say that they reverence the private parts of their director and high priest, and adore them as if belonging to a parent. Whether this is false I know not, but suspicion naturally attaches to secret and nocturnal rites. To say that a man put to death for a crime and the lethal wooden cross are objects of their veneration is to assign altars suitable for abandoned and impious men, the kind of worship they deserve. What is told of the initiation of neophytes is as detestable as it is notorious. An infant covered with spelt to deceive the unsuspecting is set before the one to be initiated in the rites. The neophyte is induced to strike what seem to be harmless blows on the surface of the spelt, and this infant is killed by his random and unsuspecting blows. Its blood—oh, shocking!—they greedily lap up; the limbs they eagerly distribute; and by this victim they league themselves, and by this complicity in crime they pledge themselves to mutual silence. . . . Their form of banqueting is notorious; everywhere all talk of it. . . . On an appointed day they assemble at a feast with all their children, sisters, and mothers, people of both sexes and every age. There, after much feasting, when the banquet has become heated and intoxication has inflamed the drunken passions of incestuous lust, a dog which has been tied to a lamp is incited to rush and leap forward after a morsel thrown beyond the range of the cord by which it was tied. The

---

23. This was also said of the Jews (cf. Tacitus, *Histories* v. iii. 4–iv. 3).

telltale light is upset and extinguished, and in the shameless dark they exchange embraces indiscriminately, and all, if not actually, yet by complicity are equally involved in incest. . . .

Furthermore, they threaten the whole world and the universe itself and its stars with fire, and work for its destruction. . . .[24] Not content with this insane notion, they add to and weave old wives' tales: they say that they are reborn after death from the cinders and ashes, and with unaccountable confidence believe in one another's lies. . . .

But you [Christians] meanwhile in anxious doubt abstain from wholesome pleasures; you do not attend the shows; you take no part in the processions; fight shy of public banquets; abhor the sacred games, meats from the sacrificial victims, drinks poured in libation on the altars.

Athenagoras,[25] *Plea for the Christians* ii. 7, 9; iii. 12–13

It is not in accord with your justice that, when others are charged with crimes they are not punished till they are convicted, but in our case the name bears more weight than the evidence at the trial, at which the judges, instead of inquiring whether the accused has committed any wrong, insult the name, as if that were itself a crime. . . . Therefore what is conceded equally to all we claim for ourselves, that we shall not be hated and punished because we are called Christians (for what bearing has the name on evil-doing?), but shall be tried on any charges anyone may bring against us, and either be released on our disproving the charges, or punished if convicted of wickedness—not for the name (for no Christian is a bad man unless he falsely profess our doctrines) but for the wrong done. . . .

Three charges are alleged against us: atheism, cannibalistic banquets, incestuous unions. But if these charges are true, spare no class; proceed at once against the crimes; kill us root and branch, with our wives and children, if any Christian is found to live like the beasts. . . . But if these things are only gossip mongering and empty slanders . . . it is left for you to make inquiry concerning our life, our beliefs, our loyalty and obedience to you [the Emperor Marcus Aurelius], your house, and the monarchy, and thus at length to accord to us nothing more than to those who persecute us.

---

24. This refers to early Christian belief in the imminent destruction of the world and the coming Day of Judgment.

25. An Athenian convert, whose pamphlet in defense of Christianity was written *c.* 177.

Tertullian, *Apology* x. 1, xxviii. 2–3, xxxv. 1, xl. 1–2; From *LCL*

"You do not," say you, "worship the gods; you do not offer sacrifice for the emperors." It follows by parity of reasoning that we do not sacrifice for others because we do not for ourselves—it follows from our not worshiping the gods. So we are accused of sacrilege and treason at once. That is the chief of the case against us—the whole of it, in fact. . . .

So now we have come to the second charge, the charge of treason against a majesty more august. For it is with greater fear and shrewder timidity that you watch Caesar than the Olympian Jove himself. . . . So that in this too you will be found irreligious to those gods of yours, when you show more fear for the rule of a man. In fact, among you perjury by all the gods together comes quicker than by the *genius* of a single Caesar. . . .

So that is why Christians are public enemies—because they will not give the emperors vain, false, and rash honors; because, being men of a true religion, they celebrate the emperors' festivals more in heart than in frolic. . . .

On the contrary, the name faction may properly be given to those who join to hate the good and honest, who shout for the blood of the innocent, who use as a pretext to defend their hatred the absurdity that they take the Christians to be the cause of every disaster to the state, of every misfortune of the people. If the Tiber reaches the walls, if the Nile does not rise to water the fields, if the sky does not move [i.e., if there is no rain] or the earth does, if there is famine, if there is plague, the cry at once arises: "The Christians to the lions!"[26]

---

26. Except in the Christian writers (see § 169). praise of the Christian way of life is practically unknown in extant ancient sources. There is evidence, however, that some independent and rational minds were not swept away by the popular anti-Christian hysteria. For example, the Greek scientist Galen (A.D. *c.* 130–*c.* 200; cf. p. 225) wrote in his summary of Plato's *Republic* (the work is lost except for some fragments preserved in an Arabic translation): "Now we see the people called Christians . . . acting in the same way [as those who philosophize]. For their contempt of death [and of its sequel] is patent to us every day, and likewise their restraint in cohabitation. For they include not only men but also women who refrain from cohabiting all through their lives; and they also number individuals who, in self-discipline and self-control in matters of food and drink, and in their keen pursuit of justice, have attained a pitch not inferior to that of genuine philosophers" (R. Walzer, *Galen on Jews and Christians* [Oxford, 1949], p. 15).

169. Defense of the Christian Way of Life

The calumnies and attacks against Christians led to the production of a body of Christian apologetic literature during the second and third centuries. The Christian apologists, such as Aristides of Athens, Justin Martyr, Athenagoras, Minucius Felix, and Tertullian, give us an idealized picture of the early Christian community, generally glossing over the numerous defections under the stress of the persecutions and the fierce internal schisms.

Tertullian, *Apology* xxx, 1, 4, xxxviii–xxxix, xlii (abridged); Adapted from *LCL*

For we invoke the eternal God, the true God, the living God for the safety of the emperors. . . . Looking up to heaven, the Christians— with hands outspread, because innocent, with head bare because we do not blush, yes! and without a prompter [cf. § 161, first selection] because we pray from the heart—are ever praying for all the emperors. We pray for a fortunate life for them, a secure rule, a safe house, brave armies, a faithful senate, a virtuous people, a peaceful world. . . .

Should not this sect have been classed among the legal associations, when it commits no such actions as are commonly feared from unlawful associations? For unless I am mistaken, the reason for prohibiting associations clearly lay in forethought for public order—to save the state from being torn into parties, a thing very likely to disturb election assemblies, public gatherings, local senates, meetings, even the public games, with the clashing and rivalry of partisans. . . .[27] We, however, whom all the passion for glory and rank leave cold, have no need to combine; nothing is more foreign to us than the state. One state we recognize for all—the universe.

Your public games, too, we renounce, as heartily as we do their origins; we know these origins lie in superstition. . . . We have nothing to do, in speech, sight, or hearing, with the madness of the circus, the shamelessness of the theater, the savagery of the arena, the vanity of the gymnasium. Why should we offend you if we assume the existence of other pleasures? . . .

I will now show you the proceedings with which the Christian association occupies itself. I have proved they are not wrong; so now I will make you see they are good. We are a society with a common

27. On the Roman government's policy toward associations, see § 51.

religious feeling, unity of discipline, a common bond of hope. We meet in gathering and congregation to approach God in prayer, massing our forces to surround Him. This violence that we do Him pleases God. We pray also for the emperors, for their ministers and those in authority, for the security of the world, for peace on earth, for postponement of the end. We meet to read the divine Scriptures. . . . Our presidents are elders of proved character, men who have reached this office not for a price[28] but by character; for nothing that is God's goes for a price.

Even if there is a treasury of a sort, it is not made up of money paid in initiation fees, as if religion were a matter of contract. Every man once a month brings some modest contribution—or whenever he wishes, and only if he does wish, and if he can; for nobody is compelled; it is a voluntary offering. You might call them the trust funds of piety. For they are not spent upon banquets[29] or drinking parties or thankless eating houses; but to feed the poor and to bury them, for boys and girls who lack property and parents, and then for slaves grown old and for shipwrecked mariners; and any who may be in mines, islands, or prisons, provided that it is for the sake of God's sect, become the pensioners of their confession. . . .

So we, who are united in mind and soul, have no hesitation about sharing property. All is common among us—except our wives. At that point we dissolve our partnership. . . .

Our dinner shows its idea in its name; it is called by the Greek name for love [i.e., *agape*]. . . . Since it turns on the duty of religion, it allows nothing vile, nothing immodest.[30] We do not take our places at table until we have first partaken of prayer to God. Only so much is eaten as satisfies hunger, only so much drunk as meets the needs of the modest. . . . After water for the hands come the lights; and then each, from what he knows of the Holy Scriptures, or from his own heart, is called before the rest to sing to God. . . . Prayer in like manner ends the banquet. . . .

This gathering of Christians may properly be called illegal, if it is like illegal gatherings; may properly be condemned, if any complaint can be made against it such as are made against factions. To whose hurt have we ever met? We are when assembled just what we are when apart; taken together the same as singly; we injure none; we grieve none.

---

28. Tertullian refers to the purchase of priesthoods among the Greeks and Romans.

29. Formal banquets were one of the principal activities of associations among the Romans (cf. § 52, first selection).

30. For the popular charges against the Christians, see § 168.

When decent people, when good men gather, when the pious and when the chaste assemble, that is not to be called a faction. . . .

But there is another charge of wrong-doing made against us. We are said to be useless in business. How so, when we are human beings and live alongside of you—men with the same ways, the same dress and furniture, the same necessities of life? . . . So not without a *forum,* not without a meat market, not without baths, shops, workshops, stalls, and market days, and the other aspects of business, we live with you— in this world. We sail ships together with you, we serve in the army, go to the country, to market with you. Our skills and yours work together; our labor is openly at your service.

EARLY CHRISTIAN WORSHIP

Justin Martyr, *First Apology* lxi, lxv–lxvii

All who are convinced and believe that what is taught and said by us is true, and promise that they are able to live accordingly, are taught to pray and with fasting to ask forgiveness of God for their former sins; and we pray and fast with them. Then they are brought by us to where there is water, and they are reborn in the same manner as we ourselves were reborn [the rite of baptism]. For in the name of God, the Father and Lord of the universe, and of our Savior Jesus Christ, and of the Holy Ghost, they then are washed in the water. . . .

After thus washing the one who has been convinced and has given his assent, we conduct him to the place where those who are called the brethren are assembled, to offer earnest prayers in common for ourselves, for him who has been enlightened, and for all others everywhere, so that we, now that we have learned the truth, may by our works also be deemed worthy of being found to be good practitioners and keepers of the commandments, and thus be saved with eternal salvation. When we end our prayers we greet each other with a kiss. Then bread and a chalice of wine mixed with water are brought to the one who presides over the brethren; and he takes it, and offers up praise and glory to the Father of the universe, through the name of the Son and the Holy Ghost; and he gives thanks at length for our being deemed worthy of these things by Him. When he has finished the prayers and thanksgiving, all the people present express their assent, saying "Amen." . . . And when he who presides has celebrated the eucharist [thanksgiving], and all the people have expressed their assent, those called among us deacons allow each one of those present to partake of the bread and wine and water for which thanks have been given, and they bring it also to those not present. And this food is called among us the eucharist. . . .

And on the day called Sunday there is a gathering in one place of all who dwell in the cities or in the country places, and the memoirs of the apostles or the writings of the prophets are read as long as time allows. Then when the reader has finished, he who presides gives oral admonition and exhortation to imitate these excellent examples. Then we all rise together, and offer prayers; and, as stated before, when we have ended our praying, bread and wine and water are brought. And he who presides similarly offers up prayers and thanksgiving, as far as lies in his power, and the people express their approval by saying "Amen." And each receives a share and partakes of the food for which thanks have been given[31] and through the deacons some is sent to those not present. The prosperous, if they so desire, each contribute what they wish, according to their own judgment, and the collection is entrusted to the one who presides. And he assists orphans and widows, and those who are in need because of illness or any other reason, and those who are in prison, and strangers sojourning with us; in short, all those in need are his care.

DENUNCIATION OF PAGAN AMUSEMENTS

Tatian,[32] *Address to the Greeks* xxii–xxiii; From M. Whittaker, *Tatian, Oratio ad Graecos* (Oxford, 1982)

What is one to make of your teaching? Your official festivals are ridiculous, celebrated in honor of evil demons and bringing shame upon human beings. I saw a certain man on many occasions; when I first saw him I was astonished, but my astonishment was replaced by contempt as I considered how he was one man in himself, but quite another in the outward mask he assumed: very affected and putting on all sorts of delicate airs, now with flashing eyes, now wringing his hands and expressing madness with a clay make-up; sometimes appearing as Aphrodite, and sometimes as Apollo; a one-man accuser of all the gods, epitome of superstition, disparager of heroism, actor of murders, dem-

---

31. Justin refers to the *agape* ("love feast").

32. Born of pagan parents in Assyria, Tatian received a Greek education, became a pupil of Justin Martyr, and was converted to Christianity in the reign of Antoninus Pius.

onstrator of adultery, repository of madness, teacher of perverts, instigator of condemned criminals—and such a one drew praise from all!
But I rejected him as a total falsehood—the godlessness, the practices
and the man! Yet you are captivated by these men and abuse those who
do not share in your activities. I refuse to stand and gape at a chanting
crowd, and I do not want to ape the antics of someone gesticulating and
writhing in an unnatural way. Is there any kind of spectacle left for you
to devise? They blow through their noses and use foul language, they
posture obscenely and demonstrate on the stage how to commit adultery
in full view of your daughters and boys. You have splendid lecture halls,
publicizing all the wickedness that goes on at night and delighting the
audiences with disgraceful speeches; and splendid poets too, liars all,
who delude their hearers with their subtle wordplay.

I saw other men who had trained to become heavyweights, and
carried round a load of superfluous flesh, to whom prizes and garlands
are offered. The judges summon them not to a display of manliness but
to a contest of violent brawling, and the garland goes to the hardest
hitter. These are the lesser evils; anyone would shrink from mentioning
the greater ones. Some men are so abandoned as to make a profession of
idleness and actually sell themselves to be murdered; the hungry man
sells himself and the rich man buys the murderers-to-be. The spectators
take their seats and the gladiators engage in single combat about nothing, and no one goes down to their aid. Are your celebrations of this
kind really a good thing? Your great man collects his camp of murderers
by promising them a bandit's keep, so bandits are what come out of it.
You all gather to watch, and while on the one hand you criticize the
president of the games for his villainy, you also criticize the gladiators
themselves. Someone who happens to miss the murder is vexed, because
he was not condemned to be a spectator of wicked and bloody acts. You
sacrifice animals in order to eat meat and you buy men to provide
human slaughter for the soul, feeding it with bloodshed of the most
impious kind. The bandit murders for the sake of what he can get, but
the rich man buys gladiators for the sake of murder.

170. Atrocities Against Christians

In the reign of Marcus Aurelius, the "philosopher on the throne," occurred the only large-scale persecution of the Christians during the second
century. Mass hysteria generated by serious internal and frontier troubles

led to violent anti-Christian outbreaks in various provinces. The cruel torture and execution of forty-eight Christians, with the approval of the emperor, at Lyons and Vienne in A.D. 177, is a gruesome commentary on the brutality of the age.

Eusebius, *Ecclesiastical History* v. i (abridged); From *LCL*

First they endured nobly all that was heaped upon them by the mob, howls and stripes and dragging about, and rapine and stoning and imprisonment, and all things that are wont to happen at the hands of an infuriated populace against its supposed enemies and foes. Then they were dragged into the market place by the tribune and by the chief authorities of the city, were indicted and confessed, and at last they were shut up until the coming of the governor. Then they were brought before the governor, and when he used all his cruelty against them, then intervened Vettius Epagathus, one of the brethren. . . . His character forbade him to endure the unreasonable judgment given against us, and, overcome with indignation, he asked to be heard himself in defense of the brethren to the effect that there was nothing atheistic or impious among us. He was howled down by those around the judgment seat— he was a man of position—and the governor would not tolerate the just requests which he had put forward but merely asked if he were a Christian himself. He then confessed in clear tones and was himself taken into the ranks of the martyrs. . . .

There were also arrested certain heathen slaves of our members, since the governor had publicly commanded that we should all be prosecuted, and these by the snare of Satan, fearing the tortures which they saw the saints suffering, when the soldiers urged them, falsely accused us of cannibalistic feasts and incestuous intercourse [cf. § 168], and things which it is not right for us either to speak of or to think of or even to believe that such things could ever happen among men. When this rumor spread, all men turned like beasts against us, so that even if any had formerly been lenient for friendship's sake, they then became furious and raged against us. . . . All the fury of the mob and of the governor and of the soldiers was raised beyond measure against Sanctus, the deacon from Vienne, and against Maturus, who was a neophyte but a noble contender, and against Attalus, a Pergamene by origin, who had always been a pillar and support of the Christians there, and against Blandina. . . . The blessed woman, like a noble athlete, kept gaining in vigor in her confession, and found comfort and rest and freedom from pain from what was done to her by saying, "I am a Christian woman and nothing wicked happens among us." . . .

But when the tyrant's torments had been brought to naught by Christ through the endurance of the blessed saints, the devil thought of other devices, imprisonment in jail in darkness and in the most horrible place, and stretching their feet in the stocks, separated to the fifth hole, and the other outrages which angry warders filled with the devil were accustomed to inflict on the prisoners. Thus most of them were strangled in prison. . . .

Maturus, Sanctus, Blandina, and Attalus were led forth to the wild beasts, to the public, and to the common exhibition of the inhumanity of the heathen, for the day of fighting with beasts was specially appointed for the Christians. Maturus and Sanctus passed again through all torture in the amphitheater. . . . Blandina was hung on a stake and offered as a prey to the wild beasts that were let in. . . . Then, when none of the beasts would touch her, she was taken down from the stake and brought back into the jail. . . .

But Attalus was himself loudly called for by the crowd, for he was well known. He went in, a ready combatant, for his conscience was clear, and he had been nobly trained in Christian discipline and had ever been a witness for truth among us. He was led round the amphitheater and a placard was carried before him on which was written in Latin, "This is Attalus, the Christian." The people were very bitter against him, but when the governor learned that he was a Roman [citizen], he commanded him to be put back with the rest, who were in the jail, about whom he had written to the emperor and was awaiting a reply. . . .

Caesar wrote that they should be tortured to death, but that if any should recant they should be let go, and at the beginning of the local feast (and this is widely attended by the concourse of all the heathen to it) the governor led them to the judgment seat, making a show and spectacle of the blessed men to the mob. He accordingly interrogated them again, beheaded all who appeared to possess Roman citizenship, and sent the rest to the beasts. . . .

Those who had been strangled in the jail they threw to the dogs, and watched carefully night and day that none should be cared for by us. Then they threw out the remains left by the beasts and by the fire, torn and charred, and for many days watched with a military guard the heads of the rest, together with their trunks, all unburied. And some raged and gnashed their teeth at the remains seeking some further vengeance from them, others laughed and jeered glorifying their idols and ascribing to them the punishment of the Christians. . . . Thus the bodies of the martyrs, after having been exposed and insulted in every way for six days, and afterwards burned and turned to ashes, were swept by the wicked into the river Rhone, which flows near by, that not even a relic of them might still appear upon the earth.

171. Interrogation of Christians

From the middle of the second century there began to be disseminated in Christian circles descriptions of the manner in which those who perished for their faith endured martyrdom. A number of the early Acts of the Martyrs—the first of which is the martyrdom of Polycarp, bishop of Smyrna, in A.D. 155/156 recorded by Eusebius, *Ecclesiastical History* IV. xv. 1–24—are contemporary literary testimonials based on official records of the legal proceedings before Roman authorities (cf. § 167). The following is an account of the interrogation of six Christians from Scillium, in the province of Africa, by the proconsul Vigellius Saturninus at Carthage in A.D. 180.

R. Knopf, *Ausgewählte Märtyrerakten,* 3d ed. (Tübingen, 1929), no. 6

In the consulship of Praesens (for the second time) and Claudianus, on July 17, Speratus, Nartzalus, Cittinus, Donata, Secunda, and Vestia were put on trial in the [governor's] council chamber at Carthage. The proconsul Saturninus said, "You can secure the indulgence of our lord the emperor if you return to your senses."

Speratus said, "We have never done any wrong; we have lent ourselves to no injustice; we have never spoken ill of anyone; but when we have been ill-treated, we have given thanks, because we honor our emperor."

The proconsul Saturninus said, "We, also, are religious, and our religion is simple; and we swear by the *genius* of our lord the emperor, and pray for his welfare, as you too ought to do."

Speratus said, "If you grant me your undivided attention, I will tell you the mystery of simplicity."

Saturninus said, "I shall not grant you a hearing, if you begin to speak evil about our sacred rites; but swear rather by the *genius* of our lord the emperor."

Speratus said, "The empire of this world I do not recognize; but rather I serve that God whom no man has seen nor can see with human eyes. I have not committed theft; if I buy anything, I pay the tax, because I recognize my Lord, the King of kings and Emperor of all peoples."

The proconsul Saturninus said to the others, "Cease to be of this persuasion."

Speratus said, "It is an evil persuasion to commit murder, or to bear false witness."

The proconsul Saturninus said, "Do not participate in this madness."

Cittinus said, "We have none other to fear except only our Lord God who is in heaven."

Donata said, "Honor to Caesar as to Caesar, but fear to God."

Vestia said, "I am a Christian."

Secunda said, "What I am, that I wish to be."

The proconsul Saturninus said to Speratus, "Do you persist in being a Christian?"

Speratus said, "I am a Christian." And they all concurred with him.

The proconsul Saturninus said, "Do you desire some time to reconsider?"

Speratus said, "In a matter so just there is no reconsidering."

The proconsul Saturninus said, "What are the things in your box?"

Speratus said, "The Books, and the letters of Paul, a just man."

The proconsul Saturninus said, "Take a postponement of thirty days and reconsider."

Speratus said again, "I am a Christian." And they all concurred with him.

The proconsul Saturninus read out the decree from the tablet: "Since Speratus, Nartzalus, Cittinus, Donata, Vestia, Secunda, and the rest who have confessed that they live according to the rite of the Christians have obstinately persevered when an opportunity was offered them to return to the practice of the Romans, it is my decision that they be punished with the sword."

Speratus said, "We give thanks to God."

Nartzalus said, "Today we are martyrs in heaven; thanks to God!"

The proconsul Saturninus ordered the herald to proclaim: "I have ordered the execution of Speratus, Nartzalus, Cittinus, Veturius, Felix, Aquilinus, Laetantius, Januaria, Generosa, Vestia, Donata, and Secunda."

They all said, "Thanks be to God!"

And so they were crowned with martyrdom all together: and they reign with the Father and the Son and the Holy Ghost forever and ever. Amen.

172. ORGANIZED PERSECUTION OF CHRISTIANITY

The statement of Orosius *(History Against the Pagans* VII. xxvi. 9), that "the Church of Christ suffered ten persecutions from Nero [see § 38] to Maximian," is unfounded. Before the middle of the third century, action against Christians was sporadic and local, undertaken as police measures in a climate of popular anti-Christian agitation and violence. But in the great crisis of the Empire, by which time the sect had developed into a powerful organization—virtually a "state within a state"—systematic Empire-wide efforts to suppress the religion as a challenge to the state were organized by imperial order.

THE PERSECUTION UNDER DECIUS:
THE LOYALTY TEST

The first systematic persecution was that conducted by the Emperor Decius in A.D. 249–251. In the course of the persecution, Decius, in an ineffective attempt to expose all Christians, issued an edict apparently requiring all inhabitants of the Empire to take a "loyalty oath" to the state cult. Local commissions were set up in all communities of the Empire to administer the loyalty test. Each individual, even priests and priestesses of pagan gods, was required to give formal evidence of religious loyalty, which was certified in writing by the commissioners. More than fifty such certificates, all from Egypt, are extant. There were many defections at this time; but considerable numbers of Christians managed to obtain certificates of loyalty *(libelli)* through influence or bribery or by performing pagan sacrifice with mental reservations. The question of readmitting such *libellatici* (certificate holders), after the persecution was over, roused vigorous discussion among Church authorities.

Michigan Papyrus No. 158; A.D. 250

To those superintending the sacrifices of the village of Theadelphia, from Aurelia Bellias, daughter of Peteres, and her daughter Capinis. We have sacrificed to the gods all along, and now in your presence according to orders I poured a libation and sacrificed and tasted of the sacred offerings, and I request you to subscribe this for us. Farewell.

[Signatures] We, Aurelius Serenus and Aurelius Hermas, saw you sacrificing. Signed by me, Hermas.

Year 1 of the Emperor Caesar Gaius Messius Quintus Trajanus DE-CIUS Pius Felix Augustus, Payni 27.

THE PERSECUTION UNDER VALERIAN

After disastrous military defeats in A.D. 257, the Emperor Valerian organized a general persecution of the Christians, seeking to destroy the Church as an organization by depriving it of its leaders and by confiscating its economic resources. Cyprian, bishop of Carthage, the author of the following letter, perished in this persecution, which lasted until 270.

Cyprian, *Letters* lxxx

Cyprian to Successus, his brother, greeting.

The reason I did not write to you at once, dearest brother, is the fact that all the clergy have been placed under stress of peril and are unable to leave here at all: all are prepared, by virtue of the devotion of their minds, for divine and heavenly glory. You should know, however, that those have come whom I sent to the city [of Rome] for the purpose of investigating and bringing back to us the truth concerning whatsoever had been decreed concerning us. For many, various, and indefinite reports are rumored about. But the truth about them is as follows: Valerian has sent an address to the senate, to the effect that bishops, presbyters, and deacons should be immediately punished,[33] but that senators, distinguished men, and Roman *equites* should lose their rank and be deprived of their property also; and if, when their goods have been taken away, they should persist in being Christians, that they should then also be punished capitally; but that matrons should be deprived of their property and relegated to exile. Moreover, persons of the imperial household who had either previously confessed or should now confess, should be expropriated and put in chains and assigned to Caesar's estates. The Emperor Valerian also appended to his address a copy of the letters he prepared for the governors of the provinces concerning us. We are daily expecting these letters to come, and we are, according to the firmness of our faith, awaiting the endurance of suffer-

33. Here begins the second edict of Valerian, issued in A.D. 258. The first, in 257, ordered bishops and priests who refused to sacrifice to the state gods to be exiled and forbade Christians to assemble or to enter their cemeteries.

ing and expecting from the help and mercy of the Lord the crown of eternal life. But know that Sixtus [the bishop of Rome] was executed in the cemetery on August 6, and four deacons with him. The prefects of the city, furthermore, are daily pressing this persecution; so that any who are brought before them are punished and their property assigned to the fisc.

I beg that these things be made known through you to our other colleagues, so that everywhere by their exhortations the brotherhood may be able to be strengthened and prepared for the spiritual struggle, that each one of our people may not be more concerned about death than about immortality, and, dedicated to the Lord with full faith and complete courage, they may rejoice rather than be afraid in this confession, in which they know that the soldiers of God and Christ are not slain but crowned. I bid you, dearest brother, ever farewell in the Lord.

THE PERSECUTION UNDER DIOCLETIAN

The persecution carried out by Diocletian and his colleagues was the last to which Christians were subjected on an Empire-wide basis, but it was also the severest, lasting from 303 to 311.

Lactantius, *On the Deaths of the Persecutors* xii–xiv

A suitable and auspicious day was sought for accomplishing this business, and the Terminalia [cf. vol. 1, pp. 515–16], which takes place on February 23, was especially chosen to put an end, as it were, to this religion. . . . When that day dawned, in the eighth and seventh consulships of the two emperors [Diocletian and Maximian], suddenly, while it was hardly light, the prefect, together with the military commanders, tribunes, and treasury officers, came to the church [in Nicomedia], and when the doors had been broken down they sought for an image of God. Scriptures were found and burnt; spoil was given to all. Rapine, confusion, and tumult reigned. The emperors, watching from a vantage point (for the church, situated on an elevation, was visible from the palace), disputed for a long time with one another whether it should be set on fire. The opinion of Diocletian prevailed, for he feared that if such a great fire should be started some part of the city might be burned; for many large dwellings surrounded the church on all sides. Accordingly, the Praetorian Guard poured in from all sides in battle array, with axes and other iron implements, and in a few hours leveled that very lofty shrine to the ground.

On the following day an edict was published providing that men of that religion should be deprived of all honors and rank; that they should be subjected to torture, from whatever rank and station they might come; that every legal action should be pressed against them, but they themselves were not to have the right to sue for any wrong or for adultery or theft; and finally, that they should be accorded no freedom and no voice. A certain person, although it was wrong, yet with great courage ripped down this edict and tore it up, saying in derision, "These are the victories of Goths and Sarmatians." Brought to judgment at once, he was not only tortured but was burned in the legal manner, and displaying admirable endurance was finally consumed by the flames.

But Galerius was not satisfied with the terms of the edict and sought another way to influence Diocletian. For to drive him to a determination to employ an excess of cruelty in persecution, he employed private agents to set the palace on fire; and when some part of it had gone up in flames, the Christians were accused as public enemies, and tremendous prejudice flared up against the very name of Christian as the palace burned. It was said that the Christians had plotted in concert with the eunuchs to destroy the princes, and that the two emperors had almost been burned alive in their own palace. But Diocletian, who always wanted to appear shrewd and intelligent, suspected nothing of the deception; inflamed with anger, he began immediately to torture all his domestics.[34]

     .   .   .   .

This document from Middle Egypt sheds light on one of the administrative modalities of the persecution: the churches were closed and their valuables confiscated to the imperial privy purse. At that time many churches were still no more than chapels maintained in private houses.

Oxyrhynchus Papyrus No. 2,673; February 5, A.D. 304

In the 9th consulship of our lord emperor Diocletian and the 8th of our lord emperor Maximian Augusti. . . . [To the officials] of the glorious and most glorious city of the Oxyrhynchites from Aurelius Ammonius son of Copres, lector of the erstwhile church of the village of Chysis. Whereas you gave me orders—in accordance with the communication

34. Not only servants in the imperial household but even Diocletian's own wife and daughter had by this time embraced Christianity.

from Aurelius Athansius, procurator of the privy purse, *vir perfectissimus*
—concerning surrender of all the goods in the said erstwhile church, and
whereas I submitted that the said church had neither gold nor silver nor
money nor vestments nor animals nor slaves nor land nor property from
gifts or from testamentary bequests, excepting only the bronze material
that was found and delivered to the *curator* to be transported down to
the most glorious Alexandria in accordance with the communication
from our prefect Claudius Culcianus, *vir perfectissimus,* I now swear by
the fortune of our lords emperors Diocletian and Maximian Augusti and
Constantius and Galerius the most noble Caesars, that this is so and that
I have not falsified anything, or may I be liable to the imperial oath.
[Date.]

[2nd hand] I, Aurelius Ammonius, swore the oath as above. I, Aurelius Seranus, wrote on behalf of him, who is illiterate.

THE PERSECUTION UNDER MAXIMINUS

Despite the promulgation of the Edict of Toleration and the "Edict of
Milan" (see § 173), persecution continued in various parts of the Empire
until A.D. 324, especially in the East. The following inscriptions from Asia
Minor are connected with renewed persecution by Maximinus Daia.

OGIS, no. 569

[Arycanda, A.D. 311/312]

To the saviors of the entire human race, the divine Augustus Caesar
Galerius Valerius MAXIMINUS, the divine Augustus Caesar Flavius Val-
lerius CONSTANTINE, and the divine Augustus Caesar Valerius Licinianus
LICINIUS. Supplication and petition from the loyal province of Lycia and
Pamphylia.

Whereas the gods, of the same family as you, have ever by deeds
displayed benevolence to all, O Most Illustrious Emperors who have
been seriously concerned with the divine worship on behalf of the
eternal safety of yourselves, our lords, conquerors of all, we have decided that it would be well to seek refuge in your immortal majesty, and
to request that the Christians, who of old have been seditious and still
persist in the same disease, should finally desist and not, by introducing
some new mischief, neglect the honor owed to the gods. This would
easily be realized if by your divine and eternal will it were ordained to
all that the wickedness of the hateful practice of the atheists be forbidden

and prohibited, and if injunctions were given for all to devote themselves steadfastly to the worship of the gods, of the same family as you, on behalf of your eternal and indestructible majesty, the extent of whose benefits to all your people is manifest.

Journal of Roman Studies (1988), 78:105–124

[*Calbasa*, A.D. *312*]

[The beginning is lost.] Let them rejoice through the quiet that has finally been granted to them. And let those rejoice especially who have been freed from those blind and deviant obscurities and have returned to upright and good thinking. And as if preserved from a sudden storm or snatched from a great illness, let them henceforth feel a more pleasant enjoyment of life. But those who have persisted in the abominable superstition are to be separated and removed from your city and territory, as you request, so that in conformity with the laudable zeal of your petition your city, separated from the stain of all impiety, may respond as has been your tradition to the rites of the immortal gods with due veneration. Moreover, so that you may know how much your petition has been welcome to us, without any decree and any requests on your part, with spontaneous favor and our just and benevolent spirit, we grant, in response to your declaration, that you request whatever benefaction you wish, in return for your religious devotion of this kind. And you may act and request this now, for you will surely obtain the same without any delay, which granted to your city for all time may both attest to our religious devotion to the immortal gods and demonstrate to your sons and grandsons that you have received rewards from our Clemency worthy of your traditions. Farewell. Given in the second consulship of the Emperors Constantine and Licinius, April 6, at Sardis to the people of Colbasa.

173. The End of the Persecutions

THE EDICT OF TOLERATION

On April 30, A.D. 311, the Emperor Galerius, stricken with a serious illness from which he died shortly after, promulgated at Nicomedia the famous Edict of Toleration. This marked a turning point in the history of

Christianity, which, by this enactment, became a fully legal religion, though sporadic persecutions continued for some time after.

Lactantius, *On the Deaths of the Persecutors* xxxiv and Eusebius, *Ecclesiastical History* VIII. xvii. 6–10

Among other measures which we are constantly formulating for the advantage and benefit of the state, we had formerly desired to set all things right in accordance with the ancient laws and public order of the Romans, and to provide that the Christians, too, who had abandoned the doctrines of their own fathers, should return to a sound mind. For somehow such obstinacy had taken possession of the said Christians and such folly had seized them that, abandoning the institutions of the ancients, which their own fathers perhaps had previously established, they made laws for themselves to observe at their own will and as it pleased the said persons, and assembled various persons in sundry places. Accordingly, when our command had gone forth to the effect that they should return to the institutions of the ancients, many indeed were subjected to danger, and many also were struck down. But since very many persevered in their determination, and we saw that the said persons were neither paying worship and reverence to the gods nor worshiping the god of the Christians, in view of our most gentle Clemency and considering our consistent practice whereby we are wont to grant pardon to all men, we have thought fit in this case, too, to extend immediate indulgence, to wit: that they may be Christians once more and that they may reconstitute their places of assembly, on condition that they do nothing contrary to public order. In another letter, moreover, we shall indicate to governors of provinces what rules they are to observe. Wherefore, in accordance with this indulgence of ours, they are bound to implore their own god for our safety, for that of the state, and for their own, so that on every side the state may be rendered secure and they may be able to live tranquilly in their own homes.

THE "EDICT OF MILAN"

Early in A.D. 313 Constantine and Licinius at a conference at Milan agreed upon an Empire-wide religious policy. As a compromise between Licinius' pagan position and Constantine's pro-Christian views, the Roman state adopted a position of neutrality and enunciated a policy of complete religious freedom. No general edict was issued at Milan, but in all probability detailed instructions were drawn up for provincial governors to implement the new policy, already in force in the West under Constantine's rule. The famous "Edict of Milan" was probably a directive of Licinius despatched several months later from Nicomedia to governors of the Eastern provinces.

Lactantius, *On the Deaths of the Persecutors* xlviii, and Eusebius, *Ecclesiastical History* X. v. 2–14

Observing that freedom of worship should not be denied, but that each one should be given the right in accordance with his conviction and will to adhere to the religion that suits his preference, we had already long since given orders that both to the Christians[35] . . . to maintain the faith of their own sect and worship. But since many and various sects seem clearly to have been appended to that rescript in which such right was granted to the said persons, it may be perchance that some of them after a short time were driven away from such observance.

When I, Constantine Augustus, and I, Licinius Augustus, met under happy auspices in Milan and had under discussion all matters that concerned the public advantage and security, among other measures that we saw would benefit most men we considered that first of all regulations should be drawn up to secure respect for divinity, to wit: to grant both to the Christians and to all men unrestricted right to follow the form of worship each desired, to the end that whatever divinity there be on the heavenly seat may be favorably disposed and propitious to us and all those placed under our authority. Accordingly, with salutary and most upright reasoning, we resolved on adopting this policy, namely that we should consider that no one whatsoever should be denied freedom to devote himself either to the cult of the Christians or to such religion as he deems best suited for himself, so that the highest divinity, to whose worship we pay allegiance with free minds, may grant us in all things his wonted favor and benevolence. Wherefore, it is fitting that Your Devotion should know that it is our will that the conditions which were contained in our previous letter sent to your office with respect to the Christians be entirely removed, and that now each one of those who possess the same desire, namely to observe the form of worship of the Christians, should proceed freely to observe the same freely and unconditionally, without any interference or molestation to himself. These matters we decided to explain very fully to Your Solicitude, so that you

35. There is a lacuna in the text. Perhaps the text read: "and to all others freedom should be given."

may know that we have granted to the said Christians free and absolute power to observe their religion. And while you perceive that this indulgence has been granted to the said persons by us, Your Devotion will understand that free and untrammeled freedom in their religion or cult has similarly been granted to others also, in keeping with the peace of our times, so that each person may have unrestricted freedom to practice the cult he has chosen. This has been done by us so that we should not appear to have detracted anything from any form of worship or religion.

And, moreover, with special regard to the Christians we have decided that the following regulation should be set down: That, as for the said places in which they were wont to assemble previously, concerning which a definite regulation was previously contained also in the letter sent to your office, if any person should appear to have purchased them in prior times either from our fisc or from any other sources, they shall restore the said places to the Christians without payment or any demand for compensation, setting aside all fraud and ambiguity; and if any persons have obtained them as gifts, they shall similarly restore the same as quickly as possible to the said Christians; and in addition, if either those who have purchased the said places or those who have obtained them as gifts make some request of our benevolence, let them make the demands of the deputy prefect [cf. chapter 6, note 65] so that we may take thought for them too through our clemency. All these things must be transferred to the organization of the Christians by your intervention at once and without delay.

And since the said Christians not only possessed those places in which they were wont to assemble but are also known to have had others belonging not to individual men but to their corporate body, that is the churches, all these, under the provisions of the law we have set forth above, you will give orders to have restored without any uncertainty at all or controversy to the said Christians, that is to the organization and to their places of assembly, observing, of course, the aforesaid regulation, that those persons who restore the same without compensation, as we have stated, may look for compensation from our benevolence.

In all these matters you shall employ your most effective intervention for the aforesaid organization of the Christians, that this directive of ours may be fulfilled with all speed, so that in this also thought may be taken for the public peace through our clemency. To this extent it will come about, as set forth above, that the divine favor toward us, which we have already enjoyed in many matters, will continue for all time with good fortune for our successes together with the public happiness.

And that, moreover, the form which this decree and benevolence of ours takes may be brought to the knowledge of all, it will be proper for you to issue your proclamation and publish this document everywhere and bring it to the knowledge of all, to the end that the decreeing of this benevolence of ours may not remain unknown.

174. THE TRIUMPH OF CHRISTIANITY

Before his conversion to Christianity in A.D. 312, Constantine had been an adherent of the syncretic solar cult. Constantine's Christianity, whether genuine or inspired by political expediency, was expressed by a series of administrative and legal acts in favor of the Christian Church. As a Christian emperor ruling a predominantly pagan world, he was compelled to move slowly; until 324, when he became sole emperor after the defeat of Licinius, he strove by his legislation to give Christianity the same privileges the pagan cults enjoyed, thus maintaining a balance between Christianity and paganism (cf. § 173). But after 324 his negative attitude toward paganism took sharper form, though there is no trustworthy evidence that he took measures for the general abolition of pagan worship and the destruction of pagan temples. This final step was taken by the Emperor Theodosius in 395.

PRIVILEGES GRANTED THE CHURCH BY CONSTANTINE

Eusebius, *Ecclesiastical History* x. vii

Greeting, our most esteemed Anulinus [proconsul of Africa in A.D. 313]. Since it appears from many things that the setting at naught of divine worship, through which the highest reverence for the most holy power of heaven is preserved, has brought great dangers to the state, and that the lawful restoration and maintenance of this have bestowed good fortune on the Roman name and extraordinary prosperity on all the affairs of mankind (for it is divine Providence which bestows these blessings), it is our decision that those men who, with due holiness and devotion to this ordinance, offer their services in the performance of divine worship, should receive rewards for their labors, most esteemed Anulinus. Wherefore it is my will that those persons in the Catholic Church presided over by Caecilianus in the province entrusted to you who devote their service to this holy worship—those who are customarily named clerics—shall once and for all be kept completely exempt from all compulsory public services. They shall not be dragged away from the worship due the Divinity through any mistake or irreverent error, nor shall they be disturbed in any way from devoting themselves completely to serving their own law. For when they render supreme service to the Deity, it seems that they confer the greatest possible benefits upon the state. Farewell, our most esteemed and dearest Anulinus.

Eusebius, Ecclesiastical History x. vi

Constantine Augustus to Caecilianus, bishop of Carthage [the date of this letter is also A.D. 313]. Whereas we have resolved that throughout all provinces, namely the African, Numidian, and Mauretanian, some additional assistance be given to certain specified ministers of the lawful and most holy Catholic religion for expenses, I have sent a letter to Ursus, the most eminent procurator of Africa, and have notified him to see to the payment of 3,000 *folles* to Your Steadfastness. Accordingly, when you obtain delivery of the aforesaid sum of money, give orders that this money be distributed among all the aforementioned persons in accordance with the schedule sent to you by Hosius. But if, nevertheless, you should find that the sum is insufficient for the fulfillment of this purpose of mine with respect to all of them, you should request without hesitation whatever you find to be necessary from Heraclides, the procurator of our estate. For indeed I gave him instructions in person that if Your Steadfastness should request any money from him, he should see to the payment of it without any hesitation. And since I have learned that certain men of unstable conviction are desirous of turning aside the laity of the most Holy and Catholic Church by some miserable seduction, know that I have personally given orders to Anulinus, the proconsul, and moreover to Patricius, prefect's deputy [cf. chapter 6, note 65], to the effect that they should give due attention to all other matters and especially to this, and not permit such an occurrence to be overlooked. Therefore if you observe any such persons continuing in this madness, do not hesitate to go to the aforementioned governors and bring this said matter before them, so that they, as I personally ordered them, may bring these persons back to the right path. May the divinity of the great God preserve you for many years.

Theodosian Code VIII. xvi. 1; A.D. 320

Those persons who were considered celibates under the old law shall be freed from the threatening terrors of the statutes[36] and shall live just as if supported by the bond of matrimony in the number of married men, and all men shall have equal status with respect to accepting what each is entitled to.[37] Nor indeed shall any person be considered childless, and the disabilities attached to that term shall not harm him. We apply this provision also with respect to women, and we release all of them indiscriminately from the legal compulsions imposed like yokes on their necks.

Theodosian Code II. viii. 1; A.D. 321

Just as it appeared most unseemly for the day of the Sun [i.e., Sunday], solemn in its veneration, to be occupied with the altercations of the law courts and the noxious controversies of contending parties, so it is gratifying and pleasing for those acts which are especially longed for to be accomplished on that day. Therefore all men shall have freedom to emancipate and manumit on a festive day, and the legal formalities concerning such matters shall not be forbidden.

Theodosian Code IV. vii. 1; A.D. 321

Any persons who with pious intention grant deserved freedom to their favorite slaves in the bosom of the Church shall be deemed to have bestowed it with the same legality as Roman citizenship has been customarily conferred under the usual formalities. But it is our pleasure that this indulgence be allowed only to persons who make such grant in the presence of the bishops. To clerics, moreover, we further grant that when they bestow freedom on their own slaves, not only shall they be said to have granted full enjoyment of such freedom [when they manumit] in the presence of the Church and the religious congregation, but also when they confer freedom in a last will or give instructions in any words whatsoever that it be conferred. Accordingly, such grant of freedom takes immediate effect on the day of the publication of the expressed intent without any witness or intermediary required by law.[38]

36. The Papian-Poppaean laws of Augustus (see vol. 1, § 204). The present enactment of Constantine was not a general repealer but affected only the clergy.

37. That is, legacies and gifts, which unmarried and childless persons were permitted under the Augustan legislation to receive only in limited amount.

38. For the usual procedures employed in manumitting slaves, see § 49.

Theodosian Code xvi. ii. 5; A.D. 323

Since we have learned that certain ecclesiastics and others who serve the Catholic sect are compelled by men of different religions to perform lustral sacrifices [cf. vol. 1, § 56], we ordain by this sanction that if any person believes that those who serve the most holy law are to be compelled to [perform] the ritual of an alien superstition, he shall be publicly beaten with clubs if his legal status so permits [cf. § 159]; or, if the consideration of honorable rank protects him from such outrage, he shall sustain the penalty of a very heavy fine, which shall be claimed by the municipalities.

Theodosian Code xvi. v. 1; A.D. 326

The privileges which have been granted in consideration of religion must benefit only the adherents of the Catholic faith. It is our will, moreover, that heretics and schismatics shall not only be excluded from these privileges but shall also be bound and subjected to the various compulsory public services.

CONSTANTINE'S OFFICIAL POSITION
TOWARD PAGANISM

Theodosian Code ix. xvi. 2; A.D. 319

We forbid soothsayers and priests and persons accustomed to serve that rite to approach a private home or under pretext of friendship to cross the threshold of another; and punishment will threaten them if they disregard the statute. You, however, who think this profits you, go to the public altars and shrines and celebrate the ceremonies of your custom; for we do not forbid the services of a bygone usage to be conducted in open view.

Theodosian Code xvi. x. 1; A.D. 320/321

If it is established that any part of our palace or of other public works has been touched by lightning, the custom of the ancient religion shall be maintained: inquiry shall be made of the soothsayers as to the portent thereof, and the written record thereof shall be very carefully collected and referred to our wisdom. Others are also to be granted freedom to practice this custom, provided they abstain from domestic sacrifices, which are specifically prohibited.

CONSTANTINE AND EMPEROR WORSHIP

As a Christian, Constantine prohibited all forms of worship of himself. He did not, however, take measures to suppress the imperial cult as an institution, for it was by this time largely secularized and offered, moreover, distinct social and political advantages. A striking illustration of what has been called "his half-Christian, half-pagan state of mind" is afforded by the following reply to a petition from the town of Hispellum, in Umbria.

CIL, vol. XI, no. 5,265 (= Dessau, no. 705); A.D. 333–337

Copy of Sacred Rescript

The Emperor Caesar Flavius CONSTANTINE Maximus Germanicus Sarmaticus Gothicus, victorious, triumphant Augustus, and Flavius CONSTANTINE, and Flavius Julius CONSTANTIUS, and Flavius CONSTANS.[39] All things which protect human society we embrace in the deliberation of our ever-watchful administration; but it is especially incumbent upon our providential care to see to it that all cities, which are distinguished among the ornaments of all the provinces and regions for their splendor and beauty, should not only retain their former distinction but should also be elevated to a better state by virtue of our beneficence.

You declare that you [Umbrians] are administratively joined to Tuscia, and that by an established ancient custom you and the aforesaid [Tuscians] in alternate years appoint the priests who present theatrical shows and gladiatorial games at Vulsinii, a municipality of Tuscia. But because the journey lies over steep and wooded mountains you earnestly request that relief be granted to your priest, so that it will not be necessary for him to proceed to Vulsinii to celebrate the spectacles. Your request is that to the municipality which is now called Hispellum and which, you state, adjoins and connects with the Flaminian Way, we grant a name from our family name; that a temple of the Flavian family

---

39. Constantine, Constantius, and Constans, the sons of Constantine the Great, held the rank of Caesar under their father and divided the empire among them after his death.

may be constructed there in magnificent style truly in keeping with the splendor of the name; and that the priest whom Umbria has provided every other year may there present an exhibition of both theatrical shows and gladiatorial games—the said custom to continue in Tuscia, where a priest chosen from that region shall celebrate the aforementioned exhibitions at Vulsinii as in the past.

To your petition and desire we have acceded with ready assent. For to the municipality of Hispellum we have granted an eternal title and revered name from our appellation, so that in the future the aforesaid city shall be called Flavia Constans; and in its midst, as you wish, we desire a temple of the Flavian family, that is, our family, to be constructed in magnificent style, with this restriction, that a temple dedicated to our name be not defiled by the evils of any contagious superstition. Accordingly, we have also given you permission to exhibit spectacles in the aforementioned city, with the understanding that, as has been stated, the periodic celebration of the spectacles shall not cease at Vulsinii, where the aforementioned celebration is to be conducted by priests to be chosen from Tuscia. Thus not very much will seem to have been detracted from old institutions, and you, who for the aforesaid reasons have appeared as suppliants before us, will rejoice to have obtained what you earnestly requested.

175. THE COUNCIL OF NICAEA, A.D. 325

"Constantine sitting amongst the Christian bishops at the oecumenical council of Nicaea is in his own person the beginning of Europe's Middle Age" (*Cambridge Ancient History*, 12:699).

Eusebius, *Life of Constantine* III. vi–x (abridged)

Constantine summoned a general synod, inviting the bishops in all parts with honorary letters to be present as soon as possible. . . . At that time there were to be seen congregated in one place persons widely different from one another not only in spirit but also in physical appearance, and in the regions, places, and provinces from which they came. . . . From all the churches which had filled all Europe, Africa, and Asia, those who held the chief place among the servants of God assembled at the same time; and one sacred hall, extended as it were by the will of God, embraced in its compass Cilicians, Phoenicians, Arabs, Palestinians,

Egyptians, Thebans, Libyans, and some coming from Mesopotamia. A bishop from Persia also participated in the synod, nor was Scythia absent from this body. Pontus, likewise Galatia, Pamphylia, and Cappadocia, Asia, too, and Phrygia provided their most carefully chosen persons. Thracians also, Macedonians, Achaeans, and Epirotes, and those who are situated at a very long distance beyond these were nonetheless present. . . . Present among the body were more than 250 bishops. . . .

But on the day fixed for the council which was to put an end to the controversies, when the various persons who composed the synod were at hand, in the very middle of the hall of the palace which seemed to surpass all the rest in size, there were many seats arranged in rows on both sides; and all who had been summoned entered and each sat down in his place. After the entire synod had seated itself with seeming modesty, all at first fell silent, awaiting the coming of the emperor. Soon one of those closest to the emperor, then a second and a third entered. Others, too, preceded—not, as customary, from among the soldiers and bodyguard, but only those of his advisers who professed the faith of Christ. And when the signal was given which announced the entry of the emperor, all rose, and finally he himself approached proceeding down the center . . . dazzling the eyes of all with the splendor of his purple robe and sparkling with fiery rays, as it were, adorned for the occasion as he was with an extraordinary splendor of gold and jewels. . . . As for his soul, it was sufficiently apparent that he was adorned with the fear of God and religion.

176. THE FOUNDATION OF CONSTANTINOPLE

Sozomen,[40] *Ecclesiastical History* book 2, ch. 3

Since everything was going according to his wishes, and he had by wars and treaties settled his relations with the barbarians, Constantine decided to found a city having the same name as himself and the same rank as Rome. [He chose a site near Troy, but] God appeared to him in the night and . . . transporting him [in his dream] to Byzantium in Thrace opposite Chalcedon in Bithynia, disclosed to him to found this as his city and honor it with the name of Constantine. Obeying the word of God, he extended the city formerly called Byzantium over a wide area

40. Sozomen (c. 380–c. 450), a lawyer in Constantinople, was a Greek author of an *Ecclesiastical History* in nine books, covering the years A.D. 324–439.

and surrounded it with very big walls. And since he thought that the local inhabitants were not enough citizens for the great size of the city, he built great houses here and there along the streets, made men of renown masters of these houses and settled them there with their households, summoning some of the men from Old Rome, others from other provinces. He imposed taxes, some for the buildings and embellishment of the city, others for feeding the citizens; he adorned it lavishly all about the city, most notably (along with everything else) with a hippodrome and fountains and porticoes and other buildings; and he named Constantinople New Rome and established it as the capital of all who inhabit land subject to Roman rule to the north, south and east and the seas in between from the cities near the Ionian Sea to Cyrene. . . . This, then, like a newly constructed city of Christ and bearing his own name, Constantine honored by adorning it with many great [Christian] houses of prayer.

THE LAST STAND OF PAGANISM AND THE CONSOLIDATION OF CHRISTIAN SOCIETY

177. THE ECONOMY IN DISORDER

EXTRAVAGANCE AND POVERTY

Anonymous, *On Military Affairs*[1] ii; From R. Ireland, *De Libris Bellicis* (Oxford, 1979)

In the age of Constantine extravagant public spending prescribed gold for petty transactions instead of bronze, which previously had been highly valued. The origin of this display of greed is believed to have sprung from the following cause. When the gold and silver and the enormous quantity of precious stones which had been hoarded many years ago in the temples reached the public, it inflamed everyone's desire to spend and possess. And although the spending of bronze itself . . . could already be seen to be excessive and difficult to control, neverthe-less, as a result of some blindness or other, there came about an increas-ingly widespread insistence on spending gold, which is understood to be more valuable. The private mansions of the powerful, filled from this flood of gold, were turned into more signal instruments for the oppres-sion of the poor, the less-well-off, obviously, being held down by brutal means. But the suffering poor, driven to attempt various acts of wicked-ness, and having before their eyes no respect for the law nor feeling of loyalty, entrusted their revenge to the criminal arts. For frequently they inflicted extremely serious damage on the Empire by laying the country-side waste, by persistently disturbing the peace with acts of brigandage, by stirring up hatreds. And they encouraged along the stages of their

---

1. Written in mid-fourth century.

criminal career the tyrants whom desperation brought forth . . . against your virtuous splendor. Your prudence, most excellent emperor, will therefore take steps to hold down public spending, and thereby both to look to the interests of the taxpayer and to extend to ages to come the splendor of your name. Last of all, think over briefly what is known of happier ages of mankind, and remember the celebrated kingdoms of the ancient times of poverty, which had learned how to cultivate the land and not covet riches, remember with what honor and praise their untainted frugality gives them a name for all time. Certainly we speak of those ages as "golden" which had absolutely no gold at all.

PRICE CONTROLS

This papyrus from Oxyrhynchus contains six sworn declarations of current prices by guilds. In the declaration given here the bakers' guild declares the price they paid for wheat, thus certifying that the legal maximum had not been exceeded. The price paid, 24 talents or 144,000 drachmas, provides for us a striking example of how far the inflation of the currency had advanced; a hundred years earlier an artab of wheat cost, at most, 20 drachmas.

SB, no. 12,648; November 26, A.D. 338

To Flavius Eusebius, *curator* of the Oxyrhynchite [nome], the guild of bakers of the same city, through us Aurelii Hatres, Achilles, Didymus, another Hatres, Marcellus and Nilus. At our own risk we declare the following to be the contract price of the purchased goods which we handle during this month, and we swear the divine [i.e., imperial] oath that we have not falsified anything. Item: wheat by the one-tenth measure, 24 talents. In the counsulship of Flavii Ursus and Polemius, *viri clarissimi*, Hathyr 30.

178. THE PAGAN ARISTOCRACY AND THE ANCESTRAL RELIGION

CIL, vol. VI, no. 499 (=Dessau, no. 4,147); Rome, A.D. 374

To the great mother of the gods Ida, parent in the highest, to Hermes and Attis, to Lord Mēn unconquered, Clodius Hermogenianus Caesarius, *vir clarissimus*, proconsul of Africa, prefect of the city of Rome, member of the Board of Fifteen for Making Sacrifices, having performed the sacrifice of a bull and a ram on the 19th of August, to the gods guardians of his soul and mind, dedicated the altar during the consulship of our Lord Gratian Augustus for the third time and of Flavius Aequitius.

CIL, vol. VI, no. 510 (=Dessau, no. 4,152); Rome, A.D. 376

To the great gods, to the mother of the gods and to Attis, Sextilius Agesilaus Aedesius, *vir clarissimus,* distinguished orator in cases of the African tribunal and in the cabinet of the emperors; likewise, in charge of petitions and judicial inquiries involving sacral law, in charge of imperial replies, in charge of records, deputy to the prefects in the Spains, alternate for investigating matters of sacral law, father of the priests of the unconquered Sun god, of Mithra, priest of Hecate, chief priest of the god Liber, reborn in eternity by the sacrifice of a bull and of a ram, dedicated the altar in the consulship of our Lords Valens for the fifth time and of Valentinian II Augusti, August 13.

CIL, vol. VI, no. 1,741 (=Dessau, no. 1,243); Rome, mid-fourth century

In honor of Memmius Vitrasius Orfitus [father-in-law of the author Symmachus], *vir clarissimus,* of noble descent, at home and abroad in the traditions of old, very distinguished by restraint, justice, constancy, foresight and all the virtues, prefect of the city, and a short time after again prefect of the city, proconsul of Africa, member of the cabinet first rank, governor of the province of Sicily, superior priest of Vesta, member of the Board of Fifteen for Making Sacrifices, priest of the Sun God, consul, praetor, candidate for the quaestorship. He accomplished all this from very youth. For his remarkable and salutary provisions in difficult times, the very ancient guild of the tax collectors of Ostia and Portus set up this statue, also for his restoration of the efficiency of the city of Rome.

CIL, vol. VI, no. 1,698 (=Dessau, no. 1,257); Rome, A.D. 377

The family of the Phosphorii. To Lucius Aurelius Avianus Symmachus [father of the author Symmachus], *vir clarissimus,* prefect of the city, consul, assistant prefect of the Praetorian Guard in the city of Rome and the neighboring provinces, prefect of the grain supply of the city of Rome, major *pontifex,* member of the Board of Fifteen for Making

Sacrifices. He engaged in many embassies to the Divine Emperors on behalf of the interests of this most distinguished order [Senate]. He was customarily the first in the Senate to be asked his view, and by his authority, prudence and eloquence on behalf of the dignity of this great order he demonstrated the greatness of his status. Accordingly, the most distinguished Senate requested in frequent decrees from our Lords and Emperors a statue lustrous with gold. The same conquerors, our Emperors, ordered this to be set up, adding an oration which contained the order and sequence of his merits. Their eternal judgment added this also to such a great benefaction, that there be set up a second statue of equal splendor also in Constantinople. Dedicated April 29 in the consulship of our Lord Gratian for the fourth time and of Merobaudes.

CIL, vol. VI, No. 1,779 (=Dessau no. 1,359); Rome, A.D. 385

To the spirits of the dead. Vettius Agorius Praetextatus, augur, priest of Vesta, priest of the Sun God, Member of the Board of Fifteen [for Making Sacrifices], district priest of Hercules, father of the college of priests. In public affairs he was candidate for the questorship, urban praetor, governor of Tuscia and Umbria, governor of Lusitania, proconsul of Achaea, prefect of the city, sent seven times as envoy by the Senate, prefect of the Praetorian Guard twice in Italy and Illyricum, designated ranking consul, and Aconia Fabia Paulina [see § 103], *femina clarissima,* consecrated to Ceres and the Eleusinian Mysteries, consecrated to Hecate at Aegina, having performed the bull sacrifice, priestess. They lived together forty years.

VESTAL VIRGINS

CIL, vol. VI, no. 2,145 (=Dessau no. 1,261); Rome, late fourth century

To Coelia Concordia, head of the Vestal Virgins. [Aconia] Fabia Paulina, *femina clarissima,* arranged for this statue [of Coelia] to be made and erected because of her scrupulous modesty and outstanding piety toward sacred rites, and because she had previously erected a statue to Vettius Agorius, her husband, *vir clarissimus,* preeminent in every way and worthy of being worshipped by the virgins of this kind and by priests.

Symmachus, *Letters* IX. cviii

Everything that is bruited about anonymously is untrustworthy. But I cannot endure that credence should be given to talk against the reputation of a Vestal Virgin. Therefore in my capacity of *pontifex* and by my integrity as a senator I am constrained to report what I have heard. You are said to desire to withdraw from the seclusion of a Vestal before the years established by the laws [thirty years; for the Vestal Virgins see § 103]. I do not yet give credence to the rumor, but I await a personal declaration from you which either confirms or repudiates the dubious rumor.

179. PAGANISM ON THE DEFENSIVE

Beginning with the Emperor Constantius "laws of unprecedented severity which had no real effect succeeded one another only to be modified from time to time, and brutal arbitrariness was followed by acts of clemency" (J. Geffcken, *The Last Days of Graeco-Roman Paganism* [Amsterdam and New York, 1978], p. 126). Cf. § 163.

DECREES AGAINST SOOTHSAYERS
AND ASTROLOGERS

Theodosian Code IX. xvi. 4; A.D. 357

The Emperor Constantius Augustus to the people: No one shall consult a soothsayer or astrologer or diviner. The evil teachings of augurs and practitioners of magic shall become silent. The Chaldeans and magicians and all the rest whom the common people call evil doers because of the greatness of their crimes shall not attempt anything of this sort. The curiosity of all men for divination shall forever cease. If any one should refuse obedience to these orders he shall suffer capital punishment, executed by the sword of vengeance.

Theodosian Code IX. XVI. 12; A.D. 409

The Emperors Honorius and Theodosius Augusti to Caecilianus, Praetorian Prefect: We decree that astrologers shall be expelled not only from the city of Rome but also from all municipalities, unless, after the books of their false teaching have been burned in flames in the presence of the bishop, they are prepared to transfer their faith to the practice of the Catholic religion and never revert to their former false teaching. But if they do not do this and, in the face of the salutary constitution of our Clemency, are apprehended in the municipalities and introduce there the secrets of their false teaching and profession, they shall be punished by deportation.

ABOLITION OF DIVINATION

Theodosian Code XVI. X. 9; A.D. 385

The same Augusti [Gratian, Valentinian, and Theodosius] to Cynegius, Praetorian Prefect: No person shall have the audacity of performing sacrifices with a view to inspection of the liver and the omens of the entrails of sacrificial victims so as to win the hope of a vain prediction, or, worse, to learn the future by heinous consultation. The retribution of a very condign punishment shall threaten those who in violation of our prohibition attempt to search into the truth of present or future events.

A PETITION FOR TOLERATION OF PAGANISM

In the face of Christian persecution of pagans, Libanius, who was devoted to the traditional religion, addressed to the Emperor Theodosius a plea for freedom of worship.

Libanius, *Orations* XXX. 8–10, 33–34; From *LCL*

You then have neither ordered the closure of temples nor banned entrance to them. From the temples and altars you have banished neither fire nor the offerings of other perfumes [i.e., incense]. But this black-robed tribe [i.e., monks], who eat more than elephants and, by the quantities of drink they consume, weary those that accompany their drinking with the singing of hymns, who hide these excesses under an artificially contrived pallor—these people, Sire, while the law yet remains in force, hasten to attack the temples with sticks and stones and bars of iron, and, in some cases, disdain these, with hands and feet. Then utter desolation follows, with the stripping of roofs, demolition of walls, the tearing down of statues and the overthrow of altars, and the priests must either keep quiet or die. After demolishing one, they scurry

to another, and to a third, and trophy is piled on trophy, in contravention of the law. Such outrages occur even in the cities, but they are most
common in the countryside. . . . They sweep across the countryside like
rivers in spate, and by ravaging the temples, they ravage the estates, for
wherever they tear out a temple from an estate, that estate is blinded and
lies murdered. Temples, Sire, are the soul of the countryside: they mark
the beginning of its settlement, and have been passed down through
many generations to the men of today. In them the farming communities rest their hopes for husbands, wives, children, for their oxen and the
soil they sow and plant. An estate that has suffered so has lost the
inspiration of the peasantry together with their hopes, for they believe
that their labor will be in vain once they are robbed of the gods who
direct their labors to their due end. . . .

If all this business of sacrifice is nonsense, then why has the nonsense
been stopped? If it is harmful, then isn't this all the more reason? But if
the stability of empire depends on the sacrifices performed there, we
must consider that sacrifice is everywhere to our advantage: the gods in
Rome grant greater blessings, those in the countryside and the other
cities, lesser ones, but any sensible man would welcome even such as
these. . . . One [god] supports the might of Rome, another protects for
her a city under her sway, another protects an estate and grants it
prosperity. Let temples everywhere remain in being, then, or else let
these people agree that you emperors are ill-disposed to Rome since you
allow her to act in a manner that will cause her harm.

180. JULIAN THE APOSTATE

PAGAN WORSHIP RESTORED

The first of these letters of Julian, written in November 361 soon after the
death of Constantius, is addressed to the philosopher Maximus, one of
Julian's teachers, who lost his life ten years later in the "witch hunts"
under Valens (see § 181). The second was written from Constantinople in
April 362 to Julian's uncle in Antioch.

Julian,[1] *Letters* viii (abridged); From *LCL*

Let me arrange what I have to tell in chronological order, though not till I have first offered thanks to the all-merciful gods, who at this present have permitted me to write and will also perhaps permit us to see one another. Directly after I had been made Emperor—against my will, as the gods know . . .—I led the army against the barbarian [Germans]. . . . I pass over many important events. Above all it is right that you should learn how I became all at once conscious of the very presence of the gods, and in what manner I escaped the multitude of those who plotted against me, though I put no man to death, deprived no man of his property, and only imprisoned those whom I caught red-handed. All this, however, I ought perhaps to tell you rather than write it, but I think you will be very glad to be informed of it. I worship the gods openly, and the whole mass of the troops who are returning with me worship the gods. I sacrifice oxen in public. I have offered many hecatombs as thank offerings. The gods command me to restore their worship in its utmost purity, and I obey them, yes, and with a good will. For they promise me great rewards for my labors, if only I am not remiss.

Julian, *Letters* xxix (abridged); From *LCL*

Be assured that with the aid of the gods I shall leave nothing undone. First of all, set up the pillars of the temple [of Apollo] at Daphne; take those that are in any palace anywhere and convey them thence; then set up in their places others taken from the recently erected church(?). And if there are not enough even from that source, let us use cheaper ones meanwhile, of baked brick and plaster, encasing them with marble [stucco], for you are well aware that piety is to be preferred to splendor.

Sozomen,[2] *Ecclesiastical History* v. iii

Julian, when he found himself in sole possession of the Empire, ordered that all pagan temples throughout the East should be reopened; that those which had been neglected should be restored; that those which had fallen into ruins should be rebuilt; and that the altars should be restored. He allotted considerable funds for this purpose. He restored the practices

1. Written in mid-fourth century.
2. See chapter 9, note 40.

of antiquity and the ancestral ceremonies in the cities, and the practice of offering sacrifice.

He himself openly offered libations and sacrificed publicly; restored the priests, hierophants and servants of the statues of the gods to their old privileges, and reaffirmed the legislation of former emperors on their behalf. He granted exemption from duties and other burdens, as they were previously entitled to, and restored the regimen, which had been rescinded, of the temple guardians, commanding them to abstain from meats and from whatever according to pagan tradition was befitting him who announced his purpose of leading a pure life.

He also ordered the Nilometer and the symbols of earlier traditional tablets to be cared for in the temple of Serapis, instead of being placed, according to the regulation established by Constantine, in the church. He wrote frequently to the inhabitants of those cities in which he knew paganism was cultivated and urged them to ask for what benefactions they might desire. Towards the Christians, on the contrary, he openly demonstrated his aversion, refusing to honor them with his presence, or to give audience to their envoys who were delegated to report their grievances.

When the inhabitants of Nisibis sent to beg his aid against the Persians, who were about to invade the Roman territories, he refused to assist them because they were wholly Christianized. He would neither reopen their temples nor resort to the sacred places, and he threatened that he would not help them, nor receive their embassy, nor come to enter their city until he had heard that they had returned to paganism.

JULIAN'S EDICT ON TEACHERS

Julian's education law, under which teachers were to be evaluated on their acceptance of the religious and moral values of Greco-Roman literature, was a calculated assault on Christian education and caused a great uproar in the Christian communities.

Julian, *Letters* xxxvi (abridged); From *LCL*

I hold that a proper education results not in laboriously acquired symmetry of phrases and language, but in a healthy condition of mind. I mean a mind that has understanding and true opinions about things good and evil, honorable and base. Therefore when a man thinks one thing and teaches his pupils another, in my opinion he fails to educate exactly in proportion as he fails to be an honest man. . . . Now, all who profess to teach anything whatever ought to be men of upright character, and ought not to harbor in their souls opinions irreconcilable with what they publicly profess; and above all I believe it is necessary that those who associate with the young and teach them rhetoric should be of that upright character; for they expound the writings of the ancients, whether they be rhetoricians or grammarians, and still more if they are sophists. For these claim to teach, in addition to other things, not only the use of words but morals also, and they assert that political philosophy is their peculiar field. . . . While I applaud them still for aspiring to such high pretensions, I should applaud them still more if they did not utter falsehoods and convict themselves of thinking one thing and teaching their pupils another. What! Was it not the gods who revealed all their learning to Homer, Hesiod, Demosthenes, Herodotus, Thucydides, Isocrates and Lysias? Did not these men think that they were consecrated, some to Hermes, others to the Muses? I think it is absurd that men who expound the works of these writers should dishonor the gods whom these men honored. Yet, though I think this absurd, I do not say that they ought to change their opinions and then instruct the young. But I give them this choice: either not to teach what they do not think admirable, or, if they wish to teach, let them first really persuade their pupils that neither Homer nor Hesiod nor any of these writers, whom they expound and have declared to be guilty of impiety, folly and error in regard to the gods, is such as they declare. For since they make a livelihood and receive pay from the works of these writers, they thereby confess that they are most shamefully greedy of gain and that, for the sake of a few drachmas, they would put up with anything. It is true that until now there were many excuses for not attending the temples, and the terror that threatened on all sides absolved men for concealing their truest beliefs about the gods. But since the gods have granted us liberty, it seems to me absurd that men should teach what they do not believe to be sound. But if they believe that those whose interpreters they are and for whom they sit, so to speak, in the seats of prophets were wise men, let them be the first to emulate their piety towards the gods. If, however, they think that those writers were in error with respect to the most honored gods, then let them betake themselves to the churches of the Galilaeans to expound Matthew and Luke, since you Galilaeans are obeying them when you ordain that men shall refrain from temple worship. For my part, I wish that your ears and tongues might be "born again," as you would say.

JULIAN'S TREATMENT OF CHRISTIANS

Julian, *Letters* xxxvii; From *LCL*

I affirm by the gods that I do not wish the Galilaeans to be either put to death or unjustly beaten, or to suffer any other injury; but nevertheless I do assert absolutely that the god-fearing must be preferred to them. For through the folly of the Galilaeans almost everything has been overturned, whereas through the grace of the gods we are all preserved. Wherefore both men and cities ought to honor the gods and the god-fearing.

Julian, *Letters* xl; From *LCL*

I have behaved to all the Galilaeans with such kindness and benevolence that none of them has suffered violence anywhere or been dragged into a temple or threatened with anything else of the sort against his own will. But the followers of the Arian church, in the insolence bred by their wealth . . . have committed in Edessa such rash acts as could never occur in a well-ordered city. Therefore, since by their most admirable law they are bidden to sell all they have and give to the poor so that they may attain more easily to the kingdom of the skies, in order to aid those persons in that effort, I have ordered that all their funds that belong to the church of Edessa are to be taken over to be given to the soldiers, and that its property be confiscated; this in order that poverty may teach them to behave properly and that they may not be deprived of the heavenly kingdom for which they still hope.

DEDICATION TO JULIAN

AE, 1969–1970, no. 631; Jordan River valley, A.D. 362

To the liberator of the Roman world, restorer of the temples, reviver of senates and of the Roman state, destroyer of barbarians, our Lord Julian forever Augustus, Alamannicus Maximus, Francicus Maximus, Sarmaticus Maximus, *pontifex maximus,* father of his country. [The rest of lost.]

AN APPRECIATION OF JULIAN

Ammianus Marcellinus, *History* XVI. i; XXII. x (abridged); From *LCL*

Some law of higher life seems to have attended his youth from his noble cradle even to his last breath. For with rapid strides he grew so conspicuous at home and abroad that in his foresight he was esteemed a second Titus, son of Vespasian, in the glorious progress of his wars as very like Trajan, mild as Antoninus Pius, and in searching out the true and perfect reason of things in harmony with Marcus Aurelius, in emulation of whom he moulded his conduct and his character. . . . Drawn from the peaceful shades of the Academy . . . to the dust of battle, he vanquished Germany, subdued the meanders of the freezing Rhine, here shed the blood of kings breathing cruel threats, and there loaded arms with chains. . . .

He also corrected some of the laws, removing ambiguities, so that they showed clearly what they demanded or forbade to be done. But this one thing was inhumane and ought to be buried in eternal silence, namely, that he forbade teachers of rhetoric and literature to practice their profession if they were followers of the Christian religion.

181. THE "WITCH HUNTS" UNDER VALENS

In the fourth century the imperial courts of Constantinople and Rome were riven by incessant intrigues, political and personal. Insecure and suspicious emperors executed many prominent persons on scanty evidence or trumped-up charges. A specially notable example is the following episode of A.D. 371–372 in which, in the name of suppressing sorcery, Valens wiped out virtually all the pagan philosophers of the Eastern empire.

Ammianus Marcellinus, *History* XXIX. i–ii (abridged); From *LCL*

Valens' monstrous savagery spread everywhere like a fiercely blazing torch, and was increased by the base flattery of many men, and in particular by that of Modestus, who was then Praetorian Prefect. . . . First, after some unimportant questions, Pergamius was called in, betrayed . . . by Palladius of having foreknowledge of certain things through criminal incantations. Since he was very eloquent and was prone to say dangerous things, while the judges were in doubt what ought to be asked first and what last, he began to speak boldly, and shouted out in an endless flood the names of a very large number of men as accomplices, demanding that some be produced from all but the ends of the earth, to be accused of great crimes. He . . . was punished with death; and after him others were executed in flocks; then finally they came to the case of Theodorus. . . .

Then Patricius and Hilarius were brought in and ordered to give a connected account of what had happened. [Compelled by torture] Hilarius said: "O most honored judges, we constructed from laurel twigs under dire auspices this unlucky little table which you see, in the likeness of the Delphic tripod, and having duly consecrated it by secret incantations, after many long-continued rehearsals we at length made it work. . . . We then and there inquired, "What man will succeed the present emperor?", since it was said that he would be perfect in every particular, and the ring leaped forward and lightly touched the two syllables THEO, adding the next letter,[3] then one of those present cried out that by the decision of inevitable fate Theodorus was meant. And there was no further investigation of the matter; for it was agreed among us that he was the man who was sought.

And when Hilarius had laid the knowledge of the whole matter so clearly before the eyes of the judges, he kindly added that Theodorus was completely ignorant of what was done. After this, being asked whether they had, from belief in the oracles which they practised, known beforehand what they were now suffering, they uttered verses which clearly announced that this work of inquiring into the superhuman would soon be fatal to them, but that nevertheless the Furies, breathing out death and fire, threatened also the emperor himself and his judges. . . . When these verses had been read, both were terribly torn by the hooks of the torturers and taken away lifeless. . . .

After all of these matters had been examined with sharp eye, the emperor, in answer to the question put by one of the judges, under one decree ordered the execution of all of the accused; and in the presence of a vast throng, who could hardly look upon the dreadful sight without inward shuddering and burdening the air with laments . . . they were all led away and wretchedly strangled except Simonides; him alone that cruel author of the verdict, maddened by his steadfast firmness, had ordered to be burned alive. . . . And after him, in the days that followed, a throng of men of almost all ranks, whom it would be difficult

3. The letters would apply equally well to Theodosius, who actually did succeed Valens.

to enumerate by name, involved in the snares of calumny, wearied the arms of the executioners after being first crippled by tortures, lead and scourge. Some were punished without breathing space or delay, while inquiry was being made whether they deserved punishment; everywhere the scene was like a slaughtering of cattle.

Then, innumerable writings and many heaps of volumes were brought together from various houses and under the eyes of the judges were burned—being pronounced unlawful, to allay the indignation at the executions, although the greater number were treatises on the liberal arts and on jurisprudence.

And not so very long afterward that famous philosopher Maximus, a man with a great reputation for learning, through whose rich discourses Julian stood out as an emperor well stocked with knowledge, was alleged to have heard the verses of the aforesaid oracle. And he admitted that he had learned of them, but out of regard for his philosophical principles had not divulged secrets, although he had volunteered the prediction that the consultors of the future would themselves perish by capital punishment. Thereupon he was taken to his native city of Ephesus and there beheaded. . . .

Diogenes also was entangled in the snares of an impious falsehood. He was a man born of noble stock, eminent for his talent, his fearless eloquence, and his charm; he was a former governor of Bithynia, but was now punished with death in order that his rich patrimony might be plundered.

Lo! even Alypius also, former vice-governor of Britain, a man amiable and gentle, after living in leisure and retirement . . . was made to wallow in utmost wretchedness; he was accused with his son Hierocles, a young man of good character, as guilty of magic, on the sole evidence of a certain Diogenes, a man of low origin, who was tortured with every degree of butchery, to lead him to give testimony agreeable to the emperor, or rather to the instigator of the charge. Diogenes, when not enough of his body was left for torture, was burned alive; Alypius himself also, after confiscation of his goods, was condemned to exile, but recovered his son, who was already being led to a wretched death, but was reprieved [because of popular outcry].

During all this time the notorious Palladius, the fomentor of all these troubles . . . entangled many persons in his lamentable nets, some of them on the ground of having stained themselves with the knowledge of magic, others as accomplices of those who were aiming at treason. And in order that even wives would have no time to weep over the

misfortunes of their husbands, men were immediately sent to put the
seal on the houses, and during the examination of the furniture . . . to
introduce privily old-wives' incantations or offensive love-potions, contrived for the ruin of innocent people. And when these were read in a
court where there was no law or scruple or justice to distinguish truth
from falsehood, without opportunity for defense young and old without
discrimination were robbed of their goods and, although they were
found stained by no fault, after being maimed in all their limbs were
carried off in litters to execution. As a result, throughout the eastern
provinces owners of books, through fear of a like fate, burned their
entire libraries; so great was the terror that had seized upon all.

182. EARLY CHRISTIANITY AND JEWS

In the third century Jews in the Diaspora in the eastern part of the Empire
were not excluded from the civic life of the cities, even if they maintained
their ancestral religious and cultural traditions. But with the triumph of
Christianity in the fourth century, the privileges that Jews had enjoyed for
centuries under Roman rule were gradually attenuated or abolished. Beginning with the reign of Constantine, while they were free to practice
their religion, Jews throughout the Roman Empire experienced increasing
restrictions as anti-Jewish measures made inroads on their traditional rights
in civil matters. Toleration was gradually replaced by anti-Jewish propaganda, repression, persecution, and finally segregation in ghettoes.

Theodosian Code XVI. ix. 2; A.D. 339

The Emperor Constantius Augustus to Evagrius: If any of the Jews
should think that he may purchase the slave of another sect or people,
such slave shall forthwith be freed to the fisc. If a Jew purchases a slave
and circumcises him, not only will he be penalized by the loss of the
slave, but he will also be punished with a capital sentence. But if a Jew
should not hesitate to purchase slaves who are adherents of the venerable
faith [i.e., Christianity], he shall forthwith be deprived of all such found
in his possession, nor shall there be any delay in his losing possession of
these men who are Christians.

Theodosian Code III. vii. 2; A.D. 388

The Emperors Valentinian, Theodosius, and Arcadius Augusti to Cynegius, Praetorian Prefect: No Jew shall take a Christian woman in marriage, nor shall a Christian contract a marriage with a Jewess. For if anyone commits an act of this kind, the charge for this misdeed shall be treated as equivalent to adultery, and freedom to bring accusation is allowed even to informers from the general public.

JULIAN THE APOSTATE AND THE JEWS

Julian displayed good will to the Jews both as an anti-Christian gesture and because he exalted the performance of sacrifices to the gods. Early in A.D. 363 he decreed the rebuilding of the Temple of Jehovah, destroyed by the Romans in A.D. 70, and planned to resettle Jews of the Diaspora in Jerusalem, from which they had been banished by Hadrian. The project, however, was soon abandoned after Julian's death that year in the war against the Persians.

Julian, *Letters* xxv

Julian to the community of the Jews: Decidedly more burdensome for you in times past than the yokes of slavery has been the fact that you were subjected to taxes without previous notice, and required to furnish untold amounts of gold to the account of the treasury. Many of the taxes I observed myself, and I learned about them in detail from examining the tax rolls kept regarding you. I prevented still another special tax again about to be levied against you, and then and there I put a stop to the sacrilege of such an offense, and I consigned to the fire the tax rolls regarding you found in my archives, so that no longer will anyone be able to level such a charge of impiety against you. . . . Throughout my entire kingdom you are now free from anxiety, so that in happiness you may offer even greater prayers for my kingdom to Almighty God, the Creator. . . . This you should do so that, after successfully completing the war against the Persians, I may rebuild at my own expense and settle the holy city of Jerusalem—as you have ardently desired to see it settled for many years—and in it I shall join you in giving praise to the Almighty.

Ammianus Marcellinus, *History* XXIII. i. 2–3

Julian planned to restore with enormous expenditures the once splendid temple at Jerusalem, which had with difficulty been taken by storm after many bloody battles through siege by Vespasian and afterwards by Titus. [The rebuilding was begun] but fearful balls of flame burst forth near the foundations with frequent explosions and made the place inaccessible to the workmen, some of whom were burned to death. Since in this way the elements persistently repelled them, the enterprise was abandoned.

183. CHRISTIAN CELIBACY AND MONASTICISM

The Christian injunction of celibacy for priests, monks, and nuns necessitated the annulment of laws fostering marriage and the family still on the books since the legislation of Augustus (vol. 1, § 204).

MONASTICISM

Sulpicius Severus,[4] *Life of St. Martin of Tours;* From R. E. Morris, *The Fathers of the Church* (Washington, 1949)

It is not within our power to describe the quality and grandeur of Martin's life, once he had assumed the office of bishop. What he had been before, he firmly continued to be. There was the same humility in his heart, the same poverty in his dress. Lacking nothing in authority and grace, he fulfilled the dignity of a bishop, yet did not abandon the virtuous resolve of a monk. So, for a while he used a cell attached to the church. Then, unable to bear up under the distraction caused by throngs of visitors, he set up for himself a monastery some two miles outside the city.

This location was so sheltered and remote that it could have been a desert solitude. On one side it was hedged in by the sheer rock of a high mountain; on the other the plain was closed in by a little bend of the River Loire. Approach was possible by a single path, and that a very narrow one. Martin himself occupied a cell built of wood. While many of the brothers had similar shelters, the majority fashioned lodgings for

4. Sulpicius Severus (*c.* 360–*c.* 420), a convert to Christianity, was a native of Gaul.

themselves carved out of the rock of the overhanging mountain. The disciples numbered about eighty, all forming themselves after the model of their blessed master. No one there had anything as his own; all property was brought together for common holding. It was illicit to buy or to sell anything (as is the practice of many monks). No art was practised there except that of the copyist, and to this work only the more youthful were assigned; the elders had their time free for prayer. Rarely was anyone found outside his own cell, except when they came together at the place of prayer. All had meals in common and after the hour of fasting. All abstained from wine, except when compelled by illness. The majority were dressed in camel's hair; the use of any softer clothing was held a serious offense. This must be regarded as all the more remarkable, in that many of the monks were thought to be nobles who, after a far different upbringing, had constrained themselves to such practices of humility and patience. A number of them we later saw as bishops. And what city or what church would not have wished for itself a bishop from Martin's monastery?

.   .   .   .

St. Paula (died 404), mother of St. Julia Eustachium (370–418/9; see § 184), founded St. Jerome's monastery and a convent at Bethlehem.

Jerome, *Letters* cviii. 20

Besides establishing a monastery for men, the charge of which she left to men, she divided into three companies and nunneries the numerous virgins whom she had gathered out of different provinces, some of whom were of noble birth while others belonged to the middle or lower classes. But, although they worked and had meals separately from each other, these three companies met together for psalm-singing and prayer. . . . At dawn, at the third, sixth, and ninth hours, at evening, and at midnight they recited the psalter each in turn. No sister was allowed to be ignorant of the psalms, and all had every day to learn a certain portion of the Holy Scriptures. On the Lord's day only, they proceeded to the church beside which they lived, each company following its own mother-superior. Returning home in the same order, they then devoted themselves to their allotted tasks, and made garments either for themselves or for others. If a virgin was of noble birth, she was not allowed to have an attendant belonging to her own household. . . . All the sisters were clothed alike. Linen was not used except for drying the hands. So strictly did Paula separate them from men that she would not allow even eunuchs to approach them. . . .

Apart from food and clothing she allowed no one to have anything she could call her own, for Paul had said, "Having food and clothing, let us therewith be content." She was afraid lest the custom of having more might breed covetousness in them, an appetite which no wealth can satisfy, for the more it has the more it requires, and neither opulence nor indigence is able to diminish it. When the sisters quarreled with one another she reconciled them with soothing words. If the younger ones were troubled with carnal desires, she broke their force by imposing redoubled fasts; for she wished her virgins to be ill in body rather than to suffer in the soul. If she chanced to notice any sister too attentive to her dress, she reproved her for her error with knitted brows and severe looks, saying, "A clean body and a clean dress mean an unclean soul." A virgin's lips should never utter an improper or an impure word, for such indicate a lascivious mind. . . .

The sin of theft she loathed as if it were sacrilege; and that which among men of the world is counted little or nothing she declared to be a crime of the deepest dye in a convent. How shall I describe her kindness and attention towards the sick or the wonderful care and devotion with which she nursed them? Yet, although when others were sick she freely gave them every indulgence, and even allowed them to eat meat, and when she fell ill herself she made no concessions to her own weakness, and seemed unfairly to change in her own case to harshness the kindness which she was always ready to show to others.

184. WOMEN IN EARLY CHRISTIANITY

Beginning with the teaching of Paul, Christian doctrine viewed the temptations of the flesh as evil, made virtues of sexual denial and celibacy, and acknowledged marriage only as necessary for carrying out God's injunction to man to be fruitful and multiply. The ideal woman was represented as a virgin, the married woman as subordinate to her husband and dedicated to being *univira* (a one-man woman) all her life.

Paul, 1 Corinthians 7–14 (excerpts), 1 Timothy 2:9–14

It is good for a man to have nothing to do with a woman. But in view of the widespread immorality, let each man have his own wife and let each woman have her own husband. Let the husband render to the wife the due affection, and likewise the wife to the husband. The wife does not have authority over her own body, but her husband does; the husband likewise does not have authority over his own body, but his wife does. Do not deny yourselves to each other, unless by agreement for a time in order that you may devote yourselves to prayer. . . .

To the unmarried and the widows I say it is good for them if they stay [single] as I myself am. But if they cannot control themselves, let them marry; it is better to marry than to be afire [with desire].

Upon the married I enjoin—not I but the Lord—that a wife not separate from her husband (but if she does separate let her remain unmarried or be reconciled to her husband), and that the husband not divorce his wife. . . .

The unmarried man cares for the work of the Lord, how he shall please the Lord, but the married man cares for the things of the world, how he shall please his wife. . . . The unmarried woman cares for the work of the Lord, in order to be dedicated to him both in body and in spirit; but the married woman cares for the things of the world, how she shall please her husband. . . .

A wife is bound to her husband as long as he lives. If the husband dies, she is free to be married to whom she wishes, only in the Lord. But she is happier if she remains [single], in my opinion. . . .

Any man praying or prophesying with head covered dishonors his head; any woman praying or prophesying bare-headed dishonors her head. . . . A man ought not cover his head, being the image and glory of God; but a woman is the glory of man. For man was not made from woman, but woman from man; nor was man created on account of woman, but woman on account of man. . . .

Let women remain silent in church, for they are not permitted to speak but to be submissive, just as the law also says. If there is anything they want to know, let them ask their own husbands at home. . . .

Women should bedeck themselves in seemly dress, modestly and with discretion, not with braided hair or gold or pearls or expensive clothes, but, as befits women who profess piety, with good deeds. Let a woman learn quietly and with all submissiveness. I do not permit a woman to teach or to assume authority over man; she is to be quiet. For Adam was formed first, then Eve; and Adam was not deceived, but the woman was deceived and in transgression.

MODESTY IN DRESS

Tertullian, *On the Apparel of Women* I. i. xi, xii

If there dwelt upon earth a faith as great as is the reward of faith which is expected in the heavens, no one of you at all, best beloved sisters, from the time she has first "known the Lord" and learned the truth concerning her own [i.e., woman's] condition, would have desired too indulgent (not to say too ostentatious) a style of dress, so as not to go about in humble garb but rather to affect meanness of appearance, walking about as Eve mourning and repentant, in order that by every garb of penitence she might more fully expiate what she derives from Eve—the ignominy, I mean, of the first sin, and the odium attaching to her as the cause of human perdition. . . . And do you know that you are such an Eve? The sentence of God on this sex of yours lives in this age; the guilt must of necessity live too. You are the devil's gateway. . . .

Moreover, what reasons have you for appearing in public in excessive splendor, removed as you are from the occasions which call for such displays? For you neither make the circuit of the temples, nor demand presence at public shows, nor have any acquaintance with the holy days of the pagans. Now it is for the sake of all these public gatherings, and of much seeing and being seen, that all the pomp of dress is exhibited before the public eye, either for transacting the trade of voluptuousness, or else inflating glory.

Let us only wish that we may be no cause for just blasphemy! But how much more provocative of blasphemy is it that you, who are called modesty's priestesses, should appear in public dressed and painted out after the manner of the immodest. . . .

The Scriptures suggest that meretricious attractiveness of form is invariably connected with and appropriate to bodily prostitution. . . . Provision must be made in every way against all immodest associations and suspicions. . . . Grant that it be lawful to assume the appearance of a modest woman.

THE EDUCATION OF A CHRISTIAN GIRL

In this letter, written A.D. 403, Jerome outlines for Laeta, a Christian, born daughter of a pagan, the education of her daughter Paula, who later became head of the nunnery at Bethlehem (see § 183).

Jerome, *Letters* cvii (abridged); From *LCL*

The blessed apostle Paul, writing to the Corinthians and instructing Christ's novice church in the ways of sacred discipline, among his other precepts laid down also the following rule: "The woman that hath an husband that believeth not, and if he be pleased to dwell with her, let her not leave him. For the unbelieving husband is sanctified by the believing wife, and the unbelieving wife is sanctified by the believing husband; else were your children unclean, but now they are holy." . . . You yourself are the child of a mixed marriage; but now you and my dear Toxotius are Paula's parents. Who would ever have believed that the granddaughter of the Roman pontiff Albinus would be born in answer to a mother's vows; that the grandfather would stand by and rejoice while the baby's yet stammering tongue cried "Alleluia"; and that even the old man would nurse in his arms one of Christ's own virgins? . . . Christians are not born but made. The gilded Capitol today looks dingy, all the temples in Rome are covered with soot and cobwebs, the city is shaken to its foundations, and the people hurry past the ruined shrines and pour out to visit the martyrs' graves. . . .

Even in Rome now heathenism languishes in solitude. Those who once were the gods of the Gentiles are left beneath their deserted pinnacles to the company of owls and night-birds. The army standards bear the emblem of the cross. The purple robes of kings and the jewels that sparkle on their diadems are adorned with the sign of the cross that has brought us salvation. Today even the Egyptian [god] Serapis has become a Christian. Marnas [a Syrian god] mourns in his prison at Gaza, and fears continually that his temple will be overthrown. From India, from Persia and from Ethiopia we welcome crowds of monks every hour. The Armenians have laid aside their quivers, the Huns are learning the psalter, the forests of Scythia are warmed by the fire of faith. The ruddy flaxen-haired Getae carry tent-churches about with their armies; and perhaps the reason why they fight with us on equal terms is that they believe in the same religion. . . .

It was my intention, in answer to your prayers and those of saintly Marcella, to direct my discourse to a mother, that is, to you, and to show you how to bring up our little Paula, who was consecrated to Christ before she was born.

Let her every day repeat to you a portion of the Scriptures as her fixed task. A good number of verses she should learn by heart in the Greek, but knowledge of the Latin should follow close after. If the tender lips are not trained from the beginning, the language is spoiled by a foreign accent and our native tongue debased by alien faults. You must be her teacher, to you her childish ignorance must look for a model. Let her never see anything in you or her father which she would do wrong to imitate. Remember that you are a virgin's parents and that you can teach her better by example than by words. . . .

Let her never appear in public without you, let her never visit the churches and the martyrs' shrines except in your company. Let no youth or curled dandy ogle her. Let our little virgin never stir a finger's breadth from her mother when she attends a vigil or an all-night service. I would not let her have a favorite maid into whose ear she might frequently whisper: what she says to one, all ought to know. . . . Set before her as a pattern some aged virgin of approved faith, character, and chastity, one who may instruct her by word, and by example accustom her to rise from her bed at night for prayer and psalm singing, to chant hymns in the morning, at the third, sixth, and ninth hour, to take her place in the ranks as one of Christ's amazons, and with kindled lamp to offer the evening sacrifice. . . .

Let her learn also to make wool, to hold the distaff, and to put the basket in her lap, to turn the spindle, to shape the thread with her thumb. Let her scorn silk fabrics, Chinese fleeces, and gold brocades. Let her have clothes which keep out the cold, not expose the limbs they pretend to cover. Let her food be vegetables and wheaten bread and occasionally a little fish. . . . . Let her meals always leave her hungry and able at once to begin reading or praying or singing the psalms.

CHRISTIAN WOMEN AND MARRIAGE

Jerome, *Letters* lxxvii. 3; From *LCL*

As at the very outset there is a rock in the path, and I am faced by the storm of censure that was directed against her for having taken a second husband and abandoned her first, I shall not praise her for her conversion until I have cleared her from this charge. We are told that her first husband was a man of such heinous vices that even a prostitute or a common slave could not have put up with them. If I describe them, I shall mar the heroism of the woman, who preferred to bear the blame of separation rather than to expose to shame the man who was one body with her, and thus reveal the stains upon his character. This only I will say, and it is a plea sufficient to excuse a chaste matron and a Christian wife. The Lord ordained that a wife must not be put away except for fornication, and that, if she was put away, she must remain unmarried. A command that is given to men applies logically also to women. It cannot be that an adulterous wife should be put away and an unfaithful husband retained. If 'he which is joined to a harlot is one body,' she who is joined to a filthy whoremonger is one body with him also. The laws of Caesar are different from the laws of Christ: Papinian[5] commands one thing, our Paul another. Among the Romans men's unchastity goes unchecked; seduction and adultery are condemned, but free permission is given to lust to range the brothels and to have slave girls, as though it were a person's rank and not the sensual pleasure that constituted the offence. With us what is unlawful for women is equally unlawful for men, and as both sexes serve God they are bound by the same conditions. Fabiola, as men say, put away a vicious husband; she put away a man who was guilty of this and that crime; she put him away because—I almost mentioned the scandal which the whole neighbourhood proclaimed but which his wife alone refused to reveal. If she is blamed because after repudiating her husband she did not remain unmarried, I will readily admit her fault, provided that I may put in the plea of necessity. 'It is better,' says the apostle, 'to marry than to burn.' She was a young weak woman and she could not remain a widow. She saw another law in her members warring against the law of her mind, and she felt herself dragged like a chained captive into carnal intercourse. She thought it better to confess her weakness openly and to accept the dark stain that such a lamentable marriage would bring, rather than to claim to be the wife of one husband and under that disguise to ply the harlot's trade. The same apostle expresses his wish that 'young widows should marry, bear children, and give no handle to calumny.' And then at once he gives his reason: 'For some are already turned aside after Satan.' Fabiola therefore had convinced herself, and thought that she was justified in putting away her husband. She did not know the Gospel's strict ordinance, which precludes Christian women from marrying again in their first husband's lifetime, whatever their case may be.

5. Famous Roman jurist of the end of the second–early third century.

CHRISTIANS ARRANGE A MARRIAGE

SB, no. 8,002; fourth century

This private letter gives us an intimate glimpse of an arranged marriage uniting two Christian families.

To my lord, my most longed-for son Ammonius, his father Paniscus (sends greetings) with success. Through the will of the Almighty and his concomintant providence, I have been able at long last to arrange a marriage for you . . . and since God has brought this into the light I write to tell you of this development, and let this be placed in your reckoning. And now that there has been as beginning of our (two families') association, they sought first of all for me to know your disposition. Rather than give them (an answer) off the top of my head I postponed concluding (the matter) until I learn your intention. Let me know if you prefer to stay away or to come back (for the arrangements), for the people will not wait (long). . . . . [The rest is lost.]

185. CHRISTIAN LEGISLATION ON WOMEN

WOMEN'S HAIR

Theodosian Code XVI. ii. 27; A.D. 390 (abridged)

Emperors Valentinian, Theodosius, and Arcadius Augusti to Tarianus, Praetorian Prefect: Women who cut off their hair, contrary to divine and human laws, through the influence and persuasion of some professed belief, shall be debarred from the doors of the churches. It shall not be lawful for them to approach the holy mysteries, nor shall they be granted, through any pleas, the privilege of being present at the altars which must be venerated by all. Moreover, if a bishop permits a woman with shorn hair to enter a church, the bishop himself shall be expelled from his post and kept away. . . . .

PROSTITUTION

Theodosian Code xv. viii. 1; A.D. 343

Emperor Constantius Augustus to Severus, Prefect of the City: If anyone should wish to subject to harlotry women who are known to have
dedicated themselves to the veneration of the holy Christian law, and if
he should arrange that such women be sold to brothels and compelled
to engage in the foul service of prostituted virtue, no other person shall
have the right to buy such women except those who are known to be
ecclesiastics or those who are shown to be Christian men, on payment
of the proper price.

RAPE

Theodosian Code ix. xxv. 1; A.D. 354

Emperor Constantius Augustus to Orfitus: Rapists of both kinds shall
be punished with equal severity: there is to be no distinction between
the man discovered to have violated the honor of sacrosanct maidens
and the man who violates the chastity of a widow. Nor shall any man
be able to deceive himself [that he will be absolved] by the later consent
of the woman whom he has violated.

ACTRESSES

Theodosian Code xv. vii. 4; A.D. 380

Emperors Gratian, Valentinian, and Theodosius Augusti to Paulinus,
Prefect of the City: If a woman who is sprung from the lower class and
is obligated to the compulsory performances of the shows should seek
to evade her compulsory service of the stage, she shall be assigned to
such theatrical services, provided that contemplation of the most holy
religion and reverence of Christian law have not yet bound her to this
faith. For we forbid women to be returned to this duty, if a better mode
of living has released them from the ties of their natural condition. We
also order that such women remain free from the ignoble mark of any
prejudice derived from the stage, if they have obtained exemption from
this compulsory public service of a coarse character by a special grant of
imperial favor of our Clemency.

186. THE AFFAIR OF THE ALTAR OF VICTORY

Around the Altar of Victory in the Senate-house there swirled for decades a determined stand of pagan resistance to Christianity by a substantial number of senators. Many of them regarded the preservation of the altar as a symbol of resistance to the eclipse of the traditional religion. In A.D. 384 St. Ambrose, bishop of Milan, addressed to the Emperor Valentinian a letter denouncing pagan symbols. This led to a response by Quintus Aurelius Symmachus, then Prefect of the City of Rome, ardent defender of paganism, who, petitioning the emperor to restore the altar, sent him a state paper (below) that has been called "one of the most poignant documents of dying paganism" (H. Bloch, in *The Conflict Between Paganism and Christianity in the Fourth Century,* ed. A. Momigliano [Oxford, 1963], p. 211).

Ambrose, Letters vii; A.D. 384 (abridged)

Not only are all under the power of Rome in your service, the emperors and princes of the earth, but you yourselves are also in the service of almighty God and of our holy faith. Salvation will not be assured unless each one truly worships the true God, that is, the God of the Christians. . . .

Since you have truly shown your faith in God, most Christian Emperor, I am amazed that your zeal for the faith, and your protection and devotion, have inspired hope in some that you are now obligated to erect altars to the gods of the pagans and to furnish funds for the upkeep of profane sacrifices. . . .

If today some pagan emperor—God forbid!—should erect an altar to idols and compel Christians to hold their meeting there, to attend the sacrifices, so that the breath and nostrils of Christians would be filled with the ashes from the altar, cinders from the sacrifice, and smoke from the wood; and if he would give his opinion in the Senate-house, where in giving their opinion they would be forced to swear at the altar of the idol (for this is how they interpret the altar erected, so that, as they think, each meeting under this oath will be held in its midst, although the Senate already has a majority of Christians [an exaggeration]), the Christian, compelled to come into Senate, would on these conditions regard it as persecution. . . . Now that you are Emperor, will Christians be forced to take their oath on an altar? . . . Are you bidding that an altar be raised and money allocated for profane sacrifices?

A decree like this cannot be enforced without sacrilege. I beg you not to make such a decree, nor pass a law, nor sign a decree of this sort. As a priest of Christ, I appeal to your faith. . . . Is it dignified in your day, a Christian day, that Christian senators be deprived of their dignity so that pagans may have deference paid to their unholy will?

Symmachus, *Petition* III (abridged); From the translation of R. H. Barrow (Oxford, 1973)

More than any other cause the fair name of our age will benefit from the defense of our ancestral practices and the rights and destiny of our fatherland. . . . We seek to have restored therefore the religious institutions that have served the state well for so long. One can of course list emperors of either belief and persuasion; the earlier practised the rites of their fathers, the latter did not abolish them. . . . Who is such a good friend of the barbarians that he does not want the Altar of Victory back? We are cautious with regard to the future and avoid omens of change. If she [Victory] cannot be honored as a goddess, at least let her name be honored. . . . No one, if he admits she is desirable, should deny her right to be worshiped. . . .

Where are we to swear loyalty to your laws and decrees? By what religious scruple will the mind of a deceiver be deterred from committing perjury? . . . The Altar binds the friendship of all, that altar guarantees the faith of individuals, and nothing gives greater authority to our decisions than the fact that our [senatorial] order passes all its decrees as if acting under oath. . . .

Let us now imagine that the figure of Rome stands before you and addresses you thus: "Best of princes, father of your country, respect my length of years which pious observation of my ritual has ensured me. Let me employ the rites my ancestors used, for they are not a matter of regret. Let me live my own way, since I am free. Through this worship I brought the whole world under the rule of my laws. These sacred objects drove Hannibal from our walls, the Gauls from the Capitol.". . .

Therefore we ask that the gods of our fathers, our native gods, be left in peace. It is reasonable that all the different gods we worship be thought of as one. We see the same stars, share the same sky, the same earth surrounds us. What does it matter what scheme of thought a man uses in his search for the truth? Man cannot come to so profound a mystery by one road alone. . . .

How much did it benefit your imperial treasury to revoke the privileges granted to the Vestal Virgins? . . . Their sole distinction lies in their payment, as it were, of chastity; just as their headbands lend glory to their heads, so their priesthood was honored in their freedom from state dues. They ask only the bare title of exemption, since they are safe from any actual payment because of their poverty. . . . It is a truth that virginity, consecrated to the public good, when lacking monetary rewards, deservedly grows in reputation. . . .

May your Clemency have the support of the unseen guardians of all religions and especially those who helped your ancestors in times past. Let them protect you, while being worshiped by us.

187. ANTIPAGAN LEGISLATION

Withdrawal of official subsidies in A.D. 394 for pagan cults effectively ended all links between the state and pagan religion. Nevertheless, pagan cults continued with private support and survived in many places well into the fifth and sixth centuries.

Zosimus, *New History* IV. lix; From the translation of R. T. Ridley (Sydney, 1982)

After his victory, Theodosius went to Rome, where he announced the proclamation of his son Honorius as emperor, and declared Stilicho Master of the Soldiers in the West, leaving him as guardian for his son. Then summoning the Senate, which remained true to ancestral rites and did not choose to join those inclined to despise the gods, he addressed it, calling on the senators to cast off their previous error, as he called it, and choose the Christian faith which promises deliverance from all sin and impiety. No one obeyed his summons or chose to abandon those ancestral rites handed down to them since the founding of the city or preferred an irrational assent to his request. By observing these rites they lived in a city which was unconquered for almost twelve hundred years, and did not know what might happen if they changed their beliefs. Theodosius then said that the treasury was burdened by the expense of rites and sacrifices and that he wished to abolish them, because not only did he disapprove of what they were doing but also the army needed more money. Although the senators said that rites not performed at public expense were not performed properly, the law concerning sacrifices was repealed and other traditions handed down from their forefathers neglected.

Theodosian Code XVI. X. 12; A.D. 392

Emperors Theodosius, Arcadius, and Honorius Augusti to Rufinus, Praetorian Prefect: No person at all, of any class or order whatsoever of men or of officials, whether he occupies a position of power or has fulfilled such offices, whether he is powerful by the accident of birth or is humble in descent, legal status and fortune, shall sacrifice an innocent victim to senseless statues in any place at all or in any city. He shall not, through more secret wickedness, venerate his household god with fire, his *genius* with wine, his Penates with fragrant essences. He shall not burn lamps to them, place incense before them, or suspend wreaths for them.

But if any one should dare to immolate a victim for the purpose of sacrifice, or to consult the entrails, he shall be reported in accordance with the example of a person guilty of high treason, such accusation being permitted to all persons. And he shall receive the appropriate penalty, even if he has made no inquiry contrary to, or with regard to, the welfare of the Emperors. . . .

But if any one should venerate images made by the work of humans, by placing incense before them . . . or should bind fillets around a tree, or should erect an altar of turf that he has dug up, or should try to honor vain statues with the offer of a gift, which, even though it be humble, still is a complete outrage against religion, such person, as guilty of the violation of religion, shall be punished by the forfeiture of the house or land in which it is proved that he served a pagan superstition. For we decree that all places be confiscated to our fisc if it is proved that they reeked with the odor of incense. . . .

Theodosian Code XVI. X. 13; A.D. 395

Emperors Arcadius and Honorius Augusti to Rufinus, Praetorian Prefect: We decree that no one shall have the right to approach any shrine or temple whatsoever, or to perform abominable sacrifices in any place or time whatsoever. All persons, therefore, who try to deviate from the dogma of the Catholic religion shall hurry to observe those regulations which we have recently decreed, and shall not dare to disregard former decrees regarding either heretics or pagans. . . . Moreover, the governors of our provinces and the assistants who serve them, the chief decurions also and the defenders of the municipalities, as well as the decurions, and the procurators of our possessions . . . shall know that if any such offense has been attempted contrary to our statutes, and if it has not been avenged at once and punished in its very beginning, they shall be subjected to all the losses and punishments established by the ancient decrees. . . .

Theodosian Code XVI. 16; A.D. 399

The same Augusti [Arcadius and Honorius] to Eutychianus, Praetorian Prefect: If there should be any temples in the country districts, they shall be torn down without disturbance or tumult. For when they are torn down and removed, the material basis for all superstition will be destroyed.

Theodosian Code XVI. x, 19; A.D. 407–409

Emperors Arcadius, Honorius, and Theodosius Augusti to Curtius, Praetorian Prefect: If any images still stand in the temples and shrines, and if they received, or do now receive, the worship of pagans anywhere, they shall be torn from their foundations, since we realize that this regulation has very often been decreed by repeated regulations.

The buildings themselves of the temples which are located in cities or towns or outside the towns shall be confiscated to public use. Altars shall be destroyed in all places, and all temples situated on our estates shall be transferred to suitable uses. The proprietors shall be compelled to destroy them.

It shall not be permitted at all to hold convivial banquets in honor of sacrilegious rites in such funereal places or to celebrate any solemn ceremony. We grant to bishops of such places also the right to use ecclesiastical power to prevent such practices. Moreover, we impose on judges a penalty of twenty pounds of gold, and on their office staffs an equal sum, if they should neglect the enforcement of these regulations by their connivance.

LEGISLATION REGARDING HOLIDAYS

Constantine had converted the Roman Day of the Sun to the Lord's Day of the Christians (A.D. 321). Later emperors increased the number of activities forbidden on Sunday.

Theodosian Code II. viii. 18; A.D. 386

Emperors Gratian, Valentinian, and Theodosius Augusti to Principius, Praetorian Prefect: On the Day of the Sun, which our ancestors rightly called the Lord's Day, the prosecution of all litigation, court business and suits, shall be entirely suspended. No person shall demand the payment of a public or private debt, nor shall there be any cognizance of controversies before abitrators, whether they have been requested in court or chosen voluntarily.

Theodosian Code II. viii. 20; A.D. 392

The same Augusti [Valentinian, Theodosius, and Arcadius] to Proculus, Prefect of the City: Contests in the circuses shall be prohibited on the festal Days of the Sun, except on the birthdays of our Clemency, in order that no concourse of people to the spectacles may divert men from the reverend mysteries of the Christian law.

Theodosian Code XVI. x. 17; A.D. 399

The same Augusti [Arcadius and Honorius] to Apollodorus, Proconsul of Africa: Just as we have already abolished profane rites by a salutary law, so we do not permit the festal assemblies of citizens and the common pleasure of all to be abolished. Hence we decree that, according to ancient custom, amusements shall be furnished to the people, but without any sacrifice or any accursed superstition, and they shall be permitted to attend festival banquets, whenever public desires so demand.

188. DECREES AGAINST HERESIES AND APOSTATES

Theodosian Code XVI. i. 2; A.D. 380

Emperors Gratian, Valentinian, and Theodosius Augusti. An edict to the people of the City of Constantinople.

It is our will that all peoples ruled by our Clemency shall practise that religion which the divine Peter the Apostle transmitted to the Romans, as the religion which he introduced makes clear even to this day. It is evident that this is the religion followed by the Pontiff Damasus and by Peter, Bishop of Alexandria, a man of apostolic sanctity; that is, according to the apostolic discipline and the evangelical doctrine, we shall believe in the single Deity of the Father, the Son, and the Holy Spirit, under the concept of equal majesty and of the Holy Trinity.

We order that those persons who follow this rule shall embrace the name of Catholic Christians. The rest, however, whom we judge demented and insane, shall have the infamy of heretical dogmas, their meeting places shall not receive the name of churches, and they shall be smitten first by divine vengeance and secondly by the retribution of our hostility, which we shall assume in accordance with divine judgment.

Theodosian Code XVI. v. 6; A.D. 381

The same Augusti [Gratian, Valentinian, and Theodosius] to Eutropius, Praetorian Prefect: No place for celebrating their mysteries, no opportunity for practicing the madness of their excessively obstinate minds shall be available to the heretics. . . .

Crowds shall be kept away from the illegal congregations of all heretics. The name of the One and Supreme God shall be celebrated everywhere; the observance, destined to remain forever, of the Nicene faith, as transmitted long ago[6] by our ancestors and confirmed by the declaration and testimony of divine religion, shall be maintained. The contamination of the Photian pestilence, the poison of the Arian sacrilege, the crime of the Dunomian perfidy, and the sectarian monstrosities, abominable because of the ill-omened names of their authors, shall be abolished even from the hearing of men. . . .

Those persons, however, who are not devoted to the aforesaid doctrine [i.e., of the Nicene Creed] shall cease to assume, with studied fraud, a name alien to the true religion, and they shall be removed and completely barred from the threshold of all churches, since we forbid all heretics to hold illegal assemblies within the towns. We order that their madness shall be banished and that they shall be driven away from the very walls of the cities, in order that the Catholic churches throughout the whole world may be restored to all orthodox bishops who hold the Nicene faith.

Theodosian Code XVI. vii. 2; A.D. 383

Emperors Gratian, Valentinian, and Theodosius Augusti to Eutropius, Praetoran Prefect: If Christians and those confirmed in the faith have turned to pagan rites and cults, we deny them all power to make a will in favor of any person whatsoever, so that they shall be outside the

---

6. In A.D. 325 at the Council of Nicaea (see § 175).

Roman law. But if any persons are Christians and catachumens only and should neglect the venerable religion and turn to altars and temples, and if they have children or brothers germane, that is, their own heirs or statutory ones, such Christians shall be deprived of the right to make a will of their own discretion in favor of any other persons whatsoever. The same general rule shall be observed regarding persons in taking property under a will. . . . They must unquestionably be excluded from all power not only to make wills but also to enjoy them under any right of acquiring an inheritance.

189. THE TENACITY OF PAGANISM

Prudentius,[7] *Against the Speech of Symmachus* I. lines 1–39; From *LCL*

I used to think that Rome which was sick with her pagan errors, had by now quite rid herself of the dangers of her old disease and that no ill remained behind, now that the emperor's healing measures had assuaged in the seat of power her grievous pains.[8] But since the plague has broken out anew and seeks to trouble the well-being of the race of Romulus, we must beg a remedy of our father [the Emperor], that he may not let Rome sink again into her filthy torpor nor suffer her great men's gowns to be stained with smoke and blood. Did the illustrious father of his country and ruler of the world achieve nothing, then, when he forbade old error to believe in shapes of gods that went about in the murky air? . . . The treatment of the usurpers applied before had been to see what order of affairs would meet the passing situation of the moment, and take no trouble about the future. Alas, ill did they serve the nation, ill complaisance did they show to the senators themselves, when they let them plunge headlong into hell in company with Jupiter and the great mob of their gods.[9] But this Emperor has extended the fame of his reign further in time by seeking to establish his people's well-being. . . . In him the race of men and the people who wear the toga have found a wise leader; Rome's commonwealth in our day thrives in blessedness because righteousness in on the throne. Obey ye a teacher who wields the sceptre; he gives warning that the wicked error and superstition of our forefathers of old be put away.

7. The Christian poet Aurelius Prudentius Clemens (A.D. 348–after 404), native of Spain, was a public servant and fervent defender of the Christian faith.

8. Theodosius I is meant.

9. Julian the Apostate is meant.

190. Paganism Defeated

Paulinus[10] of Nola, *Poems* xix (excerpted); A.D. 405; From P. G. Walsh, *The Poems of St. Paulinus of Nola* (New York/Ramsey, N.J., 1975)

Holiness has gained the ascendant in almost every nation, and life has subdued death. As faith grows strong, error is conquered and melts away; hardly any community is left abandoned to sin and death. All Rome is called by Christ's holy name, and she jeers at the falsehoods of Numa or the oracles of the Sibyl. Rome's devoted throng, in company with its sacred shepherds, answers joyfully "Amen" in the countless folds of the reigning God. Their pious shout strikes the sky with praises of the eternal Lord, and the summit of the Capitol shakes and totters. Dilapidated images in deserted temples tremble on being struck by the holy voices and smitten by the name of Christ. . . .

[In Alexandria] . . . the bull has been driven out with Jupiter, and Egypt will not stupidly worship cattle under the name of Apis; nor Crete wickedly venerate a buried citizen under the name of Jupiter; nor the Phrygians celebrate the feast of Cybele by the castration of the Galli, offering consolation to their polluted mother by such grisly wounds (thus Mount Ida could bring forth her foliage on a mountain at last purified, providing virgin pines from her peaks untroubled); nor Greece superfluously consult any longer a Delphi now silent, but rather despise and grind underfoot her own Olympus as she mounts higher to Sion, where Christ sets high His soft yoke on a lofty summit of that kindly hill. Diana, too, has fled from Ephesus. . . . She accompanied her brother [i.e., Apollo], who has himself been routed by Paul's command given in Christ's name at the expulsion of the Python.

Satan has fled from Egypt, where he had taken countless forms and countless names appropriate to different monsters. . . . God's hidden mind sent goads to prick the hearts of that devout people. They destroyed and shattered Serapis, and ended the worship of that wicked spirit. Isis does not wander through the woods of Pelusium seeking Osiris by means of shaven prophets who beat their breasts and mourn another's grief with their own sorrow, and who then in turn put their wailing to sleep and manifest empty joy like lunatics, lyingly claiming

10. Pontius Meropius Paulinus, a native of Aquitania in Gaul, member of the senatorial aristocracy (he was consul in 378), was converted to Christianity and became a devout Christian.

to have found Osiris with the same guile with which they made their wandering search for him when he was not lost. . . .

Is Isis, then, divine? Can a woman be divine? If she is a goddess she has no body, and without a body there is no sex, nor without sex any childbearing. So how did she obtain the Osiris whom she seeks? And does she not know where to look for him though she is a goddess? No, a mother or a woman can never be divine. For there is only one God.

191. FRONTIER WARS TO THE SACK OF ROME, A.D. 410

The fourth century was a time of recurrent wars on all the Roman Empire's frontiers, north, east, and south. Belief in the invincibility of the Roman army—theretofore a given—was shattered in A.D. 378, when the cavalry of the East Goths routed the Roman infantry at Adrianople in Thrace. That decisive battle marked a turning point in the history of the Western world and was a harbinger of things to come. Thirty-two years later the West Goths under Alaric sacked the city of Rome itself.

Following is a sampling of the wars on Rome's frontiers and of the peoples encountered there.

THE SARACENS

Ammianus Marcellinus, *History* XIV. iv; From *LCL*

The Saracens, however, whom we never found desirable either as friends[11] or as enemies, ranging up and down the country in a brief space of time [in A.D. 354] laid waste whatever they could find, like rapacious hawks which, whenever they have caught sight of any prey from on high, seize it with swift swoop and directly they have seized it make off. . . . I will now briefly relate a few more particulars about them. Among those tribes whose original abode extends from the Assyrians to the cataracts of the Nile and the frontiers of the Blemmyae, all alike are warriors of equal rank, half-nude, clad in dyed cloaks as far as the waist, ranging widely with the help of swift horses and slender camels in times of peace or of disorder. No man ever grasps a plow-handle or cultivates a tree, none seeks a living by tilling the soil, but they rove continually over

11. Most of the emperors of the fourth century bought them off.

wide and extensive tracts without a home, without fixed abodes or laws; they cannot long endure the same sky, nor does the sun of a single district ever content them. Their life is always on the move, and they have mercenary wives, hired under a temporary contract. But in order that there may be some semblance of matrimony, the future wife, by way of dower, offers her husband a spear and a tent, with the right to leave him after a stipulated time, if she so elect: and it is unbelievable with what ardor both sexes give themselves up to passion. Moreover, they wander so widely as long as they live that a woman marries in one place, gives birth in another, and rears her children far away, without being allowed any opportunity for rest. They all feed upon game and an abundance of milk, which is their main sustenance, on a variety of plants, as well as on such birds as they are able to take by fowling; and I have seen many of them who were wholly unacquainted with grain and wine. So much for this dangerous tribe.

BRITAIN, GAUL, GERMANY, A.D. 360

Ammianus Marcellinus, *History* xx. i

But in Britain . . . raids of the savage tribes of the Scots and the Picts, who had broken the peace that had been agreed upon, were laying waste the regions near the frontiers, so that fear seized the provincials, wearied as they were by a series of past calamities. And Julian who was passing the winter in Paris and was distracted amid many cares, was afraid to go to the aid of those across the sea . . . for fear of leaving Gaul without a ruler at a time when the Alamanni [in Germany] were already roused to rage and war.

WAR AND PEACE WITH PERSIA, A.D. 360, 364

Ammianus Marcellinus, *History* xx. vi; xxv. vii (abridged)

That savage king of the Persians [Sapor] burned with the desire of gaining possession of Mesopotamia while Constantius was busy at a distance with his army. So, having increased his arms and his power and crossed the Tigris, he proceeded to attack Singara, a town which, in the opinion of those who had charge of that region, was abundantly fortified with soldiers and with all necessities. The defenders of the city, as soon as they saw the enemy a long way off, quickly closed the gates and full of courage ran to the various towers and battlements, and got together stones and engines of war; then, when everything was prepared, they all stood fast under arms, ready to repulse the horde should it try to come near the walls.

The king on his arrival, through his grandees, who were allowed to enter, tried by peaceful mediation to bend the defenders to his will. Failing in this . . . he gave the signal and the city was assailed on every side. . . . Finally a ram of uncommon strength was brought up, which with rapidly repeated blows battered the round tower where the city was breached in the former siege. . . . The tower collapsed and a way was made into the city; the defenders, scattered by the great danger, abandoned the place; the Persian hordes, raising shouts and yells, rushed from all sides and without opposition filled every part of the city; and after a very few defenders had been slain here and there, all the rest were taken alive by Sapor's order and transported to the remotest parts of Persia.

This city was defended by two legions, the First Flavian and the First Parthian, as well as by a considerable number of natives, with the help of some horsemen who had taken refuge there because of the danger. All these (as I have said) were led off with hands bound, and none of our men could aid them, for the greater part of the army was in camp guarding Nisibis, which was a very long distance off. . . . [The Emperor Constantius tried but failed to retake Singara.]

However, the eternal power of God in heaven was on our side, and the Persians, beyond our hopes, took the first step and sent envoys for securing peace. . . . The king obstinately demanded the lands which (as he said) were his and had been taken from him long ago by Maximian; but in fact as the negotiations showed, he required, as our ransom, five provinces on the far side of the Tigris . . . with fifteen fortresses, besides Nisibis,[12] Singara and Castra Maurorum, a very important stronghold. And whereas it would have been better to fight ten battles than give up any one of these, the band of flatterers pressed upon the timid emperor [Jovian . . . who] without delay surrendered all that was asked, except that with difficulty he succeeded in bringing it about that Nisibis and Singara should pass into control of the Persians without their inhabitants, and that the Romans in the fortresses that were to be taken from us should be allowed to return to our protection. To these conditions there was added another which was destructive and impious, namely, that after the completion of these agreements Arsaces [king of Armenia],

---

12. The Persians had tried, and failed, three times to take this stronghold.

our steadfast and faithful friend, should never, if he asked for it, be given help against the Persians. This was contrived . . . that the opportunity might be left of presently invading Armenia without opposition. The result was that later this same Arsaces was taken alive, and that the Parthians [= Persians] amid various dissensions and disturbances seized a great tract of Armenia bordering on Media, along with Artaxata.

AFRICA AND ISAURIA, A.D. 364–368

Ammianus Marcellinus, *History* XXVII. ix

Africa from the very beginning of Valentinian's reign was sore distressed by the madness of the barbarians, who made daring forays and were eager for wholesale bloodshed and robbery. This evil was increased by the slackness of the army and its greed for seizing the property of others; and especially by the conduct of the governor, Romanus by name. He, having an eye to the future and being an adept in shifting odium to others, was hated by many because of his savage disposition, but especially for his haste to outdo the enemy in devastating the provinces. . . .

Since I have a free opportunity of saying what I think, I shall declare openly that Valentinian was the first of all the emperors to increase the arrogance of the military officers, to the injury of the commonwealth, by raising their rank and power to excess. . . . He punished the peccadilloes of the common soldiers with unbending severity, while sparing those of higher rank; so that these assumed that they had complete license for their sins, and were aroused to shameful and monstrous crimes. In consequence, they are so arrogant as to believe that the fortunes of all without distinction are dependent on their nod. . . .

But in Isauria bands of brigands were overrunning the neighboring places, harassing towns and rich villas with unrestrained pillage, and inflicting great losses on Pamphylia and the Cilicians. Musonius, the deputy governor of Asia at that time, who had formerly been a teacher of rhetoric in Attic Athens, perceived that, since no one resisted them, they were devastating everything with utter destruction; so at last, finding the situation deplorable and that the luxury of the soldiers made their aid feeble, he gathered together a few half-armed troops . . . and attempted to attack one band of the marauders if the opportunity should offer. But in passing through a narrow, winding and steep pass he came into an ambuscade from which he could not escape, and was slain then and there with those whom he was leading. When the brigands, highly elated by this success, with greater confidence extended their raids in various directions, at last our troops were called out and after killing some of them drove the rest to the rocky retreats in the mountains where they live.

THE HUNS

Ammianus Marcellinus, *History* XXXI. ii (in part)

The people of the Huns, but little known from ancient records, dwelling beyond the Maeotic Sea near the ice-bound ocean, exceed every degree of savagery. Since there the cheeks of the children are deeply furrowed from their very birth, in order that the growth of hair, when it appears at the proper time, may be checked by the wrinkled scars, they grow old without beards and without any beauty, like eunuchs. They all have compact, strong limbs and thick necks, and are so monstrously ugly and misshapen that one might take them for two-legged beasts. . . . They are so hardy in mode of life that they have no need of fire nor of savory food, but eat the roots of wild plants and the half-raw flesh of any kind of animal whatever, which they put between their thighs and the backs of their horses, and thus warm it a little.

They are never protected by any buildings. . . . Not even a hut thatched with reed can be found among them. But roaming at large amid the mountains and woods, they learn from the cradle to endure cold, hunger and thirst. . . . They dress in linen cloth or in the skins of field-mice sewn together, and they wear the same clothing indoors and out. But when they have once put their necks into a faded tunic, it is not taken off or changed until by long wear and tear it has been reduced to rags and fallen from them bit by bit. They cover their heads with round caps and protect their hairy legs with goatskins; their shoes are formed upon no lasts, and so prevent their walking with free step. For this reason they are not at all adapted to battles on foot, but they are almost glued to their horses, which are hardy, it is true, but ugly, and sometimes they sit them woman-fashion and thus perform their ordinary tasks. . . .

They are subject to no royal restraint, but they are content with the disorderly government of their important men, and led by them they force their way through every obstacle. . . . They enter battle drawn up in wedge-shaped masses, while their medley of voices makes a savage noise. And as they are lightly equipped for swift motion, and unexpected in action, they purposely divide suddenly into scattered bands and attack, rushing about in disorder here and there, dealing terrific slaughter; and because of their extraordinary rapidity of movement they are never seen to attack a rampart or pillage an enemy's camp. And on this account you would not hesitate to call them the most terrible of all warriors, because they fight from a distance with missiles having sharp bone (instead of metal) points, joined to the shafts with wonderful skill; then they gallop over the intervening spaces and fight hand to hand with swords, regardless of their own lives; and while the enemy are guarding against wounds from the sabre thrusts, they throw strips of cloth plaited into nooses over their opponents and so entangle them that they fetter their limbs and take from them the power of riding or walking. . . .

They are all without fixed abode, without hearth, or law, or settled mode of life, and they keep roaming from place to place, like fugitives, accompanied by the wagons in which they live; in wagons their wives weave for them their hideous garments, in wagons they cohabit with their husbands, bear children, and rear them to the age of puberty. . . . This race of untamed men, without encumbrances, aflame with an inhuman desire for plundering others' property, made their violent way amid the rapine and slaughter of the neighboring peoples as far as the Halani [on the river Don].

THE BATTLE OF ADRIANOPLE, A.D. 378

Ammianus Marcellinus, *History* XXXI. xiii, xv, xvi (abridged)

On every side armor and weapons clashed. . . . But when the barbarians, pouring forth in huge hordes, trampled down horse and man, and in the press of ranks no room for retreat could be gained anywhere, and the increased crowding left no opportunity for escape, our soldiers also, with a contempt of death which was their last feeling, received their death blows, yet struck down their assailants; and on both sides the strokes of axes split helmet and breastplate. . . . Now the sun had risen higher and . . . scorched the Romans, who were more and more exhausted by hunger and worn out by thirst, as well as distressed by the heavy burden of their armor. Finally our line was broken by the onrushing weight of the barbarians and . . . they took to their heels in disorder as best they could. . . . The barbarians, their eyes blazing with frenzy, were pursuing our men . . . ; some fell without knowing who struck them down, others were buried beneath the mere weight of their pursuers . . . nor did anyone spare those who retreated. Besides all this, the roads were blocked by many who lay mortally wounded, lamenting the torment of their wounds; and with them also mounds of fallen horses filled the plains with corpses. To these ever irreparable losses, so costly to the Roman state, a night without the bright light of the moon put an end. . . .

[The Emperor Valens was killed, but his body could not be found.]

The victorious Goths laid siege to Adrianople, where Valens had left his treasures . . . but after vainly trying every means of taking the city they withdrew unsuccessful. . . .

The Goths, after bribing the forces of the Huns and the Halani to join them . . . hastened in rapid march to Constantinople, greedy for its vast heaps of treasure. . . . [Beaten off by Saracens serving the emperor], the Goths then departed and spread everywhere over the northern provinces, which they traversed at will as far as the foot of the Julian, or as they were formerly called, the Venetic Alps.

192. THE SIEGE AND SACK OF ROME, A.D. 410

Zosimus, *New History* v. xxxvi–vi. xiii (abridged); From the translation of R. T. Ridley

[Autumn 409] Alaric sought peace on these conditions, but the emperor refused his request, even though he should have done one of two things if he were to handle the present situation successfully: he ought either to have deferred the war and made peace for a moderate sum, or chosen to fight and assembled all his legions. . . . Honorius, however, neither accepted the peace nor . . . called up the Roman army, but pinning his hopes on Olympius' advice became the cause of terrible disasters to the state. . . .

Considering Honorius' preparations laughable, Alaric began to march on Rome . . . and sent to Upper Pannonia for his wife's brother, Ataulphus, who had a considerable army of Huns and Goths. . . . He marched through Aquileia . . . then, passing through Aemilia and leaving Ravenna[13] behind, he reached and overran Ariminum, a great city in Flaminia, and all the other cities in this province. He next came to Picenum, a province

---

13. A strong Roman army and naval base.

somewhere at the end of the Ionian Bay, whence he marched for Rome, destroying all forts and cities on his way. . . .

Alaric encircled the city and all the gates, and by controlling the river Tiber he prevented supplies coming from the harbor [at Ostia]. Although the Romans realized this they were still determined to hold out, expecting that help for the city would come from Ravenna any day. When, however, no one came and their hopes were disappointed, they decided to reduce their rations and to eat only half the previous daily allowance, and later, when the scarcity continued, only a third. And when there was no means of relief, and their food was exhausted, plague not unexpectedly succeeded famine. Corpses lay everywhere, and since the bodies could not be buried outside the city with the enemy guarding every exit, the city became their tomb. The result was that the place was uninhabited for another reason: even if there had been no shortage of food, the stench from the corpses would have been enough to destroy the bodies of the living. . . . When their situation was critical and they were in danger of turning to cannibalism,[14] after trying every abomination known to man they decided to send an embassy to the enemy to say that they were ready for a reasonable peace but even more ready for war because the Roman people were armed and so well drilled that they no longer feared a confrontation. . . .

Sending ambassadors back again, after many discussions they decided that the city should give five thousand pounds of gold as well as thirty thousand of silver, four thousand silk tunics, three thousand scarlet skins and three thousand pounds' weight of pepper. Since the city had no public monies, the senators who had property undertook to contribute this on the basis of a census. . . . When the money had been raised in this way, they decided to send an embassy to the emperor to inform him about the peace and that Alaric wanted not only money but also aristocratic children as hostages; on this condition he had made not only peace but also an alliance with the emperor, promising to assist the Romans against any of their enemies. The emperor decided to make peace on these terms and the money was paid to the barbarians. Alaric then allowed the citizens a market for three days, the right of safe exit by certain gates, and facilities to bring up food from the harbor. The citizens thus had a breathing space to buy necessities, which they did either by selling whatever they had left or by exchanging other posses-

14. According to two other sources they did resort to cannibalism.

sions for food. The barbarians withdrew from Rome and pitched camp somewhere in Tuscany. Day by day almost all the slaves who were in Rome poured out of the city to join the barbarians, who now numbered about forty thousand. . . .

Jovius, the Praetorian Prefect, whose influence with the emperor was paramount, decided to send ambassadors to Alaric, urging him to come with Ataulphus as far as Ravenna to conclude the peace there. Alaric was persuaded by the emperor's and Jovius' letters to come to Ariminum, thirty miles from Ravenna. . . . Alaric demanded that a fixed amount of gold and grain be provided each year, and that he and all his followers should live in the two Venetias, the two Noricums and Dalmatia. . . . [When the emperor rejected Jovius' additional suggestion that Alaric be made a Roman general], Alaric lost his temper and ordered his barbarians to march on Rome immediately to avenge the insult to him and his whole race. . . . The emperor summoned ten thousand Huns as allies in the war against Alaric and, in order to have supplies for them when they came, ordered the Dalmatians to contribute grain, sheep and oxen. After dispatching scouts to find out how Alaric was coming to Rome, he assembled his army from all quarters. Alaric, however, repenting of his march on Rome, sent the bishops of each city as ambassadors to urge the emperor not to allow a city which had ruled the greater part of the earth for more than a thousand years to be plundered by barbarians, or to permit such great buildings to be destroyed by barbarian flames, but to make peace on reasonable terms. They said that Alaric did not want office or honor, nor did he now wish to settle in the provinces previously specified but only the two Noricums, which are on the far reaches of the Danube, are subject to continual incursions, and pay little tax to the treasury. Moreover, he would be satisfied with as much grain each year as the emperor thought sufficient, and forget about the gold. Thus there could be friendship and alliance between him and the Romans against everyone who took up arms and was roused to war against the emperor.

When Alaric made these fair and prudent proposals, everyone marveled at the man's moderation. Jovius and those who had the greatest authority after the emperor, however, declared that his demands were impossible because everyone in office had sworn not to make peace with Alaric. They claimed that if they had taken an oath by God they may well have disregarded it, relying on His kindness for forgiveness, but since they had sworn by the emperor's head it was not right for them to offend such a powerful oath. So blind were the minds of those in charge of the state at that time in the absence of the [pagan] gods' care.

When his very moderate demands were so insultingly rejected, Alaric marched on Rome with his entire force, determined to persevere in the siege of the city.

Zosimus' narrative was presumably climaxed by a description, now lost, of the capture and devastating sack of the city in August of 410.]

193. LAMENTS FOR ROME

Jerome, *Letters* lx. 16–17; From *LCL*

I come now to the frail fortunes of human life, and my soul shudders to recount the downfall of our age. For twenty years now and more the blood of Romans has every day been shed between Constantinople and the Julian Alps. Scythia, Thrace, Macedonia, Thessaly, Dardania, Dacia, Epirus, Dalmatia, and all the provinces of Pannonia, have been sacked, pillaged and plundered by Goths and Sarmatians, Quadians and Alans, Huns and Vandals and Marcomanni. How many matrons, and how many of God's virgins, ladies of gentle birth and high position, have been made the sport of these beasts! Bishops have been taken prisoners, presbyters and other clergymen of different orders murdered. Churches have been overthrown, horses stabled at Christ's altar, the relics of martyrs dug up. . . .

The Roman world is falling, and yet we hold our heads erect instead of bowing our necks. What, think you, are the feelings of Corinthians, the Athenians, the Lacedaemonians, the Arcadians, and all the other Greeks over whom barbarians now are ruling? I have only mentioned a few cities certainly, but they were once the seats of no small powers. The East seemed to be immune from these dangers and was only dismayed by the news that reached her. But lo! last year [A.D. 395] the wolves—not of Arabia, but from the far north—were let loose upon us from the distant crags of Caucasus, and in a short time they overran whole provinces. How many monasteries did they capture, how many rivers were reddened with men's blood! They besieged Antioch and all the cities on the Halys, Cydnus, Orontes, and Euphrates. They carried off troops of captives. Arabia, Phoenicia, Palestine and Egypt in their terror felt themselves already enslaved. . . .

But I did not propose to write a history: I only wished briefly to lament our miseries. In any case, if it came to telling this tale adequately, even Thucydides and Sallust would have no voice.

Lactantius, Divine Institutes VII. xxv

The fall and ruin of the world will soon take place, but it seems that nothing of the kind is to be feared as long as the city of Rome stands intact. But when the capital of the world has fallen . . . who can doubt that the end will have come for the affairs of men and the whole world?

194. ETERNAL ROME

Ammianus Marcellinus, History XVI. x. 13–15; From LCL

So then Constantius entered Rome [in 357], the home of empire and of every virtue, and when he had come to the Rostra, the most renowned forum of ancient dominion, he stood amazed; and on every side on which his eyes rested he was dazzled by the array of marvelous sights. He addressed nobles in the Senate-house and the populace from the tribunal, and being welcomed to the palace with manifold attentions, he enjoyed a longed-for pleasure; and on several occasions, when holding equestrian games, he took delight in the sallies of the commons, who were neither presumptuous nor regardless of their old-time freedom while he himself also respectfully observed the due mean. For he did not (as in the case of other cities) permit the contests to be terminated at his own discretion, but left them (as the custom is) to various chances. Then, as he surveyed the sections of the city and the suburbs, lying within the summits of the seven hills, along their slopes, or on level ground, he thought that whatever first met his gaze towered above all the rest: the sanctuaries of Tarpeian Jove so far surpassing as things divine excel those of earth; the baths built up in the manner of provinces; the huge bulk of the amphitheater, strengthened by its framework of travertine, to whose top human eyesight barely ascends; the Pantheon like a round city-district, vaulted over in lofty beauty; and the exalted columns which rise with platforms to which one may mount, and bear the likeness of former emperors; the Temple of the City; the Forum of Peace; the Theatre of Pompey, the Odeum, the Stadium, and in their midst the other adornments of the Eternal City. But when he came to the Forum of Trajan, a construction unique under the heaven, as we believe, and admirable even in the unanimous opinion of the gods, he stood fast in amazement, turning his attention to the gigantic complex about him, beggaring description and never again to be imitated by mortal men. Therefore, abandoning all hope of attempting anything like it, he said he would and could copy Trajan's steed alone, which stands in the center of the vestibule, carrying the emperor himself.

Claudian,[15] *On the Consulship of Stilicho* III, lines 130–176; A.D. 399/400; From *LCL*

Consul, all but peer of the gods, protector of a city greater than any that upon earth the air encompasseth, whose amplitude no eye can measure, whose beauty no imagination can picture, whose praise no voice can sound, who raises a golden head amid the neighboring stars and with her seven hills imitates the seven regions of heaven, mother of arms and of law, who extends her sway o'er all the earth and was the earliest cradle of justice, this is the city which, sprung from humble beginnings, has stretched to either pole, and from one small place extended its power so as to be co-terminous with the sun's light. Open to the blows of fate while at one and the same time she fought a thousand battles, conquered Spain, laid siege to the cities of Sicily, subdued Gaul by land and Carthage by sea, never did she yield to her losses nor show fear at any blow, but rose to greater heights of courage after the disasters of Cannae and Trebia, and, while the enemy's fire threatened her, and her foe [i.e., Hannibal] smote upon her walls, sent an army against the farthest Iberians. Nor did Ocean bar her way; launching upon the deep, she sought in another world for Britons to be vanquished. 'Tis she alone who has received the conquered into her bosom and like a mother, not an empress, protected the human race with a common name, summoning those whom she has defeated to share her citizenship and drawing together distant races with bonds of affection. To her rule of peace we owe it that the world is our home, that we can live where we please, and that to visit Thule and explore its once dreaded wilds is but a sport; thanks to her all and sundry may drink the waters of the Rhone and quaff Orontes' stream, thanks to her we are all one people. Nor will there ever be a limit to the empire of Rome, for luxury and its attendant vices, and pride with sequent hate have brought to ruin all kingdoms else. 'Twas thus that Sparta laid low the foolish pride of Athens but to

15. Claudius Claudianus (*c.* 370–*c.* 404), "the last poet of Classical Rome," was a sort of court poet of the Emperor Honorius and fervent admirer of the general Stilicho, famed for his victories over the Visigoths and Ostrogoths.

fall herself a victim to Thebes; thus that the Mede deprived the Assyrian of empire and the Persian the Mede. Macedonia subdued Persia and was herself to yield to Rome. But Rome found her strength in the oracles of the Sibyl, her vigor in the hallowed laws of Numa. For her Jove brandishes his thunderbolts; 'tis she to whom Minerva offers the full protection of her shield; to her Vesta brought her sacred flame, Bacchus his rites, and the turret-crowned mother of the gods her Phrygian lions. Hither to keep disease at bay came, gliding with steady motion, the snake whose home was Epidaurus, and Tiber's isle gave shelter to the Paeonian serpent [i.e., Aesculapius] from beyond the sea.

This is the city whom thou, Stilicho, and heaven guard, her thou protectest, mother of kings and generals, mother, above all, of thee.

COINS

As noted in volume 1, under Augustus the mints and the whole monetary system were reorganized. Thenceforth the emperor issued the gold and silver coinage, leaving the bronze to be authorized by the Senate on his recommendations. An imperial procurator was in charge of each mint, at least from the early second century.

The number of different Roman coins known today runs into the thousands. Many celebrate events, such as military victories, accessions to the principate, annexations of provinces or distributions of largesse. Often such coins were issued years after the event to which they refer; others were struck on anniversaries—fifth, tenth, and so forth, all the way to the coin issued in A.D. 357 to commemorate the 1,110th anniversary of the founding of Rome. Vast numbers of still other coins have legends on the reverse celebrating virtues and accomplishments, real or claimed, of the emperors: for example, clemency, concord, felicity, justice, loyalty, liberality, moderation, piety, peace, providence, munificence, recovery, safety, hope.

Legends are given in capital letters, as they appear on the coins. OBV. = Obverse, REV. = Reverse, r. = facing right, l. = facing left.

A.D. 22–23 Bronze
   OBV. Laureate head l. TI(berius) CAESAR AUGUST(us), S(on) OF
        THE DEIFIED AUG(ustus), 8 TIMES IMP(erator)
   REV. Small bust of Tiberius inside concentric laurel wreaths TO (his)
        CLEMENCY; (issued) BY D(ecree) OF THE S(enate)

The legend on the reverse is no doubt a reference to Tiberius' mildness in dealing with political dissent.

A.D. 37–38 Bronze
> OBV. Laureate head l. G(aius) CAESAR AUG(ustus) GERMANI-
> CUS PON(tifex) M(aximus) (holder of) TR(ibunician) POW(er)
> REV. Caligula's three sisters in the guise of the goddesses Security,
> Concord, and Fortune AGRIPPINA DRUSILLA JULIA; (issued)
> BY D(ecree) OF THE S(enate)

A.D. 46–47 Silver
> OBV. Laureate head r. TI(berius) CLAUD(ius) CAESAR AUG(ustus)
> P(ontifex) M(aximus) (in his) 6TH TR(ibunician) P(ower) 11 TIMES
> IMP(erator)
> REV. Winged, draped female figure r. combining attributes of Peace,
> Victory, Prosperity, Safety, and Propriety TO THE AUGUS-
> TAN PEACE

A.D. 64–66 Bronze
> OBV. Head r. EMP(eror) CAESAR AUG(ustus) PONT(ifex)
> MAX(imus) (holder of) TR(ibunician) P(ower) F(ather) OF HIS
> COUNTRY
> REV. Temple of Janus PEACE OBTAINED FOR THE R(oman)
> P(eople) ON LAND AND SEA, HE CLOSED (the temple of)
> JANUS; (issued) BY D(ecree) OF THE S(enate)

A.D. 72 Bronze
> OBV. Laureate, cuirassed bust r. T(itus) CAESAR VESPASIAN
> THRICE IMP(erator) PON(tifex maximus) (in his) 2D
> TR(ibunician) POW(er) TWICE CONSUL
> REV. Titus, laureate, holding scepter tipped with a human head, standing
> r. in a four-horse chariot (Issued) BY D(ecree) OF THE S(enate)

The scene on the reverse commemorates the triumph that Titus and
Vespasian celebrated for the suppression of the Jewish revolt. Some coins
of this period have the additional legend JUDAEA CAPTURED.

A.D. 88 Gold
> OBV. Laureate head r. DOMITIAN AUGUSTUS GERMANICUS
> REV. Herald l. carrying wand and shield 14 TIMES CONS(ul) HE
> CEL(ebrated) THE SEC(ular) GAM(es)

A.D. 97 Silver

OBV. Laureate head r. EMP(eror) NERVA CAES(ar) AUG(ustus) P(ontifex) M(aximus) THRICE CONS(ul) F(ather) OF HIS C(ountry)

REV. Liberty standing l. holding cap of freedom and scepter PUBLIC LIBERTY

The legend of the reverse makes the obvious contrast with the tyranny of Domitian's last years.

A.D. 97 Bronze

OBV. As above

REV. A modius measure filled with grain GRAIN ESTABLISHED FOR THE URBAN POPULACE; (issued) BY D(ecree) OF THE S(enate)

A.D. 104 Bronze

OBV. Laureate bust r. TO THE EMP(eror) CAES(ar) NERVA TRA-JAN AUG(ustus) GER(manicus) DAC(icus) P(ontifex) M(aximus) (holder of) TR(ibunician) P(ower) 5 TIMES CONS(ul) F(ather) OF HIS C(ountry)

REV. An arched bridge over a river [Danube] THE R(oman) S(enate) AND P(eople) TO THEIR BEST PRINCEPS; (issued) BY D(ecree) OF THE S(enate)

A.D. 116–117 Bronze

OBV. Laureate bust r. TO THE EMP(eror) CAES(ar) NER(va) TRA-JAN BEST AUG(ustus) GER(manicus) DAC(icus) PARTHICUS P(ontifex) M(aximus) (holder of) TR(ibunician) P(ower) 6 TIMES CONS(ul) F(ather) OF HIS C(ountry)

REV. Trajan standing in military dress r., holding spear and dagger; to his l. and r. the reclining river gods Euphrates and Tigris; between them Armenia seated l. ARMENIA AND MESOPOTAMIA SUBDUED TO THE POWER OF THE R(oman) P(eople); (issued) BY D(ecree) OF THE S(enate)

With the creation of the provinces of Armenia and Mesopotamia the Roman Empire reached its greatest extent.

A.D. C. 140 Bronze

OBV. Laureate head r. ANTONINUS AUG(ustus) PIUS F(elix)
C(aesar) (holder of) TR(ibunician) P(ower) THRICE CONS(ul)

REV. An imposing temple, on its roof the goddess Rome flanked by
two Victories holding diadems. TO ETERNAL ROME; (issued)
BY D(ecree) OF THE S(enate)

This coinage probably celebrates the completion of the temple of Venus
and Rome begun by Hadrian.

A.D. C. 143 Bronze

OBV. Laureate head r. ANTONINUS AUG(ustus) PIUS F(elix)
C(aesar) (holder of) TR(ibunician) P(ower) THRICE CONS(ul)

REV. Antoninus clad in toga standing l., placing tiara on head of a
smaller figure standing l. A KING GIVEN TO THE ARME-
NIANS; (issued) BY D(ecree) OF THE S(enate)

The weakness of Parthia at that time enabled the Roman emperor to put
his protege on the throne of the buffer kingdon of Armenia.

A.D. 149 Gold

OBV. Draped and garlanded bust r. TO FAUSTINA AUG(usta)
DAU(ghter) OF AUG(ustus) PIUS

REV. A goddess standing l. holding a wreath and baton. TO PUBLIC
REJOICING

This coin celebrates the birth of twins to Marcus Aurelius and Faustina.

A.D. 161 Gold

OBV. Head r. EMP(eror) CAES(ar) L(ucius) AUREL(ius) VERUS
AUG(ustus)

REV. Marcus Aurelius laureate l. clasping r. hands with Verus standing bareheaded r. TO THE CONCORD OF THE AUGUSTI
(holders of) TR(ibunician) P(ower) TWICE CONS(uls)

In this first joint reign of the Roman Empire the coin proclaims the
intention of the two *principes* to rule in harmony.

A.D. 228 Silver

OBV. Laureate, draped, cuirassed bust r. EMP(eror) C(aesar) M(arcus) AUR(elius) SEV(erus) ALEXANDER AUG(ustus)

REV. A goddess standing l. holding a globe and scepter TO THE PERPETUITY OF THE AUG(ustus)

A.D. 241–243 Bronze medallion

OBV. Laureate, draped, cuirassed bust l. EMP(eror) GORDIAN PIUS FELIX AUG(ustus)

REV. The Colosseum seen from above with animal combat inside. THE MUNIFICENCE OF GORDIAN AUG(ustus)

A.D. 243 Silver

OBV. Radiate, draped, cuirassed bust r. EMP(eror) GORDIAN PIUS FELIX AUG(ustus)

REV. Mars advancing r. holding spear and shield. MARS (our) DE-FENDER

The reference is to the war with the Persians.

A.D. 247 Silver

OBV. Laureate, draped, cuirassed bust r. EMP(eror) PHILIP AUG(ustus)

REV. A goddess standing l. holding scales and cornucopia. EQUITY OF THE AUGUSTI

A.D. 256 Gold

OBV. Laureate, draped, cuirassed bust r. EMP(eror) C(aesar) P(ublius) LIC(inius) GALLIENUS AUG(ustus)

REV. Valerian and Gallienus seated l. extending r. hands; behind them a standing figure l. [= attendant or citizen?]. 3D LARGESSE OF THE AUG(usti)

A.D. 268–270 Silver

OBV. Radiate, draped, cuirassed bust r. EMP(eror) CLAUDIUS P(ius) F(elix) AUG(ustus)

REV. A goddess standing l. holding a military standard in each hand. LOYALTY OF THE SOLD(iers)

A.D. 271–272 Silver

OBV. Radiate, draped, cuirassed bust r. EMP(eror) C(aesar) AURE-
LIAN AUG(ustus)

REV. Aurelian standing l. being crowned with a wreath by a female
figure standing r. RESTORER OF THE WORLD

A.D. 281 Silver

OBV. Laureate, mantled bust l. holding an eagle-tipped scepter.
EMP(eror) C(aesar) M(arcus) AUR(elius) PROBUS AUG(ustus)

REV. The four seasons. HAPPY TIMES

A.D. 327 Bronze, struck at Constantinople

OBV. Laureate head r. CONSTANTINE GREAT(est) AUG(ustus)

REV. Labarum surmounted by the monogram of Christ piercing a
serpent [= paganism?]. PUBLIC HOPE

This is one of only a few coin types of Constantine to include a Christian
symbol.

A.D. 348–350 Billon

OBV. Diademed, draped, cuirassed bust r. O(ur) M(aster) CON-
STANS P(ius) F(elix) AUG(ustus)

REV. A phoenix [symbol of renewal] standing r. on a globe. RE-
VIVAL OF HAP(py) TI(mes)

The reference of the reverse is probably to the 1,100th anniversary of the
founding of Rome, which was celebrated in A.D. 348.

A.D. 367–375 Bronze

OBV. Diademed, draped, cuirassed bust r. O(ur) M(aster) GRATIAN
AUG(ustus son) OF AUG(usti) [cf. the Oriental concept "king of
kings"]

REV. The emperor standing l. holding a labarum with the monogram
of Christ. GLORY OF THE NEW AGE

A.D. 383–392 Bronze

OBV. Diademed, draped, cuirassed bust r. O(ur) M(aster) THEO-
DOSIUS P(ius) F(elix) AUG(ustus)

REV. Victory advancing l. holding a trophy and dragging a captive.
PRESERVATION OF THE STATE

A.D. 409–410 Gold
    OBV. Diademed, draped, cuirassed bust r. PRISCUS ATTALUS P(ius)
        F(elix) AUG(ustus)
    REV. The Goddess Rome seated holding Victory on a globe in r. hand
        and a spear in l. hand. UNCONQUERED ETERNAL ROME

The irony of the image and legend on the reverse is acute. When Alaric
captured Rome he named Priscus Attalus as his puppet emperor and soon
after deposed him.

EPILOGUE

The optimism of the Gallo-Roman poet Rutilius Namatianus, as he wrote what has since been called "the swan song of Rome" in A.D. 416 (six years after the capture of Rome by the Goths under Alaric), stands in sharp contrast to the prophecy of doom written centuries earlier by Seneca, who, as a Stoic, held to a cyclical theory of history developed by Greek historians and philosophers.

Rutilius Namatianus, *On his Return* I. 46–66, 133–38; *Adapted from LCL*

Listen, O fairest queen of thy world, Rome, welcomed amid the starry skies, listen thou mother of men and mother of gods, thanks to thy temples we are not far from heaven. Thee do we chant, and shall, while destiny allows, forever chant. None can be safe if forgetful of thee. Sooner shall guilty oblivion overwhelm the sun than the honor due thee quit my heart; for thy benefits extend as far as the sun's rays, where are the waves of the circling Ocean-flood. For thee the very Sun-god who embraceth all doth revolve; his steeds that rise in thy domains he putteth in thy domains to rest. Thee Africa hath not stayed with scorching sands, nor hath the Bear, armed with native cold, repulsed thee. As far as habitable nature hath stretched toward the poles, so far hath earth opened a path for thy valor. For nations far apart thou hast made a single fatherland; under thy dominion conquest hath meant profit for those who knew not justice; and by offering to the vanquished a share in thine own law, thou hast made a city of what was erstwhile a world. . . . Spread forth the laws that are to last throughout the ages of Rome; thou alone needst not dread the distaffs of the Fates. . . . The span which doth remain is subject to no bounds, so long as earth shall stand and heaven uphold the stars!

Seneca, *Moral Epistles* lxxi. 15

The entire human race, both present and future, is condemned to death. All the cities that have ever held dominion or have been the splendid jewels of empires belonging to others—some day men will ask where they were. And they will be swept away by various kinds of destruction: some will be ruined by wars, others will be destroyed by idleness and a peace that ends in sloth, or by luxury, the bane of those of great wealth. All these fertile plains will be blotted out of sight by a sudden overflowing of the sea, or the subsiding of the land will sweep them away suddenly into the abyss.

GLOSSARY

ACHAEA, the Roman province of Greece.

AMPHORA, a Greek and Roman liquid measure, 8 *congii,* or *c.* 6 gallons, 7 pints.

ANNONA, the tribute in grains paid by the provinces to supply the city of Rome and the Empire's armies.

AROURA, a land measure in Roman Egypt, slightly more than ½ acre.

ARTAB, an Egyptian dry measure, varying from 3 to 6 *modii* in capacity.

AS, plur. ASSES, the smallest Roman copper coin.

ASIA, a Roman province in the western part of Asia Minor.

CAMPUS MARTIUS ("Field of Mars"), so called from the very early altar of Mars situated there, this plain between the Tiber and the Capitol was originally the meeting place of the *comitia centuriata.* In the course of time it was adorned with numerous public buildings and temples; see § 37.

CAPITAL OFFENSE, any crime for which a citizen paid with his *caput* ("head"), that is, his physical or civic existence: cf. chapter 8, note 15.

CAPITOL, the temple of Jupiter Optimus Maximus (Jupiter Best and Greatest), center of the Roman civic religion, situated on the Capitoline Hill in Rome.

CENTURION, the principal professional Roman military officer, in charge of a century (100 men at maximum strength). Each Roman legion had 60 centurions.

CENTURY: see centurion.

CHOENIX, a dry measure. *c.* 1 quart.

CIRCUS MAXIMUS, the chariot-race oval in Rome between the Palatine and Aventine hills. It was 600 m. long and 150 m. wide.

CLERUCHY ("allotment"), a numbered division of land in Egypt, originating in Ptolemaic times and continued under the Romans.

COLLEGIUM, plur. COLLEGIA, an association of any kind, especially artisan "guilds" and benevolent or burial societies.

COLONUS, (1) a tenant farmer on an imperial estate; (2) similarly, the operator of a mine on government contract.

COSMETES, in Greek cities and the nome metropolises of Egypt the officer in charge of matters concerning the ephebes (see chapter 4, note 87).

DECURION, a member of a municipal senate, comprising usually 100 decurions.

DENARIUS, a Roman silver coin, equal to 4 sesterces; it was reduced in the successive devaluations of the third century to a mere fraction of its original value.

DRACHMA, the basic silver coin of the Greek monetary system, which continued in use in the Greek-speaking Roman provinces. The drachma was equated with the Roman *denarius* (except in Egypt, where the equation was 4 drachmas = 1 *denarius,* 1 drachma = 1 *sestertius*).

DUOVIR, member of two-man board; most commonly, *duoviri iure dicundo,* "two-man board with judicial power," the two chief magistrates of Roman municipalities.

EPISTRATEGUS, head of one of the three administrative divisions in which the nomes of Egypt (each governed by a *strategus*) were grouped under Roman rule.

EQUES, pl. EQUITES, originally "cavalrymen," or "knights." The equestrian order was a social and economic class in Rome, Italy, and the provinces, second in status to the senatorial order. Members of this class, for which a minimum of 400,000 sesterces was required, served as army officers of intermediate rank and staffed important posts in the imperial civil service.

FASCES, a bundle of rods with an axe protruding from the upper part, carried by lictors in front of magistrates possessing *imperium* as symbols of the power of these magistrates to scourge (rods) or behead (axe) Roman citizens.

FISC, the privy purse of the emperor, as distinct from the state treasury, which it at first outstripped in resources and eventually superseded.

FLAMEN, priest assigned to the cult of an individual god.

FOLLIS, pl. FOLLES, a copper coin introduced in Diocletian's currency reform of A.D. 296. No fully satisfactory determination of its value has yet been made.

FORUM, the Roman Forum, civic center in Rome (also in Roman municipalities), situated between the Capitoline and Palatine hills; Rome possessed five additional fora for the transaction of public business, constructed under Julius Caesar, Augustus, Vespasian, Nerva, and Trajan.

GENIUS, a tutelary spirit that, according to Roman belief, each man was assigned at birth as his personal protecting deity and that he worshiped accordingly, especially on his birthday. Under the Empire, the worship of the *genius* of the emperor was an important aspect of the ruler cult.

GYMNASIARCH, in Greek cities and towns, the magistrate who superintended the functioning of the gymnasium.

IMPERATOR, commander-in-chief, a title bestowed on a victorious general by his soldiers. Under the Empire, it denoted the supreme power of the emperor and was, beginning with Vespasian's reign, regularly the first title in the imperial nomenclature. In addition, the emperor added after his name the number of times he was acclaimed *imperator* for military victories won by himself or his legates.

IMPERIUM, the right or power to command, supreme military and administrative power.

IUGERUM, a Roman land measure, 28,800 square Roman feet, or *c.* ⅝ acre.

LICTOR, an apparitor of a Roman magistrate invested with *imperium;* in public appearances he walked in front of the magistrate carrying the symbol of the latter's authority, the *fasces.*

LITURGY (from Greek *leitourgia,* "service to the people"), a compulsory public service, termed *munus* in Latin.

MILE, Roman, in Latin *mille passus* ("1,000 paces"), that is, 5,000 Roman feet, *c.* 4,850 English feet or *c.* 0.92 English mile.

MINA: see talent.

MODIUS, a Roman dry measure, 16 *sextarii* or *c.* 1 peck.

MUNUS: see liturgy.

NOBLES (*nobiles,* "the well known"), an unofficial term designating those families one or more of whose members had held the consulship.

NOME, an administrative district of Egypt, in charge of a *strategus.*

OBOL, the smallest Greek coin, ⅙ of a drachma.

PONTIFEX MAXIMUS, "supreme pontiff," head of the college of pontiffs and of other priests in charge of the Roman state cult. This office was always held by the emperor.

PRAETORIAN GUARD, the emperor's bodyguard, stationed in and near Rome. Its total strength is thought to have varied in the course of the Principate between 5,000 and 16,000 troops. It was headed by (usually) two prefects, who early in the Principate and increasingly in times of crisis intervened to act as emperor makers. Constantine disbanded the Guard and reorganized the office of the Praetorian Prefects, increasing their number to four and assigning to each a viceregal authority over a fourth of the Empire.

PRAETORIAN PREFECT: see PRAETORIAN GUARD.

PRIMUS INTER PARES, "first among equals," the official conceptualization of the status of the *Princeps* as established by Augustus.

PRINCEPS, "first citizen," unofficial title of the Roman emperors during the Principate.

PROCURATOR, title of a great variety of imperial middle-echelon officials, many belonging to the equestrian order. Most procurators held administrative posts connected with the far-flung imperial properties and revenues; a few were (especially in the third century) governors or acting governors of lesser provinces.

PROMAGISTRATE, the title of a consul, praetor, or quaestor after his year of office. Proconsuls and propraetors continued to exercise *imperium* in command of armies and provinces.

PUBLICAN, tax farmer.

QUINQUENNALIS, "fifth-year official," (1) title of chief magistrates of Roman municipalities who took the local census and possessed other censorial powers; (2) honorary title of officers of *collegia.*

QUIRITES, Roman citizens.

SALIANS, "leapers," an ancient priesthood of Mars, whom they celebrated with elaborate ritual dances and feasts.

SESTERTIUS, a Roman coin worth in imperial times 4 *asses,* or ¼ *denarius* (for its devaluation see DENARIUS). The English plural is sesterces.

SEXTARIUS, a Roman liquid measure, ⅙ *congius,* or *c.* 1 pint; also a dry measure, ¹⁄₁₆ *modius.*

SITOLOGUS, in Egypt a collector of grain taxes at a local granary.

STADE or STADIUM, a Greek linear measure, 625 Roman feet, or ⅛ Roman mile.

STRATEGUS, (1) in Egypt, the governor of a nome; (2) in other Greek-speaking provinces, a high city official or head of a league of cities.

TALENT, a Greek weight (80 Roman lb., or *c.* 57 lb. avoirdupois) and monetary unit worth 60 minas or 6,000 drachmas.

TRIBUNICIAN POWER, one of the constitutional bases of the Principate, granting the emperors supreme power over civil affairs in the capital. The emperors counted their regnal years from the date of the assumption of this power.

TRIUMPH, the procession—from the Campus Martius to the Capitol—of a Roman general celebrating a major victory. The victor rode in a chariot and was accompanied in the parade by his army, the magistrates and senators, and displays of the spoils (including fettered captives), all proceeding on foot. Under the Empire triumphs were reserved for the emperor; other commanders deemed worthy of such honor were awarded "triumphal decorations" *(ornamenta triumphalia).*

VIR CLARISSIMUS (literally, "most illustrious man"), an honorific appellation that became under the Empire the distinctive title of Roman senators.

VIR EGREGIUS (literally, "distinguished man"), honorary title of an *eques,* approximately equivalent in English to "the honorable."

VIR EMINENS OR EMINENTISSIMUS (literally, "prominent" or "most prominent man") the highest honorary appellation of public officials of equestrian rank. From the time of Hadrian this was the distinctive title of Praetorian Prefects.

VIR PERFECTISSIMUS (literally, "most excellent man"), honorific appellation of high-ranking equestrian officials.

SELECT BIBLIOGRAPHY

GENERAL BIBLIOGRAPHY

Included in this list are books pertinent to all or most of the period of the Empire. Books noted here are as a rule not repeated in the individual chapter bibliographies.

Boardman, J. et al., eds. *Oxford History of the Classical World*. Oxford, 1986.

Bowder, D., ed. *Who Was Who in the Roman World, 753 B.C.–A.D. 476*. Oxford and Ithaca, 1980.

Cambridge Ancient History. Vols. 10–12 and vol. 5 of Plates. Cambridge, 1934–1939.

Cary, M. *The Geographic Background of Greek and Roman History*. Oxford, 1949.

Garnsey, P. and R. Saller. *The Roman Empire: Economy, Society, and Culture*. Berkeley, 1987.

Grant, M. *The Roman Emperors: A Bibliographical Guide to the Rulers of Imperial Rome*. London and New York, 1985.

Lemprière's Classical Dictionary of Proper Names Mentioned in Ancient Authors. 3d ed., rev. by F. A. Wright. Boston, 1984.

MacDonald, W. L. *The Architecture of the Roman Empire*. New Haven, 1986.

Mattingly, H. *Man in the Roman Street*. New York, 1947.

Oxford Classical Dictionary. 2d ed. Oxford, 1970.

Reinhold, M. *History of Purple as a Status Symbol in Antiquity*. Brussels, 1970.

Rostovtzeff, M. *The Social and Economic History of the Roman Empire*. 2d ed., rev. by P. M. Fraser. 2 vols. Oxford, 1957.

Rostovtzeff, M. and E. Bickermann. *A History of the Ancient World: Rome*. New York, 1961.

Sherwin-White, A. N. *The Roman Citizenship*. 2d ed. Oxford, 1973.

Starr, C. G. *The Roman Empire 27 B.C.–A.D. 476; A Study in Survival*. Oxford and New York, 1982.

Taylor, L. R. *The Divinity of the Roman Emperor*. Middletown, Conn., 1931; reprint New York, 1975.

Waddy, L. H. *Pax Romana and World Peace*. New York, 1950.

Wylie, J. K. *Roman Constitutional History from Earliest Times to the Death of Justinian*. Pasadena, 1948.

1. THE ROMAN PEACE: IMPERIAL POLICY AND ADMINISTRATION

Allen, W., Jr. "The Political Atmosphere of the Reign of Tiberius," *Transactions of the American Philological Association* (1941), 72:1–25.

Bauman, R. A. *Impietas in Principem: A Study of Treason Against the Roman Emperor with Special Reference to the First Century* A.D. Munich, 1974.

Braund, D. C. *Rome and the Friendly Kings: The Character of Client Kingship*. London and New York, 1984.

Brunt, P. A. "Lex de Imperio Vespasiani," *Journal of Roman Studies* (1977), 67:95–116.

Brunt, P. A. "Princeps and Equites," *Journal of Roman Studies* (1983), 73:42–75.

Brunt, P. A. "The Role of the Senate in the Augustan Regime," *Classical Quarterly* (1984), 34:423–444.

Charlesworth, M. P. *"Pietas* and *Victoria:* The Emperor and the Citizen," *Journal of Roman Studies* (1943), 33:1–10.

Charlesworth, M. P. "The Virtues of the Roman Emperor: Propaganda and the Creation of Belief," *Proceedings of the British Academy* (1937), 23:105–133.

Colledge, M. A. R. *The Parthians*. London, 1967.

Ferrill, A. "The Senatorial Aristocracy in the Early Roman Empire," in *The Craft of the Ancient Historian: Essays in Honor of Chester G. Starr,* ed. J. W. Eadie and J. Ober, 353–371. Lanham, Md., 1985.

Grant, M. "Roman Coins as Propaganda," *Archaeology* (1952), 5:79–85.

Greenhalgh, P. A. L. *The Year of the Four Emperors*. London, 1975.

Hammond, M. *The Augustan Principate in Theory and Practice During the Julio-Claudian Periods*. Reprinted with appendix. New York, 1968.

Lepper. F. A. *Trajan's Parthian War*. London, 1948.

MacMullen, R. *Enemies of the Roman Order: Treason, Unrest and Alienation in the Empire*. Cambridge, Mass., 1966.

Millar, F. *The Emperor in the Roman World, 31 B.C.–A.D. 337*. London, 1977.

Millar, F. "Government and Diplomacy in the Roman Empire during the First Three Centuries," *The International History Review* (1988), 38:345–77.

Millar, F., ed. *The Roman Empire and Its Neighbours*. 2d ed. New York, 1981.

Rankin, H. D. *The Celts and the Classical World*. London, 1987.

Rogers, R. S. *Criminal Trials and Criminal Legislation Under Tiberius*. Middletown, Conn., 1935.

Smith, R. E. "The Law of Libel at Rome," *Classical Quarterly* (1951), 45:169–179.

Starr, C. G. "The Prefect Democracy of the Roman Empire," *American Historical Review* (1952–1953), 58:1–16.

Sutherland, C. H. V. *Coinage in Roman Imperial Policy, 31 B.C.–A.D. 68.* London, 1951.

Talbert, R. J. A. *The Senate of Imperial Rome.* Princeton, N.J., 1984.

Wirszubski, C. *Libertas as a Political Idea at Rome During the Late Republic and Early Principate.* Cambridge, 1950.

Yavetz, Z. *Plebs and Princeps.* Rev ed. New Brunswick, N.J., 1988.

2. THE ROMAN PEACE: ECONOMIC LIFE

Bedford, O. H. "The Silk Trade of China with the Roman Empire," *China Journal* (1938), 28:207–216.

Casson, L. "The Isis and Her Voyage," *Transactions of the American Philological Association* (1950), 81:43–56.

Casson, L. *Periplus Maris Erythraei.* Princeton, 1989.

Casson, L. *Travel in the Ancient World.* London, 1974.

Charlesworth, M. P. *Trade Routes and Commerce of the Roman Empire.* 2d ed., rev. Cambridge, 1926; reprint Chicago, 1974.

Forbes, R. J. *Metallurgy in Antiquity.* Leiden, 1950.

Forster, E. S. "Columella and His Latin Treatise on Agriculture," *Greece and Rome* (1950), 19:123–128.

Frank, T., ed. *An Economic Survey of Ancient Rome.* Vols. 2–5. Baltimore, 1936–1940; reprint Paterson, N.J., 1959.

Garnsey, P. *Famine and Food Supply in the Graeco-Roman World: Responses to Risk and Crisis.* Cambridge, 1988.

Garnsey, P. et al., eds. *Trade in the Ancient Economy.* Berkeley and London, 1983.

Heitland, W. E. *Agricola. A Study of Agriculture and Rustic Life in the Graeco-Roman World from the Point of View of Labour.* Cambridge, 1921; reprint Westport, Conn., 1970.

Jones, A. H. M. "Inflation Under the Roman Empire," *Economic History Review* (1953), 5:293–318.

Jongman, W. *The Economy and Society of Pompeii.* Amsterdam, 1988.

Wheeler, R. E. M. *Rome Beyond the Imperial Frontiers.* London, 1954.

Yeo, C. A. "The Economics of Roman and American Slavery," *Finanzarchiv* (1952), 13:445–485.

Yeo, C. A. "Land and Sea Transportation in Imperial Italy," *Transactions of the American Philological Association* (1946), 77:221–244.

Yeo, C. A. "The Overgrazing of Ranch Lands in Ancient Italy," *Transactions of the American Philological Association"* (1948), 79:275–309.

3. THE ROMAN PEACE: SOCIETY AND CULTURE

Africa, T. W. "Urban Violence in Imperial Rome," *Journal of Interdisciplinary History* (1971), 2:3–21.

Alföldy, G. *The Social History of Rome.* Totowa, N.J., 1985.

Bagnani, G. "The House of Trimalchio," *American Journal of Philology* (1954), 75:16–39.

Balsdon, J. P. V. D. *Life and Leisure in Ancient Rome.* London and New York, 1969.

Balsdon, J. P. V. D. *Romans and Aliens.* London and Chapel Hill, N.C., 1979.

Barrow, R. H. *Slavery in the Roman Empire.* London, 1928.

Bonner, S. F. *The Education of a Roman.* Liverpool, 1950.

Boren, H. C. *Roman Society: A Social, Economic and Cultural History.* Lexington, Mass., 1977.

Bradley, K. R. *Slaves and Masters in the Roman Empire: A Study in Social Control.* Brussels and New York, 1984–1987.

Brenk, F. E. "In the Light of the Moon: Demonology in the Early Imperial Period," *Aufstieg und Niedergang der römischen Welt* (1979), 2 (16.3):2068–2145.

Clark, D. L. *Rhetoric in Greco-Roman Education.* New York, 1954.

Clarke, M. L. *Rhetoric at Rome: A Historical Survey.* London, 1953.

Colish, M. L. *The Stoic Tradition from Antiquity to the Early Middle Age.* 2 vols. Leiden, 1985.

Cramer, F. H. *Astrology in Roman Law and Politics.* Philadelphia, 1954.

D'Arms, J. H. *Commerce and Social Standing in Ancient Rome.* Cambridge, Mass., 1981.

D'Arms, J. H. *Romans on the Bay of Naples.* Cambridge, Mass., 1970.

Dodds, E. R. *Pagan and Christian in an Age of Anxiety: Some Aspects of Religious Experience from Marcus Aurelius to Constantine.* Cambridge, 1965; reprint New York, 1970.

Duff. A. M. *Freedmen in the Early Roman Empire.* Oxford, 1928; reprint Cambridge, 1958.

Duff. J. W. *A Literary History of Rome in the Silver Age from Tiberius to Hadrian.* Rev. and ed. by A. M. Duff. London, 1953; reprint 1960.

Edelstein, L. *The Meaning of Stoicism.* Cambridge, 1966.

Fears, J. R. "The Cult of Virtues and Roman Imperial Ideology," *Aufstieg und Niedergang der römischen Welt* (1981), 2(17,2):827–948.

Fears, J. R. *"Princeps a deis electus:* The Divine Election of the Emperor as a Political Concept at Rome," *Papers and Monographs of the the American Academy in Rome* (1977), no. 26.

Ferguson, J. *The Religions of the Roman Empire.* Ithaca, 1970.

Fishwick, D. *The Imperial Cult in the Latin West.* Leiden, 1987.

Friedländer, L. *Roman Life and Manners Under the Early Empire.* 4 vols. New York, 1908–1915; reprint London, 1965.

Garnsey, P. "Religious Toleration in Classical Antiquity," *Studies in Church History* (1984), 21:1–27.

Garnsey, P. *Social Status and Legal Privilege in the Roman Empire.* Oxford, 1970.

Grimal, P. *Roman Cities, with a Descriptive Catalogue of Roman Cities by G. M. Woloch.* Madison, Wis., 1983.

Hermansen, G. *Ostia: Aspects of Roman City Life.* Edmonton, 1982.

Hopkins, K. *Conquerors and Slaves.* Cambridge and New York, 1978.

Hopkins, K. *Death and Renewal: Sociological Studies in Roman History.* Vol. 2. Cambridge, 1983.

Humphrey, J. H. *Roman Circuses: Arenas for Chariot Racing.* London and Berkeley, 1986.

Kennedy, G. A. *The Art of Rhetoric in the Roman World, 300 B.C.–A.D. 300.* Princeton, N.J., 1972.

Kenyon, F. G. *Books and Readers in Ancient Greece and Rome.* 2d ed. London and New York, 1951.

Keresztes, P. "The Imperial Roman Government and the Christian Church," *Aufstieg und Niedergang der römischen Welt* (1979), 2(23):247–315.

Liebeschuetz, J. H. W. G. *Continuity and Change in Roman Religion.* Oxford, 1979.

Luck, G. *Arcana Mundi: Magic and the Occult in the Greek and Roman Worlds.* Baltimore, Md., 1985.

MacMullen, R. *Paganism in the Roman Empire.* New Haven, 1981.

MacMullen, R. *Roman Social Relations, 50 B.C. to A.D. 284.* Corr. reprint New Haven and London, 1981.

Mattingly, H. B. *The Man in the Roman Street.* New York, 1966.

Neugebauer, O. *The Exact Sciences in Antiquity.* 2d ed. Providence, R.I., 1957.

Petit, P. *Pax Romana.* Berkeley, 1976.

Rawson, E., ed. *The Family in Ancient Rome.* London, 1986.

Rose, H. J. *A Handbook of Latin Literature from the Earliest Times to the Death of St. Augustine.* 3d ed. London, 1954.

Saller, R. P. *Personal Patronage Under the Early Empire.* Cambridge, 1982.

Sarton, G. *Ancient Science and Modern Civilization.* Lincoln, Neb., 1954.

Sarton, G. *Galen of Pergamon.* Lawrence, Kan., 1954.

Segar, A. P. *Judaism and Christianity in the Roman World.* Cambridge, 1986.

Simon, M. *Verus Israel: A Study of the Relations Between Christians and Jews in the Roman Empire (135–425).* Oxford, 1986.

Sherwin-White, A. N. *Racial Prejudice in Imperial Rome.* Cambridge, 1967.

Smallwood, E. M. *The Jews Under Roman Rule from Pompey to Diocletian.* Reprint with corrections. Leiden, 1981.

Sordi, M. *The Christians and the Roman Empire.* London, 1986.

Stahl, W. H. *Roman Science: Origins, Development and Influence to the Later Middle Ages.* Madison, Wis., 1962.

Starr, C. G. *Civilization and the Caesars.* Ithaca, 1954.

Wardman, A. *Religion and Statecraft Among the Romans.* Baltimore, 1982.

Whittaker, M. *Jews and Christians: Graeco-Roman Views.* Cambridge, 1984.
Wiedemann, T. *Adults and Children in the Roman Empire.* New Haven, 1989.
Wilken, R. L. *The Christians as the Romans Saw Them.* New Haven, 1984.
Witt, R. E. *Isis in the Graeco-Roman World.* Ithaca and London 1971.

4. THE ROMAN-PEACE:
LIFE IN THE MUNICIPALITIES AND PROVINCES

Arnold, W. T. *The Roman System of Provincial Administration to the Accession of Constantine the Great.* 3d ed., ed. by E. S. Bouchier. Oxford, 1914.
Ashley, A. M. "The 'Alimenta' of Nerva and His Successors," *English Historical Review* (1921), 36:5–16.
Bell, H. I. *Egypt from Alexander the Great to the Arab Conquest.* Oxford, 1948.
Birley, A. *Life in Roman Britain.* New ed. London, 1981.
Brogan, O. *Roman Gaul.* London, 1953.
Burn, A. R. *Agricola and Roman Britain.* London and New York, 1953.
Duyvendak, N. "Restraining Regulations for Roman Officials in the Roman Provinces," in *Symbolae . . . Van Oven Dedicatae.* Leiden, 1946, 333–348.
Dyson, S. L. "Native Revolt Patterns in the Roman Empire," *Aufstieg und Niedergang der römischen Welt* (1979), 2(3):138–175.
Jones, A. H. M. *The Cities of the Eastern Roman Provinces.* 2d ed.., rev. by M. Avi-Yonah, et al. Oxford, 1971.
Jones, A. H. M. *The Greek City from Alexander to Justinian.* Oxford, 1940.
Lewis, N. *Life in Egypt Under Roman Rule.* Oxford, 1983.
Magie, D. *Roman Rule in Asia Minor.* 2 vols. Princeton, 1950; reprint Salem, N.H., 1975.
Oliver, J. H. "The Ruling Power: A Study of the Roman Empire in the Second Century After Christ Through the Roman Oration of Aelius Aristides," *Transactions of the American Philosophical Society* (1953), 43:871–1003.
Reinhold, M. *Disapora: The Jews Among the Greeks and Romans.* Sarasota and Toronto, 1983.
Stevenson, G. H. *Roman Provincial Administration till the Age of the Antonines.* 2d ed. Oxford, 1949.

5. WOMEN IN THE ROMAN WORLD

Balsdon, J. P. V. D. *Roman Women, Their History and Habits.* London, 1962; reprint Westport, Conn., 1975.
Cantarella, E. *Pandora's Daughters: The Role and Status of Women in Greek and Roman Antiquity.* Baltimore, 1987.
D'Avino, M. *The Women of Pompeii.* Naples, 1967.

Dixon, S. *The Roman Mother*. London and Norman, Oklahoma, 1988.

Foley, H. P., ed. *Reflections of Women in Antiquity*. New York, 1981.

Gardner, J. F. *Women in Roman Law and Society*. London and Bloomington, Ind., 1986.

Goodwater, L. *Women in Antiquity: An Annotated Bibliography*. Metuchen, N.J., 1975.

Hallett, J. P. *Fathers and Daughters in Roman Society: Women and the Elite Family*. Princeton, 1984.

Holum, K. G. *Theodosian Empresses: Women and Imperial Dominion in Late Antiquity*. Berkeley, 1981.

Lefkowitz, M. R., and M. B. Fant. *Women's Life in Greece and Rome: A Sourcebook in Translation*. Baltimore and London, 1982.

Lightman, M., and W. Zeisel. "Univira: An Example of Continuity and Change in Roman Society," *Church History* (1977), 46:19–32.

Pomeroy, S. B. *Goddesses, Whores, Wives and Slaves: Women in Classical Antiquity*. New York, 1975.

Santirocco, M. "Sulpicia Reconsidered," *Classical Journal* (1979), 74:229–239.

Shaw, B. D. "The Age of Girls at Marriage: Some Reconsiderations," *Journal of Roman Studies* (1987), 77:30–46.

Tavard, G. H. *Women in Christian Tradition*. South Bend, Ind., 1973.

Treggiari, S. "Jobs for Women," *American Journal of Ancient History* (1976), 1:76–104.

6. THE CRISIS OF THE THIRD CENTURY AND THE EMERGENCE OF THE BYZANTINE STATE

Alföldy, G. "The Crisis of the Third Century as Seen by Contemporaries," *Greek, Roman and Byzantine Studies* (1974), 15:89–111.

Barnes, T. D. *The New Empire of Diocletian and Constantine*. Cambridge, Mass., 1982.

Baynes, N. H. *Constantine the Great and the Christian Church*. 2d ed. Oxford, 1972.

Burckhardt, J. *Constantine the Great*. New York, 1949.

Dodds. E. R. *Pagan and Christian in an Age of Anxiety: Some Aspects of Religious Experience from Marcus Aurelius to Constantine*. Cambridge, 1965; reprint New York, 1970.

Jones, A. H. M. *The Later Roman Empire 284–602: A Social, Economic and Administrative Survey*. 2 vols. Oxford, 1964; reprint Baltimore, 1986.

Keresztes, P. "The Imperial Roman Government and the Christian Church," *Aufstieg und Niedergang der römischen Welt* (1979), 2(23):247–315.

MacMullen, R. *Constantine*. New York, 1969.

MacMullen, R. "Late Roman Slavery," *Historia* (1987), 36:359–382.
MacMullen, R. "Tax Pressures in the Roman Empire," *Latomus* (1987), 46:737–754.
Magie. D. *Roman Rule in Asia Minor.* 2 vols. Princeton, 1950; reprint Salem, N.H., 1975.
Shaw, B. D. "Bandits in the Roman Empire," *Past and Present* (1984), 105:3–52.
Wardman, A. *Religion and Statecraft Among the Romans.* Baltimore, 1982.
Williams, S. *Diocletian and the Roman Recovery.* London, 1985.

7. THE ROMAN ARMY

Birley, E. *Roman Britain and the Roman Army: Collected Papers.* Kendal, 1953.
Campbell, B. "The Marriage of Soldiers under the Empire," *Journal of Roman Studies* (1978), 68:153–166.
Davies, R. W. "The Daily Life of the Roman Soldier Under the Principate," *Augstieg und Niedergang der römischen Welt* (1972), 2(1):299–338.
Davies, R. W. *Service in the Roman Army.* Ed. by D. Breeze and V. Maxfield. Edinburgh, 1987.
Fuller, J. F. C. *A Military History of the Western World.* Vol 1. New York 1954; reprint 1987.
Gilliam, J. F. "The Roman Military Feriale," *Harvard Theological Review* (1954), 47:183–196.
Grant, M. *The Army of the Caesars.* New York, 1974.
Helgeland, J. "Christians and the Roman Army from Marcus Aurelius to Constantine," *Aufstieg und Niedergang der römischen Welt* (1979), 2(23,1):724–834.
Keppie, L. *The Making of the Roman Army from Republic to Empire.* London and Totowa, N.J., 1984.
Mann, J. C. *Legionary Recruitment and Veteran Settlement during the Principate.* Ed. by M. M. Roxan. London, 1983.
Mellersh, H. E. L. *The Roman Soldier.* New York, 1965.
Starr, C. G. *The Roman Imperial Navy, 31 B.C.–A.D. 324.* 2d ed. Cambridge, 1960.
Watson, G. R. *The Roman Soldier.* London and Ithaca, 1969.
Webster, G. *The Roman Imperial Army of the First and Second Centuries A.D.* 3d ed. Totowa, N.J., 1985.
Welles, C. B. et al. *The Excavations at Dura-Europos.* Final report 5, part 1: "The Parchments and Papyri." New Haven, 1959.

8. ROMAN LAW

Berger, A. *Encyclopedic Dictionary of Roman Law*. Philadelphia, 1953.

Blatt, F. "Written and Unwritten Law in Ancient Rome," *Classica et Medievalia* (1942), 3:137–158.

Buckland, W. W. *A Text-Book of Roman Law from Augustus to Justinian*. 3d ed., rev. by P. Stein. Cambridge, 1975.

Cambridge Ancient History. Vol. 9, chapter 21; vol. 11, chapter 21. Cambridge, 1932, 1936.

Crook, J. A. *Law and Life of Rome*. London and Ithaca, 1967.

Jolowicz, H. F. *Historical Introduction to the Study of Roman Law*. 3d ed. Cambridge, 1972.

Justinian's Institutes. Translated by B. Peter and M. Grant. Ithaca and London, 1987.

Kunkel, W. *An Introduction to Roman Legal and Constitutional History*. 2d ed. Oxford, 1973.

Lee, R. W. *The Elements of Roman Law, with a Translation of the Institutes of Justinian*. Rev. ed. London, 1946.

Nicholas, J. K. B. M. *An Introduction to Roman Law*. Oxford, 1962.

Nicholson, B. *An Introduction to Roman Law*. Oxford, 1969 (reprint).

Pharr, C., ed. *The Theodosian Code*. Princeton, 1952.

Pharr, C., et al., eds. *Ancient Roman Statutes*. Austin, 1961.

Schiller, A. A. "Bureaucracy and the Roman Law," *Seminar* (1949), 7:26–48.

Schulz, F. *Classical Roman Law*. Oxford, 1951.

Scott, S. P. *The Civil Law*. 17 vols. Cincinnati, 1932.

[This work contains English translations of *The Twelve Tables*, the *Institutes* of Gaius, the *Rules* of Ulpian, the *Opinions* of Paulus, and the enactments of the Emperor Leo, as well as the entire *Corpus Juris Civilis*.]

Turner, J. W. C. *Introduction to the Study of Roman Private Law*. Cambridge, 1953.

Wolff, H. J. *Roman Law: An Historical Introduction*. Norman, Okla., 1951.

Wylie, J. K. *Roman Constitutional History from Earliest Times to the Death of Justinian*. Pasadena, 1948.

9. THE CONFLICT OF RELIGIONS AND THE TRIUMPH OF CHRISTIANITY

Alföldi, A. *The Conversion of Constantine and Pagan Rome*. New York, 1948.

Barnes, T. D. "Legislation Against the Christians," *Journal of Roman Studies* (1968), 58:32–50.

Barnes, T. D. "The Edict of Milan," *Journal of Roman Studies* (1973), 63:29–46.

Bowder, D. *The Age of Constantine and Julian.* London, 1978.

Brown, P. R. *The Body and Society: Men, Women and Sexual Renunciation in Early Christianity.* New York, 1988.

Brown, P. R. *Social Context to the Religious Crisis of the Third Century* A.D. Berkeley, 1975.

Davies, J. G. *Daily Life in the Early Church: Studies in the Church Social History of the First Five Centuries.* London, 1952.

Elliot, T. G. "The Tax Exemption Granted to Clerics by Constantine and Constantius II," *Phoenix* (1978), 32:326–336.

Fox, R. L. *Pagans and Christians in the Mediterranean World from the Second Century to the Conversion of Constantine.* London, 1987.

Jones, A. H. M. *Constantine and the Conversion of Europe.* London and New York, 1949; reprint Toronto, 1978.

Kennedy, G. A. *Classical Rhetoric and Its Christian and Secular Tradition from Ancient to Modern Times.* Chapel Hill, N.C., 1980.

Kyrtatas, D. *The Social Structure of the Early Christian Communities.* New York, 1987.

Lebreton, J., and J. Zeiller. *The History of the Primitive Church.* 2 vols. London and New York, 1949.

Legge, F. *Forerunners and Rivals of Christianity.* 2 vols. Cambridge, 1915.

Leitzmann, H. *A History of the Early Church.* 3d ed. New York and London, 1953.

MacMullen, R. *Paganism in the Roman Empire.* New Haven, 1981.

Novak, D. M. "Constantine and the Senate: An early Phase of the Christianization of the Roman Aristocracy," *Ancient Society* (1979), 10:271–310.

Pohlsander, H. A. "The Religious Policy of Decius," *Aufstieg und Niedergang der römischen Welt,* (1986), 2(16,3):1826–1842.

Segar, A. P. *Judaism and Christianity in the Roman World.* Cambridge, Mass., 1986.

Simon, M. *Verus Israel: A Study of the Relations between Christians and Jews in the Roman Empire (135–425).* New York, 1986.

Sordi, M. *The Christians and the Roman Empire.* London, 1986.

Ste. Croix, G. E. M. de. "Why Were the Early Christians Persecuted?" *Past & Present* (1963), 26:250–262.

Wilken, R. L. *The Christians as the Romans Saw Them.* New Haven, 1984.

10. THE LAST STAND OF PAGANISM AND THE CONSOLIDATION OF CHRISTIAN SOCIETY

Arnheim, M. T. W. *The Senatorial Aristocracy in the Later Roman Empire.* Oxford, 1972.

Athanassiadi-Fowden, P. *Julian and Hellenism: An Intellectual Biography.* Oxford, 1981.

Bernardi, A. "The Economic Problems of the Roman Empire at the Time of its Decline," *Studia et Documenta Historiae et Iuris* (1965), 31:110–70.

Bowder, D. *The Age of Constantine and Julian*. London, 1978.

Bowersock, G. W. "From Emperor to Bishop: The Self-conscious Transformation of Political Power in the Fourth Century," *Classical Philology* (1986), 86:298–307.

Bowersock, G. W. *Julian the Apostate*. Cambridge, Mass., 1978.

Brown, P. R. *The Making of Late Antiquity*. Cambridge, Mass., 1978.

Brown, P. R. *The World of Late Antiquity*, A.D. 150–750. London and New York, 1971.

Browning, R. *The Emperor Julian*. Berkeley and Los Angeles, 1976.

Chuvin, P. *A Chronicle of the Last Pagans*. Cambridge, Mass., 1990.

Gardner, A. *Julian, Philosopher and Emperor, and the Last Struggle of Paganism Against Christianity*. New York, 1978.

Geffcken, J. *The Last Days of Graeco-Roman Paganism*. Amsterdam and New York, 1978.

Head, C. *The Emperor Julian*. Boston, 1976.

Jones, A. H. M. *The Later Roman Empire 284–602: A Social, Economic and Administrative Survey*. Oxford, 1964; reprint 1986.

King, N. Q. *The Emperor Theodosius and the Establishment of Christianity*. London, 1961.

Ladner, G. B. "On Roman Attitudes Towards Barbarians in Late Antiquity," *Viator* (1976), 7:1–26.

MacMullen, R. *Christianizing the Roman Empire*. New Haven, 1984.

Matthews, J. F. *Political Life and Culture in Late Roman Society*. London, 1985.

Momigliano, A., et al. *The Conflict Between Paganism and Christianity in the Fourth Century*. Oxford, 1963.

O'Donnell, J. J. "The Demise of Paganism," *Traditio* (1979), 35:45–88.

The Fall of the Roman Empire

Chambers, M., ed. *The Fall of Rome: Can It be Explained?* 2d ed. New York, 1970.

Ferrill, A. *The Fall of the Roman Empire: The Military Explanation*. London, 1986.

Hodges, R. and J. W. Hayes. "Aspects of the Decline and Fall of the Roman Empire," *Journal of Roman Archaeology* (1988), 1:215–22.

Jones, A. H. M. *The Decline of the Ancient World*. London, 1966.

Kagan, D., et al. *Decline and Fall of the Roman Empire: Why Did It Collapse?* Boston, 1962.

MacMullen, R. *Corruption and the Decline of Rome*. New Haven, 1988.

Mazzarino, D. *The End of the Ancient World*. London and New York, 1966.

Perowne, S. *The End of the Roman World*. London and New York, 1966–1967.

Thompson, E. A. *Romans and Barbarians: The Decline of the Western Empire*. Madison, Wis., 1982.

Walbank, F. W. *The Awful Revolution: The Decline of the Roman Empire in the West*. New ed. Liverpool and Toronto, 1969.

11. COINS

Carson, R. A. G. *Coins of the Roman Empire*. New York, 1989.

Carson, R. A. G. *Principal Coins of the Romans*. 3 vols. London, 1978–1981.

Grant, M. "Roman Coins as Propaganda," *Archaeology* (1952), 5:79–85.

Grant, M. *Roman History from Coins*. Cambridge, 1958.

Grant, M. *Roman Imperial Money*. London, 1954.

Mattingly, H., ed. *Coins of the Roman Empire in the British Museum*. 6 vols. London, 1923–1963.

Mattingly, H., ed. *Roman Coins from the Earliest Times to the Fall of the Western Empire*. 2d ed. London, 1960.

Mattingly, H., E. A. Sydenham, C. H. V. Sutherland, et al., eds. *The Roman Imperial Coinage*. 9 vols. London, 1923–.

Robertson, A. S. *Roman Imperial Coins in the . . . University of Glasgow*. 5 vols. Oxford, 1962–1982.

Sutherland, C. H. V. *Roman History and Coinage 44 B.C.–A.D. 69*. Oxford, 1987.

INDEX

Actium, battle of, 445

Actors, 143; actresses, 367

Administration, imperial: increasing centralization of, 251, 521; child-assistance system *(alimenta)*, 255–59, 438; increasing intervention in local affairs, 239; reorganization under Augustus, 61; under Caracalla and military emperors of third and fourth centuries, 379, 379n; under Constantine, 429; under Diocletian, 416–18, 427–30; *see also* Municipalities; Provinces; Rome

Adoption: and disposition of estates, 300; imperial, 4–7

Adrianople, battle of, 623–24

Aelian-Sentian Law, 481

Africa: beset by barbarians, 621; cancellation of taxes, 400–1; and child-assistance legislation, 438; circumnavigation of, 220n; citizenship granted to an African family, 57–58; economic resources of, 84–85; grain shipped from, 61–62, 84n; Hadrian reviews garrison in, 460–62; imperial estates in, 96–99

Agentes in rebus (imperial secret service agents), 415

Agoranomi, 174, 289

Agricola, Gnaeus Julius, 278–79, 335

Agriculture: abandonment of cultivation in third century, 409; compulsory cultivation, 289, 308n; crisis in, during third and early fourth centuries, 437; crop rotation, 95n; Egyptian, 302–5; farmers' almanacs, 211–14; in frontier lands, 392; imperial estates, 95–101, 409; large estates, small farms incorporated into,

256–57; large estates, rise of tenancy on, 85–95; loans to farm owners, 255–56; manpower, growing shortage of, 96; profitableness of, 90–92; success of, in provinces, 92n; *see also* Estates; Tenant farmers

Agrippa, Marcus Vipsanius, 5; husband of Julia, 349; public works of, 72n; refusal of triumphs by, 13; and subjugation of Spain, 445n; and water supply of Rome, 136n

Agrippina, granddaughter of Augustus, 348

Agrippina, niece and wife of Claudius, 355–56

Alamanni, 619

Alaric, leader of the Visigoths: names puppet emperor of Rome, 637; and sack of Rome, 618, 624–27, 638

Alexander, Tiberius Julius, 4; edict of, 295–98

Alexander Severus (Marcus Aurelius Alexander Severus), emperor, 16n, 377–78, 400n; forms "guilds," 408; name defaced on inscription, 550

Alexandria: *annona* shipments, 63–64; capital of Egypt, 282–83, 295, 319; commercial capital of East, 83n, 117, 120–22; grain fleet, size and routes, 112–13; Jews in, 285, 287, 332; "purging" of, by Caracalla, 395–96

Alexandrians: letter of Claudius to, 285–88; privileges of, 55–56, 285, 297

Alimenta systems (child-assistance funds): imperial, 255–59; privately endowed, 259, 268–71